D0926705

THE TALMUD OF BABYLONIA

Program in Judaic Studies
Brown University
BROWN JUDAIC STUDIES
Edited by
Jacob Neusner,
Wendell S. Dietrich, Ernest S. Frerichs,
Alan Zuckerman

Project Editors (Project)

David Blumenthal, Emory University (Approaches to Medieval Judaism)
Ernest S. Frerichs, Brown University (Dissertations and Monographs)
Lenn Evan Goodman, University of Hawaii (Studies in Medieval Judaism)
William Scott Green, University of Rochester (Approaches to Ancient Judaism)
Ivan Marcus, Jewish Theological Seminary of Americas
(Texts and Studies in Medieval Judaism)
Marc L. Raphael, Ohio State University (Approaches to Judaism in Modern Times)
Jonathan Z. Smith, University of Chicago (Studia Philonica)

Number 78
THE TALMUD OF BABYLONIA
An American Translation
I: Tractate Berakhot

translated by
Jacob Neusner

THE TALMUD OF BABYLONIA
An American Translation
I: Tractate Berakhot

translated by
Jacob Neusner

Scholars Press
Chico, California

THE TALMUD OF BABYLONIA
An American Translation
I: Tractate Berakhot

translated by
Jacob Neusner

BM
499.5
.E4
1984
vol.1

© 1984
Brown University

Library of Congress Cataloging in Publication Data

Talmud. Berakhot. English.
  Tractate Berakhot.

  (The Talmud of Babylonia ; 1) (Brown Judaic studies ;
no. 78)
  Includes index.
  I. Neusner, Jacob, 1932–   . II. Title. III. Series:
Talmud. English. 1984 ; 1. IV. Series: Brown Judaic
studies ; no. 78.
BM499.5.E4 1984 vol. 1 296.1'2505 s   84–20273
[BM506.B6E5]   [296.1'2505]
ISBN 0-89130-808-3 (alk. paper)
ISBN 0-89130-809-1 (pbk. : alk. paper)

Printed in the United States of America
on acid-free paper

In Memory of
Shalom Spiegel

A great teacher, a scholar of learning and vision, when he taught us Jeremiah, he presented a great man, himself as well, the model not only of the prophet but also of the teacher. In an age in which Judaic learning was falling into the hands of small- and narrow-minded people, he kept alive and embodied the vision of Judaic learning as a venture in humanity, an expression of human greatness. When there were only a few true humanists in Judaic studies, he showed what it meant to be a humanist within the disciplines of Torah-study. So he gave us, his students for the whole of our lives, a measure and a model for ourselves.

CONTENTS

PREFACE

This is the fourth tractate to appear in this American translation, and, of course, the first tractate of the Talmud of Babylonia. The project, when completed, will consist of the following parts (number of folio pages in the original):

I.	Berakhot (64)
II.	Shabbat (157)
III.	Erubin (105)
IV.	Pesahim (121)
V.	Yoma (88)
VI.	Sukkah (56) [1984]
VII.	Besah (40)
VIII.	Rosh Hashanah (35)
IX.	Taanit (31)
X.	Megillah (32)
XI.	Moed Qatan (29)
XII.	Hagigah (27)
XIII.	Yebamot (122)
XIV.	Ketubot (112)
XV.	Nedarim (91)
XVI.	Nazir (66)
XVII.	Sotah (49) [1984]
XVIII.	Gittin (90)
XIV.	Qiddushin (82)
XX.	Baba Qamma (119)
XXI.	Baba Mesia (119)
XXII.	Baba Batra (170)
XXIII.	Sanhedrin (113)
XXIV.	Makkot (24)
XXV.	Abodah Zarah (76)
XXVI.	Horayot (14)
XXVII.	Shebuot (49)
XXVIII.	Zebahim (120)
XXIX.	Menahot (110)
XXX.	Hullin (142)
XXXI.	Bekhorot (61)
XXXII.	Arakhin (34) [1984]
XXXIII.	Temurah (34)

The several tractates will be issued when they become ready. The corps of translators hopes that the entire project will be complete by 1994, that is, within ten years of the date of the appearance of this tractate.

Tractates will be numbered by volume, then, if appearing in two or more fascicles, lettered, e.g., as follows:

THE TALMUD OF BABYLONIA. AN AMERICAN TRANSLATION

XXX.Hullin. A. Folios 2-50.
XXX.Hullin. B. Folios 51-100.
XXX.Hullin. C. Folios 101-142.

Vol. XXX.C then would contain the index for all three parts and also the reproduction of the text.

I expect to translate five tractates in all, this one and Arakhin, Sukkah, Sotah, and Sanhedrin. Translators for the other volumes already are at work.

To refer to passages of the Talmud, I have preserved my system of Mishnah-references. Thus in my translation of M. Berakhot, I followed the established system of using the first Arabic number to designate the chapter of the Mishnah, the second, the paragraph of the chapter as conventionally divided, e.g., in Albeck's edition, hence 1:1 stands for the first chapter and the first paragraph of M. Berakhot. I then proceeded to divide each paragraph into completed units of thought, whether whole sentences or parts of sentences, indicating what I conceived to be a complete thought by a letter. So 1:1A stands for the first completed thought of the first paragraph of the first chapter of the cited tractate. Now in the present work, I have marked the Mishnah-paragraphs so that they may be readily cross-referenced with my translation. To refer to the Talmudic materials, as is clear, I then use Roman numerals to signify what I believe to be a complete and whole unit of discourse of a given problem or topic, beginning to end, and then letters to mark the complete units of thought, as before. So 1:1.I.A stands for the first unit of thought of the first complete unit of discourse relevant to the first paragraph of the first chapter of the Mishnah-tractate at hand, and so throughout. The system makes possible easy reference to specific statements. I also have indicated where the folios begin and end, thus [2A], [2B], and so on throughout.

This is the second English translation of Babylonian Talmud tractate Berakhot. More than three decades ago Maurice Simon published <u>Berakhot. Translated into English with notes, glossary, and indices,</u> (London, 1948: The Soncino Press), part of a complete translation of the Talmud of Babylonia. I have consulted Simon's excellent translation and notes on every page. Where I reproduce his language in solving a problem I could not otherwise work out, I indicate it by placing his name in parentheses.

In my own case I undertake this translation because I wish to ask those questions of the Talmud of Babylonia that I raised, for the Talmud of the Land of Israel, in my Talmud of the Land of Israel. 35. Introduction. Taxonomy (Chicago, 1983: University of Chicago Press). For that purpose I require access, in my own sort of analytical translation, to a suitable statistical sample of the whole. But I do not have to translate and then construct my analytical tables for all of the tractates all together. I plan to take approximately 10% of the whole, Berakhot, Sukkah, Sotah, Sanhedrin, and Arakhin, that is, 316 folios of the total of 2,964 folios of the Talmud of Babylonia. These come from all four divisions of the Mishnah served by Bavli, plus the opening tractate, Berakhot. Some are long, some are short. Since, overall, I have the impression that the same redactional techniques characterize every tractate, with a uniform rhetoric and shared mode of constructing units of discourse commonplace throughout, the sample at hand should suffice to allow for the kind of generalizations of a literary and redactional character that I hope to be able to make.

Other translators, covering the thirty-two tractates in the thirty-one volumes I shall not translate, as I said, are already at work. But once we have a theory of the character of the document as a whole, even before the fresh translation is complete, a further set of studies, parallel to my Judaism in Society: The Evidence of the Yerushalmi (Chicago, 1984: University of Chicago Press) and Judaism: The Evidence of the Mishnah (Chicago, 1981: University of Chicago Press), should become possible. Accordingly, the present exercise fits into the larger program of my step-by-step inquiry into the formation of Judaism. Let me now spell out precisely how the theory of translation governing the present project differs from that by which Rabbi Slotki and his fellow-translators determined how to carry out their work.

The classic and enduring texts of humanity undergo translation in age succeeding age. For each new generation takes up the task of confronting and making its own the intellectual heritage of civilization. An exception to that rule until the present day has been the sacred literature of the canon of Judaism. Excluding only the Hebrew Scriptures (Tanakh, "Old Testament"), no text originally in Hebrew or Aramaic of the Judaic canon reached a foreign language, except for Latin, before the nineteenth century. The reason is that, before modern times, Jews took for granted only they would wish to receive and revere the literary heritage of their people. They further assumed that all male, worthy Jews could learn to read them in the original Hebrew or Aramaic. Learned men translated into, not out of, Hebrew. The act of translation therefore drew a certain opprobrium. Serious scholars would not bother; self-respecting male Jews would master the original language anyhow.

In the later nineteenth century in Germany and France, and in the twentieth century in Britain and the USA, by contrast, numerous scholars have turned to the task of transmitting the heritage of Judaism to an audience of Western Jews of both genders, and a considerable reception among non-Jews and Jews awaited the results. The Mishnah reached most of the Western languages, the Babylonian Talmud came into German and twice into English (Rodkinson, Soncino), and the Palestinian Talmud into French at the end of the nineteenth century and English just now. Many (though by no means all) of the compilations and compositions of scriptural exegesis produced by the rabbis of late antiquity and medieval times ("midrashim") exist in German and English. By the end of this century, all of those classics of the canon of Judaism that were completed by the end of late antiquity will have come into the English (mainly, the American) language. The reason, as is clear, is that there is a sizable audience, both Jewish and gentile, and there also is a significant corps of competent and interested translators available to do the work. (In passing, we take note also that many of the documents at hand turn out to attract the interest of translators into modern, Israeli Hebrew as well.) The substantial interest in the labor of moving the old texts from one language and system of thought into another would surprise no one, except, as I said, those many generations of male Jews who took for granted translation was neither necessary nor valuable, in the untested theory that whoever cared knew Hebrew or should learn it.

Outside of the canon of writings at hand no one debates the question of whether a given text requires more than a single translation into a given language. Great scholars who also are poets undertake the successive retranslation of every great classic of world literature, whether philosophical or dramatic or poetic. Who can count the number of translations into English alone of the Hebrew Scriptures? It is a commonplace that through the work of serious translation great literary creations have come into being, in the case, for instance, of Homer, Plato, and Euripides. None therefore need wonder why someone would translate afresh a classic text of Judaism that already exists in the English language. What requires attention is only the issue of what the latter-day translator wishes to accomplish, that has been left undone by a predecessor.

In the present context, I see no fewer than four available theories of translation, any one of which enjoys its distinctive value. Let me spell them out, so as to place into context the newest effort to translate a classic text of Judaism into the American language. These may be briefly entitled a literary translation, a reference translation, a research translation, and a conversation-translation.

A literary translation aims at presenting in English not a literal and exact rendition of the text but an elegant and poetic one. It transmits main ideas, thoughts closely related to, but not in the exact language of, the original. Such a translation aims through the power of the contemporary idiom at winning to the gist of the text a sizable audience of lay readers. Success then means a large and understanding audience. The translator serves as a partner to the original author. My impression is that all efforts at translating poetry fall into this classification.

A reference translation, the opposite of the foregoing, provides a succinct and literal account of the original, with few notes of the character of more than brief references. The utility of such a translation is to facilitate quick reference to the original text. It will serve to guide the outsider to a given passage, but not to lead into the heart of matters someone who does not know the original language. Such a purpose, for the aesthetic side, is served by the literary translation.

For the substantive side of things, the research translation, the exact opposite of the reference translation, serves admirably. Such a translation draws together into one place every piece of information that appears to pertain to the passage at hand. Philological, historical, textual issues intervene into the text. The scholar, particularly one who works in an area other than that of the text at hand, finds in such a translation enormous assistance. The research translation further will address the issue of variant text-traditions of the text at hand, so that diverse manuscripts will come to testify to the original sense and wording of the passage.

Standing apart from the first three types of translation, the conversation-translation aims at one thing only, and that is, clear comprehension not only of the words but also of the sense of the classic text. By "talking the reader through" the text, clearly distinguishing language added by the translator from the original words of the text, the translator renders accessible the distinctive message and mode of thought of the ancient text. Who will want such a translation? The same sort of reader who responds to the literary sort of translation, but with a difference. The reader at hand wants access to not only the gist of discourse but the mode and medium. It is insufficient to such a reader to know what, in general, the text wishes to tell us. Such a reader wishes to know the message in relationship to the medium.

Let me now spell out my views of these available theories of translation and explain my preference for the fourth one in particular. The reference-translation I deem inadequate, because it is essentially useless, in leaving the text unexplained. The research-translation has merit; since it stands as a convenient source for whatever is relevant (and much that is not relevant) to the particular text subject to translation. But it is not a great deal more useful than the reference-translation for those whose principal interest is in what this text says and what it means. Only a reference-translation, putting down on paper only the corresponding words in the other language so that people may look things up and pick and choose what may be useful, justifies an essentially unadorned translation, a simple "rendition" from one language to the other. A research translation meant to raise and solve all the problems, philological and linguistic, textual and lexicographical, historical and theological, ranging here, there, and everywhere, with endless notes and a dazzling display of erudition -- such a translation seems to me of equally limited use. For someone opening it will find overwhelming the limitless ranges of erudite discourse and so lose sight of the issue at hand. That issue is the protracted and brilliant exercise in practical reason and applied logic which is the Babylonian Talmud at its most interesting, if also its most difficult.

Clearly, the criterion for evaluating a translation among the available types derives in the end from the audience at hand. For whom does one translate the document anyhow? It cannot be only for those able to make sense of the document in its original language. For them, a translation is merely another commentary, lacking all canonical status, in the acutely theological and nervous atmosphere of the schools in which this particular document is studied, a translation enjoys no standing whatsoever. That does not mean it will not be used. The excellent efforts of the translators of the Babylonian Talmud into German, then into English, have hardly been neglected in the German- and English-speaking world in which the sacred writings of Judaism are studied. But it is foolish to contribute to a world with its own conventions and canonical exegesis a translation which that world claims not to need and forthrightly alleges it does not want. To that world a translation is not a commentary. It is an affront.

On the other hand, if the translator proposes to present the text "to whom it may concern," that is, to no one in particular, then the question arises of how much requires explanation. Here there can simply be no end to the matter. In the case of a document that assumes so vast a knowledge of the Hebrew Scriptures and the Mishnah as does the Talmud, even if one quotes the whole of a verse alluded to only by a word or two, should the translator then proceed to interpret that verse? Its context? Its meaning and use in the passage of the Talmud before us? Similarly, if the Talmud rests upon a pericope of the Mishnah that is not cited at all, should the translator merely allude to the passage and expect the reader to look it up? Should the translator cite the passage in full? And if so, how extensive an explanation is required?

As to the discourse of the Talmud itself, the translation, of course, constitutes a substantial judgment upon the meaning of the text. Where we put a period or a comma, or indicate the end of one major discourse and the start of another, how we break up the undifferentiated columns of words into paragraphs, the paragraphs into sentences, and the sentences into their individual, small units of cognition -- these decisions are conveyed in the very simple facts of how we present what we claim to be the meaning of the text. And yet, beyond that simple statement, it is clear, a fair amount of explanation is demanded. How much, or how little, must be explained is not self-evident, and probably will never be readily settled. It is invariably an exercise of judgment and taste. That is why, as I said, the translator has to find a balance between the requirements of intelligibility, indeed, to whom it may concern, on the one side, and the limited possibilities of full and ample presentation of a single text in a single book, on the other. Too much will overwhelm the reader, who will lose sight of the text, which is, after all, at the center of the translation. Too little will puzzle the reader, leaving the text translated but still inaccessible.

In order to show in a graphic way the different choices confronting a translator of Bavli, I set side by side the translation of Babylonian tractate Arakhin 2A-2B in, first, the version appearing in the great Soncino translation of the Babylonian Talmud produced, for the tractate at hand, by Leo Jung, and second, my version. In this way the difference in the theories governing how the work is to be done becomes vivid. Within the scheme I have laid forth, I should categorize Jung's (and the rest of the Soncino translations) as essentially a reference-translation. Mine, clearly, is meant to be a conversation-translation. In order to provide a full picture of how Jung explains what is not self-evidently clear in the text, further, I have included those of his footnotes which constitute more than mere references to other texts. The notes follow the extracts.

In order to make clear how I think my approach to translation differs, let me spell out a few of its salient traits. The single significant trait in what follows is the extensive use of square brackets to add to the flow of discourse those sources alluded to but not cited. The translation is richly augmented by understanding not made explicit and by rhetorical shifts and turns in no way indicated in the original Aramaic. To state the theory of translation of this document as simply as I can: Here I propose to talk my way through an account of what the document says -- not stated in square brackets but translated into fairly fluent American English -- and of what the document means. That is, both what we need to know to make sense of it, and also what we are supposed to conclude on the basis of what the document says and the facts added by me, are supplied. Translation here is a kind of extended conversation, an interchange within the document, with the document, and through the document, and, always, an urgent encounter with the reader.

If I had to make a guess as to what we have, I should imagine we deal with nothing more than brief notes, notations really, out of which a whole and complete discourse is supposed to be reconstructed by those essentially familiar with the (original) discourse. The Babylonian Talmud is a kind of abbreviated script, a set of cue cards drastically cut down to a minimum of words. But these metaphors are meant only to account for the theory of translation followed here, I mean the theory that out of the sherds and remnants of coherent speech we have to reconstruct and fully reconstitute the (original) coherent discourse, as best we can, whole sentences from key words, whole analyses from truncated allusions.

MISHNAH. [2a] All [persons] are fit to evaluate or to be made the subjects of valuation, are fit to vow [another's worth] or have their worth vowed: -- priests, Levites and [ordinary] Israelites, women and slaves. Persons of unknown sex and hermaphrodites are fit to vow [another's worth], or to have their worth vowed, and are fit to evaluate, but they are not fit to be made the subjects of valuation, for the subject of valuation may be only a person definitely either male or female. A deaf-mute, an imbecile, or a minor are fit to have their worth vowed or be made the subject of valuation, but they are not fit to make either a vow [of another's worth] or to evaluate, because they have no mind.

[2A]

A. All may pledge the Valuation [of others] and are subject to the pledge of Valuation [by others].

B. may vow [the worth of another] and are subject to the vow [of payment of their worth by another]:

C. priests   and   Levites   and Israelites, women and slaves.

D. A person of doubtful sexual traits and a person who exhibits traits of both sexes may vow [the worth of another] and are subject to the vow [of payment of their worth by another], may pledge the Valuation [of others], but are not subject to the pledge of Valuation by others,

E. for evaluated is only one who is certainly a male or certainly a female.

F. A deaf-mute, an imbecile, and a minor are subject to the vow [of payment of their worth by another], and are subject to the pledge of Valuation by others, but do not vow the worth, and do not pledge the Valuation, of others,

G. for   they   do   not   possess understanding.

GEMARA. What does ALL [PERSONS] ARE FIT TO EVALUATE mean to include? -- It is meant to include one close to manhood who must be examined.[1] What does [ALL[2] ARE] FIT TO BE MADE THE SUBJECTS OF VALUATION mean to include? -- It is meant to include a person disfigured, or one afflicted with boils. For one might have assumed that since Scripture says: A   vow...   according   to   thy

I.   A. [When the framer explicitly refers to] all, [in framing the Mishnah-paragraph at hand, saying All pledge....,] what [classification of persons does he intend] to include, [seeing that in what follows C, he lists the available classifications of persons in any event, and, further, at D-G specifies categories of persons that are excluded. Accordingly, to what purpose does he add the encompassing language, all, at the outset?]

valuation,[4] that only such persons as are fit to be made the subjects of a vow [as regards their worth], are fit to be made subjects of a valuation, and that persons who are unfit to be made subjects of a vow [as regards their worth], are also unfit to be made subjects of a valuation, hence Scripture informs us: of persons.[4] i.e., no matter who they be.

[1]Mufla' from the root meaning, to make clear, to examine, hence 'one to be examined' as to the purpose for which he made the valuation. Above the age of thirteen such knowledge is taken for granted. Below the age of twelve it is assumed to be absent. During the period from twelve to thirteen the boy is to be subject to questioning. If the examination establishes his knowledge of the purpose of the dedication, his dedication is considered valid, and renders payment obligatory. Otherwise no significance is to be attached during that period to his utterance of the formula: Erek peloni' alay.

[2]The first word of the Mishnah ALL is assumed to apply to the four cases enumerated. This word does not seem necessary, the Mishnah might have stated e.g., Priests, Levites and Israelites are fit etc. The additional ALL hence is assumed by the questioner to have implied the inclusion of persons whom, without this inclusion, one might have excluded. Hence the series of questions establishing the identity of the persons included in each case. This discussion leads to the consideration of other passages throughout the Mishnah, in which the word 'all' occurs, and to an explanation of who is included in each statement.

B. It serves to include a male nearing puberty [who has not yet passed puberty. Such a one is subject to examination to determine whether he grasps the meaning of a vow, such as is under discussion. A child younger than the specified age, twelve years to thirteen, is assumed not to have such understanding, and one older is taken for granted to have it.]

C. [When the framer explicitly frames matters as all] are subject to the pledge of Valuation, what [classification of persons does he intend] to include?

D. It is to include a person who is disfigured or afflicted with a skin ailment.

E. [Why in any event should one imagine that persons of that classification would be omitted?] I might have supposed that, since it is written, "A vow... according to your Valuation" (Lev. 27:2), [with Scripture using as equivalent terms "vow" and "Valuation,"] the rule is that [only] those who possess an [instrinsic] worth [e.g., whoever would be purchased for a sum of money in the marketplace, hence excluding the disfigured persons under discussion, who are worthless] also would be subject to a vow of Valuation [at fixed price, such as Scripture specified]. On the other hand, [I might have supposed that] whoever does not possess an [intrinsic] worth also would not be subject to a vow of Valuation.

F. Accordingly, [the formulation of the Mishnah-passage at hand] tells us, [to the contrary, that a pledge of Valuation is not dependent upon represents an absolute charge and is not relative to the subject's market-value.]

G. [How does Scripture so signify? When the framer of Scripture refers at

[4]A person disfigured, or afflicted with boils, would fetch no price at all on the market place. In the expression A vow according to. thy valuation, one might have inferred from this juxtaposition, that a certain fundamental agreement prevailed between cases of vow (of one's worth) and of valuation, and that therefore a person unfit to have his work vowed (because a vow was redeemable by payment of the market value, which did not exist in the case of a disfigured person) would be unfit to be made the subject of a valuation. But this inference is cancelled by another Biblical phrase, which indicates that what is required is but 'persons', independent of their physical condition: When a man shall clearly utter a vow of persons (ibid.).

Lev. 27:2 to] "persons," [the meaning is that a pledge of Valuation applies] to anyone at all.

What does [ALL PERSONS] ARE FIT TO VOW mean to include? -- [The phrase ALL] is needed only for [the clause] 'are fit to have their worth vowed'. What is to be included [in the phrase ALL] ARE FIT TO HAVE THEIR WORTH VOWED? Is it to include persons of unknown sex or hermaphrodites -- but they are expressly stated [in our Mishnah]. Again is it to include a deaf-mute, an imbecile and a minor -- they too are expressly stated! And if it is to include a person below the age of one month -- that too is expressly mentioned! And again if it is to include an idolator -- he too is expressly mentioned! -- In reality it is meant to include a person below the age of one month; and the Mishnah states it [by

H. [When the framer of the Mishnah, further, states that all] vow [the worth of another], what [classification of persons does he thereby intend] to include [seeing that at C we go over the same matter, specifying those who may make such a vow]?

I. It is necessary for him [to specify that all take such a vow to indicate that all also applies to] those concerning whom such a vow is taken.

J. [Therefore, when the framer specifies that all] are subject to a vow, what [classification of persons does he thereby intend] to include?

K. [Here matters are not so self-evident, for] if the intention is to include a person of doubtful sexual traits and a person who exhibits the traits of both sexes, both of those classifications

implication] and later on expressly mentions it.[3]

[3]By the redundant ALL, which obviously includes some person or persons, which but for this all-inclusive term, would have been excluded. The particular reason why this case rather than any other of the four here dealt with is included here Rashi finds in the fact that it is the only one concerning which a controversy exists (infra 5a), whence the statement here by implication is of importance in teaching that even the Rabbis who hold that one who is less than a month cannot be subject to evaluation, nevertheless agree that he can have his worth vowed.

are explicitly stated [in the formulation of the Mishnah-passage itself].

L. And if the intention is to include a deaf-mute, an imbecile, and a minor, these classifications also are explicitly stated. [So what can have been omitted in the explicit specification of the pertinent classifications, that the framer of the Mishnah-passage found it necessary to make use of such amplificatory language as all?]

M. If, furthermore, the intent was to include an infant less than a month old, that classification also is explicitly included [below].

N. If, furthermore, the intent was to include an idolator, that classification furthermore is explicitly included as well. [Accordingly, what classification of persons can possibly have been omitted in the framing of the Mishnah-passage at hand, that the author found it necessary to add the emphatic inclusionary are in mind?]

O. In point of fact, [the purpose of adding the emphatic language of inclusion] was to include an infant less than a month in age.

P. [The framer of the passage] taught [that such a category is included by using the word all] and then he went and stated the matter explicitly [to clearly indicate the inclusion of that category].

What does 'All persons are obliged to lay on hands' mean to include?[4] -- It is meant to include the heir, and this against the view of R. Judah.[5] What does 'All persons can effect a substitute'[6] mean to include? -- That, too, means to include the heir, in contrast to the view of R. Judah. For it

II.   A. [When at M. Men. 9:8, we find the formulation], All lay hands [on a beast to be slaughtered, that is, including not only the owner of the beast, who set it aside and consecrated it for the present sacrificial purpose, but also some other party], whom do we find included [by the inclusionary language, all]?

was taught: An heir must lay on hands, an heir can effect a substitute. R. Judah says: An heir does not lay on hands, and an heir cannot effect a substitute.

[4]The Gemara proceeds now to discuss all other cases in which a redundant 'all' is to convey some inclusion in the principle of other persons. The laying on of the hands on the head of the animal to be sacrificed conveyed the sense of ownership. It was a duty, hence a question arises in the case of several partners, or in the case of proxy.

[5]R. Judah denied this obligation to an heir. Lev. I, 3 reads: If he be a burnt offering...he shall lay his hand upon the head. This, R. Judah argues, expressly limits the duty of laying the hand to the man who offered it, not to his heir, who is freed from his obligation.

[6]Lev. XXVII, 10: He shall not alter it, nor change it, a good for a bad, or a bad for a good; and if he shall at all change beast for beast, then both it and that for which it is changed shall be holy. The dispute concerns only the case of an heir in respect of an offering dedicated by his father but all agree that an exchange made by anyone besides the original owner of the sacrifice would have no effect at all, the first animal remaining sacred, the second not being affected by the unauthorized attempt at exchange.

B. [It is used to indicate] the inclusion of the heir [of the owner of the beast who consecrated it and subsequently died. The heir of the deceased owner, may take his place vis à vis the beast, lay hands on the beast, and so derive benefit from the sacrifice of that beast, even though he did not originally designate it as holy].

C. And that inclusion does not accord with the position of R. Judah [who maintains that, since Scripture specifies at Lev. 1:3 that the person who has designated the beast as a holy sacrifice "shall lay hands on it," excluded are all other parties, who did not designate the beast as holy. Only the owner of the beast may lay hands, and no one else. In so formulating the rule by using the inclusionary language all, the framer of the passage has indicated that he rejects the position of Judah].

D. [And when, at M. Tem. 1:1, we find the formulation,] All effect an act of substitution [so consecrating the beast that is supposed to take the place of the originally consecrated beast, in line with Lev. 27:10, but leaving that originally consecrated beast in the status of consecration nonetheless], what category of person do we find included [by the use of such language]?

E. [Once more], the use of such language indicates the inclusion of the heir [of the owner of the beast, who originally consecrated it and died before sacrificing it, just as at B, above].

F. And that inclusion once more does not accord with the position of R. Judah [for Lev. 27:10 states, "He shall not alter it...," thus referring solely to the owner of the beast, and not to an heir or any other third party].

G. [Now the statements just given accord with] that which has been taught [in a tradition external to the Mishnah but deriving from authorities named in the Mishnah], as follows:

H. An heir lays hands [on a beast originally consecrated by the deceased], an heir effects an act of substitution [in regard to a beast originally consecrated by the deceased].

I. R. Judah says, "An heir does not lay on hands, an heir does not effect an act of substitution."

J. What is the Scriptural basis for the position of R. Judah?

K. "His offering..." (Lev. 3:2, 7, 13: "He shall lay his hand upon the head of his offering") -- and not the offering that was set aside by his father.

L. From the rule governing the end of the process of consecration [the laying on of hands] [R. Judah further] derives the rule governing the beginning of the process of consecrating a beast [e.g., through an act of substitution, which indicates that a given beast is substituted for, therefore shares the status, of another beast that already has been consecrated. In this way the beast put forward as a substitution is itself deemed to be sanctified. Accordingly, a single principle governs both stages in the sacrificial process, the designation of the beast as holy and therefore to be sacrificed, e.g., through an act of substitution, and the laying on of hands just prior to the act of sacrificial slaughter itself. Just as the latter action may be performed solely by the owner of the beast, who derives benefit only when the owner of the beast carries it out, so is the rule for the former action.]

What is the reason of R. Judah's view? -- [Scripture says:] His offering,[1] i.e., but not his father's offering. And he infers the rule concerning the commencement of the dedication of the animal from the rule governing its end. Just as at the end of the dedication the heir does not lay on hands, thus also at the beginning[2] he cannot effect a substitute. And the Rabbis? -- [Scripture says redundantly:] And if he shall at all change -- that included the heir. And we infer the rule concerning the end of the dedication from the rule governing the commencement of the dedication. Just as at the beginning of the dedication the heir has power to effect a substitute, so at the end is he obliged to lay his hands on the animal's head.[3] But what do the Rabbis do with 'his offering'? -- [They interpret:] 'his offering', but not the offering of an idolator; 'his offering', but not the offering of his neighbour; 'his offering', i.e., to include all who have a share[4] in the ownership of a sacrifice in the duty to lay on hands. And R. Judah?[5] -- He does not hold that all who have a share in the ownership share the obligation of laying hands thereon; or, indeed, if he should hold so [2b] he would infer [the exclusion of] idolator and neighbour from one passage,[6] so that two more would remain redundant, from one of which he would ifer that 'his offering' means 'but not that of his father', and from the other that all who have a share in the ownership of a sacrifice are obliged to perform the laying on of hands. But what does R. Judah do with 'If he shall at all change'? -- He needs that to include woman,[7] for it was taught: Since all this chapter is couched in masculine gender, what brings us eventually to include woman? The text stated: 'If he shall at all change'[8] But [whence do] the Sages [infer this]? -- From the [redundant] 'And if'. And R. Judah? -- He does not interpret 'And if'.[9]

[1] Lev. II, 2, 7 and 13 in connection with the laying on of hands in the case of peace-offerings. V. Rash and Tosaf. a.l.

[2] First an animal is separated for the purpose of being offered on the altar. That is the commencement of its sanctification. At the end, just before the slaying of the animal, the owner lays his hand on its head. R. Judah infers from the regulations at the end, viz., the prohibition for anyone but the owner to lay hands on the head, the inefficacy of the change at the beginning, i.e., his intended exchange has no effect on the animal he wanted to substitute.

[3] The Sages infer from the redundant 'shall at all change' that even another may effect the substitute and argue from the beginning of the sanctification to the end, hence permit an heir to lay hands on the animal.

M. Accordingly, just as, at the end of the process of consecration, the heir does not lay on hands, so at the beginning of the process of consecration, an heir does not carry out an act of substitution.

N. And as to the position of rabbis [vis à vis Judah, who maintain that the heir may do so, how do they read Scripture in such wise as to derive their view?]

O. [Scripture states,] "And if changing, he shall change" (Lev. 27:10) [thus intensively using the same verb twice, with one usage understood to refer to the owner himself, the other usage to some closely related person].

P. [The use of the verbal intensive therefore is meant] to include the heir, and, as before, we derive the rule governing the conclusion of the sacrificial process [with the laying on of hands] from the rule governing the commencement of the sacrificial process [the designation of the beast as holy, by its substitution for an already-consecrated beast].

Q. Accordingly, just as, at the beginning of the process of consecration, the heir does carry out an act of substitution, so at the end of the process of consecration, the heir does lay on hands.

R. Now [given rabbis' reading of the relevant verses], how do these same rabbis deal with Scripture's three references to "his offering" [which in Judah's view makes explicit that only the owner of the beast lays hands on his beast, cf. Lev. 3:2,7,13]?

S. They require that specification of Scripture to lay down the rule that [an Israelite] lays hands on his sacrifice, but not on the sacrifice of an idolator, on

[4]The phrase 'his offering' occurs three times in Lev. III, viz., vv. 2, 7 and 13, and while two of these expressions have a limiting sense, one has an inclusive meaning. Just as 'his' implies ownership, so must anyone who has a claim to ownership lay his hands on the animal's head. Therefore, every member of a group who offer the animal together must perform the laying on of hands on the part of anyone who shares in it -- for which an inclusive interpretation is necessary?

[6]The word 'his' could exclude both the fellow-Jew and the idolator, since the Scriptural 'his sacrifice' logically excludes both.

[7]That a woman can effect a substitute in her offering.

[8]Lit., 'if change he shall change' the emphasis is inclusive.

[9]He does not ascribe to that word the implications attributed to it by the Sages. About the limits of such interpretation and the basic suggestions implied in disputes thereon v. D. Hoffman, Leviticus I, 9f.

his sacrifice and not on the sacrifice of his fellow;

T. on his sacrifice, further, to include all those who own a share in the sacrificial animal, according to each the right to lay hands upon the beast [of which they are partners].

U. And as to R. Judah? He does not take the view that all those who own a share in the sacrificial animal have a right to.

V. Alternatively, [one may propose that] he does maintain the stated position [concerning the partners in a sacrificial animal].

W. [But] he derives the rule governing [2b] the idolator['s beast] and that of one's fellow from a single verse of Scripture [among the three verses that make explicit that one lays hands on his animal], leaving available for the demonstration of a quite separate proposition two [other] of these same [three] references.

X. [It follows, for Judah's position, that] one of these verses serves to indicate, "His offering" and not the offering of his father," and another of the available verses then serves to include [among those who indeed may lay hands on the sacrificial beast] all shareholders, according to each of them the right to lay hands on the beast held in common partnership.

Y. [Further exploring the thesis of Judah about the scriptural basis for his view, exactly] how does R. Judah interpret the intensive verb used at Lev. 27:10, "And if changing, he shall change"?

Z. He requires that usage to include the participation of the woman [in the process of substitution, so that if a woman makes a statement effecting an act of substitution, that statement is as valid as if a man had made it].

AA. That [view of his reading] is in accord with the following tradition assigned to Tannaitic authority:

BB. Since the entire formulation of the passage concerning an act of substitution speaks of the male, how in the end shall we include the female as well [so that an act of substitution of a woman is regarded as valid]?

CC. Scripture states, "And if changing, he shall change..." [The intensive language serves to include the woman.]

DD. And as to rabbis, [how do they prove the same position]?

EE. It is from the use of the inclusionary word, and if, in the phrase, "And if changing...."

GG. The usage, "And if...," in his view is not subject to exegesis at all [and yields no additional information about the role under discussion. Accordingly, in order to prove that a woman is involved in the process of substitution, as much as a man, Judah must refer solely to the intensive verb construction.]

What does 'All persons are obliged[5] to observe [the laws concerning] the booth' mean to include? -- That is meant to include a minor that no more needs his mother,[6] for we have learnt: A minor that no more needs his mother is obliged to observe the laws concerning the booth.

[5]The Gemara proceeds now to a systematic examination of all cases in which the word 'all' is used. Unless it can be proved that in each case that word includes something normally excluded, the argument, or rather the

III.   A. All are obligated [to carry out the religious duty of dwelling in] a tabernacle [on the Festival of Tabernacles].

B. [When the framer of the foregoing statement makes explicit use of the inclusionary language, all], what [classification of persons is] included, [that otherwise would have been omitted]?

C. It is to include a minor who does not depend upon his mother [but can take care of himself], in line with the following statement found in the Mishnah [M. Suk. 2:8:] A child who does not depend upon his mother is liable to [carry out the religious duty of dwelling in a] tabernacle.

first question posed on 2a will be
invalidated.

[6]A child which (Suk. 28b) on
awakening no more calls out 'Mother!'
but attends to his needs, dresses himself,
etc.

What does 'All are obliged to
observe the law of the lulab'[8] mean to
include? -- That includes a minor who
knows how to shake the lulab, for we
learnt: A minor who knows how to
shake[9] the lulab is obliged to observe
[the laws of] the lulab. What does 'All
are obliged to observe the [law of] the
fringes' include? -- That includes the
minor who knows how to wrap himself,
for it was taught: A minor who knows
how to wrap himself [into the tallith][10]
is obliged to observe the law of the
fringes. What does 'All are obliged to
observe the rules concerning the tefillin'
include? -- That includes a minor who
knows how to take care of the tefillin,
for it was taught: If a minor knows how
to take care of the tefillin,[11] his father
buys tefillin for him.

[8]The palm-branch forming with
citron, myrtle and willow, the cluster
taken during the Feast of Tabernacles (v.
Lev. XIII, 40) is every day waved in
every direction to symbolize the
omnipresence of God.

[9]The lulab is waved in the four
main directions: south, north, west and
east, and there are some details as to
the position of the components of the
cluster, which are known to the
worshipper, so that he may follow the
cantor's lead.

D. All are liable [to carry out the
religious duty of taking up] the palm
branch [enjoined at Lev. 23:40.

E. [When the framer of the
foregoing statement makes explicit use of
the inclusionary language, all] what
[classification of persons is] included,
[that otherwise would have been omitted]?

F. It is to include a minor who
knows how to shake [the palm-branch, so,
with proper intention, making appropriate
use of the holy object].

G. That is in line with the
following statement found in the Mishnah
[M. Suk. 3:15:] A minor who knows how to
shake [the palm branch with proper
intention] is liable to [the religious duty
of taking up] the palm branch.

H. All are liable [to carry out the
religious duty of affixing] fringes [to the
corners of garments].

I. [When the framer of the
foregoing statement makes explicit use of
the inclusionary language, all] what
[classification of persons is] included,
[that otherwise would have been omitted]?

J. It is to include a minor who
knows how to cloak himself [in a garment,
and so enters the obligation of affixing to
said cloak the required fringes].

K. For it has been taught [at T.
Hag. 1:2:] A minor who knows how to
cloak himself [in a garment] is liable to
[affix to that garment the required show]
fringes.

L. All are liable [to carry out the
religious duty of wearing] phylacteries.

M. [When the framer of the
foregoing statement makes explicit use of
the inclusionary language, all,] what
[classification of persons is] included,
[that otherwise would have been omitted]?

[10]The prayer shawl at the four corners of which the fringes are attached, and into which one wraps himself, 'in order to remember the commandments of the Lord'. The wrapping must be performed in a special manner, v. M.K. 24a.

[11]Commonly called phylacteries. The attachment, leather box and leather strap, each on left arm and forehead, containing the Shema' and other extracts from the Torah, originally worn all day, now only at the morning prayer.

What does 'All are obliged to appear' include[3] -- It is meant to include one who is half[4] slave and half freedman. According, however, to Rabina, who holds that one who is half slave and half freed is free from the obligation to appear, [the word 'All'] is meant to include one who was lame[5] on the first day of the festival and became normal again on the second day. -- That would be right according to the view that all the days of the festival may make up for each other. But according to the view that they all are but making up for the first day, what will 'All' come to include?[6] -- It will include one blind in one of his eyes. This [answer] is not in accord with the following Tanna, for it was taught: Johanan b. Dahabai said in the name of R. Judah: One blind in one eye is free from the obligation to appear, for it is said:[7] Yir'eh-yera'eh [he shall see -- he shall appear] i.e., just as He is present to see [the comer], so shall He be seen, just as His sight is complete, so shall the sight of him who appears be intact.

N. It is to include a minor who knows how to take care of phylacteries [and therefore may be entrusted with them].

O. For it has been taught [at T. Hag. 1:2:] As to a minor who knows how to take care of phylacteries, his father purchases phylacteries for him.

IV.   A.   All are obligated [on the occasion of a pilgrim festival to bring] an appearance-offering [to the Temple and to sacrifice it there in honor of the festival M. Hag. 1:1].

B.   [When the framer of the foregoing statement makes explicit use of the inclusionary language, all,] what [classification of persons is] included, [that otherwise would have been omitted]?

C.   It is to include a person who is half-slave and half-free. [Such a person is subject to the stated liability of bringing an appearance-offering. But a person who is wholly a slave is exempt from the stated requirement of making the pilgrimage and bringing the offering.]

D.   But in the view of Rabina, who has made the statement that one who is half slave and half free [also] is exempt from the obligation of bringing an appearance-offering [in celebration of the pilgrim festival and in his view], what [classification of persons] is included [by the specification that all are subject to the stated obligation]?

[3]Ex. XXIII, 17: <u>Three times in the year all thy males shall appear before the Lord God</u>. The Scriptural text is all-inclusive, hence the Mishnaic 'All' must deal with a case which, but for its redundant 'all', one would have excluded from the obligation to appear.

[4]A full slave is free because <u>'before the Lord God'</u> is interpreted to mean: only those who have but one Lord or Master, i.e., excluding the slave, who has a terrestrial master in addition to the Eternal Lord to serve. If owned by two masters, one of whom frees him, the slave becomes half freed, and stays half slave.

[5]The word <u>regel</u> in Hebrew may mean either <u>'foot'</u> or <u>'festival'</u> (on the three festivals the men <u>'footed'</u> it to Jerusalem). Hence the inference that only those who could foot it normally are obliged to appear on these three festivals, which excludes a lame man.

[6]There are two views as to the statement of the Mishnah (Hag. 9a: One who has made no offering on the first day of the feast must make up, or has the opportunity to make up for it, throughout the other days of the festival), the first holding that each day has its own obligation; hence even if the worshipper was unfit on the first day of the festival, provided he is fit on the next, he is not exempt on the other days <u>per se</u> imposing the obligation, whilst the other considers only the first day imposing the obligation of an offering. Consequently, if he was disqualified on the first day, or free of that obligation, he would be exempt a complementary offering. The practical difference, in our case, would be this: One who on the

E.   It is to include a person who is lame on the first day of the festival but is restored [to full activity] on the second day. [A lame person is exempt from the religious obligation of coming up to Jerusalem on the pilgrim festival, since he obviously cannot make the trip. If, however, as of the second day of the festival, the lame person should be healed, then, according to the formulation of the rule at hand, such a person would become obligated, retroactively, to bring the required appearance-offering, as of the first day.]

F.   [The foregoing statement rests on the position that on the successive days of the festival, one has the option of meeting an obligation incurred but not met on the earlier day. Thus if one did not make the required appearance-offering on the first day, he is obligated for it but also may make up for it on the later days of the festival. The obligation for one day pertains to, but then may be made up, on the days following, thus, on day three for day two, on day four for day three, and the like. Accordingly, at E we maintain, first, that the person becomes obligated on the second day, and, second, that the obligation then is retroactive to the first. So he can make up what he owes. But the obligation to begin with likewise is retroactive. On day two he became obligated for an appearance-offering to cover day one. Accordingly, what we have just proposed] fully accords with the position of him who said that offerings made on] all [of the days of the festival] serve as a means of carrying out the obligations incurred on each one of them [as just now explained].

G.   But in the view of him who

first day of the festival had been lame, hence not obliged to offer the festal sacrifices, would be free according to the second view, but according to the first, would be obliged to make the offering on one of the subsequent days of the festival.

[7]The massoretic text y-r-'-h may be accentuated to read either yir'eh (he will see) or yera'eh (he will be seen). The first reading applied to the Lord, the second to the Israelite appearing before Him, would be thus interpreted: Just as the Lord sees him 'with two eyes' i.e., with undisturbed vision, so shall the worshipper be one appearing with both eyes intact, i.e., with undiminished sight. For an alternative rendering v. Hag., Sonc. ed., p. 3. n. 3. Or, if you like, say this: In truth it is meant to include one who is half slave and half freed man, and if the view of Rabina should appear as the difficulty, this is no difficulty either; the first view is in accord with the former Mishnah, the second with the later Mishnah. For we learnt: One who is half slave and half freed man shall serve himself one day and his master the other -- thus Beth Hillel. Said Beth Shammai to them: You took care of the interests of his master, but you have done nothing [thereby] on his behalf. For he is unable to marry either a female slave or free woman. Shall he do without marriage? But the world was created only for propagation of the species, as it is said: He created it not a waste. He formed it to be inhabited. Rather, for the sake of the social welfare we force his master to set him free, and the slave writes out a document of indebtedness covering the other half of his value. Beth Hillel retracted and taught as Beth Shammai.

says that all of the days of the festival [may serve to make up only for an obligation] incurred on the first day [of the festival alone, so that, first, one does not incur an obligation on a later day of the festival affecting what one owes for an earlier day of the festival, and so that, second, if one is not obligated to bring an appearance-offering on the first day of the festival, he is not obligated to bring such an offering to all, what category of persons] is included [by use of the inclusionary language, all]?

H. It serves to include a person who is blind in one eye. [A person blind in both eyes is exempt from the appearance-offering on the pilgrim festival. One fully sighted, of course, is liable. The intermediate category then is dealt with in the stated formulation].

I. Now that view would not accord with the following teaching in the authority of sages of the Mishnah, as it has been taught:

J. Yohanan b. Dahabbai says in the name of R. Judah, "One who is blind in one eye is exempt from the religious duty of bringing an appearance-offering, for it is said, 'He will see... he will see...' (Ex. 23:14) [reading the scriptural language not as 'make an appearance,' but, with a shift in the vowels, 'will see,' cf. T. Hag. 1:1].

K. "[The proposed mode of reading the verse at hand yields the following consequence:] Just as one comes to see [the face of the Lord], so he comes to be seen. Just as one sees with two eyes, so one is seen with two eyes" [cf. T. Hag. 1:1F-H]. [The exegesis then excludes a person blind in one eye.]

L. If you prefer, [however, we may revert to the earlier proposal, and] state: Indeed, [the use of the inclusionary language 'all' is meant] to include a person who is half slave and half free.

M. And now as to the question you raised above [D], that that position would not accord with the opinion of Rabina, that indeed poses no problem.

N. [Why not?] The formulation at hand, [which prohibits the half-slave half-free man from bringing the necessary offering] is in line with the original formulation of the Mishnah-law [prior to the debate, cited presently, between the Houses of Shammai and Hillel]. The other formulation [which permits and hence requires the half-slave half-free person, in the intermediate status, to bring the appearance-offering] is in line with the posterior formulation of the Mishnah-law.

O. For we have learned [at M. Git. 4:5:]

P. "He who is half-slave and half-free works for his master one day and for himself one day," the words of the House of Hillel.

Q. Said to them the House of Shammai, "You have taken good care of his master, but of himself you have not taken care.

R. "To marry a slave-girl is not possible, for half of him after all is free [and free persons may marry only free persons.]

S. "[To marry] a free woman is not possible, for half of him after all is a slave [and slaves may marry only other slaves.]

T. "Shall he refrain?

U. "But was not the world made only for procreation, as it is said, 'He created it not a waste, he formed it to be inhabited' (Is. 45:18).

V.   "But: For the good order of the world,

"they force his master to free him.

W.   "And he [the slave] writes him a bond covering half his value."

X.   And the House of Hillel reverted to teach in accord with the opinion of the House of Shammai. [Accordingly, the law prior to the reversion specified at X treated one who is half-slave and half-free as in a fixed category, and such a one would not bring an appearance-offering, since he was partially a slave. But after the reversion, one who was half-slave and half-free could leave that interstitial category easily and so would not be regarded as essentially a slave. Such a one then would be obligated to bring the appearance-offering, there being no permanent lord over him except for the Lord God.]

What does 'All are obliged to sound the shofar' mean to include? -- That includes a minor who has reached the age of training, for we learnt: One does not prevent a minor from blowing the shofar on the festival.[1]

[1]R.H. 32b. The source quoted does not seem to fit the inference made, for the answer postulates evidence that a minor is obliged to sound the shofar, whereas the reference quoted refers to the fact that one does not prevent a minor from sounding the horn, which allows for the possibility of his being neither obliged nor forbidden to sound it. There is a lacuna in the text which Tosaf. s.v. 'yn m^{c}kbyn supplies, from R.H. 33a, where such obligation is definitely stated.

V.   A. **All are obligated [to the religious duty of hearing] the sounding of the ram's horn [on the New Year, T.R.H. 4:1]**

B.   [When the framer of the passage makes use of the inclusionary language, all,] what [classification of persons does he thereby] include?

C.   It is to include a minor who has reached the age [at which he is able to benefit from] instruction.

D.   For we have learned [in a teaching attributed to the authority of Mishnah-sages:] They do not prevent a minor from sounding the ram's horn on the festival day.

'All are obliged to read the scroll. All are fit to read the scroll.' What are these meant to include? -- [3a] They are meant to include women, in accord with the view of R. Joshua b. Levi; for R. Joshua b. Levi said: Women are obliged to read the scroll because they too, had a part in that miracle.[1] What does 'All are obliged to arrange zimmun[2] mean to include? -- It means to include women and slaves, for it was taught: Women are under the obligation of zimmun amongst themselves, and slaves are under the obligation of zimmun amongst themselves. What does 'All may be joined to a zimmun' mean to include? -- That includes a minor who knows to Whom one pronounces a blessing. What does 'All defile by reason of their flux' include? -- That includes a child one day old, for it was taught: [It could have said,] When a man [hath an issue out of his flesh].' Why does the text state 'any man'? That is to include a child one day old, [teaching] that he defiles by reason of his flux; this is the view of R. Judah. R. Ishmael the son of R. Johanan b. Beroka says: [This inference] is not necessary, for behold, Scripture reads: And of them that have an issue whether it be a male or a female, i.e., once he is 'a male,' however minor or major, once she is 'a female,' whether minor or major. If so, why does the Torah use [the redundant phrase] 'any man'? The Torah speaks in the language of man.[3]

[1] V. Meg. 4a, Rashi and Tosaf. Either they too were included in Haman's decree of extinction, or their

VI. A. All are subject to the religious obligation of hearing the reading of the Scroll of Esther, [T. Meg. 2:7A-B].

B. All are suitable to read the Scroll of Esther aloud [for the community, thereby fulfilling the religious obligation of all those who are present, M. Meg. 2:4].

C. [When the framer of the passage makes use of the inclusionary language, all,] what [classification of persons does he thereby] include [3A]?

D. It is to include women [who may read the Scroll of Esther aloud for the community and thereby carry out the obligation of all present to do so].

E. This view accords with the position of R. Joshua b. Levi. For R. Joshua b. Levi said, "Women are liable [to the religious duty of] the reading of the Scroll of Esther, for they too were included in the miracle [of redemption from Israel's enemies, celebrated on Purim]."

VII. A. All are liable to the religious duty of saying Grace in public quorum [if they have eaten together. They thus may not say Grace after meals by themselves, if a quorum of three persons is present. In that circumstance a public recitation, involving a call to Grace, is required, T. Ber. 5:15.]

B. [When the framer of the rule uses the inclusionary word, all,] what [classification of persons does he mean to] include?

C. He means to include women and slaves.

D. For it has been taught [in a teaching bearing the authority of Mishnah-teachers:] Women say Grace in public as a group [unto] themselves, and

merit, too, brought about the miracle of the deliverance.

[2]Ber. 45a: Three who ate together are under the obligation of <u>zimmun</u>, i.e. of saying grace together. Literally <u>zimmun</u> means appointing and may thus refer to the appointment to eat together, with the implied obligation to say grace together.

[3]The repetition of the word '<u>man</u>' is redundant. '<u>Ish</u> <u>ish</u>' means every man, any man.

slaves do likewise. [Accordingly, both classifications of persons are subject to the liability of saying a public Grace, should a quorum of appropriate persons be present].

VIII.   A.   All join in the public saying of Grace [responding to the call to say Grace].

B.   [When the framer of the ruler uses the cited inclusionary language,] what [classification of persons] does he mean to include?

C.   It is to include a minor who has knowledge on his own concerning Him to whom they say a blessing [in the Grace after meals].

D.   That is in line with what R. Nahman said, "He who knows to Whom they say a blessing [in the Grace after meals] -- they include such a one in the public call to say the Grace after meals."

IX.   A.   <u>All are subject to becoming unclean by reason of the flux [specified at Lev. 15:1ff</u>, M. Zab. 2:1].

B.   [When the framer of the rule uses the cited inclusionary language,] what [classification of persons does he mean to] include?

C.   It is to include an infant one day old [who, should he produce a flux, would be deemed subject to flux-uncleanness under appropriate circumstances. This form of genital uncleanness is not limited to an adult.]

D.   For it has been taught [in a teaching bearing the authority of Mishnah-sages:] "'[When any] man [produces flux out of his flesh]' (Lev. 15:2).

E.   "Now why does the Author of Scripture state, 'When any man...' [so indicating an inclusion of some category beyond man]?

F. "It is to include even an infant a day old, who thus is subject to the uncleanness of flux," the words of R. Judah.

G. R. Ishmael, the son of R. Yohanan b. Beroqah, says, "It is hardly necessary [to interpret Scripture in such wise]. Lo, [Scripture] says, 'And any of them who has an issue, whether it is male or female' (Lev. 15:33).

H. "[The sense is], 'Male,' meaning, whoever is male, whether minor or adult. 'Female' [means], whoever is female, whether minor or adult. [Both categories, minor and adult, male and female, fall within the classification of those subject to uncleanness through flux. Scripture is explicit in this matter, without the necessity of interpreting the language important in Judah's view.]

I. "If that is the case, then on what account does [the Author of Scripture] use the language, 'If any man...'? [The Author of] the Torah made use of the language of common speech [and did not mean to provide occasions for exegesis of minor details of formulation]."

Let me conclude by stating why I think the present approach improves upon the former one. In my view the work of transmitting an ancient text to a new generation should go on so long as new readers in successive ages come to the classic document. No great text of antiquity has ever reached English only one time, and then for all time. As I said, just as one generation after another has taken up the challenge of translating and therefore interpreting Plato and Aristotle, Euripides and Herodotus, not to mention the Hebrew Scriptures and the New Testament, so the classics of Judaism, the Mishnah, the Tosefta, the several scriptural-exegetical compilations ("midrashim"), the Talmud of the Land of Israel, and the Talmud of Babylonia demand renewed encounter in age succeeding age. The reason is not solely the possibility that a better text, better lexicographical aids, better interpretative commentaries, become available. In the case of Bavli, that presently is certainly not the case. It is that a new generation simply raises a fresh set of questions and so wants a translation that addresses its concerns in particular.

In my case and in that of my colleagues at work on the other tractates of the Talmud of Babylonia, we come with all due respect for the achievements of our predecessors. If in any aspect we improve upon their work, the reason is that, to begin with, we build upon what they already have achieved. What we want to know, which the Soncino generation did not, is several things. First, how the materials of the Bavli fall into diverse genres; second, how the framers of the document arranged their discussion of the Mishnah; third, what sorts of materials, in addition to those serving as Mishnah-exegesis, they constructed or borrowed, and fourth, how they proposed to put the whole together.

In other words, apart from occasional improvements in the understanding of a passage, though we would not claim that that is common, our principal contribution lies in the more analytical character of our translation than that which came before. We do not present long columns of undifferentiated type, broken up merely by paragraphs. We distinguish from one another the large-scale and complete discussions of problems or topics. Within these large-scale discussions we distinguish one completed thought from another. In our remarks at the end of each of the discussions of a Mishnah-paragraph, we furthermore comment on the relationship to the Mishnah-paragraph at hand of the completed units of thought of the Bavli.

For the reader who does not know Hebrew and Aramaic at all, we add an enormous quantity of explanatory language, included in square brackets in the text, to make the text readable and accessible in its own terms. The footnotes of the Soncino translators simply do not lead a reader through the text. In most instances, the Soncino translators take for granted a fundamental comprehension of the text in Aramaic that, if widely present, would have rendered the work of translation superfluous to begin with. To put matters more bluntly, where the text is not self-evidently accessible, the Soncino translators do not seem to me to make it so. My principal contribution is to attempt to remedy this enormous failing in the otherwise superb work of those who attempted the work before now.

We readily add our hope that those who in a coming generation will undertake yet another translation will improve upon what we have done. So, in all, successive ages will call forth translators who aim at making clear and readily understood in the host-language what hithertofore has been puzzling and essentially incomprehensible (however elegantly worded). In all, therefore, we do not apologize to our predecessors in the on-going work of translating the great text at hand, while we also do not for one minute denigrate their contribution. We recognize the abiding value of what they did, and we hope that for another age we may improve upon what is now available.

It goes without saying, moreover, that as scholarship in the Bavli's Aramaic becomes accessible in dictionaries, as study of the text and exegesis of its meanings reaches still higher levels, and as a critical edition and commentary come to realization, translators will bring to the text at hand a still deeper grasp of its meanings than we do. We should label this translation "preliminary," if it were not so self-evident to us that any translation of the Talmud of Babylonia at this primitive stage in our knowledge must be preliminary. We work on translation before the completion of a critical text, a competent dictionary, and a reliable commentary drawing upon the exegetical achievements of all times. On that basis, any translation must be regarded as temporary and, at best, a mere expedient.

My former student and friend, Professor Alan J. Avery-Peck, subjected my translation to a detailed comparison with the original Hebrew-Aramaic text and contributed numerous, important corrections, as well as improvements in style and in interpretation. I am grateful to him for his painstaking and prompt work in my behalf.

INTRODUCTION

The tractate at hand takes up three closely related matters of the holy life: reciting the Shema ("Hear O Israel"), reciting the Prayer, and uttering blessings said when eating various foods and in the grace after meals, as well as on other occasions besides formal prayer and meal-time. About a third of the tractate is devoted to each of the three topics. In my Judaism: The Evidence of the Mishnah (Chicago, 1981), pp. 357-8, Zahavy provides the following outline of the tractate:

I. Reciting the Shema. 1:1-3:8

    A.   The time for saying the Shema, evening and morning. 1:1-3

    B.   The liturgy of saying the Shema and the text of the Shema itself. 1:4-2:3

    C.   Special cases in which the requirement to say the Shema is suspended or does not apply. 2:4-3:8

II. Reciting the Prayer. 4:1-5:5

    A.   The time for reciting the Prayer. 4:1-2

    B.   The liturgy of the Prayer. 4:3-4

    C.   Special cases in which the requirement to say the Prayer is suspended or does not apply. 4:5-5:1

    D.   Additions to the Prayer. 5:2-5

III. Blessings for food and for meals. 6:1-8:8

    A.   Categories of foods and saying a blessing before eating them. 6:1-7

    B.   The grace after meals and its protocol. 6:8-7:5

    C.   Special rules regarding blessings at meals and other rites connected with meals. 8:1-8

IV. Other kinds of blessings and private prayers. 9:1-5

While the tractate draws upon various verses of Scripture, its principal themes do not emerge from coherent passages of Scripture. Rather, once people know that there is a requirement to recite the Shema, the Prayer, and the Grace after Meals, they find in Scripture relevant statements. Albeck in Seder Zeraim lists the following verses as the scriptural basis for tractate Berakhot:

1. The Shema (first paragraph only)

Deuteronomy 6:4-9:

"Hear, O Israel: The Lord our God is one Lord; and you shall love the Lord your God with all your heart, and with all your soul, and with all your might. And these words which I command you this day shall be upon your heart; and you shall teach them diligently to your children, and shall talk of them when you sit in your house, and when you walk by the way, and when you lie down, and when you rise. And you shall bind them as a sign upon your hand, and they shall be as frontlets between your eyes. And you shall write them on the doorposts of your house and on your gates."

2. Grace after Meals

Deuteronomy 8:10:

"And you shall eat and be full, and you shall bless the Lord your God for the good land he has given you."

3. Other Pertinent Verses

Deuteronomy 11:18-20:

"You shall therefore lay up these words of mine in your heart and in your soul; and you shall bind them as a sign upon your hand, and they shall be as frontlets between your eyes. And you shall teach them to your children, talking of them when you are sitting in your house, and when you are walking by the way, and when you lie down, and when you rise. And you shall write them upon the doorposts of your house and upon your gates..."

The translation of both the Mishnah and the Tosefta of Berakhot is by T. Zahavy. I have made extensive revisions throughout, but the division of the passages and the basic work of translating are his achievement. His Mishnah-Berakhot appears in J. Neusner,

The Mishnah. A New Translation (New Haven & London, 1985: Yale University Press), and Tosefta-Berakhot in J. Neusner and R.S. Sarason, eds., Tosefta Zeraim (New York, 1984: Ktav Publishing House).

I consulted Maurice Simon, Berakoth. Translated into English with notes, glossary, and indices (London, 1948: Soncino Press). In the text a translation taken directly from Simon is marked [Simon], and where I cite nearly verbatim a footnote of his, I indicate with a page and footnote number as well.

1:1

A. From what time do they recite the Shema in the evening?

B. From the hour that the priests [who had immersed after uncleanness and awaited sunset to complete the process of purification] enter [a state of cleanness, the sun having set, so as] to eat their heave offering --

C. "until the end of the first watch," the words of R. Eliezer.

D. And sages say, "Until midnight."

E. Rabban Gamaliel says, "Until the rise of dawn."

F. M^{C}sh s: His sons came from the banquet hall.

G. They said to him, "We do not recite the Shema."

H. He said to them, "If the morning star has not yet risen, you are obligated to recite [the Shema]."

I. And not only [in] this [case], rather, all [commandments] which sages said [may be performed] until midnight, their religious duty to do them applies until the rise of the morning star.

J. [For example], as to the offering of the fats and entrails -- the religious duty to do them applies until the rise of the morning star.

K. All [sacrifices] which are eaten for one day, their religious duty to do them applies until the rise of the morning star.

L. If so why did sages say [that these actions may be performed only] until midnight?

M. In order to keep a man far from sin.

I.

A. On what basis does the Tannaite authority stand when he begins by teaching the rule, "From what time...," [in the assumption that the religious duty to recite the Shema has somewhere been established? In point of fact, it has not been established that people have to recite the Shema at all.]

B. Furthermore, on what account does he teach the rule concerning the evening at the beginning? Why not start with the morning?

C. The Tannaite authority stands upon the authority of Scripture, [both in requiring the recitation of the Shema and in beginning with the evening], for it is written, "When you lie down and when you rise up" (Deut. 6:7).

D.   And this is the sense of the passage: When is the time for the recitation of the Shema when one lies down? It is from the hour that the priests enter [a state of cleanness so as] to eat their heave-offering [M. 1:1B].

E.   And if you prefer, I may propose that the usage derives from the order of the description of creation, for it is said, "And there was evening, and there was morning, one day" (Gen. 1:5).

F.   If there were the principal consideration, then let us take note of the formulation of the rules that occurs later on: In the morning one says two blessings before reciting the Shema and one afterward, and in the evening, one says two blessings before hand and two afterward [M. 1:4]. [The formulation therefore ignores the order of the description of creation.]

G.   [By the reasoning just now proposed,] should not the Tannaite authority speak first of evening?

H.   The Tannaite authority at hand began by discussing matters pertaining to the Shema recited in the evening, and then he proceeded to take up matters having to do with reciting the Shema at dawn. While dealing with the matters having to do with the dawn, he proceeded to spell out other rules on the same matter, and then, only at the end, he went on to spell out other matters having to do with the evening.

II.

A.   A master stated: From the hour that the priests [who had immersed after uncleanness and awaited sunset to complete the process of purification] enter [a state of cleanness, the sun having set, so as] to eat their heave-offering [M. 1:1B].

B.   In point of fact, when is it that priest actually eats food in the status of heave-offering [having completed the process of purification]? Is it not when the stars come out? So let the frame of the passage say simply, "From when the stars come out."

C.   His intent was to inform about a quite distinct matter en passent, namely, When in fact do priests eat heave-offering [once the process of purification has been completed]? It is from the time that the stars come out.

D.   And lo, what he further tells us is that the rite of atonement for having been unclean [an element of the rite of purification] is not essential [to the matter of eating food in the status of heave-offering].

E.   For it has been taught on Tannaite authority:

F.   "And when the sun sets and the day is clear [for eating heave-offering]" (Lev. 22:7).

G.   The sense is that the setting of the sun is what is essential in permitting the priest to eat food in the status of heave-offering, and the completion of the purification rite through an atonement sacrifice is not essential in permitting the priest to eat food in the status of heave-offering.

H.   How do we know that the sense of the words is, "And the sun sets so that the day is clear"?

I.   [2B] Perhaps the sense is, "When the sun comes [up the next day], then the man will be clean"?

J.   Said Rabbah bar R. Shila, "If that were the case, Scripture would have had to say, 'And he <u>will be</u> clean.' What is the sense of 'and it is clear'? The meaning is that the day clears out, as people say, 'The sun has set and the day has cleared out.'"

K.   In the West [in the Land of Israel] this statement of Rabbah b. R. Shila was not available, so they framed the matter in this way: "Does the expression, 'And the sun sets,' refer to the setting of the sun? And what is the sense of 'will be clean'? Does it mean that the day is clear, or perhaps that the appearance of the sun is such that the man becomes clean?"

L.   They went and solved the problem by reference to a Tannaite teaching, for it has been taught in a Tannaite teaching:

M.   **A mnemonic for the matter consists in the appearance of the stars [T. Ber. 1:1D].**

N.   That mnemonic then bears the implication that the reference is to sunset, with the sense of "will be clean" that the day will be clear.

III.

A.   A master has said: <u>From the hour that the priests [who had immersed after uncleanness and awaited sunset to complete the process of purification] enter [a state of cleanness, the sun having set, so as] to eat their heave-offering [M. 1:1B]</u>:

B.   An objection was raised on the basis of the following statement:

C.   From what time do people recite the <u>Shema</u> in the evening? From when a poor man goes in to eat his bread and salt, until he stands up to leave his meal.

D.   The second clause [limiting the time for reading the <u>Shema</u> to a brief interval] assuredly contradicts the Mishnah-passage before us.

E.   But as to the former passage, may we say that there is a disagreement between the cited version and the Mishnah-passage at hand?

F.   No, not necessarily so. Since the poor man and the priest are subject to the same specification of the appropriate time for eating the meal, [namely, at sunset, the two statements simply refer to the same hour in different ways].

IV.

A.   An objection was raised [from a different version of the rule at hand:]

B.   **From what time does one recite the Shema in the evening? [M. Ber. 1:1A]**

C.   **"From the time that people go to eat their meal on the eve of the Sabbath," the words of R. Meir.**

D.   **And sages say, "From the time that the priests are permitted to eat their heave-offering [M. Ber. 1:1B].**

E.   **"A mnemonic for the matter [which designates the proper time] is the emergence of the stars."**

F.   **Even though there is no [explicit Scriptural] proof for the matter, there is an allusion to the matter [in the verse,] So we labored at the work and half of them held the spears from the break of dawn till the stars came out (Neh. 4:15 [= RSV 4:21]) [T. Ber. 1:1A-E].**

G.   And Scripture further states, "That in the night they may be a guard for us and may labor in the day" (Neh. 4:16).

H. What is the sense of this further proof-text?

I. It is this: should you ask, "Now the night indeed begins with sunset, but they, for their part, got up and left early and, furthermore, came home early as well," [I prove my case with the verse, to which] you should pay heed: "That in the night they may be a guard for us and may labor in the day" (Neh. 4:16).

J. [Reverting to the point at which we begin:] Now you presumably maintain that the poor person and ordinary folk are subject to the same specification of time for supper. [Hence we take for granted that the poor man of unit III and the people of the cited passage of Tosefta eat at the same time.]

K. But if you maintain that the poor man and the priest are subject to the same specification of time [as unit III has said], then we find that sages and R. Meir say the same thing. [That is impossible, since the point of the passage at hand is that they are in disagreement.]

L. That surely proves that a poor man is subject to one specification of time, and a priest to a different specification of time.

M. No, not necessarily so. A poor man and a priest are subject to a single specification of time, but a poor man and ordinary folk are not subject to the same specification of time.

N. Is it then the case that the poor man and the priest really accord with the same specification of time [at which they eat supper]?

O. An objection was raised from the following:

P. "From what time do people start to recite the Shema in the evening? From the moment at which, on the eve of the Sabbath, the day is sanctified [by sunset]," the words of R. Eliezer.

Q. R. Joshua says, "From the time that priests have attained cleanness so as to eat their heave-offering."

R. R. Meir says, "From the time that priests immerse so as to be able to eat heave-offering."

S. Said R. Judah to him, "But do not the priests immerse while it is day?"

T. R. Hanina says, "From the time that a poor man goes in to eat his bread and salt."

U. R. Ahai, and some say, R. Aha, says, "From the time that most people go in to recline [at their meal]."

V. Now if you maintain that the poor man and the priest are subject to a single specification of time, then R. Hanina and R. Joshua are saying the same thing.

W. Does it not follow, then, that the specification of time for reciting the Shema for a poor man is different from the specification of time for the priest?

X. It does indeed follow.

Y. Which of the specified times comes later?

Z. It is reasonable to assume that that of the poor man comes later.

AA. For if you maintain that that of the poor man comes earlier [than that of the priest], it follows that R. Hanina is saying the same thing as R. Eliezer.

BB. Does it not then follow that the time for the poor man to recite the <u>Shema</u> is later than the time for the priest?

CC. It does indeed follow.

<u>V.</u>

A.   A master has said: "Said to him R. Judah, 'But do not the priests immerse while it is still day?'"

B.   R. Judah's reply to R. Meir is a good one.

C.   This is what R. Meir can reply to him, "Do you suppose that I make reference to twilight as you define it? I make reference to twilight as R. Yose defines it."

D.   R. Yose has said, "Twilight lasts for as long as the blinking of an eye. As soon as the one [night] comes in, the other [day] goes out. It is not possible to fix it exactly. [Simon, p. 5, n. 6: And consequently the priests may bathe at twilight as defined by R. Yose since it is still day, and one may also recite the <u>Shema</u> at that time since it is practically night]."

E.   [3A] The views of R. Meir appear to contradict one another [since he says people recite the <u>Shema</u> when they come home for supper on the Sabbath night, and that is after twilight, but he also sets a time that is prior to twilight].

F.   What we have in hand are the versions of two different Tannaite authorities concerning the opinion of R. Meir.

G.   The views of R. Eliezer appear to contradict one another [as before].

H.   What we have in hand are the versions of two different Tannaite authorities concerning the opinion of R. Eliezer.

I.   Or, if you prefer, I shall propose that the first of the two opinions does not belong to R. Eliezer at all.

<u>VI.</u>

A.   "<u>Until the end of the first watch</u>," the words of R. Eliezer [M. 1:1C].

B.   What is R. Eliezer's view [about the division of the night-watches]?

C.   If he takes the view that the night is divided into three watches, let him say, "Until four hours [have passed in the night]."

D.   If he takes the view that the night is divided into four watches, let him say, "Until three hours [have passed in the night]."

E.   In point of fact he takes the view that the night is divided into three watches. And by phrasing matters as he does, he informs us that there are watches in the firmament and watches on earth, [and these correspond].

F.   For it has been taught on Tannaite authority:

G.   R. Eliezer says, "The night is divided into three watches, and [in heaven] over each watch the Holy One, blessed be he, sits and roars like a lion,

H.   "as it is said, 'The Lord roars from on high and raises his voice from his holy habitation, roaring he does roar because of his fold' (Jer. 25:30).

I.   "The indication of each watch is as follows: at the first watch, an ass brays, at the second, dogs yelp, at the third, an infant sucks at its mother's breast or a woman whispers to her husband."

J.   What is R. Eliezer's reckoning?

K.   If he is reckoning from the beginning of the several watches, then what need is there to give a sign for the beginning of the first watch? It is twilight.

L.   If he is reckoning from the end of the several watches, then what need is there to give a sign for the end of the third watch? It is marked by the coming of the day.

M.   But he is reckoning at the end of the first watch, beginning of the last, and the middle of the middle watch, and that is what the specified signs indicate.

N.   Or, if you prefer, I shall propose that in all cases he reckons from the end of the watches. And, as to your question, why is it necessary to specify the end of the third watch, for what difference would it make?

O.   The answer is this: It is important for the recitation of the Shema in the case of someone who sleeps in a darkened room and does not know when it is time for reciting the Shema: When a woman whispers to her husband or an infant sucks from the breast of its mother, it is time for him to get up and to recite the Shema.

VII.

A.   Said R. Isaac bar Samuel in the name of Rab, "The night is divided into three watches, and over each watch, the Holy One, blessed be he, sits and roars like a lion.

B.   "He says, 'Woe to the children, on account of whose sins I have wiped out my house and burned my palace, and whom I have exiled among the nations of the world.'"

VIII.

A.   It has been taught on Tannaite authority:

B.   Said R. Yose, "Once I was going along the way, and I went into one of the ruins of Jerusalem to pray. Elijah, of blessed memory, came and watched over me at the door until I had finished my prayer. After I had finished my prayer, he said to me, 'Peace be to you, my lord.'

C.   "And I said to him, 'Peace be to you, my lord and teacher.'

D.   "And he said to me, 'My son, on what account did you go into this ruin?'

E.   "And I said to him, 'To pray.'

F.   "And he said to me, 'You would have done better to pray on the road.'

G.   "And I said to him, 'I was afraid lest some bypassers interrupt me.'

H.   "He said to me, 'You would have been better off to say an abbreviated form of the prayer.'

I.   "Thus I learned three lessons from him. I learned that people should not go into ruins, I learned that people may say a prayer on the road, and I learned that if one is praying on the road, he should say an abbreviated version of the prayer.

J.   "And he said to me, 'My son, what sound did you hear in this ruin?'

K.   "I said to him, 'I heard the sound of an echo moaning like a pigeon and saying, "Woe to the children, on account of whose sins I have wiped out my house and burned my palace and whom I have exiled among the nations of the world."'

L.   "He said to me, 'By your life and the life of your head, it is not only at this moment that the echo speaks in such a way, but three times daily, it says the same thing.

M.   "'And not only so, but when Israelites go into synagogues and schoolhouses and respond, "May the great name be blessed," the Holy One shakes his head and says, "Happy is the king, whom they praise in his house in such a way! What does a father have, who has exiled his children? And woe to the children who are exiled from their father's table!"'"

IX.

A.   Our rabbis have taught on Tannaite authority:

B.   For three reasons people should not go into a ruin, because of suspicion [of an assignation there], because of the danger of collapse, and because of demons."

C.   [Why mention all three reasons?] "Because of suspicion" is not needed, since it would be sufficient to give the reason of danger of a collapse.

D.   [3B] That would not apply to a new ruin.

E.   Then offer as the sole reason "on account of demons."

F.   We deal with a case in which two people go in [and demons do not bother two people].

G.   If there are two people, then there is no consideration of suspicion of an assignation.

H.   It might be two people who are known as licentious.

I.   "Because of the danger of collapse" -- but why not merely because of suspicion and demons? You might have two people who are honorable [in which case the other considerations do not apply].

J.   "Because of demons" -- And why not suffice with the considerations of suspicion or collapse?

K.   You might have the case of a new ruin, and two people who are honorable.

L.   If there are two people, then what consideration of demons is at hand?

M.   In a place which demons inhabit, there is danger [even to two].

N.   If you prefer, I shall propose that we deal only with one person and with a new ruin located in the fields. In such a case there is no consideration of suspicion of an assignation, for women do not go out by themselves to the fields. But there is surely a consideration of demons.

X.

A.   Our rabbis have taught on Tannaite authority:

B.   "The night has four watches," the words of Rabbi.

C.   Rabbi Nathan says, "Three."

D.   What is the Scriptural basis for the view of R. Nathan?

E.   As it is written, "So Gideon and the hundred men that were with him came into the outermost part of the camp in the beginning of the middle watch" (Jud. 7:19).

F.   A Tannaite authority stated, "There can be a middle watch only if there is one before it and one after it" [hence, three] [T. Ber. 1:1G-L].

G.   And, so far as Rabbi is concerned, what is the meaning of, "...middle..."? [How does he explain it?]

H.   The sense of the passage is, one of two middle ones.

I.   But R. Nathan may respond: Is "one of the middle ones" written? What is written is, "the middle one" [of three].

J.   What is the scriptural basis for the view of Rabbi?

K.   Said R. Zeriqa said R. Ammi said R. Joshua b. Levi, "One verse of Scripture says, 'At midnight I rise to give thanks to you because of your righteous ordinances' (Ps. 119:62).

L.   "And another verse of Scripture says, 'My eyes open before the watches' (Ps. 119:148).

M.   "How so [Simon, p. 8, n. 5: that somebody may rise at midnight and still have two watches before him, the minimum of the plural watches being two]?

N.   "The night is divided into four watches."

O.   And R. Nathan accords with the view of R. Joshua.

P.   For we have learned in the Mishnah:

Q.   R. Joshua says, "Until the third hour, for it is the practice of royalty to rise at the third hour" [M. Ber. 1:2E-F].

R.   Six hours of the night and two of the day add up to two watches. [Simon, p. 8, n. 7: Since the day for royal personages begins at eight a.m., that is with the third hour when they rise. David by rising at midnight forestalled them by eight hours, i.e., two watches, each have four hours.]

S.   R. Ashi said, "A watch and a half may also be called 'watches.'"

XI.

A.   And [continuing X K] R. Zeriqa said R. Ammi said R. Joshua b. Levi said, "In the presence of a corpse people may speak only about matters having to do with the deceased."

B.   Said R. Abba bar Kahana, "That rule applies only to speaking about words of Torah, but as to commonplace matters, we have no objection."

C.   And there are those who say, said R. Abba bar Kahana, "That rule applies even to words of Torah, and all the more so to commonplace matters."

XII.

A.   [Reverting to the statement at K that David got up at midnight:] Did David get up at midnight? He got up at dusk of the evening.

B.   For it is written, "I got up with the neshef and cried" (Ps. 119:147).

C.   And this word neshef speaks of the evening, for it is written, "In the neshef, in the evening of the day, in the blackness of the night and the darkness" (Prov. 7:9).

D.   Said R. Oshaiah said R. Aha, "This is the sense of the passage: 'Half the night never passed for me in sleep' [and that is the meaning of Ps. 119:162]."

E.   R. Zira said, "Up to midnight he would doze like a horse, from that point he would regain full energy like a lion.

F.   R. Ashi said, "Up to midnight he would deal with teachings of Torah. From that point he would engage in songs and praises."

G.   But does the word neshef refer to dusk? Surely the word refers to the morning light, for it is written, "And David slew them from the neshef to the evening of the next day" (1 Sam. 30:17), with the sense "from the morning to evening."

H.   No, that is not the sense. Rather, it is from dusk, to dusk on the next day.

I.   If that were the case, the passage should read, "From dusk to dusk" or "from evening to evening."

J.   Rather, said Raba, "The word neshef has two meanings. One refers to the dawn of day, when the evening disappears and the morning comes, and the other to when the day disappears and the evening comes [and neshef in this instance refers to dusk]."

XIII.

A.   Did David really know exactly when it was midnight?

B.   Now Moses, our master, did not know, for it is written, "At about midnight I will go out into the midst of Egypt" (Ex. 11:4).

C.   What is the sense of "at about midnight" cited in the preceding verse?

D.   If I should say that that is language which the Holy One, blessed be he, said to him, that is, "At about midnight," is it possible that before Heaven there is such a doubt [as to the exact time of night? That is impossible.]

E.   Rather, [God] said to him, "At midnight," but Moses is the one who came along and said, "At about midnight."

F.   It follows that he was in doubt as to exactly when it was midnight. Could David then have known exactly when it was?

G.   David had a device for telling when it was.

H.   For R. Aha bar Bizna said R. Simeon the Pious said, "David had a harp suspended over his bed, and when midnight came, the north wind would come and blow on the strings, and the harp would play on its own. David immediately got up and undertook Torah-study until dawn.

I.   "When it was dawn, the sages of Israel came into him. They said to him, 'Our lord, O king, your people Israel needs sustenance.'

J.   "He said to them, 'Let them go and make a living from one another.'

K.   "They said to him, 'A handful [of food] cannot satisfy a lion, and a hole in the ground cannot be filled up from its own clods.'

L.   "He said to them, 'Go and organize marauders.'

M.   "They forthwith took counsel with Ahitophel and sought the advice of the sanhedrin and addressed a question to the Urim and Thumim."

N.   Said R. Joseph, "What verse indicates this? 'And after Ahithofel was Jehoiada, son of Benaiah, and Abiathar, and the captain of the king's host was Joab' (1 Chr. 27:34).

O.   "'Ahithofel was counsellor,' and so it is said, 'Now the counsel of Ahithofel, which he counselled in those days, was as if a man inquired of the word of God' (2 Sam. 16:23).

P.   "[4A] 'Benaiah, son of Jehoiada' refers to the sanhedrin.

Q.   "'And Abiathar' refers to the Urim and Thumim. And so it says, 'And Benaiah, son of Jehoiada, was in charge of the Kerethi and Pelethi' (2 Sam. 20:23).

R.   "Why were the Urim and Thumim so called? They were called 'Kerethi' because their words are decisive [korethim], and 'Pelethi' because they are distinguished (muflaim) through what they say.

S. "And then comes 'the captain of the king's host, Joab.'"

T. Said R. Isaac bar Ada, and some say R. Isaac, son of R. Idid, said, "What is the verse of Scripture that makes this point? 'Awake, my glory, awake, psaltery and harp, I will awake the dawn' (Ps. 57:9)."

U. [Reverting to A-B, F] R. Zira said, "Moses most certainly knew when it was midnight, and so did David.

V. "But since David knew, what did he need a harp for? It was to wake him up from his sleep.

W. "And since Moses also knew, why did he say, 'at about midnight'?

X. "Moses thought that the astrologers of Pharoah might make a mistake and then claim that Moses was a charlatan [should the event not take place exactly when Moses predicted, if he made too close a statement for their powers of calculation]."

Y. For a master has said, "Teach your tongue to say, 'I don't know,' lest you turn out to lie.'"

Z. R. Ashi said, "[The matter of Ex. 11:4] took place at midnight on the night of the thirteenth toward dawn of the fourteenth.

AA. "And this is what Moses said to Israel: 'The Holy One, blessed be he, has said, "Tomorrow at about midnight, at around this time, I shall go forth into the midst of Egypt."'"

XIV.

A. "A prayer of David: Keep my soul, for I am pious" (Ps. 86:1-2).

B. Levi and R. Isaac.

C. One of them said, "This is what David said before the Holy One, blessed be he, 'Lord of the world, am I not pious? For all kings, east and west, sleep to the third hour, but as for me: "At midnight, I rise to give thanks to you" (Ps. 119:62).'"

D. The other said, "This is what David said before the Holy One, blessed be he, 'Lord of the world, am I not pious? For all kings, east and west, sit in all their glory with their retinues, but as for me, my hands are sloppy with menstrual blood and the blood of the foetus and placenta, which I examine so as to declare a woman clean for sexual relations with her husband.

E. "'And not only so, but, further, in whatever I do, I take counsel with Mephibosheth, my master, and I say to him, "Rabbi Mephibosheth, did I do right in the judgment I gave? Did I do right in acquitting? Did I do right in awarding an advantage? Did I do right in declaring something clean? Did I do right in declaring something unclean?" and in no way have I been ashamed [to depend on his judgment].'"

F. Said R. Joshua, son of R. Idi, "What verse of Scripture supports that view of David? 'And I recite your testimonies before kings and am not ashamed' (Ps. 119:46)."

XV.

A. A Tannaite authority stated: His name was not Mephibosheth but Ishbosheth. But why did he bear that name? Because he shamed David in criticizing his legal decisions. Therefore David gained merit so that Kileab [2 Sam. 3:3] should come forth from him."

B.   And R. Yohanan said, "His name was not Kileab but rather Daniel. Why, then, was he called Kileab? Because he shamed Mephibosheth in criticizing his legal decisions.

C.   "And concerning him said Solomon in his sagacity, 'My son, if your heart is wise, my heart will be glad, even mine' (Prov. 23:15).

D.   "And he further said, 'My son, be wise and make my heart glad, that I may answer him who taunts me' (Prov. 27:11)."

XVI.

A.   Now did David really call himself "pious"?

B.   And has it not been written, "I am not sure to see the good reward of the Lord in the land of the living" (Ps. 27:13). [How could David have been unsure, if he knew he was pious?]

C.   A Tannaite authority taught in this connection in the name of R. Yose, "Why are there dots over the word for 'not sure'?

D.   "Said David before the Holy One, blessed be he, 'Lord of the world, I am confident you pay a good reward to the righteous in the coming future, but I do not know if I shall have a share among them or not. Perhaps sin will cause [punishment for me instead of reward]'"

E.   That accords with what R. Jacob bar Idi said, for R. Jacob bar Idi contrasted two verses of Scripture, as follows: "It is written, 'And behold, I am with you and will keep you wherever you go' (Gen. 28:15), and another verse states, 'Then Jacob was greatly afraid' (Gen. 32:8).

F.   "[Why the contrast between God's promise and Jacob's fear?] [Jacob thought to himself,] 'Sin which I have done may cause [punishment for me instead]'"

G.   That accords with what has been taught on Tannaite authority:

H.   "Till your people pass over, O Lord, till your people pass over, that you have acquired" (Ex. 15:16).

I.   "Till your people pass over" refers to the first entry into the land [in Joshua's time].

J.   "Till your people pass over, that you have acquired" refers to the second entry into the land [in the time of Ezra and Nehemiah. Thus a miracle was promised not only on the first occasion, but also on the second. But it did not happen the second time around. Why not?]

K.   On the basis of this statement, sages have said, "The Israelites were worthy of having a miracle performed for them in the time of Ezra also, just as it had been performed for them in the time of Joshua b. Nun, but sin caused [the miracle to be withheld]."

XVII.

A.   And sages say, "Until midnight" [M. 1:1D]:

B.   [Since Eliezer holds that the time of "lying down" is when one goes to bed, on which account Eliezer has the Shema recited only until the end of the first watch, and since Gamaliel allows the Shema to be recited until dawn, understanding "lying down" to refer to the entire period of sleep, we ask:] Which view did sages adopt?

C.   If they take the view of R. Eliezer [that "lying down" refers to going to bed], then let them state, "... in accord with R. Eliezer."

D.   [4B] If they take the view of Rabban Gamaliel [that "lying down" refers to the time in which people sleep], then let them state, "... in accord with Rabban Gamaliel."

E.   In point of fact sages accord with the view of Rabban Gamaliel, but the reason that they have said, "until midnight" is in order to keep a man far from sin [M. 1:1M-N].

F.   This accords with that which has been taught on Tannaite authority:

G.   The sages have established a fence for their rulings.

H.   It is so that a person may not come in from the field in the evening and say, "I shall go to my house, eat a bit, drink a bit, sleep a bit, and afterward I shall recite the Shema and say the Prayer." But then sleep may overtake him, and he will end up sleeping all night long.

I.   Rather a person should come in from the field in the evening and go directly into the synagogue. If he is in the habit of reciting Scripture, then let him recite Scripture, and if he is in the habit of repeating Mishnah sayings, then let him repeat Mishnah-sayings, and then let him recite the Shema and say the Prayer. Only then should he eat his bread and say the blessing [and sleep].

J.   And whoever violates the teachings of sages is liable to death.

K.   Now why is it that in all other passages the Tannaite formulation does not include the statement that one may be liable to death, while in the present case the Tannaite formulation includes the words, "And he is liable to death"?

L.   If you wish, I shall propose that there is the consideration that sleep might come inadvertently [so ordinarily there would be no penalty, but here there is a penalty even in a case of inadvertence.]

M.   And if you wish, I shall propose that the reason is that the formulation serves, as an additional teaching, to exclude the view of him who says, "The recitation of the Prayer in the evening is an optional matter."

N.   In phrasing matters in this way, we are informed that it is obligatory.

XVIII.

A.   A Master has said, "He recites the Shema and says the Prayer."

B.   This supports the view of R. Yohanan.

C.   For R. Yohanan has said, "Who belongs to the world to come? It is one who places the recitation of the blessing for the redemption from Egypt right next to the recitation of the Prayer in the evening [and thus recites the Shema and the Prayer in sequence]."

D.   And R. Joshua b. Levi says, "The [sages] ordained that the Prayers should be said in the middle [between the two recitations of the Shema, morning and night. Thus there will be the Shema, one Prayer, then, at dark the next Prayer and then the final Shema]."

E.   What is the point at issue?

F.   If you wish, I may propose that at issue is the exegesis of a verse of Scripture, and if you wish, I shall propose that it is a point of reasoning.

G.   If you wish I shall propose that it is a point of reasoning:

H.   R. Yohanan takes the view that while the redemption from Egypt took place in the full light of day, there was an act of redemption by night as well, [on which account the blessing for the redemption from Egypt must be stated at night in sequence with the recitation of the Prayer, which, after all, includes prayers for personal and national redemption].

I.   And R. Joshua b. Levi takes the view that since the full redemption took place only by day, the redemption by night was not really of like order [with the equivalent, opposite consequence].

J.   If you wish, I shall propose that at issue is the exegesis of a verse of Scripture. In fact, both authorities interpret a single verse.

K.   It is written, "When you lie down and when you rise up" (Deut. 6:7).

L.   R. Yohanan takes the theory that Scripture therefore establishes an analogy between lying down and rising up. Just as, when one gets up, he recites the Shema and afterward says the Prayer, so when he lies down, he also says the Shema and afterward says the Prayer.

M.   R. Joshua b. Levi theorizes that the analogy serves to compare lying down to rising up. Just as when one gets up, the recitation of the Shema is accomplished close to the point at which he gets out of bed, so when he lies down, the recitation of the Shema should be close to the point at which he goes to bed.

N.   To the theory at hand Mar, son of Rabina, objected, "In the evening one recites two blessings before it and two blessings after it [M. Ber. 1:4]. Now if you maintain that one has to set one thing near the other, lo, in this case a person does not set the blessing for redemption next to the Prayer, for lo, he has to say the prayer beginning, 'Cause us to lie down in peace...' [So the reasoning of Joshua b. Levi does not work.]"

O.   One may reply as follows: Since rabbis are the ones who ordained that one should recite, "Cause us to lie down...," it is a kind of protracted prayer concerning redemption.

P.   If you do not maintain that thesis, then in the prayer at dawn, how can one place the one prayer next to the other?

Q.   For lo, R. Yohanan has said, "At the beginning of the Prayer, one says, 'O Lord, open my lips...' (Ps. 51:17). [Here too there is an interruption between the one and the other, that is, between the blessing for redemption and the recitation of the Prayer.] And at the end, one should recite, 'Let the words of my mouth be acceptable' (Ps. 19:15)."

R.   But in the case at hand, since the rabbis are the ones who ordained that one must say, "O Lord, open my lips," it is regarded as a protracted recitation of the Prayer. Here too, since rabbis have ordained that one must recite, "Cause us to lie down in peace," it falls into the category of a protracted blessing for redemption.

XIX.

A.   Said R. Eleazar bar Abina, "Whoever says the Psalm, 'Praise of David' (Ps. 145) three times a day may be assured that he belongs to the world to come."

B.   What is the scriptural basis for that view?

C.   If you should say that it is because the Psalm follows the order of the alphabet, there also is the Psalm, "Happy are they that are upright in the way" (Ps. 119) which goes through the alphabet eight times [and should be a preferred choice on that account].

D.   Rather, it is because, in Ps. 145, there is the sentence, "You open your hand and satisfy every living thing with favor" (Ps. 145:16).

E.   If that is the case, then in the Great Hallel (Ps. 136), we find the phrase, "Who gives food to all flesh" (Ps. 136:25), which one would do better to recite.

F.   Rather, it is because [in Ps. 145] there are both considerations [namely, the entire alphabet and the statement that God provides.]

XX.

A.   [Referring to Ps. 145], said R. Yohanan, "On what account is there no verse beginning with an N is Psalm 145?

B.   "It is because the N starts the verse referring to the fall of (the enemies of) Israel.

C.   "For it is written, 'Fallen (NPLH), no more to rise, is the virgin of Israel' (Amos 5:2)."

D.   In the West [the Land of Israel] the verse at hand is laid out in this way: "Fallen, and no more to fall, the virgin of Israel will arise."

E.   Said R. Nahman bar Isaac, "Even so, David went and by the Holy Spirit brought together the N with the following letter of the alphabet, S: 'The Lord upholds (SMK) all those who fall (NPL) (Ps. 145:14)."

XXI.

A.   Said Eleazar bar Abina, "What is said about Michael is greater than what is said about Gabriel.

B.   "In regard to Michael, it is written, 'Then one of the seraphim flew to me' (Is. 6:6), while in respect to Gabriel, it is written, 'The man Gabriel whom I had seen in the vision at the beginning, being cause to fly in a flight' (Dan. 9:21)."

C.   How do we know that this "one" refers in particular to Michael?

D.   Said R. Yohanan, "We draw an analogy to other references to 'one.' Here it is written, 'Then one of the seraphim flew to me' (Is. 6:6). And there it is written, 'And behold, Michael, one of the chief princes, came to help me' (Dan. 10:13)."

E.   It was taught on Tannaite authority:

F.   Michael [reaches his destination] in one [leap], Gabriel in two, Elijah in four, and the angel of death in eight, but during a time of plague, it is in one.

XXII.

A.   Said R. Joshua b. Levi, "Even though a person has recited the Shema in the synagogue, it is a religious duty to recite it in bed."

B.   Said R. Yose, "What verse of Scripture indicates it? 'Tremble and do not sin, commune with your own heart upon your bed and be still, selah' (Ps. 4:5)."

C.   Said R. Nahman, "[5A] If he is a disciple of a sage, he does not have to do so."

D. Said Abayye, "Even a disciple of a sage has [in bed] to recite one verse, to plead for mercy, for example, 'Into your hand I commit my spirit, you have redeemed me, O Lord, you God of truth' (Ps. 31:6)."

XXIII.

A. Said R. Levi bar Hama said R. Simeon b. Laqish, "A person should always provoke his impulse to do good against his impulse to do evil,

B. "as it is said, 'Provoke and do not sin' (Ps. 4:5).

C. "If [the good impulse] wins, well and good. If not, let him take up Torah-study,

D. "as it is said, 'Commune with your own heart' (Ps. 4:5).

E. "If [the good impulse] wins, well and good. If not, let him recite the Shema,

F. "as it is said, '... upon your bed' (Ps. 4:5).

G. "If [the good impulse] wins, well and good. If not, let him remember the day of death,

H. "as it is said, 'And keep silent. Sela' (Ps. 4:5)."

I. And R. Levi bar Hama said R. Simeon b. Laqish said, "What is the meaning of the verse of Scripture, 'And I will give you the tables of stone, the law and the commandment, which I have written, that you may teach them' (Ex. 24:12).

J. "'The tables' refers to the Ten Commandments.

K. "'Torah' refers to Scripture.

L. "'Commandment' refers to Mishnah.

M. "'Which I have written' refers to the Prophets and the Writings.

N. "'That you may teach them' refers to the Gemara.

O. "'This teaches that all of them were given to Moses from Sinai."

XXIV.

A. Said R. Isaac, "Whoever recites the Shema on his bed is as if he holds a two-edged sword in his hand [to fight against demons],

B. "as it is said, 'Let the high praises of God be in this mouth, and a two-edged sword in their hand' (Ps. 149:6)."

C. What is the proof [from that verse]?

D. Said Mar Zutra, and some say, R. Ashi, "It derives from the opening part of the same passage,

E. "for it is written, 'Let the saints exult in glory, let them sing for joy upon their beds' (Ps. 149:5), and then it is written, 'Let the high praises of God be in their mouth, and a two-edged sword in their hand.'"

F. And R. Isaac said, "From whoever recites the Shema on his bed demons stay away.

G. "For it is said, 'And the sons of reshef [sparks] fly upward' (Job. 5:7).

H. "The word used for 'fly' speaks only of the Torah, as it is written, 'Will you cause your eyes to close [using the same root] upon it? It is gone'" (Prov. 23:5).

I. "And the word reshef refers solely to demons, as it is said, 'The wasting of hunger and the devouring of the reshef and bitter destruction' (Deut. 32:24)."

J. Said R. Simeon b. Laqish, "From whoever takes up the study of Torah suffering stays away,

K.   "as it is said, 'And the sons of <u>reshef</u> fly upward' (Job 5:7).

L.   "The word used for 'fly' speaks only of the Torah, as it is written, 'Will you cause your eyes to close upon it? It is gone' (Prov. 23:5).

M.   "And the word <u>reshef</u> refers solely to suffering, as it is said, 'The wasting of hunger, and the devouring of the <u>reshef</u>...' (Deut. 32:24)."

N.   Said R. Yohanan to him, "Lo, even children in kindergarten know that, for it is written, 'And he said, If you will diligently hearken to the voice of the Lord your God and will do that which is right in his eyes and will give ear to his command- ments and keep all his statutes, I will put none of the diseases upon you which I have put upon the Egyptians, for I am the Lord who heals you' (Ex. 15:26).

O.   "Rather, [phrase the matter in this way:] 'Upon whoever has the possibility of taking up the study of Torah and does not do so, the Holy One, blessed be he, brings ugly and troubling suffering, as it is said, 'I was dumb with silence, I kept silence from the good thing, and so my pain was stirred up' (Ps. 39:3).

P.   "'The good thing' speaks only of the Torah, as it is said, 'For I give you a good doctrine, do not forsake my teaching' (Prov. 4:2)."

XXV.

A.   Said R. Zira, and some say, R. Hanina bar Papa, "Take note that the trait of the Holy One, blessed be he, is not like the trait of mortals."

B.   "When a mortal sells something to his fellow, the seller is sad and the buyer happy. But the Holy One, blessed be he, is not that way. He gave the Torah to Israel and was happy about it.

C.   "For it is said, 'For I give you a good doctrine, do not forsake my teaching' (Prov. 4:2)."

XXVI.

A.   Said Raba, and some say, R. Hisda, "If a person sees that sufferings afflict him, let him examine his deeds.

B.   "For it is said, 'Let us search and try our ways and return to the Lord' (Lam. 3:40).

C.   "If he examined his ways and found no cause [for his suffering], let him blame the matter on his wasting [time better spent in studying] the Torah.

D.   "For it is said, 'Happy is the man whom you chastise, O Lord, and teach out of your Torah' (Ps. 94:12).

E.   "If he blamed it on something and found [after correcting the fault] that that had not, in fact, been the cause at all, he may be sure that he suffers the afflictions that come from God's love.

F.   "For it is said, 'For the one whom the Lord loves he corrects' (Prov. 3:12)."

G.   Said Raba said R. Sehorah said R. Huna [said], "Whomever the Holy One, blessed be he, prefers he crushes with suffering.

H.   "For it is said, 'The Lord was pleased with him, hence he crushed him with disease' (Is. 53:10).

I.   "Is it possible that even if the victim did not accept the suffering with love, the same is so?

J.   "Scripture states, 'To see if his soul would offer itself in restitution' (Is. 53:10).

K.   "Just as the offering must be offered with the knowledge and consent [of the sacrifier], so sufferings must be accepted with knowledge and consent.

L.   "If one accepted them in that way, what is his reward?

M.   "'He will see his seed, prolong his days' (Is. 53:10).

N.   "Not only so, but his learning will remain with him, as it is said, 'The purpose of the Lord will prosper in his hand' (Is. 53:10)."

XXVII.

A.   R. Jacob bar Idi and R. Aha bar Hanina differed. One of them said, "What are sufferings brought on by God's love? They are any form of suffering which does not involve one's having to give up studying Torah.

B.   "For it is said, 'Happy is the man whom you chasten, O Lord, and yet teach out of your Torah' (Ps. 94:12)."

C.   The other said, "What are sufferings brought on by God's love? They are any form of suffering which does not involve having to give up praying.

D.   "For it is said, 'Blessed be God, who has not turned away my prayer nor his mercy from me' (Ps. 66:20)."

E.   Said to them R. Abba, son of R. Hiyya bar Abba, "This is what R. Hiyya bar Abba said R. Yohanan said, 'Both constitute forms of suffering brought on by God's love.

F.   "'For it is said, "For him whom the Lord loves he corrects" (Prov. 3:12).

G.   "'What is the sense of the Scripture's statement, 'And you teach him out of your Torah"? Do not read it as "You teach him," but "You teach us."

H.   "'This matter you teach us out of your law, namely, the argument [concerning the meaning of the suffering brought on by God's love] a fortiori resting on the traits of the tooth and the eye:

I.   "'Now if, on account of an injury done to the slave's tooth or eye, which are only one of a person's limbs, a slave goes forth to freedom, sufferings, which drain away the whole of a person's body, how much the more so [should a person find true freedom on their account].'"

J.   This furthermore accords with what R. Simeon b. Laqish said.

K.   For R. Simeon b. Laqish said, "A 'covenant' is stated in respect to salt, and a covenant is mentioned with respect to suffering.

L.   "With respect to a covenant with salt: 'Neither shall you allow the salt of the covenant of your God to be lacking' (Lev. 2:13).

M.   "With respect to a covenant with suffering: 'These are the words of the covenant' (Deut. 28:69) [followed by discourse on Israel's suffering].

N.   "Just as the covenant noted with salt indicates that salt sweetens meat, so the covenant noted with suffering indicates that suffering wipes away all of a person's sins."

XXVIII.

A.   It has been taught on Tannaite authority:

B. R. Simeon b. Yohai says, "Three good gifts did the Holy One, blessed be he, give to Israel, and all of them he gave only through suffering.

C. "These are they: Torah, the Land of Israel, and the world to come.

D. "How do we know that that is the case for Torah? As it is said, 'Happy is the man whom you chasten, O Lord, and teach out of your Torah' (Ps. 94:12).

E. "The Land of Israel? 'As a man chastens his son, so the Lord your God chastens you,' (Deut. 8:5), after which it is said, 'For the Lord your God brings you into a good land' (Deut. 8:7).

F. "The world to come? 'For the commandment is a lamp and the teaching is light, and reproofs of sufferings are the way of life' (Prov. 6:23)."

XXIX.

A. A Tannaite authority repeated the following statement before R. Yohanan: "Whoever devotes himself to study of the Torah or acts of loving kindness, [5B] or who buries his children, is forgiven all his sins."

B. Said to him R. Yohanan, "Now there is no issue with regard to study of the Torah or practice of deeds of loving kindness, for it is written, 'By mercy and truth iniquity is expiated' (Prov. 16:6).

C. "'Mercy' refers to acts of loving kindness, for it is said, 'He who follows after righteousness and mercy finds life, prosperity, and honor' (Prov. 21:21).

D. "'Truth' of course refers to Torah, for it is said, 'Buy the truth and do not sell it' (Prov. 23:23).

E. "But how do we know that that is the case for one who buries his children?"

F. An elder repeated for him on Tannaite authority the following statement in the name of R. Simeon b. Yohai, "We draw an analogy to the sense of the word 'sin' used in several passages.

G. "Here it is written, 'By mercy and truth iniquity is expiated' (Prov. 16:6), and elsewhere, 'And who repays the iniquity of the fathers into the bosom of their children' (Jer. 32:18)."

XXX.

A. Said R. Yohanan, "The suffering brought by skin-ailments [such as are listed at Lev. 13-14] and by the burial of one's children are not sufferings that are brought by God's love."

B. Is it really the case that the sufferings brought by the skin ailments are not [sufferings of love]?

C. And has it not been taught on Tannaite authority:

D. "Whoever has any one of the four skin-traits that indicate the presence of the skin-ailment may know that these serve solely as an altar for atonement [of his sins]"?

E. To be sure, they serve as an altar for atonement, but they are not sufferings that come on account of God's love.

F. If you prefer, I shall explain that the one teaching belongs to us [in Babylonia], the other to them [in the Land of Israel].

G. If you wish, I shall propose that the one teaching [that they are sufferings brought on by God's love] applies when the skin-ailment appears on hidden places of the body, the other, when it appears on parts of the body that people see.

H. And with respect to burying one's children is it not [a sign of suffering brought on by God's love]?

I. Now what sort of case can be in hand? If I say that one actually had the children but they died,

J. did not R. Yohanan say, "This is the bone of my tenth son [whom I buried]"? [Yohanan then regarded the death of the child as suffering brought on by God's love.]

K. Rather, the one case involves someone who never had any children at all, the other, to someone who had children who died.

XXXI.

A. R. Hiyya bar Abba got sick. R. Yohanan came to him. He said to him, "Are these sufferings precious to you?"

B. He said to him, "I don't want them, I don't want their reward."

C. He said to him, "Give me your hand."

D. He gave him his hand, and [Yohanan] raised him up [out of his sickness].

E. R. Yohanan got sick. R. Hanina came to him. He said to him, "Are these sufferings precious to you?"

F. He said to him, "I don't want them. I don't want their reward."

G. He said to him, "Give me your hand."

H. He gave him his hand and [Hanina] raised him up [out of his sickness].

I. Why so? R. Yohanan should have raised himself up?

J. They say, "A prisoner cannot get himself out of jail."

XXXII.

A. R. Eliezer got sick. R. Yohanan came to see him and found him lying in a dark room. [The dying man] uncovered his arm, and light fell [through the room]. [Yohanan] saw that R. Eliezer was weeping. He said to him, "Why are you crying? Is it because of the Torah that you did not learn sufficiently? We have learned: 'All the same are the ones who do much and do little, so long as each person will do it for the sake of heaven.'

B. "If it is because of insufficient income? Not everyone has the merit of seeing two tables [Torah and riches, as you have. You have been a master of Torah and also have enjoyed wealth].

C. "Is it because of children? Here is the bone of my tenth son [whom I buried, so it was no great loss not to have children, since you might have had to bury them]."

D. He said to him, "I am crying because of this beauty of mine which will be rotting in the ground."

E. He said to him, "For that it certainly is worth crying," and the two of them wept together.

F. He said to him, "Are these sufferings precious to you?"

G. He said to him, "I don't want them, I don't want their reward."

H.   He said to him, "Give me your hand."

I.   He gave him his hand, and [Yohanan] raised him up [out of his sickness].

XXXIII.

A.   Four hundred barrels of wine turned sour on R. Huna. R. Judah, brother of R. Sala the Pious, and rabbis came to see him (and some say it was R. Ada bar Ahba and rabbis). They said to him, "The master should take a good look at his deeds."

B.   He said to them, "And am I suspect in your eyes?"

C.   They said to him, "And is the Holy One, blessed be he, suspect of inflicting a penalty without justice?"

D.   He said to them, "Has anybody heard anything bad about me? Let him say it."

E.   They said to him, "This is what we have heard: the master does not give to his hired hand [the latter's share of] vine twigs [which are his right]."

F.   He said to them, "Does he leave me any! He steals all of them to begin with."

G.   They said to him, "This is in line with what people say: 'Go steal from a thief but taste theft too.' [Simon: If you steal from a thief, you also have a taste of it.]"

H.   He said to them, "I pledge that I'll give them to him."

I.   Some say that the vinegar turned back into wine, and some say that the price of vinegar went up so he sold it off at the price of wine.

XXXXIV.

A.   It has been taught on Tannaite authority:

B.   Abba Benjamin says, "I have been particularly attentive to two matters for my entire life, first, that my prayer should be said before my bed, second, that my bed should be placed on a north-south axis."

C.   "That my prayer should be said before my bed" -- what is the meaning of that statement?

D.   Can it be literally in front of my bed? And has not R. Judah said Rab said, (and some say R. Joshua b. Levi said it), "How do we know that there should be nothing that intervenes between one who says a prayer and the wall? As it is said, 'Then Hezekiah turned his face to the wall and prayed' (Is. 38:2)? [So prayer before the bed would be contrary to Hezekiah's practice.]

E.   Do not, therefore, maintain that it is "before my bed" but rather "near my bed."

F.   "That my bed should be placed on a north-south axis" [-- what is the meaning of that statement]?

G.   This is in line with that which R. Hama b. R. Hanina said R. Isaac said, "Whoever sets his bed on a north-south axis will have male children.

H.   "For it is said, 'And whose belly you fill at the north [lit.: with your treasure], who has sons in plenty' (Ps. 17:14)."

I.   R. Nahman bar Isaac said, "Also, his wife will not have miscarriages. It is written here, 'And whose belly you fill with your treasure' (Ps. 17:14). And elsewhere: 'And when her days to be delivered were fulfilled, behold, there were twins in her womb' (Gen. 25:24)."

XXXV.

A.   It has been taught on Tannaite authority:

B.   Abba Benjamin says, "If two people go in to say a prayer, and one of them finished saying a prayer sooner than the other and did not wait for his fellow but left, [in Heaven the angels] tear up his prayer in his very presence [and it is rejected].

C.   "For it is written, 'You tear yourself in your anger, shall the earth be forsaken for you' (Job 18:4).

D.   "Not only so, but he makes the Presence of God abandon Israel, for it is said, 'Or shall the rock be removed out of its place' (Job 18:4).

E.   "And the word 'rock' refers only to the Holy One, blessed be he, as it is said, 'Of the rock that begot you you were not mindful' (Deut. 32:18)."

F.   And if one does wait, what is his reward?

G.   [6A] Said R. Yose b. R. Hanina, "He has the merit of receiving the blessings specified in the following verse: 'Oh that you would listen to my commandments! Then your peace would be as a river, and your righteousness as the waves of the sea, your seed also would be as the sand, and the offspring of your body like the grains of the sand' (Is. 48:18-19)."

XXXVI.

A.   It has been taught on Tannaite authority:

B.   Abba Benjamin says, "If the eye had the power to see them, no creature could withstand the demons."

C.   Said Abayye, "They are more numerous than we and stand around us like a ridge around a field."

D.   Said R. Huna, "At the left hand of each one of us is a thousand of them, and at the right hand, ten thousand."

E.   Said Raba, "The crowding at the public lectures comes from them, the fact that the clothing of rabbis wears out from rubbing comes on account of them, the bruising of the feet comes from them.

F.   "If someone wants to know that they are there, take ashes and sprinkle them around the bed, and in the morning, he will see something like footprints of a cock.

G.   "If someone wants actually to see them, take the after-birth of a black she-cat, offspring of the same, first born of a first born. Roast it in fire and grind it to powder. Put the ash into his eye. He will see them.

H.   "Let him pour it into an iron tube and seal it with an iron signet [so Simon] so that they will not grab it from him.

I.   "Let him keep his mouth closed, lest they harm him."

J.   R. Bibi bar Abayye did this. He saw them but was injured. Rabbis prayed for mercy for him and he was healed.

XXXVII.

A.   It has been taught on Tannaite authority:

B.   Abba Benjamin says, "A prayer of a person is heard only if it is said in the synagogue.

C.   "For it is said, 'To hearken unto the song and to the prayer' (1 Kgs. 8:28).

D.   "Where there is song, there should the prayer take place."

E.   Said Rabin bar R. Ada said R. Isaac, "How do we know on the basis of Scripture that the Holy One, blessed be he, is found in the synagogue? As it is said, 'God stands in the congregation of God' (Ps. 82:1).

F.   "And how do we know that when ten are praying, the Presence of God is with them? As it is said, 'God stands in the congregation of God [which is ten]' (Ps. 82:1).

G.   "And how do we know that where three are sitting in judgment the Presence of God is with them? As it is said, 'In the midst of the judges he judges' (Ps. 82:1).

H.   "And how do we know that where two are sitting and studying the Torah, the Presence of God is with them? As it is said, 'Then they that feared the Lord spoke one with another, and the Lord hearkened and heard, and a book of remembrance was written before him, for them that feared the Lord and that thought upon his name' (Mal. 3:16)."

I.   What is the meaning of "Who thought upon his name"?

J.   Said R. Ashi, "If a person gave thought to doing a religious deed but perforce was not able to do it, Scripture credits it to him as if he had actually done it."

K.   [Continuing Isaac's statement,] "And how do we know that even if one person alone is sitting and studying the Torah, the Presence of God is with him? As it is said, 'In every place where I cause my name to be mentioned I will come to you and bless you' (Ex. 20:21)."

L.   Now since it is the case that even if one is studying by himself [the Presence is with him], why was it necessary to make the statement concerning two?

M.   The words of two are written down in the book of remembrances, while the words of one are not written down in the book of remembrances.

N.   And since it is the case that even if two are studying [the Presence is with them], why was it necessary to make the statement concerning three?

O.   What might you have said? Judging cases serves only for the purpose of making peace in this world, and the Presence of God would not come on that account. So we are informed that that is not the case, for judging a case also is an act of Torah.

P.   And since it is the case that even when three [are studying Torah, the Presence is with them], what need was there to speak of ten?

Q.   In the case of ten, the Presence of God comes first, while in the case of three, the Presence comes only when the people actually go into session.

XXXVIII.

A.   Said R. Abin bar Ada said R. Isaac, "How do we know on the basis of Scripture that the Holy One, blessed be he, puts on phylacteries? As it is said, 'The Lord has sworn by his right hand, and by the arm of his strength' (Is. 62:8).

B.   "'By his right hand' refers to Torah, as it is said, 'At his right hand was a fiery law for them' (Deut. 33:2).

C.   "'And by the arm of his strength' refers to phylacteries, as it is said, 'The Lord will give strength to his people' (Ps. 29:11).

D.   "And how do we know that phylacteries are a strength for Israel? For it is written, 'And all the peoples of the earth shall see that the name of the Lord is called upon you and they shall be afraid of you' (Deut. 28:10)."

E.   And it has been taught on Tannaite authority:

F.   R. Eliezer the Great says, "This [Deut. 28:10] refers to the phylacteries that are put on the head."

XXXIX.

A.   Said R. Nahman bar Isaac to R. Hiyya bar Abin, "As to the phylacteries of the Lord of the world, what is written in them?"

B.   He said to him, "'And who is like your people Israel, a singular nation on earth' (1 Chr. 17:21)."

C.   "And does the Holy One, blessed be he, sing praises for Israel?"

D.   "Yes, for it is written, 'You have avouched the Lord this day... and the Lord has avouched you this day' (Deut. 26:17, 18).

E.   "Said the Holy One, blessed be he, to Israel, 'You have made me a singular entity in the world, and I shall make you a singular entity in the world.

F.   "'You have made me a singular entity in the world,' as it is said, 'Hear O Israel, the Lord, our God, the Lord is one' (Deut. 6:4).

G.   "'And I shall make you a singular entity in the world,' as it is said, 'And who is like your people, Israel, a singular nation in the earth' (1 Chr. 17:21)."

H.   Said R. Aha, son of Raba to R. Ashi, "That takes care of one of the four subdivisions of the phylactery. What is written in the others?"

I.   He said to him, "'For what great nation is there... And what great nation is there...' (Deut. 4:7, 8), 'Happy are you, O Israel...' (Deut. 33:29), 'Or has God tried...,' (Deut. 4:34). And 'To make you high above all nations' (Deut. 26:19)."

J.   "If so, there are too many boxes!

K.   "But the verses, 'For what great nation is there' and 'And what great nation is there,' which are equivalent, are in one box, and 'Happy are you, O Israel' and 'Who is like your people Israel' are in one box, and 'Or has God tried...,' in one box, and 'To make you high' in one box.

L.   [6B] "And all of them are written in the phylactery that is on the arm."

XL.

A.   Said Rabin bar R. Ada said R. Isaac, "About anyone who regularly comes to the synagogue, but does not come one day, the Holy One, blessed be he, inquires.

B.   "For it is said, 'Who is among you who fears the Lord, who obeys the voice of his servant, and now walks in darkness and has no light' (Is. 50:10).

C.   "If it was on account of a matter of religious duty that the person has gone away [from regular synagogue attendance], he nonetheless 'will have light.'

D.   "But if it was on account of an optional matter that he did so, he 'has no light.'

E.   "'Let him trust in the name of the Lord' (Is. 50:10).

F.   "Why so? Because he should have trusted in the name of the Lord but did not."

XLI.

A. Said R. Yohanan, "When the Holy One, blessed be he, comes to a synagogue and does not find ten present, he forthwith becomes angry.

B. "For it is said, 'Why when I came was there no one there? When I called, there was no answer' (Is. 50:2)."

XLII.

A. Said R. Helbo said R. Huna, "For whoever arranges a regular place for praying, the God of Abraham is a help, and when he dies, they say for him, 'Woe for the humble man, woe for the pious man, one of the disciples of Abraham, our father.'

B. "And how do we know in the case of Abraham, our father, that he arranged a regular place for praying?

C. "For it is written, 'And Abraham got up early in the morning on the place where he had stood' (Gen. 19:27).

D. "'Standing' refers only to praying, for it is said, 'Then Phinehas stood up and prayed' (Ps. 106:30)."

E. Said R. Helbo to R. Huna, "He who leaves the synagogue should not take large steps."

F. Said Abayye, "That statement applies only when one leaves, but when he enters, it is a religious duty to run [to the synagogue].

G. "For it is said, 'Let us run to know the Lord' (Hos. 6:3)."

H. Said R. Zira, "When in the beginning I saw rabbis running to the lesson on the Sabbath, I thought that the rabbis were profaning the Sabbath. But now that I have heard what R. Tanhum said R. Joshua b. Levi said,

I. "namely, 'A person should always run to take up a matter of law, and even on the Sabbath, as it is said, "They shall walk after the Lord who shall roar like a lion [for he shall roar, and the children shall come hurrying]" (Hos. 11:10),'

J. "I too run."

XLIII.

A. Said R. Zira, "The reward for attending the lesson is on account of running [to hear the lesson, not necessarily on account of what one has learned.]"

B. Said Abayye, "The reward for attending the periodic public assembly [of rabbis] is on account of the crowding together."

C. Said Raba [to the contrary], "The reward for repeating what one has heard is in reasoning about it."

D. Said R. Papa, "The reward for attending a house of mourning is on account of one's preserving silence there."

E. Said Mar Zutra, "The reward for observing a fast-day lies in the acts of charity one performs on that day."

F. Said R. Sheshet, "The reward for delivering a eulogy lies in raising the voice."

G. Said R. Ashi, "The reward for attending a wedding lies in the words [of compliment paid to the bride and groom]."

XLIV.

A.   Said R. Huna, "Whoever prays behind the synagogue is called wicked,

B.   "as it is said, 'The wicked walk round about' (Ps. 12:9)."

C.   Said Abayye, "That statement applies only in the case of one who does not turn his face toward the synagogue, but if he turns his face toward the synagogue, we have no objection."

D.   There was a certain man who would say his prayers behind the synagogue and did not turn his face toward the synagogue. Elijah came by and saw him. He appeared to him in the guise of a Tai Arab.

E.   He said to him, "Are you now standing with your back toward your master?" He drew his sword and killed him.

F.   One of the rabbis asked R. Bibi bar Abayye, and some say, R. Bibi asked R. Nahman bar Isaac, "What is the meaning of the verse, 'When vileness is exalted among the sons of men' (Ps. 12:9)?"

G.   He said to him, "This refers to matters that are exalted, which people treat with contempt."

H.   R. Yohanan and R. Eleazar both say, "When a person falls into need of the help of other people, his face changes color like the kerum, for it is said, 'As the kerum is to be reviled among the sons of men' (Ps. 12:9)."

I.   What is the meaning of kerum?

J.   When R. Dimi came, he said, "There is a certain bird among the coast towns, called the kerum. When the sun shines, it turns many colors."

K.   R. Ammi and R. Assi both say, "[When a person turns to others for support], it is as if he is judged to suffer the penalties of both fire and water.

L.   "For it is said, 'When you caused men to ride over our heads, we went through fire and through water' (Ps. 66:12)."

XLV.

A.   And R. Helbo said R. Huna said, "A person should always be attentive at the afternoon prayer.

B.   "For lo, Elijah was answered only at the afternoon prayer.

C.   "For it is said, 'And it came to pass at the time of the offering of the late afternoon offering, that Elijah the prophet came near and said, "Hear me, O Lord, hear me"' (1 Kgs. 18:36-7)."

D.   "Hear me" so fire will come down from heaven.

E.   "Hear me" that people not say it is merely witchcraft.

F.   R. Yohanan said, "[A person should also be attentive about] the evening prayer.

G.   "For it is said, 'Let my prayer be set forth as incense before you, the lifting up of my hands as the evening sacrifice' (Ps. 141:2)."

H.   R. Nahman bar Isaac said, "[A person should also be attentive about] the morning prayer.

I.   "For it is said, 'O Lord, in the morning you shall hear my voice, in the morning I shall order my prayer to you, and will look forward' (Ps. 5:4)."

XLVI.

A. And R. Helbo said R. Huna said, "Whoever enjoys a marriage banquet and does not felicitate the bridal couple violates five 'voices.'

B. "For it is said, 'The voice of joy and the voice of gladness, the voice of the bridegroom and the voice of the bride, the voice of those who say, "Give thanks to the Lord of hosts"' (Jer. 33:11)."

C. And if he does felicitate the couple, what reward does he get?

D. Said R. Joshua b. Levi, "He acquires the merit of the Torah, which was handed down with five voices.

E. "For it is said, 'And it came to pass on the third day, when it was morning, that there were voices [thus two], and lightnings, and a thick cloud upon the mount, and the voice of a horn, and when the voice of the horn waxed louder, ... Moses spoke and God answered him by a voice...' (Ex. 19:16, 19) [thus five voices in all]."

F. Is it so [that there were only five voices]?

G. And lo, it is written, "And all the people saw the voices" (Ex. 20:15). [So this would make seven voices.]

H. These voices came before the giving of the Torah [and do not count].

I. R. Abbahu said, "It is as if the one [who felicitated the bridal couple] offered a thanksgiving offering.

J. "For it is said, 'Even of them that bring thanksgiving-offerings into the house of the Lord' (Jer. 33:11)."

K. R. Nahman bar Isaac said, "It is as if he rebuilt one of the ruins of Jerusalem.

L. "For it is said, 'For I will cause the captivity of the land to return as at the first, says the Lord' (Jer. 33:11)."

XLVII.

A. And R. Helbo said R. Huna said, "The words of any person in whom is fear of Heaven are heard.

B. "For it is said, 'The end of the matter, all having been heard: fear God and keep his commandments, for this is the whole man' (Qoh. 12:13)."

C. What is the meaning of the phrase, "For this is the whole man" (Qoh. 12:13)?

D. Said R. Eleazar, "Said the Holy One, blessed be he, 'The entire world has been created only on account of this one.'"

E. R. Abba bar Kahana said, "This one is worth the whole world."

F. Simeon b. Zoma says, "The entire world was created only to accompany this one."

XLVIII.

A. And R. Helbo said R. Huna said, "Whoever knows that his fellow regularly greets him should greet the other first.

B. "For it is said, 'Seek peace and pursue it' (Ps. 34:15).

C. "If he greeted him and the other did not reply, the latter is called a thief.

D. "For it is said, 'It is you who have eaten up the vineyard, the spoil of the poor is in your houses' (Is. 3:14)."

XLIX.

A.   [7A] Said R. Yohanan in the name of R. Yose, "How do we know that the Holy One, blessed be he, says prayers?

B.   "Since it is said, 'Even them will I bring to my holy mountain and make them joyful in my house of prayer' (Is. 56:7).

C.   "'Their house of prayer' is not stated, but rather, 'my house of prayer.'

D.   "On the basis of that usage we see that the Holy One, blessed be he, says prayers."

E.   What prayers does he say?

F.   Said R. Zutra bar Tobiah said Rab, "'May it be my will that my mercy overcome my anger, and that my mercy prevail over my attributes, so that I may treat my children in accord with the trait of mercy and in their regard go beyond the strict measure of the law.'"

L.

A.   It has been taught on Tannaite authority:

B.   Said R. Ishmael b. Elisha, "One time I went in to offer up incense on the innermost altar, and I saw the Crown of the Lord, enthroned on the highest throne, and he said to me, 'Ishmael, my son, bless me.'

C.   "I said to him, 'May it be your will that your mercy overcome your anger, and that your mercy prevail over your attributes, so that you treat your children in accord with the trait of mercy and in their regard go beyond the strict measure of the law.'

D.   "And he nodded his head to me."

E.   And from that story we learn that the blessing of a common son should not be negligible in your view.

LI.

A.   And said R. Yohanan in the name of R. Yose, "How do we know that one should not placate a person when he is angry?

B.   "It is in line with the following verse of Scripture: 'My face will go and then I will give you rest' (Ex. 33:14).

C.   "Said the Holy One, blessed be he, to Moses, 'Wait until my angry countenance passes, and then I shall give you rest.'"

D.   But does the Holy One, blessed be he, get angry?

E.   Indeed so.

F.   For it has been taught on Tannaite authority:

G.   "A God that is angry every day" (Ps. 7:12).

H.   And how long is this anger going to last?

I.   A moment.

J.   And how long is a moment?

K.   It is one fifty-eight thousand eight hundred and eighty-eighth part of an hour.

L.   And no creature except for the wicked Balaam has ever been able to fix the moment exactly.

M.   For concerning him it has been written, "He knows the knowledge of the Most High" (Num. 24:16).

N. Now if Balaam did not even know what his beast was thinking, was he likely to know what the Most High is thinking?

O. But this teaches that he knew exactly how to reckon the very moment that the Holy One, blessed be he, would be angry.

P. That is in line with what the prophet said to Israel, "O my people, remember now what Balak, king of Moab, devised, and what Balaam, son of Beor, answered him... that you may know the righteous acts of the Lord" (Mic. 6:5).

Q. Said R. Eleazar, "The Holy One, blessed be he, said to Israel, 'Know that I did any number of acts of righteousness with you, for I did not get angry in the time of the wicked Balaam. For had I gotten angry, not one of (the enemies of) Israel would have survived, not a remnant.'

R. "That is in line with what Balaam said to Balak, 'How shall I curse whom God has not cursed, and how shall I execrate whom the Lord has not execrated?' (Num. 23:8).

S. "This teaches that for that entire time [God] did not get mad."

T. And how long is God's anger?

U. It is a moment.

V. And how long is a moment?

W. Said R. Abin, and some say, R. Abina, "A moment lasts as long as it takes to say 'a moment.'"

X. And how do we know that a moment is how long God is angry?

Y. For it is said, "For his anger is but for a moment, his favor is for a lifetime" (Ps. 30:6).

Z. If you like, you may derive the lesson from the following: "Hide yourself for a little while until the anger be past" (Is. 26:20).

AA. And when is God angry?

BB. Said Abayye, "It is during the first three hours of the day, when the comb of the cock is white, and it stands on one foot."

CC. But it stands on one foot every hour.

DD. To be sure, it stands on its foot every hour, but in all the others it has red streaks, and in the moment at hand there are no red streaks [in the comb of the cock].

LII.

A. A certain Sadducean who lived in R. Joshua b. Levi's neighborhood would give him plenty of trouble by citing verses of Scripture. One day [Joshua] took a cock and put it between the legs of his bed and watched it. He thought, "When that very moment comes [that the comb is unstreaked], I shall curse him."

B. When that very moment came, [Joshua] was dozing. He said to him, "That fact implies that it is not proper to do things this way."

C. "'And his tender mercies are over all his works' (Ps. 155:9), and it is written, 'Neither is it good for the righteous to punish' (Prov. 17:26)."

LIII.

A. It has been taught on Tannaite authority in the name of R. Meir, "When the sun comes up, and all kings, east and west, put their crowns on their heads and bow down to the sun, forthwith the Holy One, blessed be he, grows angry."

LIV.

A. And R. Yohanan said in the name of R. Yose, "Better is one self-reproach that a person sets in his own heart [on account of what he has done] than a great many scourgings.

B. "For it is said, 'And she shall run after her lovers... then shall she say [in her heart], I shall go and return to my first husband, for then it was better for me than now' (Hos. 2:9)."

C. And R. Simeon b. Laqish said, "It is better than a hundred scourgings,

D. "as it is said, 'A rebuke enters deeper into a man of understanding than a hundred stripes into a fool' (Prov. 17:10)."

LV.

A. And R. Yohanan said in the name of R. Yose, "There were three things that Moses sought from the Holy One, blessed be he, and he gave them to him.

B. "He asked that the Presence of God should come to rest on Israel, and he gave him his request, as it is said, 'Is it not in that you go with us...' (Ex. 33:16).

C. "He asked that the Presence of God not come to rest on idolators, and he gave him his request, as it is said, 'So we are distinguished, I and your people' (Ex. 33:16).

D. "He asked that he teach him the ways of the Holy One, blessed be he, and he gave him his request, as it is said, 'Show me now your ways' (Ex. 33:13).

E. "He said before him, 'Lord of the world, on what account can there be a righteous man who has it good, a righteous man who has it bad, a wicked man who has it good, and a wicked man who has it bad?'

F. "He said to him, 'Moses, in the case of a righteous man who has it good, it is a righteous man, son of a righteous man, a righteous man who has it bad is a righteous man, son of a wicked man, a wicked man who has it good is a wicked man, son of a righteous man, and a wicked man who has it bad is a wicked man, son of a wicked man.'"

G. A master has said, "A righteous man who has it good is a righteous man, son of a righteous man, a righteous man who has it bad is a righteous man, son of a wicked man."

H. But is this so? And lo, it is written, "Visiting the wickedness of the fathers upon the children" (Ex. 34:7), and it also is written, "Neither shall the children be put to death for the fathers" (Deut. 24:16).

I. These two verses were set into contrast with one another, and we learned, "It is not a contradiction. The one verse speaks of a case in which the sons take hold of the deeds of the fathers and do them, and the other speaks of a case in which the sons do not take hold of the deeds of the fathers and do them."

J. Rather, this is what he said to him, "A righteous man who has it good is a totally righteous man. A righteous man who has it bad is a righteous man who is not totally righteous. A wicked man who has it good is a wicked man who is not totally wicked. A wicked man who has it bad is a totally wicked man."

K. What R. Yohanan has said differs from what R. Meir said

L.   For R. Meir said, "Two [of the three] requests were granted to him, and one was not.

M.   "For it is said, 'For I shall be gracious to whom I shall be gracious' (Ex. 33:19), even though he may not be worthy of it, 'And I will show mercy on whom I will show mercy' (Ex. 33:19), even though he may not be worthy of it."

LVI.

A.   "And he said, 'You cannot see my face'" (Ex. 33:20).

B.   It was taught on Tannaite authority in the name of R. Joshua b. Qorha, "This is what the Holy One, blessed be he, said to Moses:

C.   "'When I wanted [you to see my face], you did not want to, now that you want to see my face, I do not want you to.'"

D.   This differs from what R. Samuel bar Nahmani said R. Jonathan said.

E.   For R. Samuel bar Nahmani said R. Jonathan said, "As a reward for three things he received the merit of three things.

F.   "As a reward for: 'And Moses hid his face,' (Ex. 3:6), he had the merit of having a glistening face.

G.   "As a reward for: 'Because he was afraid to' (Ex. 3:6), he had the merit that 'They were afraid to come near him' (Ex. 34:30).

H.   "As a reward for: 'To look upon God' (Ex. 3:6), he had the merit: 'The similitude of the Lord does he behold' (Num. 12:8)."

LVII.

A.   "And I shall remove my hand and you shall see my back" (Ex. 33:23).

B.   Said R. Hana bar Bizna said R. Simeon the Pious, "This teaches that the Holy One, blessed be he, showed Moses [how to tie] the knot of the phylacteries."

LVIII.

A.   And R. Yohanan said in the name of R. Yose, "Every word containing a blessing that came forth from the Mouth of the Holy One, blessed be he, even if stated conditionally, was never retracted.

B.   "How do we know it? It is from Moses, our master.

C.   "For it is said, 'Let me alone, that I may destroy them and blot out their name from under heaven, and I will make of you a nation mightier and greater than they' (Deut. 9:14).

D.   "Even though Moses prayed for mercy, so that the matter was nullified, even so, [the blessing] was carried out in his seed.

E.   "For it is said, 'The sons of Moses, Gershom and Eliezer... and the sons of Eliezer were Rehabia the chief... and the sons of Rehabiah were very many' (1 Chr. 23:15-17)."

F.   And in this regard R. Joseph stated on Tannaite authority, "They were more than sixty myriads."

G.   "This is to be derived from an analogy between two uses of the word 'many.'

H.   "Here it is written, 'They were very many' (1 Chr. 23:17).

I.   "And elsewhere it is written, 'And the children of Israel were very fruitful and increased abundantly and became very many' (Ex. 1:7). [At that time they were sixty myriads.]"

LIX.

A.   [7B] Said R. Yohanan in the name of R. Simeon b. Yohai, "From the day on which the Holy One, blessed be he, created the world, there was no man who called the Holy One, blessed be he, 'Lord,' until Abraham came along and called him Lord.

B.   "For it is said, 'And he said, O Lord, God, whereby shall I know that I shall inherit it' (Gen. 15:8)."

C.   Said Rab, "Daniel too was answered only on account of Abraham.

D.   "For it is said, 'Now therefore, O our God, hearken to the prayer of your servant and to his supplications and cause your face to shine upon your sanctuary that is desolate, for the Lord's sake' (Dan. 9:17).

E.   "'For your sake' is what he should have said, but the sense is, 'For the sake of Abraham, who called you 'Lord.'"

LX.

A.   And R. Yohanan said in the name of R. Simeon b. Yohai, "How do we know that people should not seek to appease someone when he is mad?

B.   "As it is said, 'My face will go and then I will give you rest' (Ex. 33:14)."

LXI.

A.   And R. Yohanan said in the name of R. Simeon b. Yohai, "From the day on which the Holy One, blessed be he, created his world, there was no one who praised the Holy One, blessed be he, until Leah came along and praised him.

B.   "For it is said, 'This time I will praise the Lord' (Gen. 29:35)."

C.   As to Reuben, said R. Eleazar, "Leah said, 'See what is the difference [the name of Reuben yielding reu, see, and ben, between] between my son and the son of my father-in-law.

D.   "The son of my father-in-law, even knowingly, sold off his birthright, for it is written, 'And he sold his birthright to Jacob' (Gen. 25:33).

E.   "See what is written concerning him: 'And Esau hated Jacob' (Gen. 27:41), and it is written, 'And he said, is not he rightly named Jacob? for he has supplanted me these two times' (Gen. 27:36).

F.   "My son, by contrast, even though Joseph forcibly took away his birthright, as it is written, 'But for as much as he defiled his father's couch, his birthright was given to the sons of Joseph' (1 Chr. 5:1), did not become jealous of him, for it is written, 'And Reuben heard it and delivered him out of their hand' (Gen. 37:21)."

G.   As to the meaning of the name of Ruth, said R. Yohanan, "It was because she had the merit that David would come forth from her, who saturated (RWH) the Holy One, blessed be he, with songs and praises."

H.   How do we know that a person's name affects [his life]?

I.   Said R. Eleazar, "It is in line with the verse of Scripture: 'Come, behold the works of the Lord, who has made desolations in the earth' (Ps. 46:9).

J.   "Do not read 'desolations' but 'names' [which the same root yields]."

LXII.

A.   And R. Yohanan said in the name of R. Simeon b. Yohai, "Bringing a child up badly is worse in a person's house than the war of Gog and Magog.

B.   "For it is said, 'A Psalm of David, when he fled from Absalom, his son' (Ps. 3:1), after which it is written, 'Lord how many are my adversaries become, many are they that rise up against me' (Ps. 3:2).

C.   "By contrast, in regard to the war of Gog and Magog it is written, 'Why are the nations in an uproar? And why do the peoples mutter in vain' (Ps. 2:1).

D.   "But it is not written in that connection, 'How many are my adversaries become.'"

E.   "A Psalm of David, when he fled from Absalom, his son" (Ps. 3:1):

F.   "A Psalm of David"? It should be, "A lamentation of David"!

G.   Said R. Simeon b. Abishalom, "The matter may be compared to the case of a man, against whom an outstanding bond was issued. Before he had paid it, he was sad. After he had paid it, he was glad.

H.   "So too with David, when he the Holy One had said to him, 'Behold, I will raise up evil against you out of your own house,' (2 Sam. 2:11), he was sad.

I.   "He thought to himself, 'Perhaps it will be a slave or a bastard child, who will not have pity on me.

J.   "When he saw that it was Absalom, he was happy. On that account, he said a psalm."

LXIII.

A.   And R. Yohanan said in the name of R. Simeon b. Yohai, "It is permitted to contend with the wicked in this world,

B.   For it is said, 'Those who forsake the Torah praise the wicked, but those who keep the Torah contend with them' (Prov. 28:4)."

C.   It has been taught on Tannaite authority along these same lines:

D.   R. Dosetai bar Matun says, "It is permitted to contend with the wicked in this world, for it is said, 'Those who forsake the Torah praise the wicked, but those who keep the Torah contend with them' (Prov. 28:4)."

E.   And if someone should whisper to you, "But is it not written, 'Do not contend with evil-doers, nor be envious against those who work unrighteousness' (Ps. 37:1)," say to him, "Someone whose conscience bothers him thinks so."

F.   "In fact, 'Do not contend with evil-doers' means, do not be like them, 'nor be envious against those who work unrighteousness,' means, do not be like them.

G.   "And so it is said, 'Let your heart not envy sinners, but fear the Lord all day' (Prov. 23:17)."

H.   Is this the case? And lo, R. Isaac has said, "If you see a wicked person for whom the hour seems to shine, do not contend with him, for it is said, 'His ways prosper at all times' (Ps. 10:5).

I.   "Not only so, but he wins in court, as it is said, 'Your judgments are far above, out of his sight' (Ps. 10:5).

J.   "Not only so, but he overcomes his enemies, for it is said, 'As for all his enemies, he farts at them' (Ps. 10:5)."

K.   There is no contradiction. The one [Isaac] addresses one's own private matters [in which case one should not contend with the wicked], but the other speaks of matters having to do with heaven [in which case one should contend with them].

L. And if you wish, I shall propose that both parties speak of matters having to do with Heaven. There is, nonetheless, no contradiction. The one [Isaac] speaks of a wicked person on whom the hour shines, the other of a wicked person on whom the hour does not shine.

M. And if you wish, I shall propose that both parties speak of a wicked person on whom the hour shines, and there still is no contradiction.

N. The one [Yohanan, who says the righteous may contend with the wicked] speaks of a completely righteous person, the other [Isaac] speaks of someone who is not completely righteous.

O. For R. Huna said, "What is the meaning of this verse of Scripture: 'Why do you look, when they deal treacherously, and hold your peace, when the wicked swallows up the man that is more righteous than he' (Hab. 1:13)?

P. "Now can a wicked person swallow up a righteous one?

Q. "And lo, it is written, 'The Lord will not leave him in his hand' (Ps. 37:33). And it is further written, 'No mischief shall befall the righteous' (Prov. 12:21).

R. "The fact therefore is that he may swallow up someone who is more righteous than he, but he cannot swallow up a completely righteous man."

S. And if you wish, I shall propose that, when the hour shines for him, the situation is different.

LXIV.

A. And R. Yohanan said in the name of R. Simeon b. Yohai, "Beneath anyone who establishes a regular place for praying do that person's enemies fall.

B. "For it is said, 'And I will appoint a place for my people Israel, and I will plant them, that they may dwell in their own place and be disquieted no more, neither shall the children of wickedness afflict them any more as at the first' (2 Sam. 7:10)."

C. R. Huna pointed to a contradiction between two verses of Scripture: "It is written, 'To afflict them,' and elsewhere, 'To exterminate them' (1 Chr. 17:9).

D. "To begin with, merely to afflict them, but, at the end, to exterminate them."

LXV.

A. And R. Yohanan said in the name of R. Simeon b. Yohai, "Greater is personal service to Torah than learning in Torah, [so doing favors for a sage is of greater value than studying with him].

B. "For it is said, 'Here is Elisha, the son of Shaphat, who poured water on the hands of Elijah' (2 Kgs. 3:11).

C. "It is not said, 'who learned' but 'who poured water.'

D. "This teaches that greater is service to Torah than learning in Torah."

LXVI.

A. Said R. Isaac to R. Nahman, "What is the reason that the master did not come to the synagogue to say his prayers?"

B. He said to him, "I could not do it."

C. He said to him, "Let the master gather ten to say prayers [at home]."

D. He said to him, "It was too much trouble for me."

E. "And let the master ask the agent of the community to let him know when the congregation prays [so he could do so at the same time]?"

F. He said to him, "Why all this bother?"

G. He said to him, "For R. Yohanan said in the name of R. Simeon b. Yohnai, [8A], 'What is the meaning of that which is written, "But as for me, let my prayer be made to you, O Lord, in an acceptable time" (Ps. 69:14)? When is an acceptable time? It is the time that the community is saying its prayers.'"

H. R. Yose b. R. Hanina said, "The proof of the same principle derives from here: 'Thus says the Lord, in an acceptable time I have answered you' (Is. 49:8)."

I. R. Aha b. R. Hanina said, "From here: 'Behold, God does not despise the mighty' (Job 36:5). And it is written, 'He has redeemed my soul in peace so that none came near me, for they were many with me' (Ps. 55:19) [showing that when many pray together, they are listened to]."

J. It has been taught along these same lines on Tannaite authority:

K. R. Nathan says, "How do we know that the Holy One, blessed be he, does not reject the prayer of the community?

L. "As it is said, 'Behold, God does not despise the mighty' (Job 36:5), and it is further said, 'He has redeemed my soul in peace so that none came near me, for they were many with me' (Ps. 55:19).

M. "Said the Holy One, blessed be he, 'Whoever is occupied with study of the Torah and with the doing of deeds of loving kindness and who prays with the community do I regard as though he had redeemed me and my children from among the nations of the world.'"

LXVII.

A. Said R. Simeon b. Laqish, "Whoever has a synagogue in his town and does not go in there to pray is called a bad neighbor.

B. "For it is said, 'Thus says the Lord, as for all my evil neighbors, who touch the inheritance that I have caused my people Israel to inherit' (Jer. 12:14).

C. "Not only so, but he causes himself and his children to go into exile, as it is said, 'Behold, I will pluck them up from off their land and will pluck up the house of Judah from among them' (Jer. 12:14)."

LXVIII.

A. They told R. Yohanan that there are old men in Babylonia. He was amazed. He said, "'That your days may be multiplied, and the days of your children, upon the land' (Deut. 11:21) -- and not outside the land."

B. When they told him that the people came early and left late so as to attend upon synagogue worship, he said, "This is what gives them the advantage [that permits them to live a long time]."

C. That accords with what R. Joshua b. Levi said to his children, "Come up early and go home late so as to attend upon synagogue worship, so that you will live for a long time."

D. Said R. Aha b. R. Hanina, "What proves the same point? 'Happy is the man who hearkens to me, watching daily at my gates, waiting at the posts of my doors' (Prov. 8:34), followed by, 'For whoever finds me finds life' (Prov. 8:35)."

E. Said R. Hisda, "A person should always enter two doors to the synagogue."

F. "Two doors" is what you think?

G. Rather, I should say, "A distance of two doors, and afterward he should say his prayer."

LXIX.

A. "For this let every one who is pious pray to you in the time of finding' (Ps. 32:6).

B. Said R. Hanina, "'The time of finding' refers to a wife, as it is said, 'Who has found a wife has found a great good' (Prov. 18:22)."

C. In the West when a man married a woman, they would say this to him: "'Found' or 'find'?"

D. "Found" as it is written, "Who has found a wife has found a great good" (Prov. 18:22).

E. "Find" as it is written, "And I find more bitter than death the woman" (Qoh. 7:26).

F. R. Nathan says, "'The time of finding' refers to Torah, as it is said, 'For who finds me finds life' (Prov. 8:35)."

G. R. Nahman bar Isaac said, "'The time of finding' refers to death, as it is said, 'The findings of death' (Ps. 68:22)."

H. It has been taught along these same lines on Tannaite authority:

I. Nine hundred and three sorts of death were created in the world, as it is said, "The findings of death" (Ps. 68:22), and the numerical value of the letters in the word for findings is nine hundred three.

J. The most difficult death of all is croup, and the easiest, a kiss.

K. Croup is like [Simon:] a thorn in a ball of wool pulled out backwards.

L. Some say, "It is like [pulling] a rope through the loop-holes of a ship."

M. The kind by a kiss is like drawing a hair out of milk.

N. R. Yohanan said, "'The time of finding' refers to burial."

O. Said R. Hanina, "What is the proof-text for that proposition? 'Who rejoice unto exultation and are glad when they can find the grave' (Job 3:22)."

P. Said Rabbah bar R. Shila, "That is in line with what people say: 'People should pray for peace even as the last clod of earth [is thrown upon the grave].'"

Q. Mar Zutra said, "'The time of finding' refers to finding a toilet."

R. In the West they say, "This statement of Mar Zutra is the best of the lot."

LXX.

A. Said Raba to Rafram bar Papa, "Let the master tell us some of those excellent sayings having to do with the synagogue which were said in the name of R. Hisda."

B. He said to him, "This is what R. Hisda said: 'What is the meaning of the verse of Scripture, "The Lord loves the gates of Zion (SYN) more than all the dwellings of Jacob" (Ps. 87:2)? The Lord loves the gates that are distinguished (SYN) in law more than synagogues and school-houses.'"

C.   That is in line with what R. Hiyya bar Ami said in the name of Ulla, "From the day
      on which the house of the sanctuary was destroyed, the Holy One, blessed be he, has
      had in his world only the four cubits of the law alone."

D.   And Abayye said, "To begin with I would study at home and pray in the synagogue.
      Once I heard this statement that R. Hiyya bar Ammi stated in the name of Ulla,
      'From the day on which the house of the sanctuary was destroyed, the Holy One,
      blessed be he, has had in his world only the four cubits of the law alone,' I have had
      the practice of saying my prayers only in the place in which I study."

E.   Even though they had thirteen synagogues in Tiberias, R. Ammi and R. Assi would
      pray only among the columns [of the basilica] where they were studying.

LXXI.

A.   And R. Hiyya bar Ammi said in the name of Ulla, "Greater is the status of one who
      derives benefit from his own labor than one who fears heaven.

B.   "For with regard to one who fears heaven, it is written, 'Happy is the man who fears
      the Lord' (Ps. 112:1).

C.   "With regard to the one who derives benefit from his own labor, by contrast, it is
      written, 'When you eat the work of your hands, happy you shall be, and it shall be
      well with you' (Ps. 128:2).

D.   "'Happy are you' in this world and 'it shall be well with you' in the world to come.

E.   "With respect to the one who fears heaven, 'And it shall be well with you' is not
      written."

LXXII.

A.   And R. Hiyya bar Ami said in the name of Ulla, "A person should always live in the
      place in which his master lives.

B.   "For so long as Shimei, son of Gera, was alive, Solomon did not marry the daughter
      of Pharaoh."

C.   But has it not been taught on Tannaite authority: One should not dwell [where his
      master does]?

D.   There is no contradiction. The one [saying one should live near the master] speaks
      of a disciple who is submissive, the other of one who is not.

LXXIII.

A.   Said R. Huna bar Judah said R. Menahem said R. Ammi, "What is the meaning of the
      verse that follows: 'And they who forsake the Lord shall be consumed' (Is. 1:28)?

B.   "This refers to one who leaves the scroll of the Torah [when it is read] and goes out
      [of the synagogue]."

C.   R. Abbahu would go out [at the breaks in the lections] between the reading of one
      person and the next.

D.   R. Pappa asked about the law governing leaving the synagogue between the reading
      of one verse and the next.

E.   The question stands.

F.   R. Sheshet would turn his face away and study [his legal traditions during the
      reading of the Torah-lection].

G. He said, "We with our [Torah], they with theirs."

LXXIV.

A. Said R. Huna bar Judah said R. Ammi, "A person should always complete the reading of his passage of Scripture along with the congregation [studying the same lection from the Pentateuch as is read in the synagogue], following the practice of repeating the verse of Scripture two times, with one reading from the translation of the same verse into Aramaic.

B. [8B] "And that is the case even with "Ataroth and Digon" (Num. 32:3). [Simon, p. 42, n. 5: Even strings of names which are left untranslated in the Targum should be recited in Hebrew and in the Aramaic version.]"

C. "For whoever completes the reading of his passage of Scripture along with the congregation is given long days and a lengthy life."

D. R. Bibi bar Abayye considered completing his recitation of the entire Scriptural lections for the year on the eve of the Day of Atonement.

E. Hiyya b. Rab of Difti recited to him on Tannaite authority: "It is written, 'And you shall afflict your souls, on the ninth day of the month at evening' (Lev. 23:32). Now do people fast on the ninth of the month? Do they not fast on the tenth of the month? But the passage serves to tell you the following:

F. "Whoever eats and drinks on the ninth of the month is regarded by Scripture as if he had fasted on the ninth and the tenth."

G. He thereupon considered completing them still sooner. A certain elder said to him, "It has been taught on Tannaite authority: 'However, he should not recite [the verses of the lections] either before or after [the congregation does]."

H. This accords with what R. Joshua b. Levi said to his children, "Complete your lections with the congregation, reading each verse twice as written in Scripture and once as written in the Aramaic translation.

I. "And be careful to deal with the jugular veins [in slaughtering a beast] in accord with the teaching of R. Judah, for we have learned in the Mishnah: R. Judah says, '[An act of slaughter is valid] only if one cuts through the jugular veins' [M. Hul. 2:1].

J. "And be attentive to an old man who has forgotten his learning on account of some untoward condition [through no fault of his own].

K. "For we say: 'The tablets [of the law] as well as the broken sherds of the tablets were put away in the ark.'"

LXXV.

A. Said Raba to his children, "When you cut meat, do not cut it while holding it in your hand."

B. Some say it is because of the danger of injury, and some say it is because of ruining the food for the meal.

C. [Raba continues,] "And do not sit on the bed of an Aramean woman, and do not pass behind a synagogue when the community is saying its prayers."

D.   "Do not sit on the bed of an Aramean woman:" Some say his meaning was not to go
     to bed without saying the Shema; some say his meaning was not to marry a female
     proselyte; and some say he referred to an actual Aramean woman, on account of the
     story involving R. Papa.

E.   For R. Papa went to visit an Aramean woman. She brought out a bed for him, saying
     to him, "Sit."

F.   He said to her, "I shall not sit down until you raise up the bed [so that I can see what
     is underneath it]."

G.   She raised up the bed and they found a dead child there.

H.   On the basis of that incident, sages said, "It is forbidden to sit on the bed of an
     Aramean woman."

I.   "Do not pass behind a synagogue when the community is saying its prayers:"

J.   That statement supports the view of R. Joshua b. Levi.

K.   For R. Joshua b. Levi said, "It is forbidden for someone to pass behind a synagogue
     when the community is saying its prayers."

L.   Said Abayye, "But that statement has been made only where there is no other entry.
     But if there is another entry, there is no objection to doing so.

M.   "And that objection applies when there is no other synagogue, but if there is another
     synagogue, there is no objection to doing so.

N.   "And that objection applies, finally, when one is not carrying a burden, not running,
     or not wearing phylacteries. But if one of these conditions applies, there is no
     objection to doing so."

LXXVI.

A.   It has been taught on Tannaite authority:

B.   Said R. Aqiba, "On three counts I admire the Medes:

C.   "When they cut meat, they cut it only on a table.

D.   "When they kiss, they kiss only on the hand.

E.   "When they take counsel, they take counsel only in a field."

F.   Said R. Ada bar Ahba, "What verse of Scripture [proves E]? 'And Jacob sent and
     called Rachel and Leah to the field, to his flock' (Gen. 31:4)."

G.   It has been taught on Tannaite authority:

H.   Said Rabban Gamaliel, "On three counts I admire the Persians:

I.   "They are modest when they eat.

J.   "They are modest in the privy.

K.   "They are modest in conducting another matter [sexual relations]."

L.   [By contrast to the foregoing:] "I have commanded my consecrated ones" (Is. 13:3):

M.   R. Joseph repeated on Tannaite authority, "This refers to the Persians, who are
     consecrated and designated for Gehenna."

LXXVII.

A.   Rabban Gamaliel says, etc. [M. Ber. 1:1E]:

B.   Said R. Judah said Samuel, "The law accords with the view of Rabban Gamaliel."

LXXVIII.

A. It has been taught on Tannaite authority:

B. R. Simeon b. Yohai says, "There are occasions on which a person recites the Shema twice in a single night, once before dawn, the other time afterward, and thereby carries out his obligation for both day and night."

C. The statement as formulated contains a contradiction, for you have said, "There are occasions on which a person recites the Shema twice in a single night," which bears the implication that after the morning star rises, it is still night.

D. And then the cited passage continues, "... and thereby carries out his obligation for both day and night," which bears the implication that it then is day.

E. Indeed, there is no real contradiction. It is really night, and the reason that one may call it "day" is that there are people who get up at that time.

F. Said R. Aha bar Hanina said R. Joshua b. Levi, "The decided law accords with the view of R. Simeon b. Yohai."

G. There are some who repeat that statement of R. Aha bar Hanina in regard to the following, which has been taught on Tannaite authority:

H. R. Simeon b. Yohai says in the name of R. Aqiba, "There are occasions on which a person may recite the Shema twice by day, once before sunrise, once after sunrise, and he thereby carries out his obligation for both day and night."

I. Lo, there is a contradiction in the framing of that statement:

J. You have said, "There are occasions on which a person may recite the Shema twice by day," which bears the implication that the time prior to sunrise is regarded as day.

K. Then the passage proceeds to state, "... and thereby carries out his obligation for both day and night," which bears the implication that it is night.

L. [9A] No, there is no real contradiction. It really is day, and the reason that it is called "night" is that there are people who are in bed at that time.

M. Said R. Aha bar Hanina said R. Joshua b. Levi, "The decided law is in accord with what R. Simeon has said in the name of R. Aqiba."

N. Said R. Zira, "And that is the case so long as the person not recite the prayer, 'Cause us to lie down in peace...'" [That prayer is said only by night.]

O. When R. Isaac bar Judah came, he said, "The statement of R. Aha bar Hanina that R. Joshua b. Levi said was not made explicitly but rather made on the basis of inference.

P. "For there was a pair of scholars who got drunk at the wedding banquet of R. Joshua b. Levi's son. They came before R. Joshua b. Levi. He ruled, 'R. Simeon is sufficiently reliable for an emergency [but under ordinary circumstances, one cannot recite the Shema two times, once before, once after sunrise, and so carry out his obligation for night and day].'"

LXXIX.

A. M^CSH S: His sons came [M. 1:1F]:

B. And up to that point had they never heard that statement from Rabban Gamaliel?!

C.   This is what they had to say to him, "Rabbis differ from you, and in the case where there is an individual view against that of the majority, the decided law follows the majority.

D.   "But is it possible that rabbis really concur with you, and the reason that they say, Up to midnight is only to keep a man far from sin [and that is the question they addressed to him]?"

E.   He said to them, "Rabbis concur with me, and you are liable [to recite the Shema].

F.   "And the reason that they say, Up to midnight is only to keep a man far from sin."

LXXX.

A.   And not only in this case [M. 1:11]:

B.   [Inquiring into the formulation of the matter at hand, we ask:] Has Rabban Gamaliel stated, "To midnight," that he should then add, "And not only in this case have they stated matters..."? [The cited clause is not connected to Gamaliel's lemma.]

C.   This is the sense of what Rabban Gamaliel said to his sons, "Even in accord with rabbis, who take the view that the recitation is to take place before midnight, the religious duty pertaining to the recitation applies until dawn.

D.   "And the reason that they have said, Until midnight is in order to keep a man far from sin."

LXXXI.

A.   The offering of the fats [M. 1:1K]:

B.   Now we note that the framer of the Mishnah does not make mention of the rule governing the eating of the Passover-sacrifices [which by inference may not be done up to dawn but must be completed before midnight].

C.   The following then was adduced as an objection to the inference yielded by the present formulation.

D.   The religious duty governing the recitation of the Shema at night, the recitation of Hallel on Passover night, and the eating of the Passover sacrifice, applies until dawn. [So there is a clear contradiction between the framing of the Mishnah-passage and the cited Tannaite teaching.]

E.   Said R. Joseph, "There is no contradiction. The one represents the view of R. Eleazar b. Azariah, the other, of R. Aqiba."

F.   For it has been taught on Tannaite authority:

G.   "And they shall eat the meat in that night" (Ex. 12:8).

H.   R. Eleazar b. Azariah says, "Here it is stated, 'In that night,' and later on it is stated, 'For I shall pass through the land of Egypt in that night' (Ex. 12:12).

I.   "Just as, in the latter usage, the reference is to the period up to midnight, so here the reference is to the period up to midnight."

J.   Said to him R. Aqiba, "And has it not already been stated, 'You shall eat it in haste' (Ex. 12:11)? The meaning is, 'until the time of haste' [which was dawn, at which point they scurried out of Egypt].

K.   "Why then does Scripture say, 'By night'? One might suppose that the Passover sacrifice may be eaten by day, as is the case with Holy Things. Accordingly,

Scripture says, 'By night,' meaning, 'It is by night that the Passover sacrifice is eaten, and not by day.'"

L. Now with respect to the view of R. Eleazar b. Azariah, who argues by constructing an analogy [between the references to "night,"] it was necessary for Scripture to make explicit references to "that" [night]. But how does R. Aqiba deal with the reference to "that"?

M. He regards it as important to exclude reference to another night.

N. [How so?] I might have thought that, since the Passover sacrifice falls into the category of Lesser Holy Things, and peace-offerings fall into the category of Lesser Holy Things,

O. just as peace-offerings may be eaten over a span of two days and the intervening night [from the time that they are slaughtered], so a Passover offering may be eaten [not for one night only] but over a space of two nights as the counterpart to the two days, so that it may be eaten for two nights and the intervening day.

P. Accordingly, we are informed that it must be eaten "in that night," that is, in that night it must be eaten, and it may not be eaten on yet another night [following].

Q. And R. Eleazar b. Azariah? He derives the same lesson from the explicit statement, "You shall not leave any of it over until the morning" (Ex. 12:10).

R. And R. Aqiba? If it were necessary to derive the lesson from that statement, I might have argued, What is the sense of "Morning"? It is the second morning [after slaughter].

S. And R. Eleazar would say to you, "Whenever reference is made to 'morning,' it means the first morning only [after the event that has taken place, not the second morning. So the meaning imputed by Aqiba is impossible anyhow.]"

T. The dispute among the Tannaite authorities just now cited follows the same lines as the dispute among these Tannaite authorities:

U. "There you shall sacrifice the Passover-offering in the evening, at the going down of the sun, at the season that you came forth out of Egypt" (Deut. 16:6).

V. R. Eliezer says, "'At evening' [in the afternoon] you make the sacrifice, 'at sunset' you eat the meat, and 'at the season that you came forth from Egypt' [midnight] you must burn what is left over."

W. R. Joshua says, "'At evening' you make the sacrifice, 'at sunset' you eat the meat, and until how long may you continue eating? Until 'the season that you came forth from Egypt' [midnight]."

X. Said R. Abba, "All concur that when the Israelites were redeemed from Egypt, they were redeemed only in the evening.

Y. "For it is said, 'The Lord your God brought you forth out of Egypt by night' (Deut. 16:1).

Z. "And when they came forth, they came forth only by day, as it is said, 'On the morrow after the Passover the children of Israel went out with a high hand' (Num. 33:3).

AA. "Concerning what point is there a disagreement?

BB. "They disagree concerning the 'time of haste.'

CC. "R. Eleazar b. Azariah takes the view that the sense of 'haste' pertains [not to the Israelites but] to the Egyptians, and R. Aqiba supposes that the sense of 'haste' pertains to the Israelites. [At midnight the Egyptians hastened to go out. That is the basis for the disagreement on the time in which it is permitted to eat the Passover sacrifice, so Simon, p. 47, ns. 7-9]."

DD. It has been taught along these same lines on Tannaite authority:

EE. "The Lord your God brought you forth out of Egypt by night" (Deut. 16:1):

FF. Now did they go forth by night? And was it not by day that they went forth, as it is said, "On the morrow after the Passover the children of Israel went out with a high hand" (Num. 33:3)?

GG. But the passage teaches that the redemption began for them by night.

LXXXIII.

A. "Speak now in the ears of the people" (Ex. 11:2).

B. In the house of R. Yannai they say, "The word for 'now' bears the implication of a request ['by your leave'].

C. "Said the Holy One, blessed be he, to Moses, 'By your leave, go and say to the Israelites,' [and] 'By your leave, ask of the Egyptians utensils of silver and gold.'

D. "[God continues,] 'It is so that that righteous man [Abraham] may not say [9B], "the promise, 'And they shall serve them and they shall afflict them' (Gen. 15:14) he indeed carried out, but the promise, 'And afterward they shall come out with great wealth' (Gen. 15:14) he did not carry out for them.'"

E. "They said to [Moses], 'Would that we can get out with our very lives.'"

F. The case may be compared to that of a man who was imprisoned, and they said to him, "People are coming tomorrow to take you out from prison and they are going to give you a great deal of money."

G. He will answer them, "By your leave, just get me out of here today, and I won't ask for anything else."

LXXXIV.

A. "And they let them have what they asked" (Ex. 12:36):

B. Said R. Ammi, "This teaches that they handed over [property] to them against their wills."

C. There are those who say that it was against the will of the Egyptians.

D. And there are those who say that it was against the will of the Israelites.

E. He who says that it was against the will of the Egyptians points to what is written, "And she who tarries at home divides the spoil." (Ps. 68:13).

F. And he who says that it was against the will of the Israelites explains that it was on account of the burden of carrying the spoil [that the Israelites did not want it].

G. "And they spoiled Egypt" (Ex. 12:36):

H. R. Ammi said, "This teaches that they made it like a snare without grain [to trap birds]."

I. R. Simeon b. Laqish said, "They made it like a pond without fish."

LXXXV.

A. "I am that I am" (Ex. 3:14):

B. Said the Holy One, blessed be he, to Moses, "Go, say to the Israelites: 'I was with you in this subjugation, and I shall be with you when you are subjugated to the [pagan] kingdoms.'"

C. He said to him, "Lord of the world, sufficient for the hour is the trouble [in its own time. Why mention other troubles that are coming?]'

D. Said the Holy One, blessed be he, to him, "Go, say to them, '"I am" has sent me to you' (Ex. 3:14)."

LXXXVI.

A. "Hear me, O Lord, hear me" (1 Kgs. 18:37):

B. Said R. Abbahu, "Why did Elijah say, 'Hear me,' two times?

C. "It teaches that Elijah said before the Holy One, blessed be he, 'Lord of the universe, Answer me, so that fire may come down from heaven and eat what is on the altar.

D. "'And answer me that you may divert them so that they will not say that it was mere enchantment.'

E. "For it is said, 'You did turn their heart backward' (1 Kgs. 18:37)."

To understand how the redactors have arranged this vast array of materials, let us divide matters up among Mishnah-sentences, to see the points at which the units of discourse take up the exegesis or amplification of the Mishnah:

M. 1:1A-B: From what time... from the hour that the priest...

    I-V

M. 1:1C: Until the end of the first watch, so Eliezer.

    VI

M. 1:1D: Sages say, "Until midnight."

    XVII-XVIII

M. 1:1E-N: Gamaliel, "Until dawn."

    LXXVII-LXXXI

Clearly, several very large blocks of materials have been collected and inserted without regard to the requirements of either close exegesis or secondary amplification of the Mishnah passage at hand. These are three: VII-XVI, XIX-LXXVI, and LXXXIII-LXXXVI.

If we begin with the shortest set, we see that the attached constructions deal with the redemption from Egypt, to which the immediately preceding unit of discourse is addressed. So it is a thematic amplification. Why the passage on Abbahu is tacked on (since it has already occurred) I cannot say.

Moving then to the second shortest, VII-XVI, we find the following topics:

VII: The night has three watches, ending "Woe to the children"

VIII: Do not pray in a ruin, ending "Woe to the children"

IX: Do not go into a ruin.

X: The night has three watches or four watches,

XI: Continues X K

XII: Continues X K

XIII: Continues established theme, David, study at midnight

XIV: David's prayer. Mephiboshet.

XV: Mephibosheth.

XVI: Continues foregoing

Accordingly, what we have is really an effort to complement materials directly relevant to the Mishnah-passage. Secondary continuation of discussion of the materials introduced for Mishnah-expansion is added. Thus VII-XVI have in common the single theme of the watches of the night (VIII is tacked on because of sharing the key-phrase, and IX then complements VIII), and, finally, the issue of David's conduct during the night and secondary amplifications of that theme. The person who gathered and organized these materials followed a rather simple plan. Explain the Mishnah-passage, expand upon it, then expand upon the expansions, in sequence and very systematically.

This brings us to the much more complicated mass of material, XIX-LXXVI, an amazingly protracted discussion of many things. Can we account for this unit, which would form about the third of the volume of a small Talmud-tractate? Let us begin by outlining the topics, then see how we may group the topics into a set of large thematic constructions:

XIX: Ps. 145 XX: Ps. 145	Joined to XVIII because of interest in who belongs to the world to come, including one who recites Ps. 145.
XXI: Michael and Gabriel	No clear connection.
XXII: Reciting the Shema in bed	Yohanan at XVIII has insisted one should say the Shema in the evening. Now we stress that it must be done, in addition, in bed. Proof-text: Ps. 4:5.
XXIII: Ps. 4:5	Continues discourse on proof-text.
XXIV: Reciting the Shema in bed keeps demons away.	Continues XXII. Proof-text: Ps. 4:2.
XXV: Ps. 4:2	Continues discourse on proof-text.
XXVI: Causes of suffering	XXIV has referred to the suffering of someone who could study Torah but does not do so. This leads to the notion that study of Torah keeps one from suffering.
XXVII: Suffering brought on by God's love.	Continues foregoing theme.
XXVIII: God gave Israel gifts through suffering.	Continues foregoing theme.
XXIX: He who studies Torah or does acts of loving kindness or buries his children is forgiven all his sins.	Continues foregoing theme.

XXX: Suffering brought on by skin-ailments is a sign of God's love.

Continues foregoing theme.

XXXI: Stories of sick rabbis.

Continues foregoing theme.

XXXII: Stories of sick rabbis.

Continues foregoing theme.

XXXIII: Stories of rabbi's loss of property.

Continues foregoing theme.

XXXIV: Say a prayer before one's bed, place bed on north-south axis.

Now begins a new theme: rules on where and how to say prayers. Abba Benjamin.

XXXV: If two people pray together, they should stay together until both have finished.

Rules on praying. Abba Benjamin.

XXXVI: Demons are numerous.

Abba Benjamin. Same authority, new topic.

XXXVII: Prayer of a person is heard only in the synagogue.

Rules on praying. Abba Benjamin.

XXXVIII: Rules on phylacteries. God puts them on.

Rules on phylacteries. Abin bar Ada/Isaac.

XXXIX: Rules on phylacteries: What is in God's phylacteries?

Nahman bar Isaac to Hiyya bar Abin on theme of phylacteries.

XL: Importance of praying in synagogue.

Rules on praying. Rabin bar Ada/Isaac.

XLI: God is angry when he finds fewer than ten in a synagogue.

Continues the foregoing.

XLII: Set up a regular place in which to pray.

Rules on praying. Helbo, Huna.

XLIII: Reward for attending a lesson, etc.

This continues the immediately preceding item, on running to hear a discourse on law.

XLIV: Not praying behind a synagogue.

Rules on praying, Huna.

XLV: Attentive at afternoon prayer.

Helbo, Huna.

XLVI: Felicitate bridal couple.

Helbo, Huna. Same authority, new topic.

XLVII: Heaven hears words of one who fears heaven.

Rules on praying. Helbo, Huna.

XLVIII: One should greet his friend without waiting to be greeted.

Helbo, Huna. Same authority, new topic.

XLIX: God says prayers.

New topic, related to the theme of praying. Now we speak of God saying prayers. Yohanan/Yose. Continues foregoing.

L: God's prayer.   Continues foregoing.

L I: God's anger.   Continues theme begun at XLIX.

L II: Importance of mercy.   Continues foregoing.

LIII: God's anger.   Continues foregoing.

L IV: Person should reproach   New theme, same authorities, Yohanan/
himself.   Yose.

L V: God gave Moses three things   New theme, same authorities, Yohanan/
that he asked for.   Yose.

L VI: Expansion on one of the   Continues foregoing theme.
things Moses asked for, with ref-
erence to Ex. 33:20.

L VII: Expansion on the theme of   Continues foregoing theme.
Moses' requests.

L VIII: God never retracted a   New theme, same authorities, Yohanan/
conditional promise to do good for   Yose.
Israel.

LIX: Abraham was the first to   New theme, same authority, now Yohanan/
call God "Lord."   Simeon b. Yohai.

L X: How do we know not to   New theme, same authority, now Yohanan/
appease someone when he is angry?   Simeon b. Yohai.

LXI: Leah was the first to   Same theme as LIX, same authorities,
praise God.   Yohanan/Simeon b. Yohai.

LXII: Bringing up a child badly   New theme, same authorities, Yohanan/
is worse than war of Gog and Magog.   Simeon b. Yohai.

LXIII: One may contend with the   New theme, same authorities, Yohanan/
wicked in this world.   Simeon b. Yohai.

L XIV: Anyone who has a regular   New theme, same authorities, Yohanan/
place for praying vanquishes his   Simeon b. Yohai.
enemies.

L XV: Personal service to a sage   New theme, same authorities, Yohanan/
more important than studying with   Simeon b. Yohai.
him.

L XVI: Importance of saying   New theme: rules for saying prayers
prayers with the community, not by   with the community.
self.

L XVII: One who does not say   Rules for saying prayers with the
prayers with the community is a   community.
bad neighbor.

L XVIII: People live long who say   As above.
prayers with the community.

LXIX: Praying at the right time.	Meaning of "the right time." But this "right time" is now interpreted as having to do with something other than praying. It stands at the head of a series on what is more important than praying.
LXX: God loves study of law more than praying.	Continues established theme.
LXXI: Greater is one who works for his own living than one who fears heaven.	No clear relationship to foregoing. Saying of Hiyya bar Ami/Ulla.
LXXII: Person should live where his master does.	No clear relationship to foregoing. Saying of Hiyya bar Ami/Ulla.
LXXIII: One should not leave synagogue when Torah is being read.	New topic: importance of reading the Torah along with the community.
LXXIV: One should read the same Scripture at home that the community is reading in the synagogue.	Continues established topic. Ends with Joshua b. Levi's advice to his children.
LXXV: Raba's advice to his children.	I take it the connection is that Raba accords with a statement that Joshua b. Levi has made. But it is not the same statement that occurs at LXXIV.
LXXVI: Reasons for admiring Medes, Persians.	I see no connection to the foregoing.

If we now seek to group the foregoing, we find the following principles of conglomeration and organization:

1. Common theme, spelled out over a number of distinct units of discourse on aspects of the one theme: 21.

    XIX-XX; XXI-XXXIII; LXVI-LXX; LXXIII

2. Common authorities behind a number of statements on discrete topics: 37.
    Abba Benjamin: XXXIV-XXXVII; Abin bar Ada/Isaac: XXXVIII-XLI; Helbo-Huna, XLII-XLVIII; Yohanan/Yose, XLIX-LVIII; Yohanan/Simeon b. Yohai, LIX-LXV; Hiyya bar Ami/Ulla, LXX-LXXII; Joshua b. Levi, LXXIV-LXXV

3. No clear explanation: 2.
    XXI; LXXVI

The upshot is that there were two principles for the redaction of large conglomerates of materials, the one, thematic, the other, the name of the authority and tradent (X says Y says). In this second principle, the tradent's name will predominate, thus Yohanan/Yose and Yohana/Simeon b. Yohai materials are grouped, XLIX-LXIX, 21 units of discourse, to which we should attach Ulla's set, added because Ulla's name occurs in the foregoing composite. Can we then rigidly differentiate thematic or topical compositions, e.g., rules on public prayer or on praying in synagogues, from tradental compositions, e.g., sayings in the name of a given tradent and authority? Yes and no. What all topical compositions have in common, of course, is focus on a given topic. But some tradental compositions are arranged around a single topic, and in most a given subject will predominate, even though tangentially or not-at-all related topics will enter. So while we may say that all topical compositions as a group differ from all tradental ones, we may not rigidly distinguish tradental compositions from topical ones. What we have to recognize as the distinctive trait of the tradental composition is the predominance of a given tradent's name, which will explain the insertion of a thematically irrelevant (or, at best, neutral) item. It follows that the Talmud of Babylonia is made up, so far as our protracted sample is concerned, of four types of material: Mishnah-exegesis, expansion of Mishnah-exegesis, topical compositions in some way relevant to the largest themes of the Mishnah-tractate, or the Mishnah-paragraph, at hand, and tradental compositions possibly relevant in the same way, possibly not.

1:2

A.   From what time do they recite the Shema in the morning?
B.   From the hour that one can distinguish between blue and white.
C.   R. Eliezer says, "Between blue and green."
D.   And one completes it by sunrise.
E.   R. Joshua says, "By the third hour.
F.   "For it is the practice of royalty to rise [at] the third hour."
G.   One who recites the Shema from then on has not lost [the merit of the act entirely, since he is] like one who recites from the Torah.

I.
A.   What is the meaning of "between blue and white?"
B.   If I should propose that it means the difference between a white piece of wool and a blue piece of wool, that difference can be discerned by night [as much as by day].
C.   Rather, [the sense is to distinguish] between the blue and the white [threads in the same piece of wool].

II.
A.   It has been taught on Tannaite authority:
B.   R. Meir says, "Once one can tell the difference between a wolf and a dog."
C.   R. Aqiba says, "... between an ass and a wild ass."
D.   **Others say, "Once one can see his fellow four cubits away and recognize who it is"** [T. Ber. 1:2B].
E.   Said R. Huna, "The decided law accords with the position of 'others.'"
F.   Said Abayye, "The law as to the phylacteries accords with the view of 'others,' while the law on reciting the Shema accords with the view of the old-timers."

G.   For R. Yohanan said, "The old-timers would complete the recitation of the Shema by dawn."

III.

A.   It has been taught on Tannaite authority along these same lines:

B.   The old-timers would complete the recitation of Shema exactly at dawn so as to place the prayer for redemption [with which the Shema closes] right next to the Prayer [of supplication], and one will turn out to say the Prayer in daylight."

C.   Said R. Zira, "What verse of Scripture supports this practice? 'They shall fear you with the sun and so long as the moon throughout all generations' (Ps. 82:5)."

D.   R. Yose b. Eliaqim gave testimony in behalf of the holy community of Jerusalem, "Whoever recites the prayer for Redemption immediately prior to the Prayer [of supplication] will not suffer injury that entire day."

E.   Said R. Zira, "Is that so? But lo, I joined the two but I still was injured that day."

F.   He said to him, "What went wrong with you? Was it that you had to carry a myrtle branch into the royal palace? In that case that was no injury at all, because you should have had to pay a fee to have the right to see the face of the king! [It was no injury at all to have to pay the corvee under such circumstances.]"

G.   For R. Yohanan said, "A person should always try to run to meet the kings of Israel, and not the kings of Israel alone, but even the kings of the idolators,

H.   "so that if one should have the merit, he may know the difference between the kings of Israel and the kings of the idolators [living so long as to see the restoration of the Israelite monarchy]."

IV.

A.   Said R. Ila to Ulla, "When you go up there, greet my brother, R. Berona, in the presence of the entire community [of scholars], for he is a great man and takes great joy in carrying out religious duties.

B.   "Once he managed to join the recitation of the prayer for redemption to the Prayer [of supplication], and he did not stop smiling the whole day."

V.

A.   But how is it possible to join the two prayers without interruption.

B.   For R. Yohanan said, "At the beginning [of the Prayer], a person has to recite, 'O Lord, open my lips' (Ps. 51:17), and at the end, 'Let the words of my mouth be acceptable' (Ps. 19:15). [So at the beginning there is a prayer that intervenes between the blessing for redemption and the Prayer itself.]"

C.   Said R. Eleazar, "The inclusion of the cited verses must be only at the Prayer said in the evening."

D.   But did not R. Yohanan say, "Who belongs to the category of the world to come? It is a person who joins the prayer for redemption said at night to the Prayer that is recited at night"?

E.   Rather, said R. Eleazar, "The added verses should come in the Prayer when it is recited in the late afternoon."

F.   R. Ashi said, "You may take the position that the additional verses of Scripture belong in the Prayer when it is said throughout the day [morning, afternoon, night]. For since rabbis have ordained that these verses should be added to the Prayer, it is as if the Prayer itself has simply been protracted.

G.   "For if you do not take this position, how in the Prayer said at night can we join the prayer for redemption to the Prayer. For in any event a person has in the middle to recite, 'Cause us to lie down....'

H.   "Rather, the operative principle is that, since rabbis have ordained that we say, 'Cause us to lie down...,' it is in the category of a protracted prayer for Redemption.

I.   "Here too, since rabbis have ordained the inclusion of the verses of Psalms in the Prayer, it is as if the Prayer had been lengthened."

VI.

A.   Since the verse, "May the words of my mouth be acceptable" (Ps. 19:15) would serve equally well at the end of the Prayer as much as at the beginning, why did rabbis ordain that it was to be said at the end of the Eighteen Blessings [the Prayer]? Why not say it at the beginning?

B.   Said R. Judah, son of R. Simeon b. Pazzi, "Since David said that verse only at the end of eighteen chapters [of Psalms, namely, at the end of Psalm 19], rabbis on that account ordained that it should come at the end of the Eighteen Blessings."

C.   But the eighteen Psalms [to which reference has just been made] in fact are nineteen!

D.   "Happy is the man" and "Why are the nations in an uproar" (Ps. 1:1, 2:1) constitute a single chapter.

E.   For R. Judah, son of R. Simeon b. Pazzi said, "David recited 103 Psalms, and he never said 'Halleluyah' until he had witnessed the downfall of the wicked.

F.   "For it has been said, 'Let sinners cease out of the earth, and let the wicked be no more. Bless the Lord, O my soul. Halleluyah' (Ps. 104:35)."

G.   These 103 Psalms in fact are 104 Psalms.

H.   That then yields the inference that "Happy is the man" and "Why are the nations in an uproar" (Ps. 1:1, 2:1) constitute a single chapter.

I.   For R. Samuel bar Nahmani said R. Yohanan said, "[10A] Every chapter that was particularly beloved for David did he open by saying 'Happy' and close by saying 'Happy.'

J.   "He began with 'Happy,' as Scriptures states, 'Happy is the man' (Ps. 1:1) and he closed with 'Happy,' as Scriptures states, 'Happy are all who trust in him' (Ps. 2:11)."

VII.

A.   There were some thugs in R. Meir's neighborhood, who gave him a lot of trouble. R. Meir prayed for mercy for himself so that they would die. His wife, Beruriah, said to him, "What is on your mind? [Do you pray that they should die] because it is written [at Ps. 104:35], 'Let sins die'? Is it written 'sinners'? What is written is 'sins.'

B.   "And at the end of the verse, moreover, it is written, 'And let wicked men be no more' (Ps. 104:35).

C.   "Since my sins will stop, there will be no more wicked men.

D.   "Rather, pray for mercy concerning them that they will revert in repentance and not be wicked any more."

E.   He prayed for mercy concerning them, and they did revert in repentance.

VIII.

A.   A certain min said to Beruriah, "It is written, 'Sing, O barren woman, who has not born...' (Is. 54:1).

B.   "Because the woman is barren, should she rejoice?"

C.   She said to him, "Idiot, look at the end of the same verse of Scripture, for it is written, 'For the children of the desolate shall be more than the children of the married woman, says the Lord' (Is. 54:1).

D.   "What then is the sense of, 'Barren woman, who has not born'?

E.   "Rejoice, O congregation of Israel, which is like a barren woman [that is,] who has not born children destined for Gehenna such as yourself."

IX.

A.   A certain min said to R. Abbahu, "It is written, 'A Psalm of David when he fled from Absalom, his son' (Ps. 3:1). And it is written, 'A mihtam of David, when he fled from Saul in the cave' (Ps. 57:1).

B.   "Which incident took place first? Since it was the incident with Saul, it should have been written first."

C.   He said to him, "You, who do not execute an exegesis of Scripture based on the juxtaposition of passages, find the issue a problem. We, who execute exegeses based on the juxtaposition of verses, do not find the matter a problem."

D.   For R. Yohanan said, "The principle of the exegesis of passages based on juxtapositions derives from the Torah itself.

E.   "Whence do we know that fact? As it is written, "They are joined together forever and ever they are done in truth and uprightness" (Ps. 111:8).

F.   [Reverting to Abbahu:] "Why is the passage concerning Absalom placed in juxtaposition with the passage dealing with Gog and Magog [that is, Ps. 2]? For if someone should say to you, 'Is there such a thing as a slave that rebels against his master,' you may say to him, 'Is there such a thing as a son who rebels against his father?' But just as the one thing happened so did the other."

X.

A.   Said R. Yohanan in the name of R. Simeon b. Yohai, "What is the meaning of the Scripture, 'She opens her mouth with wisdom, and the Torah of kindness is on her tongue' (Prov. 31:26)?

B.   "With regard to whom did Solomon say this verse? He said it only with reference to his father, David, who dwelled in five worlds and said a song [in each].

C.   "He dwelled in the belly of his mother and said a song, as it is said, 'Bless the Lord, O my soul, and all my inwards bless his holy name' (Ps. 103:1).

D. "He came forth into the world and looked at the stars and planets and said a song, as it is said, 'Bless the Lord, you angels of his, you mighty in strength that fulfill his word, hearkening to the voice of his word. Bless the Lord, all you his hosts' (Ps. 103:20, 21).

E. "He sucked at the tit of his mother and looked at her breasts and said a song, as it is said, 'Bless the Lord, O my soul, and forget not all his benefits' (Ps. 103:21)."

F. What is the meaning of "all his benefits"?

G. Said R. Abbahu, "That God put the breasts at the place of understanding [the heart]."

H. What is the reason?

I. Said R. Judah, "So that one should not gaze upon the woman's sexual parts."

J. R. Mattena said, "So that one should not suck from a smelly place."

K. [Resuming Simeon b. Yohai's statement:] "He saw the catastrophe that came upon the wicked and said a song, as it is said, 'Let sinners cease out of the earth and let the wicked be no more. Bless the Lord, O my soul, Halleluyah' (Ps. 104:35).

L. "He looked upon the day of death and said a song, as it is said, 'Bless the Lord, O my soul. O Lord my God, you are very great, you are clothed with glory and majesty' (Ps. 104:1)."

M. How do we know that the cited verse refers to the day of death?

N. Said Rabbah bar R. Shila, "We derive that information from the latter part of the same clause: 'You hide your face, they vanish, you withdraw their breath, they perish' (Ps. 104:29)."

XI.

A. R. Shimi bar Uqba, and some say, Mar Uqba, often was in session before R. Simeon b. Pazzi, who had laid forth exegeses before R. Joshua b. Levi. He said to him, "What is the meaning of the verse of Scripture, 'Bless the Lord, O my soul, and all that is within me bless his holy name' (Ps. 103:1)?"

B. He said to him, "Come and take note of the fact that the trait of the Holy One, blessed be he, is not like the trait of mortals.

C. "If a mortal makes a drawing on the wall, he cannot put into it spirit and breath, bowels and intestines. But the Holy One, blessed be he is, is not that way. He can make a drawing within a drawing and put into it spirit and breath, bowels and intestines.

D. "And that is in line with what Hannah said, 'There is none holy as the Lord, for this is none beside you, neither is there any form (SR) like our God' (1 Sam. 2:2).

E. "What is the sense of, 'neither is there any form like our God'?

F. "There is no artist (SYR) like our God."

G. What is the meaning of, "For there is none beside you" (Ps. 1 Sam. 2:2)?

H. Said R. Judah bar Menassia, "Do not read it as if it says, 'There is none beside you,' but rather, 'There is none to outlive you.'

I. "For the trait of the Holy One, blessed be he, is not like the trait of mortals.

J. "The trait of mortals is that what mortals create outlives them.

K. "But the Holy One, blessed be he, outlives his own creations."

L.   He said to him, "This is what I meant to say to you: As to these five references to 'Bless the Lord, O my soul' [which David said], to whom did David allude when he said them?

M.   "He alluded only to the Holy One blessed be he, and to the soul.

N.   "Just as the Holy One, blessed be he, fills the whole world, so the soul fills the whole body.

O.   "Just as the Holy One, blessed be he, sees but is not seen, so the soul sees but is not seen.

P.   "Just as the Holy One, blessed be he, sustains the whole world, so the soul sustains the whole body.

Q.   "Just as the Holy One, blessed be he, is pure, so the soul is pure.

R.   "Just as the Holy One, blessed be he, sits in the innermost chambers, so the soul dwells in the innermost chambers.

S.   "Let that which bears all these five traits come and give praise to the One in whom are all these five traits."

XII.

A.   Said R. Hamnuna, "What is the meaning of the verse of Scripture, 'Who is as the wise man? And who knows the interpretation of a matter?' (Qoh. 8:1)?

B.   "Who is like the Holy One, blessed be he, who knows how to accomplish a mediating interpretation of the claims of two righteous men, Hezekiah and Isaiah.

C.   "Hezekiah said, 'Let Isaiah come to me, for we find in the case of Elijah that he came to Ahab.'

D.   "Isaiah said, 'Let Hezekiah come to me, for we find in the case of Jehoram, son of Ahab, that he came to Elisha.'

E.   "What did the Holy One, blessed be he, do? He brought suffering upon Hezekiah and said to Isaiah, 'Go and pay a call on the sick man.'

F.   "For it is said, 'In those days Hezekiah was sick unto death. And Isaiah the prophet, son of Amoz, came to him and said to him, Thus says the Lord, Set your house in order, for you will die and not live' (Is. 38:1)."

G.   What is the meaning of, "You shall die and not live"?

H.   "You shall die" in this world "and shall not live" in the world to come.

I.   [Resuming the interrupted narrative:] "He said to him, 'Why all this?'

J.   "He said to him, 'Because you did not engage in carrying out the religious duty to be fruitful and multiply.'

K.   "He said to him, 'It was because I saw by the Holy Spirit that from me would go forth sons who were not worthy.'

L.   "He said to him, 'What business is it of yours to get involved with the secrets of the All-Merciful? What you are commanded to do is what you have to do, and what pleases the Holy One, blessed be he, he will do.'

M.   "He said to him, 'Then give me your daughter. Perhaps the merit that has accrued to me and the merit that has accrued to you will serve so that out of me worthy sons will come forth.'

N.   "He said to him, 'The decree has already been made against you.'

O.   "He said to him, 'Ben Amoz, finish your prophecy and leave. Thus have I received as a tradition from the house of the father of my father: "Even if a sharp sword is lying on a man's neck, he should not refrain from praying for mercy."'"

P.   It has been stated on Amoraic authority along these same lines:

Q.   R. Yohanan and R. Eleazar both say, "Even if a sharp sword is resting on a man's neck, he should not refrain from praying for mercy,

R.   "For it is said, 'Though he slay me, yet I will trust in him' (Job 13:15)."

S.   [10B] Said R. Hanan, "Even if the master of dreams says to a man that he will die tomorrow, he should not refrain from praying for mercy.

T.   "For it is said, 'For in the multitude of dreams are vanities, and also many words, but fear you God' (Qoh. 5:6)."

U.   [Resuming the interrupted narrative:] "Forthwith, 'Hezekiah turned his face to the wall and prayed to the Lord' (Is. 38:2)."

V.   What is the sense of "wall"?

W.   Said R. Simeon b. Laqish, "[He prayed] from the innermost walls of his heart, as it is said, 'My bowels, my bowels, I writhe in pain. The walls of my heart...' (Jer. 4:19)."

X.   R. Levi said, "He prayed concerning matters having to do with a wall. He said before him, 'Lord of the world, now if for the Shunamit woman, who only made a small wall[ed hut], you brought her son back to life, for father's father, who covered the entire house with silver and gold, all the more so [should you restore me to life].'"

Y.   "'Remember now, O Lord, I beseech you, how I have walked before you in truth and with a whole heart and have done that which is good in your sight" (Is. 38:3).

Z.   What is the meaning of, "I have done that which is good in your sight"?

AA.   Said R. Judah said Rab, "What he did was to juxtapose the prayer for redemption to the Prayer."

BB.   R. Levi said, "He hid away the scroll containing cures."

XIII.

A.   Our rabbis have taught on Tannaite authority:

B.   King Hezekiah did six things. On account of three of them [sages] praised him, and on account of three they did not praise him.

C.   On account of three they praised him:

D.   He hid away the book of cures and they praised him.

E.   He pulverized the copper snake and they praised him.

F.   He dragged the bones of his father on a bed of ropes and they praised him.

G.   On account of three they did not praise him.

H.   He shut off the waters of Gihon, and they did not praise him.

I.   He cut off the gold from the doors of the Temple and sent it to the king of Assyria, and they did not praise him.

J.   He intercalated the month of Nisan during the month of Nisan itself and they did not praise him.

K. But did Hezekiah not concur with the law, "'This month shall be unto you the beginning of months' (Ex. 12:2), which means that this month is Nisan, and no other month can be declared Nisan [so that one may not intercalate a month into the year and call it Nisan]"?

L. But he erred with respect to the matter that is framed in the teaching of Samuel.

M. For Samuel said, "People may not intercalate the year on the thirtieth day of Adar, since that day may belong to Nisan" [Simon, p. 57, n. 1: if the new moon is observed on it].

N. He said, "We do not invoke the possibility that it might belong [to Nisan], [so he intercalated a second Adar in that year, doing so on the thirtieth day of the first Adar]."

XIV.

A. R. Yohanan said in the name of R. Yose b. Zimra, "Whoever relies [in his petition to Heaven] on his own merit is made to depend upon the merit of others, and whoever relies on the merit of others is made to depend upon his own merit.

B. "Moses depended upon the merit of others, as it is said, 'Remember Abraham, Isaac, and Israel, your servants' (Ex. 32:13), so the matter was made to depend upon his own merit, as it is said, 'Therefore he said that he would destroy them, had not Moses his chosen stood before him in the breach to turn back his wrath, lest he should destroy them' (Ps. 106:23).

C. "Hezekiah depended upon his own merit, as it is said, 'Remember, now O Lord, I beseech you, how I have walked before you' (Is. 38:3). So he was made to depend upon the merit of others, for it says, 'I will defend this city to save it, for my own sake and for my servant David's sake' (Is. 37:35)."

D. That is in line with what R. Joshua b. Levi said.

E. For R. Joshua b. Levi said, "What is the meaning of the following verse of Scripture: 'Behold for my peace I had great bitterness' (Is. 38:17)?

F. "Even when the Holy One, blessed be he, sent him peace, it was bitter to him [Simon, p. 57, n. 8: because it was not made to depend on his own merit]."

XV.

A. "Let us make, I pray you, a little walled chamber on the roof" (2 Kgs. 4:10):

B. Rab and Samuel:

C. One said, "There was an upper chamber there, and they made a roof for it."

D. The other said, "There was a large veranda, and they divided it into two."

E. Now in the view of him who said there was a veranda, that is why it is written, "...wall...," [which is to say, they added another wall].

F. But in the view of him who says that it was a chamber, why does it say "...wall... (QYR)"?

G. For they roofed (QYR) it.

H. Now in the view of him who says there was an upper chamber (CLH), that is why it is written "chamber (CLH)."

I. But in the view of him who says it was a veranda, why does it say "chamber"?

J.   It was the best (^CLH) of all the rooms.

K.   "And let us set a bed for him there, a table, stool, and candlestick" (2 Kgs. 4:10):

L.   Said Abayye, and some say, R. Isaac, "He who wants to derive benefit [from hospitality] should do so as did Elisha, and he who does not wish to derive benefit should not do so, in the model of Samuel of Ramah.

M.   "For it is said, 'And his return was to Ramah, for there was his house' (1 Sam. 7:17).'"

N.   And R. Yohanan said, "Wherever he went, there his house was with him."

O.   "And she said to her husband, Behold now, I perceive that he is a holy man of God" (2 Kgs. 4:9):

P.   Said R. Yose bar Hanina, "This proves that a woman recognizes the character of guests more accurately than does her husband."

Q.   "A holy man" (2 Kgs. 4:9):

R.   How did she know?

S.   Rab and Samuel:

T.   One said, "Because she never saw a fly passing the table on which he [ate]."

U.   And the other said, "Because she spread a linen sheet on his bed, and she did not see a drop of semen on it."

V.   "He is holy" (2 Kgs. 4:9):

W.   Said R. Yose b. R. Hanina, "He is holy, but his servant is not holy.

X.   "For it is said, 'And Gehazi came near to thrust her away' (2 Kgs. 4:27).

Y.   R. Yose b. R. Hanina said, "He grabbed her by the breast."

Z.   "He passes by us all the time" (2 Kgs. 4:9):

AA.   Said R. Yose b. R. Hanina in the name of R. Eliezer b. Jacob, "Whoever provides hospitality in his own home for a disciple of a sage and provides for him from his prosperity is regarded by Scripture as though he had offered daily whole offerings."

XVI.

A.   And R. Yose b. R. Hanina said in the name of R. Eliezer b. Jacob, "A person should not stand in a high place and say his prayer, but he should stand in a low place and say his prayer.

B.   "For it is said, 'Out of the depths I have called to you, O Lord' (Ps. 130:1)."

C.   It has been taught on Tannaite authority along the same lines:

D.   A person should not stand either on a chair or on a stool or on a high place and say his prayers, but he should stand on a low place and say his prayers.

E.   For there is no such thing as elevation before the Omnipresent.

F.   For it is said, "Out of the depths I have called to you, O Lord" (Ps. 130:1).

G.   And it is written, "A prayer of the afflicted, when he faints" (Ps. 102:1).

H.   And R. Yose b. R. Hanina said in the name of R. Eliezer b. Jacob, "He who says the Prayer has to line up his feet [side by side],

I.   "as it is said, 'And their feet were straight' (Ez. 1:7)."

J.   And R. Yose b. R. Hanina said in the name of R. Eliezer b. Jacob, "What is the meaning of this verse of Scripture: 'You shall not eat with the blood' (Lev. 19:26)?

K.   "Do not eat before you have said your prayer concerning your own blood [so pray as to save your own life]."

L.   And R. Isaac said R. Yohanan said R. Yose b. R. Hanina said in the name of R. Eliezer b. Jacob, "Whoever eats, drinks, and only then says his prayers is regarded by Scripture as follows: 'And me have you cast beyond your back' (1 Kgs. 14:9).

M.   "Do not read the letters as though they say 'your back' but rather, 'your pride.'

N.   "Said the Holy One, blessed be he, 'After this one has taken pride in himself, only then has he accepted the dominion of heaven.'"

XVII.

A.   Said R. Joshua, "By the third hour" [M. 1:2E]:

B.   Said R. Judah said Samuel, "The decided law accords with the position of R. Joshua."

XVIII.

A.   One who recites the Shema from then on has not lost... [M. 1:2G]:

B.   Said R. Hisda said Mar Uqba, "But that is on condition that one not say the blessing, '... who forms the light'."

C.   An objection was raised from the following statement: He who recites the Shema from then on has not lost [the merit of the act entirely, since he is] like one who recites from the Torah. But he has to say two blessings [including 'who forms light'] before reciting the Shema and one afterward.

D.   Is this not a refutation of R. Hisda's view?

E.   It is an explicit refutation.

F.   Some report the matter as follows:

G.   Said R. Hisda said Mar Uqba, "What is the sense of '... he has not lost...'? That he has not lost the blessings [recited prior to, and following, the recitation of the Shema]."

H.   It has been taught along these same lines on Tannaite authority:

I.   He who recites the Shema from then on has not lost [the merit of the act entirely, since he is] like one who recites from the Torah. But he has to say two blessings before reciting the Shema and one afterward.

XIX.

A.   Said R. Mani, "Greater is the merit according to him who recites the Shema at its proper time than that accruing to one who takes up study of the Torah.

B.   "Since the Mishnah states, 'He who recites the Shema from then on has not lost the merit of the act entirely, since he is like one who recites from the Torah, there is the implication that the one who recites it in its proper time is still better off.

The sizable portion at hand includes materials brought together to serve as exegesis of the Mishnah, others worked out on a single theme and proposition, and still others conglomerated around the name of a single authority and tradent. Units I, II, complemented by III, serve the opening phrase of the Mishnah. Units IV, V take up a detail of unit III, juxtaposition of the Shema to the Prayer. Since unit V has referred to Ps. 19:15, unit VI proceeds to develop ideas on that verse. Since unit VI has included a reference to

Ps. 104:35, unit VII tells a story in which that verse figures. Since unit VII refers to Beruriah, unit VIII tells another story about Beruriah. Since unit VIII's story refers to a min, unit IX introduces another story about a min.

I am not entirely sure why unit X is introduced. It does not seem to me that including Yohanan at IX D accounts for introducing a sizable unit of discourse of his. My best guess is that what we have is another instance of building an exegesis based on the juxtaposition of verses. The appearance, at X C, of Ps. 103:1, however, certainly explains the introduction of unit XI.

Unit XII does strike me as a random insertion. I see no connection whatever to what has gone before, nor any to what will follow after the completion of unit XI in units XII, XIII, XIV -- more on Hezekiah. Unit XV is introduced because of XII V-X, that is, the reference to the word 'wall,' on the one side, and the Shunamit woman, on the other. Now we have a rather elaborate treatment of that and subsequent verses.

Because we end with Yose b. R. Hanina's citation of Eliezer, we are given the entire construction of which XV X is the opening line, that is, unit XVI, a tradental construction.

We end, XVII-XIX, with a reversion to Mishnah-commentary.

My sense of the purpose of inserting everything between III and XVI is that the redactor simply gathered together masses of connected materials and placed them where he did as a way of providing them with a home. Why were the materials connected to begin with? Once more we see that entire sets were assembled around sequential verses of Scripture, on the one side, or around the name of a tradent and authority, on the other. A dominant theme, third, will account for the gathering of yet other materials. It seems to me the set at hand is more clearly meant to form a continuous -- if somewhat meandering -- discourse than the foregoing.

1:3

A.   The House of Shammai say, "In the evening everyone should recline to recite the Shema, and in the morning they should stand.

B.   "As it says, 'When you lie down and when you rise up' (Deut. 6:7)."

C.   And the House of Hillel say, "Everyone recites according to his usual manner.

D.   "As it says, 'And as you walk by the way' (ibid.)."

E.   "If so why does [the verse] say, 'When you lie down and when you rise up'?

F.   "[It means, recite the Shema] at the hour that people lie down [at night] and at the hour that people rise [in the morning]."

G.   Said R. Tarfon, "I was coming on the road and I reclined, so as to recite the Shema, according to the words of the House of Shammai. And I placed myself in danger of [being attacked by] thugs."

H.   They said to him, "You have only yourself to blame [for what might have befallen you], for you violated the ruling of the House of Hillel."

I.

A.   [11A] Now [at M. 1:3C-F] the House of Hillel explain their position and also deal with the reason behind the position of the House of Shammai.

B.   But what is the reason that the House of Shammai do not rule as do the House of Hillel?

C.   The House of Shammai will say to you, "If [matters were] as [you state, at M. 1:3D-E], Scripture should say merely, 'In the morning... and at night.' Why does Scripture say, 'When you lie down and when you rise up' (Deut. 6:7)? It is to indicate that one recites the <u>Shema</u> at the time that one actually lies down, and at the time that one actually gets up."

D.   Then how do the House of Shammai interpret the words, "And when you walk by the way" (Deut. 6:7)?

E.   They require it for support for the following proposition, which has been taught on Tannaite authority:

F.   "When you sit in your house" thus excluding [from the requirement to recite the <u>Shema</u>] one who is engaged in carrying out a religious duty.

G.   "When you walk by the way" further is meant to exclude the newly-wed [who does not have to recite the <u>Shema</u>].

H.   On the basis of the foregoing exegesis, sages have ruled:

I.   He who marries a virgin-woman is exempt from the obligation to recite the <u>Shema</u>, but he who marries a widow is obligated.

J.   What is the force of the proof-text at hand?

K.   Said R. Papa, "The word 'way' contains this implication: Just as one goes on the way [and makes a journey] as an optional matter, so anyone involved in a merely optional matter [is obligated to recite the <u>Shema</u>, but one engaged in a religious duty is exempt].

L.   But do we not deal with someone who may be en route to carry out a religious duty, and here too, the All-Merciful has said that such a one should recite the <u>Shema</u>?

M.   If so, the All-Merciful should have stated, "While sitting... while walking...." Why has it made explicit reference to <u>your</u> sitting and <u>your</u> going? When you are sitting and involved in your own affairs, when you are going on the way for your own purposes, is that point at which you are obligated. But if what you are doing concerns a religious duty, you are exempt.

N.   If that is the operative consideration, then should not even one who marries a widow also be exempt [from reciting the <u>Shema</u>, since it is a religious duty to engage in procreation]?

O.   The one who marries a virgin is preoccupied [with the sexual act], and the one who marries a widow is not preoccupied.

P.   If the operative consideration is whether or not one is preoccupied, then even if one's boat is sinking at sea, he should also be exempt from the obligation to recite the <u>Shema</u>.

Q.   And if you say, that indeed is the rule, then take account of what R. Abba bar Zabeda said Rab said, "A mourner is liable to carry out all of the religious duties that are stated in the Torah,

R.   "exempt for the duty of putting on phylacteries.

S.   "For lo, in their regard, the word 'glory' is used, as it says, 'Put your glory upon you' (Ez. 24:17). [Ezekiel was a mourner but was told, as a matter of exception, to put on his head-covering. What this means is that under ordinary circumstances a mourner does not put on his head-covering, understood to refer to the phylacteries]." [Accordingly, it cannot be the case that one who is preoccupied with a major financial loss is exempt from the obligation to recite the Shema.]

T.   There [with respect to marriage to a virgin], the groom is preoccupied with concerns brought about in the performance of a religious duty, while here [with reference to the one whose ship is sinking], he is preoccupied with concerns brought about by an optional [and personal] matter.

U.   And how do the House of Shammai [deal with the words, "and when you walk along the way"]?

V.   That phrase excludes from the requirement to recite the Shema those who are messengers carrying out religious duties.

W.   And the House of Hillel [deal with the verse in the same way, in which case, how can they also use the verse to prove their point as at M. 1:3D]?

X.   They will respond, "Quite tangentially the phrase at hand bears the implication that, even when one is on the way, he also has to recite the Shema."

II.

A.   It has been taught on Tannaite authority:

B.   The House of Shammai say, "People may stand and recite the Shema, sit and recite the Shema, recline and recite the Shema, go along the way and recite the Shema, do their work and recite the Shema.

C.   M^{C}sh b: R. Ishmael and R. Eleazar ben Azariah were staying in the same place. R. Ishmael was reclining and R. Eleazar ben Azariah was standing upright. When the time came to recite the Shema, R. Ishmael arose and R. Eleazar ben Azariah reclined.

D.   [Following T.:] Said R. Ishmael, "What is this, Eleazar?"

E.   R. Eleazar b. Azariah said to R. Ishmael, "Ishmael, my brother, I shall offer an analogy: they say to one, 'Why is your beard grown long?', and he says to them, 'Let it serve [as a protest] against the destroyers.'

F.   "[Just so,] I, who was standing, reclined; and you, who were reclining, arose."

G.   He [Ishmael] said to him, "You reclined to carry out the words of the House of Shammai, and I arose to carry out [the words of] the House of Hillel [M. Ber. 1:3]."

H.   "And not only so, but [I arose] so that the students should not behold and establish the law for all generations according to your words" [T. Ber. 1:4].

I.   What is the sense of "Not only so..."?

J.   "And if you should say that the House of Hillel also approve reclining, I have to reply that that ruling applies to one who has been reclining all along. But here, since up to this point you were standing upright and now you have chosen to recline, people will rule that that action bears the implication that the law accords with the House of Hillel."

K.   Hence it is said, "...lest the disciples see and establish the law for all generations according to your words."

III.

A.   R. Ezekiel taught on Tannaite authority: "If one has acted in accord with the view of the House of Shammai, or if he has acted in accord with the view of the House of Hillel, he has done what is required."

B.   R. Joseph said, "If one has acted in accord with the view of the House of Shammai, he has done nothing whatsoever.

C.   For we have learned in the Mishnah:

D.   He whose head and the greater part of whose body are in the sukkah, but whose table is in the house -- the House of Shammai declare invalid, and the House of Hillel declare valid.

E.   Said the House of Hillel to the House of Shammai, "Was not the precedent so, that the elders of the House of Shammai and the elders of the House of Hillel went to pay a sick-call on R. Yohanan b. Hahorani, and they found him sitting with his head and the greater part of his body in the sukkah, and his table in the house, and they said nothing at all to him!"

F.   Said the House of Shammai to them, "Is there proof from that story? But in point of fact they did say to him, 'If this is how you act, you have never in your whole life fulfilled the religious requirement of dwelling in a sukkah!'" [M. Suk. 2:7].

G.   R. Nahman bar Isaac said, "If one has acted in accord with the view of the House of Shammai, he is liable to the death penalty.

H.   "For we have learned in the Mishnah:

I.   "Said R. Tarfon, 'I was coming on the road and I reclined so as to recite the Shema according to the words of the House of Shammai. And I placed myself in danger of being attacked by thugs.'

J.   "They said to him, 'You have only yourself to blame for what might have befallen you, for you violated the ruling of the House of Hillel' [M. 1:3G-H]."

Unit I explores the exegetical foundations for the position of the two Houses, filling in the gap left by the Mishnah's version's failure to account for the Shammaites' rule. Unit II complements the Mishnah-paragraph. Unit III does the same, now placing Tarfon's statement into a larger context.

1:4

A.   In the morning one recites two [blessings] before it and one blessing after it.

B.   And in the evening two blessings before it and two blessings after it,

C.   one long and one short [blessing]:

D.   Where sages have said to say a long one, one is not permitted to say a short one.

E.   [Where they said] to say a short one, one is not permitted to say a long one.

F.   [Where they said] to conclude [with an appropriate blessing] one is not permitted not to conclude with one.

G.   [Where they said] not to conclude with a blessing, one is not permitted to do so.

I.

A.   [In the morning] what blessing does one say?

B.   Said R. Jacob said R. Oshaia, "[11B] '... who forms light and creates darkness.'"

C.   But why not say, "... who forms light and creates brightness"?

D.   As the verse is written in Scripture [Is. 45:7], so we recite it.

E.   If so, what about the following: "Who makes peace and creates evil" (Is. 45:7)? Do we say these words as they are written? Rather, it is written, "Evil," but in the blessing we recite "all things."

F.   What we have, in point of fact, is the use of a more suitable formulation.

G.   But here too, why not say "brightness," which is a more suitable formulation?

H.   Rather, said Raba, "Matters are so phrased as to make mention of the character of day by night and the character of night by day."

I.   Now there is no problem in the claim that we mention the character of night by day, for it is as we say, "Who creates light and forms darkness."

J.   But where do we find that we mention the character of day by night?

K.   Said Abayye, "It is in the phrase, '... who rolls away the light before the darkness, and the darkness before the light.'"

II.

A.   What is the other blessing [that is recited in the morning before the Shema]?

B.   Said R. Judah said Samuel, "It is the prayer beginning, '... with great love....'"

C.   And so did R. Eleazar teach R. Pedat his son, "It is, '... with great love....'"

D.   So too has it been taught on Tannaite authority: People do not say, "'... with everlasting love...,' but '... with great love....'"

E.   But rabbis say, "It is, '... with everlasting love.'

F.   "And so Scripture says, 'Yes, I have loved you with an everlasting love, therefore with affection I have drawn you' (Jer. 31:3)."

III.

A.   Said R. Judah said Samuel, "If one has gotten up early to repeat Mishnah-traditions before reciting the Shema, he has to say a blessing [for the act of study].

B.   "If he has recited the Shema, he does not have to say a blessing, for he has already carried out his obligation to say a blessing for the study by reciting the prayer, '... With great love....'"

IV.

A.   Said R. Huna, "For the study of Scripture, one has to say a blessing, for the study of scriptural exegesis, one does not have to say a blessing."

B.   And R. Eleazar said, "For the study of Scripture and scriptural exegesis, it is necessary to say a blessing, but for the study of Mishnah it is not necessary to say a blessing."

C.   And R. Yohanan said, "Also for the study of Mishnah it is necessary to say a blessing, but for the study of the Talmud it is not necessary to say a blessing."

D.   And Raba said, "Also for the study of the Talmud it is necessary to say a blessing."

E.   For R. Hiyya bar Ashi said, "Many times I stood before Rab to repeat our passage in the Sifra of the house of Rab, and he would go ahead and wash his hands and say a blessing and then he would repeat our chapter for us [proving that Eleazar is right, B, about saying a blessing before the study of scriptural exegesis]."

V.

A.   What is the blessing [before study of the Torah]?

B.   Said R. Judah said Samuel, "'... who has sanctified us by his commandments and commanded us to take up the study of words of the Torah.'"

C.   And R. Yohanan concludes with the following: "Make pleasant, I ask, O Lord our God, the words of your Torah, in our mouth and in the mouth of your people, the House of Israel, so that we, our heirs, and the heirs of our heirs, your people, the House of Israel, all may be those who know your name and take up the study of your Torah. Blessed are you, O Lord, who teaches Torah to his people, Israel.'"

D.   And R. Hamnuna said, "'... who has chosen us from among all peoples and given us his Torah. Blessed are you, O Lord, who gives the Torah.

E.   Said R. Hamnuna, "That is the best of all blessings."

F.   Therefore let us say all of them.

VI.

A.   There we have learned in the Mishnah:

B.   The superintendent said to them, "Say one blessing." They said a blessing, pronounced the Ten Commandments, the Shema, "And it shall come to pass if you shall hearken" (Deut. 11:13-21), and "And the Lord spoke to Moses" (Num. 15:37-41). They blessed the people with three blessings: "True and Sure," "Abodah," and the blessing of priests. And on the Sabbath they add a blessing for the outgoing priestly watch [M. Tam. 5:1].

C.   What is this added blessing?

D.   It accords with the following:

E.   R. Abba and R. Yose bar Abba happened to come along to a certain place. The people asked them, "What is the additional blessing?" The answer was not in their hands, so they came and asked R. Mattenah.

F.   The answer was not in his hands, so they came and asked R. Judah. He said to them, "This is what Samuel said: 'It is "... With great love..."'."

G.   And R. Zeriqa said R. Ammi said R. Simeon b. Laqish said, "It is '... who creates light....'"

H.   When R. Isaac bar Joseph came, he said, "This statement attributed to R. Zeriqa was
      not stated explicitly, but it derives from inference based on something else that he
      said."

I.   For R. Zeriqa said R. Ammi said R. Simeon b. Laqish said, "[The fact (B) that they
      said only one blessing (Simeon)] indicates that reciting one blessing is not essential
      for reciting another blessing [but one may recite one without then going on to the
      next]."

J.   [Continuing the inferential argument:] Now if you maintain that the additional
      blessing that they would say was, "Who creates light" [= G], that would be in line
      with the principle that the recitation of one blessing is not essential in the
      recitation of some other blessing, for, under the stated conditions, the people did
      not recite also, "With great love," [which, we know, goes along with the former
      blessing in the recitation of the Shema, as we see at M. 1:4B].

K.   [12A] But if you maintain that it was, "With great love," that the priests said, how
      would it follow that the recitation of one blessing is not essential in the recitation
      of some other blessing? [Perhaps there is a quite separate consideration for
      omitting the other blessing, while under ordinary circumstances, it is necessary to
      recite groups of blessings together. That other consideration then would be that]
      the reason they did not recite "Who creates light" is that the time for reciting the
      blessing, "Who creates light," had not come. But when the time for saying "Who
      creates light" comes, the priests would recite that blessing as well.

L.   [Granted, then, that Zeriqa's statement was imputed to him only by inference,] what
      difference does it make?

M.   If it was only an inference, I should be able to refute it as follows: In point of fact,
      the priests did say, "With great love." And when the time for reciting "Who creates
      light" came, the people would indeed recite it.

N.   And what, then, is the sense of the phrase, "The recitation of the blessings is not
      essential, so that if one says one blessing, he need not say the other"?

O.   The sense of that principle is only with respect to the fixed order of the blessings.
      [One can say the several blessings in an order different from the established one, but
      one must recite all of the blessings, and omission of one of them invalidates the
      recitation of all the others.]

VII.

A.   They pronounced the Ten Commandments, the Shema, "And it shall come to pass if
      you shall hearken" (Deut. 11:13-21), and "And the Lord spoke to Moses" (Num.
      15:37-41). They blessed the people with three blessings: True and sure, Abodah, and
      the blessing of the priests [M. Tam. 5:1].

B.   Said R. Judah said Samuel, "They proposed to conduct the same rite [reciting the
      Ten Commandments in worship] in the outlying districts, but the practice was
      annulled on account of the claim of the minim [that only the Ten Commandments
      had been received at Sinai]."

C.   It has been taught along these same lines on Tannaite authority:

D. R. Nathan says, "They proposed to conduct the same rite in the outlying districts, but the practice was annulled on account of the claim of the minim."

E. Rabbah b. b. Hana considered establishing such a rite in Sura. Said R. Hisda to him, "They already have annulled the practice on account of the claim of the minim."

F. Amemar considered establishing such a rite in Nehardea. Said R. Ashi to him, "They already have annulled the practice on account of the claim of the minim."

VIII.

A. And on the Sabbath they add a blessing for the outgoing priestly watch [M. Tam. 5:1]:

B. What was the blessing that they said?

C. Said R. Helbo, "The outgoing priestly clan would say to the incoming priestly clan, "May he who brought his name to dwell in this house bring to dwell among you love, brotherhood, peace, and friendship."

IX.

A. Where sages have said to say a long one... [M. 1:4D]:

B. It is self-evident that in a case in which someone took a cup of wine in his hand, and, thinking that it was beer, went ahead in the notion that it was beer and said the blessing for beer, but concluded the blessing with the words appropriate for wine, that the person has carried out his obligation.

C. [The reason is that] even if he had said the blessing, "... by whose word all things come into being," he would have carried out his obligation.

D. For we have learned in the Mishnah: Over all things, if one says the blessing, "... by whose word all things come into being," he has fulfilled his obligation [to say a blessing] [M. Ber. 6:2A].

E. But in a case in which one took a cup of beer in hand thinking that it was wine, and began to say the blessing in the mistaken opinion that it was wine, but concluded that act with the blessing for the beer, what is the rule? [In this case the blessing that the man had had in mind -- for wine -- would have served only wine and not beer.]

F. Do we invoke the criterion of the body of the blessing that the man has said [which was the blessing for beer, therefore not in fulfillment of the obligation for wine]?

G. Or do we impose the criterion of the concluding statement of the blessing [which was for wine, and, if so, the man has carried out his obligation]?

H. Come and take note of the principle of the following:

I. If in the recitation of the morning service one commenced with "Who forms light" [which is the proper blessing for the Shema in the morning], but then finished, "Who brings on evening" [which is what is said at night], he has not carried out his obligation. If he began, "Who brings on evening" but concluded with, "Who creates light," he has carried out his obligation. [So we follow the criterion of what the person says at the very end, and, since what he said at the end was valid, we regard that statement as having served in fulfillment of the obligation].

J. If in the recitation of the evening service one commenced with "Who brings on evening," but completed with, "Who creates light," he has not carried out his obligation. If he began, "Who creates light," and finished with, "Who brings on evening," he has carried out his obligation.

K. The governing principle throughout is this: All things follow the status of the concluding statement [which tells us the upshot of the entire prayer].

L. The case just now adduced is different from the case involving beer or wine, for in that case, at the end, he concludes, "Blessed... who creates the heavenly lights" [Simon, p. 68, n. 1: which is the concluding formula of the morning benediction and is a complete blessing by itself. Hence we can disregard the beginning. The same is not the case with wine and beer, where there was no benediction to rectify the error made at the beginning].

M. That argument is entirely valid from the viewpoint of Rab, who has said, "Any blessing that lacks the mention of the divine name is null" [but if the divine name is mentioned, it is valid]. There is no problem then, [for a valid blessing has been said].

N. But in the view of R. Yohanan, who has said, "Any blessing which lacks all mention of God's rule is null," what is there to be said [to distinguish the two cases]? [In this case, since the blessing does not refer to God as "king of the University," it is not a complete benediction. Hence what we argued was the complete blessing by itself, "Blessed... who creates the heavenly lights," was in fact null. Then the argument above does not effectively distinguish the two cases at all.]

O. [There is a simple solution to this objection, which] accords with what Rabbah bar Ulla has said, "It is so as to make mention of the trait of day by night and the trait of night by day." [Hence, when to begin with the man stated a blessing inclusive of the allusion to God's rule of the world, that statement affected both elements of the blessing. Accordingly, God's rule has been introduced, and the blessing is valid. The matter remains as argued above, because the cases cannot be distinguished from one another.]

P. Come and take note of the end of the cited passage:

Q. "The governing principle throughout is this: All things follow the status of the concluding statement."

R. What does the phrase, "The governing principle throughout" serve to include?

S. Is it not to include the case with which we began [involving beer and wine]? [That would accord with the original intent in adducing in evidence the entire cited passage.]

T. No, it serves to include a case involving bread and dates.

U. [If so], what would such a case amount to? If we say that someone ate bread, and, thinking that he ate dates, began to say a blessing with the notion that he had eaten dates but then concluded the blessing with the appropriate language for bread, then what we have in hand is nothing more than the case which, to begin with, we have already addressed.

V. No, such an inclusive statement would be required for a case in which one had eaten dates and, thinking that he had eaten bread, began with the notion that he had eaten bread and completed saying the appropriate blessing for dates. In such an event [in line with R] the man has carried out his obligation.

W. [Why so]? For even if he had completed the transaction with the blessing for bread, he would in any event have carried out his obligation.

X. Why so? Because dates also provide food.

X.

A. Said Rabbah bar Hinena, the elder, in the name of Rab, "Whoever has omitted the blessing, 'True and firm,' in the morning service, or 'True and faithful,' in the evening service, has not carried out his obligation.

B. "For it is said, 'To declare your lovingkindness in the morning, and your faithfulness by night' (Ps. 92:3).

XI.

A. And Rabbah bar Hinena, the elder, said in the name of Rab, "When one bows during the recitation of the Prayer, he bows when he says the word, 'Blessed,' and he straightens up when he says the divine name."

B. Said Samuel, "What is the scriptural basis for the rule of Rab? It is in line with that which is written, 'The name [of the Lord] raises up those who are bowed down' (Ps. 146:8)."

C. An objection was raised on the basis of the following verse: "And was bowed before my name" (Mal. 2:5).

D. Is it written, "At my name"? What is written is "before my name."

E. Said Samuel to Hiyya bar Rab, "Son of our Torah, Come and I shall repeat to you an excellent statement which your father made.

F. "This is what your father said, 'When one bows during the recitation of the Prayer, he bows when he says the word, "Be Blessed," and he straightens up when he says the divine name.'"

G. [12B] When R. Sheshet would bow, he would bend like a reed [all at once] and when he stood up, he would stand up like a snake [slowly].

XII.

A. And Rabbah bar Hinena, the elder, said in the name of Rab, "Throughout the year a person says in the Prayer, "'The holy God,' 'King who loves righteousness and justice.' The exception is on the ten days between the New Year and the Day of Atonement, on which one says in the Prayer, 'The Holy King,' 'The King of justice.'"

B. And R. Eleazar said, "Even if one has said, 'The Holy God,' he has carried out his obligation.

C. "For it is said, 'But the Lord of hosts is exalted through justice, and the holy God is sanctified through righteousness' (Is. 5:16).

D. "When is it that 'the Lord of hosts is exalted through justice'? It is during the ten days between the New Year and the Day of Atonement.

E "Yet nonetheless it says 'the holy God.'"

F.   What is the upshot of the matter?

G.   Said R. Joseph, "'The holy God' and 'King who loves righteousness and justice.'"

H.   Rabbah said, "'The Holy King,' and 'King who loves righteousness and justice.'"

I.   And the decided law accords with the view of Rabbah.

XIII.

A.   And Rabbah bar Hinena, the elder, said in the name of Rab, "Whoever has the possibility of seeking mercy for his fellow and does not do so is called a sinner.

B.   "For it is said, 'And as for me, far be it from me that I should sin against the Lord in ceasing to pray for you' (1 Sam. 12:23)."

C.   Said Raba, "If he is a disciple of a sage, he has to make himself sick in praying for him.

D.   "What is the scriptural basis for that view? If I should say that it is because it is written, "There is none of you that is sick for me or discloses to me" (1 Sam. 22:8), the answer is that the case of a king is different.

E.   "Rather, the scriptural evidence is from the following: 'But as for me, when they were sick, my clothing was sackcloth, I afflicted my soul with fasting' (Ps. 35:13)."

XIV.

A.   And Rab bar Hinena, the elder, said in the name of Rab, "Whoever commits a transgression but is ashamed on that account is forgiven all his transgressions.

B.   "For it is said, 'That you may remember and be ashamed and never open your mouth any more because of your shame; when I have forgiven you all that you have done, says the Lord God' (Ez. 16:63)."

C.   But perhaps the sin of the community is different [and the remission on account of shame would not apply to the individual]?

D.   Rather, proof derives from here: "And Samuel said to Saul, Why have you disturbed me to bring me up? And Saul answered, I am sore distressed, for the Philistines make war against me, and God has left me and does not answer me any more, neither by prophets nor by dreams; therefore I called you that you may tell me what I should do" (1 Sam. 28:15).

E.   Now he does not mention the Urim and Thummim because he destroyed Nob, the town of the priests [and he was ashamed to mention that fact].

F.   And how do we know that he was forgiven by Heaven?

G.   As it is said, 'And Samuel said, 'Tomorrow you and your sons will be with me" (1 Sam. 28:16, 19)."

H.   And R. Yohanan said, "'With me' means 'in my category [in Heaven].'"

I.   And rabbis derive proof from the following: "'We will hang them up to the Lord in Gibeath of Saul, the chosen of the Lord' (2 Sam. 21:6)."

J.   "An echo came forth and said, 'He was the chosen of the Lord.'"

XV.

A.   Said R. Abbahu b. Zutrati said R. Judah bar Zebida, "[Sages] proposed to include the pericope of Balak [Num. 22-24] in the recitation of the Shema [along with the blessings fore and aft mentioned at M. 1:4A-B].

B. "On what account did they not do so? It was because it is too much bother for the community."

C. What is the scriptural basis for proposing to do so?

D. If we say that it is because in that pericope it is written, "God brought them forth from Egypt" (Num. 23:22),

E. then one should include in the recitation of the Shema the pericope having to do with usury and the pericope having to do with just weights, which also mention the Exodus from Egypt [Lev. 23:35-38, Lev. 19:36].

F. Rather, said R. Yose bar Abin, "It is because in that passage the following verse of Scripture appears: 'He couched, he lay down as a lion and as a lioness, who will rouse him up' (Num. 24:9). [The passage refers to lying down and rising up.]"

G. [If that is the operative consideration, then] why not say that verse alone?

H. We have learned that, in the case of every pericope which Moses treated as distinct, we treat the same pericope as distinct, but in the case of any one that Moses did not treat as distinct, we do not treat as distinct. [The verse is not distinct.]

I. In the case of the pericope on the show-fringes [Num. 15:37-41], on what account did sages include reciting that in the Shema?

J. Said R. Judah bar Habiba, "It is because five [six] important matters are mentioned in it:

K. "The religious duty of wearing show-fringes, the Exodus from Egypt, the yoke of the religious duties, the admonition against the position of the minim, and the admonitions against yearning for transgression, and against yearning for idolatry."

L. Now as to the first three, these are explicitly mentioned in the passage at hand.

M. As to the yoke of the commandments, it is written, "And you make look upon it and remember all the commandments of the Lord" (Num. 15:39).

N. As to the show-fringes, it is written, "That they make for themselves show-fringes" (Num. 15:38).

O. As to the Exodus from Egypt, it is written, "Who brought you out of the land of Egypt" (Num. 15:31).

P. But as to the admonition against the position of the minim and the admonitions against yearning for transgression and yearning for idolatry, whence do we derive these [from the passage at hand]?

Q. It is in accord with what has been taught on Tannaite authority:

R. "After your own heart" (Num. 15:39) speaks of the position of the minim, and so Scripture says, "The fool has said in his heart, There is no God" (Ps. 14:1).

S. "After your own eyes" refers to yearning for transgression, as it says, "And Samson said to his father, Get her for me, for she is pleasing in my eyes" (Jud. 14:3).

T. "After which you used to go astray" (Num. 15:39) refers to yearning for idolatry, and so Scripture says, "And they went astray after the Baalim" (Jud. 8:33).

We find clarification of the Mishnah-paragraph at units I and II. Unit III is a secondary expansion on the theme of M. 1:4, namely, blessings one says in the morning.

Once we mention what must be said in connection with reciting the Shema, we proceed to ask about other blessings to be said in the morning, now not in connection with the Shema. Unit IV continues unit III, so too unit V. My sense is that unit VI, devoted to M. Tam. 5:1, is inserted because it deals with blessings subject to inferential discussion at M. 1:4, namely, blessings having to do with the Shema. So once the Mishnah-passage deals with a subject, other Mishnah-passages dealing with the same subject are inserted as well. These then produce their own protracted discussion. Then units VII and VIII, carry forward the exegesis of M. Tam. 5:1.

Unit IX does not treat the Mishnah-clause at IX A. It takes up its own subject. But the reference at IX I to the blessings to which M. 1:4 refers accounts for inclusion of the sizable, quite autonomous discourse. The same consideration accounts for unit X, once more a reference to a blessing said after the Shema. Since the tradental construction has encompassed numerous sayings of Rabbah bar Hinena in Rab's name, the whole set, X-XIV, is inserted. Unit XV complements the Mishnah in only a general way, since it speaks of passages that do not form part of the recitation of the Shema. If we should ask the framer of the whole whether every element of what he has given us pertains to the Mishnah-paragraph at hand, he would answer that, for one reason or another, that is the case. But the reasons are not always the same.

1:5

A.   They mention the exodus from Egypt at night.

B.   Said R. Eleazar ben Azariah, "I am about seventy years old and I have not been worthy [of understanding why] the exodus from Egypt is recounted at night, until Ben Zoma expounded it.

C.   "As it says, 'So that you may remember the day on which you left Egypt all the days of your life' (Deut. 16:3).

D.   "'The days of your life' [implies only] the days. 'All the days of your life' [includes] the nights."

E.   And sages say, "'The days of your life' [includes only] this world. 'All the days of your life' -- encompasses the messianic age."

I.

A.   It has been taught on Tannaite authority:

B.   Said Ben Zoma to sages, "But does one mention the exodus from Egypt in the messianic age?

C.   "For has it not already been said, 'Therefore, behold, the days are coming, says the Lord, when men shall no longer say 'As the Lord lives who brought up the people of Israel out of the land of Egypt,' but, 'As the Lord lives who brought up and led the descendents of the house of Israel out of the north country [and out of all the countries where he had driven them'] (Jer. 23:7-8)?"

D. They said to him, "It is not that [mention of] the exodus from Egypt will be removed from its place [in the liturgy], but that [mention of the people of Israel's release from] servitude to [other] nations will be primary and the exodus from Egypt [will be] secondary [cf. T. Ber. 2:1].

E. Similarly, No longer shall your name be called Jacob, but Israel shall be your name (Gen. 35:10). [13A] It is not that the name Jacob will be taken from him but that [he shall be called Jacob in addition to Israel.] Israel will be [his] primary [name] and Jacob [his] secondary [name]. [T. Ber. 1:10F-I].

F. Similarly, Remember not the former things, nor consider the things of old (Isa. 43:18). Remember not the former things -- these are [God's mighty acts in saving Israel] from the [various] kingdoms; nor consider things of old -- these are [God's mighty acts in saving Israel] from Egypt.

G. Behold, I am doing a new thing; now it springs forth (Isa. 43:19).

H. R. Joseph taught on Tannaite authority, this refers to the war of God and Magog [at the end of time]."

I. They drew a parable, to what may the matter be compared? To one who was walking in the way and a wolf attacked him, but he was saved from it. He would go on telling about the incident of the wolf. Later a lion attacked him, but he was saved from it. He forgot the incident of the wolf and told about the incident of the lion. Later still a serpent attacked him, but he was saved from it. He forgot the other two incidents and went along telling about the incident of the serpent.

J. So, too is Israel: current sufferings make them forget about earlier ones [T. Ber. 1:11J-M].

K. Similarly, "No longer shall your name be Abram, but your name shall be Abraham" (Gen. 17:5). At first you were the father of Aram [the Arameans]. Now you are the father of the entire world, [T. adds:] as Scripture states, For I have made you the father of a multitude of nations (ibid).

L. [T. adds: Similarly, As for Sarai, your wife, you shall not call her name Sarai, but Sarah shall be her name (Gen. 17:15).] At first she was the ruler of her nation. Now she rules over all the world, [as it says, But Sarah [princess] shall be her name] [T. Ber. 1:13].

II.

A. Bar Qappara repeated on Tannaite authority, "Whoever calls Abraham 'Abram' violates an affirmative commandment.

B. "For it is said, 'And your name will be Abraham' (Gen. 17:5)."

C. R. Eliezer says, "He violates a negative one, for it says, 'Nor shall your name be called Abram any more' (Gen. 17:5)."

D. But if that is so, does the same rule apply to one who calls Sarah "Sarai"?

E. In that case the Holy One, blessed be he, is the one who said to Abraham, "'As to Sarai, your wife, you shall not call her Sarai but her name shall be Sarah' (Gen. 17:15). [Abraham was so commanded, others were not.]"

F. Then would the same rule apply to one who calls Jacob "Jacob" [since God changed his name to Israel]?

G.   That case too is different, for it was Scripture itself who later on reversed itself,

H.   for it is written, "And God spoke to Israel in visions of the night and said, Jacob, Jacob" (Gen. 46:2).

I.   R. Joseph bar Abin, and some say, R. Yose bar Zabeda, objected, "'You are the Lord, the God who chose Abram' (Neh. 9:7)."

J.   It was said to him, "In that case it was the prophet himself who recounted the praise of the All-Merciful, referring to how matters had originally been framed."

The Talmud adds to M. 1:5 its Toseftan complement, unit I, and unit II expands on the theme of unit I.

2:1-2

A. As to one who was reading [the verses of the Shema] in the Torah and the
    time for the recitation [of the Shema] arrived:

B. if he directed his heart [to read in order to carry out his obligation to
    recite the Shema], he fulfilled his obligation [to recite the Shema].

C. [B lacks: And if [he did] not, he has not fulfilled his obligation.]

D. "At the breaks [between the paragraphs of the Shema] one may greet [his
    fellow] out of respect,

E. "and respond [to a greeting extended to him].

F. "And in the middle [of a paragraph] one may give a greeting out of fear,

G. "and respond,"

H. the words of R. Meir.

I. R. Judah says, "In the middle [of a paragraph] one may give a greeting
    out of fear,

J. "and respond out of respect.

K. "In the breaks [between the paragraphs] one may greet out of respect and

L. "respond to the greeting of any man."

M. 2:1

A. The following are [those places referred to as breaks] "between the
    paragraphs":

B. Between the first blessing and the second [of those which precede the
    Shema];

C. or between the second blessing and [the paragraph which begins] Shema
    (Deut. 6:4-9);

D. or between [the two sections which begins] Shema and "And it shall come
    to pass if you shall hearken" (Deut. 11:13-21);

E. Between [the two sections beginning] "And it shall come to pass" and
    "And God said to Moses" (Num. 15:37-41);

F. Between [the two sections] "And the Lord said" and "True and upright."

G. R. Judah said, "Between [the two sections] 'And the Lord said' and 'True
    and upright' one may not interrupt."

H. Said R. Joshua b. Qorha, "Why does Shema precede 'And it shall come to
    pass' [in the order of this liturgy]?

I.   "So that one should first accept upon himself the yoke of the kingdom of heaven and afterwards accept the yoke of the commandments.

J.   "[Why does] 'And it shall come to pass' [precede]: 'And the Lord said'?

K.   "For 'And it shall come to pass' is customarily [recited] by both day and night.

L.   "And 'And the Lord said' is customarily [recited] only by day.

M. 2:2

I.

A.   [The statement at M. 2:1A-C] bears the implication that carrying out religious duties requires the intention to do just that [since it is clearly stated that only if the person directed his heart to the fulfillment of his obligation to recite the Shema when he actually read the words of the Shema has he carried out that obligation].

B.   [That is not necessarily the proper inference to draw, for] what is the sense of, If he directed his heart?

C.   It is "to recite the Scripture."

D.   But how can that be the case, since lo, the person is already reciting the Scripture? [The proposed sense of the statement is impossible.]

E.   No, we deal with a case of one who is reciting the Scripture only so as to see that the letters of the text at hand are correctly written [and is not reciting it as to meaning. But if he were then to recite the text only so as to make an intelligible statement, rather than merely to proof-read, that would suffice in carrying out his obligation, even though the man did not intend to carry out that obligation in reciting the passage at hand.]

II.

A.   Our rabbis have taught on Tannaite authority:

B.   "The recitation of the Shema must be as it is written [in the Hebrew language]," the words of Rabbi.

C.   And sages say, "In any language."

D.   What is the scriptural basis for the view of Rabbi?

E.   Scripture has said, "And they shall be..." (Deut. 6:6), meaning, "Just as they are," [that is, in Hebrew].

F.   And as to rabbis, what is the scriptural basis for their view?

G.   Scripture has said, "Hear..." (Deut. 6:4), meaning, in any language that you understand.

H.   And as to Rabbi, lo, it indeed is written "Hear"?

I.   He requires that statement to make its own point, which is that one should make his ears hear what his mouth says [and so has to say the Shema out loud].

J.   And rabbis? They take the position of the one who has said, "If one has not made his ear hear what his mouth has said, he has nonetheless carried out his obligation."

K.   And in the view of rabbis, lo, it is written, "And they shall be...."

L.   They require that statement to prove that a person should not read the passage backward.

M.   And as to Rabbi, how does he prove that one should not read the passage backward?

N.   He proves that proposition from the use of the definite article in the word, "words," thus, "these words" [in the sense of, these words, in this order].

O.   And rabbis? They draw no conclusions from the use of the definite article [in "words"].

P.   Now the foregoing dispute bears the implication that, so far as Rabbi is concerned, the entire Torah was stated in all languages. For if you think that it was stated only in the Holy Language [of Hebrew], what need was there for the All-Merciful to stipulate, "They shall be"? [If it were in Hebrew, Scripture would not have to insist that this passage in particular be read in Hebrew, as Rabbi maintains is the sense of the passage].

Q.   It was indeed necessary to make that explicit reference to "They shall be," because, after all, it also is written, "Hear," [which bears the implication rabbis have said. Accordingly, Scripture had to make explicit that, despite the implication of the word, "Hear," these words must be said only in Hebrew.]

R.   And does not the passage at hand further bear the implication that, so far as rabbis are concerned, the entire Torah was written in Hebrew?

S.   For if you take the view that it was written in all languages, what was the point of having the All-Merciful stipulate, "Hear"?

T.   It was necessary to say exactly that, because, after all, the words, "And they shall be..." have been written down. [Accordingly, rabbis explain the reference without implying their view on the original language of composition of Scripture as a whole.]

III.

A.   Our rabbis have taught on Tannaite authority:

B.   "'And they shall be' means that one should not read the passage backward.

C.   "'These words upon your heart':

D.   "One might have taken the view that the recitation of the entire passage requires that the one who says it intend thereby to carry out his obligation.

E.   "Accordingly, Scripture states, '... these...,' meaning, up to this passage in the recitation of the Shema, one has to have the intention of carrying out his obligation to recite the Shema by stating these words. From that point onward it is not necessary to have that intention," the words of R. Eliezer.

F.   Said to him R. Aqiba, "Lo, Scripture says, [13B] 'Which I command you this day upon your heart' (Deut. 6:6). This means that the recitation of the entire passage must be accompanied by the intention to carry out one's obligation to recite the Shema [if one is to fulfill that obligation]."

G.   Said Rabbah b. b. Hana said R. Yohanan, "The law accords with the position of R. Aqiba."

H.   There are those who repeat the passage on Tannaite authority in the following terms, for it has been taught on Tannaite authority:

I.   One who recites the shema must direct his heart [so as to intend to carry out his obligation] [cf. M. Ber. 2:1].

J.   R. Aha says in the name of R. Judah, "If he did so during [his recitation of] the first paragraph [even though he did not concentrate during his recitation of the last paragraph, he has fulfilled his obligation] and need not do so further." [T. Ber. 2:2A-B].

K.   Said Rabbah b. b. Hana said R. Yohanan, "The decided law accords with the view of R. Aha, which he said in the name of R. Judah."

IV.

A.   A further teaching on Tannaite authority:

B.   "And they shall be" means that one should not read them backward.

C.   "Upon your heart":

D.   R. Zutra says, "Up to this point, the religious duty involves correct intention [to fulfill one's obligation to read the Shema by the recitation at hand]. From that point, the religious duty is simply one of reading the words [aloud, without necessarily having the intention of thereby carrying out one's religious obligation to recite the Shema]."

E.   R. Josiah says, "Up to that point the religious duty involves simply reciting the words aloud. From that point, the religious duty involves having the correct intention to fulfill one's duty to recite the Shema, [not merely to read the words at hand]."

F.   What differentiates the two passages, so that, from that point it is a religious duty only to read the words [as Zutra has said]?

G.   It is written, "To speak of them" (Deut. 6:11) [which bears the commandment to recite the words aloud].

H.   Here too it is written, "And you shall speak of them" [so the same implication applies to both parts of the passage under discussion].

I.   This is the sense of the wording:

J.   Up to this point the religious duty involves the obligation to have the proper intention to recite the Shema and so carry out one's obligation, and also to read the words at hand. From this point onward, the duty involves only the recitation of the words at hand, without the further intention of fulfilling one's religious duty to say the Shema.

K.   And what differentiates the passage, so that, up to the designated point, it is a religious duty both to have the intention to fulfill his obligation to recite the Shema and also to recite aloud the words at hand?

L.   For it is written, "Upon your heart, and you shall speak of them..." (Deut. 6:6).

M.   But there too it is written, "Upon your heart, to speak of them" (Deut. 11:18).

N.   That other reference [has no bearing upon the present problem, for] it is required to prove the proposition of R. Isaac, who has said, "'And you shall put these words of mine upon your heart' (Deut. 11:18). This proves that the location of [one of the phylacteries] should be opposite the heart."

V.

A.   A master stated: R. Josiah says, "Up to that point the religious duty involves simply reciting the words. From that point, the religious duty involves having the correct intention to fulfill one's duty to recite the Shema."

B.   What differentiates the passage at hand to indicate that, from that point onward, it is an issue of having the proper intention to recite the Shema and so to carry out one's obligation?

C.   It is because it is written, "Upon your heart."

D.   Here too, lo, it is written, "Upon your heart" [as above].

E.   This is the sense of the passage: Up to that point the religious duty involves both reciting the words and also having the proper intention to carry out one's obligation to recite the Shema. From that point forward what is required is the intention to carry out one's religious duty to recite the Shema without necessarily having the intention to recite the words aloud [for one may just follow them and read silently].

F.   And what distinguishes the passage so that, up to that point it is a religious duty up to the stated passage to both recite the words aloud and also to have the intention thereby to recite the Shema?

G.   For it is written, "Upon your heart, and you shall speak of them."

H.   But elsewhere it also is written, "Upon your heart, to speak of them"?

I.   That latter statement concerns words of Torah, and this is the sense of the All-Merciful: "Teach your children Torah, so that they may be knowledgeable in it."

VI.

A.   Our rabbis have taught on Tannaite authority:

B.   "'Hear O Israel, the Lord our God, the Lord is one' (Deut. 6:4):

C.   "Up to that point in the recitation of the Shema it is necessary that the heart be directed [toward the fulfillment of one's religious duty to recite the Shema]," the words of R. Meir.

D.   Said Raba, "The decided law accords with the position of R. Meir."

VII.

A.   It has been taught on Tannaite authority:

B.   Sumkhos says, "Whoever lengthens the recitation of the word 'one' [ehad] has his days and years lengthened as well."

C.   Said R. Aha bar Jacob, "And that applies, in particular, to lengthening the letter D in the word for one."

D.   Said R. Ashi, "And that is on condition that one not slur the letter H."

E.   R. Jeremiah was in session before R. Hiyya bar Abba. He noticed that someone prolonged the letters too much. He instructed him, "Once you have [in your heart] declared God to be king above and below and in the four quarters of heaven, you do not have to persist in the matter."

VIII.

A.   Said R. Nathan bar Mar Uqba said R. Judah, "'Upon your heart' means that that passage must be said standing "

B. "Upon your heart" alone is what you think? Rather, I should say, "Up to the passage, 'Upon your heart,' must be said standing. From that point it is not necessary."

C. R. Yohanan said, "The entire passage must be said standing."

D. And R. Yohanan is consistent with other views, for Rabbah bar bar Hanah said R. Yohanan said, "The decided law accords with the view of R. Aha, which he stated in the name of R. Judah."

IX.

A. Our rabbis have taught on Tannaite authority:

B. "Hear O Israel, the Lord our God, the Lord is one" (Deut. 6:4) -- this is the form of the Shema as it was recited [early, prior to prayer] by R. Judah the Patriarch.

C. Said Rab to R. Hiyya, "I did not see Rabbi [Judah] accept upon himself the dominion of heaven."

D. He said to him, "Son of the nobility, at the very moment at which he passes his hands across his face, he accepts the dominion of Heaven."

E. Does [Judah the Patriarch] later on go back and complete the recitation of the Shema [which he said only incompletely earlier], or does he not do so?

F. Bar Qappara says, "He does not go back and complete it."

G. R. Simeon b. Rabbi says, "He does go back and complete the recitation."

H. Said Bar Qappara to R. Simeon b. Rabbi, "Now there is no problem with my view, for I maintain that he does not go back and complete [the recitation of the Shema]. That is why Rabbi always reviews in his public study a passage which makes reference to the Exodus from Egypt. [This one must mention, so if it is not in the Shema, it will occur in the study materials].

I. "But from your viewpoint, since you maintain that Rabbi does go back and complete the recitation of the Shema, why should Rabbi find it necessary to include in his review of traditions a passage involving the Exodus from Egypt [since that is included in the Shema in any case]?"

J. [He replied,] "It is so that he may make mention of the Exodus from Egypt at the right time [namely, at the time of day at which the Exodus took place.]"

X.

A. Said R. Ela, son of R. Samuel bar Marta, in the name of Rab, "If one has recited, 'Hear O Israel, the Lord our God, the Lord is one,' and then was overcome by sleep, he has carried out his obligation."

B. Said R. Nahman to Daro his slave, "Keep us awake for the recitation of the first verse, but from that point, do not both to keep us awake."

C. Said R. Joseph to R. Joseph son of Rabbah, "How did your father do it?"

D. He said to him, "For the recitation of the first verse he would take trouble [to stay awake], but for more than that he would not take trouble."

XI.

A. Said R. Joseph, "Someone lying on his back should not recite the Shema."

B. That statement then implies that in that position he may not recite the Shema, but he may indeed sleep in that position.

C. But lo, R. Joshua b. Levi cursed anyone who slept lying on his back.

D. They replied, "As to sleeping on one's back, so long as one turns to the side, that is all right, but as to reciting the Shema, even though one turns to the side, it is also forbidden."

E. And lo, R. Yohanan would turn to his side and recite the Shema!

F. R. Yohanan was a special case, because he was fat.

XII.

A. At the break one may greet, etc. [M. 2:1D]:

B. [And respond to a greeting extended to him, M. 2:1E:] On what account may he respond?

C. If I say that it is on account of respect owing to the other, [then I must ask the following question:]

D. If one may to begin with greet his fellow, is there any question that he may also reply to him?

E. Rather, he greets his fellow on account of respect, and he replies with a greeting to anyone [whether out of respect or not].

F. Then I may point to the concluding passage of the same unit:

G. In the middle one may give a greeting out of fear and respond [so Meir] [M. 2:1F-G].

H. Now on what account should one reply? If I say it is because of fear, now lo, if one may greet a person out of fear, is there any question of whether he may reply to him? [Of course he may!]

I. Rather it is because of respect.

J. But that is the opinion of R. Judah! For we have learned in the Mishnah:

K. R. Judah says, "In the middle of a paragraph one may give a greeting out of fear and respond out of respect. In the breaks between the paragraphs one may greet out of respect and respond to the greeting of any man" [M. 2:1I-L].

L. Something is missing in the formulation of the passage at hand, and this is how the passage should be repeated:

M. "At the breaks one may greet someone out of respect, and, it is not necessary to add that he may reply to him. In the middle of a paragraph one may greet someone out of fear, and it is not necessary to add, that he may, of course, reply," the words of R. Meir.

N. R. Judah says, "In the middle of a paragraph one may greet a person out of fear and reply to him out of respect.

O. "[14A] And in the breaks between the paragraphs one may greet a person out of respect and reply with a greeting to anybody."

P. It has been taught on Tannaite authority along these same lines:

Q. "He who is reciting the Shema and his master or someone of higher status than he met him, at the breaks between paragraphs he gives a greeting out of respect, and it is not necessary to say that he replies to a greeting, and in the middle of a paragraph he gives a greeting only out of fear, and it is not necessary to add that he responds to a greeting," the words of R. Meir.

R.   R. Judah says, "In the middle of a paragraph he gives a greeting out of fear and responds out of respect, and at the breaks between paragraphs he gives a greeting out of respect and responds with a greeting to anyone at all."

XIII.

A.   Ahi, the Tannaite authority at the house of R. Hiyya, asked R. Hiyya, "In the case of reciting the Hallel-psalms or the Scroll of Esther, what is the law about interrupting [his recitation to greet someone]?

B.   "Do we rule that it is an argument a fortiori:

C.   "In the case of reciting the Shema, which derives from the authority of the Torah, one interrupts his reading, so is it any issue about interrupting the recitation of the Hallel-Psalms, which rest upon the authority of rabbis?

D.   "Or since the purpose of reciting the Psalms is to make a miracle known, the recitation of the Hallel-psalms is more important."

E.   He said to him, "One interrupts the recitation [to give a greeting], and there is no objection to doing so."

F.   Said Rabbah, "On days on which an individual praying by himself says the entire Hallel-Psalms, one may interrupt to give a greeting between one passage and another, but in the middle of a given passage he may not interrupt to give a greeting.

G.   "And on days on which the individual does not complete the recitation of the Hallel-psalms, even in the middle of a passage he may interrupt the recitation to give a greeting."

H.   Is that really the case? And lo, Rab bar Sheba happened by the house of Rabina. It was on one of the days on which the individual does not complete the recitation of the Hallel-Psalms, and yet he did not interrupt his recitation to greet him.

I.   Rab bar Sheba was a special case, because Rabina had held him of no account.

XIV.

A.   Asyan, the Tannaite authority of the house of R. Ami, asked R. Ammi, "If someone is fasting, what is the law about his tasting food or drink [to test the food]?

B.   "Has he accepted the discipline of the fast, and in such a taste there is no violation of the basic fast?

C.   "Or perhaps he has undertaken the discipline of not gaining any enjoyment of food or drink whatsoever, and in such a taste, there would be benefit?"

D.   He said to him, "One may take a taste and there is no objection whatever to doing so."

E.   It has been taught along these same lines on Tannaite authority:

F.   If one takes a mere taste, it is not necessary to say a blessing.

G.   One who is fasting may take a taste and there is no objection to his doing so.

H.   How much?

I.   R. Ami and R. Asi took a taste to the measure of a quarter-log.

XV.

A.   Said Rab, "Whoever greets his fellow before saying the Prayer is as if he treated him as a high place.

B. "For it is said, 'Cease from man in whose nostrils is a breath, for how little is he to be accounted' (Is. 2:22).

C. "Read the word for 'how little' with different vowels as 'high place.'"

D. Samuel said, "[Reading the word differently:] 'On what account have you esteemed this one, and not God.'"

E. R. Sheshet objected: "In the breaks one may greet his fellow out of respect and respond [M. 2:1D-E]. [All the more so doing so before saying the Prayer]."

F. R. Abba interprets [the statement of Rab and Samuel] to refer to someone who gets up early in the morning to go to the other's door.

G. Said R. Idi bar Abin said R. Isaac bar Asyan, "It is forbidden for a person to do his own business before he says his Prayer.

H. "For it is said, 'Righteousness shall go before him and then he shall set his steps on his own way' (Ps. 85:14)."

I. And R. Idi bar Abin said R. Isaac bar Isyan said, "Whoever says his Prayer and afterward goes out to the public way has the Holy One, blessed be he, to do his business.

J. "For it is said, 'Righteousness shall go before him and then he shall set his steps on his own way' (Ps. 85:14)."

XVI.

A. Said R. Jonah said R. Zira, "Whoever sleeps for seven days without a dream is called wicked.

B. "For it is said, 'And he that has it shall abide satisfied, he shall not be visited with evil' (Prov. 19:23).

C. "Do not read the word for 'satisfied' but the word for 'seven.'" [Simon, p. 82, n. 12: And render, "If he abides seven days without and is not visited with a dream, this shows that he is evil."]

D. Said R. Aha, son of R. Hiyya bar Abba, "This is what R. Hiyya said R. Yohanan said, 'Whoever is sated with words of Torah and goes to sleep will not be told bad news [in a dream].

E. "For it is said, 'And if he abides sated he shall not be visited with evil' (Prov. 19:23)."

XVII.

A. The following are those places referred to as breaks between the paragraphs [M. 2:2A]:

B. Said R. Abbahu said R. Yohanan, "The decided law accords with the view of R. Judah, who has said, 'Between the two sections, "And the Lord said" and "True and upright" one may not interrupt' [M. 2:2G]."

C. Said R. Abbahu said R. Yohanan, "What is the scriptural basis for the view of R. Judah?

D. "It is because it is written, "[14B] 'The Lord God is truth' (Jer. 10:10)."

E. [Simon, p. 83, n. 2: After concluding the Shema with the word true,] does one have to repeat the word true [which is really the beginning of the next paragraph in the prayers], or does one not do so?

F.   Said R. Abbahu said R. Yohanan, "One has to go back and repeat the word, 'True.'"

G.   Rabbah said, "One does not do so."

H.   Someone went down [to lead the prayers] in the presence of Rabbah, and Rabbah heard him say, "True... true..." two times. Said Rabbah, "[Simon:] The whole of truth has got hold of this man."

XVIII.

A.   Said R. Joseph, "How lovely is this tradition which, when R. Samuel bar Judah came, he reported that they say in the West: 'In the evening they say, "Speak to the children of Israel and you shall say to them, I am the Lord your God. True."' [They thus omit reference to the middle part of the third paragraph of the Shema, which deals with show-fringes. That requirement is not applicable by night, so the people do not say the prayer referring to them by night.]"

B.   Abayye said to him, "What is so lovely about that tradition? Lo, R. Kahana said Rab said, '[In the evening] one does not have to begin [to recite that section of the Shema at all, although] if he did begin to recite it, he must complete it.'

C.   "And should you maintain that the words, 'And you shall say to them,' do not constitute the beginning of the third paragraph of the Shema,

D.   "has not R. Samuel bar Isaac said Rab said, 'The phrase, "Speak to the children of Israel" does not constitute the beginning of the paragraph, but "You shall say to them" does constitute the beginning of the paragraph'?"

E.   Said R. Papa, "In the West they maintain that the phrase, 'And you shall say to them' does not constitute the beginning of the third paragraph of the Shema. It begins only at 'That they make for themselves show-fringes.'"

F.   Said Abayye, "Therefore we [in Babylonia] begin [to recite the section], for they do so in the West. But once we begin it, we also complete it.

G.   "For lo, R. Kahana said Rab said, 'One should not begin to recite the third paragraph of the Shema, but if he did so, he must complete it.'"

H.   Hiyya bar Rab said, "If [in the evening] one has said, 'I am the Lord your God,' he also has to say, 'True.'

I.   "If he did not say, 'I am the Lord your God,' he does not have to say, 'True.'"

J.   But lo, one has to make mention of the Exodus from Egypt [which is included in the paragraph beginning, "True"]?

K.   One may say this prayer: "We give thanks to you, Lord our God, because you took us out of the land of Egypt and redeemed us from the house of slavery and performed miracles and wonders for us at the sea, where we sang a song to you."

XIX.

A.   Said R. Joshua b. Qorha, "Why does the Shema precede, etc. [M. 2:2H]:

B.   It has been taught on Tannaite authority:

C.   R. Simeon b. Yohai says, "It is quite proper that one should say, 'Hear O Israel,' before the paragraph, 'And it shall come to pass, if you listen...,' for the former speaks of learning, the latter of teaching.

D.   "And the paragraph, 'It shall come to pass...,' should come before, 'And he said...,' for the former speaks of teaching and the latter of doing."

E.   But is it the case that the Shema speaks of learning but not of teaching and doing? And lo, it is written, "And you shall teach them diligently... and shall bind them and shall write them..."

F.   And is it the case that the paragraph beginning, "It shall come to pass" speaks of teaching but not of doing? And lo, it is written in that very paragraph, "And you shall bind them... and you shall write them..."

G.   But this is the sense of his statement: "It is quite proper that one should say, 'Hear O Israel,' before the paragraph, 'And it shall come to pass, if you listen,' for the former speaks of learning, teaching, and doing, [the latter only of teaching and doing].

H.   "And the paragraph, 'It shall come to pass...,' should come before, 'And he said...,' for the former speaks of teaching and doing and the latter speaks only of doing."

I.   But can one not explain matters satisfactorily through the reasons given by R. Joshua b. Qorhah [at M. 2:2I-L]?

J.   [Simeon's] point is to say, "There are both this consideration and yet another one."

K.   That is, "First, so that one should first accept upon himself the yoke of the kingdom of heaven and afterwards accept the yoke of the commandments [M. 2:2I],

L.   "And, furthermore, because in the passage at hand are these several other matters as well."

XX.

A.   Rab washed his hands, recited the Shema, put on phylacteries, and then said the Prayer.

B.   How could he have done it this way?

C.   And has it not been stated on Tannaite authority:

D.   He who digs a burial niche for a corpse in a grave-area is exempt from the requirement to recite the Shema and from having to say the Prayer and from having to put on phylacteries and from all of the religious duties that are listed in the Torah. Once the time for reciting the Shema comes, he comes up [out of the hole], washes his hands, puts on his phylacteries, recites the Shema and says the Prayer.

E.   Lo, there is a contradiction in the cited passage itself, which announces at the beginning that one is exempt and at the end that he is obligated [to carry out the rites].

F.   That indeed is no contradiction, since the latter part deals with a case in which there are two ditch-diggers, and the former part a case in which there is only one.

G.   In any event the cited passage presents a contradiction to the position of Rab [at A].

H.   Rab accords with R. Joshua b. Qorhah, who has said, "First comes accepting the yoke of the kingdom of Heaven and afterward comes accepting the yoke of the commandments [on which account the phylacteries, which serve to carry out a commandment, come after reciting the Shema]."

I.   Now I can well understand that R. Joshua b. Qorhah had the idea of reciting one passage before reciting another passage. But does he mean to imply that one should place a recitation of a passage before the actual carrying out of one's religious duty [with reference to the phylacteries]?

J.   And, furthermore, does he really accord with the view of R. Joshua b. Qorhah?

K.   And has not R. Hiyya bar Ashi said, "Many times I stood before Rab, and he would first of all wash his hands and say a blessing, then he would repeat our chapter to us, then he would put on his phylacteries, then recite the Shema."

L.   Now if you say that he referred to the time before the hour for reciting the Shema had come, if that were the case, what would be the purpose of the testimony of R. Hiyya bar Ashi?

M.   It would serve to exclude the position of one who maintains that it is not necessary to say a blessing in connection with Mishnah-study.

N.   Thus [Hiyya] has informed us that also for Mishnah-study it is required to say a blessing.

O.   In any event it is a contradiction to the position of Rab [outlined at the outset].

P.   His messenger was the one who made the mistake [and brought his phylacteries too late that day. Normally he put them on first.]

XXI.

A.   Said Ulla, "Whoever recites the Shema without putting on phylacteries is as if he gave false testimony against himself."

B.   Said R. Hiyya bar Abba said R. Yohanan, "It is as if he brought a burnt-offering without added a meal-offering, or a sacrifice without drink-offerings."

XXII.

A.   And R. Yohanan said, "He who wants to accept upon himself the yoke of the kingdom of Heaven in a full way [15A] should first empty his bowel, then wash his hands, put on his phylacteries, recite the Shema, and say the Prayer, and this constitutes accepting the kingdom of Heaven in a full way."

B.   And R. Hiyya bar Abba said R. Yohanan said, "Whoever empties his bowel, then washes his hands, puts on his phylacteries, recites the Shema and says the Prayer is regarded by Scripture as if he had built an altar and offering an offering on it.

C.   "For it is written, 'I will wash my hands in cleanliness and I will walk around your altar, O Lord' (Ps. 26:6)."

D.   Said Raba to him, "Does not the master maintain that it is as if he had immersed,

E.   "for it is written, 'I shall wash in cleanliness, and not, 'I shall wash my hands.'"

F.   Said Rabina to Raba, "See, master, how this neophyte among the rabbis who has come from the West has said, 'He who has no water to wash his hands may dry his hands in dirt or pebbles or sawdust.'"

G.   He said to him, "What he says is quite correct. Is it written, 'I shall wash in innocence in water'? What is written is merely, 'In cleanliness,' meaning, 'anything that serves to clean [the hands].'"

H.   For lo, R. Hisda cursed anyone who went in search of water at the time of prayer [maintaining that dirt would do.]

I.   But the rule at hand applies to the recitation of the Shema. As to cleaning the hands for saying the Prayer, one does have to go in search of water.

J.   How far must one search? To a parasang.

K.   And that applies to a forward search [for water prior to saying the Prayer].

L.   But as to backtracking, he may not go back even a mil.

M.   He may not backtrack by a mil, but if it is less than a mil, he may indeed backtrack [in search of water].

Unit I clarifies the meaning of the Mishnah-rule. It seems to me that unit II carries forward the theme of understanding what one recites and doing so for the purpose of fulfilling one's religious duty. Unit III continues unit II. Unit IV takes up the same theme as the Mishnah-paragraph, and unit V carries forward unit IV and repeats its ideas. Unit VI concludes the matter begun with the Mishnah's insistence that the Shema be recited with the intent of fulfilling one's religious obligation to do so, not merely mechanically. Units VII, VIII, IX, X, XI then complement the foregoing with thematically relevant materials, other rules for the recitation of the Shema. Unit XII reverts to the Mishnah-paragraph. Unit XIII then takes up the same theme as the Mishnah, namely, interrupting the recitation of sacred writ. I am not sure why unit XIV is inserted, since it makes no sense in context. Unit XV, by contrast, does go over the basic principle of the Mishnah-paragraph, namely, the matter of greeting one's fellow in the setting of reciting the Shema and saying the Prayer. I cannot see why anyone would have added unit XVI. Unit XVII reverts to the Mishnah-paragraph. I take it that unit XVIII is added as a supplement to information on what constitute the paragraphs of the Shema. Unit XIX clearly complements the Mishnah-paragraph. Unit XX is included because it makes reference to Joshua b. Qorhah's statement in the Mishnah. Units XXI and XXII then complement unit XX. In all, therefore, the rather protracted discussion at hand has focused mainly on the Mishnah-paragraph, with a fair amount of complementary material pertinent to the themes of that paragraph.

2:3

A.   One who recites the Shema but did not recite it audibly -- [still] has fulfilled his obligation.

B.   R. Yose says, "He has not fulfilled his obligation."

C.   One who recited and did not articulate the letters precisely --

D.   R. Yose says, "He has fulfilled his obligation."

E.   And R. Judah says, "He has not fulfilled his obligation."

F.   One who recites in improper order has not fulfilled his obligation.

G.   One who recited and erred [in the recitation, later realizing his error] should return to the place where he erred [and continue reciting from there to the conclusion].

I.

A.   What is the scriptural basis for the view of R. Yose?

B.   It is because it is written, "Hear" (Deut. 6:4), meaning: "Let your ear hear what your mouth says."

C.   And the first authority [at M. 2:3A]?

D.   He takes the view that the sense of "Hear" is to say the Shema in any language that you hear [and understand].

E.   And R. Yose? He derives two lessons from the same word.

II.

A.   There we have learned:

B.   A deaf person who can speak but not hear may not separate heave-offering. But if he separated heave-offering, that which he has separated is valid heave-offering [M. Ter. 1:2, Peck, p. 30].

C.   Now who so construes Tannaite teaching to maintain that a deaf person who can speak but not hear [who does such a deed] post facto [is credited after the fact with a valid action] but de novo is not [credited to begin with with a valid action]?

D.   Said R. Hisda, "It represents the view of R. Yose. For we have learned in the Mishnah:

E.   "'One who recites the Shema but did not recite it audibly has carried out his obligation,' the words of R. Judah.

F.   "R. Yose says, 'He has not carried out his obligation' [M. 2:3A-B]."

G.   [No, it need not be Yose at all], for R. Yose takes the position that one has not carried out his obligation only with regard to the recitation of the Shema, which rests upon the authority of the Torah. But in the matter of the separation of heave-offering, the operative consideration is the recitation of the blessing over the separation of heave-offering [which the one who says must hear]. But the recitation of the blessing is required only upon the authority of rabbis [so, in that case, Yose might well concur that a deaf-person may conduct the action validly, post facto].

H.   [The reason is that] the matter does not depend upon the validity of the blessing [but only upon the actual physical action of designating that portion of the crop that is to be regarded as heave-offering].

I.   Now why maintain that the rule accords with the principle of R. Yose? Why not maintain the possibility that it is R. Judah.

J.   And he has taken the view that, even with reference to the recitation of the Shema, post facto [a deaf-mute] may indeed [recite the Shema, even though he does not actually hear the words], while only de novo he may not [validly do so].

K.   You may derive evidence from the framing of the Mishnah-passage itself that that is the case, for it is framed in this language: One who recites, yielding the sense, "Post facto, it is a valid act, though de novo it is not."

L.   To that possibility I may say the following:

M.   The point of framing the Mishnah-passage in terms of, One who recites in fact is to show you the extent to which R. Yose will go. For he takes the view that, even after the fact, the deaf-mute who has recited the Shema has not carried out his obligation.

N.   For if you maintain that it is R. Judah's view, then even de novo he would maintain that such a one has carried out his obligation.

O.   In that case, what is the upshot of the matter? It is that the cited passage [at M. Ter.] accords with the view of R. Yose.

P.   In that case, how do you deal with the following Tannaite tradition:

Q.   A person should not say the Grace after Meals silently [in his heart], but if he has done so, he has carried out his obligation.

R.   According to whom is the cited teaching? It cannot be either R. Yose or R. Judah.

S.   For in the view of R. Judah, he has maintained the position that even de novo, one has carried out his obligation [if he has said a prayer silently] while in the view of R. Yose, he maintains the view that even post facto one has not carried out his obligation [if he has said a prayer silently].

T.   What then is the outcome?

U.   It is R. Judah's view, and he takes the position that post facto one has [carried out his obligation if he has said a prayer silently], while de novo he has not.

V.   Then let us turn to the following teaching on Tannaite authority of R. Judah, son of R. Simeon b. Pazzi: "A deaf-mute who can speak but not hear may to begin with separate heave-offering."

W.   In accord with which of the two authorities is that teaching? It can be neither R. Judah nor R. Yose.

X.   If it were R. Judah, lo, he has taken the position that, de facto one may indeed do so, but only de novo he may not, and in the view of R. Yose, lo, he has said that even de facto one may not do so.

Y.   Then the upshot is that it must accord with R. Judah, and even de novo one may also [carry out the action, even though he cannot hear the blessing].

Z.   And there is no real contradiction [between the versions of R. Judah's views, for] the one is his own view, and the other is the view of his master.

AA.   For we have learned on Tannaite authority: Judah says in the name of R. Eleazar b. Azariah, "He who recites the Shema has to do so audibly, as it is said, 'Hear O Israel, the Lord our God, the Lord is one.'"

BB.   Said to him R. Meir, "Lo, Scripture says, 'Which I command you this day shall be upon your heart' (Deut. 6:5).

CC.   "Matters follow the intention of the heart [and not what your lips speak, so one need not actually say the Shema audibly]."

DD.   Now that you have reached this point, you may as well take the view that R. Judah concurs with the position of his master. There is still no contradiction among the several passages, since on the one side we have the view of R. Judah, on the other, R. Meir [who holds that even de novo a deaf-mute who cannot hear but can speak may carry out the several actions].

III.

A.   We have learned in the following Mishnah-passage:

B.   All are valid to read the Esther-Scroll on Purim, except for a deaf-mute, an idiot, and a minor. R. Judah declares valid in the case of a minor [M. Meg. 2:4A-B].

C.   Who takes the view on Tannaite authority that a deaf-mute even de facto may not [read the Esther-scroll]?

D. Said R. Matenah, "It is R. Yose, for we have learned in the Mishnah:

E. "'One who recites the Shema but did not recite it audibly has carried out his obligation,' the words of R. Judah.

F. "R. Yose says, 'He has not carried out his obligation' [M. 2:3A-B]."

G. Why take the view that it is the position of R. Yose [that is represented in the anonymous clause of M. Meg. 2:4A], and that even post facto, the deaf-mute also may not read the Esther-scroll?

H. [15B] Perhaps the position at hand belongs to R. Judah, and it is de novo that he maintains a deaf-mute may not read the Esther-scroll in public, but de facto it is quite all right.

I. Let that proposition not enter your mind! For the passage at hand treats the deaf-mute as equivalent to an idiot and a minor. Just as, in the case of an idiot and a minor, even post facto the action is null, also with respect to the deaf-mute, what is post facto also is invalid.

J. And perhaps we may maintain that one category follows the rule applying to that category, and the other the rule applying to a different category.

K. But can you actually conclude that the passage at hand is to be assigned to R. Judah? And lo, since the concluding clause of the construction states, R. Judah declares valid in the case of a minor, surely it follows that the opening clause of the same construction cannot represent the view of R. Judah! [He should not be arguing with himself.]

L. But perhaps the entire construction indeed does follow the view of R. Judah, and at issue are two categories of minor. The passage, then, exhibits a flaw, and this is the way it is to be repeated on Tannaite authority:

M. "All are valid to read the Esther-scroll except for a deaf-mute, an idiot, and a minor.

N. "Under what circumstances [may a minor not read the Esther-scroll]? It is a minor who is not yet of age to be taught. But in the case of a minor who has reached the age at which he may be taught, even to begin with he is valid to recite the Esther-scroll," the words of R. Judah.

O. For R. Judah declares valid in the case of a minor.

P. What then is the outcome? It is R. Judah's view, and he takes the position that, post facto, one has [carried out his obligation], while, de novo, he has not.

Q. Then let us turn to the following teaching on Tannaite authority of R. Judah, son of R. Simeon b. Pazzi: "A deaf-mute who can speak but not hear may to begin with separate heave-offering."

R. In accord with which of the two authorities is that teaching? It can be neither R. Judah nor R. Yose.

S. If it were R. Judah, lo, he has taken the position that, de facto one may indeed do so, but only de novo he may not, and, in the view of R. Yose, lo, he has said that even de facto one may not do so.

T. Then the upshot is that it must accord with R. Judah, and even de novo one may also [carry out the action].

U. Then let us consider the following, that is taught on Tannaite authority:

V. A person should not say the Grace after Meals silently [in his heart], but if he has done so, he has carried [post facto] out his obligation.

W. According to whom is the cited teaching? It cannot be either R. Yose or R. Judah.

X. For in the view of R. Judah, he has maintained the position that even de novo, one has carried out his obligation [if he has said a prayer silently], while in the view of R. Yose, he has the position that even post facto one has not carried out his obligation.

Y. What then is the outcome?

Z. It is R. Judah's view, and he takes the position that even de novo one has [carried out his obligation if he has said a prayer silently].

AA. And there is no contradiction between the versions of R. Judah's views, for the one is his own view, and the other is the view of his master..

BB. For we have learned on Tannaite authority: R. Judah says in the name of R. Eleazar b. Azariah, "He who recites the Shema has to do so audibly, as it is said, 'Hear O Israel, the Lord our God, the Lord is one.'"

CC. Said to him R. Meir, "Lo, Scripture says, 'Which I command you this day shall be upon your heart' (Deut. 6:5).

DD. "Matters follow the intention of the heart."

EE. Now that you have reached this point, you may take the view that R. Judah concurs with the position of his master. There is, then, no contradiction among the several passages, since, on the one side, we have the view of R. Judah, on the other, R. Meir.

FF. Said R. Hisda said R. Shila, "The decided law accords with the position of R. Judah stated in the name of R. Eleazar b. Azariah.

GG. "And the law accords with R. Judah."

HH. And it is necessary to have both statements of the decided law in hand, for had we heard only that the law accords with R. Judah, I might have supposed that that is the case even de novo. Accordingly we are told [that that is not the case], but the decided law accords with R. Judah as he stated matters in the name of R. Eleazar b. Azariah.

II. And had we learned only that the law accords with R. Judah as he stated it in the name of R. Eleazar b. Azariah, I should have reached the conclusion that it is necessary to do things that way, and there is no remedy if one did not do it that way.

JJ. Accordingly we are informed also that the law accords with R. Judah [so there is a remedy if one has not done things properly].

IV.

A. Said R. Joseph, "The dispute concerns only the recitation of the Shema. But as to all other religious duties, all parties concur that if the prayer is not heard, one has not carried out his obligation.

B. "For it is said, 'Attend and hear, O Israel' (Deut. 27:9)."

C. An objection was raised from the following: A person should not say Grace after Meals silently, but if he did so, he has carried out his obligation. [So the Foregoing is impossible.]

D.   But if the matter was stated on Amoraic authority, this is how it was phrased:

E.   Said R. Joseph, "The dispute concerns the recitation of the <u>Shema</u>, because it is written, 'Hear O Israel.'

F.   "But as to all other religious duties, all parties concur that one does carry out his obligation [even if the blessing is said inaudibly]."

G.   But has it not been written, "Attend and hear, O Israel" (Deut. 27:9)?

H.   That verse refers only to teachings of Torah [which must be learned and transmitted audibly].

<u>V.</u>

A.   <u>One who recited the Shema and did not articulate the letters precisely [M. 2:3C]:</u>

B.   Said R. Tabi said R. Josiah, "The law accords with the views of both authorities [named in the Mishnah-paragraph] when it comes to imposing a lenient ruling [so: Judah as to audibility, Yose as to pronunciation]."

C.   And R. Tabi taught in the name of R. Josiah, "What is the sense of the verse of Scripture: 'There are three things which are never satisfied... the grave and the barren womb' (Prov. 30:15, 16)?

D.   "What is the connection between the grave and the womb?

E.   "It is to tell you, Just as the womb receives and gives forth, so Sheol receives and gives forth.

F.   "And that moreover yields an argument <u>a fortiori</u>: If the womb receives in secret but gives forth with loud cries, Sheol, which receives with loud cries [of mourning] surely should give forth [the dead] with great noise indeed!

G.   "On the basis of that argument there is an answer to those who say that, on the basis of the teachings of the Torah in particular, there is no basis for expecting the resurrection of the dead."

<u>VI.</u>

A.   R. Oshaiah taught on Tannaite authority before Raba, "'And you shall write them' (Deut. 6:9) means that everything must be written down [in the <u>mezuzah</u> and in the phylacteries,] even the commands [to do so, that is, the words 'And you shall write them and you shall bind them']."

B.   He said to him, "Who is the authority for this view of yours [that a text is required to prove that even the command to write must be written down]?

C.   "This is the view of R. Judah, who has said with reference to the rite of the accused wife, 'The curses one writes down on the scroll of the accused wife, but the commandments one does not write down.' [Hence it is necessary, following Judah's line of reasoning, to find a proof-text for writing the commandment that indicates one has to inscribe in the document at hand not only the body of the document, but also the commandment. Ordinarily one would not write it down.]

D.   "But [Raba continues in the exposition of Judah's reasoning] in that case [namely, the matter of the accused wife], there is a particular text which states, 'And he shall write these curses' (Num. 5:23).

E.   "But here [with regard to the <u>Shema</u>], since it is written, 'And you shall write them,' even the commandments are included.

F. [Raba now objects to this thesis:] "But was the scriptural basis for the view of R. Judah the fact that it is written, 'And he shall write...' (Num. 5:23)?

G. "The real reason for R. Judah's view is that it is written, 'Curses,' meaning, 'One does write the curses, but not the commandment attached to them to write them down.' [Simon, p. 92, n. 3: And but for that implied limitation the expression 'he shall write' by itself would have included commands]."

H. [A reply to Raba's view of matters follows:] Nonetheless, a proof-text is needed [to show that one must write down the commandment to write down in the phylacteries and mezuzah not only the formula but also the commandment too].

I. [Why so?] It might have entered your mind to derive the sense of "writing" from the use of the word "writing" in that other passage. Just as, in that other passage, one writes down the curses, but not the commandment to write down the curses, so here too one might have understood that one does not write down the commandment to write down the commandment.

J. Accordingly, the All-Merciful has said, "And you will write them," meaning, "even the commandments [to write the formula]."

VII.

A. It has been taught on Tannaite authority by R. Obadiah before Raba, "'And you shall teach them' (Deut. 11:19) means that your teaching should be perfect [Simon, p. 92, n. 6: 'And you shall train them' is read as 'and the teaching shall be perfect'].

B. "So one must pause between the joints [so that if one word ends with the same letter with which the next begins, one should pause between one word and the next]."

C. [Agreeing,] Raba responded along the lines of what he said, "For example, 'Upon your heart,' 'Upon your heart [pl.]', 'With all your heart,' and the like."

VIII.

A. Said R. Hama b. Hanina, "For whoever recites the Shema and pronounces the letters distinctly they cool down the fires of Gehenna.

B. "For it is said, 'When the Almighty scatters kings therein, it snows in Zalmon' (Ps. 68:15).

C. "Read the word 'when he scatters' as 'when one pronounces distinctly,' and read the word 'in Zalmon' as 'in the shadow of death.'"

D. And R. Hama b. R. Hanina said, "Why is the word 'tents' [16A] juxtaposed to the word 'streams'?

E. "For it says, '[How goodly are your tents, O Jacob...], as streams stretched out and as gardens by the riverside, as aloes planted...' (Num. 24:5).

F. "Just as a stream raises a person from a state of uncleanness to a state of cultic cleanness, so sitting in tents [in study of Torah] raises a person from the scale of guilt to the scale of merit."

IX.

A. One who recites in improper order has not carried out his obligation [M. 2:3F]:

B. R. Ammi and R. Assi were decorating the bridal chamber of R. Eleazar.

C. He said to them, "While you are doing this, I'll go and listen to what is being taught in the study-house and I'll come back and report it to you."

D.   He went and found the Tannaite authority of the study-house repeating before R.
       Yohanan:

E.   If one was reciting the Shema and erred and does not know where he erred, if it was
       in the middle of a paragraph, he should go back to the beginning of the paragraph. If
       it was between one paragraph and the next, he should go back to the beginning of
       the first of the two paragraphs. If it was between one reference to 'writing' and the
       other reference to 'writing' [in the Shema], he should go back to the first reference
       to 'writing.' [T. Ber. 2:5].

F.   Said to him R. Yohanan, "That rule applies only if one has not begun to read the
       words, 'In order that your days may be lengthened.' But if one has reached the
       words, 'In order that your days may be lengthened,' he has [presumably] taken his
       habitual course [and said things right]."

G.   He came and reported this to them. They said to him, "Had we come only to hear
       this fine teaching, it would have been enough for us."

The Talmud's exposition of the Mishnah concludes with unit I, with some further
glosses at units V and IX. The Talmud really has its own autonomous program of inquiry,
which intersects with the Mishnah-passage. This is expressed in the large and beautifully
articulated constructions of units II and III-IV. These go over the same ground and should
be regarded as a single, protracted discourse. Units VI, VII seem to me only remotely
relevant to the larger construction into which they have been inserted. I can understand
why unit VIII has been added, since it provides a supplement to M. 2:3C. Perhaps the idea
that things must be done perfectly and with great care accounts for unit VII as well, that
is, carefully pronouncing words is what M. 2:3C-E require. What then do units VI and VII
have in common? The shared formula about teaching before Raba and also the theme of
perfect replication of the commandment. If on that slender reed we rely in explaining the
joining of VI to VII and the introduction of both here, we can account for the entire
composition.

2:4-5

A.   Craftsmen recite the Shema while atop a tree or a scaffold,

B.   something which they are not permitted to do with respect to the Prayer
       [i.e., the eighteen benedictions].

M. 2:4

A.   A bridegroom is exempt from the recitation of the Shema on the first
       night [after the wedding] until after the Sabbath [following the wedding],

B.   if he did not yet consummate the marriage.

C.   M^CSH B: Rabban Gamaliel who was married and recited the Shema on
       the first night of his marriage.

D. [His students] said to him, "Did our master not teach us: 'A bridegroom is exempt from the recitation of the Shema on the first night'?"

E. He said to them, "I cannot accede to you so as to suspend myself from [accepting] the kingdom of heaven [even] for one hour."

M. 2:5

I.

A. Our rabbis have taught on Tannaite authority:

B. Craftsmen recite [the shema] while in a treetop or a scaffold and recite the Prayer while atop an olive tree or atop a fig tree.

C. [As for] all the other kinds of trees -- they must climb down [first] and [then] recite the Prayer.

D. But a householder must always climb down and [then] recite the Prayer [since the height will] distract him. [T. Ber. 2:8].

E. R. Mari, son of the daughter of Samuel, objected to Raba, "We have learned in the Mishnah: Craftsmen recite the Shema while atop a tree or a scaffold [M. 2:4A]. It then follows that in the recitation of the Shema one does not have to direct his heart [to the recitation of the Shema in fulfillment of his obligation to do so. Merely saying the words suffices.]

F. "Now note the contrast: 'He who recites the Shema has to direct his heart, since it is said, "Hear O Israel," (Deut. 6:4) and elsewhere it says, "Pay attention and hear O Israel" (Deut. 27:9). Just as in that latter passage one has to be attentive, so here one has to be attentive.'"

G. [Raba] remained silent.

H. [Mari] said to him, "Have you heard anything about this problem?"

I. He said to him, "This is what R. Sheshet said, 'And [the law at M. 2:4A] applies to a case in which the workers stop working and recite the Shema.' [Hence there is no conflict between the cited passage of the Mishnah and the contrasting teaching, since the former takes for granted the workers stop working and direct their hearts to the recitation of the Shema, rather than doing so mechanically.]"

J. But has it not been taught on Tannaite authority:

K. "The House of Hillel say, 'Workers may continue their work and recite the Shema'"?

L. There is no problem, since the former teaching [that one has to direct his heart to what he is doing] applies to the first paragraph of the recitation of the Shema, and the latter teaching [that one does not have to do so] applies to the second.

II.

A. Our rabbis have taught on Tannaite authority:

B. Workers who were at work at a household [take time to] recite the Shema and recite the benedictions before it and after it,

C. and eat their bread and recite the benedictions before it [the meal] and after it [cf. T. Ber. 5:24].

D.   and recite [three times daily] the Prayer of eighteen [blessings].

E.   But they do not descend before the ark [to lead the recitations of the Prayer in a synagogue].

F.   And they do not lift up their hands [in the priestly benediction] [T. Ber. 2:9].

G.   But has it not been taught on Tannaite authority: "[They say not the complete Prayer but only] an abbreviation of the eighteen benedictions"?

H.   Said R. Sheshet, "There is no contradiction. The one position represents the position of Rabban Gamaliel, the other of R. Joshua [at M. Ber. 4:3]."

I.   If it is R. Joshua's view [represented at G], why specify that the rule applies to workers? [In Joshua's view, the same law] pertains even to ordinary people.

J.   Rather, both positions represent the view of Rabban Gamaliel, and there still is no contradiction between the two statements, for the statement [permitting the workers to say only the abbreviated version] speaks of workers who are laboring for a wage, while the other speaks of workers who are working for their keep [and the latter may take longer in reciting the Prayer].

K.   And [in proof of the foregoing distinction] has it not been taught on Tannaite authority:

L.   Workers who were at work at a household take time to recite the Shema and recite the benedictions before it and after it and eat their bread but do not recite a benediction before it but they do recite the benedictions after it, stating both required blessings. How so? They recite the first of the two blessings as it is laid down, and in the second one, one opens with a blessing for the Land, then including "who builds Jerusalem" in the blessing of the Land. Under what circumstances [does this rule apply]? It applies to workers who are working for a wage, but in the case of those who are working for their keep, or with whom the householder was joined in the meal, one says the entire blessing as it has been laid down.

III.

A.   A bridegroom is exempt from the recitation of the Shema [M. 2:5A]:

B.   Our rabbis have taught on Tannaite authority:

C.   "When you sit in your house" (Deut. 6:6) serves to exclude from the requirement to recite the Shema one who is engaged in carrying out a religious duty.

D.   "And when you walk by the way" (Deut. 6:6) serves to exclude a bridegroom from the requirement to recite the Shema.

E.   On this basis [sages] have ruled, "He who marries a virgin is exempt from the requirement of reciting the Shema, but if he marries a widow, he is liable."

F.   What is the proof for that distinction?

G.   Said R. Papa, "The matter derives from the analogy supplied by the word 'way.' Just as going on the way is an optional matter, so here to it is an optional matter."

H.   Do we not in fact deal with one who is on the way to carry out a religious duty? And even so, the All-Merciful has said that one should recite the Shema.

I.   If that were the appropriate conclusion, Scripture should have said, "While walking." Why does it specify, "In your walking on the way"? That yields the inference that

one is going on a trip on his own volition in which case one is liable to recite the
Shema. But if he should be on a trip in connection with carrying out a religious
duty, he is exempt.

J.   [16B] If that is the operative consideration, then why emphasize that the exemption
applies only to one who marries a virgin? Even one who marries a widow should also
be exempt.

K.   In the one case the bridegroom is preoccupied, in the other he is not.

L.   If the operative consideration is whether or not the groom is preoccupied, then even
if one's ship is sinking in the sea, he should also be exempt.

M.   But on what account, then, did R. Abba bar Zabeda say Rab said, "A mourner is
liable to carry out all of the religious duties that are listed in the Torah except for
the religious duty of putting on phylacteries.

N.   "For lo, in their regard, it is said, 'Glory,' as it is stated, 'Your glory bound upon
your head' (Ez. 24:26)."

O.   One may reply, In that case we deal with a preoccupation involving an optional
matter, here it involves a religious duty.

Unit I supplies Tosefta's complement to the Mishnah-passage and analyzes that
passage, and unit II does the same. Unit III then goes over familiar ground, appropriate to
the passage at hand because it supplies a proof-text for the Mishnah's proposition.

2:6-8

A.   [Gamaliel] washed on the first night after the death of his wife.

B.   [His students] said to him, "Did not our master teach us that it is
forbidden for a mourner to wash?"

C.   He said to them, "I am not like other men, I am frail."

M. 2:6

A.   And when Tabi, [Gamaliel's] servant, died [Gamaliel] received condolences on his account.

B.   Said to him [his students], "Did not our master teach us that one does not
receive condolences for [the loss of] slaves?"

C.   He said to them, "Tabi my slave was not like other slaves. He was
proper (ksr)."

M. 2:7

A.   If a bridegroom wishes to receive the Shema on the first night [after his
wedding] -- he may recite it.

B.   Rabban Simeon b. Gamaliel says, "Not all who wish to take the name [so claiming high rank as a sage] may do so."

M. 2:8

I.

A.   What is the basis for Rabban Gamaliel's action [described at M. 2:6A]?

B.   He took the view that the rules of mourning by night derive solely from the authority of rabbis [and that mourning rites apply only by day, so far as the requirement of the Torah is concerned].

C.   For it is written, "[And I will make it as the mourning for an only son] and the end thereof as a bitter day" (Amos 8:10). [Thus it is only by day that the bitterness of mourning applies].

D.   In a case in which one is frail, rabbis made no such decree [on which account Gamaliel felt free not to mourn by night, so he washed up].

II.

A.   And when Tabi his servant died etc. [M. 2:7A]:

B.   Our rabbis have taught on Tannaite authority:

C.   As to man-servants and woman-servants, one may not on their account stand in line [to receive condolences] or express on their account either the blessing for mourners or the condolence for mourners.

D.   M^cSH W: The serving woman of R. Eliezer died. His disciples came to comfort him. When he saw them, he went up to the upper room. They went up after him. He entered the anteroom. They went after him. He went into the dining hall. They went after him. He said to them, "I supposed that you would be scalded by warm water, but you are not affected even by boiling water.

E.   "Have I not repeated for you the following: 'As to man-servants and woman-servants, one may not on their account stand in line [to receive condolences] or express on their account either the blessing for mourners or the condolence for mourners'?

F.   "'What then do they say in their regard? They say what people say to someone on account of his ox or ass who have died, namely, "May the Omnipresent replace your loss." So they say to someone on account of the death of his man-servant or woman-servant: "May the Omnipresent replace your loss."'"

G.   It has been further taught on Tannaite authority:

H.   As to man-servants and woman-servants they do not make a funeral lamentation for them.

I.   R. Yose says, "If it was a suitable servant, they do make a funeral lamentation on his account, in these terms: 'Woe for the good and faithful man, who lived from his own labor.'"

J.   They said to him, "If that is the case, then what do you leave for suitable [people who are not slaves at all]?"

III.

A.   Our rabbis have taught on Tannaite authority:

B.   People may call "fathers" only the three patriarchs, and "mothers" only the four matriarchs. [The others of the early generations do not merit those titles.]

C.   What is the reason? Is it because we do not know whether we come from Reuben or Simeon? If so, then the same problem applies to the matriarchs, since we do not know whether we come from Rachel or from Leah.

D.   Rather the reason is this: To that point the ancestors are regarded as worthy, and from that point they are not regarded as worthy.

E.   It has further been taught on Tannaite authority:

F.   As to man servants and woman servants, they do not call them, "Father So-and-so" or "Mother So-and-so."

G.   But the one of Rabban Gamaliel they called "Father So-and-so" or "Mother So-and-so" [as at M. 2:7C].

H.   Does the precedent contradict the rule?

I.   [No, it is] because [Tabi] was important.

IV.

A.   Said R. Eleazar, "What is the meaning of the verse of Scripture: 'So will I bless you as long as I live, in your name I will lift up my hands' (Ps. 63:5)?

B.   "'I will bless you as long as I live' refers to the Shema.

C.   "'In your name I will lift up my hands' speaks of the Prayer.

D.   "If one does so, Scripture says of such a one, 'My soul is satisfied as with marrow and fat' (Ps. 63:6).

E.   "Not only so, but such a one inherits two worlds, this and the next, as it says, 'And my mouth praises you with [two] joyful lips' (Ps. 63:6)."

V.

A.   When R. Eleazar finished saying his prayer, this is what he said: "May it be pleasing before you, O Lord our God, to bring to dwell within our lot love, brotherhood, peace, and friendship, and make our territories rich in disciples, and make our destiny succeed with a future and a hope, and place our portion in the Garden of Eden, and provide us with a good colleague and good impulse in your world. And may we get up in the morning and find the yearning of our heart to fear your name. And may the serenity of our souls come before you for good."

B.   When R. Yohanan had finished saying his Prayer, this is what he said: "May it be pleasing before you, O Lord our God, to look upon our shame and see our suffering, and clothe yourself in mercy, cover yourself in your strength, and cloak yourself in your loyalty, and gird yourself in your compassion, and may the attribute of goodness come before you and that of your gentleness."

C.   When R. Zira had finished saying his Prayer, this is what he said: "May it be pleasing before you, O Lord our God, that we not sin or be ashamed or disgrace ourselves more than did our fathers."

D.   When R. Hiyya had finished saying his Prayer, this is what he said: "May it be pleasing before you, O Lord our God, that your Torah will be our craft, and that our heart not get sick or our eyes grow dim."

E.   When Rab had finished saying his Prayer, this is what he said: "May it be pleasing before you, O Lord our God, to give us long life, peaceful life, good life, blessed life, abundant life, secure life, a life of fear of sin, a life not marred by shame or humiliation, a life of wealth and honor, a life of love of Torah and fear of Heaven, a life in which you fill all the desires of our hearts for good."

F.   When Rabbi had finished saying his Prayer, this is what he said: "May it be pleasing before you, O Lord our God and God of our fathers, that you save us from those who are arrogant and from arrogance, from a bad man and a bad encounter, from the evil impulse and a bad associate, from a bad neighbor and from the destructive Satan, from a bad judgment and from a difficult litigant, whether a member of the covenant or not."

G.   [He said that prayer] even though there were guards standing over Rabbi.

H.   When R. Safra finished saying his Prayer, this is what he said, "May it be pleasing before you, O Lord our God, to make peace [17A] in the heavenly family and in the earthly family and among the disciples who are occupied with your Torah, whether they are occupied with it for its own sake or not for its own sake.

I.   "And as to all those who are occupied with Torah not for its own sake, may it be pleasing before you that they should be occupied with it for its own sake."

J.   When R. Alexandri had finished saying his Prayer, this is what he said: "May it be pleasing before you, O Lord our God, to set us up in a well-lit corner and not in a dark one, and may our hearts not grow sick, or our eyes dim."

K.   There are those who report that R. Hamnuna said that prayer.

L.   And when R. Alexandri had finished saying his Prayer, this is what he said: "Lord of the ages, it is perfectly obvious to you that our will is to do your will. But what prevents it? It is the leaven in the dough, the subjugation to the pagan kingdoms. May it be pleasing before you, O Lord our God, to save us from their power so that we may return to carry out the rules that please you with a whole heart."

M.   When Raba finished saying his Prayer, this is what he said: "My God, before I was created, I was unworthy, and now that I have been created, it is as if I had not been created. I am dust in my life, all the more so in my death. Lo, I am before you as a utensil filled with shame and humiliation. May it be pleasing before you, O Lord my God, that I not sin again, and as to the sins that I have committed before you, wipe them out in your great mercies. But this should not be done through suffering or painful ailments."

N.   This is, moreover, the form of the Confession that was said by the younger R. Hamnuna on the Day of Atonement.

O.   When Mar, son of Rabina, finished saying his Prayer, this is what he said: "My God, guard my tongue from gossiping and my lips from deceit. To those who curse me, may my soul be silent, and may my soul be as dust to everyone. Open my heart to your Torah, and let my soul pursue your religious duties. Keep me from a bad encounter, a bad impulse, a bad woman, and from all sorts of bad events that may come into the world. Quickly nullify the counsel of all who plan to do me ill and frustrate their plans. May what my mouth says and what my heart reflects be pleasing before you, O Lord, my rock and redeemer."

P.   When R. Sheshet would sit fasting, after he had said his Prayer, he would say this: "Lord of the ages, it is perfectly obvious to you that, when the house of the sanctuary stood, a person who had sinned would make an offering. And of that offering the priests would offer up only the fat and blood, yet atonement would be attained for that person. Now I have sat in a fast, and so my fat and blood have become less. May it be pleasing before you that my fat and blood that have become less be received as if I had offered them up before you on the altar and so be reconciled with me."

Q.   When R. Yohanan would finish [the study of] the book of Job, this is what he said: "The destiny of a person is to die, and the destiny of a beast is to be slaughtered, so all are destined to death. Happy is the one who grows in knowledge of Torah, whose labor is in Torah, who thereby brings pleasure to his Creator, who grows in good repute, and who dies in good repute in this world. Concerning such a one Solomon said, 'A good name is better than precious oil, and the day of death than the day of one's birth' (Qoh. 7:1)."

VI.

A.   A pearl in R. Meir's mouth: "Learn with all your heart and with all your soul to know my ways and to attend upon the entries of my Torah. Keep my Torah in your heart and let awe of me be before your eyes. Keep your mouth from every sort of sin, purify and sanctify yourself from all guilt and transgression. Then I shall be with you everywhere."

B.   A pearl in the mouth of rabbis of Yabneh: "I am mortal and so is my fellow. But my labor is in town, and his is in the field. I get up early to do my work and he gets up early to do his work. Just as he does not infringe upon my work, so I do not infringe upon his work. And perhaps you might suppose that I do much and he does little? We have learned to repeat: 'All the same is the one who does much and the one who does little, so long as a person directs his heart to Heaven.'"

C.   A pearl in the mouth of Abayye: "A person should always be subtle [in finding ways to] fear [Heaven]. 'A soft answer turns away anger' (Prov. 15:1). One should increase peace with his brethren and relatives and everyone, even with a gentile in the marketplace, so that he may be beloved above and pleasing below and accepted by people."

D.   They said about Rabban Yohanan ben Zakkai that no person ever greeted him first, even a gentile in the marketplace.

E.   A pearl in the mouth of Raba: "The concrete realization of wisdom lies in repentance and good deeds. So a person should not study Scripture and repeat Mishnah traditions but at the same time abuse his father, his mother, his master, or someone greater than himself in wisdom and in years [Simon: rank], as it is said, 'The fear of the Lord is the beginning of wisdom, a good understanding have all they who do thereafter' (Ps. 111:10). It is not said, 'To those who do,' but 'Those who do thereafter,' meaning, those who do for their own sake and not for those who do them not for their own sake. And whoever does not for its own sake would have been better off not having been created."

F.   A pearl in the mouth of Rab: "The world to come is not like this world. In the world to come there is neither eating nor drinking nor procreating nor give and take nor envy nor hatred nor competition. But the righteous are enthroned with their crowns on their heads, enjoying the splendor of the Presence of God. For it is said, 'And they beheld God and [it was that that they] ate and drank' (Ex. 24:11)."

VII.

A.   The promise made by the Holy One, blessed be he, to women is greater than that to the men, for it is said, "Rise up, you women that are at ease, you confident daughters, give ear to my speech" (Is. 32:9).

B.   Said Rab to R. Hiyya, "How do women gain merit? It is by having their children learn to recite Scripture in the synagogue, and having their husbands learn to repeat Mishnah-traditions at the rabbis' house, and by watching for their husbands until they come from the rabbis' house."

VIII.

A.   When rabbis took their leave of the house of R. Ammi, and some say, from the house of R. Hanina, this is what they said to him: "May you see to your world[ly needs] in your lifetime and your future in the world to come and your hope in the generations to follow. May your heart attain understanding, your mouth speak wisdom, your tongue express song, your eyelids look straight before you [Simon, p. 103, n. 3: The meaning here seems to be, 'may you have a correct insight into the meaning of the Torah'], may your eyes be illumined in the light of the Torah, your faith glisten in the glow of the firmament, your lips speak knowledge, your reins rejoice in uprightness, and your feet run to listen to the words of the Ancient of Days."

B.   When rabbis took their leave of the house of R. Hisda, and some say, from the house of R. Samuel bar Nahmani, this is what they said to him: "'We are instructed, we are well laden' (Ps. 144:14)."

IX.

A.   "We are instructed, we are well laden" (Ps. 144:14):

B.   Rab and Samuel, and some say it was R. Yohanan and R. Eleazar:

C.   One said, "'We are instructed' in Torah and 'we are well-laden' with religious duties."

D.   The other said, "'We are instructed' in Torah and in religious duties,' and we are well laden' in suffering."

E.   [17B] "There is no breach" (Ps. 144:14): May our class not be like the class of David, from which Ahitophel went forth.

F.   "And no going forth" (Ps. 144:14): May our class not be like the class of Saul, from which Doeg the Edomite went forth.

G. "And no outcry" (Ps. 144:14): May our class not be like the class of Elisha, from which Gehazi went forth.

H. "In our broad places" (Ps. 144:14): May we have no son or disciple who humiliates himself in public.

X.

A. "Listen to me, you stout-hearted, who are far from charity" (Is. 46:12):

B. Rab and Samuel, and some say it was R. Yohanan and R. Eleazar:

C. One said, "The entire world is sustained through charity, but they are sustained by force."

D. And one said, "The entire world is sustained on their merit, but as to them, even on the basis of their own merit they are not sustained."

E. This accords with what R. Judah said in the name of Rab,

F. For R. Judah said Rab said, "Every day an echo goes forth from Mount Horeb and says, 'The entire world is sustained on account of my son, Hanina, and my son Hanina finds sufficient a gab of carobs from one week to the next.'"

G. This explanation [of the reference of Is. 46:12] differs from what R. Judah said.

H. For R. Judah said, "Who are the stout-hearted? They are the stupid Gubeans."

I. Said R. Joseph, "You may know that that is so, for out of that group a proselyte has never come."

J. Said R. Ashi, "The people who live in Mata Mehasia are the 'stout-hearted,' for lo, they witness the glory of the Torah twice a year [when the sages assemble there], and yet a single proselyte has never come forth from among them."

XI.

A. If a bridegroom wishes to recite the Shema [M. 2:8A]:

B. [Does the statement of Rabban Simeon b. Gamaliel at M. 2:8B] bear the implication that Rabban Simeon b. Gamaliel takes account of the possibility of showing off, and the rabbis do not?

C. But lo, we have heard exactly the opposite views imputed to both parties.

D. For we have learned in the Mishnah:

E. Where they are accustomed to do work on the ninth of Ab, they do it. Where they are accustomed not to do work, they do not do it. And in every place disciples of sages refrain from labor.

F. Rabban Simeon b. Gamaliel says, "Under all circumstances should a man act on his own like a disciple of a sage" [M. Pes. 4:5A-D].

G. There is then a contradiction between the two sayings assigned to rabbis, and there is a contradiction between the two sayings assigned to Rabban Simeon b. Gamaliel.

H. Said R. Yohanan, "Reverse the theories [assigned to the respective parties]."

I. R. Sisha, son of R. Idi, said, "There is no need to make such an exchange. The position of rabbis in the one passage does not present a contradiction to the position of the rabbis in the other.

J. "As to the recitation of the Shema, since everyone says it, if the bridegroom also says it, it will not look as though he is acting in a self-important way. But here,

   since everyone else does work, if he does not do work, it will appear as though he is
   acting in a self-important way.

K.   "The views of Rabban Simeon b. Gamaliel likewise do not contradict one another. In
     that other matter [involving the recitation of the Shema], the matter depends upon
     proper attitude, and we can give testimony that under the conditions [of new-
     ly-weds], the man cannot properly attain the right attitude.

L.   "But here [in the matter of refraining from work, which Simeon permits anyone to
     do], one who sees [the man refrain from work] will say, 'He simply does not have a
     job.' For go and see how many unemployed people there are in the market-place."

Once more we deal with sizable units of discourse -- IV-X -- assembled without any
concern for Mishnah-exegesis. Units I, II and XI deal with the Mishnah. Unit III clearly
complements unit II's treatment of the Mishnah's reference to special honor accorded to
Tabi. Now if we were not interested in the Mishnah at all, how would we account for the
conglomeration of the units that follow? Clearly someone has composed a long and
reasonably cogent tractate not so much on reciting the Shema and saying the Prayer, as
on supplementing the received Prayer with individually composed liturgies. Unit IV then
serves as a rather elegant prologue, on the Shema and the Prayer. Unit V moves on to a
long and important account of the individual prayers of various great authorities. Unit VI
proceeds to sayings on the importance of Torah-study and wisdom, the sayings are joined
by the formal reference to all of them as "pearls." Unit VII proceeds to further material
on Torah-study, and unit VIII explains why unit VII is included. That is to say, VII serves as
a prologue to VIII, prayers said by disciples when they left their master's house. So units
V and VIII form the centerpiece of the composition as a whole. Because VIII B refers to
Ps. 144:14, further exegesis of that verse is appended at unit IX, and, since unit IX has as
its tradents Rab/Samuel or Yohanan/Eleazar, unit X adds a further exegesis in their
names. So we can account by reference either to theme or to tradent for the conglomeration of the several parts, units IV-X, into a single extended discussion. The execution
on the stated theme, moreover, serves as a kind of conclusion to the Talmud's treatment
of the matter of Shema and the Prayer, by supplying the inevitable theme of Torah-study
in the present context, on the one side, and of the exemplary character of the rabbi and
his distinctive prayer, on the other. None of this serves as Mishnah-commentary. In no
way do we recognize an interest in a secondary expansion on the specific allegations made
in the Mishnah-passage. What we have is Talmud "for its own sake," that is, protracted
and acute discussion of an important theme, out of all relationship with the Mishnah's
statements on the same theme. Such little "tractates" clearly were composed over a long
period of time and then found their way into the larger work of composition that yielded
the Talmud in hand.

3:1-2

A. He whose deceased relative is lying before him [before burial of the body] is exempt from

    1.   the recitation of the Shema.

    2.   from the Prayer,

    3.   and from [wearing] phylacteries, and from all religious duties listed in the Torah.

B. Pallbearers and they who replace them and they who replace their replacements --

C. as to those who go before the bier and those who go behind the bier --

D. as to they who go before the bier, they who are necessary for [carrying] the bier are exempt [from the Shema and phylacteries].

E. As to those who go behind the bier, they who are necessary for the bier are obligated.

F. Both parties are exempt from the Prayer.

M. 3:1

A. Once they have buried the deceased and returned [from the gravesite] --

B. if they have time to begin and complete [the recitation of the Shema] before they reach the line [of those who have come to console the mourners], they should begin.

C. And if not, they should not begin.

D. [Concerning] they who are standing in line [to comfort the mourner],

E. those on the inside [line] are exempt [from the recitation of the Shema],

F. and those on the outer [line] are obligated [to recite it].

M. 3:2

I.

A. [If] the deceased actually lies before [the mourner], then [the laws] do [apply], and if not, they do not.

B. An objection then is to be raised from the following:

C.   As to one whose deceased [actually] lies before him, he eats in a different room. If
     he does not have another room, he eats in the room of his fellow. If he has no
     access to the room of his fellow, he makes a partition and eats [separate from the
     corpse]. If he has nothing with which to make a partition, he turns his face away
     and eats. He does not recline and eat, he does not eat meat, he does not drink wine,
     he does not say a blessing before the meal, he does not serve to form a quorum,
     [18A] and people do not say a blessing for him or include him in a quorum. He is
     exempt from the requirement to recite the Shema and from the Prayer and from the
     requirement of wearing phylacteries and from all of the religious duties that are
     listed in the Torah. But on the Sabbath he does recline and eat, he does eat meat,
     he does drink wine, he does say a blessing before the meal, he does serve to form a
     quorum and people do say a blessing for him and include him in a quorum. And he is
     liable to carry out all of the religious duties that are listed in the Torah. Rabban
     Simeon b. Gamaliel says, "Since he is liable for these [religious duties], he is liable
     to carry out all of them."

D.   And [in connection with the dispute just now recorded], R. Yohanan said, "What is at
     issue between [Simeon and the anonymous authority]? At issue is the matter of
     having sexual relations. [Simeon maintains that the mourner on the Sabbath has the
     religious obligation to have sexual relations with his wife, and the anonymous
     authority does not include that requirement, since during the mourning period it
     does not apply.]"

E.   In any event, the cited passage does state that the one whose corpse is lying before
     him is exempt from the requirement to recite the Shema and say the Prayer and
     wear phylacteries and from all of the religious duties that are listed in the Torah.
     [But we noted, A, that if the corpse was not actually present, these obligations
     would pertain.]

F.   Said R. Papa, "Interpret the cited passage [M. 3:1] to apply to the requirement of
     turning away one's face and eating. [Such a one has no other place in which to eat,
     and he would be exempt from the various obligations. Anyone else would be liable.
     The Mishnah-passage at hand speaks only of this narrow case.]"

G.   R. Ashi said, "Since the mourner bears the obligation to bury the deceased, it is as if
     the deceased is [actually] lying before him, for it is said, 'And Abraham rose up from
     before his dead' (Gen. 23:3), and it says, 'That I may bury my dead out of my sight'
     (Gen. 23:4). [Since at that moment, Abraham was not actually gazing upon the
     deceased, the implication is that, so long as the responsibility of burying the
     deceased applies, it is as if the deceased is present, and that makes Papa's
     explanation impossible. But in fact the implication is that, at M. 3:1, the corpse is
     not to be understood to be actually present, and the sense of the language of M. 3:1
     is simply that the obligation to bury the deceased applies.]"

II.

A.   [Since the Mishnah refers to a deceased relative, I offer the inference that] if it is
     one's deceased relative, the law applies, but if one is obligated only to guard the
     corpse [but it is not one's deceased relative], the law does not apply.

B. And has it not been taught on Tannaite authority:

C. He who watches over a corpse, even though it is not a corpse belonging to one's own family, is exempt from the requirement to recite the <u>Shema</u> and to say the Prayer, to put on phylacteries, and to do any of all of the religious duties that are listed in the Torah.

D. Accordingly, the law applies to one who guards the corpse, even though it is not a relation, or to one who has the obligation to bury a corpse, even though he does not actually have to guard it.

E. [Now we may further infer:] the law applies to one who guards the corpse, but not to one who is walking in a cemetery.

F. But has it not been taught on Tannaite authority:

G. A person should not walk in a cemetery with phylacteries on his head and a scroll of the Torah in his arm and recite the <u>Shema</u>. And if one should do so, he violates the principle, "He who mocks the poor [deceased] blasphemes his maker" (Prov. 17:5).

H. The prohibition applies to one standing within four cubits of a corpse, but one who stands outside of the space of four cubits is liable.

I. For a master has said, "A corpse affects four cubits of space round about for the purposes of recitation of the <u>Shema</u> [which should not be carried out within that space].

J. In the present case, then, if one is four cubits outside of that space, he also is exempt.

III.

A. [Returning to the] body [of the text just now cited]:

B. He who watches over a corpse, even though it is not a corpse belonging to one's own family, is exempt from the requirement to recite the <u>Shema</u> and to say the Prayer, to put on phylacteries, and to do any of all of the religious duties that are listed in the Torah.

C. If there were two together, one guards the corpse while the other recites the <u>Shema</u>, then the other guards the corpse while the one recites the <u>Shema</u>.

D. Ben Azzai says, "If they are coming by boat, one may leave the deceased in one corner and the two of them may say their Prayer in another corner."

E. What is at issue between the [anonymous authority and Ben Azzai]?

F. Said Rabina, "At issue is whether we take account of the threat [to the corpse] posed by mice. One authority holds that we take account of that threat [on which account the corpse is never left untended, even while the guard says his Prayer], and the other authority maintains that we do not take account of that concern."

IV.

A. It has been taught on Tannaite authority:

B. He who brings bones from one place to another, lo, such a one should not put them into saddle-bags and put them on his ass and then ride on them, because one would thereby treat them in a contemptuous manner.

C. But if he was afraid on account of the threat of gentiles or thugs, it is permitted to do so.

D. And in the manner in which they have said one must handle bones, so they have said one must handle a scroll of the Torah.

E. To which matter [B, C] does that statement refer? If we say it refers to the first clause [B], who would have thought that a scroll of the Torah was to be treated with less respect than bones?

F. Rather, it refers to the latter clause [that one may do so if there is threat from gentiles or thugs].

V.

A. Said Rahba said R. Judah, "Whoever sees a corpse and does not accompany it violates the principle, 'He who mocks the poor blasphemes his maker' (Prov. 17:5)."

B. And if one accompanies a corpse, what reward does he get?

C. Said R. Assi, "In his regard Scripture states, 'He who is gracious to the poor lends to the Lord' (Prov. 19:17) and 'He who is gracious to the needy honors him' (Prov. 14:31)."

VI.

A. R. Hiyya and R. Jonathan were discoursing while walking in a cemetery. The blue fringes [of the show-fringes] of R. Jonathan were trailing on the ground. Said R. Hiyya to him, "Lift them up, so that [the dead] should not say, 'Tomorrow they are coming to us, and now they are ridiculing us.'"

B. He said to him, "Do the dead know so much as that? And lo, it is written, 'But the dead do not know a thing' (Qoh. 9:5)."

C. He said to him, "If you have studied Scripture, you have not reviewed what you learned, and if you reviewed what you learned, you failed to do it a third time, and if you did it a third time, then people did not explain the meaning to you.

D. "'For the living know that they shall die' (Qoh. 9:5) refers to the righteous, for, when they have died, they still are called the living.

E. "For it is said, 'And Benaiah, son of Jehoiada, son of a living man from Kabzeel, who had done mighty deeds, smote the two altar-hearths of Moab; he went down and also slew a lion in the midst of a pit in the time of snow' (2 Sam. 23:20).

F. "[18B] 'The son of a living man:' Then were all other people sons of corpses? Rather, the sense of 'son of a living man' is that, even after he had died, he was called 'living.'

G. "'From Kabzeel, who had done mighty deeds:' for he did much in collecting works for the Torah.

H. "'He smote two altar-hearths of Moab:' He did not leave behind anyone like himself, either in the time of the first sanctuary or in the time of the second sanctuary.

I. "'He went down and also slew a lion in the midst of a pit in the time of snow:' some say he broke through blocks of ice and went down and immersed, and some say that he repeated the Sifra of the house of Rab in a single winter day.

J.   "'But the dead know nothing:' This refers to the wicked, who, even while they are alive, are called dead, as it is said, 'And you, wicked one, who are slain, the prince of Israel' (Ezek. 21:30).

K.   "If you wish, I shall offer proof from the following verse: 'At the mouth of two witnesses shall the dead be put to death' (Deut. 17:6). Now he is still alive, but the sense is that, since he is wicked, he is regarded as if he were dead."

VII.

A.   The sons of R. Hiyya went out to their villages, and their learning became difficult for them. They made great efforts to remember. One said to his fellow, "Does father know about this trouble of ours?"

B.   The other said to him, "How would he know? And lo, it is written, 'His sons come to honor and he does not know it' (Job 14:21)."

C.   He said to him, "But does he not know? Is it not written, 'But his flesh grieves for him and his soul mourns over him' (Job 14:22). And [commenting on this passage], R. Isaac said, 'The worm causes pain for the corpse as much as does a needle in the flesh of a living person.'"

D.   [The other answered], "They know their own suffering but not the suffering of others."

VIII.

A.   And that is not so [that the deceased know the suffering of others]. For has it not been taught on Tannaite authority:

B.   M^{C}SH B: A certain pious man gave a <u>denar</u> to a poor person on the event of the New Year during a time of failure. His wife scolded him, so he went and spent the night in a cemetery. He heard two spirits talking with one another. One said to her friend, "My friend, come and let us flit through the world and listen behind the veil to learn what sort of punishment is going to come upon the world."

C.   Her friend said to her, "I cannot do so, since I am buried in a mat of reeds [and not in linen]. But you go, and tell me whatever you hear."

D.   She went and flirted about and came back, and [the one who had remained] said to her friend, "My friend, what did you hear from behind the veil?"

E.   She said to her, "I heard that whoever sows his seed in the time of the first rain [will lose out, for] the crop will be ruined by hail."

F.   The man went and sowed at the time of the second rains. The crops of everyone else were smitten but his were not smitten.

G.   The next year he went and spent the night in the cemetery and heard those same two spirits talking with one another. One said to her friend, "Come and let us flit about the world and listen from behind the veil to find out what sort of punishment is coming upon the world."

H.   Her friend said to her, "My friend, did I not tell you that I cannot do so, for I am buried in matting of reeds? But you go and come back and tell me what you hear."

I.   She went and flitted about and came back, and her friend said to her, "My friend, what did you hear from behind the veil?"

J.   She said to her, "I heard that whoever sows his crop in the time of the second rain [will lose out, for] the crop will be smitten with blight."

K.   The man went and sowed his seed in the time of the first rain. The crop of everyone else was smitten with blight, but his was not smitten with blight.

L.   His wife said to him, "How is it the case that last year everyone's crop was smitten and yours was not smitten, and this year too, everyone else's crop was blighted and yours was not blighted?

M.   He told her this entire story. They say that the days were only a few before there was a quarrel between the wife of that pious man and the mother of that girl [who had died and whose spirit had been heard by the pious man in conversation]. The woman said, "Go, and I shall show you your daughter, buried in matting of reeds!"

N.   The next year the man went and spent the night in the cemetery and heard the spirits talking with one another. One said to the other, "My friend, come and let us flit about the world and listen from behind the veil to find out what sort of punishment is coming upon the world."

O.   She said to her, "My friend, leave me alone. The things that were said between you and me have already been heard among the living."

P.   What follows from this story is that the dead do know [what goes on].

Q.   Perhaps someone else died and went and told them what had happened.

IX.

A.   Come and take note of the following relevant story:

B.   Zeiri left some money with his landlady while he went to the school house. She died. He followed after her to the graveyard. He said to her, "Where is my money?"

C.   She said to him, "Go and take them from beneath the ground, in the hole of the doorpost, in such and such a place. Tell me mother, also, to send me my comb and my tube of eye-paint, along with Miss Such-and-so, who is coming here tomorrow [when she dies]."

D.   Thus it follows that the deceased do know what is going on among the living.

E.   Perhaps Dumah [the angel of death] comes along and lets them know [but the deceased do not know it on their own].

X.

A.   Come and take note of the following:

B.   The father of Samuel held some money for an estate. When he died, Samuel was not with him [so he did not know where the money was]. People called him, "The son of someone who robs estates."

C.   Samuel came after [his father] to the cemetery. He said to them, "I want father."

D.   They said to him, "There are lots of fathers here."

E.   He said to them, "I want Father, son of Father."

F.   They said to him, "There are lots of fathers, sons of fathers, here too."

G.   He said to them, "I want Father, son of Father, the father of Samuel. Where is he?"

H.   They said to him, "He has gone up to the academy in the firmament."

I.   In the meantime he saw Levi, who was seated outside [away from the rest of the deceased].

J.   He said to him, "Why are you seated outside? Why did you not go up?"

K.   He said to him, "They told me that for as many years as you did not go up to the session of R. Efes and so you injured his feelings, we are not going to take you up to the academy in the firmament."

L.   Meanwhile the father [of Samuel] came along. [Samuel] saw that he was both weeping and smiling. He said, "Why are you weeping?"

M.   He said to him, "Because soon you are coming here."

N.   "Why are you smiling?"

O.   "Because you are highly regarded in this world."

P.   He said to him, "If I am highly regarded, then let them take up Levi." So they took Levi up.

Q.   He said to him, "As to the money belonging to the estate, where is it?"

R.   He said to him, "Go and take it out of the case of the millstones. The money at the top and bottom belongs to us, and what is in the middle belongs to the estate."

S.   He said to him, "Why did you do it that way?"

T.   He said to him, "If thieves come, they will steal ours. If the earth rots the money, it will rot ours."

U.   This story again proves that the deceased know what is going on.

V.   But perhaps the case of Samuel is different, since he is highly regarded.

W.   Since that was the case, [in heaven] they went ahead and announced, "Make room for him."

XI.

A.   Furthermore, R. Jonathan retracted his view [at VI B]. For R. Samuel bar Nahmani said R. Jonathan [said], "How do we know that the deceased do talk with one another? As it is said, 'And the Lord said to him, This is the land which I swore to Abraham, Isaac, and Jacob, saying...' (Deut. 34:4). What is the sense of 'saying'?

B.   "Said the Holy One, blessed be he, to Moses, 'Go and tell Abraham, Isaac, and Jacob, "The oath that I took to you have I now carried out for your children."'"

C.   [19A] Now if you imagine that the deceased do not know, then if Moses did go and inform them, what difference would it make?

D.   What follows? It is that the deceased do know [what is going on].

E.   [If so,] what reason was there to inform them?

F.   It was to make them grateful to Moses.

XII.

A.   Said R. Isaac, "Whoever tells [stories] after the deceased [has died] is as if he tells stories about a stone."

B.   There are those who say it is because the dead do not know it, and there are those who say that they do know it but it does not matter to them.

C.   Is that the case? And lo, R. Papa said, "Someone made nasty remarks after the death of Mar Samuel, and a log fell from the roof and broke his head. [So he heard and avenged himself.]

D.   The case of a "twig of the rabbis" is different, for the Holy One, blessed be he, follows up on matters of honor affecting him.

E.   Said R. Joshua b. Levi, "Whoever tells [stories] after a deceased disciple of sages [has died] will fall into Gehenna.

F.   "For it is said, 'But as for such as turn aside into their crooked ways, the Lord will lead them away with the workers of iniquity. Peace be upon Israel' (Ps. 125:5).

G.   "Even when 'Israel has peace,' 'the Lord will lead them away with the workers of iniquity.'"

H.   It was taught on Tannaite authority in the house of R. Ishmael, "If you have seen a disciple of a sage who committed a transgression by night, do not pursue the matter by day, for he might have repented."

I.   Do you think he merely "might" have repented? Rather, he assuredly <u>has</u> repented.

J.   And that judgment pertains to carnal matters.

K.   But as to financial matters, [one should pursue the matter] until he returns the money to its owner."

XIII.

A.   And R. Joshua b. Levi said, "In twenty-four passages a court excommunicates [a person] on account of the honor owing to a master. And all of them we repeat in our learning of the Mishnah."

B.   Said to him R. Eleazar, "Where?"

C.   He said to him, "Go, find them."

D.   He went and looked with care and found three cases: involving him who treats lightly the washing of the hands, one who tells [stories] after the burial of disciples of sages, and one who acted in a familiar way toward heaven.

E.   What is the case involving one who tells [stories] after the burial of disciples of sages?

F.   It is as we have learned in the Mishnah:

G.   <u>He would say, "They do not administer bitter water [to test the woman accused of adultery] in the case of a proselyte-woman or in the case of a freed-slave girl."</u>

H.   <u>And sages say, "They do administer the test."</u>

I.   <u>They said to him, M^CSH B: "Karkemit, a freed slave-girl, was in Jerusalem, and Shemaiah and Abtalion administered the bitter water to her."</u>

J.   <u>He said to them, "They administered it to her to make her into an example."</u>

K.   <u>They excommunicated him, and he died while he was subject to the excommunication, so the court stoned his bier [M. Ed. 5:6I-M].</u>

L.   What is the case of him who treats lightly the washing of the hands?

M.   It is as we have learned in the Mishnah:

N.   <u>Said R. Judah, "God forbid that ^CAqabia was excommunicated.</u>

O.   <u>"For the courtyard is never locked before any Israelite of the wisdom, purity, and fear of sin of a man like ^CAqabia b. Mahalalel.</u>

P.   <u>"But whom did they excommunicate? It was Eliezer b. Hanokh, who cast doubt on [the sages' ruling about] the cleanness of hands.</u>

Q. "And when he died, the court sent and put a stone on his bier."

R. This teaches that whoever is excommunicated and dies while he is subject to the excommunication -- they stone his bier [M. Ed. 5:6N-R].

S. What is the case of one who acted in a familiar way toward heaven?

T. It is as we have learned in the Mishnah:

U. Simeon b. Shatah sent to Honi, the circle-maker, "You ought to be excommunicated. And were you not Honi, I should decree excommunication against you. But what can I do? For you importune the Omnipresent and he does what you want, just as a son importunes his father so that he will do what he wants. And concerning you, Scripture says, 'Let your father and mother be glad, and let her who bore you rejoice' (Prov. 23:25)" [M. Ta. 3:8].

V. And are there no more such instances? And lo, there is the one that R. Joseph stated on Tannaite authority:

W. "Todos of Rome led the Roman [Jews] to eat lambs roasted helmut-style on the night of Passover. Simeon b. Shatah sent a message to him, 'Were you not Todos, I should decree excommunication against you, because you have the Israelites eat Holy Things outside [of the Temple, which is forbidden to do].'"

X. What we said was, "in our Mishnah," [and the cited tale is not found in the Mishnah], but in a Tannaite teaching external to the Mishnah.

Y. And are there no more such cases in the Mishnah? And lo, we have learned in the Mishnah: If one cut up an oven into circles and put sand between one ring and the next, R. Eliezer declares the construction insusceptible to uncleanness [since it is broken down into useless sherds], and sages declare it susceptible. This is the oven of Aknai [M. Kel. 5:10].

Z. What is the meaning of Akhnai?

AA. Said R. Judah said Samuel, "It teaches that they surrounded [that sort of oven] with legal rulings like a snake [Akhnai] and thereby declared it unclean."

BB. And it has been taught on Tannaite authority [concerning the point at issue, excommunication:]

CC. On that day they brought all of the things that R. Eliezer had declared insusceptible to uncleanness and burned them in his presence [as though they had been susceptible to uncleanness and then been made unclean], and in the end they even "blessed" [= cursed] him.

DD. Even though, as to excommunication in particular, there is no reference in the Mishnah-passage to that matter, [this item counts].

EE. Accordingly, [to revert to the point at which we started,] where in the world do we find so many as twenty-four examples?

FF. R. Joshua b. Levi compares one thing to another [Simon, p. 116, n. 1: He takes count of all the cases where the ruling of the rabbis was disregarded by an individual and excommunication should have been incurred, even if this is not mentioned].

GG. But R. Eleazar does not compare one thing to another.

XIV.

A. Pall-bearers and they who replace them [M. 3:1B]:

B.   Our rabbis have taught on Tannaite authority:

C.   They do not bring out the corpse for burial near the time for reciting the <u>Shema</u>, but if they have begun the rite, they do not interrupt it [for the recitation of the <u>Shema</u>].

D.   Is this the case? And lo, as to R. Joseph, they brought out his corpse near the time for reciting the <u>Shema</u>.

E.   An important man is subject to a different rule.

XV.

A.   <u>As to those who go before the bier and those who go behind the bier [M. 3:1C]</u>:

B.   As to those who are occupied with the mourning, when the corpse is lying before them, they take off one by one and recite the <u>Shema</u>.

C.   If, on the other hand, the corpse is not lying before them, they sit down and recite the <u>Shema</u>, and [the mourner] remains seated and silent.

D.   They arise and recite the Prayer, and he stands and [as his prayer] accepts the righteousness of the judgment and says, "Lord of the ages, I have sinned in many things before you, and [the punishment for] not even one in a thousand has been exacted from me. May it be pleasing before you, O Lord our God, that you may heal the breach that has afflicted us and the breaches that have afflicted all of your people, the House of Israel, in mercy."

E.   Said Abayye, "It is not necessary for someone to say such a prayer.

F.   "For R. Simeon b. Laqish said, and so it has been taught on Tannaite authority in the name of R. Yose, 'A person should never open an entry for Satan.'"

G.   And R. Joseph said, "What is the proof-text for that proposition? As it is said, 'We were almost like Sodom' (Is. 1:9). What then does the prophet reply to them? 'Hear the word of the Lord, you rulers of Sodom' (Is. 1:10)."

XVI.

A.   <u>Once they have buried the deceased and returned from the gravesite [M. 3:2A]</u>:

B.   <u>If they have time to begin and complete the recitation of the Shema</u>, then they do so, but if it is only time to recite one paragraph or one verse, they do not do so.

C.   The following was cited as a contradiction of that statement:

D.   <u>Once they have buried the deceased and returned from the gravesite, if they have time to begin and complete [M. 3:2A-B]</u> -- even one paragraph or one verse, [they do so].

E.   The sense of the passage is to indicate that that indeed is the case, namely: If before they reach the line of mourners, they can begin and complete even one paragraph or one verse, they should do so, and if not, they should not begin.

XVII.

A.   [19B] <u>Concerning those who are standing in line [M. 3:2D]</u>:

B.   Our rabbis have taught on Tannaite authority:

C.   The row that can see the mourners at the inner circle is exempt [from the obligation to recite the <u>Shema</u>], and those who cannot see the inner area [where the mourners are located] is liable.

D. R. Judah says, "Those who come in order to honor the deceased are exempt, and those who come on their own account are liable" [T. Ber. 2:11A-I].

XVIII.

A. Said R. Judah said Rab, "He who discovers in his garment the presence of mixed kinds [linen and wool] must take it off even if he finds out when he is in the marketplace.

B. "What is the scriptural basis for that view? 'There is no wisdom, nor understanding, nor counsel against the Lord' (Prov. 21:30).

C. "In any circumstance in which there is a profanation of the divine Name, people must not pay honor to the master."

D. An objection was raised on the basis of the following passage:

E. If people have buried the deceased and are en route back, and before them are two paths, one that is not contaminated by corpse-uncleanness and the other that is contaminated by corpse-uncleanness, if the mourner takes the clean one, the others may go along with him in a state of cleanness. If he takes the unclean one, the others come along with him in a state of uncleanness, on account of the honor owing to him.

F. Now why should this be the case? Should we not invoke the principle, "There is no wisdom, nor understanding, nor counsel against the Lord" (Prov. 21:30)?

G. R. Abba explained the cited rule to speak of a grave-area of dubious status [in which we are not sure whether or not there is corpse-matter in the area], which derives its uncleanness only because of a decree of rabbis."

H. For R. Judah said Samuel said, "In a grave-area of dubious status, one puffs away before him as he walks along [to blow the small bones out of the way]."

I. And R. Judah bar Ashi said in the name of Rab, "A grave-area that has been trodden down is regarded as not affected by corpse-uncleanness."

J. Come and hear [another relevant case].

K. For R. Eleazar bar Sadoq said, "We used to skip across the biers of corpses in order to greet the kings of Israel, and not only to greet the kings of Israel alone have they made that rule, but even to greet kings of the gentiles, so that if one should have the merit [of witnessing the coming of the Messianic king], he may know how to tell the difference between Israelite and pagan kings."

L. Now why should this be the case? Should we not invoke the principle, "There is no wisdom, nor understanding, nor counsel, against the Lord" (Prov. 21:30?

M. The answer accords with what Raba said.

N. For Raba said, "As a matter of law on the authority of the Torah, in the case of a Tent [for purposes of conveying corpse-uncleanness through overshadowing], in the case of any object that has a contained inner space of a handbreadth, such an object interposes against corpse-uncleanness [so that if one overshadows such a container, he will not be affected by the corpse-uncleanness], and in the case of any that does not have a contained space of a handbreadth, the object will not serve to interpose against uncleanness, [and one who overshadows such an object will receive corpse-uncleanness from corpse-matter contained within the object].

O.   "Now most coffins do contain a contained space of a handbreadth, but the sages made a decree concerning those that do contain such a space on account of those that do not [and that is why one who overshadows any coffin, whatever its size, is deemed affected by corpse-uncleanness]."

P.   But in the case of paying the honor owing to kings, rabbis made no such decree [in which case the vast majority of coffins are of sufficient size to contain the corpse-matter's uncleanness and those who skip over them to see kings will not be regarded as unclean].

Q.   [Pursuing the same inquiry] come and take note: So great is the honor owing to people that it overrides a negative commandment that is contained in the Torah.

R.   Now why should this be the case? Should we not invoke the principle, "There is no wisdom, nor understanding, nor counsel, against the Lord" (Prov. 21:30)?

S.   Rab bar Sheba explained the matter before R. Kahana, "It speaks of the negative commandment, 'You shall not turn aside' (Deut. 17:11) [and not to all negative commandments]."

T.   The others laughed at him, for the negative commandment, "You shall not turn aside" itself derives from the Torah [so this is no solution to any problem].

U.   Said R. Kahana, "When an eminent person makes a statement, you have no business laughing at him. All matters that derive from the authority of rabbis were made to depend upon the negative commandment of 'You shall not turn aside,' and on account of the honor owing to a person, rabbis permitted one to violate that rule."

V.   Come and take note: "And hide yourself from them" (Deut. 22:1, 4): [stated twice] the sense is that there are occasions on which you may hide yourself from them, and there are occasions on which you may not hide yourself from them. How so? If one was a priest and the ass was in a cemetery, or if one was a sage and it is not in accord with his dignity, or if one has had more work than his fellow, in such a case, it is said, "And you will hide yourself from him" [and not help out, since the one party would lose more than the other would gain if the former dropped his work to help the latter].

W.   Now why should this be the case? Should we not invoke the principle, "There is no wisdom nor understanding nor counsel against the Lord" (Prov. 21:30)?

X.   The present case is different, since it is explicitly stated, "And you will hide yourself from them" (Deut. 22:1).

Y.   And why not derive the rule applying here from the case of the rule governing mixed kinds [of fabrics in the garment, which one must remove even in the marketplace]?

Z.   We do not derive a rule affecting a matter that is prohibited from a rule governing a property-matter.

AA. Come and take note: "Or for his sister" (Num. 6:7) [that is, a Nazirite may not contract corpse-uncleanness even so as to bury his sister].

BB. Why does Scripture make this point?

CC. Lo, if [a Nazirite, who was also a priest] was going along to slaughter an animal as his Passover-offering, or to circumcize his son, and he got the news that he had suffered a bereavement, is it possible to suppose that he should go back and contract corpse-uncleanness [rather than carrying out the specified acts, which must be done at a specific time and cannot be postponed until he once more regains cleanness from the corpse-uncleanness involved in the burial]?

DD.   You must rule that he should not contract corpse-uncleanness.

EE.   Is it possible to suppose that, just as he may not contract corpse-uncleanness for them, so he may not contract corpse-uncleanness for a neglected corpse?

FF.   Scripture says, "For his sister" (Num. 6:7).

GG.   The meaning, then, is that, while for his sister he may not contract corpse-uncleanness, [20A], he must contract corpse-uncleanness to take care of a neglected corpse.

HH.   Now why should this be the case? Should we not invoke the principle, "There is no wisdom, nor understanding, nor counsel, against the Lord" (Prov. 21:30)?

II.   That case is distinguished from others, because it is written, "And for his sister" (Num. 6:7).

JJ.   And let us derive the besought principle from that case?

KK.   It is a case in which one has merely to do nothing at all, and that is different [from the case of wearing mixed kinds, which involves violation of the rule through an affirmative action].

XIX.

A.   Said R. Papa to Abayye, "What makes the difference that the former authorities have miracles done for them, while miracles are not done for us?

B.   "If it is because of the issue of learning Tannaite traditions, in the time of R. Judah, all they learned to repeat was the matter of Damages, while, for our part, we repeat all six divisions [of the Mishnah, and their associated Tannaite traditions].

C.   "And when R. Judah would come to the passage in tractate Uqsin, 'A woman who presses vegetables in a pot' (M. Uqs. 2:1), or, some say, 'Olives pressed with their leaves are clean' (M. Uqs. 2:1), he would say, 'Here I see the issues raised by Rab and Samuel for reflection.' But when we repeat tractate Uqsin, we have thirteen sessions [to devote to the matter].

D.   "Yet when R. Judah would take off one sandal [in preparation for a fast for rain], it would rain right away, while we torture ourselves and cry out, and no one [in heaven] pays attention to us."

E.   [Abayye] said to [Papa], "The former authorities would give their lives for the sanctification of the Divine Name, while we do not give our lives for the sanctification of the Divine Name."

XX.

A.   There was, for example, the case of R. Ada bar Ahba. He saw a Samaritan woman who was wearing a red cloak. Thinking that she was an Israelite woman, he went and tore it off her. It turned out that she was a Samaritan, and he had to pay a fine of four hundred zuz.

B.   He said to her, "What is your name?"

C.   She said to him, "Matun."

D.   He said to her, "Matun? Matun [the letters of which add up to four hundred in numerical value] is worth four hundred <u>zuz</u>."

XXI.

A.   R. Giddal had the habit of going and sitting at the gates of the ritual bath. He would say to [the women], "This is how to immerse [for purposes of cleanness], that is how to bathe."

B.   Rabbis said to him, "Does not the Master fear that his evil impulse will be aroused?"

C.   He said to them, "To me they look like so many white geese."

XXI.

A.   R. Yohanan had the habit of going and sitting at the gates of the ritual bath. He explained, "When the Israelite women go and come up from the immersion [thus preparing for sexual relations after their period of menstruation], they gaze at me, so they will have seed which is as beautiful as I am."

B.   Rabbis said to him, "Does not the Master fear on account of the evil eye [of envy]?"

C.   He said to them, "I come from the seed of Joseph, over which the evil eye does not rule.

D.   "For it is written, 'Joseph is a fruitful vine, a fruitful vine above the eye' (Gen. 49:22).'

E.   "And R. Abbahu said, 'Do not read what is written, but rather, 'superior to the evil eye.'"

F.   R. Yose b. R. Hanina said, "Proof comes from here: 'And let them multiply like fishes in the midst of the earth' (Gen. 48:16). Just as the fish of the sea are covered by water so that the evil eye cannot get at them, so the evil eye cannot get at the seed of Joseph.'

G.   "And if you wish, I shall say, 'Over an eye [namely, Joseph's,] which did not want to feast upon what did not belong to him the evil eye has no power."

Once more we have to distinguish those units of discourse which treat the Mishnah's exegesis from others composed out of relationship to the Mishnah. In the former classification fall units I, II (continued at III), XIV, XV, XVI, XVII. The following units amplify the theme at hand, that is to say, the disposition and burial of a corpse, but do not address the particular interest of the Mishnah-paragraph in that theme, the recitation of the <u>Shema</u> and related prayers by pall-bearers: units IV, V. Unit VI then moves on to a quite separate problem and in no way has been composed with the Mishnah's interests in mind. It treats the subject of whether or not the deceased know what is going on on earth. It seems to me that the theme arises because of the assertion in unit V that one must not mock a corpse. That bears the implication that the corpse will know the difference. Then the rest follows. Units VII, VIII, IX, X, XI complete the discussion. The reason for the inclusion of unit XII is that here too the theme of what the dead know of what happens on earth defines discourse. Once the topic of the honor owing to disciples of sages comes up, penalties for not paying that respect are discussed, and that accounts for the continuation of unit XII by unit XIII. That leaves only unit XVIII. The reason that rather extended discussion is included may be found at XVIII E. That entry directly relates to XVII, which amplifies the Mishnah. So what we have, in all, is a set of materials that explain or amplify the Mishnah, vastly augmented by other materials that pick up on themes or suggestions contained within those explanatory units.

3:3

A. Women, and slaves, and minors are exempt from the recitation of the Shema [20B] and from [the obligation of wearing] phylacteries,

B. but are obligated [to recite] the Prayer,

C. and [are obligated to post] the mezuzah and to recite Grace after meals.

I.

A. As to [the exemption from reciting the Shema], that is self-evident, since it is a religious duty of commission that has to be done at a particular time, and from the obligations to carry out religious duties of commission that have to be done at a particular time women are exempt.

B. What might you have said? Since in the recitation of the Shema is the act of accepting the dominion of Heaven, [they might be obligated to recite the Shema], even though they are exempt from other religious duties in that classification].

C. So we are informed that that is not the case.

II.

A. And from the obligation of wearing phylacteries [M. 3:3A]:

B. That is self-evident [since the Shema is not required].

C. What might you have maintained? Since the matter at hand is comparable to the placing of the mezuzah [on the doorpost], [a woman might be obligated in the present matter].

D. So we are informed that that is not the case.

III.

A. But they are obligated to recite the Prayer [M. 3:3B]:

B. It is because the Prayer involves beseeching God's mercy.

C. What might you have thought [to lead you to the conclusion that a woman is exempt here too]? Since it is written in connection [with the Prayer], "Evening and morning and at noonday" (Ps. 55:18), the matter at hand falls into the classification of a religious duty of commission that has to be done at a particular time.

D. So we are informed that that is not the case.

IV.

A. And are obligated to post the mezuzah [M. 3:3C]:

B. That is self-evident.

C. What might you have thought [to lead you to the conclusion that a woman is exempt here too]?

D. Since this matter is comparable to the study of Torah, [which is required only of males, a woman might be thought to be exempt].

E. So we are informed that that is not the case.

V.

A. And Grace after Meals [M. 3:3C]:

B. That is self-evident.

C. What might you have thought [to lead you to the conclusion that a woman is exempt here too]?

D. Since it is written, "When the Lord shall give you in the evening meat to eat and in the morning enough bread" (Ex. 16:8), I might have thought that the present matter falls into the classification of a religious duty that has to be carried out at a particular time.

E. Accordingly we are informed that that is not the case.

VI.

A. Said R. Ada bar Ahba, "As a matter of Torah-law, women are liable to recite the sanctification of the [Sabbath-] day."

B. Why should that be the case? Is this not a religious duty of commission that has to be done at a particular time, and from all religious duties of commission that have to be done at a particular time women are exempt?

C. Said Abayye, "It is only on the authority of rabbis [and not on the authority of the Torah, and rabbis are the ones who imposed the obligation]."

D. Said Raba to him, "But [the prior authority indeed] stated, 'As a matter of Torah-law'!

E. "And furthermore, by authority of the rabbis women are indeed obligated to carry out all religious duties of commission. [So why single out this one item?]"

F. Rather, said Raba, "Scripture has said, 'Remember' and 'Observe' (Ex. 20:8, Deut. 5:12) [with regard to the Sabbath]. Thus: Whoever is subject to the commandment of 'keeping' is subject to the commandment of 'remembering' [which is carried out through the prayer of sanctification of the Sabbath day], and, since women are indeed subject to the commandment of keeping the Sabbath, they also are subject to the commandment of remembering it [by reciting the prayer of sanctification of the day]."

VII.

A. Said Rabina to Raba, "Is the obligation of women to recite the Grace after Meals upon the authority of the Torah or of the rabbis?"

B. What difference does it make?

C. It pertains to whether women can fulfill the obligation of the community [to recite the prayer].

D. If you maintain that the obligation of women to say Grace after Meals is on the authority of the Torah, then one who is subject to the requirement on the authority of the Torah may come along and carry out the obligation of another whose obligation to recite the prayer is on the authority of the Torah.

E.   If the woman is subject to the obligation to recite the Grace after Meals only by the authority of the rabbis, then the woman falls into the category of one who is not obligated [by Torah-law] to carry out the matter, and whoever is not obligated to carry out a religious duty is not able to fulfill the obligations of the community in carrying out that same religious deed [not being of the same status as the male community at large].

F.   What then is the law?

G.   Come and hear:

H.   A son may say the blessing in behalf of his father, a slave in behalf of his master, a woman in behalf of her husband. But sages have said, "May a curse come upon a man whose wife and children say the blessing for him."

I.   Now, if you maintain that the woman's obligation is on the authority of the Torah, then one who is obligated on the authority of the Torah may come and carry out the obligation for another who is obligated on the authority of the Torah.

J.   But if you maintain that the woman's obligation is merely on the authority of rabbis, can someone who is obligated only on the authority of rabbis come and carry out the obligation of another whose obligation is on the authority of the Torah?

K.   But in accord with this reasoning, do you maintain that a minor is subject to the stated obligation?

L.   But here, with what sort of case do we deal? It is with one who has eaten merely the volume of food defined by the rabbis as subject to the requirement to say Grace after meals, [and that volume of food is much smaller than the volume that one must eat in order to be liable on the authority of the Torah to say Grace after meals].

M.   In this case one may come along who is obligated only on the authority of rabbis and carry out the obligation of another person who is obligated [by reason of the small volume of food consumed] only on the authority of rabbis.

VIII.

A.   R. Avira gave an exposition, sometimes in the name of R. Ammi and sometimes in the name of R. Assi, "The ministering angels said before the Holy One, blessed be he, 'Lord of the ages'! It is written in your Torah, "Who does not regard persons or take a reward" (Deut. 10:17).

B.   "'But do you not regard persons in the case of Israel, for it is written, "May the Lord lift up his face to you" (Num. 6:26)?'

C.   "He says to them, 'Should I not then have special regard for Israel, for whom I have written in the Torah, "And you will eat and be satisfied and bless the Lord your God" (Deut. 8:10), and they are so careful about what they do that [they recite Grace after meals even if they eat a volume of] only so much as an olive's bulk or an egg's bulk [as at VII L]!'"

The several units are laid out in accord with an obvious plan. First, we have a sequence of close exegeses of the text at hand, units I-V, which surely form a protracted and unified discourse. Unit VI then takes up the principle introduced in the foregoing, concerning women's obligation to carry out religious duties of commission which one has to do at a particular time. Unit VII forms a secondary expansion of the Mishnah's statement at M. 3:3C. The established theme, Grace after Meals, accounts then for the inclusion of unit VIII. So the entire sequence is logical and well composed.

3:4

A. One who has had a seminal discharge may silently meditate but may not recite the blessings out loud,

B. either [those blessings] before [the Shema] or [those blessings] after it.

C. And as to those for the meal, he may recite the blessing after it, but not before.

D. R. Judah says, "He may say the blessings both before them [i.e., the Shema and the meal] and after them."

I.

A. Said Rabina, "That then suggests that meditation is equivalent to speech [since at M. 3:4A, one may say the blessings in his heart but may not say them out loud, yet that suffices for the purpose].

B. "For if you maintain that the meditation does not fall into the classification of actual recitation, then why should one meditate [and say the blessings silently at all]?

C. "So what conclusion is to be drawn? Meditation falls into the same classification as speech."

D. [But if that is the case, then] let the man say the blessings with his lips [out loud]. For so we find at Sinai [Simon, p. 124, n. 1: Moses ordered the Israelites to keep away from woman before receiving the Torah, but those who were unclean could still accept it mentally].

E. And [contrary to A] R. Hisda said, "Meditation is not equivalent to speech. For if you maintain that meditation does fall into the classification of recitation, let someone actually say the blessings with his lips [out loud].

F. "So what conclusion is to be drawn? Meditation does not fall into the same classification as speech."

G. Why then should one meditate [on the blessings but not say them]?

H. Said R. Eleazar, "It is so that, while everyone is engaged in [the blessings at hand], he should not sit and do nothing."

I. But let him study some other teaching?

J. Said R. Adda bar Ahba, "He should be engaged with something with which the community also is dealing."

K. [21A] But there is the matter of the Prayer, which is something with which the community is dealing, and we have learned in the Mishnah:

L. One who was standing in recitation of the Prayer and remembered that he had had a seminal emission should not interrupt his recitation. Rather he should shorten the prayer [M. 3:5A-D].

M. The operative consideration, then, is that he had begun. Lo, if he had not begun, he should not begin [and that is the case even though everyone else is saying the Prayer. That would appear to contradict Adda bar Ahba's view].

N. The case of the Prayer is different, because it contains no mention of the dominion of Heaven [on which account it is not essential that a man participate in it when the community says it].

O. But lo, there is the matter of the Grace after Meals, which does not contain a mention of the dominion of Heaven, and yet we have learned in the Mishnah:

P. As to those for the meal, he may recite the blessing after it but not before [M. 3:4C]. [So that applies even to the one who has had a seminal emission.]

Q. But the operative distinction is that the recitation of the _Shema_ and the Grace after Meals rests upon the authority of the Torah, while saying the Prayer rests on the authority of rabbis [and that is why, in the latter case, one need not engage in the same matter with which the community at large is occupied].

II.

A. Said R. Judah, "How do we know on the basis of statements in the Torah that there is a requirement to say the Grace after Meals?

B. "It is in line with what is written, 'And you shall eat and be satisfied and say a blessing' (Deut. 8:10).

C. "And how do we know on the basis of statements in the Torah that there is a requirement to say a blessing before studying Torah-sayings?

D. "Because it says, 'When I proclaim the name of the Lord, ascribe greatness to our God' (Deut. 32:3)."

E. R. Yohanan said, "[Rather than a proof-text,] we derive evidence that one must say a blessing after studying the Torah by an argument _a fortiori_ built upon the requirement to say Grace after meals. We furthermore learn that one should say a blessing before eating food from an argument _a fortiori_ based upon the requirement to say a blessing before one studies Torah-sayings.

F. "Now in the case of food, which does not require the recitation of Grace before hand, there is a requirement of Grace afterward, study of the Torah, which does require the recitation of a blessing before hand, surely should require a blessing afterward.

G. "And the requirement to say a blessing for food before eating derives on the basis of an argument _a fortiori_ from the case of the blessing said over the Torah:

H. "Now if in the case of the study of the Torah, which does not require recitation of a blessing afterward, there is the requirement of the recitation of a blessing beforehand, food, which does require the saying of a blessing [Grace after meals] afterward, surely should require the recitation of a blessing before hand."

I. One may raise the following objections:

J. The distinctive trait of food [F] is that one derives physical benefit from it.

K. The distinctive trait of study of the Torah [G-H] is that it leads to eternal life.

L. And furthermore, we have learned in the Mishnah: And as to those for the meal, he may recite the blessing after it but not before [M. 3:4C].

M. This accordingly constitutes a refutation of the proposed argument.

N. It indeed refutes that argument.

III.

A. Said R. Judah, "If one is in doubt whether or not he has recited the Shema, he should not go back and recite it. If one is in doubt whether or not he has said the prayer, 'True and established....,' he should go back and recite it."

B. What is the reason?

C. The recitation of the Shema derives from the authority of rabbis, while reciting the prayer, "True and firm" derives from the authority of the Torah.

D. R. Joseph objected, "'And in your lying down and in your rising' (Deut. 6:5). [Surely that constitutes the Torah's requirement to recite the Shema.]"

E. Said Abayye to him, "That refers to study of words of Torah [and not to recitation of the Shema]."

F. We have learned in the Mishnah: One who has had a seminal discharge may silently meditate but may not recite the blessings out loud, either those blessings before the Shema or those blessings after it. And as to those for the meal, he may recite the blessing after it but not before [M. 3:4A-C].

G. Now if you take the view that the prayer, "True and firm" [and this is the blessing after the Shema] derives from the authority of the Torah, the man [noted at the cited passage of the Mishnah] surely should say the blessing after the Shema. [Just as the Grace after meals is said on the authority of the Torah, so any other prayer that is imposed on the authority of the Torah should be said. Not saying "True and firm" is a sign that that prayer is not imposed on the authority of the Torah.]

H. But what is the reason that he should say that blessing? If it is because the Exodus from Egypt is mentioned in it, lo, the Exodus is mentioned in the body of the recitation of the Shema.

I. If that is the case, then let a person say this one and he need not say the other [that is, let him say "True and firm" aloud and not recite the Shema in his mind].

J. The recitation of the Shema is preferable, because it contains two important matters [specifically, allusions to the dominion of Heaven and the Exodus from Egypt, with the former not included in the prayer, "True and firm."]

K. And [reverting back to A], R. Eleazar said, "If one is in doubt whether or not he has recited the Shema, let him go back and recite the Shema. If he is in doubt as to whether or not he has said the Prayer, he should not go back and say the Prayer."

L. And R. Yohanan said, "Would that a person would say the Prayer for the entire day."

IV.

A. And R. Judah said Samuel said, "If one was standing and reciting the Prayer and then realizes that he has already said the Prayer, he should stop, and even in the middle of a blessing [of the eighteen blessings of which the Prayer is composed]."

B. Is this the case? And lo, R. Nahman said, "When we were at the house of Rabbah bar Abbuha, we asked him about the students who, making an error, made mention of the weekday blessings [in the Prayer] on the Sabbath, asking the law as to their completing the Prayer. And he told us, 'They should complete that entire blessing.'"

C. But the two cases are hardly parallel. In that case, the person who says the prayer is obligated to say it [that is, the weekday Prayer], and the rabbis did not impose on him the bother of saying it on account of the honor owing to the Sabbath.

D. But in the present case, the man has already said the prayer.

E. And R. Judah said Samuel said, "If one had said the Prayer and entered a synagogue and found the community saying the Prayer, if he can say something new in the Prayer, he should go and say the Prayer again, and if not, he should not go and say the Prayer again."

F. And the two rulings are necessary [the present one, involving a case in which the person has already said the Prayer, and the one in which one recalls in the midst of saying the Prayer that he has already said it].

G. For had we learned the law applying in the first case, we might have supposed that that ruling applies only to an individual who had said the Prayer all by himself and now is in a position of repeating it all by himself.

H. [21B] Or it would apply only where a man had said the Prayer with the community and now is to repeat it with the community.

I. But in the case of an individual who then joins the community at Prayer, I might have supposed that he would fall into the category of one who has not said the Prayer at all.

J. Accordingly, we are informed that that is not the case.

K. And had we learned the present rule, we might have supposed that that applies because the man had not commenced the Prayer, but in the other case, in which he had already commenced reciting the Prayer, I might have supposed that that rule then would not apply.

L. Accordingly, it is necessary to have both statements in hand.

V.

A. Said R. Huna, "He who enters the synagogue and finds the community saying the Prayer, if he can begin and complete the Prayer before the leader of the community in his repetition, reaches the blessing, 'We acknowledge...,' should say the Prayer, and if not, he should not say the Prayer.

B. And R. Joshua b. Levi said, "If he can begin and complete the Prayer before the leader of the community in his repetition reaches the Sanctification, he should say the Prayer, and if not, he should not say the Prayer."

C. Concerning what principle do they differ?

D. One master [A] takes the view that an individual may say the Sanctification-prayer [by himself].

E. The other [B] takes the view that the individual may not say the Sanctification-prayer [by himself].

F.   So too [B] did R. Ada bar Ahba say, "How do we know on the basis of Scripture that an individual [praying by himself] does not say the Sanctification-prayer? As it is said, 'And I shall be sanctified among the children of Israel' (Lev. 22:32). Every matter involving sanctification may be conducted among no fewer than ten men."

G.   How does the besought proof derive from the cited verse?

H.   It accords with that which Rabbinai, brother of R. Hiyya bar Abba, taught on Tannaite authority, "An analogy is drawn on the use of the word 'among.'

I.   "Here it is written, 'And I shall be sanctified among the children of Israel' (Lev. 22:32), and elsewhere it is written, 'Separate yourselves from among this congregation' (Num. 16:21). Just as, in the latter instance, 'among' involves ten men, so here ten are required."

J.   Both authorities concur, in the end, that one does not interrupt [the Prayer. If a person has begun to recite the Prayer, when the congregation comes to recite the Sanctification, the person does not interrupt his prayer to recite the Sanctification with the congregation.]

VI.

A.   The question was raised: What is the law on interrupting [the Prayer] to respond [in the Qaddish with] "May his great name be blessed"?

B.   When R. Dimi came, he said R. Judah and R. Simeon, disciples of R. Yohanan, said, "For no purpose do people interrupt [the recitation of the Prayer], except for saying, 'May his great name be blessed.'

C.   "For even if one dealing with the [teachings concerning] the Works of the Chariot, one interrupts [his study to respond, 'May his great name be blessed.']"

D.   But the law does not accord with his view.

VII.

A.   R. Judah says, "He may say the blessings both before them and after them" [M. 3:4D]:

B.   Does that position bear the implication that R. Judah takes the view that one who has had a seminal discharge may indeed study Torah?

C.   And has not R. Joshua b. Levi said, "How do we know that one who has had a seminal discharge may not study Torah?

D.   "As it is said, 'Make them known to your children and your children's children' (Deut. 4:9) and, right afterward, 'The day that you stood before the Lord your God in Horeb' (Deut. 4:10).

E.   "Just as, in the latter setting, those who have had a seminal emission are prohibited [from participating], so here, those who have had a seminal emission are prohibited [from participating, that is, in that instance, in 'making the Torah known']."

F.   And if you propose to maintain that R. Judah does not derive lessons from the juxtaposition of verses [as in the above exegesis],

G.   has not R. Joseph said, "Even someone who does not derive exegetical lessons from the juxtaposition of verses in the rest of the entire Torah in the setting of the Book of Deuteronomy will derive such lessons,

H.   "for lo, [Joseph's saying continues] R. Judah does not derive exegetical lesson from the juxtaposition of verses in the entire Torah, but in the setting of the Book of Deuteronomy he does do so"?

I.   And how do we know that in the rest of the entire Torah, he does not derive exegeses in the stated manner?

J.   It accords with what has been taught on Tannaite authority:

K.   Ben Azzai says, "It is stated, 'You shall not suffer a sorceress to live' (Ex. 22:17), and immediately beyond, 'Whosoever lies with a beast shall surely be put to death' (Ex. 22:18).

L.   "The juxtaposition of the two topics is to indicate that, just as one who lies with a beast is put to death through stoning, so a sorceress also is put to death through stoning."

M.   Said to him R. Judah, "And merely because one matter is juxtaposed to the next, shall we take this person out for execution through stoning?! [There must be better proof.]

N.   "Rather, those who divine by a ghost or by a familiar spirit fall into the classification of all sorts of sorcery. Why were they singled out? It was so as to draw an analogy to them, so as to tell you, 'Just as those who divine by a ghost or by a familiar spirit are put to death through stoning, so a sorceress who is to be executed is put to death through stoning.' [So Judah clearly rejects the other form of proof for the proposition that, for his part, he accepts.]"

O.   And how do we know that, when it comes to the book of Deuteronomy he does provide an exegesis through the juxtaposition of verses?

P.   For it has been taught on Tannaite authority:

Q.   R. Eliezer says, "A man may marry a woman whom his father has raped or seduced, or whom his son has raped or seduced."

R.   R. Judah prohibits in the case of a woman whom one's father has raped or seduced.

S.   And R. Giddal said Rab said, "What is the scriptural basis for the position of R. Judah? As it is written, 'A man shall not take his father's wife and shall not uncover his father's skirt' (Deut. 23:1), meaning that he may not uncover a skirt which his father has seen.

T.   "And how do we know that the text speaks of a woman whom his father has raped?

U.   "It is written, 'Then the man that lay with her shall give to the father' (Deut. 22:29). [Simon, p. 129, n. 2: This shows that R. Judah derives lessons from juxtaposed texts in Deuteronomy.]"

V.   [Accordingly, we revert to the question of how Judah can permit one who has had a seminal emission to study the Torah, as against the exegesis to the contrary deriving from the juxtaposition of Deut. 4:9-10?] One may reply that indeed, in the Book of Deuteronomy he does derive lessons from the juxtaposition of verses, but as to the juxtaposition of verses at hand, he requires that passage [for a different purpose, namely,] to prove the case for yet another teaching assigned to R. Joshua b. Levi.

W.   For R. Joshua b. Levi has said, "Whoever teaches his son Torah is credited by
       Scripture as though he had received [Torah] from Mount Horeb.

X.   "For it is said, 'And you shall make them known to your children and your children's
       children' (Deut. 4:9), and, juxtaposed next, it is written, 'The day that you stood
       before the Lord your God in Horeb' (Deut. 4:10)."

VIII.

A.   We have learned in the Mishnah: One who had experienced a flux who also produced
       semen, a menstruating women who discharged semen, and a woman engaged in
       intercourse who produced a menstrual discharge require immersion before they may
       recite the Shema. And R. Judah exempts them from the requirement of immersion
       [M. 3:6].

B.   Now when R. declares the man exempt, he does so only in the case of a man who has
       suffered a flux and who then has had a seminal emission. For to begin with, such a
       person is not served by immersion in any event [since he is unclean for seven days by
       reason of flux]. [So there is no call for immersion.]

C.   But in the case of one who has suffered a seminal emission [but is not in the status
       of one who has, in addition, suffered a flux], [Judah] imposes the liability [of
       immersion].

D.   And should you say that the same rule applies, so that even in the case of one who
       has had a seminal emission [but is not in the status of one who has also suffered a
       flux], R. Judah also declares the man exempt [from having to immerse],

E.   and the reason that there is a dispute concerning one who has suffered a flux and
       also had a seminal emission is to tell you how far rabbis are prepared to go [in
       imposing the requirement of immersion prior to reciting the Shema],

F.   may I point to the concluding part of the same passage: And a woman engaged in
       intercourse who produced a menstrual discharge has to immerse.

G.   Now on what account would it be necessary to include in the Mishnah's rule the
       cited detail? If I should say that that detail is needed for the exposition of the
       principle of rabbis, that fact is self-evident [and hardly needs articulation].

H.   For if one who has suffered a flux and has produced a seminal emission, who to begin
       with is not served by immersion, is required by rabbis to immerse, a woman who has
       produced a drop of menstrual blood while she is having sexual relations, who to begin
       with will be served by immersion [on account of the semen that issued prior to the
       blood], all the more so [should have to take a ritual bath. There is then no need
       from rabbis' perspective to include the explicit detail that a woman in the stated
       status has to do so, since that fact is self-evident.]

I.   Therefore does it not represent a detail added to deal with the position of R. Judah?

J.   And the framing of the Mishnah-passage is such as to speak to the specific case at
       hand:

K.   [22A] A woman who during sexual relations produced a drop of menstrual blood does
       not have to immerse, but one who has had a seminal emission alone [but is not
       suffering from the uncleanness of flux] for his part [is held by Judah to be] liable.

L. [In reciting the Mishnah,] do not say, [in Judah's name] He says the blessing but rather, "He recites it silently."

M. But does R. Judah take the view that silent recitation [is ever required]?

N. And has it not been taught on Tannaite authority: He who has had a seminal emission and has no water for immersion recites the Shema but does not say the blessings either before it or after it. He eats his bread and says a blessing after it but he does not say a blessing before it, but only does so in his heart and does not say it aloud," the words of R. Meir.

O. R. Judah says, "One way or the other, he says it out loud" [cf. T. Ber. 2:13]. [So Judah does not require silent recitation.]

P. Said R. Nahman bar Isaac, "R. Judah treated these matters as equivalent to the laws of proper conduct of lower standing" [as will be seen below, at Z].

Q. For it has been taught on Tannaite authority:

R. "And you shall make them known to your children and your children's children" (Deut. 4:9), and immediately afterward, "The day on which you stood before the Lord your God in Horeb" (Deut. 4:10).

S. Just as in the latter case there are fear, trembling, dread and awe, so in this case [study of Torah] there must be fear, trembling, dread and awe.

T. On the basis of the exegesis at hand they have said, "Those who have suffered a flux, those who are afflicted with the skin disease [of Lev. 13-14], those who have had sexual relations with menstruating women are permitted to recite the Torah, prophets, and writings, to repeat teachings of the Mishnah and the Gemara and the laws and lore, but those who have had a seminal emission are forbidden to do so. [Sexual relations are not a sign that one has the proper spirit of solemnity such as is required by the cited verses, while those who have suffered the other listed forms of uncleanness are appropriately solemn.]

U. R. Yose says, "One may repeat passages he already knows, so long as he does not then lay out and expound upon the Mishnah."

V. R. Jonathan b. Joseph says, "He expounds upon the Mishnah, but he may not expound upon the Gemara."

W. R. Nathan Abishalom says, "He may also expound upon the Gemara, so long as he does not make mention of the divine name that may be included in a given passage."

X. R. Yohanan, the sandal-maker, disciple of R. Aqiba, in the name of R. Aqiba, says, "In no way may he enter into problems of exegesis."

Y. And some say, "He may not enter the school house under any circumstances."

Z. R. Judah says, "He may repeat the laws of proper conduct" [which is the position ascribed to him above].

AA. There was the case in which R. Judah had a seminal emission, and he was walking by the river. His disciples said to him, "Our master, repeat for us a chapter of the laws of proper conduct."

BB. He went down to the river, immersed, and then repeated the chapter for them.

CC.   They said to him, "Did our master not teach us, 'One may repeat laws of proper conduct [without immersion, even though he has had a seminal emission]'?"

DD.   He said to them, "Even though I impose a lenient rule upon others, I impose a strict rule upon myself."

IX.

A.   It has been taught on Tannaite authority:

B.   R. Judah b. Batera would say, "Words of Torah do not receive uncleanness [if they are repeated by an unclean person]."

C.   There was the case of a disciple, who was repeating traditions in a stuttering manner toward R. Judah b. Batera. He said to him, "My son, open your mouth and let your words give light, for words of Torah are not susceptible to uncleanness, [and so, even though you have had a seminal emission and are unclean, you still may participate in Torah-study]."

X.

A.   A master has said [VIII V], "He may expound the Mishnah but he may not expound the Gemara."

B.   That statement supports the view of R. Ilai.

C.   For R. Ilai said R. Aha bar Jacob said in the name of our rabbi, "The law is that he may expound the Mishnah but he may not expound the Gemara."

D.   The matter accords with a Tannaite dispute:

E.   "He may expound the Mishnah but he may not expound the Gemara," the words of R. Meir.

F.   R. Judah b. Gamaliel says in the name of R. Hanina b. Gamaliel, "Both this and that he is forbidden [to expound]."

G.   And some say, "Both this and that he is permitted [to expound]."

H.   He who maintains that the ruling is that both this and that he may not expound accords with the view of R. Yohanan, the sandal-maker.

I.   The one who says, "This and this it is permitted for him to expound" accords with the position of R. Judah b. Batera.

XI.

A.   R. Nahman bar Isaac said, "Everyone is accustomed to accord with these three elders, with R. Ilai in the rule on the first fleece, R. Josiah in the matter of mixed kinds, and R. Judah b. Batera in the matter of words of Torah."

B.   With R. Ilai in the matter of the tithe of the first fleece, for it has been taught on Tannaite authority:

C.   R. Ilai says, "The law governing the first fleece applies only in the [Holy] Land."

D.   With R. Josiah in the matter of mixed kinds, as follows:

E.   It is written, "You shall not sow your vineyard with two kinds of seeds" (Deut. 22:9).

F.   R. Josiah says, "One is liable only if he sows wheat, barley, and grape kernels in a single fist."

G.   According to R. Judah b. Batera in teachings of Torah.

H.   For it has been taught on Tannaite authority:

I. R. Judah b. Batera says, "Words of Torah do not receive uncleanness."

XII.

A. When Zeiri came, he said, "They have abolished immersion."

B. Some say he said, "They have abolished the washing of the hands."

C. He who has said the tradition in the version, "They have abolished immersion" accords with R. Judah b. Batera [at XI I].

D. He who says that the version is, "They have abolished the washing of the hands" accords with the position of R. Hisda.

E. For he cursed anyone who went looking for water at the time of prayer [maintaining that it is no longer necessary to do so].

XIII.

A. Our rabbis have taught on Tannaite authority:

B. One who has had a seminal emission upon whom nine qabs of water are poured is clean.

C. Nahum of Gim Zo whispered this tradition to R. Aqiba, R. Aqiba whispered it to Ben Azzai, Ben Azzai went out and repeated it to his disciples in the market place.

D. Concerning the wording of this passage there was a disagreement between two Amoraic masters in the West, R. Yose bar Abin and R. Yose bar Zabeda.

E. One of them stated it as, "He repeated it," and the other stated it as, "He whispered it."

F. The one who maintained that he taught it aloud held that the rule [making the return to cleanness after sexual relations so easy] was on account of avoiding the abrogation of Torah-study and avoiding the cessation of sexual relations [if it were made so inconvenient as to require formal immersion in a pool, rather than a mere dousing with water].

G. The one who repeated it in the version, "He whispered it," maintained that the rule must be kept quiet so that disciples of the sages should not be always upon their wives like cocks.

H. Said R. Yannai, "I heard that they impose a lenient ruling in this matter, and I heard that they impose a strict ruling in this matter.

I. "And whoever imposes a strict ruling on himself is given lengthened days and years."

XIV.

A. Said R. Joshua b. Levi, "What value is it for those who immerse at dawn?"

B. What is the value? Lo, he himself is the one who has said that one has had a seminal emission is forbidden to study Torah [so the obvious value of immersion is to permit the man to study Torah].

C. This is the sense of his statement: "What is the value of those who immerse in forty seahs of water [in a regular immersion pool]. It is possible to accept the same end with nine qabs of water.

D. "What is the value of actual immersion, when it is possible to achieve the same end with a mere dousing."

E. Said R. Hanina, "[By using forty seahs of water in a regular pool, sages have] made a great fence."

F. For it has been taught on Tannaite authority:

G. There was the case of a man who propositioned a woman. She said to him, "Empty head! Do you have immediate access to a proper immersion pool containing forty seahs of water, in which you can immerse afterward?"

H. He forthwith gave up.

XV.

A. Said R. Huna to rabbis, "My masters, on what account do you treat lightly this matter of immersion? Is it because of the cold? It is possible to make use of the baths."

B. Said R. Hisda to him, "And may one immerse in hot water?"

C. He said to him, "R. Ada bar Ahba takes your view."

D. R. Zira would sit in a pool of water in the baths and say to his attendant, "Go and bring nine qabs of water and toss it over me."

E. Said to him R. Hiyya bar Abba, "Why does the master do it this way? Lo, he is sitting right in [that volume of water anyhow]."

F. He said to him, "It is in direct contrast to the matter of forty seahs [of proper water in an immersion pool]. Just as, in the case of forty seahs of water, the pool must be entered through immersion and not through tossing, so in the case of the nine qabs, it should be through tossing and not through immersion."

XVI.

A. R. Nahman had a ewer for nine qabs of water prepared. When R. Dimi came, he said, "R. Aqiba and R. Judah, the locksmith, have ruled, 'That law applies [that the dunking in nine qabs of tossed water suffices] only for a sick man who has an involuntary emission. But if it is a sick man who has it through intercourse, what is required is immersion in forty seahs."

B. Said R. Joseph, "The ewer of R. Nahman has been broken."

C. When Rabin came, he said, "The case came to Usha, to [22B] the anteroom of R. Oshaia. They came and asked R. Assi. He said to them, 'The rule applies only for a sick man who has an emission through intercourse, but a sick man who has an involuntary emission is exempt from all [necessity to immerse, either in a regular emission pool or in nine qabs of water]."

D. Said R. Joseph, "The ewer of R. Nahman has been fixed."

XVII.

A. Since all of the cited Amoraic and Tannaite masters differ as to the actions of Ezra, let us see precisely what Ezra ordained.

B. Said Abayye, "Ezra ordained that in the case of a healthy person who had a seminal emission through normal intercourse, immersion in forty seahs [of water in a proper immersion pool is required]. And a healthy person who unwittingly had a seminal emission may attain purification by having nine qabs of water doused on him.

C. "And the Amoraic authorities then came along and differed as to the case of a sick man.

D. "One authority maintained that a sick man who did matters in the normal way is in the category of a healthy person who did matters in the normal way, and a sick man who had an emission unwittingly is in the category of a healthy person who had one in the same way.

E. "And the other authority takes the view that a sick man who had an emission in the normal way through intercourse is in the status of a healthy man who had an emission unwittingly, while a sick man who had an emission unwittingly is exempt from all rites of purification."

F. Said Raba, "While, to be sure, Ezra did ordain the rite of immersion, did he ordain the rite of dousing water [at all, as the provision of nine qabs requires]?

G. "And did not a master state, 'Ezra ordained immersion for those men who have had a seminal emission.'"

H. Rather, said Raba, "Ezra ordained immersion in forty seahs of water for a healthy man who had a seminal emission in the normal way, and rabbis were the ones who came along and made the ordinance that a healthy man who had a seminal emission unwittingly may attain purification through having nine qabs of water doused on him. Then Amoraim came along and had a dispute as to the status of a sick man.

I. "One master maintained the view that a sick man who had an emission in the normal way is in the status of a healthy man who has had a seminal emission in the normal way, and a sick man who had an emission unwittingly is in the category of a healthy man who had the same.

J. "And the other master maintained that in the case of a healthy person who had a seminal emission in the normal way, an immersion in forty seahs of water is required, and a sick person who has had a seminal emission in the normal way is in the status of a healthy person who has had an emission unwittingly and so suffices with nine qabs of water.

K. "But a sick man who had a seminal emission unwittingly is exempt from all modes of purification."

L. Said Raba, "The decided law is that a healthy man who had a seminal emission in the normal way and a sick man who had an emission in the normal way are to immerse in forty seahs of waters, and a healthy man who had a seminal emission unwittingly purifies himself in nine qabs of water. But a sick man who had a seminal emission unwittingly is exempt from all modes of purification.

XVIII.

A. Our rabbis have taught on Tannaite authority:

B. One who had a seminal discharge [on account of illness] upon whom one poured nine qabs of water is clean.

C. T. adds: behold he recites [cf. M. Ber. 3:4] for what purpose?

D. For himself. But he cannot exempt others from their obligation [to recite the Shema] unless he first immerses himself in [a pool of] forty seahs [of water]

E.	R. Judah says, "[He must immerse himself in] forty seahs in all cases [whether to recite the Shema for himself or to exempt others from the recitation]" [T. Ber. 2:12].

F.	R. Yohanan and R. Joshua b. Levi, R. Eleazar and R. Yose b. R. Hanina:

G.	One of the former of the two pairs and one of the latter made a statement on the opening clause of the cited passage.

H.	One of them said, "The statement that you have made, For what purpose? For himself. But he cannot exempt others from their obligation to recite the Shema unless he first immerses himself in a pool of forty seahs of water, applies only to a case in which there was a sick man who had an emission in the ordinary way. But a sick man who had an emission unwittingly suffices with a dousing of nine qabs of water."

I.	The other of them said, "In the case of anyone who proposes to recite the Shema in behalf of others, even if it is a sick man who has had a seminal emission unwillingly, the man may not do so unless he has immersed in forty seahs of water."

J.	And one of the former pair and one of the latter pair made a statement on the latter part of the same passage.

K.	One said, "As to this statement that R. Judah says, 'He must immerse himself in forty seahs in all cases, [whether to recite the Shema for himself or to exempt others from the recitation],' that statement applies to water in the ground [e.g., in a river or well]. But as to water in a utensil, that may not be used [for the purpose]."

L.	The other said, "That statement applies even to water drawn in a utensil."

M.	Now in the view of him who has said, "Even in utensils," that accords with that which has been taught on Tannaite authority: R. Judah says, "Forty seahs in all cases."

N.	But in the view of him who has said, "That rule applies to water on the ground, but not to water in utensils," what further datum is encompassed by the language, "in all cases"?

O.	It serves to encompass water that has been drawn [and does not come from a spring].

XIX.

A.	R. Papa, R. Huna, son of R. Joshua, and Raba bar Samuel, broke bread together. Said R. Papa to them, "Give me the honor of saying the blessing, for nine qabs of water have fallen on me."

B.	Said to them Raba bar Samuel, "We have learned on Tannaite authority: For what purpose? For himself. But he cannot exempt others from their obligation unless he first immerses himself in a pool of forty seahs of water. Rather, give me the honor of saying the blessing, for forty seahs of water have fallen on me."

C.	Said to them R. Huna, "Give me the honor of saying the blessing. For neither the one nor the other has fallen on me, [since I had no seminal emission to begin with]."

D.	R. Hama immersed on the eve of the Passover so as to carry out the obligation [of saying grace] in behalf of the community [gathered for the Passover rite].

E.	But the law does not follow that view.

These units of discourse take up the exegesis of phrases in the Mishnah-paragraph: I, continued at II, and, in the principle examined at II, at III-VI. VII takes up M. 3:4D. Then VIII occurs, I assume, because it intersects with the interests of the Mishnah-paragraph at VII N. Unit IX undertakes the secondary amplification of the Mishnah-paragraph's principle, about saying words indistinctly when one is unclean. Unit X then carries forward the theme and problem of IX, and XI, XII do the same. Unit XIII goes on to a fresh topic, namely, the way in which one who has had a seminal discharge attains purification. This is a further secondary amplification of the topic of the Mishnah-paragraph. The provision of a distinctive mode of purification -- not immersion in a proper pool but mere dunking in a few qabs of water in buckets (that is, water that could not serve in a proper pool) -- defines the issue. The topic is expanded at XIV through XIX. So the entire, rather protracted Talmudic composition flows from the Mishnah-paragraph at hand and either explains its language or expands upon and completes its theme.

3:5

A. If a man was standing [and reciting] the Prayer

B. and remembered that he had had a seminal emission,

C. he should not interrupt [his recitation].

D. Rather he should abbreviate [the Prayer].

E. If one went down to immerse himself,

F. If he can come up [from the pool] and cover himself and recite [the Shema] before the sun rises,

G. he should come up and cover himself and recite.

H. And if not, he should cover himself in the water and recite.

I. But he should cover himself neither in foul water nor in water used for soaking [flax],

J. uunless he has poured [some fresh] water into it.

K. And how far should one distance himself from it [from foul water] and from excrement [before he may recite the Shema]?

L. Four cubits.

I.

A. Our rabbis have taught on Tannaite authority:

B. If a man was standing [and reciting] the Prayer and remembered that he had had a seminal emission, he should not interrupt his recitation. Rather, he should abbreviate [the Prayer] [M. 3:5A-D].

C. If he was reciting the Torah and remembered that he had had a seminal emission, he should not interrupt the reading and go up [from the reader's stand]. Rather, he reads in a halting manner.

D. R. Meir says, "A man who has had a seminal emission is not permitted to read more than three verses in the Torah. [Beyond that point, he should stop and leave.]"

E.   A further teaching on Tannaite authority is as follows:

F.   If a man was standing [and reciting] the Prayer and saw excrement nearby, he should walk forward until it is left four cubits behind him.

G.   And has it not been taught, "He should walk to one side"?

H.   There is no contradiction. The one version speaks of a case in which it is possible [to walk forward], the other in which it is not possible to do so.

I.   If a man was saying the Prayer and found excrement where he was standing,

J.   said Rabbah, "Even though he has committed a sin, his recitation of the Prayer is valid.

K.   Raba objected to him, "Lo, [it is said], 'The sacrifice of the wicked is an abomination' (Prov. 21:27)."

L.   Rather, said Raba, "Since he has committed a sin, even though he has said the Prayer, his Prayer is an abomination."

II.

A.   It has been taught on Tannaite authority:

B.   If a man was standing [and reciting] the Prayer and urine dripped onto his knees, he should suspend his praying until the urine stops dripping and then goes back and continues reciting the Prayer.

C.   To what point should he return and take up the Prayer?

D.   R. Hisda and R. Hamnuna:

E.   One of them said, "He goes back to the beginning [of the Prayer]."

F.   The other said, "He goes back to the point at which he broke off."

G.   May we then propose that this is the principle at issue:

H.   [23A] One authority takes the view that, if he suspended the Prayer for sufficient time to complete reciting the whole of it, he goes back to the beginning.

I.   The other party maintains that he goes back to the place at which he suspended [the praying].

J.   Said R. Ashi, "[If that is at issue, then] it was necessary for the framer of the passage to specify both, 'If he suspended' [and] 'If he did not suspend [saying the prayer long enough to complete the whole thing].' [So the formulation of the passage does not accord with the specification of what is at issue.]

K.   "Rather, all parties concur that, if the man stopped praying long enough to complete saying the whole of the Prayer, he goes back to the beginning of the Prayer.

L.   "At issue now is when the man did not suspend praying at all.

M.   "One authority takes the view that the man was unfit to say the prayer [since he could not hold his urine] and it would be inappropriate, so that his recitation of the Prayer is invalid.

N.   "The other authority maintains that the man is suitable, and his recitation of the Prayer is valid."

III.

A.   Our rabbis have taught on Tannaite authority:

B.   He who has to defecate should not say the Prayer. And if, in that condition, he said the Prayer, his Prayer is an abomination.

C.   Said R. Zebid and some say, R. Judah, "That statement applies only to a case of a man who cannot hold himself in. But if he can hold himself in, his recitation of the Prayer is valid."

D.   How much [must he be able to hold himself in]? Said R. Sheshet, "Sufficient time to walk a parasang."

E.   There are those who repeat the foregoing tradition with reference to a Tannaite teaching, as follows:

F.   When is it [the case that his Prayer is an abomination]?

G.   When he cannot hold himself in.

H.   But if he can hold himself in, his recitation of the Prayer is valid.

I.   How much [must he be able to hold himself in]?

J.   Said R. Zebid, "For a parasang."

IV.

A.   Said R. Samuel bar Nahmani said R. Jonathan, "He who has to defecate, lo, such a one should not recite the Prayer.

B.   "For it is said, 'Prepare to meet your God, O Israel' (Amos 4:12) [T. Ber. 2:18]."

C.   And R. Samuel bar Nahmani said R. Jonathan said, "What is the sense of the following verse: 'Guard your foot when you go to the house of God' (Qoh. 4:17)?

D.   "Guard yourself that you not sin, but if you do sin, bring an offering before me."

E.   "And come near to listen" (Qoh. 4:17):

F.   Said Raba, "Be sure to draw near to listen to the teachings of sages, for if they sin, they bring an offering and repent."

G.   "It is better than when fools give" (Qoh. 4:17):

H.   Do not be like fools, who when they sin bring an offering but do not repent.

I.   "For they do not know to do evil" (Qoh. 4:17).

J.   If so, they are righteous!

K.   "Rather: Do not be like the fools who sin and then bring an offering but do not know whether it is on account of a good deed that they bring it or on account of a bad deed that they bring it.

L.   Said the Holy One, blessed be he, "They do not know how to distinguish between good and evil, and yet they bring an offering before me."

M.   [Interpreting the cited verse], R. Ashi, and some say, R. Hanina bar Papa, said, "Guard your bowels when you stand to recite the Prayer before me."

V.

A.   Our rabbis have taught on Tannaite authority:

B.   He who goes into a privy should first remove his phylacteries at a distance of four cubits and only then go in.

C.   Said R. Aha bar R. Huna said R. Sheshet, "That statement applies only to a permanent privy, but as to one that is temporary, one may take off his phylacteries and relieve himself forthwith."

D.   "Then, when he leaves the place, he goes for cubits before putting them on, because, by using the privy, he has turned it into a permanent one."

E.   The following question was raised: What is the law as to a man's wearing his phylacteries in a permanent privy when he goes in only to urinate?

F.   Rabina permitted doing so.

G.   R. Ada bar Mattena forbade doing so.

H.   They came and asked Raba.

I.   He said to them, "It is forbidden to do so, since we take account of the possibility that one may also defecate while wearing them."

J.   And some repeat the statement in this way: "Perhaps he may fart while wearing them."

VI.

A.   A further teaching on Tannaite authority:

B.   "He who enters a permanent privy must remove his phylacteries while at a distance of four cubits and put them on the window at the side of the public road. Then he goes in. And when he comes out, he goes the distance of four cubits and then he puts them on," the words of the House of Shammai.

C.   And the House of Hillel say, "He holds them in his hand and goes in [and does not have to leave them on the window sill.]"

D.   R. Aqiba says, "He holds them in his garment and goes in."

E.   Do you think one may hold them in his garment? But there may be times in which they may slip out and fall!

F.   Rather, "He holds them in his garment with his hand and enters."

G.   And he puts them in a hole at the side of the privy, but he should not put them in a hole at the side of the public road, lest passers-by take them and he become suspect.

H.   There was the case of a disciple who left his phylacteries in a hole at the side of the public way, and a whore came along and took them and came to the study-house and said, "See what So-and-so paid me."

I.   When the disciple heard this, he went up to the top of the roof and threw himself off and died.

J.   On that occasion sages ordained that one should hold the phylacteries in his garment with his hand and then go into the privy.

VII.

A.   Our rabbis have taught on Tannaite authority:

B.   At first people would leave phylacteries in a hole at the side of the privy. But mice came and took them.

C.   They ordained that people should leave them in the windows nearest the public road. But passers-by came along and took them.

D.   They then ordained that a person should hold them in his hand and then enter the privy.

E.   Said R. Miasha, son of R. Joshua b. Levi, "The decided law is that one should roll them up like a scroll and hold them in his right hand next to his heart."

F. Said R. Joseph bar Minyomi said R. Nahman, "That is on condition that a strap of the phylactery not protrude below his hand by so much as a handbreadth."

G. Said R. Jacob bar Aha said R. Zira, "That rule has been taught if there is yet daylight for the man to put them back on. But if there is no daylight for the man to put them back on, then he makes for them a kind of pocket the size of a handbreadth and puts them away."

H. Said Rabbah bar bar Hana said R. Yohanan, "By day one rolls them up like a scroll and puts them against his heart, and by night he makes for them a kind of pocket the size of a handbreadth and puts them away."

I. Said Abayye, "The rule applies only to a case that is meant to serve to hold them, but in the case of something not meant to hold them, even if it is less than a handbreadth [that suffices]."

J. Mar Zutra, and some say, R. Ashi, said, "You may know that that is the case, for lo, small utensils afford protection from the entry of corpse-uncleanness in a tent that overshadows a corpse [if they are tightly sealed, and that is so even though they are less than a handbreadth in volume]."

VIII.

A. And Rabbah bar bar Hana said, "When we followed after R. Yohanan, when he wanted to go into a privy, if he had a scroll containing lore, he would give it to us. When he had in hand phylacteries, he would not give them to us.

B. "He said, 'Since rabbis have permitted [holding them in hand], [23B] [the phylacteries] will guard us [in the privy]."

C. Said Raba, "When we went after R. Nahman, if he had a scroll containing lore, he would give it to us. When he hand in hand phylacteries, he would not give them to us.

D. "He said, 'Since rabbis have permitted [holding them in hand], they will guard us [in the privy]."

IX.

A. Our rabbis have taught on Tannaite authority:

B. A man should not hold phylacteries in his hand and a scroll of the Torah in his arm and say the Prayer.

C. Nor should he urinate while holding them or sleep with them either for a regular nap or for a brief snooze.

D. Said Samuel, "One's knife, money, dish, or a loaf of bread -- lo, they fall into the same category."

E. Said Raba said R. Sheshet, "The law does not accord with the cited teaching on Tannaite authority, for it represents the principle of the House of Shammai.

F. "For, from the viewpoint of the House of Hillel, if in their view it is permitted [to take some of these objects] into a permanent privy, is there any issue as to taking them into a temporary one [e.g., urinating while holding them? Surely the House of Hillel would permit such an act. So an argument a fortiori requires us to assign the law at hand to the Shammaites.]"

G.   An objection was raised as follows:

H.   [A teaching on Tannaite authority is phrased as follows:] "Things that I have permitted to you in one setting I have forbidden in another."

I.   Does the cited statement not refer to phylacteries? [Surely it does.]

J.   Now from the viewpoint of the House of Hillel, the cited statement may be interpreted in the following way: I have permitted to you here, in a permanent privy, what I have forbidden to you there, in a random privy [namely, use of phylacteries].

K.   But if it should follow the position of the House of Shammai, [it would make no sense,] for they permit nothing [under either circumstance].

L.   The cited statement [H] was taught on Tannaite authority with reference to the baring of a handbreadth and two handbreadths.

M.   For it has been taught on Tannaite authority as follows:

N.   When a person defecates, he bares a handbreadth behind and two in front.

O.   And a further teaching on Tannaite authority has a handbreadth behind and nothing in front.

P.   Now is it not the case that both statements refer to a man, and do not contradict one another, for the one statement refers to defecating and the other urinating.

Q.   But does that stand to reason? For if reference is made only to urinating, then what sense is there in referring to "a handbreadth behind"?

R.   Rather, both statements refer to defecation, and there still is no contradiction between them, for one refers to a man, the other to a woman.

S.   If it is so [that the statement, "Things permitted... prohibited..." refers to a man and a woman], then note what has been taught on Tannaite authority in this connection:

T.   "This is an argument a fortiori that cannot be refuted."

U.   What sense is there in claiming that that statement cannot be refuted? It is the way things are!

V.   Rather does this not refer to phylacteries and constitute a refutation of what Raba said R. Sheshet said?

W.   It does indeed refute what he said.

X.   In any event there is this problem:

Y.   Now if a permanent privy is a forbidden place for use of phylacteries, will not a temporary privy all the more so be a place forbidden for use of phylacteries?

Z.   This is the sense of the matter: In a permanent privy, in which there is no splashing, it is permitted [to carry phylacteries].

AA. In a temporary one, in which there is splashing, it is forbidden [to carry phylacteries].

BB. If that is the case, then what sort of claim is it that there is no refutation? There is a perfectly valid refutation for such a statement.

CC. This is the sense of the passage:

DD. This matter [permitting phylacteries in a permanent privy and prohibiting them in a temporary one] is founded upon a reason [namely, the issue of splashing], and not on an argument a fortiori.

EE.   For if it rested on an argument <u>a fortiori</u>, this is an argument <u>a fortiori</u> which could not be refuted [that is, an argument constructed on the regular privy and the temporary one].

X.

A.   Our rabbis have taught on Tannaite authority:

B.   He who wants to join in a regular meal [but has to relieve himself first] should walk four cubits ten times or ten cubits four times, and defecate, and afterward join the meal.

C.   Said R. Isaac, "He who joins in a regular meal should remove his phylacteries and then go in to the meal."

D.   And this differs from the view of R. Hiyya.

E.   For R. Hiyya said, "He may leave them on his table, and they serve as an ornament for him."

F.   How long?

G.   Said R. Nahman bar Isaac, "To the time of the blessing [of the food in the Grace after Meals]."

XI.

A.   One Tannaite teaching states: One may tie up his phylacteries with his money in his undergarment."

B.   Another Tannaite teaching says, "One may not do so."

C.   There is no contradiction. In the one case [in which one <u>may</u> do so], it is because he has designated the place for that purpose, and in the other instance, he did not designate it for that purpose.

D.   For R. Hisda said, "As to a scarf which one designated for tying up his phylacteries, when he has tied up his phylacteries in it, it is forbidden then to tie up his money in it.

E.   "If he designated it, but did not tie up his phylacteries in it, or tied them up but did not designate the cloth for that purpose, it is permitted to tie up money in that cloth."

F.   And in the view of Abayye, who has said, "Designation by itself [without actual use of the thing for the designated purpose] is of consequence,"

G.   if he designated the cloth even though he did not tie up his phylacteries in it, it is forbidden to tie up money in it. If he did not designate it for phylacteries, it is not forbidden to tie up money in it.

XII.

A.   R. Joseph, son of R. Nehunia, asked R. Judah, "What is the law on a man's leaving his phylacteries under his pillow?

B.   "As to leaving them under one's feet, that poses no question to me, for doing so would be to treat them contemptuously.

C.   "What interests me as to the law about putting them under one's pillow."

D.   He said to him, "This is what Samuel said, 'It is permitted, and that is the case even if his wife is with him in bed.'"

E. An objection was raised from the following formulation: A man should not leave his phylacteries under his feet, because doing so is to treat them contemptuously, but he may leave them under his pillow, though if his wife was in bed with him, it is forbidden. If there is a place [projecting from the bed] three handbreadths higher or lower, it is permitted [to put the phylacteries in that place].

F. Is this not a refutation of the ruling of Samuel?

G. It indeed is a refutation.

H. Said Raba, "Even though it has been taught on Tannaite authority in refutation of the position of Samuel, nonetheless the law accords with his position.

I. "What is the reason?

J. "[24A] Whatever serves to guard [the phylacteries] to a greater degree is to be preferred [without reference to the issue of disrespect]."

K. And where does one leave them?

L. Said R. Jeremiah, "Between the blanket and the pillow, but not directly beneath one's head."

M. And lo, R. Hiyya taught on Tannaite authority, "One leaves them in a cover under his pillow. [That would indicate one puts the bag under his head.]"

N. The sense is that one makes the top of the cover [at which the phylacteries are located] project outside [the area of the pillow].

O. Bar Qappara would [Simon:] tie them in the bed-curtain and make them project outside.

P. R. Shisha, son of R. Idi, left them on a stool and spread a cloth over them.

Q. R. Hamnuna, son of R. Joseph, said, "Once I was standing before Raba, and he said to me, 'Go and bring me my phylacteries.' I found them between the blankets and the pillow, but not directly beneath the head. So I realized that it was the day on which his wife was to immerse [having had sexual relations with him], and he had sent me so as to learn how the law is actually practiced."

XIII.

A. R. Joseph, son of R. Nehunia, asked R. Judah, "In the case of two people who slept in a single bed, what is the law as to having this one turn away and recite the Shema, and that one do the same?"

B. He said to him, "This is what Samuel said, "Even if one's wife is with him [it is permitted to do so]."

C. R. Joseph objected, "'His wife' and one need not ask about someone else? [That is, if his wife may be present, anyone else likewise would fall under the same rule.] To the contrary, his wife is in the status of himself, while another is not in the status of himself, [and hence Samuel's view of the rule governing the presence of the wife does not reply to the question]."

D. An objection was raised from the following formulation of the law:

E. In the case of two who were sleeping in one bed, this one turns his face away and recites the Shema, and so does the other [T. Ber. 2:15C-D].

F. Another Tannaite teaching states: He who is sleeping in bed, with his children and members of his household by his side -- lo, this one should not recite the <u>Shema</u> unless there was a cloak intervening between them. But if his children and dependents were minors, it is permitted [to do so without a partition].

G. Now from the perspective of R. Joseph, there is no contradiction between these two formulations of the rule [at E, F]. One would speak of the presence of his wife, the other of the presence of some other party.

H. But from the perspective of Samuel, there surely is a contradiction [between the two statements].

I. Samuel may reply to you, "And do things really work out for R. Joseph? Has it not been taught on Tannaite authority: 'If he was sleeping in bed, with his children and dependents in bed, he should not recite the <u>Shema</u> unless a cloak intervened between them. [That statement surely would encompass the presence of his wife, so from Joseph's viewpoint, the contradiction is still blatant, as much as it is from Samuel's.]

J. "Rather, what can you say? It is a dispute among Tannaite authorities, and, from my perspective too, we have a dispute among Tannaite authorities."

XIV.

A. A master has said, "This one turns his face away and recites the <u>Shema</u>...."

B. And lo, there is contact at the buttocks!

C. That supports the view of R. Huna, for R. Huna said, "Contact at the buttocks is not subject to the consideration of sexuality."

D. May I say that the following supports the view of R. Huna:

E. <u>A woman may sit naked and cut off her dough-offering, because she can cover up her 'face' [sexual parts] on the ground, but a man may not [do so] [M. Hal. 2:3].</u>

F. R. Nahman bar Isaac explained, "The case would involve one in which her 'face' [including the buttocks] was covered by the ground, [and the passage then would not necessarily support Huna's position]."

XV.

A. A master said, "If his children and dependents were minors, it is permitted."

B. Up to what age?

C. Said R. Hisda, "In the case of girls, up to three years and on one day, and in the case of boys, up to nine years and one day."

D. There are those who say, "In the case of girls up to eleven years and one day, and in the case of boys up to twelve years and one day."

E. And with both of them it is up to the time that "Your breasts were fashioned and your hair was grown" (Ez. 16:7).

F. Said R. Kahana to R. Ashi, "In the other case Raba has said that even though there is a refutation of the position of Samuel, the law follows Samuel. Here what is the law?"

G. He said to him, "Are all of them spun of a single web? But where such a statement has been made it has been made and applies. And where such a statement has not been made it has not been made."

H.   Said R. Mari to R. Papa, "If a hair protrudes through a garment, what is the law [as to regarding it as indecent exposure (Simon)]?"

I.   He called it "a hair, a hair." [We do not take account of it.]

XVI.

A.   Said R. Isaac, "An exposed handbreadth [of flesh] in the case of a woman is regarded as a matter of sexuality [and not to be permitted]."

B.   For what purpose?

C.   If I say that the rule treats the matter of gazing upon such a thing, lo, said R. Sheshet, "Why did Scripture list ornaments worn outside clothing along with those worn inside [at Num. 31:5]? It was to tell you that whoever looks even at the little finger of a woman is as if he stared at her sexual parts."

D.   Rather, the rule relates to one's own wife, and it pertains to the recitation of the Shema [so that if one's wife exposes so much as a handbreadth of flesh, one may not recite the Shema in her presence].

E.   Said R. Hisda, "A woman's leg is a matter of sexuality, as it is said, 'Uncover the leg, pass through the rivers' (Is. 47:2), and thereafter, 'Your nakedness shall be uncovered, yes, your shame shall be seen' (Is. 47:43)."

F.   Said Samuel, "A woman's voice is a matter of sexuality, as it is said, 'For your voice is sweet and your face pretty' (Song 2:14)."

G.   R. Sheshet said, "A woman's hair is a matter of sexuality, as it is said, 'Your hair is as a flock of goats' (Song 2:14)."

XVII.

A.   Said R. Hanina, "I saw Rabbi [Judah the Patriarch] hang up his phylacteries [on a peg]."

B.   It was objected: He who hangs up his phylacteries will have his life suspended."

C.   Those who expound the main point stated, "'And your life will hang in doubt before you' (Deut. 28:66) refers to those who hang up their phylacteries."

D.   There is no contradiction. The one [Hanina] refers to hanging them up by the strap, the other [B, C] refers to hanging them up by the box.

E.   And if you wish, I shall propose that there is no difference between hanging them up by the strap and by the box. In both cases it is forbidden.

F.   But when Rabbi hung up his, it was by the case [in which he kept them].

G.   If that is so, then what do we learn from that fact?

H.   What might you have maintained? That phylacteries must be carefully laid away, like a scroll of the Torah? So we are informed that that is not the rule.

XVIII.

A.   And R. Hanina said, "I saw Rabbi [while reciting the Prayer] belch, yawn, sneeze, spit, [24B] and shift his clothes. But he did not cloak himself [pulling the cloak over his head].

B.   "And when he burped, he put his hand to his chin [Simon]."

C.   An objection was raised on the basis of the following rule: One who makes his voice heard when he recites the Prayer -- lo, he is one of those of little faith. He who raises his voice while saying his Prayer, lo, he is one of the false prophets. He who belches and yawns is one of the arrogant people. He who sneezes during the recitation of his Prayer is under a bad omen. And some say, It is a sign that he is a vile person. One who spits while reciting his Prayer is as if he spit before the King.

D.   Now with reference to belching and yawning, there is no contradiction [between what Rabbi did and the cited rule], for the one did so perforce and the other speaks of doing so deliberately.

E.   But surely there is a contradiction between the two statements in regard to sneezing.

F.   No, there is no contradiction with regard to sneezing. The one [Rabbi's case] speaks of doing so above [through the nose], the other below [as a fart].

G.   For R. Zira said, "The following teaching was tangentially reported to me in the house of R. Hamnuna, and is worth everything else I have ever learned:

H.   "'He who sneezes while he is reciting his Prayer is subject to a good omen. Just as here below that gives him relief, so up above he will be given relief.'"

I.   But the two statements as regards spitting do present a contradiction.

J.   The two statements concerning spitting pose no contradiction at all.

K.   For R. Judah said, "If one was standing and reciting his Prayer and spit came to his mouth, he absorbs it in his cloak, or, if it is a good cloak, in his scarf."

L.   Rabina was standing before R. Ashi.. Spit collected. He spat behind himself. R. Ashi said to him, "Does the Master not concur with what R. Judah said, that he covers it up with his scarf?"

M.   He said to him, "I am squeamish [Simon]."

XIX.

A.   One who makes his voice heard when he recites the Prayer -- lo, he is one of those of little faith.

B.   Said R. Huna, "That statement applies only to one who can properly direct his heart if he says the prayer in a whisper. But if he cannot direct his heart if he says the Prayer in a whisper, it is permitted.

C.   "But that ruling applies when an individual is by himself. In the case of the community, he may [not] disturb the other people."

XX.

A.   R. Abba was avoiding R. Judah, for [the former] wanted to go up to the Land of Israel, while R. Judah held, "Whoever goes up from Babylonia to the Land of Israel violates a positive commandment, for it is said, 'They shall be brought to Babylonia and there they shall be until the day that I remember them, says the Lord' (Jer. 27:22)."

B.   He said, "I shall go and hear what he is saying in the meeting house."

C.   He went and found the Tannaite authority reciting before R. Judah, "If a person was standing and reciting the Prayer and he farted, he should wait until the stink passes and then go back and say the Prayer."

D. "There are those who say, 'If one was standing and reciting the Prayer and he wanted to fart, he steps four cubits back and farts and then he waits until the stink passes and returns and says the Prayer.'

E. "And he says, 'Lord of the universe, You have formed us with various holes and vents. You know full well our shame and humiliation, in our lives and in our destinies, in worms and maggots.'

F. "Then he begins from the place at which he had interrupted the prayer."

G. He said, "Had I come only to hear this, it would have been enough for me."

XXI.

A. Our rabbis have taught on Tannaite authority:

B. If who was sleeping in his cloak and cannot put his head out because of the cold makes a partition with his cloak around his neck and then recites the Shema.

C. And some say, "Around his heart."

D. Now from the viewpoint of the version of the first of the two Tannaite authorities, lo, his heart is in sight of his sexual parts.

E. He takes the view that if his heart is in sight of his sexual parts, it is still permitted.

XXII.

A. Said R. Huna said R. Yohanan, "If one was walking in dirty alleys, he puts his hand over his mouth and recites the Shema."

B. Said to him R. Hisda, "By God! Were R. Hisda to make that statement to me with his own mouth, I should pay no attention to him."

C. There are those who say, Said Rabbah bar bar Hana said R. Joshua b. Levi, "If someone was walking in dirty alleyways, he puts his hand over his mouth and recites the Shema."

D. Said to him R. Hisda, "By God! If R. Joshua b. Levi made that statement to me with his own mouth, I would not pay any attention to him."

E. But did R. Huna make that statement?

F. And did R. Huna not say, "It is forbidden for a disciple of sages to stand in a dirty place, because he cannot stand without meditation on Torah teachings."

G. There is no contradiction. The one statement speaks of merely standing, the other of walking [and the latter is permitted].

H. And did R. Yohanan make such a statement?

I. And has not Rabbah bar bar Hana said R. Yohanan said, "In every place it is permitted to meditate on Torah-teachings, except for the bath-house and privy"?

J. And if you should say here too, the one statement speaks of standing there, the other of merely walking,

K. can this be so?

L. For lo, R. Abbahu followed after R. Yohanan, and [Abbahu] was reciting the Shema. When he came to dirty alleyways, he fell silent.

M. He said to R. Yohanan, "Where do I pick up the recitation?"

N. He said to him, "If you suspended the recitation for long enough to complete reciting the whole thing, you go back to the beginning."

O. This is the sense of his statement: "In my view, I do not agree [that you had to cease reciting the Shema at all], but in your view, holding as you do that you must cease the recitation, then if you suspended the recitation for long enough to complete reciting the entire passage, you must go back to the beginning."

P. There is a Tannaite teaching according to the view of R. Huna and another according to the view of R. Hisda.

Q. The Tannaite teaching according to the view of R. Huna is as follows:

R. He who is walking through dirty alleyways puts his hand over his mouth and recites the Shema.

S. The Tannaite formulation in accord with R. Hisda is as follows:

T. He who is walking through dirty alleyways should not recite the Shema.

U. And not only so, but if he was reciting the Shema and came to such a place, he should stop reciting.

V. If he did not stop, what is the law?

W. Said Miasha, son of the son of R. Joshua b. Levi, "Concerning such a person Scripture says, 'Wherefore I gave them also statutes that were not good and ordinances whereby they should not live' (Ez. 20:25)."

X. R. Assi said, "'Woe to them who draw iniquity with cords of vanity' (Is. 5:18)."

Y. R. Adda b. Ahba said, "'Because he has despised the word of the Lord' (Num. 15:31)."

Z. And if he does stop reciting, what is his reward?

AA. R. Abbahu said, "In his regard Scripture states, 'Through this word you prolong your days' (Deut. 32:47)."

XXIII.

A. Said R. Huna, "If one's cloak was tied around his waist [leaving his upper body naked], it is permitted to recite the Shema."

B. It has been taught on Tannaite authority along these same lines:

C. **If one's garment, whether of cloth, leather, or sacking, is tied around his waist, it is permitted to recite the Shema.**

D. **[25A] But as to the recitation of the Prayer, one may do so only if he covers his heart** [T. 2:14H-I].

XXV.

A. And R. Huna said, "If one forgot and went into the privy while wearing his phylacteries, he puts his hand over them until he completes [his defecation]."

B. "Until he completes it" what do you think?!

C. Rather said R. Nahman bar Isaac, "Until he finishes his first discharge."

D. But let the man stop immediately and hold it in?

E. It is on account of what R. Simeon b. Gamaliel said, For it has been taught on Tannaite authority:

F. Rabban Simeon b. Gamaliel says, "Holding in the faeces causes dropsy, holding in urine causes jaundice."

XXIV.

A. It has been stated on Amoraic authority:

B.   [If there is] excrement on one's body, or one's hand was [poked through a window] into a privy,

C.   R. Huna said, "It is permitted to recite the Shema."

D.   R. Hisda said, "It is forbidden to recite the Shema."

E.   Said Raba, "What is the scriptural basis for the position of R. Huna? It is written, 'Let everything that has breath praise the Lord' (Ps. 150:6)."

F.   And R. Hisda said, "It is forbidden to recite the Shema."

G.   What is the scriptural basis for the view of R. Hisda? It is written, 'All my bones shall say, Lord, who is like you' (Ps. 35:10)."

XXV.

A.   It has been stated on Amoraic authority:

B.   As to a stench coming from some tangible source [Simon],

C.   R. Huna said, "One gets four cubits away from it and recites the Shema."

D.   And R. Hisda said, "One gets four cubits away from the place at which the stench ceases and recites the Shema."

E.   There is a teaching on Tannaite authority in accord with the view of R. Hisda:

F.   A person should not recite the Shema in the presence of excrement of man, dogs, pigs, chickens, or of a garbage dump that stinks.

G.   And if it was a place ten handbreadths high or ten handbreadths deep, one may sit beside it and recite the Shema.

H.   If not, he should get out of sight of it.

I.   And so is the rule for reciting the Prayer.

J.   As to a stench that comes from some tangible source, one gets four cubits away from the place of the stench and recites the Shema.

K.   Said Raba, "The law does not accord with the foregoing statement on Tannaite authority but rather in accord with that which follows:

L.   "A person should not recite the Shema in the presence of excrement of man, dogs, or pigs when he puts skins in them [for tanning]."

M.   People asked R. Sheshet, "What about a stench that comes from no tangible source [that is, a fart]?"

N.   He said to them, "Take a look at the mats in the school house. Some are sleeping [and farting], while others are studying.

O.   "And that ruling applies to words of Torah [which one may continue to recite]. But as to the recitation of the Shema, one may not [go ahead in the presence of such a stench].

P.   "And as to studying the Torah, the rule that one may continue studying in the presence of a stench applies only to the fart of one's fellow, but as to one's own fart, he may not [continue studying but must wait until the stench passes]."

XXVI.

A.   It has been stated on Amoraic authority:

B.   As to excrement that is passing by [in a dung-cart].

C.   Abayye said, "It is permitted to recite the Shema [while the stench is going by]."

D. Raba said, "It is forbidden to recite the Shema."

E. Said Abayye, "On what basis do I make this statement? As it we have learned in the Mishnah:

F. "If an unclean [bit of corpse-matter] is located still under a tree and a clean person is passing by, the latter becomes unclean. If the clean person is standing still under a tree and [a bit of corpse-matter, which is] unclean [and transmits uncleanness through overshadowing] is carried by, the clean person remains clean. But if the corpse-matter was left to stand still [under the same tree], the clean person becomes unclean. So too is the rule for a stone afflicted with a nega [M. Neg. 13:7]."

G. And Raba may reply to you, "The rule in that case is such because the matter depends upon what is permanently set in place, for it is written, 'He shall dwell alone, outside of the camp shall his dwelling be' (Lev. 13:46). But in this case, the All-Merciful has said, 'Therefore your camp shall be holy' (Deut. 23:15), and that stipulation has not been met."

XXVII.

A. Said R. Papa, "A pig's snout is in the category of excrement that is being carried by."

B. That is self-evident.

C. No, it was necessary to make that point explicit.

D. [Why? It pertains] even though the pig is coming up out of the river.

XXVIII.

A. Said R. Judah, "In a case of doubt concerning the presence of excrement, the doubt is resolved in favor of prohibition [of recitation of the Shema]. In a case of doubt concerning the presence of urine, the doubt is resolved in favor of permission [to recite the Shema]."

B. There are those who report the saying as follows:

C. Said R. Judah, "In a case of doubt concerning the presence of excrement, if it is in the house, it is resolved in favor of permission, and if it is on the dung heap, it is resolved in favor of prohibition. In a case of doubt concerning the presence of urine, even if it is on the dung heap, it is resolved in favor of permission."

D. The foregoing principle accords with the teaching of R. Hamnuna.

E. For R. Hamnuna said, "[The Torah] has prohibited [reciting the Shema] only in the very presence of an actual stream [of urine]."

F. And it accords with what R. Jonathan said, for R. Jonathan contrasted verses, "It is written, 'You shall have a place also outside of the camp, to which you shall go out' (Deut. 23:13), and it also is written, 'And you shall have a paddle.. and you shall cover what excretes from you' (Deut. 23:14). [Thus in the one case one has to leave the camp, in the other he has merely to bury excretions]."

G. "How so? The one speaks of defecation, the other of urine."

H. "Therefore in the case of urine the Torah has prohibited [reciting the Shema] only in the very presence of the actual stream of urine.

I.   "But as to what falls to the ground, that is permitted [as a location in which one may recite the Shema], and it is rabbis who have made a decree against reciting the Shema in that case. But the decree pertains only to where such urine is assuredly present. Where it is merely a matter of doubt, rabbis made no such decree."

J.   And in the case in which urine is assuredly present, to what extent [must urine be present for the recitation of the Shema to be prohibited]?

K.   Said R. Judah said Samuel, "So long as the urine remains moist."

L.   And so said Rabbah bar bar Hana said R. Yohanan, "So long as the urine remains moist."

M.   And so said Ulla, "So long as the urine remains moist."

N.   Geniba said in the name of Rab, "So long as the mark of the urine can be made out."

O.   Said R. Joseph, "May the master of Geniba forgive him. If in the case of excrement, R. Judah said Rab said, 'Once the surface of the excrement has dried up, it is permitted [to recite the Shema,] is there any question about the matter of urine?"

P.   Said Abayye to him, "Why rely on that version of his view? Rely on this version:

Q.   "For Rabbah bar R. Huna said Rab said, 'In the case of excrement, even if it is as hard as a potsherd, it is still forbidden [to recite the Shema in its vicinity]' [Hence the criticism of Joseph need not stand at all.]"

R.   And what is the definition of excrement as hard as a potsherd?

S.   Said Rabbah bar bar Hana said R. Yohanan, "[If] it does not break even when one throws it [onto the ground], [it is not as hard as a potsherd]."

T.   And there are those who say, "[If] one rolls it along the ground and it does not break, [it is not as hard as a potsherd]."

U.   Said Rabina, "I was standing before R. Judah of Difti and saw a piece of excrement. He said to me, 'Examine it to see whether or not the surface has hardened.'"

V.   Some say he said to him, "See if it has formed cracks."

W.   What is the upshot of the matter?

X.   It has been stated on Amoraic authority:

Y.   Excrement like potsherd:

Z.   Amemar said, "It is forbidden [to recite the Shema in its presence]."

AA. And Mar Zutra said, "It is permitted."

BB. Said Raba, "The decided law is that it is forbidden to recite the Shema in the presence of excrement as hard as potsherd, and as to urine, so long as the urine is yet moist, [it is forbidden to recite the Shema in its presence]."

CC. People objected by citing the following: "As to urine, so long as it is moist, it is forbidden [to recite the Shema in its vicinity]. Once it is absorbed by the ground or dried up, it is permitted to do so."

DD. Now is it not the case that we draw an analogy between the urine's being absorbed and its drying up? Just as, in the case of urine's drying up, it is no longer to be discerned, so, if it is absorbed, it no longer can be discerned. In that case, if it still can be discerned, it is prohibited to recite the Shema in its vicinity, and that is the case even though the urine is not moist any more! [So the rule at hand bears the implication contrary to the decision cited by Raba].

EE. But by your own reasoning, I may call attention to the opening clause: So long as it is moist is the time that it is forbidden to recite the Shema. Lo, if the mark of the urine yet is to be discerned, it is permitted to recite the Shema.

FF. Accordingly, from the cited passage no inferences may be drawn.

XXIX.

A. May I propose that we have at hand a dispute among Tannaite authorities:

B. As to a utensil from which urine has been poured out, it is forbidden to recite the Shema in its vicinity. But as to the urine itself which has been poured out, once the urine has been absorbed by the ground, it is permitted to recite the Shema. But while the urine has not yet been absorbed into the ground, it is forbidden to recite the Shema.

C. R. Yose says, "So long as the urine is moist [it is forbidden to recite the Shema]."

D. What is the sense of "absorbed" and what is the sense of "not absorbed" to which the former of the two authorities makes reference?

E. If I should say, it is "absorbed" in the sense that the urine is not any longer moist and "not absorbed" in the sense that the urine is yet moist, and R. Yose takes the view that so long as the urine is moist is the time at which it is forbidden to recite the Shema in the vicinity of the urine, while if the presence of the urine is to be discerned [but it is not moist], it is permitted to recite the Shema, then, well, that is the position of the first of the two authorities in any event!

F. Rather, the sense of "absorbed" must be that the presence of the urine is not to be discerned, and "not absorbed" means that the presence of the urine is to be discerned.

G. Then R. Yose's contribution is to make the point that so long as the urine is moist it is forbidden to recite the Shema, but if the urine is to be discerned [but it is not moist], it is permitted to recite the Shema.

H. No [that interpretation of the cited passage is not correct]. All parties concur that, so long as the urine is moist, it is forbidden to recite the Shema. If the presence of urine is to be discerned, it is permitted to recite the Shema.

I. [25B] But here at issue between the two authorities is a case in which the urine must be wet enough to wet down something else. [Simon, p. 152, n. 3: Only in this case does the first Tanna forbid, but R. Yose is more stringent].

XXX.

A. If one went down to immerse himself, [if he can come up from the pool and cover himself and recite the Shema before the sun rises, he should come up and cover himself and recite it] [M. 3:5E-G]:

B. May one propose that the Tannaite authority who is anonymous accords with the view of R. Eliezer, who said, "[One recites the Shema] until sunrise" [M. Ber. 1:2]?

C. You may even hold that it is in accord with the view of R. Joshua but framed in terms of the practice of the oldtimers.

D. For R. Yohanan said, "The oldtimers would complete the recitation of the Shema prior to sunrise."

XXXI.

A.   And if not, he should cover himself in the water and recite [the Shema] [M. 3:5H]:

B.   But lo, his heart is in sight of his sexual parts!

C.   Said R. Eleazar, or, some say, R. Aha bar Abba bar Aha in the name of Our Rabbi, "The authorities have taught the passage with reference to cloudy water, which is in the category of solid earth,

D.   "so that his heart should not be in sight of his sexual parts."

XXXII.

A.   Our rabbis have taught on Tannaite authority:

B.   In the case of clear water one may crouch down up to his neck and recite the Shema.

C.   And some say, "He stirs them up with his foot."

D.   But in the view of the fi st Tannaite authority, lo, his heart will be in sight of his sexual parts!

E.   He takes the view that if his heart is in sight of his sexual parts, it is nonetheless permitted to recite the Shema.

F.   But lo, his heel is in sight of his sexual parts.

G.   He takes the view that if his heel is in sight of his sexual parts, it is permitted to recite the Shema.

H.   It has been stated on Amoraic authority:

I.   If one's heel is in sight of his sexual parts, it is permitted to recite the Shema.

J.   If it is actually touching,

K.   Abayye said, "It is forbidden to recite the Shema.

L.   And Raba said, "It is permitted to do so."

M.   That is how R. Zebid repeated this passage.

N.   By contrast, this is the version of R. Hinena, son of R. Iqa:

O.   If the heel is touching, all parties concur that it is forbidden to recite the Shema.

P.   If it is within sight.

Q.   Abayye said, "It is forbidden to recite the Shema."

R.   Raba said, "It is permitted. The Torah was not given over to [disembodied] angels."

S.   The decided law is that if it touches it is forbidden, but if it is within sight, it is permitted.

XXXIV.

A.   Said Raba, "As to excrement seen through a mirror, it is permitted to recite the Shema in it presence.

B.   "If he sees sexual parts in that way, he must not recite the Shema in its presence."

C.   "If one sees excrement through a mirror, it is permitted to recite the Shema in its presence," because the issue of excrement depends on the matter's being covered up, and lo, this is covered up.

D.   "If one sees sexual parts in that way, he must not recite the Shema in its presence," because "That he see no unseemly thing in you" (Deut. 23:15) is what the All-Merciful has said, and here it is seen.

XXXIV.

A.   Said Abayye, "Excrement in any volume at all one may annul with a bit of spit."

B.   Said Raba, "It must be thick spit."

C.   Said Raba, "If there is a bit of excrement in a hole, one puts his sandal over it and recites the Shema."

D.   Mar, son of Rabina, asked, "If there is excrement clinging to one's sandal, what is the rule?"

E.   The question stands.

XXXV.

A.   Said R. Judah, "It is forbidden to recite the Shema in the presence of a naked gentile."

B.   Why specify a naked gentile? It is also forbidden to do so in the presence of a naked Israelite.

C.   It is self-evident to him that it is forbidden to do so before a naked Israelite. The question was pressing only with regard to a gentile.

D.   What might you have maintained? Since it is written in their regard, "Whose flesh is as the flesh of asses and whose issue is as the issue of horses" (Ez. 23:20), I might have supposed that the gentile is in the status of a mere ass.

E.   So we are informed that they too fall into the category of sexuality.

F.   For it is written, "And the sexual parts of their father they did not see" (Gen. 9:23).

XXXVI.

A.   But he should cover himself neither in foul water nor in water used for soaking flax unless he has poured some fresh water in it [M. 3:5I-J]:

B.   How much water does a person have to keep pouring in?!

C.   Rather, this is the sense of the passage:

D.   One should under no circumstances cover himself either in foul water or in water used for soaking flax.

E.   And as to urine, one may do so only if he pours fresh water in; then he may recite the Shema.

XXXVII.

A.   Our rabbis have taught on Tannaite authority:

B.   How much water should one pour in? Any volume whatsoever.

C.   R. Zakkai says, "A quarter-log of water."

D.   Said R. Nahman, "There is a dispute in a case in which the water is poured in at the end [after the urine is there], but if the water is there first [before urine], then any amount of water will do."

E.   R. Joseph said, "The dispute concerns the volume of water that must be present to begin with. But if the urine is there first and then the water is put in, all parties concur that it must be quarter-log."

F.   Said R. Joseph to his servant, "Bring me a quarter-log of water, in accord with the view of R. Zakkai."

XXXVIII.

A.   Our rabbis have taught on Tannaite authority:

B.   As to a chamber pot for excrement and a piss-pot, it is forbidden to recite the Shema in their presence, and that is the case even though there is nothing in them.

C.   As to urine itself, one may recite the Shema in its presence only if one will put water in.

D.   And how much water must he put in?

E.   Any amount of water.

F.   R. Zakkai says, "A quarter log of water."

G.   The foregoing rule applies whether the chamber-pot or piss-pot is located in front of the bed or behind the bed.

H.   Rabban Simeon b. Gamaliel says, "If it is behind the bed, one may recite the Shema, If it is in front of the bed, one may not recite the Shema, unless he goes four cubits away from the pot, and he may then recite the Shema.

I.   R. Simeon b. Eleazar says, "Even in a room a hundred cubits wide, one may recite the Shema only if he removes the pots or if he puts them under the bed" [cf. T. Ber. 2:16E-L].

J.   The following question was raised:

K.   What is the sense of [Simeon b. Gamaliel's] statement?

L.   Did he mean that if it is behind the bed, one may recite the Shema forthwith, while if it is in front of the bed, he has to go a distance of four cubits and then he may recite the Shema?

M.   Or perhaps this is the sense of his statement: If it is behind the bed, he must go a distance of four cubits before reciting the Shema. If it is before the bed, he may not recite the Shema at all.

N.   Come and take note, for it has been taught on Tannaite authority:

O.   R. Simeon b. Eleazar says, "If it is behind the bed one may recite the Shema forthwith. If it is in front of the bed, one has to go a distance of four cubits [before reciting the Shema]."

P.   Rabban Simeon b. Gamaliel says, "Even if the room is a hundred cubits, one should not recite the Shema unless he removes them or leaves them under the bed."

Q.   That answers our questions, but the Tannaite traditions contradict one another.

R.   Reverse the [names] in the latter of the two statements.

S.   Why reverse the names in the latter version, rather reverse the names in the former of the two versions!

T.   In whose opinion have you heard it said that the whole of a room may be constituted by four cubits [which accounts for the instruction to go four cubits away from the piss-pot]?

U.   It is R. Simeon b. Eleazar.

XXXIX.

A.   Said R. Joseph, "I asked R. Huna as follows:

B.   "In the case of a bed lower than three handbreadths in height it is self-evident to me that it is as if it were attached to the ground. [Whatever is located underneath it is as if it were buried in the ground.] In the case of one that is three, four, five, six, seven, eight, or nine high, what is the law?

C.   He said to him, "I do not know. But there is no question in my mind as to the status of one that is ten handbreadths high."

D.   Said Abayye, "You did well not to ask about one ten handbreadths high, for any domain that is ten handbreadths above the ground constitutes a distinct domain."

E.   Said Raba, "The decided law is that a bed three handbreadths high is regarded as attached to the ground. One that is ten handbreadths high constitutes a distinct domain. As to a bed that is from three to ten handbreadths high, this is the question that R. Joseph addressed to R. Huna, and he did not know the answer."

XL.

A.   Said Rab, "The law is in accord with the view of R. Simeon b. Eleazar, and so did Bali say."

B.   Said R. Jacob, son of the daughter of Samuel, "The law is in accord with R. Simeon b. Eleazar."

C.   And Raba said, "The law is not in accord with R. Simeon b. Eleazar."

XLI.

A.   R. Ahai made a match for his son with a daughter of the household of R. Isaac bar Samuel bar Marta. He went into the marriage canopy but nothing came of it. [The father] went in to see what was going on and spied a scroll of the Torah lying there.

B.   He said to the people, "How now! Had I not come in you would have endangered my son's life."

C.   For it has been taught on Tannaite authority:

D.   "As to a room in which a scroll of the Torah or phylacteries are located, it is forbidden to have sexual relations in such a room unless one removes them or places them so that one utensil is put away inside another utensil."

E.   Said Abayye, "That rule applies only in the case of a utensil that is not meant to serve for those objects in particular.

F.   "But in the case of a utensil that is meant to serve for those objects in particular, even ten utensils are deemed a single utensil [and no better than one]."

G.   Said Raba, "A covering [26A] over a chest is in the status of a receptable within a receptable."

XLII.

A.   Said R. Joshua b. Levi, "For a scroll of the Torah it is necessary to make a partition ten handbreadths high."

B.   Mar Zutra happened to come to the house of R. Ashi. He saw that in the place in which Mar, son of R. Ashi, slept, there was a scroll of the Torah, for which a partition ten handbreadths high had been made.

C.   He said to them, "In accord with whom have you acted? Is it in accord with R. Joshua b. Levi?

D.   "Granted that the rule applies as R. Joshua b. Levi stated it in a case in which one
     has no other room. But the master has another room [for the scroll of the Torah, so
     it should not be kept here anyhow]."

E.   He said to him, "It never entered my mind."

XLIII.

A.   And how far should one distance himself from them and from excrement? Four
     cubits [M. 3:5K-L].

B.   Said Raba said R. Sehorah said R. Huna, "The law has been taught only if one leaves
     the water behind. But if [the water] is in front of him, he has to go such a distance
     that it is out of sight."

XLVI.

A.   The same rule [as at M. 3:5K-L] applies to reciting the Prayer.

B.   Is that the case? And lo, Rafram bar Papa said R. Hisda said, "A man may stand
     facing a privy [within four cubits] and say his prayer."

C.   With what circumstance do we deal [in that saying]?

D.   With a privy in which there is no excrement.

E.   Can that be so? And has not R. Joseph bar Hanina said, "A privy of which they
     spoke is one even though it has no excrement, and a bathhouse of which they spoke
     is one even though no one is in it."

F.   Rather, with what circumstance do we deal here? It is with a new one. [In such a
     case, one may recite the Prayer nearby.]

G.   But that is exactly what was troubling Rabina: "If one has designated a place for a
     privy, what is the law? Does the matter of designation apply or not?"

H.   When Rabina raised that question, it concerned standing nearby to say the Prayer.
     But as to saying the Prayer while facing it, he did not raise the question, [since he
     knew that one might do so if he stood four cubits away].

I.   Said Raba, "The privies built by the Persians, even though they contain excrement,
     are as if they were sealed up [since the excrement rolled down into a hole]."

Once more we deal with a protracted construction, in which the exegesis and
amplification of the Mishnah do not define the whole of discourse. Let us begin by listing
those units of discourse that provide word for word explanation of the Mishnah-paragraph: I, XXX-XXXIII, XXXVI-XXXVIII, and XLIII. The following, further, amplify or
extend discussion of the theme of the Mishnah-paragraph: II, III, IV; on appropriate
circumstances in which to recite the Shema: XIII-XV (continued at XVI); on appropriate
conduct in reciting the Prayer: XVIII-XX; the Shema again: XXI-XXIX, XXXIV-XXXV.
The following units of discourse apply the principle expressed in the Mishnah-paragraph to
cases separate and distinct from those at hand: V-IX (proper respect for phylacteries in
connection with performance of natural functions), X-XII (proper respect for phylacteries
in general); and XXXIX-XLII (proper respect for a scroll of the Torah). What the Talmud
does, therefore, is only two things: expound the principle and details of the Mishnah and
amplify the principle of the Mishnah by applying it to other closely relevant cases. The

protracted character of the discussion should not, therefore obscure the purposeful and well-proportioned plan for exposition of principle and theme.

3:6

A.   A man who has produced a flux [in line with Lev. 15] who then had a seminal emission,

B.   a menstruating woman who discharged semen,

C.   and a woman who during sexual relations produced menstrual blood [all of whom by definition are unclean without respect to the presence of semen,

D.   must immerse [in a proper ritual pool].

E.   R. Judah exempts [them from having to do so, since they are in any event cultically unclean].

I.

A.   The following question was raised: If one who had a seminal emission produced flux [to indicate uncleanness in the classification of Lev. 15], what is the rule so far as R. Judah is concerned? [That is, the opposite of A's entry].

B.   When R. Judah declared the man [unclean by reason of flux who had a seminal emission] to be exempt from the requirement of immersing, it was because to begin with he was not subject to immersion in any event. [He would remain unclean even after the immersion so there would be no reason to require immersion on account of the uncleanness of the semen.]

C.   But one who has had a seminal emission who then produced flux, who to begin with is subject to immersion [which can remove the uncleanness produced by the seminal emission], would [in Judah's view] be liable.

D.   Or perhaps in his view there is no distinction to be drawn.

E.   Come and take note of the following: A woman who during sexual relations produced menstrual blood must immerse. R. Judah exempts [M. 3:6A-B].

F.   Now a woman who during sexual relations produced a drop of menstrual blood is in the category of one who has produced a seminal emission and then produced flux, and R. Judah exempts one in that category. [Accordingly, the answer is as specified at B.]

G.   That proves it.

H.   R. Hiyya explicitly repeated the matter on Tannaite authority in exactly that manner: "One who has had a seminal emission who then produced flux has to immerse, but R. Judah exempts [him from having to do so]."

The Talmud clarifies a secondary question presented by the Mishnah's rule.

CHAPTER FOUR
BAVLI BERAKHOT CHAPTER FOUR

A.   The morning Prayer [may be done] until midday.

B.   R. Judah says, "Until four hours [of the day]."

C.   The afternoon recitation of the Prayer [may be done] until the evening.

D.   R. Judah says, "Until mid-afternoon."

E.   The recitation of the Prayer in the evening has no fixed rule.

F.   And [the recitation] of the additional Prayers [on Sabbath and festival days] [may be done] throughout the day.

G.   R. Judah says, "Until seven hours [of the day]."

I.

A.   An objection was raised [to the statement that the recitation of the Prayer in the morning must be done by midday]:

B.   The religious duty governing [recitation of the Shema] must be carried out at dawn, so that one may juxtapose redemption to the Prayer and turn out to recite the Prayer by day [just after daybreak].

C.   When that passage was repeated on Tannaite authority, it concerned only the old-timers.

D.   For R. Yohanan said, "The old-timers would complete [the recitation of Shema] with dawn, but everyone must do so by mid-day."

II.

A.   And [may people not say it] later [in the day]?

B.   And has not R. Mari, son of R. Huna, son of R. Jeremiah bar Abba, said R. Yohanan said, "If one made an error and did not say the Prayer in the evening [when he should have done so], he says the Prayer at dawn two times [once for the Prayer he failed to recite in the evening, the other time for the dawn]. If he missed at dawn, he says the Prayer twice in the afternoon"? [So why can people not say the Prayer past midday?]

C.   Indeed someone may say the Prayer all day long. But if he does so by midday, he gets the reward for saying the Prayer at the proper time. If he says it thereafter, the reward he gets is for saying the Prayer, but the reward for saying the Prayer at the proper time he does not get.

III.

A.   The following question was raised:

B.   If one made an error and did not say the Prayer in the afternoon, what is the law as to his saying the Prayer in the evening two times?

C.   If you wish, we may reply in the following way:

D.   If one made an error and did not say the Prayer in the evening, he may say the Prayer in the morning two times, for it remains a single day, as it is written, "And there was evening, and there was morning, one day" (Gen. 1:5).

E.   But here, the recitation of the Prayer is to serve as a counterpart to the making of an offering. Since the day on which [the offering was to be made] has passed, the offering for that day is annulled. [So one would not recite the Prayer twice to make it up under the specified circumstances].

F.   Or perhaps, since the recitation of the Prayer is to seek divine mercy, whenever a person wants, he may go ahead and say the Prayer.

G.   [As to choosing between those two approaches to the problem], come and take note of the following:

H.   Said R. Huna bar Judah said R. Isaac said R. Yohanan, "If one made a mistake and did not say the Prayer in the afternoon, he says the Prayer twice in the evening, and in such a procedure we do not invoke the principle that if the day on which an offering is to be made has passed, the requirement of making an offering for that day has passed."

I.   An objection was raised: "That which is crooked cannot be made straight, and that which is wanting cannot be numbered" (Qoh. 1:15):

J.   "That which is crooked cannot be made straight": this speaks of one who has failed to recite the Shema in the evening or in the morning, or the Prayer in the evening or in the morning.

K.   "And that which is wanting cannot be numbered": This speaks of one whose friends formed an association to carry out a religious duty in common, and who was not counted with them [so did not get the share of the reward for the deed].

L.   Said R. Isaac said R. Yohanan, "With what sort of case [J] do we deal in fact? It is one who deliberately abrogated the matter."

M.   Said R. Ashi, "Take note of the wording of the passage, which is, 'failed,' and not merely 'erred.'"

N.   That proves the case.

IV.

A.   [26B] Our rabbis have taught on Tannaite authority:

B.   If one made a mistake and did not recite the Prayer in the afternoon on the eve of the Sabbath [Friday], he recites the Prayer on Sabbath night two times.

B.   If he made a mistake and did not recite the Prayer at the afternoon of the Sabbath, he recites the Prayer on Saturday night at the end of the Sabbath two times.

C.   [In the recitation of the Prayer] on the weekday [after the Sabbath has ended], he says the Prayer of Division [between the Sabbath and the weekday] in the first of the two recitations of the Prayer [which he is reciting to make up for the one he missed on the Sabbath], but he does not recite the Prayer of Division in the second recitation of the Prayer.

D.   But if he recited the Prayer of Division in the second of the two recitations of the Prayer and not in the first, that which he recited in the second recitation of the Prayer goes to his credit, while the first recitation does not go to his credit at all.

E.   Does this then imply that, since he has not said the Prayer of Division in the first recitation of the Prayer, it is as if he did not recite the Prayer at all, and we require him to go back and recite it?

F.   Then the following is to be raised in objection to this statement:

G.   If one made a mistake and did not recite the prayer concerning the miracle of rain in the prayer on the resurrection of the dead [in the recitation of the Prayer], but instead prayed for [rain] in the prayer on the blessing of the years, [the authorities] make him go back and repeat the Prayer properly.

H.   But if he inserted the Prayer of Division in the paragraph, "Who graciously grants knowledge," he is not made to repeat the matter, because he can say the Prayer of Division over wine [as against D].

I.   This assuredly presents a contradiction [to the proposition specified above, at D].

V.

A.   It has been stated on Amoraic authority:

B.   R. Yose b. R. Hanina said, "As to the recitation of Prayer, the patriarchs ordained them."

C.   R. Joshua b. Levi said, "As to the recitation of the Prayers, they were ordained as the counterpart of the daily whole-offering."

D.   It has been taught on Tannaite authority in accord with R. Yose b. R. Hanina, and it has been taught on Tannaite authority in accord with R. Joshua b. Levi.

E.   It has been taught on Tannaite authority in accord with R. Yose b. R. Hanina:

F.   Abraham ordained the recitation of the Prayer in the morning, as it is said, "And Abraham got up early in the morning to the place where he had stood" (Gen. 19:27), and "standing" refers only to reciting the Prayer, as it is said, "Then Phineas stood up and prayed" (Ps. 106:30).

G.   Isaac ordained the recitation of the Prayer in the afternoon, as it is said, "And Isaac went out to meditate in the field at eventide" (Gen. 24:63), and "meditation" refers to prayer, as it is said, "A prayer of the afflicted when he faints and pours out his meditation before the Lord" (Ps. 203:1).

H.   Jacob ordained the recitation of the Prayer in the evening, as it is said, "And he lighted upon the place" (Gen. 28:11), and "lighting" refers only to prayer, as it is said, "Therefore do not pray for this people nor lift up pray nor cry for them nor light upon me in their regard" (Jer. 7:16).

I.   And it has been taught on Tannaite authority in accord with the view of R. Joshua b. Levi:

J.   Why did they say, The morning Prayer [may be recited] until midday [M. Ber. 4:1A]?

K.   For so the daily morning sacrifice was offered until midday.

L.   R. Judah says, "[It may be offered] until the fourth hour [M. Ber. 4:1B] for so the daily morning sacrifice was offered until the fourth hour."

M.   Why did they say, The afternoon Prayer [may be recited] until the evening [M. Ber. 4:1C]?

N.   For so the daily afternoon sacrifice was offered until the evening.

O.   R. Judah says, "Until the mid-afternoon [M. Ber. 4:1D] for so the daily afternoon sacrifice was offered until the mid-afternoon."

P.   And why did they say, "The evening Prayer had no fixed time" [M. Ber. 4:1E]?

Q.   For so the limbs and fat pieces not burned up in the evening were offered all night.

R.   And why did they say, "The additional Prayer [may be recited] all day" [M. Ber. 4:1F]?

S.   For so the additional sacrifice was offered all day.

T.   R. Judah says, "Until the seventh hour [M. Ber. 4:1G], for so the additional sacrifice was offered until the seventh hour."

U.   And what is [considered] the greater part of the afternoon?

V.   From six and one-half hours onward [i.e., from 12:30 p.m., since daylight is reckoned at 6 a.m.]

W.   When is the mid-afternoon?

X.   [At] the eleventh hour less a quarter [-hour] [i.e., 4:45p.m.] [T. Ber. 3:1B-I].

VI.

A.   The following question was raised: When [at M. 4:1D] R. Judah referred to mid-afternoon, did he mean the former afternoontide or the latter afternoontide? [Simon, p. 161, n. 4: Does he in his statement in the Mishnah mean midway between 12:30 and 6 or between 3:30 and 6?]

B.   Come and take note, for it has been taught on Tannaite authority:

C.   R. Judah says, "They spoke of the middle of the latter afternoontide, which is eleven hours less a quarter" [Simon, p. 161, n. 5: midway between 9 1/2 hours and 12].

VII.

A.   Does this then refute the position of R. Yose b. R. Hanina? [If the patriarchs ordained the time of reciting the prayers, why should there be any relevance to the time of sacrifice at all?]

B.   R. Yose b. R. Hanina may say to you, "In any event I maintain that the patriarchs instituted the recitation of the Prayers. It then was the rabbis who went and joined them to the matter of the sacrifices."

C.   If you do not maintain this view, in the view of R. Yose b. R. Hanina, who ordained the requirement of reciting an Additional Prayer?

D.   What happened was that the patriarches ordained the requirement of reciting the Prayers, and rabbis came along and joined them to the matter of the sacrifices.

VIII.

A.   R. Judah says, "Until four hours [of the day]" [M. Ber. 4:1B]:

B. The question was raised: Is it measured inclusive of the specified time at hand or exclusive of that time? [Simon, p. 161, n. 9: Does he mean the beginning or the end of the fourth hour?]

C. Come and take note of the following:

D. R. Judah says, "Until mid-afternoon" [M. 4:1D].

E. Now, if you maintain that the meaning is up to, but not including the specified hour, then we can understand what is at issue between R. Judah and rabbis [Simon, p. 161-2, n. 10: assuming that Judah meant the middle of the latter afternoontide, i.e., eleven hours less a quarter].

F. But if you maintain that the meaning is up to and including the specified hour, the view of R. Judah [27A] is the same as that of rabbis [at C].

G. Then what is the proposed conclusion? That the sense is up to, but not including, the specified hour? Then I point to the concluding part of the same passage:

H. And the recitation of the additional Prayers [on Sabbath and festival days] may be done throughout the day. R. Judah says, "Until seven hours" [M. 4:1F-G].

I. And it has been taught on Tannaite authority:

J. If a person had the choice of saying two different recitations of the Prayer, one for the Additional Prayer, the other for the Afternoon, he says the Prayer for the afternoon and afterward says the Additional Prayer, for the obligation to say the former is perpetual [applying every day], and the obligation to say the latter is not perpetual [applying as it does only on Sabbaths and festivals]. R. Judah says, "One says the Additional Prayer and afterward the Prayer for the afternoon, for the time of the one passes [after seven hours], and the time of the other does not pass [but continues all day long, up to eleven hours less a quarter]."

K. Now if you take the view that the sense of "up to" is "up to and including the specified hour," you can find a case in which one may have to recite two distinct Prayers at the same time.

L. But if you take the view that the sense of "up to" is "up to but not including the specified hour," how can you find a case in which one has to recite two Prayers at the same time? For once the time for reciting the Prayer for the afternoon has come, the time for reciting the Additional Prayer will have lapsed.

M. What is the conclusion then? That the sense of "Until" is "until and including the specified hour"?

N. But there is, then, the difficulty introduced in connection with the opening clause, specifically, what difference is there between the view of R. Judah and that of rabbis?

O. [The solution to that problem is now given.] Do you, in fact, maintain that the sense of "mid-afternoon" is the middle of the latter afternoontide? It is the middle of the former afternoontide.

P. This, then, is the sense of the matter: When the former afternoon tide passes and the latter afternoon tide comes? It is at the end of eleven hours less a quarter.

Q. Said R. Nahman, "We too have learned in Tannaite teaching:

R.   "R. Judah b. Baba gave testimony concerning five matters:

S.   "that they instruct women married while minors to exercise the right of refusal;

T.   "that they permit a woman to remarry on the testimony of a single witness [that her husband has died];

U.   "that a chicken was stoned in Jerusalem because it had killed a human being;

V.   "concerning wine forty-days old, that it may be poured out as a libation-offering on the altar of the Temple;

W.   "and concerning the morning daily whole offering, that it is offered at the fourth hour" [M. Eduyyot 6:1].

X.   That final statement proves [that, in Judah's view, the word "until" encompasses the time to which reference is made, that is, up to the end, not the beginning, of four hours].

Y.   It does indeed prove it.

Z.   Said R. Kahana, "The decided law accords with R. Judah, since we have learned in the Mishnah-tractate containing select laws [namely, tractate Eduyyot] that the law is stated by him."

IX.

A.   And concerning the morning daily whole offering, that it is offered at the fourth hour [M. Ed. 6:1]:

B.   Who stands behind the Tannaite teaching that follows?

C.   "And as the sun got hot it melted" (Ex. 16:21) [with reference to the manna]. This was at four hours.

D.   You say it was at four hours. But could it have been only at six hours?

E.   When it says, "In the heat of the day," (Gen. 18:1) lo, reference is made to six hours. So how can I interpret the statement, "And as the sun got hot it melted" (Ex. 16:21)? It must mean to speak of four hours [of the day].

F.   Now [as we started to ask earlier], in accord with whom is the statement at hand? It cannot be either R. Judah or rabbis.

G.   It cannot be R. Judah, since, in his view, the time "up to four hours" also is still morning. [Simon, p. 163, n. 8: It says that the Israelites gathered the manna every morning. Why then had they stopped at this hour if it was still morning?]

H.   It cannot be rabbis, since the time up to mid-day [six hours] still falls into the category of morning.

I.   If you wish, I shall propose that it is R. Judah, and if you wish, I shall propose that it is rabbis.

J.   If you wish, I shall explain that it is rabbis. Scripture has said, "Morning by morning" (Ex. 16:21), thus dividing the morning into two [and the Israelites gathered the manna in the first of the two periods].

K.   If you wish, I shall explain that it is R. Judah, for the additional reference to the morning serves to indicate that the people pushed up the time of gathering by one hour.

L.   But all parties, in any event, concur that the statement, "As the sun waxed hot it melted" (Ex. 16:21) speaks of four hours. On what basis?

M.   Said R. Aha bar Jacob, "Scripture has said, 'As the sun waxed hot, it melted' (Ex. 16:21). At what time is the sun hot and the shade yet cool? One has to say that it is at four hours."

X.

A.   The afternoon recitation of the Prayer may be done until the evening [M. 4:1C]:

B.   Said R. Hisda to R. Isaac, "In that other passage, R. Kahana said, 'The decided law accords with R. Judah, since we have learned in the Mishnah-tractate containing select laws that the law is stated by him.'

C.   "Here what is the law?"

D.   He remained silent and said nothing in reply.

E.   Said R. Hisda, "Let us see. Since Rab says the Prayer for the Sabbath on Friday afternoon while it is still daylight it must follow that the law accords with R. Judah. [Simon, p. 164, n. 1: After the middle of the afternoontide, the afternoon Prayer can no longer be said, and evening begins.]"

F.   To the contrary, since R. Huna and rabbis did not say the Prayer until night, it follows that the law does not follow the view of R. Judah.

G.   Now since it has not been stated that the law followed either this party or that party, it must follow that one who acts in accord with one authority acts properly, and one who acts in accord with the other party acts properly.

XI.

A.   Rab came to the house of Geniba and said the Prayer of the Sabbath on the eve of the Sabbath [on Friday afternoon]. R. Jeremiah bar Abba was saying the Prayer behind Rab. Rab completed saying the Prayer but did not interrupt the recitation of the Prayer by R. Jeremiah [by not resuming his seat].

B.   Three things are to be learned from the incident.

C.   First of all, the incident yields that fact that a person says the Prayer for the Sabbath on the eve of the Sabbath [Friday afternoon, before dark].

D.   It further follows that a disciple says the Prayer while standing behind his master.

E.   And it follows that it is forbidden to cross in front of people who are saying the Prayer.

XII.

A.   That further supports the view of R. Joshua b. Levi.

B.   For R. Joshua b. Levi said, "It is forbidden to pass in front of people who are saying the Prayer."

C.   Is that so? And lo, R. Ammi and R. Assi would pass [in that way].

D.   R. Ammi and R. Assi would pass outside of a space of four cubits [before those who were saying the Prayer].

E.   And how did R. Jeremiah act in this way? And lo, said R. Judah said Rab, "A person should never say the Prayer [27B] either in front of his master or behind his master."

F.   And it has been taught on Tannaite authority:

G.   R. Eliezer says, "He who says the Prayer behind his master, he who greets his master, he who returns a greeting to his master, he who differs from the conclusion reached in session by his master, and he who says something that he has not heard directly from his master causes the Presence of God to depart from Israel."

H.   The case of R. Jeremiah is different, for he was a fellow disciple.

I.   This is in line with what R. Jeremiah bar Abba said to Rab, "Have you ceased [to work, that you now say the Prayer for the Sabbath while it is still light on Friday]?"

J.   He said to him, "Yes, I have ceased [to work]."

K.   But he did not phrase the question as, "Has the master ceased to work"?

L.   And has not R. Abin said, "One time my Master said the Prayer for the Sabbath on the eve of the Sabbath, and then he went into the bath and came out and taught us our Mishnah-chapter, while it had not yet gotten dark."

M.   Said Raba, "When he went in, it was only to perspire, and it was before the decree [not to do so]."

N.   And is that the case? And lo, Abayye permitted R. Dimi bar Livai to fumigate baskets [after saying the Sabbath prayer on Friday afternoon].

O.   That was a mistake [since it had gotten dark early, and people wrongly assumed that the Sabbath had begun, when, in fact, it had not. So once it was clear that it was yet light, Abayye permitted the work to be done.]

P.   And can one go back on an error [and resume work under such conditions]?

Q.   And lo, Abidan said, "One time the heavens grew thick with clouds. The people supposed that it had gotten dark. They entered the synagogue and said the Prayer applying to the end of the Sabbath [Saturday night after dark] on the Sabbath itself. Then the clouds scattered and the sun shone. The people came and asked Rabbi. He said, "Since they have said the Prayer, they have indeed done it once for all.'"

R.   The case of an error on the part of the community is different, for we do not impose upon the congregation unnecessary burdens [and thus Rabbi did not require the people to repeat the Prayer, but an individual would be required to do so].

XIII.

A.   Said R. Hiyya b. Abin, "Rab said the Prayer for the Sabbath on the eve of the Sabbath."

B.   R. Josiah said the Prayer for after the Sabbath on the Sabbath.

C.   Rab said the Prayer for the Sabbath on the eve of the Sabbath.

D.   Does one say the sanctification over the cup of wine or not?

E.   Come and take note:

F.   R. Nahman said Samuel said, "A person says the Prayer for the Sabbath on the eve of the Sabbath and says the sanctification of the Sabbath day over a cup of wine."

G.   And the law accords with his view.

H.   R. Josiah said the Prayer for after the Sabbath on the Sabbath.

I.   Does one say the Prayer of Division after a cup of wine or not?

J.   Come and take note:

K.   R. Judah said Samuel said, "A person says the Prayer for after the Sabbath on the Sabbath and says the Prayer of Division over a cup of wine."

XIV.

A. Said R. Zira said R. Assi said R. Eleazar said R. Hanina said Rab, "On the side of this pillar R. Ishmael, son of R. Yose, said the prayer for the Sabbath on the eve of the Sabbath."

B. When Ulla came, he said, "It was on the side of a date tree and not on the side of a column.

C. "It was not R. Ishmael, son of R. Yose, but R. Eleazar, son of R. Yose.

D. "It was not the Prayer for the Sabbath on the eve of the Sabbath, but it was the Prayer for after the Sabbath on the Sabbath."

XV.

A. The recitation of the Prayer in the evening has no fixed rule [M. 4:1E]:

B. What is the sense of the statement, "... has no fixed rule"?

C. If I say that the sense is that if one wants to say the Prayer at any time during the night, [he may do so], then the framer of the passage should state, "The recitation of the Prayer in the evening may take place throughout the night."

D. Rather, what is the sense of, "... has no fixed rule"?

E. It accords with the position of him who said, "Recitation of the Prayer in the evening is an optional matter [and not subject to legal requirement at all]."

F. For R. Judah said Samuel said, "As to the recitation of the Prayer by night, Rabban Gamaliel says, 'It is obligatory.' R. Joshua says, 'It is optional.'"

G. Said Abayye, "The decided law accords with him who says that it is obligatory."

H. And Raba said, "The decided law accords with the view of him who says it is optional."

XVI.

A. [The translation of the following unit is by Shamai Kanter, Rabban Gamaliel II: The Legal Traditions (Chico, 1980), pp. 21-24.] Our rabbis taught (M^CSH B : A certain student came before R. Joshua. He said to him, "Is the evening Tefillah optional or obligatory?" he said to him, "Optional."

B. He came before Rabban Gamaliel. He said to him, "Is the evening Tefillah optional or obligatory?" He said to him, "Obligatory."

C. He said to him, "But did not R. Joshua say, 'Optional'?" [Rabban Gamaliel] said to him, "Wait until the Shield-bearers enter the house of study."

D. When the Shield-bearers entered, the questioner stood and asked, "Is the evening Tefillah optional or obligatory?" Rabban Gamaliel said to him, "Obligatory."

E. Rabban Gamaliel said to the Sages, "Is there anyone who disagrees in this matter?" R. Joshua said to him, "No."

F. He said to him, "But did they not tell me 'Optional' in your name?" He said to him, "Joshua, stand on your feet, and let them bear witness against you."

G. R. Joshua rose to his feet and said, "If I were alive and he [the witness] were dead, the living can contradict the dead. But now that I am alive and he is alive, how can the living contradict the living?"

H.   And Rabban Gamaliel sat and expounded, and R. Joshua remained standing, until the whole assembly shouted and said to Huspit the Turegeman, "Stop!" So he stopped.

I.   They said, "How long will he go on insulting him? Last year he insulted him (on Rosh Hashanah), he insulted him in the incident of R. Sadoq (in Bekhorot), and now he has insulted him again. Let us remove him! Whom shall we appoint (NWQYM)? Shall we appoint R. Joshua? He is a party to the dispute. Shall we appoint R. Aqiba? He might be punished, since he has not ancestral merit. Let us rather appoint R. Eleazar b. 'Azariah, since he is wise, and he is rich, and he is tenth in descent from Ezra."

J.   (He is wise, [that is] if questioned, he can answer; he is rich, [that is] if [Rabban Gamaliel] has to go pay honor to Caesar, he too can go pay honor; he is tenth in descent from Ezra, [that is] he has ancestral merit, and he cannot be punished.)

K.   They came and said to him, "Would the Master consent to become head of the Academy?"

L.   He said to them, "Let me go consult my household." He went and consulted his wife.

M.   She said to him, [28A] "They may remove you." He said to her, "Let a man use a valuable cup one day, and let it be broken the next."

N.   She said to him, "You have no white hair." That day he was eighteen years old. A miracle occurred to him and eighteen rows of his hair turned white.

O.   (That is [why] R. Eleazar b. 'Azariah said, "Behold, I resemble one [lit., am like] seventy years old," and not, "am seventy years old".)

P.   It was taught (TN'): That day ('WTW HYWM) they removed the doorkeeper, and the students were given permission to enter. For Rabban Gamaliel used to proclaim and say, "Any student whose outside is not like his inside shall not enter the house of study."

Q.   (On that day a number of benches was added. R. Yohanan said, "The matter is disputed by 'Abba Joseph b. Dostai and the rabbis: one holds four hundred benches were added, and the other, seven hundred.")

R.   Rabban Gamaliel was greatly disturbed, and said, "Perhaps, God forbid, I have withheld Torah from Israel!" In a dream, he was shown white casks filled with ashes [to indicate that he had acted correctly]. But that was not [the case]. He was shown that just to calm his mind.

S.   It was taught (TN'): 'Eduyot was reviewed on that day.

T.   (and wherever it says "on that day" the reference is to that day)

U.   and there was no law which had been left pending in the house of study which was not decided.

V.   And even Rabban Gamaliel did not absent himself from the study house for as much as one hour, as we learn: On that day (BW BYWM) Judah, an Ammonite proselyte, came before them in the house of study. He said to them, "Am I permitted to enter the congregation?" Said to him Rabban Gamaliel, "You are forbidden to enter the congregation." Said to him R. Joshua, "You are permitted to enter the congregation."

W.   Said to him Rabban Gamaliel, "But has it not already been said, 'An Ammonite or a Moabite shall not enter the congregation of the Lord' (Deut. 25:4)?"

X.   Said to him R. Joshua, "Then do Ammon and Moab dwell in their own places? Sennacherib, King of Assyria, has already come up and mixed together all the nations, as it is said, 'And I have removed the boundaries of the peoples, and have plundered their treasures; like a bull I have brought down those who sat on thrones' (Is. 10:13) -- and anything which comes out [of a composite mass is assumed to have] come from its largest element."

Y.   Said to him Rabban Gamaliel, "But has it not already been said, 'And afterwards I shall restore the former condition of the children of Ammon, says the Lord' (Jer. 49:6) -- so they have returned!"

Z.   Said to him R. Joshua, "But has it not already been said, 'And I shall restore the former condition of my people Israel (Amos 9:14)'? And they have not yet returned!"

AA.   They immediately permitted him to enter the congregation.

BB.   Said Rabban Gamaliel, "Such being the case, I shall go and appease R. Joshua."

CC.   When he got to his house, he saw that its walls were black. He said to him, "From the walls of your house, I see that you are a charcoal-maker." He said to him, "Woe to the generation whose steward (PRNS) you are! You do not know of the troubles of the scholars and how they support and sustain themselves."

DD.   [Rabban Gamaliel] said to him, "I submit to you; forgive me." He paid him no attention.

EE.   "Do it out of respect for my father." [R. Joshua] was appeased.

FF.   They said, "Who will go and inform the rabbis?" A certain laundry-worker (KWBS) said to them, "I shall go."

GG.   So R. Joshua sent [a message] to the house of study, "Let him who wears the garment wear the garment; should he who does not wear the garment say to him who wears it, 'Take off your garment and let me wear it'?"

HH.   Said R. 'Aqiba to the rabbis, "Shut the doors, so that Rabban Gamaliel's servants do not come and disturb the rabbis."

II.   Said R. Joshua, "I had better go to them myself."

JJ.   He came and knocked on the door and said to them, "The sprinkler, son of a sprinkler, should sprinkle; should he who is neither a sprinkler nor the son of a sprinkler, say to the sprinkler, son of a sprinkler, 'Your water comes from a cave, and your ashes from roasting'?"

KK.   Said R. Aqiba to him, "R. Joshua, have you been appeased? We have done nothing except for your honor. Tomorrow, you and I shall wait at [Rabban Gamaliel's] door."

LL.   They said, "How shall we act? Shall we remove Eleazar b. Azariah? Tradition holds that one may increase the holiness of an object, but not diminish it. Should each Master expound one Sabbath [alternately]? That will lead to jealousy. Rather let Rabban Gamaliel expound three Sabbaths and R. Eleazar b. 'Azariah one Sabbath."

MM.   That is what the Master meant when he said, "Whose Sabbath was it? R. Eleazar b. 'Azariah's."

NN.   And that student who started the whole episode was R. Simeon b. Yohai.

XVII.

A. And the recitation of the additional Prayer on Sabbath and Festival days may be done throughout the day [M. 4:1F]:

B. Said R. Yohanan, "But such a person is called a sinner."

XIII.

A. Our rabbis have taught on Tannaite authority:

B. If a person had the obligation of reciting the Prayer for two purposes, one the Prayer for the afternoon, the other the Prayer of the Additional Service, he says the Prayer for the afternoon and afterward he says the Prayer for the Additional Service, for the obligation to say the former is perpetual, and the obligation to say the latter is not perpetual.

C. R. Judah says, "He says the Prayer for the Additional Service and afterward he says the Prayer for the afternoon, for the former is a religious duty that will pass [and cannot be postponed] and the latter is a religious duty that does not pass [and can be postponed]."

D. Said R. Yohanan, "The decided law is that one says the Prayer for the afternoon and then he says the Prayer for the Additional Service."

XIX.

A. When R. Zira would get tired from his studying, he would go sit at the door of the house of R. Nathan bar Tobi. He said, "When the rabbis come by, then I shall get up before them and receive a reward [in Heaven for honoring them]."

B. R. Nathan bar Tobi came by. He said to him, "Who reported a decided law in the house of learning?"

C. He said to him, "This is what R. Yohanan said, 'The law does not follow R. Judah, who has said, "A person says the Prayer for the Additional Service and afterward he says the Prayer for the afternoon."'"

D. He said to him, "Did R. Yohanan say this?"

E. He said to him, "Yes."

F. He repeated it after him forty times.

G. He said to him, "Is this the one thing you have [from him], or is this a new teaching you have from him?"

H. He said to him, "It is new to me. I was in doubt that it might have come [not from him but from] R. Joshua b. Levi."

XX.

A. Said R. Joshua b. Levi, "Whoever says the Prayer for the Additional Service later than seven hours, in accord with the view of R. Judah [that one may do so], is the object of the following verse of Scripture:

B. "'I will gather them that are destroyed because of the appointed season, who are of you' (Zeph. 3:18).

C. "How do you know that the word at hand means 'destruction'?

D. "It accords with the explanation of R. Joseph, 'Destruction will come on (the enemies of) the house of Israel, because they put off [the prayers for] the festivals in Jerusalem.'"

XXI.

A.   Said R. Eleazar, "Who says the Prayer for the morning after four hours, following the opinion of R. Judah [that one may do so], is the object of the following verse of Scripture:

B.   "'I will gather them that sorrow because of the appointed season, who are of you' (Zeph. 3:18).

C.   "How do you know that the word at hand means 'sorrow'?

D.   "Because it is written, 'My soul melts away for heaviness' (Ps. 119:28) [using the same word]."

E.   R. Nahman b. Isaac said, "We derive the same fact from the following verse: 'Her virgins are afflicted [at which the word at hand is used] and she herself is in bitterness' (Lam. 1:4)."

XXI.

A.   [28B] R. Avia was sick and did not come to the session of R. Joseph. The next day, when he came, Abayye wanted to appease R. Joseph [by showing that Avia's absence was not an insult].

B.   [Abayye] said to [Avia], "What is the reason that the master did not come to the session?"

C.   He said to him, "Because I was weak and couldn't."

D.   He said to him, "Why did you not eat something and come?"

E.   He said to him, "Does not the master concur with what R. Huna said?

F.   "For R. Huna said, 'It is forbidden for someone to eat a thing before he says the Prayer for the Additional Service.' [Since I was at home and not with the congregation, I did not say the Prayer for the Additional Service, so I could not eat either.]"

G.   [Abayye] said to [Avia], "The master should have said the Prayer for the Additional Service by himself and then eaten something and come."

H.   He said to him, "Does the master not concur with what R. Yohanan said, 'It is forbidden for someone to recite the Prayer prior to the recitation of the Prayer by the community'?"

I.   He said to him, "But has it not been said in interpretation of that statement, 'Said R. Abba, "That statement has been made with reference to conduct in the congregation"'?"

J.   But the decided law accords with neither R. Huna nor R. Joshua b. Levi.

K.   Not with R. Huna, as we have stated.

L.   As to R. Joshua b. Levi, R. Joshua b. Levi said, "Once the time for reciting the Prayer for the afternoon has come, it is forbidden for someone to taste a thing before he recites the Prayer for the afternoon."

These units of discourse serve to expound elements of the Mishnah-paragraph: I-II, VI (inserted in the on-going construction of V, VII), VIII, IX, X, XV, and XVII. These units of discourse raise questions that develop or amplify problems suggested by the law of the Mishnah: III, IV, XI (continues X), XII (continues XI), XIII-XIV, XVI (continues and vastly amplifies the simple dispute reported at XV in connection with the exegesis of the Mishnah's language), XVIII-XXII (the issue of the precedence of the Prayer for the Additional Service when it is said later in the day). The following provides materials in no way proposing to add to the exposition of the Mishnah-paragraph: V (who ordained the recitation of the Prayers?) and VII (continuing V). So far as I can see, therefore, the entire, rather sizable repertoire of materials is so organized as either to expound the Mishnah-paragraph or amplify elements of the exposition of the Mishnah-paragraph.

4:2

A. R. Nehuniah b. Haqanah would say a short prayer on his entry to the study hall and upon his exit.

B. They said to him, "What place is there for this prayer [in the liturgy]?"

C. He said to them, "Upon my entry I pray that no mishap will occur on my account.

D. "And upon my exit I give thanks for my portion."

I.

A. Our rabbis have taught on Tannaite authority:

B. When he goes in, what does he say?

"May it please you, Lord my God, that no mishap will occur on my account [M. 4:2C], that I not err in a matter of law, that my colleagues may rejoice in me, that I may not call something unclean clean or something clean unclean, that my colleagues not err in a matter of law, and that I may take pleasure in them."

C. When he goes out, what does he say?

D. "I thank you, Lord my God, that you have set my portion among those who sit in the school house and have not set my portion among those who sit idly on street corners.

E. "For I get up in the morning and they get up in the morning. I get up to words of Torah, and they get up to nonsense.

F. "I work and they work. I work and receive a reward, and they work and do not receive a reward.

G. "I run and they run. I run to the life of the world to come, and they run to the pit of destruction.

II.

A. Our rabbis have taught on Tannaite authority:

B. When R. Eliezer fell ill, his disciples came in to pay a call on him. They said to him, "Our master, teach us the ways of life, so that through them we may merit the world to come."

C. He said to them, "Be attentive to the honor owing to your fellows, keep your children from excessive reflection and set them among the knees of disciples of sages, and when you pray, know before whom you stand, and on that account you will merit the life of the world to come."

D. And when R. Yohanan b. Zakkai fell ill, his disciples came in to pay a call on him. When he saw them, he began to cry. His disciples said to him, "Light of Israel! Pillar at the right hand! Mighty hammer! On what account are you crying?"

E. He said to them, "If I were going to be brought before a mortal king, who is here today and tomorrow gone to the grave, who, should he be angry with me, will not be angry forever, and, if he should imprison me, will not imprison me forever, and if he should put me to death, whose sentence of death is not for eternity, and whom I can appease with the right words or bribe with money, even so, I should weep.

F. "But now that I am being brought before the King of kings of kings, the Holy One, blessed be he, who endures forever and ever, who, should he be angry with me, will be angry forever, and if he should imprison me, will imprison me forever, and if he should put me to death, whose sentence of death is for eternity, and whom I cannot appease with the right words or bribe with money,

G. "and not only so, but before me are two paths, one to the Garden of Eden and the other to Gehenna, and I do not know by which path I shall be brought,

H. "and should I not weep?"

I. They said to him, "Our master, bless us."

J. He said to them, "May it be God's will that the fear of Heaven be upon you as much as the fear of mortal man."

K. His disciples said, "Just so much?"

L. He said to them, "Would that it were that much. You should know that, when a person commits a transgression, he says, 'I hope no man sees me.'"

M. When he was dying, he said to them, "Clear out utensils from the house, because of the uncleanness [of the corpse, which I am about to impart when I die], and prepare a throne for Hezekiah king of Judah, who is coming."

Unit I amplifies the statement of the Mishnah. I am not sure why the framer of the passage found unit II relevant.

4:3-6

A. R. Gamaliel says, "Each day one should recite the Prayer consisting of eighteen [benedictions]."

B. R. Joshua says, "[Each day one says] an abbreviation of the eighteen benedictions."

C. R. Aqiba says, "If one's prayer is fluent he says the eighteen benedictions."

D. "And if not, [one says] an abbreviation of them."

M. 4:3

A. R. Eliezer says, "One who recites his prayers in a routine manner -- his prayers are not supplications (thnwnym)."

B. R. Joshua says, "One who walks in a place of danger says a short prayer [an abbreviation of the eighteen benedictions:]."

C. "And he says, 'God save your nation, [the remnant of] Israel. At all critical times, let their needs be before you. Blessed are you, O God, who hearkens to prayer.'"

M. 4:4

A. One who was riding on an ass should dismount [to pray].

B. And if he cannot dismount, he should turn his face [towards the Temple in Jerusalem].

C. And if he cannot turn his face, he should direct his heart towards the chamber of the Holy of Holies [in the Temple of Jerusalem].

M. 4:5

A. One who was travelling in a ship [(K omits:) or in a wagon] or on a raft should direct his heart towards the Chamber of the Holy of Holies [in the Temple of Jerusalem].

M. 4:6

I.

A. As to the eighteen benedictions, to what do they correspond?

B. Said R. Hillel, son of R. Samuel bar Nahmani, "They correspond to the eighteen times that David mentioned God's name in the psalm, 'Ascribe to the Lord, sons of might' (Ps. 29:1)."

C. R. Joseph said, "They correspond to the eighteen times that God is mentioned in the recitation of the Shema."

D. Said R. Tanhuma said R. Joshua b. Levi, "They correspond to the eighteen vertebrae in the backbone."

II.

A. And R. Tanhuma said R. Joshua b. Levi [said], "He who says the Prayer has to bend down until all of the vertebrae in his backbone are loosened."

B. Ulla said, "... until an issar of flesh can be seen opposite his heart [Simon: until the flesh bulges]."

C. R. Hanina said, "Once one has simply nodded his head, he does not have to do more."

D. Said Raba, "But that is the case only if it hurts him to bend over and he indicates that he thereby bends down [as much as he can]."

III.

A. The so-called eighteen benedictions are nineteen.

B. Said R. Levi, "The blessing [that is, the curse] against the Sadducees did they ordain in Yavneh."

C. On what account did they ordain it?

D. Said R. Levi, "In the view of R. Hillel, son of R. Samuel bar Nahmani, it corresponds to the verse, 'The God of Glory thunders' (Ps. 29:3)."

E. "In the view of R. Joseph, it corresponds to the word 'One' in the Shema.

F. "In the view of R. Tanhum in the name of R. Joshua, it corresponds to the small vertebrae in the spinal column."

IV.

A. Our rabbis have taught on Tannaite authority:

B. Simeon Happaquli in Yavneh laid out the eighteen benedictions before Rabban Gamaliel in proper order.

C. Said Rabban Gamaliel to sages, "Does anyone know how to ordain a 'blessing' [curse] against the Sadducees [minim]?'

D. Samuel the younger went and ordained it.

E. A year later he forgot it [29A], and for two or three hours he attempted to recover it. But they did not remove him [as leader of the worship-service].

F. But did not R. Judah say Rab said, "If someone made an error in any of the benedictions, they do not remove him, but if he did so in the 'blessing' against the Sadducees, they do remove him, suspecting that he too is a min [and is sympathetic to them]."

G. The case of Samuel is different, because he himself was the one who had ordained the curse.

H. But should they not take account of the possibility that he had reverted [and was no longer trustworthy]?

I. Said Abayye, "There is a tradition that a good man does not turn bad."

J. But is that the case? Is it not written, "But when the righteous turns away from his righteousness and commits iniquity" (Ez. 18:24)?

K. That verse refers to someone who was to begin with wicked. But if someone was to begin with righteous, he will not turn bad.

L. Is that the case?

M. And lo, we have learned in the Mishnah: Do not trust yourself until the day you die, for lo, Yohanan, high priest, served in the high priesthood for eighty years but at the end he became a Sadducee [M. Abot 2:4].

N. Said Abayye, "Yannai was the same as Yohanan."

O. Raba said, "Yannai was one person and Yohanan was a different person."

P. Yannai was wicked to begin with, and Yohanan was righteous to begin with.

Q. That view poses no problems to Abayye.

R. But in the view of Raba it poses a problem.

S. Raba may reply to you, "To begin with he also was righteous. But he reverted [to evil ways]."

T.   If so, why did they not remove [Samuel the younger]?

U.   Samuel the younger was different because he had already begun [to recite the benediction against the heretics].

V.   For R. Judah said Rab said, and some say R. Joshua b. Levi [said], "The rule applies only in a case in which one had not yet begun to recite the curse, but if one had begun to recite the curse, he is permitted to complete it."

V.

A.   As to the seven benedictions [of which the Prayer] for the Sabbath is made up, to what do they correspond?

B.   Said R. Halapta b. Saul, "They correspond to the seven voices that David said [at Psalm 29] were over the waters."

C.   As to the nine benedictions [of which the Additional Prayer] for the New Year is made up, to what do they correspond?

D.   Said R. Isaac of Qartigenin, "They correspond to the seven times that Hannah mentioned the name of God in her prayer."

E.   For a master said, "On the New Year were Sarah, Rachel, and Hannah remembered [and given children]."

F.   As to the twenty-four benedictions of the Prayer said on fast days, to what do they correspond?

G.   Said R. Helbo, "They correspond to the twenty-four times that Solomon used the expression, 'prayer' [Simon] when he brought the ark to the house of the holy of holies [1 Kgs. 8:23-53]."

H.   If so, should we not also say them?

I.   When did Solomon say them? On a day of supplication [Simon, p. 176, n. 12: because the gates would not open]. We too say them on a day of supplication [namely, a fast for rain].

VI.

A.   R. Joshua says, "Each day one says an abbreviation of the eighteen benedictions" [M. 4:3B]:

B.   What is this abbreviation of the eighteen benedictions?

C.   Rab said, "A précis of each of the blessings [individually]."

D.   Samuel said, "'Make us, Lord our God, know your ways, circumcize our hearts to fear you, forgive us so that we may be redeemed, take us far away from our anguish, give us prosperity in the pastures of your land, gather our scattered ones from the four corners of the world; may those who err in knowledge of you be judged, wave your hand against the wicked, let the righteous rejoice in the rebuilding of your city, the restoration of your temple, the growth of the horn of David your servant, and the kindling of a light for the son of Jesse, your Me⋅iah. Before we call you may you answer us. Blessed are you, Lord, who listens to prayer.'"

VII.

A.   Abayye would curse anyone who said the Prayer, "Make us know...."

B. Said R. Nahman said Samuel, "For the entire year a person may say the Prayer in the form of 'Make us know...,' except for the Prayer to be said at the end of the Sabbath and at the end of Festivals, because on those occasions it is necessary to insert the Prayer of Division in the paragraph of the Eighteen Benedictions, ending, 'Who graciously gives knowledge.'"

C. Rabbah bar Samuel objected to that view, "But let a person recite the fourth benediction by itself. Have we not learned on Tannaite authority: R. Aqiba says, 'One says it as a fourth blessing unto itself.' R. Eliezer says, 'One says it in the thanksgiving' [M. Ber. 5:2]."

D. The reply: "Is it the case that throughout the year we act in accord with the views of R. Aqiba, that on this item too we should act in accord with his view?"

E. What is the reason that for the entire year we do not act in accord with R. Aqiba?

F. It is because eighteen benedictions were ordained, and not nineteen.

G. Here too seven blessings were ordained and not eight [with 'Make us know...' as the center. If the fourth benediction were set by itself, there would be eight. So the same reason applies throughout.]

H. To that view Mar Zutra objected, "But why not include the Prayer of Division in the prayer, 'Make us know...,' as follows: 'Make us know, O Lord our God... who divides the holy from the ordinary.'"

I. That indeed presents a problem.

VIII.

A. Said R. Bibi bar Abayye, "Throughout the entire year a person may recite, as the Prayer, the paragraph, 'Make us know...,' except for the rainy season, because one has to express the request for rain in the blessing for the years."

B. To this Mar Zutra objected, "But why not include it in the prayer, 'Give us prosperity in the pastures of your land,' adding, 'and give dew and rain....'"

C. One might be confused [if required to alter the text].

D. If so, stating the Prayer of Division in the blessing, "Make us know..." likewise will cause confusion.

E. I may reply that, in that case, since the addition comes at the beginning of the recitation of the Prayer, a person will not be confused, but here since the addition comes in the middle of the Prayer, he will be confused.

F. To this R. Ashi objected, "Then why not add the statement in the phrase, '"... who hears prayer'?

G. "For R. Tanhum said R. Assi said, 'If someone erred and did not make mention of 'the power of making rain' in the prayer for the resurrection of the dead he is made to go back [and repeat the matter]. But if he included it in the blessing of the years, he is not made to go back, because he can yet add it in the blessing ending, '... who hears prayer.' If he omitted the inclusion of the Prayer of Division in the blessing ending, '... who graciously gives knowledge,' he is not made to go back, because he can say the same prayer over the cup of wine.

H. "But if one made an error, the rule is different [from that applying to a case in which we prescribe the prayer under ordinary circumstances]."

IX.

A.   Returning to the main text just now cited:

B.   R. Tanhum said R. Assi said, "If someone erred and did not make mention of 'the power of making rain' in the prayer for the resurrection of the dead, he is made to go back [and repeat the matter]. But if he included it in the blessing of the years, he is not made to go back, because he can yet add it in the blessing ending, '... who hears prayer.' If he omitted the inclusion of the Prayer of Division in the blessing ending, '... who graciously gives knowledge,' he is not made to go back, because he can say the same prayer over the cup of wine."

C.   An objection was raised on the basis of the following:

D.   If one did not mention the mightiness of [God's deeds in causing] the rains [to fall] in [the second benediction of the Prayer, which deals with] the resurrection of the dead, they make him go back.

E.   If one did not petition for rainfall in the benediction for the years [viz., the ninth benediction of the Prayer, the petition for a fruitful and prosperous year],

F.   they make him begin [reciting the entire Prayer] again.

G.   If he did not recite habdalah ["separation," acknowledging the distinctiveness and sanctity of the people Israel and the Sabbath day] in [the fourth benediction, which concludes,] "gracious giver of knowledge," they do not make him go back, for he may recite it over a cup [of wine; cf. M. Ber. 5:2] [T. Ber. 3:9A-D (Zahavy)].

H.   This is no problem. [The contradiction between the view that if one omitted the prayer in the blessing of the years he is not made to go back, and the view that he is, may be resolved.] The one speaks of prayer of an individual by himself, the other of prayer in the community.

I.   And when one is reciting the Prayer with the community, why is he not made to go back?

J.   Is it not because he hears the prayer properly phrased when the leader of the community prayer repeats it?

K.   If that were the reason, then the stated reason, "Because he can include it in the blessing ending..., '... who hears prayer,'" should be stated differently, namely, "because he may hear it when the leader of the prayers for the community repeats it."

L.   Rather, both passages speak of an individual praying by himself. There still is no contradiction between the two passages.

M.   The one speaks of a case in which the man remembers [what he has omitted] before he comes to the benediction, "... who hears prayer," [29B] while the other speaks of a case after he has said that benediction.

X.

A.   Said R. Tanhum said R. Assi said R. Joshua b. Levi, "If one made a mistake and did not make mention of the New Moon in the benediction on the sacrificial service, he goes back to repeat the benediction on the sacrificial service [and includes the necessary language]. If when he is reciting the benediction of thanksgiving he remembers what he has omitted, he goes back to the benediction for the sacrificial service.

B.   "If he remembers what he has omitted only when he is reciting benediction, 'Give peace,' he goes back to the benediction for the sacrificial service. But if he remembers only when he has completed the entire recitation of the Prayer, he goes back to the beginning."

C.   Said R. Papa, son of R. Aha bar Ada, "As to this statement that we have made, 'If he completed the entire Prayer, he goes back to the beginning,' it applies only to a case in which one has already moved his feet [after concluding the prayer]. But if he has not yet moved his feet, he may go back only to the benediction on the sacrificial service."

D.   He said to him, "How do you know that?"

E.   He said to him, "I heard it from my master, my father, and my master, my father, heard it from Rab."

F.   Said R. Nahman bar Isaac, "As to this statement that we have made, 'If he moved his feet, he goes back to the beginning,' that statement applies only in a case in which one does not usually recite a prayer of supplication after the recitation of his Prayer. But if he is accustomed to recite a prayer of supplication after he has recited the Prayer, he may go back to the benediction for the sacrificial service.'"

G.   There are those who report matters as follows:

H.   Said R. Nahman bar Isaac, "That which we have said, 'If he has not moved his feet, he goes back only to the prayer for the sacrificial service,' applies only to a case in which one is used to inserting a prayer of supplication after the recitation of his Prayer. But if he is not used to adding a prayer of supplication after his recitation of the Prayer, he goes back to the beginning."

XI.

A.   R. Eliezer says, "One who recites his prayers in a routine manner..." [M. 4:4A]:

B.   What is meant by "a routine manner"?

C.   Said R. Jacob bar Idi said R. Oshaia, "It is any case in which one's recitation of the Prayer seems to a person to be a burden."

D.   And rabbis say, "It is any case in which one does not recite the Prayer in a language of supplication."

E.   Rabbah and R. Joseph both maintain, "It is any case in which one cannot say something new [when he is reciting the Prayer]."

F.   Said R. Zira, "I can say something new in it, but I am concerned that I not become confused."

G.   Abayye bar Abin and R. Hanina bar Abin both said, "It is any case in which one does not say the Prayer at the first and last appearance of the sun."

H.   For R. Hiyya bar Abba said R. Yohanan said, "It is a religious duty to say the Prayer at the first and last appearance of the sun."

I.   And R. Zira said, "What is the scriptural verse that indicates it? 'They shall fear you with the sun and before the moon throughout all generations' (Ps. 72:5)."

J.   In the West people curse someone who says the Prayer with the last appearance of
      the sun. Why? It is possible that he will miss saying the Prayer at exactly the right
      moment.

XII.

A.   R. Joshua says, "One who walks in a place of danger says a short prayer.... at all
      critical times...'" [M. 4:4B-C]:

B.   What is the sense of at all critical times?

C.   Said R. Hisda said Mar Uqba, "'Even at a time at which you are filled with criticism
      of them as a woman who is pregnant, may all their needs be before you.'"

D.   There are those who say: Said R. Hisda said Mar Uqba, "'Even when they transgress
      the teachings of Torah let all their needs be before you.'"

XIII.

A.   Our rabbis have taught on Tannaite authority:

B.   One who was walking in a place of wild beasts or bandits recites a brief prayer [M.
      Ber. 4:4B].

C.   What is this brief prayer?

D.   R. Eliezer says, "May thy will be done in the heavens above, and grant ease to those
      who fear you, and do what is good in thine own eyes. Praised [be Thou, O Lord,] who
      hearkens to prayer."

E.   R. Joshua says, "Hearken to the prayer of thy people Israel and quickly fulfill their
      requests. Praised [be thou, O Lord,] who hearkens to prayer."

F.   R. Eliezer b. R. Sadok says, "Hearken to the sound of the cries of your people Israel
      and quickly fulfill their requests. Praised [be Thou, O Lord,] who hearkens to
      prayer."]

G.   Others say, "The needs of thy people are many and they are impatient. May it be
      thy will, Lord our God, to give to each and every one according to his needs, and to
      each and every creature that which he lacks. Praised [be Thou, O Lord,] who
      hearkens to prayer" [T. Ber. 3:7A-F].

H.   Said R. Huna, "The decided law follows the view of 'others.'"

XIV.

A.   Said Elijah to R. Judah, brother of R. Sala Hasida, "Do not lust and you will not sin,
      do not get drunk and you will not sin.

B.   "And when you go out on the way, take counsel with your creator and go forth."

C.   What is the sense of "Take counsel with your creator and go forth"?

D.   Said R. Jacob said R. Hisda, "This refers to the prayer for wayfarers."

E.   And R. Jacob said R. Hisda said, "Whoever goes forth on a trip has to recite the
      prayer for wayfarers."

F.   What is that prayer?

G.   "May it please you, Lord my God, to lead me in peace, guide my steps in peace,
      sustain me in peace, save me from the power of every enemy and bandit on the
      way. Send a blessing on what I do in your sight and in the sight of all who see me
      give me grace and lovingkindness and mercy. Blessed are you, who hears prayer."

H. Said Abayye, "A person should always [30A] join himself [in prayer] with the community."

I. What then should one say?

J. "May it please you, Lord our God, to lead us in peace..." etc.

K. When does one say [the prayer for wayfarers]?

L. Said R. Jacob said R. Hisda, "At the time that one leaves on the trip."

M. Up to what point [may one say it]?

N. Said R. Jacob said R. Hisda, "For a _parasang_."

O. How does one say the prayer?

P. R. Hisda said, "Standing."

Q. R. Sheshet said, "Even walking along."

R. R. Hisda and R. Sheshet were going along the way. R. Hisda stopped and said the prayer.

S. Said R. Sheshet [who was blind] to his servant, "What is R. Hisda doing?"

T. He said to him, "He is standing and saying a prayer."

U. He said to him, "Let me stand by myself and say the prayer. If you can be good, do not be called wicked [since saying the prayer while standing still is the better way]."

XV.

A. What is the difference between [the précis of the eighteen benedictions beginning] "Make us know...," and the abbreviated version of the Prayer [of the eighteen benedictions]?

B. The précis beginning, "Make us know" requires the recitation of the three blessings at the beginning and the three at the end, and, when a person gets home, he does not have to go back and recite the Prayer again.

C. In the case of the abbreviated version of the Prayer, one does not have to recite the first and the last three blessings, but when one gets home, he has to go back and recite the Prayer.

XVI.

A. And the decided law is this:

B. One has to say "Make us know" while standing [and silently praying], while the abbreviated version of the Prayer may be said either standing or walking along.

XVII.

A. One who was riding an ass should dismount [M. 4:5A]:

B. Our rabbis have taught on Tannaite authority:

C. One who was riding on an ass [M. Ber. 4:5],

D. if there is someone who can hold the ass [so that it will not run away], he should dismount and pray,

E. and if not, then he stays where he is [i.e., mounted on the ass] and says the Prayer.

F. Rabbi says, "In either case he stays where he is and says the Prayer,

G. "since otherwise he cannot concentrate [properly]" [T. Ber. 3:18].

H. Said Raba, and some say, R. Joshua b. Levi, "The decided law accords with Rabbi."

XVIII.

A. Our rabbis have taught on Tannaite authority:

B. A blind man and one with no sense of direction [both of whom cannot figure out the direction of Jerusalem] turn their hearts toward their Father in heaven and pray [cf. M. Ber. 4:5-6],

C. as it is written, And they pray to the Lord [toward the city which thou hast chosen and the house which I have built for thy name] (I Kings 8:44) [T. Ber. 3:14].

XIX.

A. Those who are outside the Land turn toward the Land of Israel,

B. as Scripture states, And pray toward their land [which thou gavest to their fathers, the city which thou has chosen, and the house which I have built for thy name] (II Chron. 6:38).

C. Those who are in the Land of Israel turn toward Jerusalem,

D. as Scripture states, And they pray to thee toward this city which thou hast chosen [and the house which I have built for thy name] (II Chron. 6:34) [T. Ber. 3:15].

E. Those who are in Jerusalem turn toward the Temple,

F. as Scripture states, When he comes and prays toward this house (II Chron. 6:32).

G. Those who are in the Temple turn toward the Chamber of the Holy of Holies and pray,

H. as Scripture states, When they pray toward this place (I Kings 8:30).

I. [Following T.:] It turns out that those standing in the north face south, those in the south face north, those in the east face west, and those in the west face east.

J. Thus all Israel turn out to be praying toward one place [cf. M. Ber. 4:5-6] [T. Ber. 3:16A-F].

K. Said R. Abin, and some say, R. Abina, "What verse of Scripture makes this point? 'Thy neck is like the tower of David built with turrets (talpiot)' (Song 4:4)."

L. "It is the height (tal) to   ' ich all mouths (piyot) turn."

XX.

A. When Samuel's father and Levi wanted to go out on a trip, they would first say the Prayer. When time came to recite the Shema, they recited it.

B. In accord with which authority did they do so?

C. It was in accord with the following Tannaite authority,

D. for it has been taught on Tannaite authority:

E. One who arose early to go on a journey --

F. lo, they bring him a shofar and he blows it, a lulab and he waves it, the scroll [of Esther, or Purim] and he reads from it [before he leaves his house].

G. But when the time comes for the recitation of the Shema he must recite it [where he is, even if already on the road].

H. One who arose early to travel in a wagon or on a boat,

I. recites the Prayer [before he departs],

J. but when the time comes for the recitation of the Shema, he must recite it [where he is, even if already traveling] [T. Ber. 3:1A-F].

K.   R. Simeon b. Eleazar says, "One way or the other he recites the Shema and then he
      says the Prayer, so that he may juxtapose the prayer in which redemption is
      mentioned to the recitation of the Prayer."

L.   What is at issue between the authorities?

M.   One authority takes the view that saying the Prayer while standing is more
      important.

N.   The other authority takes the view that joining a mention of redemption to the
      recitation of the Prayer is more important.

XXI.

A.   Maremar and Mar Zutra would collect ten people on the Sabbath prior to a festival
      [Simon, p. 183, n. 14: when they preached in public before daybreak], and they
      would recite the Prayer and then they would go out to the public discourse.

B.   While yet seated, R. Ashi would say the Prayer even while the community [listened
      to the restatement by the loud-speaker of what he had said], and then, when he got
      home, he would go back and say it again standing.

C.   Rabbis said to him, "Why should the master not conduct himself like Maremar and
      Mar Zutra?"

D.   He said to them, "I never saw any masters who were older than I acting in such a
      way."

The Talmud's contribution is to broaden the range of discourse on the themes of the
Mishnah-paragraph at hand. Thus unit I explains not the issue of M. 4:3, but its topic, the
eighteen benedictions. The topic then dominates through unit IV. Unit V is continuous
with the foregoing, in that it provides for other versions of the Prayer exactly the
information with which we began at unit I. Then unit VI continues the amplification of
the materials of the Mishnah. Units VII-X are continuous, either dealing with the
established topic or with materials introduced in connection with that topic. Unit XI then
reverts to the Mishnah and explains its language and sense. Unit XII does the same. Units
XIII-XVI proceed to expand by introducing and working out the pertinent materials of
Tosefta, with these materials intersecting with the Mishnah. Unit XVII returns us to the
Mishnah, once more calling upon Tosefta's amplificatory materials. These continue
through unit XIX. The theme of praying while on a trip accounts for the inclusion of unit
XX, and unit XXI deals with the theme of saying the Prayer while seated, relevant to M.
4:5B. In all, no important component of the Talmud fails to relate either to the Mishnah
or to materials introduced to amplify the statements in the Mishnah.

                                          4:7

A.   R. Eleazar b. Azariah says, "The Additional Prayer is said only by the
      town association [not by any individual]."

B.   And the sages say, "Either with the town association or not with the
      town association."

C.   R. Judah says in his name, "Wherever there is a town association, the
individual is free from the obligation to recite the Additional Prayer."

I.

A.   R. Judah says what the first of the three authorities says [at A].

B.   At issue between them is the case of an individual in a town in which there is no
town association.

C.   The first authority takes the view that he is exempt [from the obligation of reciting
the Additional Prayer].

D.   And R. Judah maintains that he is liable to do so.

E.   Said R. Huna bar Hinena said R. Hiyya bar Rab, "The decided law accords with the
view of R. Judah as he has stated it in the name of R. Eleazar b. Azariah."

F.   Said to him R. Hiyya bar Abin, "You have made a good statement.

G.   "For Samuel said, 'I never said the Additional Prayer all by myself [but only with the
congregation] [30B] in Nehardea, except for the day on which a royal regiment came
to the place and bothered the rabbis, so that they did not say the Prayer, and I said
the Prayer by myself. In that case I was an individual in a place in which there was
no town association."

H.   R. Hanina was in session reciting before R. Yannai, and, in session, he made the
following statement: "The law accords with the view of R. Judah stated in the name
of R. Eleazar b. Azariah."

I.   He said to him, "Go and proclaim what you are reciting outside, [for] the law does
not accord with the view of R. Eleazar b. Azariah as stated by R. Judah."

J.   Said R. Yohanan, "I saw R. Yannai say the Prayer and then go and say it again."

K.   Said R. Jeremiah to R. Zira, "Perhaps the first time around he did not adequately
concentrate on the Prayer, and the second time he did?"

L.   He said to him, "Take note that it is a great man [namely, Yohanan], who gives
testimony about what he did [and hence it is a reliable report]."

II.

A.   As to R. Ammi and R. Assi, even though they had thirteen synagogues in Tiberias,
they recited the Prayers only among the columns [of the basilica at which] they
were carrying on their studies.

III.

A.   It has been stated on Tannaite authority:

B.   R. Isaac b. Abdimi said in the name of our master [Rab], "The law accords with the
view of R. Judah as stated in the name of R. Eleazar b. Azariah."

C.   R. Hiyya bar Abba said the Prayer and went and repeated it.

D.   Said R. Zira to him, "Why has the master done it this way? If I should say that it is
because the master did not properly concentrate on the prayer at hand, has not R.
Eleazar said, 'A person should always take his own measure. If he can properly
concentrate, he should say the Prayer, and if not, he should not say the Prayer'?

E.   "But it must be because the master does not recall that it is the new moon.

F.   "But in that case, has it not been taught on Tannaite authority: 'If one erred and did
     not make mention of the New Month in the evening prayer recitation of the Prayer
     in the evening, he does not have to go back and repeat it, because he can make
     mention of it in the recitation of the Prayer in the morning. If this happened in the
     morning, they do not make him go back and repeat it, because he can make mention
     of it in the Additional Prayer. If he neglected it in the Additional Prayer, they do
     not make him go back and repeat it, because he can make mention of it in the
     recitation of the Prayer in the afternoon.'"

G.   He said to him, "Has it not been stated in this connection: 'R. Yohanan says, "This
     applies only to congregational prayer [but an individual has to repeat the Prayer if
     he has left something out]"'? [And I had indeed omitted the reference.]"

IV.

A.   [If one has to recite the Prayer twice], what interval should there be between one
     recitation of the Prayer and the next?

B.   R. Huna and R. Hisda --

C.   One said, "Sufficient for him [Simon:] to fall into a suppliant frame of mind."

D.   The other said, "Sufficient for him [Simon:] to fall into an interceding frame of
     mind."

E.   The one who said, "Sufficient for him to fall into a suppliant frame of mind" cites
     the following verse: "And I supplicated the Lord" (Deut. 3:23).

F.   The one who said, "Sufficient for him to fall into an interceding frame of mind"
     cites the following verse: "And Moses interceded" (Ex. 32:11).

V.

A.   Said R. Anan said Rab, If one made a mistake and did not make mention of the New
     Moon in the recitation of the Prayer in the evening, they do not make him repeat it,
     since in any event the court declares the month sanctified only by day [and not by
     night]."

B.   Said Amemar, "The statement of Rab makes sense in connection with a full month
     [of thirty days], but in a defective month [of twenty-nine days] they do make him go
     back." [Simon, p. 186, n. 4: When the preceding month is thirty days, two new moon
     days are observed, viz., the concluding day of the old month and the next day, which
     is the first of the next; in this case if he omitted reference on one evening, he can
     rectify the error on the next.]

C.   Said R. Ashi to Amemar, "Since Rab gave a reason [for his view] what difference
     does it make to me whether the month is defective or full, since there is no
     difference?"

Unit I clarifies the relationship of M. 4:7A and C, as does unit III. I do not know why
unit II is here. Units IV and V pursue a theme in the antecedent materials, namely, going
back and repeating a Prayer that has not been properly recited. So the entire passage
provides exegesis of the Mishnah-paragraph or of materials adduced to begin with in
connection with that exegesis.

CHAPTER FIVE

BAVLI BERAKHOT CHAPTER FIVE

5:1

A. One rises to recite "The Prayer" only in a solemn frame of mind.

B. The pious men of old used to tarry one hour before praying,

C. so that they could direct their hearts to their father in heaven.

D. [If one was praying], even if the king greets him, he may not respond.

E. And even if a serpent is entwined around his heel, he may not interrupt [his prayer].

I.

A. Whence [in Scripture] do we find evidence for this rule [of M. 5:1A]?

B. Said R. Eleazar, "It is in line with the following verse of Scripture: 'And she was in bitterness of soul' (I Sam. 1:10)."

C. But how does that verse prove the point? Perhaps the case of Hannah is different, because her heart was unusually bitter.

D. Rather, said R. Yose b. R. Hanina, "It derives from this verse: 'But as for me, in the abundance of your lovingkindness will I come into your house, I will bow down toward your holy temple in fear of you' (Ps. 5:8)."

E. But how does that verse prove the point? Perhaps the case of David is different, for in praying he troubled himself more than [most people].

F. Rather, said R. Joshua b. Levi, "It derives from this verse: 'Worship the Lord in the beauty of holiness' (Ps. 29:2). Do not read the word used for beauty as its vowels indicate, but rather, impose the vowels to give the meaning of 'trembling.'"

G. But how does that verse prove the point? Perhaps I should read the cited word literally, as "beauty."

H. This would be in line with the practice of R. Judah, who would dress up elegantly and only then would say the Prayer.

I. Rather, said R. Nahman bar Isaac, "It derives from this verse: 'Serve the Lord with fear and rejoice with trembling' (Ps. 2:11). [That proves the point of M. 5:1A]."

J. What is the sense of "rejoice with trembling"?

K. Said R. Adda bar Matena said Rabbah, "Where there is rejoicing, there should also be trembling."

II.

A. Abayye was in session before Rabbah. He saw someone making merry. He said to him, "'Rejoice with trembling' is what is written."

B. The other said to him, "I put on phylacteries."

III.

A. R. Jeremiah was in session before R. Zira. He saw that he was making merry. He said to him, "'In all sorrow there is profit' (Prov. 14:23)."

B. He said to him, "I put on phylacteries."

IV.

A. Mar, son of Rabina, made a celebration for the marriage of his son. He saw that the rabbis were making merry.

B. [31A] He brought a cup worth four hundred zuz and broke it before them. They were upset.

V.

A. R. Ashi made a celebration for the marriage of his son. He saw the rabbis making jokes.

B. He brought a cup of white crystal and broke it. They were upset.

VI.

A. Rabbis said to R. Hamnuna, the younger, at the wedding feast of Mar, son of Rabina, "May the master sing for us."

B. He said to them, "'Woe for us, for we are going to die, woe for us, for we are going to die.'"

C. They said to him, "What are we supposed to respond to these verses of yours?"

D. He said to them, "'Where is the Torah-learning, where is the merit for doing a religious duty! That will protect us!'"

VII.

A. Said R. Yohanan in the name of R. Simeon b. Yohai, "It is forbidden for a person to fill his mouth with laughter in this world, for it is said, 'Then [in time to come] laughter will fill our mouths and song our tongues' (Ps. 126:2).

B. "When? At the time that 'the gentiles will say, "The Lord has done great things with these"' (Ps. 126:3)."

C. They said concerning R. Simeon b. Laqish that, from the time that he heard this teaching from R. Yohanan, his master, he never again allowed laughter to fill his mouth.

VIII.

A. Our rabbis have taught on Tannaite authority:

B. People should not arise to say the Prayer either forthwith after judging a case or after discussing a matter of law, but after having dealt with a decided law.

C. What is an example of having a decided law?

D. Said Abayye, "It would, for example, accord with that which R. Zira said."

E. R. Zira said, "Israelite women imposed a strict rule on themselves. If they produce a drop of blood as small as a mustard seed, they refrain from having sexual relations on its account until seven clean days [on which no further blood appeared] have passed."

F. Raba said, "It would be illustrated by the statement of R. Hoshaia."

G. For R. Hoshaia said, "A farmer may practice deception with the crop [and avoid rendering it liable to the separation of tithes] by bringing it into the barn while the grain is still in the chaff [and so not yet liable to the separation of tithe]. Then his beast may eat the produce [as is, while it is yet] exempt from tithing."

H. If you wish, I may propose that the same matter is illustrated by the statement of R. Huna.

I. For R. Huna said R. Zeira said, "He who lets blood in the case of a beast that has been set aside for sacred purposes -- the blood may not be used for private benefit, and the laws of sacrilege apply to the blood."

IX.

A. Rabbis in practice accord with the law of the Mishnah-passage at hand [M. 5:1A].

B. R. Ashi in practice accords with the law of the Tannaite teaching [at VIII B].

X.

A. Our rabbis have taught on Tannaite authority:

B. People should not rise to say the Prayer from a moment of sadness or idleness, laughter or babbling or silliness or idle talk, but only out of rejoicing at the fulfillment of a religious duty.

C. And along these same lines, a person should not take leave of his fellow from a moment of babbling or laughter or silliness or idle talk, but only out of discourse on a matter of law.

D. For so we note that the earlier prophets concluded their teachings with words of praise and consolation [T. Ber. 3:21P-C].

E. And so did Mari, son of the son of R. Huna b. R. Jeremiah bar Abba, teach on Tannaite authority, "A person should take leave of his fellow only out of discourse on a matter of law. For on that account one will remember him."

F. It is illustrated by the case of R. Kahana. He accompanied R. Shimi bar Ashi from the head of the canal to the palm-district of Babylonia. When he got there, he said to him, "Master is it so that people say that these palm-trees of Babylonia have been since the time of the first man to the present?"

G. He said to him, "You remind me of what R. Yose b. R. Hanina said. For R. Yose b. R. Hanina said, 'What is the meaning of the verse, "Through a land that no man passed through and where no man dwelled" (Jer. 2:6)? And if no one passed through, how would someone have dwelled there anyhow? But his meaning is this: Any land which the first man decreed should be settled was settled, and any land which the first man decreed should not be settled has never been settled.'"

H. R. Mordecai accompanied R. Shimi bar Ashi from Hageronia to Be Kipi, and some say, to Be Dura.

XI.

A. Our rabbis have taught on Tannaite authority:

B. He who recites the Prayer must concentrate his heart on Heaven [cf. M. Ber. 5:1].

C. Abba Saul says, "A [Scriptural] allusion to prayer [and its requisite act of concentration] is, Thou wilt strengthen their heart, thou wilt incline thine ear (Ps. 10:17)" [T. Ber. 3:4E-F].

XII.

A.   It has been taught on Tannaite authority:

B.   Said R. Judah, "This was R. Aqiba's custom. When [R. Aqiba] would pray with the
     congregation [in public], he would shorten [the prayer] and go up [from the reader's
     pit] on account of excessively burdening the community.

C.   "And when he would pray by himself, one would leave him in one corner [of the
     room] and find him [later] in another corner.

D.   "Why so? On account of his [repeated] bowing and prostration [during his lengthy
     prayer]" [cf. M. Ber. 4:3] [T. Ber. 3:5A-C].

XIII.

A.   Said R. Hiyya bar Abba, "A person should always recite the Prayer in a room in
     which there are windows.

B.   "For it is said, 'Now his windows were open' (Dan. 6:11)."

XIV.

A.   [In T.'s version] May one think that he may pray continuously all day long?
     [Scripture specifies to the contrary] in the case of Daniel, [And he got down upon his
     knees] three times a day [and prayed and gave thanks before his God...] (Dan. 6:11
     [RSV: 6:10]). [ed. princ. adds: "Lest one think that he may pray facing any
     direction he wishes, Scripture states [to the contrary], He had windows in his upper
     chamber open towards Jerusalem (ibid.).]

B.   May one think [that Daniel prayed only] when he came to the [lands of the]
     dispersion? Scripture states [to the contrary], As he had done previously (ibid.).

C.   May one think that he must pray out loud? Scripture specifies [to the contrary] in
     the case of Hannah, as it says, Hannah was speaking in her heart (I Sam. 1:13).

D.   May one think that he may recite all [the three daily Prayers] at one time?
     Scripture specifies [to the contrary] in the case of David, as it says, Evening and
     morning and noon I utter my complaint and moan (Ps. 55:18 [= RSV 55:17]):

E.   [B. omits:] evening -- this is the evening Prayer; morning -- this is the morning
     Prayer; noon -- this is the afternoon Prayer.

F.   May one think that he may present his petition and [then immediately] recite the
     Prayer? Scripture specifies [to the contrary] of Solomon, as it says, [Yet have
     regard to the prayer of thy servant and to his supplication, O Lord my God]
     hearkening to the cry and to the prayer [which thy servant prays before thee this
     day] (I Kings 8:28):

G.   the cry -- this is the cry [of praise and rejoicing which must accompany petitionary
     prayer], [B. lacks:] as it says, Rejoice in the Lord O ye righteous! Praise befits the
     upright (Ps. 33:1);

H.   prayer -- this is petition.

I.   One does not utter words [of private petition and supplication] after "True and firm"
     [the benediction recited after the Shema, immediately before reciting the Prayer],
     but he may utter words [of petition] after [reciting] the Prayer [cf. M. Ber. 2:2, T.
     Ber. 1:2C],

J.   even if the petition is as [long as] the order of the confession on the Day of Atonement [J. Ber. 3:6].

XV.

A.   It has been stated as well on Amoraic authority:

B.   Said R. Hiyya bar Ashi said Rab, "Even though authorities have stated, 'A person should ask for what he needs in the benediction ending, "Who hears prayer,"'

C.   "if one comes to state [those needs] after he has recited the Prayer, even [if the petition is long] as the order of confession on the Day of Atonement, he may do so."

XVI.

A.   Said R. Hamnuna, "How many important laws concerning prayer are there to be derived from the verses of Scripture stated in connection with Hannah.

B.   "'Now Hannah spoke from her heart' (1 Sam. 1:10). On the basis of this verse [we learn] that one who recites the Prayer has to direct his heart [to Heaven].

C.   "'Only her lips moved.' On the basis of this verse [we learn] that one who recites the Prayer must mouth the words.

D.   "'But her voice could not be heard.' On the basis of this verse [we learn] that it is forbidden to raise one's voice when he recites the Prayer.

E.   "'Therefore Eli thought she was drunk.' On the basis of this verse [we learn] that one who is drunk may not recite the Prayer."

F.   "And Eli said to her, How long will you be drunk" (1 Sam. 1:14):

G.   Said R. Eleazar, "On the basis of this verse [we learn] that one who observes something improper in his fellow [31B] has the obligation to reprove him."

XVII.

A.   "And Hannah answered and said, No my lord" (1 Sam. 1:15).

B.   Said Ulla, and some say R. Yose b. R. Hanina, "She said to him, 'You are not a lord in this matter, and the holy spirit does not rest on you, that you should suspect me of doing such a thing.'"

C.   There are those who say that this is what she said to him: "You are not a lord. The Presence of God and the holy spirit are not with you, for you have judged me without charity and did not judge me charitably. Do you not know that 'I am a woman of sorrowful spirit, I have drunk neither wine nor strong drink.'"

D.   Said R. Eleazar, "On the basis of this passage [we learn] that one who is suspect of something that he has not done has to inform [the other that the accusation is false]."

XVIII.

A.   "Count not your handmaid for a daughter of Belial:"

B.   Said R. Eleazar, "On the basis of this passage [we learn] that a drunkard who says a prayer is like one who worships an idol.

C.   "Here it is written, 'Count not your handmaid for a daughter of Belial' and elsewhere: 'Certain sons of Belial have gone forth from the midst of you' (Deut. 13:14).

D.   "Just as in that latter passage the reference is to idolatry, so here it is to idolatry."

XIX.

A. "Then Eli answered and said, Go in peace" (1 Sam. 1:17):

B. Said R. Eleazar, "On the basis of this passage [we learn that] one who suspects his fellow of something which in fact is not true has to appease him and not only so, but he also has to bless him.

C. "For it is said, 'And the God of Israel grant your petition' (1 Sam. 1:17)."

XX.

A. "And she vowed a vow and said, O Lord of hosts" (1 Sam. 1:11):

B. Said R. Eleazar, "From the day on which the Holy One, blessed be he, created his world, no one ever called the Holy One, blessed be he, 'hosts,' until Hannah came along and called him 'hosts.'

C. "Hannah said before the Holy One, blessed be he, 'Lord of the world, among all the hosts of hosts which you have created in your world, is it such a hard thing in your sight to give me a single son?'

D. "To what may the matter be compared? To the case of a mortal king who made a banquet for his staff. A poor man came and stood at the door. He said to them, 'Give me a piece of bread.' But the people paid no attention to him.

E. "He pushed his way in and went before the king. He said to him, 'My lord, O King, in this entire banquet which you have prepared, is it such a hard thing in your sight to give me a single piece of bread?'"

F. "If you will indeed look" (1 Sam. 1:11):

G. Said R. Eleazar, "Said Hannah before the Holy One, blessed be he, 'Lord of the world, If you see, well and good. If you will not see, then I shall go and be alone [with another man] in the full knowledge of Elkanah, my husband. And since I shall go aside with another man, they will make me drink the water inflicted on the suspected wife. Now you are not going to falsify your own Torah, for it is said, "She shall be cleared and shall conceive seed" (Num. 5:28).'"

H. That tale accords well with the view of him who has said, "If the wife was barren, she will be remembered [and will conceive]." [Hannah would then conceive in consequence of her surviving the rite of the bitter water.]

I. But in the view of him who said, "If formerly the accused wife had born children in pain, she will bear easily, if she had born females, she will bear males, if she had born dark-skinned children, she will bear light skinned ones, if she had born short ones, she will bear tall ones," what can one say? [Now there is no provision for the pregnancy of the formerly barren wife who has been vindicated.]

J. For it has been taught on Tannaite authority:

K. "'She shall be cleared and shall conceive seed' (Num. 5:28), so that if she had been barren, she will be remembered," the words of R. Ishmael.

L. Said to him R. Aqiba, "If so, all barren women will go and go aside with a strange man, and the one who did not actually do anything wrong will then be remembered [and become pregnant with her husband]. Rather, the cited passage teachings that if formerly the accused wife had born females, she will bear males, if she had born dark-skinned children, she will bear light skinned ones, if she had born short ones, she will bear tall ones, if she had born only one at a time, she will bear two at a time."

M. What then is the sense of "If you will indeed look"?

N. The Torah used commonplace language [and did not mean to provide the basis for any exegesis at all].

XXI.

A. "If you will indeed look on the affliction of your handmaid and will not forget your handmaid but will give to your handmaid..." (1 Sam. 1:11).

B. Said R. Yose b. R. Hanina, "What is the sense of these three references to 'hand-maid'?

C. "Hannah said before the Holy One, blessed be he, 'Lord of the world, there are three criteria which you have created in a woman, by which one may become liable to the death penalty, and some say, three armor joints [Simon] [at which a woman is vulnerable], and these are they: the matter of avoiding sexual relations when one is menstruating, the matter of separating the dough-offering, and the matter of kindling the Sabbath lamp. Have I violated any one of these?'"

XXII.

A. "But will you give your handmaid a seed for a male" (1 Sam. 1:12):

B. What is the sense of "seed for a male"?

C. Said Rab, "A man among men."

D. Said Samuel, "Seed that will anoint two men, and who are they? Saul and David."

E. And R. Yohanan said, "Seed that is worth two other men, and who are they? Moses and Aaron.

F. "For it is said, 'Moses and Aaron are among his priests, and Samuel among those who call upon his name' (Ps. 99:6)."

G. And rabbis say, "Seed that will be assimilated among other men [and not be conspicuous]."

H When R. Dimi came, he said, "Not tall or short, not thin nor fat, not pale nor ruddy, not too smart nor too dumb."

XXIII.

A. "I am the woman that stood by you here" (1 Sam. 1:26):

B. Said R. Joshua b. Levi, "On the basis of that verse [we learn] that it is forbidden to sit within four cubits of [someone who is reciting] the Prayer."

XXIV.

A. "For this child I prayed" (1 Sam. 1:27):

B. Said R. Eleazar, "Samuel taught law in the presence of his master. For it is said, 'And when the bullock was slain, the child was brought to Eli' (1 Sam. 1:25). Is it because 'when the bullock was slain' that 'the child was brought to Eli'?

C. "Rather, this is the sense of the matter.

D. "Eli said to them, 'Call a priest and bring him to slaughter the beast.'

E. "Samuel saw that they were looking for a priest to slaughter the beast. He said to them, 'Why are you looking for a priest to slaughter the beast? An act of slaughter that is done by a non-priest is valid just as well.'

F. "They brought him to Eli, who said to him, 'How do you know this?'

G. "He said to him, 'Is it written, "And the priest will slaughter"? What is written is: 'The priests shall offer up the blood' (Lev. 1:5). The point is that from the moment of receiving the blood onward, the religious duty is to be carried out by the priesthood. On the basis of this exegesis, we learn that the act of slaughter is valid even when done by a non-priest.'

H. "He said to him, 'You have made a perfectly valid statement. But at the same time you are teaching a matter of law in the presence of your master, and whoever teaches a matter of law before his master is liable to the death-penalty.'

I. "Hannah came and cried out before him, 'I am the woman that stood by you here.'

J. "He said to her, 'Let me punish him and I shall pray for you and a greater son than this one will be given to you.'

K. "She said to him, 'For this particular child I prayed.'"

XXV.

A. "Now Hannah spoke upon her heart" (1 Sam. 1:13):

B. Said R. Eleazar in the name of R. Yose b. Zimra, "She spoke concerning matters upon her heart before him: 'Lord of the world, whatever you created in woman you have not created purposelessly. You created eyes to see, ears to hear, a nose to smell, a mouth to speak, hands to do work, feet for walking, breasts for suckling. These breasts that you have placed upon my heart are for what? Are they not for suckling? Give me a son so that I may give suck with them.'"

C. And R. Eleazar said in the name of R. Yose b. Zimra, "For whoever keeps a fast on the Sabbath they tear up a decree of seventy years standing.

D. "And even so, they go back and exact it from him on account of his failure to rejoice in the Sabbath."

E. What is his remedy?

F. Said R. Nahman bar Isaac, "Let him fast on account of the fast [that he kept on the Sabbath]."

XXVI.

A. And R. Eleazar said, "Hannah spoke insolently against the heights.

B. "For it is said, 'And Hannah prayed against the Lord' (1 Sam. 1:10).

C. "This indicates that she spoke insolently against the heights [of God]."

D. And R. Eleazar said, "Elijah spoke insolently against the heights, as it says, 'For you turned their heart backwards' (1 Kgs. 18:37)."

E. Said R. Samuel bar R. Isaac, "How do we know that the Holy One, blessed be he, went and conceded that Elijah was right?

F. [32A] As it is written, 'And whom I have wronged' (Mic. 4:6)."

XXVII.

A. Said R. Hama b. R. Hanina, "Were it not for these three verses of Scripture [Simon, p. 195, n. 6: which show that God is responsible for the evil impulse], the feet of (the enemies of) Israel should be moved [for Israel would bear the blame for its sinfulness].

B.   "One: 'Whom I have wronged' (Mic. 4:6).

C.   "The second: 'Behold as the clay in the potter's hand, so are you in my hand, house of Israel' (Jer. 18:6).

D.   "The third: 'I will take out of your flesh the heart of stone, and give you a heart of flesh' (Ez. 36:26).

E.   R. Papa said, "The matter derives from here: 'And I will put my spirit within you and cause you to walk in my statutes' (Ex. 36:27). [So God causes one thing or the other.]"

XXVIII.

A.   And R. Eleazar said, "Moses spoke insolently toward the height [God], as it is said, 'And Moses prayed to the Lord' (Num. 11:2).

B.   "Do not read 'to the Lord' but [shifting a letter] 'against the Lord.'"

C.   For so in the house of R. Eliezer b. Jacob people pronounce the letter alef as an ayin and an ayin as an alef [both silently]. [That explains B.]

D.   The house of R. Yannai say, "Proof [that it was God's fault] derives from the following: 'And enough gold' (Deut. 1:1)."

E.   What is the meaning of "enough gold"?

F.   They say in the house of R. Yannai, "This is what Moses said before the Holy One, blessed be he, 'Lord of the age, it was on account of the silver and gold that you lavished upon Israel until they said, "Enough," that caused them to make the golden calf.'"

G.   They say in the house of R. Yannai, "A lion roars not over a basket of straw but over a basket of meat."

H.   Said R. Oshaia, "The matter may be compared to the case of a man who had a cow that was thin but had good limbs. [To fatten it] he fed it lupines, and it bucked.

I.   "He said to it, 'What made you buck against me? It was only the lupines that I fed you.'"

J.   Said R. Hiyya bar Abba said R. Yohanan, "The matter may be compared to the case of a man who had a son. He washed him, anointed him, gave him food and drink, and hung a purse around his neck and sat him at the door of a whorehouse. What could the son do so as not to sin?"

K.   Said R. Aha son of R. Huna said R. Sheshet, "That is in line with what people say: 'Full stomach, bad impulse,' as it is said, 'When they were fed, they became full, they were filled and their heart was exalted, therefore they have forgotten me' (Hos. 13:6)."

L.   R. Nahman said, "Proof derives from the following: 'Then your heart was lifted up and you forgot the Lord' (Deut. 8:14)."

M.   Rabbis say, "Proof derives from the following: 'And they shall have eaten their fill and gotten fat and turned to other gods' (Deut. 31:20)."

N.   If you prefer, I can derive proof from the following: "But Jeshurun waxed fat and kicked" (Deut. 32:15).

O.   Said R. Samuel bar Nahmani said R. Jonathan, "How do we know that the Holy One, blessed be he, retracted and conceded that Moses was right?

P.   "As it is said, 'And [I] multiplied to her silver and gold which they used for Baal' (Hos. 2:10)."

XXIX.

A.   "And the Lord spoke to Moses, Go, get you down" (Ex. 32:7):

B.   What is the meaning of "Go, get you down"?

C.   Said R. Eleazar, "Said the Holy One, blessed be he, to Moses, 'Moses, go down from your position of greatness. Have I made you great for any reason other than for Israel? Now that Israel have sinned, what do I need you for?'

D.   "Forthwith Moses grew weak and did not have the power to speak.

E.   "When he said to him, 'Let me alone that I may destroy them' (Deut. 9:14), Moses thought, 'This matter now depends on me.'

F.   "Forthwith he stood and become strong in prayer and sought mercy.

G.   "The matter may be compared to the case of a king who grew angry with his son and was giving him hard blows. The king's friend was sitting before him, afraid to say anything to him. The king said, 'Were my friend not here, sitting before me, I should have killed him.'

H.   "The other realized, 'This matter depends on me.' Forthwith he stood up and saved [the son]."

XXX.

A.   "Now therefore let me alone that my wrath may wax hot against them and that I may consume them, and I will make of you a great nation" (Ex. 32:10):

B.   Said R. Abbahu, "Were it not a verse of Scripture fully spelled it, it would never have been possible to make such a statement.

C.   "The verse teaches that Moses seized the Holy One, blessed be he, like a man who grabs his friend by his garment.

D.   "He said to him, 'Lord of the world, I shall not let you go until you forgive and pardon them.'"

XXXI.

A.   "And I will make of you a great nation" (Ex. 32:10):

B.   Said R. Eleazar, "Said Moses before the Holy One, blessed be he, 'Lord of the age, 'Now if a stool with three legs cannot stand against you when you are angry, a stool with only one leg [that is, Moses] surely should not be able to stand!

C.   "'Not only so, but I have to be ashamed before my forefathers, for now they will say, "See how the provider whom he set up over them seeks greatness for himself and does not seek mercy for them!"'"

XXXII.

A.   "And Moses besought the Lord his God" (Ex. 32:11):

B.   Said R. Eleazar, "This verse teaches that Moses stood in prayer before the Holy One, blessed be he, until he had exhausted him."

C.   And Rab said, "It was until he had released him from his vow.

D.   "Here it is written, 'He besought,' and [in connection with vows], he shall not break his word' [using the same verb] (Num. 30:3).

E.   "And a master has said, 'He cannot break the vow, but others may break the vow for him.' [Moses thus released God's vow.]"

F.   And Samuel said, "This verse teaches that he gave himself up to death in their behalf.

G.   "For it is said, 'And if not, blot me, I pray you, out of the book which you have written' (Ex. 32:32)."

H.   Raba said in the name of R. Isaac, "This verse teaches that he made the attribute of mercy rest on them."

I.   And rabbis say, "This verse teaches that Moses said before the Holy One, blessed be he, 'Lord of the age, it would be perfectly common of you to do such a thing.'"

J.   "And Moses besought the Lord" (Ex. 32:11):

K.   It has been taught on Tannaite authority:

L.   R. Eliezer the elder says, "This verse teaches that Moses stood in prayer before the Holy One, blessed be he, until he was seized by a fever."

M.   What is this fever?

N.   Said R. Eleazar, "It is a burning in the bones."

O.   What is a "burning in the bones"?

P.   Said Abayye, "A fire in the bones."

XXXIII.

A.   "Remember Abraham, Isaac and Israel, your servants, to whom you swore by yourself" (Ex. 32:13):

B.   What is the meaning of "by yourself"?

C.   Said R. Eleazar, "Said Moses before the Holy One, blessed be he, 'Lord of the age, Had you taken the oath to them by heaven and earth, I might have said that just as heaven and earth shall be null, so your oath will be null. But now that you have taken your oath by your great name, just as your great name lives and endures forever and ever, so your oath endures forever and ever.'"

XXXIV.

A.   "And said to them, I will multiply your seed as the stars of heaven and all this land of which I have spoken" (Ex. 32:13):

B.   This expression, "Of which I have spoken" should be "of which you have spoken"!

C.   Said R. Eleazar, "Up to this point we have the words of the disciple [Moses]. From this point forward we have the words of the master [God]."

D.   And R. Samuel bar Nahman said, "Both clauses are the words of the disciple. But this is what Moses said before the Holy One, blessed be he, 'Lord of the world, As to the words that you have spoken to me, telling me to go and say them to the Israelites in my name, indeed I did go and speak to them in your name. Now what shall I say to them.'"

XXXV.

A.   "Because the Lord was not able" (Num. 14:16):

B.   [Since the word for "able" is given in the feminine form, it is asked,] Should not the word be given in the masculine form?

C.   Said R. Eleazar, "Said Moses before the Holy One, blessed be he, 'Lord of the age, now the nations of the world will say that his strength has become weak like a woman's, so he cannot save [them].'

D.   "Said the Holy One, blessed be he, to Moses, 'But did they not already see the miracles and mighty deeds which I did for them at the sea?'

E.   "He said to him, 'Lord of the age, But they still can say, "Against a single king he can stand, but against thirty-one kings he cannot stand."'"

F.   Said R. Yohanan, "How do we know that the Holy One, blessed be he, retracted and conceded that Moses was right?

G.   "As it is said, 'And the Lord said, I have pardoned according to your word' (Ex. 32:20)."

H.   On Tannaite authority in the house of R. Ishmael: "'In accord with your word' (Ex. 32:20):

I.   "The nations of the world are going to say this: 'Happy is the disciple with whom his master concurs.'"

XXXVI.

A.   "But in very deed, as I live" (Ex. 32:21):

B.   Said Raba said R. Isaac, "This teaches that the Holy One, blessed be he, said to Moses, 'Moses, you have given me life through your words.'"

XXXVII.

A.   R. Simlai expounded, "A person should always lay out words of praise for the Holy One, blessed be he, first of all, and then he should say the Prayer.

B.   "How do we know it?

C.   "It is from Moses, for it is written, 'And I besought the Lord at that time' (Deut. 3:23).

D.   "And then it says, 'O Lord God, you have begun to show your servant your greatness and your strong hand, for what god is there in heaven and earth who can do according to your deeds and according to your mighty acts.' And then it is written, 'Let me go over, I pray you, and see the good land' (Deut. 3:23ff.)."

XXXVIII.

A.   [32B] Said R. Eleazar, "Prayer is more important than good deeds.

B.   "For you have no one who excelled in good deeds more than Moses, our master.

C.   "Even so, he was answered only when he prayed.

D.   "For it is said, 'Speak no more to me' (Deut. 3:26), and forthwith, 'Get you up to the top of Pisgah' (Ex. Deut. 3:27)."

E.   And R. Eleazar said, "Fasting is more important than philanthropy.

F.   "What is the reason?

G.   "This is done with one's body, while that, only with his money."

H.   And R. Eleazar said, "Prayer is more important than offerings,

I.   "for it is said, 'To what purpose is the multitude of your sacrifices to me' (Is. 1:11).

J. "And forthwith: 'And when you spread forth your hands' (Is. 1:15). [Simon, p. 199, n. 6: Since spreading of hands is mentioned after sacrifice, it must be regarded as more efficacious.]"

K. Said R. Yohanan, "Any priest who has killed a person may not raise his hands.

L. "For it is said, 'Your hands are full of blood' (Is. 1:15)."

XXXIX.

A. And R. Eleazar said, "From the day on which the house of the sanctuary was destroyed, the gates of prayer have been locked.

B. "For it is said, 'Yes, when I cry and call for help, he shuts out my prayer' (Lam. 3:8).

C. "But even though the gates of prayer are locked, the gates of tears are not locked.

D. "For it is said, 'Hear my prayer, Lord, and give ear to my cry, keep not silence at my tears' (Ps. 39:13)."

E. Raba did not decree a fast on a cloudy day, because it is said, 'You have covered yourself with a cloud so that no prayer can pass through' (Lam. 3:44)."

XL.

A. And R. Eleazar said, "From the day on which the house of the sanctuary was destroyed, an iron wall came down to separate Israel and their father in heaven.

B. "For it is said, 'And take you for yourself an iron griddle and set it for a wall of iron between you and the city' (Ez. 4:3)."

XLI.

A. Said R. Hanin said R. Hanina, "Whoever takes a long time in reciting his Prayer [will find that] his prayer does not come back empty.

B. "How do we know it? From the case of Moses, our master.

C. "For it is said, 'And I prayed to the Lord' (Deut. 9:26) [Simon: This seems to be quoted in error, instead of 'And I fell down before the Lord forty days and forty nights' (Deut. 9:18)].

D. "And afterward it is written, 'And the Lord hearkened to me that time also' (Deut. 9:19)."

E. Is this the case?

F. And lo, said R. Hiyya bar Abba said R. Yohanan, "Whoever takes a long time in saying his Prayer and looks for the prayer to be fulfilled [will find that] in the end he comes to heartache.

G. "For it is said, 'Hope deferred makes the heart sick' (Prov. 13:12)."

H. What is the remedy for such a person?

I. Let him engage in Torah-study, as it says, "But desire fulfilled is a tree of life" (Prov. 13:12).

J. And the tree of life is nothing other than the Torah, as it says, "It is a tree of life to those that lay hold of it" (Prov. 3:18).

K. There is indeed no contradiction between the two statements [A, F]. The one speaks of a case in which one takes a long time in saying his prayer and looks for the prayer to be fulfilled, the other speaks of someone who takes a long time in saying his prayer but does not look for the prayer to be fulfilled.

L.   Said R. Hama bar Hanina, "If a person should see that he says a prayer and is not answered, he should go back and say the prayer again.

M.   "For it is said, 'Wait for the Lord, be strong and let your heart take courage, yes, wait for the Lord' (Ps. 37:14)."

XLII.

A.   Our rabbis have taught on Tannaite authority:

B.   Four require strengthening, and these are they: study of Torah, practice of good deeds, praying, and doing one's daily work.

C.   How do we know that that is the case for Torah and good deeds?

D.   As it is said, "Only be strong and very courageous to observe to do according to all the Torah" (Josh. 1:7).

E.   "Be strong" in Torah, and "be courageous" in good deeds.

F.   How do we know that that is the case for praying?

G.   As it is said, "Wait for the Lord, be strong and let your heart take courage, yes, wait for the Lord" (Ps. 37:14).

H.   How do we know that that is the case for one's work?

I.   As it is said, "Be of good courage and let us prove strong for our people" (2 Sam. 10:12).

XLIII.

A.   "But Zion said, The Lord has forsaken me, and the Lord has forgotten me" (Is. 49:14).

B.   Being forsaken is surely the same thing as being forgotten!

C.   Said R. Simeon b. Laqish, "Said the community of Israel before the Holy One, blessed be he,

D.   "'Lord of the age, if a man takes a second wife after the first, he remembers the deeds of the first wife. But you have forsaken me and forgotten me.'

E.   "Said the Holy One, blessed be he, to her, 'My daughter, I have created twelve constellations in the sky, and for each constellation, I have created thirty hosts, and for each host, thirty legions, and for each legion, thirty cohorts, and for each cohort, thirty maniples, and for each maniple, thirty camps, and to each camp I have attached three hundred sixty-five thousands of myriads of stars, matching the days of the solar year, and it is only for your sake that I created all of them. Yet you say, 'You have forgotten men and forsaken me'!

F.   "'Can a woman forsake her suckling child' (Is. 49:15)?

G.   "Said the Holy One, blessed be he, 'Can I ever forget the burnt-offerings of rams and the firstborn of animals which you offered me in the wilderness?'

H.   "[The community of Israel] said, 'Lord of the age, since there is no possibility of forgetfulness before the throne of your glory, can you then forget what I did with the golden calf?'

I.   "He said to her, 'Yes, "these" will be forgotten' [that is, the statement, "These are your gods", Ex. 32:4]."

J.   "She said to him, 'Lord of the age, since there is the possibility of forgetting before the throne of your glory, is it possible that you will forget what "I" did at Sinai?'

K. "He said to her, 'Yet the "I" [referring to 'I am the Lord your God' of Ex. 20:1] will not forget you' (Is. 49:15)."

L. This is in line with what R. Eleazar said R. Oshaia said, "What is the meaning of the verse of Scripture, 'Yes, "these" will be forgotten' (Is. 49:15)?

M. "This refers to the sin of the golden calf.

N. "'But the "I" will not forget you' (Is. 49:15) --

XLIV.

A. The pious men of old used to tarry one hour before praying [M. 5:1B]:

B. What is the source for that rule?

C. Said R. Joshua b. Levi, "Said Scripture, 'Happy are those who dwell in your house' (Ps. 84:5)."

D. And said R. Joshua b. Levi, "He who says a prayer has to tarry an hour after he recites the Prayer, for it is said, 'Surely the righteous shall give thanks to your name, the upright shall sit in your presence' (Ps. 140:14)."

E. It has been taught on Tannaite authority along these same lines:

F. He who recites the Prayer has to tarry an hour before he recites the Prayer and an hour after he recites the Prayer.

G. How do we know that one must do so before he recites the Prayer?

H. As it is said, "Happy are those who dwell in your house" (Ps. 84:5).

I. How do we know that one must do so after he recites the Prayer?

J. As it is said, "Surely the righteous shall give thanks to your name, the upright shall sit in your presence" (Ps. 140:14).

XLV.

A. Our rabbis have taught on Tannaite authority:

B. The pious men of old would tarry for another hour, and then recite the Prayer for an hour, then they would go and tarry for another hour.

C. But if they tarry for nine hours a day [in reciting the Prayer three times], what will become of their study of the Torah and how will their daily work be done?

D. Since they are pious men, their study of Torah is protected and their daily work is blessed.

XLVI.

A. If one was praying, even if the king greets him, he may not respond [M. 5:1D]:

B. Said R. Joseph, "That rule has been taught only with reference to Israelite kings, but as to gentile kings, one has to interrupt [and pay one's respect to the gentile king]."

C. It was objected:

D. He who is reciting the Prayer and saw a thug coming toward him or a carriage coming toward him may not interrupt reciting the Prayer but abbreviates it and goes away.

E. There is no contradiction between the two rules. One speaks of a case in which it is possible to abbreviate the recitation, [the other in which it is not possible to do so].

XLVII.

A. Our rabbis have taught on Tannaite authority:

B.   There was the case of a pious man who was saying the Prayer on the road. An officer came and greeted him but he did not reply to him with a greeting. The officer waited until he had finished reciting his Prayer.

C.   After he had finished reciting his Prayer, he said to him, "Fool! Is it not written in your Torah, 'Only take heed to yourself and keep your soul diligently' (Deut. 4:9), and it is written, 'Take you therefore good care of your souls' (Deut. 4:15). [So one has to protect his life, but you endangered yours.]

D.   "Now when I greeted you, why did you not greet me back? If I had cut off your head with a sword, who would have demanded recompense for your blood [since it would have been your own fault]?"

E.   He said to him, "Wait until I explain the matter to your satisfaction. If you were standing before a mortal king, and your friend had come and greeted you, would you have [33A] replied to him?"

F.   [The officer] said, "No."

G.   "And if you had replied to him, what would they have done to you?"

H.   He said to him, "They would have cut off my head with a sword."

I.   [The Israelite then] said to him, "Now is it not an argument a fortiori?

J.   "If you had been standing before a mortal king, who is here today and tomorrow in the grave, you would have behaved in such a way.

K.   "I, who was standing before the King of kings of kings, the Holy One, blessed be he, who lives and endures for ever and ever, how much the more so [that I must concentrate on my petition to him and not break off to greet you]."

L.   The officer found the answer satisfactory, and the pious man went on to his home in peace.

XLVIII.

A.   And even if a serpent is entwined around his heel [M. 5:1E]:

B.   Said R. Sheshet, "The law has been taught only with regard to a snake, but in the case of a scorpion, one may interrupt [the recitation of the Prayer]."

C.   An objection was raised:

D.   If a man fell into a den of lions, people may not [assume that he has died and] testify in his regard that he has died. But if he fell into a ditch filled with snakes or scorpions [people may assume that he has died] and give testimony concerning him that he has died. [Therefore the rule for snakes and scorpions should be the same.]

E.   The cited case is different, since, because the man has fallen [on the snakes,] they go and bite him, [but otherwise they would not. Scorpions, by contrast, always bite.]

F.   Said R. Isaac, "If one saw oxen [running toward him], he may interrupt the recitation of the Prayer]."

G.   For R. Oshaia taught on Tannaite authority: "People should go a distance of fifty cubits from an ox that has not been known to gore, and as far as one can see from an ox that has been known to gore."

H.   It has been taught on Tannaite authority in the name of R. Meir, "If the head of the ox is in the fodder basket, climb up to the roof and kick away the ladder behind you."

I.   Said Samuel, "That rule applies to a black ox in Nisan, because, at that time, Satan dances between its horns."

XLIX.

A.   Our rabbis have taught on Tannaite authority:

B.   There was the case concerning a certain place in which a lizard was going around and biting people. They came and told R. Hanina b. Dosa.

C.   He said to them, "Show me its hole."

D.   They showed him its hole. He put his heel over the mouth of the hole. The lizard came out and bit him and died.

E.   He took it on his shoulder and brought it to the school house. He said to them, "See, my sons, it is not the lizard that kills but sin that kills."

F.   At that moment they said, "Woe to the man who meets a lizard, and woe to the lizard that meets up with R. Hanina b. Dosa [cf. T. Ber. 3:20C-E].

This rather protracted passage, covering Talmud pages 30B-33A, is carefully arranged and follows a perfectly clear program. It is only partly intended to expound the statements of the Mishnah-paragraph in particular. The bulk of the passage takes up the theme of the Mishnah-paragraph, rather than its particular rules. The redactors draw into contact with that theme, prayer, a sizable and well-composed corpus of biblical verses. If, therefore, I had to define the intent of the redactors of the present passage of the Talmud as a whole, I should propose a simple explanation. They wished to explain the Mishnah's language, to introduce materials from Tosefta to amplify or expand upon the Mishnah's specific allegations, and, finally and to them clearly most important, to introduce a vast repertoire of biblical verses on exactly the theme at hand. What we have is a kind of biblical encyclopedia on Mishnaic themes. These biblical supplements are drawn upon in accord with a clear program. They in no way prove random or lacking in clear purpose. Let me explain why I think that the entire passage at hand proceeds in a thoughtful and well-conceived program to spell out the Talmud's message on the nature and conduct of prayer.

What the redactors have done is to illustrate the matter of praying by referring to two important examples, in Scripture's narratives, of prayers and how they were offered and answered. In this rather vast construction the biblical precedents on praying turn out to be far more important than amplification or clarification of sentences in the Mishnah-paragraph. Hence we look first at the major subdivisions of the whole, that is to say, biblical precedents of how to pray and the exegesis of relevant verses.

1.   Hannah's prayer

This occurs at unit I, which explicitly explains why the passage is invoked to begin with, namely, Hannah sets the example of praying in an appropriate spirit, I B. We note, also, that Eleazar, who turns out to be the principal tradent for the entire protracted passage, makes his first appearance here. Units II-VII are tacked on to unit I because of the proof-text, Ps. 2:11, at I. Hannah's prayer is then explicitly presented as the paradigm at XVI, and the verses of that passage are systematically worked through from

XVI through XXVI (+ XVII, which complements XXVI F). That is no small sequence but a rich and dense one.

2.   The Prayer of Moses

This passage occurs, to begin with, in a rather subtle bridge. How so? The basic idea of XXVIII, at which Moses first occurs, is the same as at XXVI-XXVII, namely, the notion that God is responsible for human sin, because he put the impulse to do evil into human beings. That expression of the theme carefully continues what was said above. But we forthwith see that the framer has then built a firm transition from Hannah and her prayer to the figure of Moses and his prayer. That theme is made explicit at XXIX (for Ex. 32) and goes on through unit XXXVI. Then comes yet another prayer of Moses, this one at Deut. 3:23, occurring at unit XXXVII-XXXVIII.

Once the two important examples of effective prayer are worked out, the framers proceed to a set of statements of a more abstract and general character on the same theme. These occur at XXXIX through XL, for Eleazar; XLI, praying for a long time; XLII, praying with vigor; XLIII, Is. 49:14, with stress that God will never abandon Israel. These are fairly routine complements to the main discussion -- Hannah and Moses.

We note that once the rather sizable construction on biblical teachings relevant to prayer has been worked out, the redactors do introduce verbatim citations and exegeses of the Mishnah-paragraph, at XLIV and XLVIII. There seems at the end to be a slight interest in presenting, in sequence, exegesis of the Mishnah's language, then amplification through Tosefta's materials of the Mishnah-sentence at hand, that is, XLIV/XLV, XLVII/XLIX. But that is only a tendency. We turn, finally, to amplifications through Tosefta's supplements of the rules given in the Mishnah-paragraph. These occur at units VIII-XII + XIII, XIV + XV, then, for later components, XLV, XLVII, and XLIX. So the established pattern is followed when Mishnah-exegesis and Tosefta's supplements come into play.

5:2

A.   They mention the "power of the rain" in [the blessing concerning] "the resurrection of the dead," [the second blessing in the eighteen benedictions].

B.   And they ask for rain in the blessing of the years [the ninth blessing].

C.   And [they insert] Prayer of Division [habdalah, i.e., the blessing which marks the end of the Sabbath or festival] in [the blessing concluding] "who graciously gives knowledge," [the fourth blessing].

D.   R. Aqiba says, "One says it as a fourth blessing, by itself."

E.   R. Eliezer says, "[One says it] in the thanksgiving [the eighteenth blessing in the prayer]."

I.

A.   They mention the "power of rain" [M. 5:2A]:

B. Why [is this benediction included in particular in the one for the resurrection for the dead]?

C. Said R. Joseph, "Because [rain] is equivalent to the resurrection of the dead, therefore [sages] gave it its place in the blessing for the resurrection of the dead."

II.

A. And they ask for rain in the blessing of the years [M. 5:2B]:

B. Why [is this benediction included in particular in the one for the blessing of the years]?

C. Said R. Joseph, "Because it concerns making a living, therefore [sages] gave it its place in the blessing concerning making a living."

III.

A. And they insert the Prayer of Division in the blessing concluding, "who graciously gives knowledge" [M. 5:2C]:

B. Why [is this benediction included in particular in the one having to do with knowledge]?

C. Said R. Joseph, "Because it concerns wisdom, so [sages] gave it its place in the blessing concerning wisdom."

D. And rabbis say, "Because it deals with an ordinary day, therefore [sages] gave it its place in a blessing having to do with an ordinary day."

IV.

A. Said R. Ammi, "The importance of knowledge is indicated by the fact that it is given its place at the beginning of the first blessing [of the Prayer, beyond the obligatory opening three, said on all occasions] having to do with a weekday."

B. And R. Ammi said, "The greatness of knowledge is indicated by the fact that it is placed between two references to the divine name.

C. "For it is said, 'For a God of knowledge is the Lord' (1 Sam. 2:3).

D. "And it is forbidden to have pity on anyone who has no knowledge, as it is said, 'For it is a people of no understanding, therefore he that made them will have no compassion upon them' (Is. 27:11)."

E. Said R. Eleazar, the elder, "The greatness of the sanctuary is indicated by the fact that it is placed between two references to the divine name, for it is said, 'You have made, O Lord, the sanctuary, O Lord' (Ex. 15:17)."

F. And R. Eleazar said, "As to any person in whom is knowledge, it is as if the house of the sanctuary had been built in his days.

G. "Knowledge is located between two references to the divine name, and the sanctuary likewise is situated between two references to the divine name."

H. R. Aha Karhinaah objected, "But what about the following:

I. "'The greatness of vengeance is indicated by the fact that it is situated between two references to the divine name,

K. "'as it is said, "God of vengeance, O Lord" (Ps. 94:1).'"

L. [Eleazar] said to him, "Indeed [vengeance] too is a great thing."

M. That is in line with what Ulla said, "Why is vengeance indicated twice here? One is for good, one for evil.

N.   "For good, as it is written, 'He shines forth from Mount Paran' (Deut. 33:2).

O.   "For evil, as it is written, 'God of vengeance, O Lord, God of vengeance, shine forth'
      (Ps. 94:1).

V.

A.   R. Aqiba says, "One says it as a fourth blessing, by itself" [M. 5:2D]:

B.   Said R. Shemen bar Abba to R. Yohanan, "Since the men of the great assembly
      ordained for Israel the recitation of the blessings, Prayers, rites of sanctification
      and Prayers of Division, let us see in what place they ordained [that these prayers
      should be recited]."

C.   He said to him, "To begin with, they gave it its place in the recitation of the
      Prayer. When they got richer, they gave it its place as a prayer to be recited over a
      cup of wine. When they became poorer, they went and once more gave it its place
      in the recitation of the Prayer.

D.   "And they ruled: He who says the Prayer of Division when he recites the Prayer has
      also to say the Prayer of Division over a cup of wine."

E.   It also has been stated on Amoraic authority:

F.   Said R. Hiyya bar Abba said R. Yohanan, "To begin with, they gave it its place in the
      recitation of the Prayer. When they got richer, they gave it its place as a prayer to
      be recited over a cup of wine. When they became poorer, they went and once more
      gave it its place in the recitation of the Prayer.

G.   "And they ruled: He who says the Prayer of Division when he recites the Prayer has
      also to say the Prayer of Division over a cup of wine."

VI.

A.   It has also been stated on Amoraic authority:

B.   Rabbah and R. Joseph both say, "He who says the Prayer of Division when he recites
      the Prayer has also to say the Prayer of Division over a cup of wine."

C.   Said Raba, "We may propose an objection to the matter on the basis of that which
      we have learned:

D.   "'If one made a mistake and did not make mention of the blessing 'power of rain' in
      the blessing for the resurrection of the dead, or the petition for rain in the blessing
      for the years, they make the person go back. [But if he did not make mention of]
      the Prayer of Division in the blessing, 'who graciously gives knowledge, they do not
      make him go back, because he can recite it over a cup of wine' [cf. T. Ber. 3:9].
      [This would show that one does not have to say the Prayer of Division both in the
      recitation of the Prayer and also over a cup of wine, as against Rabbah and R.
      Joseph's view that one does.]

E.   [The reply:] Do not recite the language, "Because he can recite it over a cup of
      wine," but rather say, "Because he says it over a cup of wine" [but that is not the
      best way to do it].

F.   It has also been stated on Amoraic authority:

G.   Said R. Benjamin bar Japheth, "R. Yose asked R. Yohanan in Sidon, and some say, R.
      Simeon b. Jacob of Tyre asked R. Yohanan, 'But I have heard: 'He who says the

Prayer of Division when he recites the Prayer has also to say the Prayer of Division over a cup of wine. Or does one not have to do so?'

H.   "'He said to him, "He has to say the Prayer of Division over a cup of wine."'"

VII.

A.   The question was raised: What is the law as to one who has said the Prayer of Division over a cup of wine having also to say the Prayer of Division when he recites the Prayer?

B.   Said R. Nahman bar Isaac, "It is an argument a fortiori on the basis of the recitation of the Prayer.

C.   "Now if in the case of the recitation of the Prayer, which is the principal location for the recitation of the Prayer of Division, [sages] have said, 'He who recites the Prayer of Division in the recitation of the Prayer has also to recite the Prayer of Division over a cup of wine,

D.   "then in the case of one who recites the Prayer of Division over a cup of wine, which is not the principal locus for the recitation of that prayer at all, is it not an argument a fortiori [that he should also have to recite the Prayer of Division when he recites the Prayer]?"

VIII.

A.   R. Aha the tall repeated on Tannaite authority before R. Hinena, "He who recites the Prayer of Division in his recitation of the Prayer is more to be praised than is he who recites the Prayer of Division over a cup of wine.

B.   "And if one recited the Prayer of Division both in the one liturgy and in the other, blessings will come to rest on his head."

C.   Now the body of the cited statement bears a contradiction.

D.   You have said, "He who recites the Prayer of Division in the recitation of the Prayer is more to be praised than is he who recites the Prayer of Division over a cup of wine."

E.   Therefore saying the Prayer of Division in the recitation of the Prayer by itself is sufficient [to carry out one's obligation].

F.   But then the continuation of the tradition claims: If one has recited the Prayer of Division both in the one and in the other liturgy, blessings will come to rest on his head.

G.   Now if it is the fact that one has carried out his obligation to recite the Prayer of Division by doing it one time only, then we have a case in which one recites a blessing which is not called for, and Rab said, and some say, R. Simeon b. Laqish, and some say, R. Yohanan and R. Simeon b. Laqish both say, "Whoever says a blessing that is not called for violates the intent of the verse, 'You shall not take the name of the Lord your God in vain' (Ex. 20:7)."

H.   Hence I should revise the passage to read as follows:

I.   If one has said the Prayer of Division in the one place but did not say the Prayer of Division in the other, blessings will [nonetheless] come to rest on his head."

IX.

A. R. Hisda asked R. Sheshet, "If one erred both in the one case and in the other, what
    is the law?"

B. He said to him, "If one erred in both the one place and the other, he goes back to the
    beginning [and recites the Prayer and also the blessing over the cup of wine]."

C. [33B] Said Rabina to Raba, "What is the decided law?"

D. He said to him, "It is comparable to the recitation of the Prayer of Sanctification.

E. "Just as, in the Prayer for Sanctification, even though one has recited the Sancti-
    fication-Prayer in his recitation of the Prayer, he also recites the Sanctifica-
    tion-Prayer over a cup of wine,

F. "so is the rule governing the Prayer of Division. Even though one has recited the
    Prayer of Division in his recitation of the Prayer, he has also to recite the Prayer of
    Division over a cup of wine."

X.

A. R. Eliezer says, "One says it in the thanksgiving" [M. 5:2E]:

B. R. Zira was riding on an ass, and R. Hiyya bar Abin was going along behind him. He
    said to him, "Is it the case that you have said in the name of R. Yohanan, 'The law
    accords with the view of R. Eliezer on the occasion of a festival day which coincides
    with a Sunday [after the Sabbath], [at which point in the recitation of the Prayer
    there is no mention of the weekday blessing, 'who graciously grants knowledge]'?

C. He said to him, "Yes, that is the decided law."

D. "Then may one infer that rabbis differ?"

E. "And do they not differ? Lo, rabbis do differ."

F. "I might suppose that rabbis differ with respect to the other days of the year, but do
    they differ in the case of a festival day that coincides with a Sunday [for the reason
    explained, there would be no choice for such an occasion]?"

G. "But lo, R. Aqiba does differ [since he allows for the Prayer of Division to stand as a
    benediction by itself, so he cannot accord with Eliezer's view of the special case at
    hand.]"

H. "Do we follow the view of R. Aqiba throughout the year, that now too we should go
    and follow his view as well!"

I. "What is the reason that for the entire year we do not follow the practice of R.
    Aqiba? It is because eighteen benedictions have been ordained, but nineteen have
    not been ordained [on which account Aqiba's view is rejected]. Here too, seven
    benedictions have been ordained, but eight have not been ordained."

J. [Zira] said to him, "It has not been stated as a decided law, but merely as an
    inclination [and a preference]."

K. For it has been stated on Amoraic authority:

L. R. Isaac bar Abdimi said in the name of our master [Rab], "It is the law."

M. And some say, "It is an inclination."

N. R. Yohanan said, "[Rabbis] concur [with Eliezer]."

O. And R. Hiyya bar Abba said, "Matters appear [to accord with Eliezer's view]."

P. Said R. Zira, "Take hold of the version of R. Hiyya bar Abba, because he is meticulous about learning traditions from the mouth of the master [who formulated them], just as is Rahba of Pumbedita."

Q. For Rahba said R. Judah said, "The Temple Mount was a double stoa, one within the other." [In this formulation, Rahba used a less familiar word. Hence it is assumed that he carefully memorized and repeated exactly what he had heard]."

R. Said R. Joseph, "I know neither this version nor that version. But I know that Rab and Samuel ordained for us in Babylonia the following pearl:

S. "'And you have made known to us, Lord our God, your righteous judgments, taught us to carry out the ordinances that please you, and given us as a heritage seasons of rejoicing and festivals of giving. You have handed on to us the sanctity of the Sabbath and the glory of the festival and the celebration of the feast-day. You have made a division between the sanctity of the Sabbath and the sanctity of the festival-day. You have sanctified the seventh day more than the six days of labor. You have set aside and sanctified your people Israel through your sanctity and given us...,' etc."

Units I-III gloss the Mishnah-paragraph, as indicated; they form a single discourse. Unit IV is tacked on as a further amplification and extension. Unit V proposes to settle the dispute of the Mishnah's three authorities. Unit VI is relevant to the foregoing and units VII, VIII and IX follow in its wake. Unit X then reverts to the problem of deciding the law. So the entire construction serves either to unpack statements of the Mishnah or to expand upon materials introduced to begin with to explain the Mishnah-paragraph.

5:3A-D

A. He who says, "May your mercy extend to the nest of a bird,"

B. or "For goodness may your name be invoked,"

C. [or] "We give thanks, we give thanks" [two times] --

D. they silence him.

I.

A. Now with regard to the one who says, "We give thanks we give thanks," they silence him, because it appears that there are two dominions [in Heaven].

B. And "For goodness may your name be invoked," also [they silence him], because he implies that [we give thanks] for the good and not for the bad.

C. And we have learned A person is obligated to say a blessing for the bad just as he is obligated to say a blessing for the good [M. Ber. 9:1].

D. But what is the reason [that they silence one who says], "May your mercy extend to the nest of a bird"?

E. Two Amoraic authorities in the West, R. Yose bar Abin and R. Yose bar Zebida, differed on that matter.

F.   One said, "Because that formulation causes jealousy among the works of creation [singling out one for special concern]."

G.   The other said, "Because it represents the traits of the Holy One, blessed be he, as deriving from mercy, while they derive only from divine decrees."

II.

A.   A certain man went down [to lead prayer] before Rabbah and said, "You have shown pity to birds in the nest. Show pity and mercy to us."

B.   Said Rabbah, "How well does this neophyte rabbi know how to win the favor of his Master."

C.   Said Abbaye to him, "But lo, what we have learned in the Mishnah is: They silence him!"

D.   But what Rabbah really wanted to do was to sharpen Abayye's wits.

III.

A.   A certain man went down [to lead prayer] before R. Hanina. He said, "'...the great, mighty, fearful, majestic, powerful, awful, strong, fearless, sure, and honored God....'"

B.   [Hanina] waited for him to finish. When he had finished, he said to him, "Have you totally completed the list of all praiseworthy traits of your Master? Why are all of these additional adjectives needed?

C.   "As to the three traits that we do mention [Great, mighty, fearful], were it not that Moses, our master, had stated them in the Torah and that the men of the great assembly came along and ordained them to be included in the recitation of the Prayer, we should not recite even those adjectives. And yet you go on and on to say all of this!

D.   "The matter may be compared to a mortal king who had a thousand thousands of golden denars, and people praised him for having some in silver.

E.   "Is this not an insult to him?"

IV.

A.   And R. Hanina said, "Everything is in the hands of heaven except fear of heaven.

B.   "For it is said, 'And now, Israel, what does the Lord, your God, require of you but to fear' (Deut. 10:12)."

C.   Is fear of heaven such a small thing?

D.   And has not R. Hanina said in the name of R. Simeon b. Yohai, "What the Holy One, blessed be he, has in his treasury is only a treasure of fear of heaven.

E.   "For it is said, 'The fear of the Lord is his treasure' (Is. 33:6)."

F.   Indeed so, for so far as Moses was concerned, it was a small thing.

G.   For R. Hanina said, "The matter to be compared to a man from whom people sought a big thing. If he has it, to him it seems a small thing. If they ask a small thing and he does not have it, to him it seems a big thing."

V.

A.   "We give thanks, we give thanks" -- they silence him [M. 5:3C-D]:

B.   Said R. Zira, "Whoever says, 'Hear, hear' [in the Shema] is like one who says, 'We give thanks, we give thanks.'"

C. The objection was raised:

D. He who recites the Shema and repeats it -- lo, this is improper.

E. Thus it is, to be sure, improper, but people do not silence him.

F. There is no contradiction. In the one case ["Hear, hear"] the person says a word and repeats it, in the other, he says a whole sentence ["We give thanks", "we give thanks"] and repeats it.

G. Said R. Pappa to Abayye, "And perhaps the man to begin with did not pay attention to what he was saying, but in the end he did pay attention. [So why is this improper at all?]"

H. He said to him, [34A], "Is it proper to act in so informal a way toward heaven? If one did not pay attention to begin with, we poke him with a smith's hammer until he does pay attention."

The Talmud's units are devoted to the illustration or explanation of the Mishnah. Units I and V explain the rules, units II, III illustrate them. I assume that unit IV is tacked on because the two tales of Hanina were joined together before insertion here.

5:3E-5:4

E. He who came before the ark [to recite the prayers] and erred -- they replace him with another.

F. And one may not be stubborn at this time [if asked to serve as replacement for the one who errs].

G. Whence does he begin [if he replaces another who erred]?

H. From the beginning of the blessing in which the [previous] one had erred.

M. 5:3

A. One who goes before the ark [to lead the prayer] shall not answer "Amen" after the [blessing of the] priests.

B. because of [possible] confusion [which might arise].

C. And if [the leader] is the only priest there, he should not raise his hands [to recite the priestly blessing].

D. But if he is sure that he can raise his hands [to bless] and return to his prayer, he is permitted [to do so].

M. 5:4

I.

A. Our rabbis have taught on Tannaite authority:

B. He who passes before the ark [to lead the congregation in prayer] has first of all to decline [the honor], and if he does not decline the honor, he is like a dish without salt.

C.   But if he declines too much, he is like a dish that has been spoiled by salt.

D.   What does one then do?

E.   The first time [he is asked] he should modestly decline. The second time he should waver.

F.   The third time he should stretch out his feet and go down [to lead the prayers].

II.

A.   Our rabbis have taught on Tannaite authority:

B.   There are three things, too much of which is bad but a bit of which is good,

C.   and these are they: yeast, salt, and declining [a public honor].

III.

A.   Said R. Huna, "If one erred in the recitation of the first three blessings, he goes back to the beginning. If it was in the middle blessings, he goes back to 'You favor man with knowledge.'

B.   "If it was in the last three blessings, he goes back to the passage on the sacrificial service."

C.   And R. Assi said, "If he errs in the middle benedictions, there is no longer any order [applicable to the sequence of blessings]."

D.   R. Sheshet objected, "Whence does he begin? From the beginning of the blessing in which the previous one had erred [M. 5:3G-H]. That serves as a refutation of the view of R. Huna."

E.   R. Huna may say to you, "The benedictions in the middle all constitute a single benediction."

IV.

A.   Said R. Judah, "A person should ask for what he personally needs not in the first three blessings nor in the last three but in the middle ones."

B.   For R. Hanina said, "In the first three blessings one is like a slave, who eulogizes his master; in the middle ones he is like a slave who seeks a reward from his master. The last one is like a servant who has received a reward from his master and is planning to take his leave of him."

V.

A.   Our rabbis have taught on Tannaite authority:

B.   There is the case of a disciple who went down before the ark [to lead prayer] in the presence of R. Eliezer, and he took too long.

C.   His disciples said to [Eliezer], "Our master, this one certainly is a slow-poke."

D.   He said to them, "Does he take any longer than did Moses, our master, concerning whom it is written, 'The forty days and the forty nights...' (Deut. 9:25)."

E.   On another occasion there was a disciple who went down before the ark in the presence of R. Eliezer and he rushed through things very rapidly.

F.   His disciples said to him, "This one certainly cuts it short."

G.   He said to them, "Does he cut things any shorter than did Moses, our master, for it is written [as a complete prayer], 'O God, heal please' (Num. 12:13)."

H.   Said R. Hisda, "Whoever seeks mercy for his fellow does not even have to mention the latter's name, for it is said, 'O God, heal please' (Num. 12:13), and he does not even mention the name of Miriam."

VI.

A.   Our rabbis have taught on Tannaite authority:

B.   In connection with these benedictions a person has to bow, in the recitation of the benediction of the fathers, beginning and end, in the thanksgiving, beginning and end.

C.   If someone proposes to bow down at the end of every benediction or at the beginning of every benediction, they teach him not to bow down.

D.   Said R. Simeon b. Pazzi said R. Joshua b. Levi in the name of Bar Qappara, "An ordinary person must conduct himself as we have said.

E.   [34B] "A high priest does it at the end of every benediction. A king does it at the beginning of every benediction and at the end of every benediction."

F.   Said R. Isaac bar Nahmani, "To me did R. Joshua b. Levi explain matters as follows:

G.   "An ordinary person does things as we have said.

H.   "A high priest bows at the beginning of every benediction.

I.   "As to a king, once he has bowed down, he does not again genuflect, for it is said, 'And it was so that when Solomon has made an end of praying... he arose from before the altar of the Lord, from kneeling on his knees' (1 Kgs. 8:54)."

VII.

A.   Our rabbis have taught on Tannaite authority:

B.   Bowing is [to fall] on one's face, as it is said, "And Bath Sheba fell on her face to the ground" (1 Kgs. 1:31).

C.   Kneeling is to go down on one's knees, as it is said, "From kneeling on his knees" (1 Kgs. 8:54).

D.   Prostrating oneself is to spread out one's hands and feet on the ground, as it is said, "Shall I and your mother and brothers come to prostrate ourselves before you on the ground" (Gen. 37:10).

VIII.

A.   Said R. Hiyya, son of R. Huna, "I saw Abayye and Raba [Simon:] bending to one side."

B.   One teaching on Tannaite authority states: He who kneels down in reciting the thanksgiving benediction -- lo, this is one is to be praised.

C.   And another teaching on Tannaite authority states: Lo, this is improper.

D.   There is no contradiction, since the one speaks of what one does at the beginning of reciting the blessing, the other at the end.

E.   Raba kneeled down in reciting the thanksgiving benediction both at the beginning and at the end.

F.   Rabbis said to him, "Why does the master do it this way?"

G.   He said to them, "I saw R. Nahman kneel down, and I saw R. Sheshet do it this way."

H.   But lo, it has been taught on Tannaite authority: He who kneels down in reciting the thanksgiving benediction -- lo, this is improper.

I.   That refers to the thanksgiving prayer that is contained within the Hallel-psalms
       [Ps. 113-118].

J.   But lo, it has been taught on Tannaite authority:

K.   He who kneels down in reciting the thanksgiving benediction as well as in the
       thanksgiving prayer of the Hallel-psalms [thus explicitly including the item just now
       cited] -- lo, this is improper.

L.   When that Tannaite teaching was framed, it referred to the thanksgiving prayer that
       is contained in the Grace after Meals.

Unit I, continued by unit II, provides some secondary amplification for M. 5:3E, the
right conduct in being called to replace a reader who has erred. Unit III takes up M.
5:3G-H. Unit IV is inserted, I believe, because of III E. Otherwise I do not see why anyone
would have thought of including that composition. Unit V then continues the theme of
unit IV, namely, petitions of a personal character. To skip ahead, unit VII is inserted
because of its relevance to unit VI's theme, bowing, and so too unit VIII. But why is unit
VI added? Since there is no reference to bowing either in the Mishnah-paragraph or in the
antecedent Talmud-unit, that is, IV-V, I see no compelling reason for adding the rather
sizable discussion at just this point. My guess is that the person who inserted the rather
substantial and well-composed set had in mind simply amplifying the matter of how one
recites the several benedictions of the Prayer, which is, after all, precisely the point of
interest of IV-V. But the connection seems to me not so tight as others we have seen.

                                        5:5

A.   He who erred when reciting the Prayer -- it is a bad sign for him.

B.   And if he is representing the community [leading the prayer, and erred],
       it is a bad sign for them that appointed him,

C.   [on the principle that] a man's appointed agent is in his stead.

D.   They said concerning R. Haninah b. Dosa, that he used to pray for the
       sick and say "This one shall live" or "This one shall die."

E.   They said to him, "Whence do you know?"

F.   He said to them, "If my prayer is fluent, then I know that he [for whom I
       pray] is accepted.

G.   "And if not, then I know that he is rejected."

I.

A.   [With reference to M. 5:5A], in which benediction [is it a bad sign to make an error]?

B.   Said R. Hiyya said R. Safra in the name of one of the members of the house of
       Rabbi, "In the benediction for the patriarchs."

C.   There are those who repeat the tradition just now cited with reference to the
       following Tannaite teaching:

D. He who is reciting the Prayer has to direct his heart [to Heaven when reciting] all of [the blessings]. But if he cannot direct his heart rightly in the case of all of them, then let him direct his heart to heaven in the case of one of them.

E. Said R. Hiyya said R. Safra in the name of one of the members of the house of Rabbi, "It should be in the benediction on the patriarchs."

II.

A. They said concerning R. Hanina... [M. 5:5D]:

B. What is the source for [his view]?

C. Said R. Joshua b. Levi, "It is because Scripture has said, 'Peace to him that is far off and to him that is near, saith the Lord who creates the fruit of the lips, and I will heal him' (Is. 57:19)."

III.

A. Said R. Hiyya bar Abba said R. Yohanan, "All of the prophets prophesied only for him who marries off his daughter to a disciple of a sage, for him who conducts the business affairs of a disciple of a sage, and for him who gives benefit from his property to a disciple of a sage.

B. "But as to disciples of sages themselves, 'Eye has not seen, God, beside you, what he will do for him who waits for him (Is. 54:3)."

C. And R. Hiyya bar Abba said R. Yohanan said, "All of the prophets prophesied only concerning the days of the Messiah, but as to the world that will come [thereafter], 'Eye has not seen, God, beside you.'"

D. That view differs from the position of Samuel.

E. For Samuel said, "There is no difference between this age and the days of the Messiah except for [the end of Israel's subjugation to] the pagan kingdoms alone.

F. "For it is said, 'For the poor shall never cease out of the land' (Deut. 15:11)."

G. And R. Hiyya bar Abba said R. Yohanan said, "All of the prophets prophesied only concerning those who repent, but as to those who are entirely righteous, 'Eye has not seen, God, beside you.'"

H. That view differs from the position of R. Abbahu.

I. For R. Abbahu said, "In a place in which those who repent stand, those who are completely righteous cannot stand, as it is said, 'Peace, peace to him that was far and to him that is near' (Is. 57:19).

J. "That is to say, 'To one that was distant at the beginning but has repented and now is near.'"

K. But R. Yohanan may say to you, "What is the sense of 'distant'? That such a one was distant from transgression to begin with. And what is the sense of 'near'"? It is one who was near transgression but then became distant from it."

L. What then is the sense of, "Eye has not seen"?

M. Said R. Joshua b. Levi, "This refers to wine that was kept in its grapes from the six days of creation."

N. R. Samuel bar Nahmani said, "This refers to Eden, which no human eye has seen."

O. Now should you say, Then where was the first man [if not in Eden]?

P.   He was in the garden.

Q.   Now should you say, "But are the garden and Eden not the same?"

R.   [The answer is no,] for Scripture says, "And a river went out of Eden to water the garden" (Gen. 2:10).

S.   "The meaning is that the garden was one thing, Eden another."

IV.

A.   Our rabbis have taught on Tannaite authority:

B.   There was the case in which the son of Rabban Gamaliel fell ill. He sent two disciples of sages to R. Hanina b. Dosa to pray for mercy for him. When he saw them, he went up to his upper room and prayed for mercy for him.

C.   When he came down, he said to them, "Go, for his fever has left him."

D.   They said to him, "Are you a prophet?"

E.   He said to them, "I am not a prophet nor a disciple of a prophet, but this is what I have received as a tradition: If my prayer is fluent, then I know that he [for whom I pray] is accepted, and if not, then I know that he is rejected" [M. 5:5F-G].

F.   They sat down and wrote down the hour, and when they came back to Rabban Gamaliel, he said to them "By the Temple service! You were neither early nor late, but that is just how it happened. At that very moment, his fever left him and he asked us for water to drink."

G.   There was the further case involving R. Hanina b. Dosa. He went to study Torah with R. Yohanan b. Zakkai, and the son of R. Yohanan b. Zakkai fell ill.

H.   He said to him, "Hanina, my son, pray for mercy for him so that he will live."

I.   He put his head between his knees and prayed for mercy for him, and he lived.

J.   Said R. Yohanan b. Zakkai, "If Ben Zakkai had put his head between his knees all day long, they would not pay attention to him [in Heaven]."

K.   Said his wife to him, "And is Hanina greater than you?"

L.   He said to her, "No. But he is like a slave before the king, and I am like a prince before the king."

V.

A.   And R. Hiyya bar Abba said R. Yohanan said, "A person should pray only in a room that has windows.

B.   "For it is said, 'Now his windows were open in his upper chamber towards Jerusalem' (Dan. 6:11)."

C.   R. Kahana said, "I find nervy someone who prays in a valley [when there is much traffic]."

D.   And R. Kahana said, "I find nervy someone who spells out his sins [in his prayers], as it is said, 'Happy is he whose transgression is forgiven, whose sin is covered' (Ps. 32:1)."

Once more the principle of conglomeration of materials is not entirely clear. On the one side, we have the sequence of sayings of Hiyya bar Abba-Yohanan, III, V. On the other, we have units I, II, and IV, which clearly refer to the Mishnah-paragraph. So the issue is why units III, V have been inserted.

My first guess (of three) is that the rather miscellaneous collection of material on rules for praying, begun in the foregoing passage, continues with Hiyya-Yohanan materials. If so, then unit V explains why unit III has been included, with the two sets forming a single construction.

An alternative hypothesis is that the issue of the status of Hanina b. Dosa explains why unit III is included. He is asked, at unit IV, whether he is a prophet, and denies it. But once the topic of prophecy emerges, sayings about the relevance of prophecy will find a natural place. That is an especially suggestive consideration since these sayings underline the stress of the Mishnah itself: that Hanina is no prophet nor a miracle-worker, but simply guided by the character of his own praying. So the basic message is uniform, through both the Mishnah-passage and the miscellaneous sayings collected at III. What seems to me to lend a measure of support to this hypothesis is the fact that unit III is inserted in particular after the topic of Hanina, M. 5:5D, has been raised. What that seems to me to mean is that in the mind of the redactors, the topic of Hanina provokes the theme of prophecy and miracle-working, and then the message of unit III, particularly at III Aff., proves remarkably apt.

I fear, however, that there is a third and far simpler reason for the insertion of the whole of III, V. It is at III I, at which the proof-text of II C is given further development. The redactor will have taken the whole of III on account of III I and joined it to II because of II C. Or, still more simply, the formation of the whole of II, III, and V took place prior to the composition of the Talmud as we have it. Then, once the final compositors selected unit II, they carried in its wake III, V. The insertion of IV between III and V poses no difficulty to this theory. Among the three explanations spelled out just now, I of course prefer the second but concede that the third is the most likely.

BAVLI BERAKHOT CHAPTER SIX

A. [35A] How does one say a blessing over produce?

B. Over produce of a tree one says, "Creator of the fruit of the tree,"

C. except for wine.

D. For over wine one says, "Creator of the fruit of the vine."

E. And over produce of the earth, one says, "Creator of fruit of the ground,"

F. except for a bread.

G. For over bread one says, "He who brings forth bread from the earth,"

H. And over vegetables one says, "Creator of the fruit of the ground."

I. R. Judah says, "Creator of diverse kinds of herbs."

I.

A. What is the source of this rule [that one must say a blessing before eating produce]?

B. It is in accord with what our rabbis have taught on Tannaite authority:

C. "The fruit thereof shall be holy, for giving praise to the Lord" (Lev. 19:24). [This verse refers to produce in the fourth year after planting a given tree.]

D. This teaches that [produce] requires the recitation of a blessing, both before and after eating.

E. On the basis of the foregoing exegesis, R. Aqiba said, "It is forbidden for a person to taste anything before reciting a blessing."

F. Now does the exegesis, "for giving praise...," serve the purpose just now specified?

G. It serves [two purposes], for the All-Merciful has stated, "Redeem [the produce of the fourth year, if it is not eaten in Jerusalem], and, second, [to apply the stated rule only to the fruit of the vine by indicating that] what requires a song [of praise] requires redemption, and what does not require a song does not require redemption [thus speaking only of wine, which alone is subject to the rule governing produce of the first year].

H. And the foregoing further accords with what R. Samuel bar Nahmani said R. Jonathan said.

I. For R. Samuel bar Nahmani said R. Jonathan said, "How do we know that a song [of praise] is sung only over wine?

J. "As it is said, 'And the vine said to them, Should I leave my wine, which cheers God and man' (Jud. 9:13).

K. "If wine cheers man, how does it cheer God?

L. "It is on the basis of that statement that we learn that people may sing a song [of praise] only over a cup of wine."

II.

A. The foregoing exegesis [proving that we derive the requirement to say a blessing from the use of the word 'praise'] poses no problem to him who repeats the tradition in the form of "the planting of the fourth year." [Then the cited verse speaks of all produce that reaches the fourth year of growth, and does not refer only to wine. Simon, p. 218, n. 4: In this case the word for praise cannot be used to prove that only the vine requires redemption and is available for teaching that a blessing must be said over fruit.]

B. But for him who repeats the version as "the vineyard in the fourth year of its growth" [in which case the cited verse speaks only of fruit of the vine, wine], what is there to be said?

C. For it has been stated on Amoraic authority:

D. R. Hiyya and R. Simeon, son of Rabbi:

E. One authority repeated: "Vineyard in the fourth year [speaking then only of wine]."

F. The other of them repeated, "Planting in the fourth year" [speaking of all sorts of produce]."

G. But for the one who repeated, "Vineyard in the fourth year after planting, there is no problem after all, if one derives by an exegesis based on analogy [the rule governing all produce from that governing wine].

H. For it has been taught on Tannaite authority:

I. Rabbi says, "Here it states, 'That it may yield to you more richly the increase thereof' (Lev. 19:25). And elsewhere it says, 'The increase of the vineyard' (Deut. 22:9).

J. "Just as the word 'increase' used in the latter passage refers to the vineyard, so here it refers to the vineyard."

K. What follows is that one of the meanings to be imputed to the word "praise" remains available to prove that one must recite a blessing.

III.

A. [The solution to the problem is not adequate.] For if one does not derive the lesson from the argument from analogy just now worked out, how, then, do we know that one has to recite a blessing at all?

B. And even if one does derive the required proof from the argument from analogy, then we know only that a blessing has to be said after eating [produce]. How do we prove that one has to say a blessing before eating produce?

C. That indeed is no problem, for there is the possibility of demonstrating that requirement on the basis of an argument a fortiori:

D. If when one is full, one says a blessing, when one is hungry, is it not all the more so that one says a blessing?

E. Accordingly, we have found proof that one has to say a blessing before and after consuming produce of the vineyard.

F. How do we know that one must do so for all other varieties of produce?

G. It must be derived from the case of fruit of the vineyard.

H. Just as, in the case of produce of a vineyard, something from which one derives benefit, one has to say a blessing, so in the case of any thing from which one derives benefit, one has to say a blessing.

I. No, there is a weak point in that argument:

J. The distinctive trait of the vineyard [which accounts for the special requirement of saying a blessing] is that it is subject to the rule governing gleanings [which must be left for the poor, so Lev. 19:10].

K. But then the case of grain will prove the case [since it is not subject to the rule governing gleanings, but is subject to the recitation of a blessing, as stated at Deut. 8:10].

L. But the special trait of grain is that it is liable to dough-offering [which must be separated from dough].

M. The case of the vineyard will prove the matter [since it is not subject to dough-offering].

O. So we come full circle. The special trait characteristic of the one is not characteristic of the other, and vice versa. What they have in common, then, is that both of them are things from which people derive benefit, and both require the recitation of a blessing. So anything from which people derive benefit demands a blessing.

P. [No, that is not conclusive either, for] what the two [wine, grain] have in common is that both of them are used on the altar. [What is not analogous will not require a blessing.]

Q. Then there is the case of the olive, which also is offered on the altar.

R. But does proof derive from the fact that the olive is offered on the altar [and that is why we derive the rule that a blessing is required]?

S. Lo, in the case of the olive, it is described in Scripture as a "vineyard."

T. For it is written, "And he burned up the shocks and the standing grain and also the vineyard of olives" (Jud. 15:5).

U. Said R. Pappa, "While it may be called 'a vineyard of olives,' it is never called merely, 'a vineyard.'" [When we see the word 'vineyard,' without further reference to olives, we do not imagine that it is a vineyard of olives]."

V. In any event we have a problem, for all that the three have in common is that they are offered on the altar.

W. Rather, one must derive [the requirement of saying a blessing] from the case of the seven species [specified at Deut. 8:8 as the produce of the Land of Israel].

X. Just as, in the case of the seven species, that from which people derive benefit requires a blessing, so any thing from which people derive benefit requires a blessing.

Y. [No, that will not do, for] the distinctive trait of the seven species is that they are liable for the presentation of the first fruits [which must be brought to the priest in the Temple].

Z. And furthermore, [what you could prove in any event] involves the blessing to be said after eating such produce. How do we learn that one has to say a blessing before hand?

AA. That is no problem, for proof derives from an argument a fortiori:

BB. Now if one has to say a blessing once he is full, when he is hungry, all the more so!

CC. Now as to the cited proof, how does one who repeats the language in terms of what is planted and reaches the fourth year of growth prove that something that is not planted, for example, meat, eggs, and fish, also requires a blessing?

DD. But it is simply a matter of principle:

EE. It is forbidden for someone to derive benefit from this world without reciting a blessing.

IV.

A. Our rabbis have taught on Tannaite authority:

B. **It is forbidden for someone to derive benefit from any thing in this world without reciting a blessing, and whoever derives benefit from this world without reciting a blessing thereby commits sacrilege [T. Ber. 4:1A-C].**

C. What is the remedy [for doing so]?

D. Let the person go to a sage.

E. If he goes to a sage, what will [the sage] do for him? Lo, the man has already violated a prohibition!

F. Rather, said Raba, "Let him go to a sage to begin with, so that [the sage] will teach him the requisite blessings to be recited, so that one will not come to commit sacrilege."

G. Said R. Judah said Samuel, "Whoever derives benefit in this world without reciting a blessing is as if he derived benefit from Holy Things that belong to Heaven [and so has committed sacrilege].

H. "For it is said, 'The earth belongs to the Lord, and everything that fills it' (Ps. 24:1)."

I. R. Levi contrasted verses of Scripture: "It is written, 'The earth belongs to the Lord, and everything that fills it' (Ps. 24:1).

J. "And it is written, 'The heaven belongs to the Lord, but the earth he has given to men' (Ps. 115:16).

K. But there is no contradiction. The former verse refers to the case before one has recited a blessing, [35B] and the latter verse refers to the case after one has recited a blessing."

V.

A. Said R. Hanina bar Pappa, "Whoever derives benefit in this world without reciting a blessing is as if he mugged the Holy One blessed be he, and the community of Israel.

B. "For it is said, 'Whoever robs from his father or mother and says, It is no transgression, is the companion of a destroyer' (Prov. 28:24).

C. "And 'father' refers only to the Holy One, blessed be he, as it says, 'Is not he your father who has gotten you' (Deut. 32:6).

D. "And 'mother' refers only to the community of Israel, as it says, "Hear, my son, the instruction of your father, and do not forsake the teaching of your mother' (Prov. 1:8)."

E. What is the sense of, "He is the companion of a destroyer"?

F. Said R. Hanina bar Pappa, "He is a companion of Jereboam b. Nabat, who destroyed Israel [for] their father in heaven."

VI.

A. R. Hanina bar Pappa contrasted these verses: "It is written, 'Therefore I will take back my grain in its time' (Hos. 2:11), and it is further written, 'And you shall gather in your grain' (Deut. 11:14).

B. "There is no contradiction between the two verses. One speaks of a time in which the Israelites carry out the will of the Omnipresent. The other speaks of a time in which the Israelites do not carry out the will of the Omnipresent."

VII.

A. Our rabbis have taught on Tannaite authority:

B. "'And you shall gather in your grain' (Deut. 11:14).

C. "What is the sense of this passage?

D. "Since it is said, 'This book of the Torah shall not depart out of your mouth' (Jos. 1:8), one might have thought that the teaching must be understood exactly as it is written down [literally].

E. "Scripture therefore says, 'And you shall gather in your grain,' meaning that you are to conduct a worldly occupation along with teachings of Torah, [both making a living and also studying Torah]," the words of R. Ishmael.

F. R. Simeon b. Yohai says, "Should it come about that a person ploughs in the time of ploughing, sows in the time of sowing, reaps in the time of reaping, threshes in the time of threshing, winnow in the time of winnowing, what then will become of the Torah [and when will he study it]?

G. "Rather, when the Israelites do what pleases the Omnipresent, their work is done by others.

H. "For it is said, 'And strangers shall stand and feed your flocks' (Is. 61:5).

I. "When the Israelites do not do what pleases the Omnipresent, they have to do their work themselves, as it says, 'And you yourself will gather in your grain' (Deut. 11:14).

J. "And not only so, but the work of others has to be done by them, as it says, 'And you shall work for your enemy' (Deut. 28:48)."

K. Said Abayye, "Many acted in accord with the opinion of R. Ishmael and things worked out for them, in accord with R. Simeon b. Yohai and things did not work out for them."

L. Said Raba to rabbis, "By your leave, in the time of Nisan and Tishri do not appear before me, so that you will not have to worry about your food for the entire year [but take care of the necessary tasks during the seasons of the ripening of the grain, in the spring, and the vintage and olive press in the fall]."

VIII.

A. Said Rabbah bar bar Hana said R. Yohanan in the name of R. Judah bar Ilai, "Come and take note that the latter generations are not like the former generations.

B. As to the former generations, they treated their study of Torah as their principal obligation, and their everyday work as their occasional task, and both this and that worked out well for them.

C. "The latter generations treat their everyday work as their principal obligation, and their study of Torah as their occasional task, and neither this nor that has worked out well for them."

D. And Rabbah bar bar Hana said R. Yohanan said in the name of R. Judah bar Ilai, "Come and take note that the latter generations are not like the former generations.

E. "The former generations would bring their produce into the courtyard by way of their kitchen-garden [through the front door], so as to impose upon the produce the liability to tithes.

F. "The latter generations bring their produce in over roofs, courtyards, or enclosures, so as to keep it exempt from the obligation of tithing."

G. For R. Yannai said, "Produce that is as yet untithed does not become liable to tithing until it appears before the household [of the farmer].

H. "For it is said, 'I have put away holy things out of my house' (Deut. 26:13)."

I. But R. Yohanan said, "Even [entry into] the courtyard imposes liability for tithing upon untithed produce, for it is said, 'And you will eat within your gates and be satisfied' (Deut. 26:12)."

IX.

A. Except for wine [M. 6:1C]:

B. What distinguishes wine [so that it gets a blessing distinctive to itself, while other produce is covered by blessings that serve a great many species]?

C. If I say that it is because, through processing, it is improved, so it is set apart through the provision of a distinctive blessing, lo, there is the case of olive oil, which through processing also is improved. Yet it is not set apart through the provision of a distinctive blessing.

D. For R. Judah said Samuel said, and so R. Isaac said R. Yohanan said, "In the case of olive oil, people recite the blessing, '... who has created the fruit of the tree.'"

E. May one say that in that case [of olive oil] it is because it is not possible [to say a special blessing]? For what blessing might one say? Should it be, "... who creates the fruit of the olive"? The fruit itself [and not only the tree] is called "olive."

F. And so we can say the blessing, "... who creates the fruit of the tree of olives."

G. Rather, said Mar Zutra, "Wine has food value, but oil does not have food value."

H. But does oil not have food value?

I. And have we not learned in the Mishnah: He who vows to abstain from food is permitted to consume water and salt [M. Er. 3:1E].

J. And reflecting on that passage, we said, "Water and salt are the things not regarded as food, but all other things are regarded as food."

K. May we not maintain, moreover, that the passage at hand refutes the view of Rab and Samuel, who have said, "People say the blessing, '... who creates various kinds of food' only prior to eating five species of cereals alone [wheat, barley, oats, spelt, and rye]."

L.   And R. Huna said, "The Mishnah [at M. Er. 3:1] speaks of a case of one who says, "'I vow to abstain from eating anything that sustains [life]."

M.   This then proves that oil has food value.

N.   Hence, wine sustains life [Simon, p. 223, n. 5: And has more than merely food value], while oil does not sustain life.

O.   But does wine sustain life?

P.   And lo, Raba would drink all afternoon prior to the Passover so as to develop his appetite to be able to eat a great deal of unleavened bread, [and that snows that wine does not fill you up but merely gives you an appetite].

Q.   A great deal of wine gives an appetite, a small quantity of wine sustains life.

R.   And does it sustain life at all?

S.   And has it not been written, "And wine that gladdens the heart of man... and bread that stays the heart of man..." (Ps. 104:15), which means that it is bread that sustains life, while wine does not sustain life.

T.   But the distinguishing trait of wine is twofold: first, it sustains, and, second, it also gladdens [a person], while bread sustains but does not gladden.

U.   If so, should we say the three blessings [after drinking wine, as one does after eating bread]?

V.   People do not make wine the basis for their meal.

W.   Said R. Nahman bar Isaac to Raba, "And if one does make it the basis for a meal, what is the law?"

X.   He said to him, "When Elijah comes, he will indicate whether it can serve as the basis for a meal. But as of now, that person's opinion [that wine, not bread, is the basis of his meal] is null as against the opinion of ordinary people [and we do not take account of, and make a ruling for, such a case]."

X.

A.   Returning to the body of the preceding passage:

B.   R. Judah said Samuel said, and so R. Isaac said R. Yohanan said, "In the case of olive oil, people recite the blessing, '... who has created the fruit of the tree.'"

C.   Now how shall we interpret the case at hand?

D.   Should we say that someone has drunk it? But it does injury.

E.   For it has been taught on Tannaite authority:

F.   He who drinks oil in the status of heave-offering has to pay the value of the principle but does not have to pay an added fifth [having derived no benefit from the oil]. He who anoints himself with oil in the status of heave-offering has to pay both the value of the principal and the added fifth [since he has derived benefit from the oil]. [Hence consuming olive oil by itself does not impart food value, for the added fifth applies as a fine only to eating food, for Lev. 22:14 speaks of eating].

G.   Would we then deal with a case in which one consumes the olive oil along with bread? If so, we have a case in which the bread is principal and the oil secondary.

H.   And we have learned in the Mishnah: This is the general rule: In the case of any primary food accompanied by a secondary food, one says the blessing over the primary food, which thereby exempts what is secondary [M. 6:7D].

I.   Then we deal with a case in which one has drunk it with elaiogaron.

J.   For Rabbah bar Samuel said, "Elaiogaron is juice of beet roots, oxygaron is juice of [36A] any other boiled vegetables."

K.   If so, then the elaiogaron would be the principal food, and the oil secondary.

L.   And we have learned in the Mishnah: This is the general rule: In the case of any primary food accompanied by a secondary food, one says the blessing over the primary food, which thereby exempts what is secondary [M. 6:7D].

M.   In the case at hand, what is the situation with which we deal?

N.   It is with someone who has a sore throat.

O.   For it has been taught on Tannaite authority:

P.   He who has a sore throat should not on the Sabbath directly soothe it with oil, but he should put much oil into elaiogaron and swallow it, [since the man does not thereby take the oil as a medicine, which he must not do on the Sabbath except in case of danger to life].

Q.   It is then self-evident [Simon, p. 224, n. 7: that in this case one should make a blessing over the oil, because the oil is here the principal item].

R.   [Nonetheless, the rule had to be spelled out, for] what might you have thought? Since in the present case the man has the intent of using the oil for medicinal purposes, he should not say a blessing over it at all.

S.   So we are informed that, since the man derives benefit from the oil [even in addition to the oil's soothing effects upon his sore throat], he does have to recite a blessing."

XI.

A.   Over wheat flour [eaten raw] --

B.   R. Judah says, "One has to say, 'Who creates the fruit of the earth' [just as is the case for crushed wheat]."

C.   And R. Nahman said, "'By whose word all things come into being.'"

D.   Said Raba to R. Nahman, "Do not differ from R. Judah, for both R. Yohanan and Samuel concur with his view.

E.   "For R. Judah said Samuel said, and so R. Isaac said R. Yohanan said, 'As to olive oil, people say the blessing, "... who creates the fruit of the tree."'

F.   "Therefore even though, in processing, the produce changes form [from solid to liquid], it remains in the same classification.

G.   "Here too [in the case of wheat flour], even though, in processing, the produce changes form, it remains in the same classification."

H.   But are the cases parallel? In the other case [involving olive oil], there is no further improvement [to be expected through processing], while here there is further improvement, specifically [when the flour is made] into bread. When, therefore, there will be further improvement [through processing], we do not recite the blessing, "Who has created the fruit of the ground" but rather "By whose word."

I.   But has not R. Zira said R. Mattena said Samuel said, "For raw cabbage and barley flour we say the blessing, 'By whose word all things come into being.'" Does that statement [by omitting wheat flour] not yield the inference that for wheat flour [the correct blessing is], "Who creates the fruit of the earth"?

J. No, the correct blessing for wheat flour also is "By whose word all things come into being." The purpose of the cited statement is to inform us the rule for wheat-flour, all the more so for barley.

K. For if we had learned the rule only for wheat flour, one might have supposed that that rule pertains to wheat. But as to barley-flour, one does not say any blessing at all. So we are informed [that that inference is false].

L. But [is barley flour] less in importance than salt or brine? For it has been taught on Tannaite authority, "For salt and brine one says the blessing, 'By whose word all things come into being.'" [Why would anyone have imagined that no blessing, therefore, is to be recited over barley-flour?]

M. It was, nonetheless, necessary to make the case of barley-flour explicit. [Why?] It might have entered your mind to reason as follows: Someone might toss salt or brine into his mouth, but as to barley flour, since it is harmful [Simon:] in creating tapeworms, one need not say any blessing over it at all.

N. So we are informed that, since one derives a measure of benefit from it, it is necessary to say a blessing.

XII.

A. Over the palm-heart --

B. R. Judah said, "'Who creates the fruit of the ground.'"

C. And Samuel said, "'By whose word all things come into being.'"

D. R. Judah said, "'Who creates the fruit of the ground,' because it is fruit."

E. Samuel said, "'By whose word all things come into being,' because in the end it will harden."

F. Said Samuel to R. Judah, "Sharp-witted one! Indeed it is reasonable to take your view, for lo, there is the case of the radish, which ends up getting hard, and yet we say the blessing for it, 'Who creates the fruit of the ground.'

G. "But [in point of fact] that is not the criterion. In the case of the radish, a person will plant them for the sake of the tuber [which will be eaten before it grows wooden]. But a person does not plant the palm tree with the palm-heart in mind."

H. But is it so that, in any case in which a person does not plant something with the stated use in mind, we do not say a blessing for that other use?

I. And lo, there is the case of the caperbush, which people plant for its blossom. Yet we have learned on Tannaite authority: For the various edible parts of the caperbush, the leaves, and the young shoots, one says, "Who creates the fruit of the ground." And for the berries and buds, one says, "Who creates the fruit of the tree."

J. Said R. Nahman bar Isaac, "People plant a caperbush with the shoots in mind, but people do not plant palms for the sake of the heart."

K. And even though Samuel praised R. Judah, the decided law accords with the view of Samuel.

XIII.

A. Said R. Judah said Rab, "As to a caperbush in the first three years of its growth that is located [even] outside of the Land of Israel [where the rule that one may not make use of the produce of a tree in the first three years of its growth applies], one throws out the berries and eats the buds."

B. Does this then suggest that the berries are fruit [and so may not be eaten], while the buds are not fruit?

C. An objection was raised from the following:

D. For the various edible parts of the caperbush, the leaves and the young shoots, one says, "Who creates the fruit of the ground." And for the berries and buds, one says, "Who creates the fruit of the tree." [This indicates that both the berries and the buds fall into the same category, namely, fruit.]

E. [Judah's view] accords with what R. Aqiba has said.

F. For we have learned in the Mishnah:

G. R. Eliezer says, "The caperbush is subject to the law of tithes in regard to its stalks, berries, and blossoms." R. Aqiba says, "No part of the caperbush is subject to the law of tithes except the berries, for they are the fruit [the part normally harvested for use as food]" [M. Ma. 4:6, Jaffee, p. 134].

H. [If Judah's intent is simply to restate Aqiba's view], then let him say, "The law accords with the view of R. Aqiba."

I. Had he said, "The law accords with R. Aqiba," I might have concluded that that same rule applies in the Land [of Israel].

J. Accordingly, [by stating matters as he does,] he informs us that the decided law in connection with rules for outside of the Land [of Israel] accords with him who gives the more lenient ruling for matters that pertain to territory inside of the Land [of Israel] [thus, Aqiba's ruling for the Land is deemed normative for territory outside of the Land], but [his view is] not [normative] for the Land [of Israel].

K. Then let him state, "The law accords with the view of R. Aqiba for the territory outside of the Land, for whoever gives the more lenient ruling for the Land of Israel is deemed to give the normative ruling for the territory outside of the Land of Israel."

L. Had the matter been phrased in this way, I might have reached the conclusion that the same rule applies to tithing produce of trees in the Land of Israel itself, which, in point of fact, is a ruling deriving only from the authority of rabbis [since Scripture requires tithing only grain, oil, and wine]. But so far as produce of the trees during the first three years of growth in the Land of Israel, which, of course, rests upon the authority of the Torah, [not only on the authority of rabbis], I might have said that, for produce in that status even outside of the Land of Israel, we should make a decree [imposing on trees outside of the Land the rule pertaining to trees in the Land].

M. By phrasing matters in the way he did, [Judah] informed us that that is not the case.

XIV.

A. Rabina found Mar, son of R. Ashi, who was throwing away the berries and eating the buds [of a caperbush].

B. He said to him, "What is your view? Do you concur with R. Aqiba [XIII G], who imposes a lenient ruling [treating the berries alone as fruit in the case of the caperbush]?

C. "Then let the master act in accord with the view of the House of Shammai, which imposes a still more lenient rule.

D. "For we have learned on Tannaite authority:

E. "As to the caperbush,

F. "The House of Shammai say, 'It is considered diverse kinds in the vineyard.'

G. "The House of Hillel say, 'It is not considered diverse kinds in the vineyard.'

H. "And both agree that the caperbush is liable in respect to the laws prohibiting use of produce in the first three years of growth [T. Kil. 3:17, Mandelbaum, p. 196].

I. "Now the passage itself contains a contradiction. You have stated, 'As to a caperbush, the House of Shammai say, "It is considered diverse kinds in the vineyard."' So therefore it is regarded as in the category of vegetables. Then it goes and teaches, 'And both agree that the caperbush is liable in respect to the laws prohibiting use of produce in the first three years of growth.' Therefore it falls into the category of fruit.

J. "But there is indeed no contradiction. The House of Shammai are in doubt [as to the appropriate category], so they impose the more stringent rule in each classification."

K. In any event, from the viewpoint of the House of Shammai, it is a case of doubt in regard to the application of the rule prohibiting use of produce in the first three years of a tree's growth.

L. And we have learned in the Mishnah:

M. Where there is a doubt concerning the status of produce in the first three years of its growth, in the Land of Israel the fruit in question is forbidden; and in Syria the fruit is permitted; and outside of the Land of Israel, one goes down [36B] to the orchard and purchases such fruit, provided that the purchaser does not see the seller pick the fruit [M. Orl. 3:9, Essner, p. 143]. [Simon, p. 228, n. 1: Consequently, Mar, son of R. Ashi, should have eaten also the berries.]

N. When there is an opinion of R. Aqiba alongside one of R. Eliezer, we follow [Aqiba's] view, and when there is an opinion of the House of Shammai alongside one of the House of Hillel, the former is not regarded as a valid Mishnah-law. [So the caperbud is subject to the law prohibiting produce of a tree in the first three years of its growth.]

O. But derive the rule from the fact that the bud serves as the protection for the fruit, and the All-Merciful has said, "And you shall observe its uncircumcision along with its fruit" (Lev. 19:23). The sense is, "With that which is secondary to its fruit." And what might that be? It is what protects its fruit. [Simon, p. 228, n. 4: How then did Raba eat the buds?]

P. Said Raba, "In what case do we invoke the rule that the bud serves as protection to the fruit? It is in a case in which the protection serves both when the fruit is plucked and also when it is attached to the tree. In the present case, when the fruit is attached to the tree, however, the bud serves, but when it is plucked, it does not serve."

Q. Abayye objected, "'<u>The nipple of the pomegranate joins together</u> [with it to form the <u>bulk requisite to regard the entire piece of fruit as susceptible to uncleanness</u>], and its blossom [sprouting hair] does not join together' [M. Uqs. 2:3C-D].

R. "What follows from the statement that the blossom does not join together is that it is not food [and so does not fall into the category of the nipple].

S. "Now it has been taught with regard to the rules of prohibition of fruit of a tree in the first three years after it is planted: '<u>The rinds of a pomegranate and its young bud, walnut shells and fruit pits, are forbidden for use under the laws prohibiting produce of a tree in the first three years after it is planted</u>' [M. Orl. 1:8J]. [Simon, p. 228, n. 7: although the blossom of the pomegranate does not protect it after it is plucked. The same should apply to the caperbud.]"

T. Rather, said Raba, "Where do we rule that [the bud] serves as a protection for the fruit? It is a case in which the bud is present at the time that the fruit reaches full ripeness. But the caperbud falls off when the fruit becomes fully ripe. [That explains why one may eat the bud.]"

U. Is this the case? And has not R. Nahman said Rabbah bar Abbahu said, "[Simon:] The calyces surrounding dates in the state of <u>orlah</u> are forbidden, since they are the protection to the fruit."

V. Now when is it that they serve as a protection of the fruit? It is in the early stages of growth, and he calls them "a protection for the fruit."

W. R. Nahman takes the view of R. Yose.

X. For we have learned in the Mishnah:

Y. <u>R. Yose says, "The budding berry is forbidden, because it is a fruit"</u> [M. Orl. 1:7C].

Z. But rabbis differ from him. [Simon, p. 228, n. 8: And the decided law follows the rabbis, who are the majority. And similarly the caperbud is not subject to the prohibition of fruit of a tree for the first three years after it is planted.]

AA. R. Shimi of Nehardea objected, "And in the case of other species of fruit trees, do rabbis indeed differ from [Yose]?

BB. "And have we not learned in the Mishnah:

CC. "<u>After what time during the Sabbatical year may they not cut down a fruitbearing tree</u> [for by doing so one would prevent fruit that already is growing on the branch from ripening?]

DD. "<u>The House of Shammai say, 'Regarding all trees -- after they have produced recognizable fruit.</u>'

EE. "<u>The House of Hillel say, 'Regarding carob trees, after their branches begin to droop; regarding vines, after they produce berries; regarding olive trees, after they blossom; and regarding all other trees, after they produce recognizable fruit</u>' [M. Sheb. 4:10A-C, Newman, p. 108].

FF. "And said R. Assi, 'The following fall into the same classification: <u>Boser, garua</u>, and white bean.'

GG. 'Do you include 'white bean'? Rather, repeat the statement as, "the size of them is that of the white bean."

HH. "Now from whom have you heard the view that <u>boser</u> falls into the category of fruit and the bud does not? It is rabbis [who differ from Yose at M. Orl. 1:7].

II. "And yet, it is taught, '<u>And regarding all other trees, after they produce recognizable fruit</u>' [Simon, p. 229, n. 6: which shows that in other cases the decided law is according to R. Yose]."

JJ. Rather, said Raba, "In what case do we rule that it serves as protection for the fruit? It is a case in which, when one removes the protection, the produce dies. But in a case in which, if one removes the protection, the fruit does not die, [as in the case of the caperbud, we do not invoke that rule]."

KK. There was a case in which they removed the blossom from a pomegranate and the fruit withered. They removed the flower of the pomegranate and it endured. [So the two do not fall into the same category.]

XV.

A. As to pepper,

B. R. Sheshet said, "'By whose word.'"

C. Raba said, "There is no blessing to be said."

D. Raba is consistent with his views.

E. For Raba said, "One who chews pepper on the Day of Atonement is exempt [from punishment]. If he chewed ginger on the Day of Atonement, he is exempt."

F. An objection was raised:

G. R. Meir would say, "Since it is said, 'You shall count the fruit thereof as forbidden' (Lev. 19:23), do I not know whether it falls into the category of a tree that is used for food? But what is the sense of the statement of Scripture, 'A tree that is eaten'? It serves to encompass a tree, the taste of the wood and the fruit of which is the same. And what would that be? It is pepper.

H. "It thereby teaches you that pepper trees are liable to the prohibition of the fruit of a tree in the first three years after it is planted.

I. "And it serves to teach you that the Land of Israel lacks for nothing, for it says, 'And land wherein you shall eat bread without scarcity, you shall not lack anything in it' (Deut. 8:9)." [Thus pepper falls into the category of produce of a tree that yields food, as against Raba's view that pepper is not food.]

J. There is no contradiction anyhow, since the one statement [treating pepper as food] speaks of moist [pepper], the other to dried pepper.

K. Rabbis said to Maremer, "If one chewed ginger on the Day of Atonement, he is exempt [from penalty]."

L. But lo, has not Raba said, "Preserved ginger which comes from India is permitted, and we recite the blessing, 'Who creates the fruit of the ground'"? [This shows that ginger is food, so one <u>should</u> be liable for chewing it on the Day of Atonement.]

M. As before, there is no contradiction, since the statement [prohibiting ginger] speaks of moist, the one permitting it speaks of dry [ginger].

XVI.

A. As to habis [a pulp of flour, honey and oil] boiled in a pot and as to pounded grain,

B.   R. Judah said, "'By whose word all things come into being.'"

C.   R. Kahana said, "'Who creates diverse kinds of food.'"

D.   All parties occur in the matter of pounded grain by itself, that the proper blessing is, "Who creates diverse kinds of food."

E.   Where there is a dispute, it concerns pounded grain prepared like boiled habis.

F.   R. Judah said, "'By whose word,'" since he treats the honey as the principal ingredient.

G.   R. Kahana said, "'Who creates diverse kinds of foods,'" since in his view the flour is the principal ingredient.

H.   Said R. Joseph, "The view of R. Kahana is more reasonable, for both Rab and Samuel say, 'Whatever contains any one of the five species gets the blessing, 'Who creates diverse kinds of foods.' [Since the pounded grain falls into that category, the blessing proposed by Kahana must be the right one.]"

XVII.

A.   Returning to the body of the text just now cited: Both Rab and Samuel say, "Whatever contains any one of the five species gets the blessing, 'Who creates diverse kinds of foods.'"

B.   And it also has been stated on Amoraic authority:

C.   Both Rab and Samuel say, "Whatever is made of any one of the five species gets the blessing, '... who creates diverse kinds of foods.'"

D.   It was necessary to report both versions of their statement.

E.   For had we had in hand only the version framed as "Whatever is made of...," I might have reached the conclusion that the rule is as given because the cereal still can be seen. But if the cereal is in a mixture [and cannot be seen], I might have concluded that the rule is not the same.

F.   [37A] So we are informed that that is not the case when the rule is stated, "Whatever is made of"

G.   And had we had in hand the creation only in the version, "Whatever is made of...," I might have reached the conclusion that the cited blessing applies to whatever is made of the five species.

H.   But as to what is made of rice and millet, when they are part of a mixture, that would not be the appropriate blessing. And if they can be distinguished, I might have held that, even in the case of rice and millet, we also say the blessing, "... who has made various species of food."

I.   So we are informed that it is only over something that is made of one of the five species that we recite the blessing, "Who has created various species of food."

J.   That then excludes the case of rice and millet, for even though they can still be discerned, we do not recite the blessing, "Who creates various species of food."

XVIII.

A.   And is it the case that over rice or millet we do not recite the blessing, "... who creates various kinds of foods"?

B.   And has it not been taught on Tannaite authority:

C. If people brought before someone a piece of bread made from rice, or a piece of bread made from millet, he says the blessings for such food before and afterward as one does for a cooked dish [made of one of the five species].

D. And as to a cooked dish, it has been taught on Tannaite authority:

E. Before eating one says the blessing, "Who creates various kinds of food." And at the end one says the single blessing that summarizes the three requisite blessings [of the Grace after Meals].

F. [In reply:] It falls into the category of a cooked dish, and at the same time it does not fall into that category.

G. It falls into the category of a cooked dish, in that people say a blessing for such food both before eating and afterward.

H. But it does not fall into the category of a cooked dish, for in the case of a cooked dish, one says beforehand, "Who creates various kinds of food," and at the end one says a single blessing that encompasses the three [of Grace after Meals], while in this case, one says before eating, "By whose word all things come into being," and at the end, one says, "Who creates many living things with their wants, for all of which he has created...."

XIX.

A. And how does rice not fall into the category of a cooked dish?

B. And has it not been taught on Tannaite authority:

C. What are those things that fall into the category of a cooked dish?

D. Spelt groats, wheat groats, fine flour, split grain, barley groats, and rice. [This states clearly that rice falls into the category of a cooked dish.]

E. Lo, who is the authority behind this statement? It is R. Yohanan b. Nuri.

F. For it has been taught on Tannaite authority:

G. R. Yohanan b. Nuri says, "Rice falls into the category of grain. On Passover people are liable for preserving leaven made of rice to the penalty of extirpation, and someone may fulfill his obligation to eat unleavened bread on Passover by eating unleavened bread made of rice.

H. But rabbis do not hold this view.

I. And do not rabbis hold this view?

J. And has it not been taught on Tannaite authority:

K. One who chews grains of wheat recites over it the benediction, "Creator of types of seeds."

L. If he baked or cooked [a dish using pieces of wheat bread in the recipe] --

M. if pieces [of bread] remain intact, he must recite over [the dish, before eating it], the benediction, "Who brings forth bread from the earth,"

N. and after [eating] it, he must recite three benedictions [i.e., the full grace after meals].

O. If no pieces [of bread] remain intact, he recites over it [the dish] the benediction, "Creator of types of foodstuffs,"

P.   and after [eating] it, he recites one benediction [an abbreviated grace after meals] [T. Ber. 4:6].

Q.   One who chews grains of rice recites over them the benediction, "Creator of the fruit of the ground."

R.   If he baked or cooked [a dish using pieces of rice bread in the recipe] --

S.   even if pieces [of bread] remain intact, he recites over [the dish] the benediction, "Creator of types of foodstuffs,"

T.   and need not recite any benediction after [eating] it [T. Ber. 4:7].

U.   Now whose opinion is at hand? Should we say that it is R. Yohanan b. Nuri, who has held that rice falls into the category of grain? Then one should indeed say, "Who brings forth bread from the earth" as well as the Grace after Meals that summarizes in one blessing the three [ordinarily said after eating bread].

V.   Rather, it must be rabbis.

W.   This then would constitute a refutation of the view of Rab and Samuel [at XVII A].

X.   It would indeed refute their view.

XX.

A.   A master has said, "One who chews grains of rice recites over them the benediction, 'Creates the fruit of the ground.'"

B.   And has it not been taught on Tannaite authority:

C.   [The appropriate blessing is,] "Who creates diverse kinds of herbs"?

D.   There is no contradiction, since the one represents the view of R. Judah, and the other, of rabbis.

E.   For we have learned in the Mishnah:

F.   Over greens one says, "Creator of the fruit of the ground."

G.   R. Judah says, "Creator of diverse kinds of herbs" [M. 6:1H-I].

XXI.

A.   A master has said, "One who chews grains of rice recites over them the benediction, 'Creator of the fruit of the ground.'

B.   "If he bakes or cooked a dish using pieces of rice bread in the recipe, even if pieces of bread remain intact, in the beginning he recites over the dish the benediction, 'Creator of types of foodstuffs.'

C.   "And at the end he recites no benediction at all.'"

D.   But has it not been taught, And at the end he need not recite any benediction after eating it?

E.   Said R. Sheshet, "There is no contradiction. The one view is that of Rabban Gamaliel, the other, of rabbis."

F.   For it has been taught on Tannaite authority:

G.   This is the general rule:

H.   [Regarding] any food that is [made from one] of the seven kinds [of produce or a kind of breadstuff] --

I.   Rabban Gamaliel says, "One recites three benedictions [i.e., the full grace after meals] after [eating] it.

J. And sages say, "[He recites] one benediction [viz., an abbreviated grace]" [cf. M. Ber. 6:8].

K. There is this precedent: Rabban Gamaliel and the elders were seated at table in an upper room in Jericho.

L. They [attendants] brought before them dates [after they had finished the meal], and they ate them. Rabban Gamaliel gave R. Aqiba the honor of reciting the blessing.

M. R. Aqiba precipitously recited one [blessing] abbreviating the three, after [eating] them.

N. Said to him Rabban Gamaliel, "Aqiba, why do you poke your head into disputes?"

O. He [Aqiba] said to him, "Our master, even though you and your colleagues take that view, thus did you not teach us, 'One should follow the majority'? [cf. Exod. 23:2], Where there is an individual and a majority, the law follows the majority [T.: Even though you rule one way and your fellows rule another way, the halakhah follows the ruling of the majority.]"

P. R. Judah says in his name, "[Regarding] any food that is [made from one] of the seven kinds [of produce] [37B] but is not a kind of breadstuff.

Q. "or [which is made from a kind of] breadstuff but was not made into a loaf --

R. "Rabban Gamaliel says, 'One recites three benedictions after [eating] it,'

S. "and sages say, '[He recites] one benediction.'

T. "And [regarding] any food that is [made] neither [from one] of the seven kinds [of produce] nor a kind of breadstuff, for instance, bread of rice or millet,

U. "Rabban Gamaliel says, 'One recites one benediction abbreviating the three after [eating] it.'

V. "And sages say, '[He recites] no benediction [after eating it]'" [T. Ber. 4:15/O-EE].

W. How, then, do you determine which authority stands behind the statement [that after rice, one has to say the single blessing that abbreviates the three]?

X. Is it to be given to Rabban Gamaliel?

Y. Then I point to the concluding part of the first statement [about chewing wheat grains], "If the pieces are not whole, before eating one says the blessing, "Who creates various kinds of food," and after eating one says the blessing that is a single benediction summarizing the three.

Z. Who can this be? It surely cannot be Rabban Gamaliel. For if in the case of eating dates and pounded grain [grain that has not been made into bread], Rabban Gamaliel requires reciting the three blessings [of Grace after Meals], should there be any question about his position in the case of a mixture in which the pieces of bread are no longer in evidence? [Surely not! He will require the complete recitation of grace, not merely the single benediction that summarizes the three of the Grace after Meals].

AA. Rather, it is self evident that at hand is the view of rabbis [Simon, p. 234, n. 4: who hold that after pounded grain only the one blessing which includes the three is said, and where the pieces are no longer whole, the cooked wheat is treated like pounded grain.]

BB. But if so, then the rabbis' statements contradict one another. [Simon, p. 234, n. 5: There the rabbis declare that after bread made of rice, no benediction is necessary, while in the previously cited passage they are said to require one benediction which includes three.]

CC. In any event the view is that of rabbis, and one should repeat the tradition regarding rice as follows: After eating one does not say any blessing at all.

XXII.

A. Said Raba, "Prior to eating <u>rihata</u> made for field workers, which has a great deal of flour, one says the blessing, 'Who creates various kinds of foods.'

B. "What is the reason? It is that the principal ingredient is the flour.

C. "Over that which is made for townsfolk, in which people do not put in a great deal of flour, one says the blessing, 'By whose word all things come into being.'

D. "What is the reason? It is that the honey is the principal ingredient."

E. And Raba retracted and ruled, "For both sorts one says, 'Who creates diverse kinds of food.'

F. "For both Rab and Samuel say, 'Whatever contains one of the five species gets the blessing, 'Who creates diverse kinds of food.'"

XXIII.

A. Said R. Joseph, "As to <u>habisa</u>, if it contains pieces of bread an olive bulk in size, to begin with one says the blessing over it, 'Who brings forth bread from the earth.' And at the end one says [the Grace after Meals consisting of] three blessings.

B. "If it does not contain pieces of bread the size of an olive, to begin with one says the blessing over it, 'Who creates various kinds of food.' And at the end one says the single blessing that abbreviates the three [of the Grace after Meals]."

C. Said R. Joseph, "How do I know it? For it has been taught on Tannaite authority:

D. "'If [a priest] was standing and making meal offerings in [The Temple in] Jerusalem, he says the blessing, 'Blessed... who has kept us in life and sustained us and brought us to this season.'

E. "'When he takes them to eat them, he says the blessing, "Who brings forth bread from the earth."'

F. "And it has been taught in connection with this statement: 'And all meal offerings are chopped up to the size of an olive's bulk.' [So if the crumbs are the size of an olive's bulk, one says, 'Who brings forth...,' but if not, one says the alternate blessing.]"

G. Said to him Abayye, "But from the viewpoint of the Tannaite authority of the house of R. Ishmael, who has said, 'One chops up [the pieces of meal-offering] until they revert to the status of flour,' in such a case also does a person not have to say the blessing, 'He brings forth bread from the earth'?

H. "And if you say that is indeed the case, has it not been taught, 'If one gathered together among bread crumbs so much as an olive's bulk in size and ate them [on Passover], if it is leavened bread, one is subject to the penalty of extirpation, but if it is unleavened, then a person fulfills his obligation to eat unleavened bread on

Passover through what has been scraped together. [And in that case, one has to say the blessing, "Who brings forth bread from the earth."]' [That is so even though the bread crumbs themselves are not of the volume of an olive. So the position of Joseph would be contradicted by the Tannaite authority at hand.]'

I.   Under what circumstances [does the rule just now stated apply]? It is to a case in which one rekneaded the crumbs [and made them into a compact mass (Simon)].

J.   If so, then let us proceed to the next clause [of the same Tannaite teaching]: "And the stated rule applies in a case in which one ate them [that is, the crumbs] in the interval of time sufficient for eating a half-loaf of bread. But if we deal with a case in which one has kneaded the crumbs into a compact mass, the phrase, "ate them" should be, "ate it."

K.   Rather, with what situation do we deal? It is with crumbs that come from a large loaf of bread. [Some of the bread remains unbroken, even though the crumbs were not rekneaded (Simon). In such a case, the blessing, "Who brings forth bread from the earth" applies on account of the origin of the crumbs.]

L.   What is the upshot of the matter?

M.   Said R. Sheshet, "As to _habisa_, even though it does not contain pieces of bread an olive's bulk in size, one says the blessing before eating it, 'Who brings forth bread from the earth.'"

N.   Said Raba, "But that is the case only if the bits of bread still look like bread."

XXIV.

A.   Teroqenin is liable for the separation of dough-offering.

B.   And when Rabin came, he said R. Yohanan [said], "Teroqenin is exempt from the requirement of the separation of dough-offering."

C.   What is teroqenin?

D.   Said Abayye, "[Dough baked] in a hole in the ground."

XXV.

A.   And Abayye said, "Tarita is exempt from the requirement of the separation of dough-offering [since it does not fall into the category of bread]."

B.   What is tarita?

C.   Some say [Simon:] "Dough just lightly baked [by being poured on the hot hearth and formed into fritters]."

D.   Others say, "Bread baked on a spit."

E.   Others say, "Bread used for kuttah [Simon: a dish made of bread mixed with sour milk and baked in the sun]."

F.   R. Hiyya taught on Tannaite authority, "Bread that is used for kuttah is exempt from the requirement of the separation of dough-offering."

G.   And lo, it has been taught on Tannaite authority: It is liable for the separation of dough-offering.

H.   In that case the reason is made explicit, namely:

I.   R. Judah says, "The way in which it is prepared defines its character. If one made it [38A] like cakes, it is liable to the separation of dough-offering. If it was made like boards [in flat pieces and so it does not look like bread], it is exempt."

XXVI.

A. Said Abayye to R. Joseph, "As to bread baked in a hole in the ground, what is the blessing that people say before eating it?"

B. He said to him, "Do you think it falls into the category of bread at all? It is merely a glob of dough, and people say the blessing before eating it, 'Who creates various kinds of food.'"

C. Mar Zutra treated it as the principal element of his meal and said the blessing over it, "Who brings forth bread from the earth," as well as [the Grace after Meals consisting of] three blessings.

D. Said Mar, son of R. Ashi, "And a person carries out his obligation on Passover [to eat unleavened bread] by eating that form of bread.

E. "What is the basis for that view? We call it 'bread of affliction.'"

XXVII.

A. And Mar, son of R. Ashi, said, "As to the honey that comes from the date-palm, people say the blessing before eating it, 'By whose word all things come into being.'

B. "What is the reason? It is merely the tree's sweat."

C. In accord with what Tannaite authority is that view?

D. It accords with the following Tannaite authority, as we have learned in the Mishnah:

E. As regards any of the following which have the status of heave-offering: honey made from dates, wine made from apples, vinegar made from winter grapes, or any other fruit juice in the status of heave-offering, R. Eliezer obligates a non-priest who unintentionally drinks any of these to payment of the principal and added fifth, but R. Joshua exempts [M. Ter. 11:2, Avery-Peck, p. 299].

XXVIII.

A. Said one of the rabbis to Raba, "What is the law as to trimma [Simon, p. 237, n. 2: a brew of pounded fruit]?"

B. Raba did not quite grasp what he had said to him. Rabina was in session before Raba. He said [to the one who had asked,] "Do you mean the kind made of sesame, of saffron, or of grape-pits?"

C. Meanwhile Raba realized what was at issue. He said to him, "You surely refer to hashilta [Simon: a brew made with pounded date pits]. Now you call to mind something which R. Assi said, 'As to dates in the status of heave-offering, it is permitted to make trimma out of them, but it is forbidden to make mead out of them."

D. And the decided law is that in the case of dates of which one has made trimma, people say the blessing over them, "Who creates the fruit of the tree."

E. What is the reason? It is because in the present condition they remain essentially as they were to begin with [in their natural state].

XXIX.

A. As to shatita [Simon, p. 237, n. 11: flour of dried barleyseeds mixed with honey]:

B. Rab said, "[The blessing is,] 'By whose word all things come into being.'"

C. And Samuel said, "'Who creates various kinds of food.'"

D.   Said R. Hisda, "They do not really differ. The one speaks of the thick kind [Samuel], the other of the thin [Rab].

E.   "The thick kind is made for eating, the thin kind is made as a medicine."

F.   R. Joseph objected, "All parties concur that people stir up a shatita drink on the Sabbath and drink Egyptian beer.' Now if you maintain that it is for healing, are people permitted to prepare medicine on the Sabbath? [Surely not!]."

G.   Said to him Abayye, "And do you not think that that is the case? And lo, we have learned in the Mishnah:

H.   "All sorts of foods a person may eat [on the Sabbath, including those that incidentally serve for] healing, and all sorts of drinks a person may drink [M. Shab. 14:3D-E].

I.   "What is there for you to say? Is it that the person intends [the food] for mere eating [and not as medicine]?

J.   "Here too the person intends it for food [and any other effect is entirely incidental]."

K.   Another version of the same discourse:

L.   "The person intends it for food, and the aspect of healing is entirely incidental. Here too, the person intends it as food, and the aspect of healing is merely incidental."

M.   Now the statement of Rab and Samuel [Simon, p. 238, n. 1: shatita, though used for medicinal purpose, is treated as food and requires a benediction, in addition to the available teaching (F) that it is regarded as food and may be partaken of on the Sabbath] is required.

N.   For if we had had in hand only the statement [Simon: that all foods may be consumed on the Sabbath for medical purposes] I should have supposed that that rule applies where the person had in mind eating merely for food, and the healing aspect was purely incidental. But in the present case, since the fundamental intention is for healing, one need not say any blessing at all.

O.   So we are informed that, since the person derives benefit from the mixture, he has to say a blessing [even though the intent is to use the food as medicine].

XXX.

A.   For over bread one says, "He who brings forth bread from the earth" [M. 6:1G]:

B.   Our rabbis have taught on Tannaite authority:

C.   What does one say?

D.   "Who brings forth bread from the earth."

E.   R. Nehemiah says, "Bringing forth bread from the earth."

F.   Said Raba, "As to the word, 'bringing forth,' all parties concur that it has the sense of 'who has brought forth.' For it is written, 'God who brought them forth from Egypt' (Num. 23:22).

G.   "Where there is a difference, it has to do with the sense of 'who brings forth.'

H.   "Rabbis hold that the sense of 'who brings forth' is also 'who has brought forth.'

I.   "For it is written, 'Who brings you forth water out of the rock of flint' (Deut. 8:15) [and this refers to a completed action, hence the past tense].

J.   "And R. Nehemiah maintains the view that 'who brings forth' has the sense of 'he
      who will bring forth,' as it is said, 'He who will bring you out from under the burden
      of the Egyptians' (Ex. 6:7).

K.   "And as to rabbis? They take the view that the Holy One, blessed be he, made that
      statement to the Israelites in this sense:

L.   "'When I shall bring you forth, I shall do something for you which will make it clear
      to you that I am the one who 'brought you forth' from Egypt,

M.   "as it is written, 'And you shall know that I am the Lord your God who has brought
      you out' (Ex. 6:7)."

XXXI.

A.   Rabbis were reporting to R. Zira praise concerning the son of R. Zebid, brother of
      R. Simeon, son of R. Zebid, saying that he is a great man, expert in what blessings
      are to be said. He said to them, "When he comes to you, bring him to me."

B.   One time he happened to come by. They brought him a loaf of bread. He gave the
      blessing, "Brings forth" [leaving out "who"].

C.   He said, "Is this the one about whom you said, 'He is a great man and expert in what
      blessings are to be said'?

D.   "Now if he has said, 'Who brings forth,' [38B] he would have implied the sense of the
      text at hand, and he would have given an indication that the law accords with rabbis
      [as against Nehemiah].

E.   "But since he has said merely, 'bringing forth,' what does he indicate to us?"

F.   But he acted as he did to avoid contention.

G.   And the decided law is that the blessing is, "He who brings forth bread from the
      earth."

H.   For we take the view of rabbis, who have said that the word bears the meaning,
      "who has brought forth."

XXXII.

A.   Over vegetables, one says... [M. 6:1H]:

B.   The framer of the passage treats vegetables as in the same category as bread.

C.   Therefore just as bread that has been changed in character by cooking [remains
      subject to the same blessing], so vegetables that have been changed in character by
      cooking [get the same blessing that raw vegetables get].

D.   Said Rabbinai in the name of Abayye, "That is to say that over boiled vegetables,
      one says the blessing, 'Who creates the fruit of the ground.'"

XXXIII.

A.   R. Hisda gave an exposition in the name of our rabbi, and who is that? It is Rab:
      "'Over boiled vegetables people say the blessing, "Who creates the fruit of the
      ground [= XXXII D]."'

B.   "And 'our rabbis' who go down from the Land of Israel, and who is that? It is Ulla, in
      the name of R. Yohanan, [who says], 'Over boiled vegetables one says the blessing,
      "By whose word all things come into being."'"

C.   "I say, 'In the case of anything over which, to begin with [in raw state], one says the blessing, "Who creates the fruit of the ground," in its boiled state it gets the blessing, "By whose word all things come into being."

D.   "'And in the case of anything which to begin with gets the blessing, "By whose word all things come into being," when it is boiled, it gets the blessing, "Who creates the fruit of the ground."'"

E.   Now the rule that whatever to begin with gets the blessing, "By whose word all things come into being," and in its boiled state gets the blessing, "Who has created the fruit of the ground," poses no problems. For we can have such examples in the case of cabbage, beets, and pumpkins.

F.   But what sort of example can you give so for something which, to begin with, gets the blessing, "Who creates the fruit of the ground," and when boiled, gets the blessing, "By whose word all things come into being"?

G.   Said R. Nahman b. Isaac, "There is the case of garlic and leek."

XXXIV.

A.   R. Hisda gave an exposition in the name of our rabbi, and who is it? It is Samuel: "'As to boiled vegetables, one says the blessing, "Who creates the fruit of the ground."'"

B.   "But our colleagues who go down from the Land of Israel, and who are they? They are Ulla in the name of R. Yohanan, take the view, 'As to boiled vegetables, one says the blessing, "By whose word all things come into being."'"

C.   "But I take the view that the matter is subject to dispute."

D.   For it has been taught on Tannaite authority:

E.   **"People fulfill their obligation to eat unleavened bread by eating an unleavened wafer that is soaked or boiled, but that has not dissolved in the process,"** the words of R. Meir.

F.   **R. Yose says, "They fulfill their obligation by eating an unleavened wafer that is soaked, but they do not fulfill their obligation by eating an unleavened wafer that is boiled, even though it has not dissolved"** [T. Pes. 2:19]." [It is no longer in its original condition, so Yose concurs with Yohanan that a different blessing is required].

G.   All parties concur that in the case of boiled vegetables people recite the blessing, "Who creates the fruit of the ground" [just as they do for raw vegetables].

H.   In the present case, R. Yose takes the position he does only because we require [for unleavened bread to fulfill the Passover obligation] the flavor of unleavened bread, and it will be a lacking. But in the present case, even R. Yose will concur [that the same blessing is acceptable for vegetables whatever their condition].

XXXV.

A.   Said R. Hiyya bar Abba said R. Yohanan, "As to boiled vegetables, before eating them people say the blessing, 'Who creates the fruit of the ground.'"

B.   And R. Benjamin bar Japheth said R. Yohanan [said], "As to boiled vegetables, before eating them people say the blessing, 'By whose word all things come into being.'"

C.   Said R. Nahman bar Isaac, "Ulla has made his mistake permanent by ruling in accord with R. Benjamin bar Japheth."

D.   R. Zira [Simon:] expressed his astonishment [Simon: that this difference of opinion should have been recorded], "Now what has R. Benjamin bar Japheth to do with R. Hiyya bar Abba? For R. Hiyya bar Abba was meticulous in learning the tradition of his master, R. Yohanan, while R. Benjamin bar Japheth was not so meticulous.

E.   "And furthermore, as to R. Hiyya bar Abba, he would review his learning before R. Yohanan, his master, every thirty days. R. Benjamin bar Japheth did not review it.

F.   "And furthermore, in addition to these two reasons, there was the case of beets, which people had boiled seven times in a pot and eaten as dessert [requiring a blessing by themselves]. They came and inquired of R. Yohanan [about what blessing was to be said,] and he told them, 'People say the blessing, "Who creates the fruit of the ground." [Even though boiled, they retain their natural condition.]'

G.   "And furthermore, R. Hiyya bar Abba said, 'I saw R. Yohanan eat a salted olive and say the blessing before and afterward as well.'

H.   "Now if you take the view that boiled vegetables remain in their essential state, then, before eating, one says the blessing over it, 'Who creates the fruit of the tree,' and at the end, one says the blessing over it which is a single blessing that abbreviates the three [of the Grace after meals].

I.   "But if you take the view [as does Benjamin] that the [processed vegetables] do not remain in their essential state [but are transformed and so require some other blessing than the one given them when they are in their natural state], then, to be sure, while to begin with [before eating] one says the blessing, 'By whose word all things come into being,' what in the world should one say at the end?"

J.   [The reply:] Perhaps, "Who creates many living things and their requirements for all that he has created."

K.   R. Isaac bar Samuel objected, "As to vegetables with which one is able to carry out his obligation on Passover to eat bitter herbs, one may make use, for that purpose, of the vegetable and its stalk, but not if these are pickled, boiled, or seethed.

L.   "But if you take the view that they remain essentially as they were [even after being processed], why should one not be able to make use, for fulfilling his obligation, of those that are boiled?"

M.   That case is different, for in the matter of eating bitter herbs on Passover, we require the bitter taste, and [if the vegetables are boiled] it will not be present. [The consideration is quite separate from the issue at hand.]

N.   Said R. Jeremiah to R. Zira, "How could R. Yohanan have said a blessing over a salted olive? Once the pit has been removed, [39A] surely it is reduced to a size less than the requisite minimum for the recitation of a blessing?"

O.   He said to him, "Do you think that what we require is the minimum size of a large olive? We require the minimum size of a medium olive. The one that they brought to R. Yohanan was a large olive, so that, even though its pit had been removed, the minimum requisite size [for the requirement of reciting the blessing] still was present."

P. For we have learned in the Mishnah:

Q. The measure of the olive of which they have spoken is not a large one or a small one but a middle sized one, that is, one that is fit for storage [M. Kel. 17:8A-B].

R. And said R. Abbahu, "It is not called 'fit for storage' but 'abruti,'" or, some say, "samrusi."

S. Why is it called "fit for storage"? Because its oil collects within it.

XXXVI.

A. [As to the dispute about what blessing to be said for boiled vegetables], may one propose that there is a disagreement among Tannaite authorities on the same matter?

B. For there were two disciples in session before Bar Qappara. They brought him cabbage, Damascene plums, and poultry.

C. Bar Qappara gave the honor to one of the disciples to say the blessing. He went and said the blessing appropriate to poultry.

D. His fellow ridiculed him.

E. Bar Qappara grew angry, explaining, "It is not against the one who said the blessing that I am angry, but against the one who made fun. If your fellow is like someone who has never in his life had a taste of meat [and so regards it as preferable and chooses that for the blessing], what right have you to ridicule him?"

F. Then he retracted and said, "I am not angry at the one who made fun but at the one who said the blessing."

G. And he said, "If there is no knowledge here, is there no claim to the dignity of age [since you did not pay me the courtesy of asking me what to do]?"

H. A Tannaite authority [stated]: And neither one of them lived out their year.

I. Now is it not the case that the dispute concerning this matter:

J. The one who said the blessing took the view that for boiled vegetables and poultry one says the blessing, "By whose word all things come into being."

K. [Since both got the same blessing], therefore the one that he preferred [the chicken] was the one that he selected [for the blessing].

L. The one who ridiculed took the view that boiled vegetables get the blessing, "Who creates the fruit of the ground," while poultry gets the blessing, "By whose word all things come into being." Therefore the produce [the boiled vegetables] take precedence [Simon, p. 242, n. 5: even though he liked the poultry better, because the blessing over vegetables is more dignified].

M. No, [that is not what is at issue]. All parties concur that the blessing for both boiled vegetables and poultry is, "By whose word all things come into being."

N. But here, what is at issue is the following matter of theory:

O. One authority takes the view that the food one prefers takes precedence.

P. The other authority takes the view that the cabbage should take precedence, because it is more nourishing.

XXXVII.

A Said R. Zira, "When we were at the house of R. Huna, he said to us, 'As to turnip-tops, if they are cut into big pieces, the blessing is, "Who creates the fruit of the ground." When they are cut into small pieces, the blessing is, "By whose word all things come into being.'

B. "And when we came to the house of R. Judah, he said to us, 'For both the one and the other, the blessing is, "Who creates the fruit of the ground." And the reason that people chop them up more is so that they will taste sweeter.'"

XXXVIII.

A. Said R. Ashi, "When we were at the house of R. Kahana, he said to us, "as to beet borscht, into which people do not put much flour, the blessing is, "Who creates the fruit of the ground."

B. "'As to turnip borscht, into which much flour is mixed, the blessing is, "Who creates various kinds of food."'

C. "Then he retracted and said, 'The blessing for both sorts of borscht is, "Who creates the fruit of the ground." And as to the fact that people put a lot of flour in, it is only to make it cohere better.'"

XXXIX.

A. Said R. Hisda, "Beet borscht is good for the heart and good for the eyes, and all the more so, for the intestines."

B. Said Abayye, "And that is the case if one lets it sit on the stove until it says, 'tuk tuk.'"

XL.

A. Said R. Pappa, "It is perfectly obvious to me that beet-water falls into the category of beets, and turnip-water into the category of turnips, and the water of any vegetables is in the category of that vegetable."

B. R. Pappa raised the question, "What is the status of aniseed water?"

C. "Do people use it to sweeten the taste or to remove the smell. [In the former case, if it is used for sweetening, the blessing is, 'Who creates the fruit of the ground.' In the latter case, the blessing is, 'By whose word....']"

D. Come and take note of the following:

E. As to aniseed, once its taste has changed in the pot, it is not subject to the separation of heave-offering and it does not fall into the classification of food that is subject to uncleanness [M. Uqs. 3:4].

F. Does that not contain the inference that it is used to sweeten the taste of the food?

G. It does indeed contain that inference.

XLI.

A. Said R. Hiyya bar Ashi, "As to a dry piece of bread that has been soaked in a pot, before eating it people say the blessing, 'Who brings forth.'"

B. And that view [that the soaked bread remains in its original classification] differs from the view of R. Hiyya.

C. For R. Hiyya said, "It is necessary to break off a piece of bread when one finishes the recitation of the blessing [but that is not possible in the case of the dry piece of bread that is now in the pot. So the proper blessing would have to be, 'By whose word all things come into being.']"

D.   Raba objected to this reasoning, "Why then should one not [say the blessing, 'He who brings forth bread from the earth']? It is because, when the blessing is concluded, one has to conclude the recitation over a broken piece of bread. Here too, when one completes the recitation of the blessing, he may complete the recitation over a piece of bread."

E.   [39B] Rather, said Raba, "One says the blessing and afterward breaks the loaf."

F.   The Nehardeans acted in accord with R. Hiyya, and rabbis acted in accord with Raba.

G.   Said Rabina, "My mother told me, 'Your father acted in accord with R. Hiyya, for R. Hiyya has said, "It is necessary to complete the recitation of the blessing over a piece of bread that has been broken."

H.   "'And rabbis act in accord with Raba.

I.   "'And the decided law is in accord with Raba, who has said, "One recites the blessing and then breaks the bread."'"

XLII.

A.   It has been stated on Amoraic authority:

B.   If people brought before [the diners] both pieces of bread and whole loaves,

C.   said R. Huna, "One says the blessing for the pieces and thereby covers the whole loaves."

D.   And R. Yohanan says, "It is the best mode of carrying out the religious duty [to say the blessing over] the whole loaf."

E.   "But if there is a piece of a loaf of bread made from wheat, and a whole loaf of bread made from barley, all parties concur that one says the blessing over the piece of bread made from wheat and thereby covers the whole loaf made from barley."

F.   Said R. Jeremiah bar Abba, "The foregoing dispute follows the lines of the following dispute among Tannaite authorities.

G.   "They separate a whole small onion as heave-offering for other produce, but not half of a large onion.

H.   "R. Judah says, 'No, rather, they separate half of a large onion as heave-offering for other produce' [M. Ter. 2:5I-J, Peck, p. 91].

I.   "Is this not what is at issue? One authority takes the view that what is the more important takes precedence, while the other master takes the view that what is whole [and complete] takes precedence?"

J.   Where a priest is on hand [to take the produce set aside as heave-offering forthwith] there is no dispute that what is more important [and more valuable] takes precedence.

K.   Where there is a dispute, it is a case in which a priest is absent.

L.   For we have learned in the Mishnah: Wherever there is a priest to receive the heave-offering at once, the householder separates heave-offering from the choicest produce. Wherever there is no priest to receive the heave-offering immediately, he separates heave-offering from that which keeps.

M. R. Judah says, "He always should separate heave-offering from the choicest produce" [M. Ter. 2:4F-H].

N. Said R. Nahman bar Isaac, "And those who truly fear heaven so conduct themselves as to act in accord with both authorities [Huna's and Yohanan's]."

O. And who would such a person be? It would be Mar, son of Rabina. For Mar, son of Rabina would put a piece of bread under the whole loaf and break it.

P. A Tannaite authority repeated before R. Nahman bar Isaac, "One puts a broken piece of bread under the whole one and breaks it and says the blessing."

Q. He said to him, "What is your name?"

R. He said to him, "Shalman."

S. He said to him, "You are whole [shalom], and your repetition of Mishnah-teachings is whole, for you have made peace between disciples."

XLIII.

A. Said R. Pappa, "All parties concur that on Passover one puts a broken piece of unleavened bread underneath a whole piece of unleavened bread and then breaks the two.

B. "What is the scriptural basis for this view?

C. "'Bread of poverty' (Deut. 16:3) is what is written."

D. Said R. Abba, "And on the Sabbath one is liable to break bread using two loaves.

E. "What is the scriptural basis? 'Double bread' (Ex. 16:22) is what is written."

F. Said R. Ashi, "I saw R. Kahana take two loaves of bread and break only one of them."

G. R. Zira would break off bread sufficient for the entire meal.

H. Said Rabina to R. Ashi, "Does this not appear gluttonous?"

I. He said to him, "Since on ordinary days he does not do it this way, but he does it this way only now [on the Sabbath], it will not appear to be gluttony."

J. When R. Ammi and R. Assi got hold of a piece of bread that had served for a symbolic meal in joining distinct domains [as part of an erub-meal], they would say the blessing for it, "Who brings forth bread from the earth."

K. They explained, "Since one religious duty has been carried out with this loaf of bread, let us carry out with it yet another."

XLIV.

A. [40A] Said Rab, "[If the householder said to the guests, having already recited a blessing over the food for all assembled, 'Now] you take for it has been blessed, take, for it has been blessed,' one does not have to say the blessing [again]. [Simon, p. 245, n. 9: In spite of the fact that there has been an interruption between the saying and the eating, because the words spoken have reference to the benediction]."

B. "If he said [between his recitation of a blessing and the actual eating of the bread], 'Pass the salt,' 'Pass the relish,' the [guest] has to recite a blessing [for the food, since now there has been an interval between the recitation of the blessing and the eating of the food; the words do not refer to the benediction in particular]."

C. And R. Yohanan said, "Even if he said, 'Pass the salt,' 'Pass the relish,' one does not have to repeat the blessing. [If he said,] 'Mix fodder for the cattle, mix fodder for the cattle,' he has to repeat the blessing."

D.   And R. Sheshet said, "[Even if he said,] 'Mix fodder for the cattle,' he also does not
      have to recite a blessing.

E.   "For R. Judah said Rab said, 'It is forbidden for a person to eat anything before he
      gives food to his cattle,

F.   "'as it is said, "And I will give grass in your fields for your cattle," and only then,
      "You shall eat and be satisfied" (Deut. 11:15).'"

XLV.

A.   Said Raba bar Samuel in the name of R. Hiyya, "The one who breaks bread may not
      do so before [the servants] bring salt or relish to each one [of the guests]."

B.   Raba bar Samuel happened by the house of the exilarch. They brought him bread,
      and he broke it right away. They said to him, "Has the master retracted his
      teaching?"

C.   He said to him, "This bread does not need condiment."

XLVI.

A.   And said Raba bar Samuel in the name of R. Hiyya, "One fully discharges [Simon]
      urine only if he does so sitting down."

B.   Said R. Kahana, "But if it is into soft dirt, then even when one is standing, [one does
      so].

C.   "And if there is no soft ground, one should stand on a high spot and urinate
      downward [so that the drops do not flow back]."

XLVII.

A.   And said Raba bar Samuel in the name of R. Hiyya, "After eating any sort of food
      you like, eat salt, and after drinking any sort of drink, drink water, and you will
      never be harmed."

B.   It has also been taught on Tannaite authority to the same effect:

C.   After eating any sort of food you like, eat salt, and after drinking any sort of drink,
      drink water, and you will never be harmed.

D.   There is a further teaching on Tannaite authority:

E.   If a person ate any sort of food and did not eat salt, drank any sort of drink and did
      not drink water, by day he will be afflicted with bad breath, and by night he will be
      afflicted with croup.

XLVIII.

A.   Our rabbis have taught on Tannaite authority:

B.   He who drinks a great deal along with his food will not have bowel trouble.

C.   And how much?

D.   Said R. Hisda, "A cupful to a loaf of bread."

XLIX.

A.   Said R. Meri said R. Yohanan, "He who regularly eats lentils once in thirty days
      keeps croup away from his house.

B.   "But one should not do so every day.

C.   "Why not? Because it is bad for the breath."

D. And said R. Meri said R. Yohanan, "He who regularly eats mustard once in thirty days keeps ailments away from his house.

E. "But he should not [have mustard] every day.

F. "Why not? Because it weakens the heart."

G. Said R. Hiyya bar Ashi said Rab, "He who eats small fish [e.g., tunnies] will not suffer from bowel ailments, and not only so, but eating small fish makes one be fruitful and multiply and brings good health to a person's whole body."

H. Said R. Hama b. R. Hanina, "He who regularly uses black cumin will not have heartburn."

I. People objected: Rabban Simon b. Gamaliel says, "Black cumin is one of the sixty poisons, and he who sleeps to the east of a storage bin [of black cumin] -- his blood is on his own head."

J. There is no contradiction. The one speaks of its smell [when stored], the other of its taste [when used].

K. The mother of R. Jeremiah baked bread for him and put [black cumin] on it [to impart flavor] and then scraped it off [to take away the odor].

XL.

A. R. Judah says, "Creator of diverse kinds of herbs" [M. 6:11]:

B. Said R. Zira, and some say, R. Hinena bar Pappa, "The decided law does not accord with R. Judah's view."

C. And said R. Zira and some say, R. Hinena bar Pappa, "What is the scriptural basis for the view of R. Judah?

D. "Scripture says, 'Blessed be the Lord, by day' (Ps. 68:20).

E. "Now is it the case that people bless him by day and not by night? What it means is that every day one should give him [in a blessing] what is appropriate to the blessings one has received that day.

F. "Here too: for every species one should specify the appropriate blessing [and hence Judah differentiates in the language of the blessing as he prescribes it]."

LI.

A. And said R. Zira, and some say, R. Hinena bar Pappa, "Come and take note that the trait of the Holy One, blessed be he, is not like the trait of a mortal.

B. "The trait of a mortal is that an empty vessel can hold something, but a full one cannot.

C. "But the Holy One, blessed be he, is not that way. A full utensil can hold something, an empty one cannot.

D. "For it is said, 'If listening you will listen' (Ex. 15:26).

E. "[That is], if listening, you will hear [more], and if not, you will hear [nothing].

F. "Another matter: If you have been listening to what is old [reviewing your studies], you will listen to what is new, but if you are distracted, you will not hear anything any more."

The first unifying trait is in theory. At the center of this very long passage, covering more than five folios, is a rather subtle question of physics discussed only by indirection. It is whether we regard a change in the character of a substance as a change in the essence of that substance. For example, if bread is soaked as to lose its definitive traits in both taste and physical characteristics, do we still regard it as bread? Or has it become something else, that is, does it fall into a different classification? The way in which the issue is phrased, of course, is hardly so abstract. The physics are translated into theology, so to speak, since the point at issue is whether we recite the blessing appropriate to bread (hence the soaked and changed bread remains what it was) or whether we recite the blessing appropriate to other solid food than bread. The issue also is framed extensively in terms of soaked vegetables, and it recurs elsewhere. A second center of interest for us is in the way in which the rather limited statement of the theme supplied by the Mishnah provokes a most extensive and well-composed discourse on the same theme in the Talmud. Clearly, nearly everything at hand proves relevant to the Mishnah-paragraph. But the needs of the close exegesis of the Mishnah-paragraph in no way dominate. The theme is a shared one, but the framers of the Talmud have gone their own way, far exceeding in depth and theoretical sophistication the simple allegations, as to fact, that the Mishnah-paragraph provides.

Let us now see how, in detail, the Talmud at hand organizes its materials. First, we look for the passages that supply a close reading to the Mishnah-paragraph itself. These are as follows: I (+II-III), IV (+X), XXX (+XXXI), XXXII, XL. In the following units of discourse, the principal problem is the one of physics to which I alluded at the outset: when does something become something else: XI, XIII, XIV, XV, XVI (+XVII-XXI), XXII, XXIII-XXVI, XXVII-XXIX; XXXIII-XLI (+XLII). These units of discourse are included because of formal, not substantive, traits, e.g., the same tradents as appear in a prior (and relevant) unit: XLVI-XLVII (+XLVIII, XLIX; LI). Finally, these units of discourse develop the Mishnah's theme but do not deal with its detailed allegations: IV, V, VI, VII, VIII (carrying forward I-III; XLIV (how to say the blessing), XLV.

6:2

A. If one has recited the blessing over the produce of the trees, "Who creates the fruit of the ground," he has fulfilled his obligation [to say a blessing over the fruit of the trees as well, since the trees grow from the ground].

B. But if he said the blessing over the produce of the ground, "Who creates the fruit of the tree," he has not fulfilled his obligation [to say a blessing over the fruit of the ground, since the produce of the ground by definition does not grow on trees].

C. And as to everything, if one has recited the blessing, "By whose word all things come into being," he has in any event carried out his obligation.

I.

A. What Tannaite authority takes the view that the principal trait of the tree is that it grows from the ground [as at M. 6:1A]?

B. Said R. Nahman bar Isaac, "It is R. Judah."

C. For we have learned in the Mishnah: If a spring went dry or a tree was cut down [but one had gathered first fruits of the tree before it was cut down], one brings first fruits but does not make the required declaration [that they are the first fruits of the ground, since the tree has been cut down].

D. R. Judah says, "One brings the first fruits and makes the declaration [Simon, p. 248, n. 4: because the land is the essence, not the tree. That is, the land has produced the produce, and the tree has served as the instrument of the land. So one declares the first fruits to come from the land, as they do. That is in line with M. 6:2A] [M. Bik. 1:6].

II.

A. But if he said the blessing over the fruit of the ground [M. 6:2B]:

B. That is self-evident.

C. Said R. Nahman bar Isaac, "No, it was necessary to make the point explicit, in particular on account of the view of R. Judah. He maintains that wheat falls into the category of trees [And that position is excluded by the formulation of M. 6:2B]."

D. For it has been taught on Tannaite authority:

E. As to the tree from which the first man ate [and was cursed],

F. R. Meir says, "It was a vine, for there is nothing that causes for man so much wailing as wine, as it says, 'And he drank of the wine and got drunk' (Gen. 9:21)."

G. R. Nehemiah says, "It was a fig tree, for the source of the curse proved also to be the remedy, as it is said, 'And they sewed fig leaves together' (Gen. 3:7).

H. R. Judah says, "It was wheat, for a child does not know how to call his mother and father by name before he can taste wheat, [so wheat is the source of knowledge, hence the Tree of Knowledge]."

I. Now it might have entered your mind to think that, because R. Judah maintains that wheat falls into the category of trees, one should say over it the blessing, 'Who creates the fruit of the tree.'

J. "So we are informed that we recite the blessing, 'Who creates the fruit of the tree' in any case in which, when one picks the fruit, the stem remains and goes and produces more fruit.

K. [40B] "But where, when one picks the fruit, the stem does not remain to go and produce more fruit, we do not recite the blessing, 'Who creates the fruit of the tree,' but rather, 'Who creates the fruit of the ground.'"

III.

A. And as to everything, if one has recited the blessing... [M. 6:2C]:

B. It has been stated on Amoraic authority:

C. R. Huna said, "[That is so] except for wine and bread."

D. And R. Yohanan said, "Even for wine and bread."

E.   May we say that the dispute at hand is along the lines of the dispute among the following Tannaite authorities?

F.   "If one saw a loaf [of bread] and said, 'How fine is this bread! Praised be He who created this loaf,' that serves [as its benediction].

G.   "[Or] if one saw figs and said, 'How fine are these figs! Praised be He who created them,' that serves as their benediction," the words of R. Meir.

H.   R. Yose says, "Anyone who departs from the formula which the sages have established for benedictions has not fulfilled his obligation" [T. Ber. 4:4F, 4:5G-H].

I.   May we then propose that R. Huna rules as does R. Yose, and R. Yohanan as R. Meir?

J.   R. Huna may reply to you, "I take the view that even R. Meir supports my position. R. Meir takes the view he does in the cited instance only where the person actually makes explicit reference to the bread. But if the person does not make reference to the bread, then even R. Meir would concur [that the person has not carried out his obligation]."

K.   And R. Yohanan may say to you, "I take the position that even R. Yose supports my ruling. R. Yose says what he says in the case at hand only because the man has recited a blessing which rabbis have not ordained. But if he had said, 'By whose word all things come into being,' a blessing which rabbis have ordained, then even R. Yose would concur with my view."

IV.

A.   Benjamin, a shepherd, doubled over a piece of bread and said, "Blessed be the master of this piece of bread."

B.   Said Rab, "He has carried out his obligation."

C.   But has not Rab stated, "Any form of a blessing which does not make mention of God's name does not serve as a blessing at all"?

D.   In the case at hand, he said, "Blessed is the All-Merciful, the master of this piece of bread."

E.   But do we not require the recitation of the three blessings [of Grace after Meals]?

F.   What is the sense of "has carried out his obligation" as Rab has said?

G.   It is that he has carried out his obligation to recite the blessing prior to eating the bread.

H.   What then does the account tell us?

I.   It is that even though one says [the blessing] in secular language [Aramaic, rather than in the sacred formulation in Hebrew, it is valid in fulfillment of one's obligation].

J.   But we have learned on Tannaite authority: These statements may be made in any language [not only in Hebrew]: the pericope of the accused wife, the confession that the tithe has been properly disposed of, the recitation of the Shema and the Prayer, the Grace after Meals [encompassing the blessing over bread, as we have seen] [M. Sot. 8:1].

K.   It is, nonetheless, necessary to provide the information given above.

L. Why? Because you might have supposed that the rule [that reciting the blessing] in secular language [not Hebrew] is acceptable if one does so in the formula that rabbis ordained in the Holy Language.

M. But if one did not make the statement using in secular language the formula which the rabbis ordained in the Holy Language, one has not carried out his obligation.

N. So we are informed that that is not the case.

V.

A. Returning to the body of the aforecited passage:

B. Said Rab, "Any blessing which does not make mention of the divine name does not constitute a valid blessing."

C. And R. Yohanan said, "Any blessing which does not make mention of God's sovereignty is not regarded as a blessing."

D. Said Abayye, "The position taken by Rab is the more reasonable.

E. "For it has been taught on Tannaite authority:

F. "'"I have not transgressed any one of your commandments, nor have I forgotten" (Deut. 26:13).

G. "'"And I have not forgotten," to mention your name.'

H. "But the matter of the sovereignty of Heaven is not raised at all in this Tannaite statement."

I. And as to R. Yohanan?

J. "It has been taught on Tannaite authority, '"Neither have I forgotten" to mention your name <u>and your sovereignty</u>.'"

Units I, II, and III cite and explain passages of the Mishnah-paragraph. Unit IV, continued by unit V, expands upon its rule and raising an important secondary question.

6:3

A. <u>And over something that does not grow from the ground one says, "By whose word all things come into being."</u>

B. <u>Over vinegar, unripe fruit, and edible locusts one says, "By whose word all things come into being."</u>

C. <u>R. Judah says, "Over anything which results from a destructive effect, one does not say a blessing."</u>

<u>M. 6:3</u>

A. <u>If one had before him many different types [of food] --</u>

B. <u>R. Judah says, "If there are among them [foodstuffs] of the seven types [of foods of the Land of Israel] -- he says a blessing over that [particular foodstuff]."</u>

C.   And sages say, "[He says a blessing] over whichever type he desires."

M. 6:4

I.

A.   Our rabbis have taught on Tannaite authority:

B.   Before eating anything that does not grow from the ground, for example, meat deriving from domesticated beasts, wild beasts, fowl, and fish, one says, "By whose word all things have come into being."

C.   For milk, eggs, and cheese, one says, "By whose word."

D.   Before eating bread that has rotted, wine covered by a film, or cooked food that has spoiled, one says, "By whose word."

E.   For salt, brine, morils, and truffles, one says, "By whose word."

F.   Does that [list, E] then bear the implication that [like salt and brine] morils and truffles do not grow from the ground?

G.   But it has been taught on Tannaite authority:

H.   He who takes a vow not to eat the fruit of the earth is forbidden to eat the fruit of the earth but permitted to eat morils and truffles.

I.   But if he had said, "Whatever grows from the ground is forbidden to me," he is forbidden also to eat morils and truffles.

J.   Said Abayye, "To be sure, they grow from the ground, but they do not derive sustenance from the earth."

K.   But lo, what is taught on Tannaite authority is, "For everything that does not grow from the earth."

L.   Repeat the version as: "For anything that does not draw sustenance from the earth."

II.

A.   Unripe fruit [M. 6:3B]:

B.   What is the definition of unripe fruit?

C.   R. Zira and R. Ilaa:

D.   One said, "It is fruit [Simon] parched by the sun [while still on the tree]."

E.   The other said, "Dates [Simon:] blown by the wind."

F.   We have learned in the Mishnah: R. Judah says, "Over anything which results from a destructive effect, one does not say a blessing" [M. 6:3C].

G.   Now from the viewpoint of him who says that it is fruit parched by the sun, that fits with the notion of calling them something that results from a destructive effect.

H.   But in the view of him who says that they are dates blown by the wind, what sort of destructive effect is at hand?

I.   [The statement about the result of a destructive effect] refers to the other things [on the list, but not to the produce under discussion].

J.   There are those who report the discourse as follows:

K.   Now from the viewpoint of him who says that it is fruit parched by the sun, that is why one says the blessing before eating them, "By whose word...."

L. But from the viewpoint of him who says that they are dates parched by the wind, should people say, "By whose word"? Surely what is required is "Who creates the fruit of the tree."

M. Rather, with respect to unripe fruit in general, all parties concur that what is under discussion is fruit parched by the sun.

N. Where there is a dispute, it concerns fruit parched by the sun deriving from a date palm.

O. For we have learned in the Mishnah:

P. These kinds of produce are dealt with leniently [and exempted from tithing when they are in the status of doubtfully tithed produce]: unripe figs, wild jujuba, hawthorn berries, pine cones, sycamore figs, unripe dates of the palm tree, fennel, and caperfruit [M. Dem. 1:1, Sarason, p. 24].

Q. As to unripe figs, said Rabbah bar bar Hana said R. Yohanan, "They are a kind of fig."

R. Wild jujuba is lote [Simon].

S. Hawthorn berries are crab apples [Simon].

T. Pine cones --

U. Said Rabbah bar bar Hana said R. Yohanan, "They are white figs."

V. Sycamore figs --

W. Said Rabbah bar bar Hana said R. Yohanan, "They are what their name says they are, sycamore figs."

X. Unripe dates are winter grapes.

Y. Fennel is caper-fruit.

Z. As to fruit of the date palm, we have opinions of R. Ilaa and R. Zira.

AA. One said, "It is fruit that has been dried by the sun."

BB. The other said, "It is fruit that has been dried by the wind."

CC. Now with respect to the opinion of him who says that it is fruit that has been dried by the sun, that is in line with that which has been taught in Tannaite tradition:

DD. As to those categories of produce subjected to a lenient ruling when in the status of doubtfully tithed produce, when they themselves are subject to doubt, they are exempt from further tithing. Lo, if they are assuredly beyond doubt, they are liable to tithing.

EE. But in the view of him who says that it is fruit that has been dried by the wind, why should they be subject to tithing if they are assuredly in the specified status? They are in fact deemed to be ownerless property [and worthless, so exempt from all requirement of tithing].

FF. What sort of case do we have at hand? It is a case in which [despite their allegedly lacking all value and hence being regarded as ownerless,] one has stored them up.

GG. For said R. Isaac said R. Yohanan in the name of R. Eliezer b. Jacob, "In the case of produce in the category of gleanings, forgotten sheaves, and produce left in the corner of the field [all of which is ownerless and left for the poor,] if one has stored them up, [by that action the poor man who has gathered them] has imposed upon them the obligation to be tithed. [He has shown that they are of value to him and hence they become subject to tithe].

HH. There are those, further, who report the matter in this way: [41A] Now in the view of him who says that they are pieces of fruit dried by the wind, that is why in the present context they are called simply <u>unripe dates</u> [without qualification] and, in the other passage [M. Dem. 1:1] <u>unripe dates of the palm tree,</u> [Simon, p. 253, n. 6: because it is necessary to distinguish the two kinds].

II. But in the view of him who has said that it is fruit parched by the sun, in both cases should not one repeat the tradition as "dates of a palm tree" or "dates" without further specification?

JJ. That indeed is a problem for the person who holds that view.

III.

A. <u>If one had before him many different types of food</u> [M. 6:3A]:

B. Said Ulla, "The dispute concerns a case in which the blessings that apply to the diverse foods are the same.

C. "For in such a case, R. Judah takes the view that food deriving from one of the seven species [for which the Land is favored] takes precedence, while rabbis take the position that the kind of food that the person likes the most takes preference [in the person's recitation of the blessing, so that he will intend the blessing to apply to that food].

D. "But in a case in which the diverse kinds of food are subject to different blessings [each applying to its own species of food], all parties maintain that one says a blessing for one kind of food and then goes and says a blessing for another kind of food."

E. An objection was raised on the basis of the following:

F. If before someone were radishes and olives, he says the blessings for the radishes and that covers the olives as well. [But the two are not subject to the same blessing!]

G. With what sort of a case do we deal? It is a meal in which the radishes are the main course.

H. If so, let me then cite the concluding words:

I. R. Judah says, "One says the blessing over the olives, for the olives are one of the seven species [for which the Land is noted]. [Simon, p. 253, n. 10: This shows that we are not dealing with the case where one of the two articles is more important.]

J. Does R. Judah not take the position of that which we have learned on Tannaite authority:

K. In the case of any portion of the meal which is the principal dish, along with something that is secondary, one says the blessing over the main dish and thereby covers the secondary dish. [And that would surely mean one says the blessing over the radishes, which are the main dish, since the olives were eaten only [Simon: to counteract the sharp taste].

L.   And if you wish to propose that he indeed does not hold that view, then has it not been taught on Tannaite authority:

M.   R. Judah says, "If it is on account of the radishes that the olives are served, one says the blessing over the radishes and thereby exempts the olives from requiring a blessing as well."

N.   Indeed we do deal with a meal in which the radishes are the main dish. And where R. Judah and rabbis differ, it is with respect to a different aspect entirely. The statement of the dispute lacks a clause, and this is the way in which it should be repeated:

O.   "If there were before someone both radishes and olives, one says the blessing for the radishes and thereby takes care of the olives.

P.   "Under what circumstances?

Q.   "In a meal in which the radishes are the main dish.

R.   "But if the radishes are not the main dish, all parties concur that one says a blessing for this species and then goes and says a blessing for that one.

S.   "And as to two varieties of food in general [Simon, p. 254, n. 2: one of which is of the seven species, e.g., olives], both of which have exactly the same blessing, one says the blessing over whichever one he wishes.

T.   "R. Judah says, 'One says the blessing over the olives, for the olives are one of the seven species [for which the Land is noted].'"

U.   There was a dispute in this matter between R. Ammi and R. Isaac Nappaha.

V.   One of them said, "The dispute pertains to a case in which the blessings pertinent to the different kinds of food were the same.

W.   "For R. Judah takes the view that one of the seven species takes precedence [over any other sort of food], while rabbis maintain that the kind of food that one prefers is the one that takes precedence.

X.   "But in a case in which the blessings to be said for the diverse kinds of foods are not the same, then all parties take the view that one says the blessing over one sort of food and then goes and says the blessing for the other sort of food."

Y.   The other party said, "Also in a case in which the blessings for the various kinds of food are not the same, there is a dispute."

Z.   Now there is no difficulty with the view of him who has said that the dispute pertains to a case in which the blessings that apply to the diverse kinds of food are the same.

AA. But in the view of him who has said that the dispute applies to a case in which the blessings applicable to the diverse kinds of food are not the same, what sort of principle can be subject to dispute?

BB. Said R. Jeremiah, "It pertains to which of the food gets the blessing first."

IV.

A.   For R. Joseph, and some say, R. Isaac, said, "Whichever species comes first in the following verse comes first when it comes to saying a blessing over food [when several of the items are eaten in the same meal].

B.   "For it is said, 'A land of wheat, barley, wine, figtrees, pomegranates, a land of olive trees and honey' (Deut. 8:8)." [Simon, p. 254, n. 4: R. Judah agrees with R. Isaac, and therefore a fortiori holds that any of these species should have precedence over other species, whereas rabbis agree with the view of R. Hanan, which follows.]

C.   [Isaac] differs from the view of R. Hanan. For R. Hanan said, "The entire verse has been stated only with respect to supply minimum standards for requisite measurements."

D.   Wheat:

E.   As we have learned in the Mishnah:

F.   He who entered a house afflicted with plague, with his garments slung over his shoulder and his sandals and rings in his hands -- he and they are unclean forthwith. If he was dressed in his garments, with his sandals on his feet and his rings on his fingers, he is unclean forthwith. But they are clean until he will remain for a time sufficient to eat a piece of bread -- a piece of bread of wheat and not a piece of bread of barley, reclining and eating it with condiment [M. Neg. 13:9].

G.   Barley:

H.   As we have learned in the Mishnah: A piece of a bone as large as a barley imparts uncleanness when it is touched or carried but does not impart uncleanness when it is overshadowed [being too small for that purpose] [M. Oh. 2:3].

I.   Wine:

J.   A quarter-log of wine is the volume prohibited for use by a Nazirite.

K.   Figs:

L.   The volume of a substance in the volume of a dried fig is the measure for what may be carried out [from one domain to another] on the Sabbath.

M.   A pomegranate:

N.   As we have learned in the Mishnah:

O.   As to the volume that indicates that a utensil is useful, therefore susceptible to uncleanness, for those utensils that belong to householders [41B] the requisite measure is at least a pomegranate in size [M. Kel. 16:1].

P.   A land of olive trees:

Q.   Said R. Rose b. R. Hanina, "A land which uses, for all measures of requisite volume, the size of an olive."

R.   All measures do you say? Lo, there are the ones that we have just now specified [that are other than an olive's bulk].

S.   Rather, A land, the greater number of the requisite measures of which are specified in terms of the volume of an olive.

T.   Honey [of dates]:

U.   A honey-date of large size provides the measure of the volume of food which, if eaten on the Day of Atonement, imposes liability for violating the rule about fasting.

V.   And the other party?

W. [He would reply], "Are the listed requisite measures written down explicitly? They are merely based on rabbis' authority, and the verse of Scripture supplies simply additional support."

V.

A. R. Hisda and R. Hamnuna were seated at a meal. They brought before them dates and pomegranates.

B. R. Hamnuna took some and said the blessing for dates first.

C. Said to him R. Hisda, "Does not the master take the view that is expressed by R. Joseph, and some say, R. Isaac, 'Whatever is listed first in the cited verse gets its blessing first at a meal'?"

D. He said to him, "This [the date] comes second after the word land and that [the pomegranate] comes fifth" [Simon]. [Simon, p. 256, n. 1: The verse referred to is Deut. 8:8, where two lists are given of the produce of the Land of Israel, each introduced with the word 'land,' and in the first, pomegranates are mentioned fifth, while in the second, honey -- date honey -- is mentioned second.]

E. He said to him, "Who will give us feet of iron so that we may [run and] hear what you have to say."

VI.

A. It has been stated on Amoraic authority:

B. If the waiters brought before the guests figs and grapes during the meal,

C. said R. Huna, "They require a blessing before they are eaten, but they do not require a blessing afterward [since the Grace after Meals suffices]."

D. And so did R. Nahman say, "They require a blessing before they are eaten, but they do not require a blessing after they are eaten."

E. But R. Sheshet said, "They require a blessing both before they are eaten and after they are eaten.

F. "For there is nothing that requires a blessing before it is eaten and yet does not require a blessing after it is eaten, except for the bread that is eaten with things that are nibbled [Simon, such as nuts or dates brought in to nibble after the Grace after Meals]."

G. Now this differs from the view of R. Hiyya.

H. For R. Hiyya said, "A blessing said over bread takes care of all kinds of food, and a blessing said for wine takes care of all kinds of drink."

I. Said R. Pappa, "The decided law is that in the case of things that are during the meal brought on account of the meal, do not require the recitation of a blessing either before they are eaten or after they are eaten.

J. "And as to things that are not brought on account of the meal [Simon: "form an integral part of the meal"],

K. "if they are brought during the meal, they require the recitation of a blessing before they are eaten and do not require the recitation of a blessing after they are eaten.

L. "If they are brought after the meal, they require the recitation of a blessing both before they are eaten and after they are eaten."

VII.

A. People asked Ben Zoma, "Why have they said, "Those that during the meal are brought on account of the meal do not require a blessing either before they are eaten or after they are eaten'?"

B. He said to them, "Because the blessing said for the bread takes care of them."

C. "If so, let the wine be taken care of by the blessing said for bread?"

D. "Wine falls into its own category, [42A] for drinking it causes the requirement that a blessing be said for the wine by itself."

VIII.

A. R. Huna ate thirteen rolls of three to a qab [Simon], without reciting a blessing.

B. Said to him R. Nahman, "Is this hunger? [Simon: Such is enough to satisfy any hunger and therefore should necessitate grace after it]."

C. But: Anything which people in general regard as the basis for a meal requires the recitation of a blessing.

IX.

A. R. Judah provided a wedding feast for his son at the home of R. Judah bar Habiba. They brought before them bread that comes along with the nasherei [nibblings after the meal].

B. When he came in, he heard the people reciting the blessing, 'Who brings forth bread...." (hamosi)."

C. He said to them, "What is this sisi that I hear? Is it possible that you are reciting the blessing, 'Who brings forth...'?"

D. They said to him, "Indeed so. For it has been taught on Tannaite authority:

E. "R. Muna said in the name of R. Judah, 'As to the bread that comes along with the nasherei, people say the blessing before eating it, "Who brings forth...."'"

F. "And Samuel said, 'The decided law accords with the view of R. Muna.'"

G. He said to them, "The decided law does not accord with R. Muna is what has been stated on Amoraic authority."

H. They said to him, "And lo, it is the master himself who has said in the name of Samuel, 'Rolls serve for the preparation of the symbolic meal that unites distinct domains [the erub meal, in which case they are regarded as bread], and, furthermore, people say, 'Who brings forth bread before eating them.' [So they are regarded as bread, even though they are served only as nasherei after the meal.]"

I. [He replied,] "That case is different, because people base their entire meal on them. But in a case in which people do not regard them as the basis for the meal, that is not the law."

X.

A. R. Pappa came to the home of R. Huna, son of R. Nathan. After their meal was done, they brought before them nasherei.

B. R. Pappa took something and began to nibble.

C. They said to him, "Does the master not take the view, 'One has completed the meal, it is forbidden to eat any more'?"

D.   He replied, 'The formulation of the rule is in terms of 'removed.' [That is, once the table has been taken away, then it is forbidden to eat any more]."

XI.

A.   Rabbah and R. Zira came as guests to the house of the exilarch. After they had removed the tray from before them, they sent them a gift of fruit from the household of the exilarch. Rabbah ate some, but R. Zira did not.

B.   He said to him, "Does not the master take the view, 'Once the tray has been removed, it is forbidden to eat any more'?"

C.   He said to him, "We rely on the tray of the exilarch. [Simon: p. 258, n. 1: We can be sure that more food will come.] [So the meal is not over, and there is no call just yet to say grace.]"

XII.

A.   Said Rab, "He who is used to rub his hands with oil after a meal is held back [from having to complete the meal and say grace, even if the table has been cleared away] until the oil is brought."

B.   Said R. Ashi, "When we were at the home of R. Kahana, he said to us, 'For example, we who are used to rubbing our hands in oil are held back [from having to complete the meal] until the oil has been brought.'"

C.   But the law does not accord with all of these various versions.

D.   Rather, it accords with that which R. Hiyya bar Ashi said Rab said, "There are three things that must come immediately upon one another:

E.   "Immediately after the laying of hands upon the beast must come the act of slaughter [of the beast for sacrificial purposes].

F.   "Immediately upon recitation of the prayer referring to redemption should come the recitation of the Prayer.

G.   "Immediately after the washing of the hands should come the recitation of the blessing [of Grace after Meals]." [Simon, p. 258, n. 4: This washing is the signal that the meal is finished, whether or not the table has been cleared.]"

H.   Said Abayye, "Furthermore, we say another:

I.   "Immediately after [entertaining] disciples of sages [in one's home] comes a blessing [to enrich the host].

J.   "For it has been said, 'The Lord has blessed me for your sake' (Gen. 30:27).

K.   "If you like, I offer proof from the following: 'And the Lord blessed the Egyptian's house on account of Joseph' (Gen. 39:5)."

The bulk of the units of discourse at hand remains close to the Mishnah-paragraph's interest in the blessings to be said prior to eating ("over") various sorts of foods. Units I, II, III (complemented by IV-V) all deal with the specific allegations of sentences in the Mishnah-paragraph. Unit VI moves on to a secondary question, namely, blessings required after certain foods. The premise of the question is that the people have eaten bread, in which case the blessing for bread both before and after the meal suffices for everything else that has been eaten. Units VII-XII pursue this same topic, mainly through the exhibition of pertinent stories.

6:5-6

A.   If one said a blessing over the wine before the meal, he thereby exempts the wine after the meal [i.e., need not say another blessing].

B.   If one said a blessing over the appetizer before the meal, he exempts the appetizer after the meal.

C.   If one said a blessing over the loaf [of bread], he exempts the appetizer.

D.   [If one said a blessing] over the appetizer, he does not exempt the loaf.

E.   And the House of Shammai say, "[He exempts] not even [cooked food] [made in a pot]."

M. 6:5

A.   [If] people were sitting down [to eat], each one says a blessing for himself.

B.   [If] they reclined at a common table one says a blessing for all of them.

C.   [42B] [If] wine was brought to them in the midst of the meal, each says a blessing on his own.

D.   [If wine was brought to them] after the meal, one says a blessing for all.

E.   And he says [the blessing] over the perfume,

F.   even though they bring the perfume only after the dinner.

M. 6:6

I.

A.   Said Rabbah bar bar Hana said R. Yohanan, "[The rule of M. 6:5A] pertains only to [wine served] on Sabbaths and festivals, since [on those occasions] a person treats wine as a principal part of his meal.

B.   "But on other days of the year, one says a blessing for each cup of wine [as it comes, since he will not (Simon:) linger at the table after the meal and drink wine]."

C.   It also has been stated on Amoraic authority:

D.   Said Rabbah bar Meri said R. Joshua b. Levi, "The cited rule applies only to Sabbaths and festivals, to the time that someone leaves the bath house, and also to the time one has blood let, since [on those occasions] a person regards wine as a principal part of his meal.

E.   "But on other days of the year, one says a blessing for each cup of wine [as it comes]."

II.

A.   Rabbah bar Meri came to the house of Raba on an ordinary day [not a Sabbath or festival]. He saw that he said a blessing [for wine drunk] before the meal, and that he went and said a blessing afterward as well.

B.   He said to him, "Quite properly so, and that is what R. Joshua b. Levi said [one should do]."

III.

A.   R. Isaac bar Joseph came to the home of Abayye on a Festival day. He saw that he said a blessing [for wine] for each cup [as it came along]. He said to him, "Does not the matter concur with the ruling of R. Joshua b. Levi?"

B.   He said to him, "I changed my mind [Simon, p. 259, n. 6: to drink an additional cup, as I did not intend at first to take more wine after the meal.]"

IV.

A.   The question was raised: If wine came to people during the meal, what is the rule as to [the blessing said for that wine] serving to exempt from the obligation [for yet another blessing] wine that is served after the meal?

B.   If you should propose to cite this statement: If one said a blessing over the wine before the meal, he thereby exempts the wine after the meal [M. 6:5A], [I may reply] that [both cups of wine] serve only for drinking.

C.   Here, by contrast, where one cup of wine serves for drinking and the other for steeping, that rule may not apply. [The different purpose of the other cup of wine subjects that cup to a different rule, namely, to a blessing for that wine alone.]

D.   Or perhaps that makes no difference.

E.   Rab said, "It exempts [the wine served later from the requirement of having another blessing said.]"

F.   And R. Kahana said, "It does not exempt it."

G.   R. Nahman said, "It exempts it."

H.   And R. Sheshet said, "It does not exempt it."

I.   R. Huna, R. Judah, and all the disciples of Rab say, "It does not exempt it."

J.   Raba objected to R. Nahman, "If wine was brought to them in the midst of the meal, each says a blessing on his own. If wine was brought to them after the meal, one says a blessing for all [M. 6:6C-D]. [Would this not indicate that a blessing said for wine drunk during the meal does not cover wine drunk after the meal]?"

K.   He said to him, "This is the sense of the passage: 'If wine was not served to them during the meal but only after the meal, one of the participants says the blessing over that cup of wine in behalf of all of them.'"

V.

A.   If one said a blessing over the loaf of bread, he exempts the appetizer. If he said a blessing over the appetizer, he does not exempt the loaf. And the House of Shammai say, "He exempts not even cooked food" [M. 6:5C-E].

B.   The question was asked as follows:

C.   Do the House of Shammai differ with the first clause or the second one?

D.   That is to say: The opening authority states, If one said a blessing over the loaf of bread, he exempts the appetizer, and all the more so cooked food. Then the House of Shammai come along to take the contrary view: it is not merely that a blessing said over the bread has not taken care of the appetizer, but it has not taken care even of cooked food.

E. Or perhaps the disagreement concerns the concluding clause, as it is taught: <u>If he said a blessing over the appetizer, he does not exempt the loaf.</u> The implication then is that it is the loaf of bread alone that has not been covered by the blessing said for the appetizer, but as to cooked food, the blessing said for the appetizer <u>does</u> take care of the cooked food.

F. Then the House of Shammai come along to state, "Even cooked food has not been covered by that blessing."

G. The question stands.

VI.

A. <u>If people were sitting down to eat, each one says a blessing for himself [M. 6:6A]:</u>

B. Is it the sense, then, that only if they sat down to eat one follows the stated procedure [and one serves for all only if they reclined], but if not, one does not?

C. An objection was raised on the basis of the following passage:

D. **Ten men who were traveling [together] on the road, even if all were eating from the same loaf, each one recites the benediction [after meals] himself.**

E. **[If] they sat down to eat [together], even if each one was eating from his own loaf, one man recites the benediction [afterwards] for all of them [cf. M. Ber. 6:6] [T. Ber. 5:23A-B].**

F. Now the passage states that [one may say a blessing for all of them if they merely] sat down, even though they were not reclining.

G. Said R. Nahman bar Isaac, "The rule [of Tosefta] speaks of a case in which the people have said, 'Let us go and eat bread in that spot [Simon, p. 261, n. 1: which is equivalent to making a party].' [On that basis one may serve to say the blessing for all of them, even though they merely sat down and did not actually recline for a banquet.]"

VII.

A. When Rab died, his disciples went after his [bier to the grave]. When they came back, they said, "Let's go and eat bread at the Danak canal."

B. After they had broken bread, they went into session and raised the question: "We have learned in the Mishnah that the cited rule applies only when the people had actually reclined. If they sat down, it does not. Or perhaps it is the case that, once people say, 'Let us go and eat bread in such and such a place,' it is as if they had reclined."

C. They did not have in hand an answer to their conundrum.

D. R. Adda bar Ahbah rose and [43A] took the tear in his garment [which he made when he heard the master had died] and put it in the back and made a new tear, saying, "Rab has died, and we have not learned even the simple laws governing the Grace after Meals!"

E. Then an elder came along and contrasted the rules as framed in the Mishnah and in the external version [given in Tosefta] and taught them, "Because the people have said to one another, 'Let us go and eat bread in that spot,' it is as if they have reclined [for a banquet, and an individual may serve the needs of all]."

VIII.

A. If they reclined at a common table, one says a blessing for all of them [M. 6:6B]:

B. Said Rab, "The rule pertains only to a blessing for bread [that is to serve all assembled], in which case, the act of reclining is necessary [to indicate that they form a common party]. But as to a blessing said for wine [to serve all assembled], there is no need for an act of reclining. [Even if the people are not reclining, a single individual may say the blessing for everyone.]"

C. And R. Yohanan said, "Even for wine, there must be reclining [so as to constitute a common party to be served by a single person's benediction]."

D. There are those who report the matter as follows:

E. Said Rab, "The rule has been taught only in connection with eating bread, which is served by reclining [since when eating bread, people will constitute a party only if they are reclining], but in the case of wine, in which reclining does not matter, [the individual may say a blessing for all assembled even if the group as a whole is not reclining as a banquet party."

F. And R. Yohanan said, "Reclining serves also in the case of wine."

G. An objective was raised from the following:

H. What is the order of reclining [at a communal meal]?

I. As the guests enter, they are seated on benches or chairs while all [the guests] assemble [and are seated together].

J. Once all have assembled, the attendants give them [water] for [washing] their hands.

K. Each [guest] washes one hand.

L. [When] they [the attendants] mix for them the cup [of wine], each one recites the benediction [over wine] for himself.

M. [T. adds:] [When] they have brought before them appetizers, each one recites the benediction [over appetizers] for himself.

N. [When] they have arisen [from the benches or seats] and reclined [to the second stage of the meal], and [the attendants] have [again] given them [water] for their hands,

O. even though each has already washed one hand, he now must wash both hands.

P. When they [the attendants] have [again] mixed for them the cup, even though each has recited a benediction over the first [cup], one person recites a benediction for the wine for all of them.

Q. [T. adds: When (the attendants) have brought before them appetizers, even though each has recited a benediction over the first (appetizers), he recites a benediction over the second, and one person recites the benediction for all of them [at this stage of the meal]. One who arrives after three (courses of) appetizers [have been served] is not allowed to enter (to join the meal)] [T. Ber. 4:8A-L].

R.   Now when we turn to the version of Rab's opinion which has Rab say, "The rule
      pertains only to a blessing for bread in which case the act of reclining is necessary.
      But as to a blessing said for wine, there is no need for an act of reclining," there is
      surely a problem in the opening part [of the Tosefta passage]. [For the cited
      Tosefta-passage is explicit that one person says the blessing in behalf of all only
      after the people have reclined.]

S.   Guests fall into a separate category, for to begin with they expect to shift their
      position.

T.   And as to the other version of Rab's statement, which imputes to him the following:
      "The rule has been taught only in connection with eating bread, which is served by
      reclining, but in the case of wine, in which reclining does not matter, the individual
      may say a blessing for all assembled], "the latter part [of the Tosefta-passage] poses
      a problem [Simon, p. 262, n. 4: which says that having reclined, one says a blessing
      on behalf of all also for wine].

U.   That passage also may be distinguished [from the generally prevailing situation], for,
      since reclining serves to form the company into a single group for purposes of a
      blessing for bread, reclining serves the same purpose as to wine.

IX.

A.   If wine was brought to them in the midst of the meal [M. 6:6C]:

B.   **They asked Ben Zoma, "Why did they say [If] wine was brought to them during the
      meal, each one recites the benediction for himself [M. 6:6C]?"**

C.   **He said to them, "Because one's throat is not clear [and he might choke if he tried
      to respond 'Amen' to the benediction]" [T. Ber. 4:12A-B].**

X.

A.   And he says the blessing over the perfume [M. 6:6E]:

B.   Since the framer of the passage stresses, "And he is the one who says the blessing
      for the perfume," it must follow that there is someone present who is more
      important than he. Why then does [the one who says the blessing for the wine say
      this blessing as well]?

C.   Since he was the one to wash his hands first at the end of the meal [he says all the
      blessings].

D.   This view supports the position of Rab.

E.   For R. Hiyya bar Ashi said Rab said, "He who washes his hands first at the end of
      the meal is the one who is designated to recite the blessings."

F.   Rab and R. Hiyya were in session before Rabbi at a meal. Said Rabbi to Rab, "Rise,
      wash your hand."

G.   [Rabbi] saw that he was trembling. Said to him R. Hiyya, "Son of the aristocracy,
      review the Grace after Meals is what [Rabbi] meant to tell you, [since he wants you
      to recite it]."

XI.

A.   Said R. Zira said Raba bar Jeremiah, "At what point do people say the blessing for
      incense?

B.   "When the column of smoke goes up."

C.   Said R. Zira to Raba bar Jeremiah, "But lo, at that point, the person will not yet have smelled the incense."

D.   He said to him, "And by that same principle of yours, as to 'He who brings forth bread from the earth,' which one says, lo, the one who says the blessing has not yet actually tasted the bread but only has in mind to taste the bread.

E.   "Here too he has in mind to smell the incense [so he says the blessing]."

XII.

A.   Said R. Hiyya, son of Abba bar Nahmani said R. Hisda said Rab, and some say, said R. Hisda said Zeiri, "As to all sorts of incense, people say over all of them the blessing, 'Who creates fragrant sorts of wood,' except over musk.

B.   "Over musk, which comes from a living creature, people say the blessing, 'Who creates various sorts of spices.'"

C.   An objection was raised on the basis of the following statement: People say the blessing, "Who creates fragrant sorts of wood" only for balsam that comes from the house of Rabbi and from the house of Caesar, and for myrtle which derives from any location.

D.   That indeed refutes the foregoing.

XIII.

A.   Said R. Hisda to R. Isaac, "As to balsam oil, what is the blessing that people say over it?"

B.   He said to him, "This is what R. Judah said, 'Who creates the oil of our land.'"

C.   He said to him, "But [what do other people,] besides R. Judah, say, for the Land of Israel is particularly precious in his view. But what is it that people in general say?"

D.   He said to him, "This is what R. Yohanan said, 'Who creates fragrant oil.'"

XIV.

A.   Said R. Adda bar Ahba, "As to custom, people say the blessing over it, 'Who creates various kinds of fragrant wood.'

B.   "But as to oil in which it is steeped, people do not say [a blessing]."

C.   And R. Kahana said, "[People says a blessing] even over the oil in which it is steeped, but not over the oil in which it is ground [Simon]."

D.   Nehardeans say, "Even over the oil in which it is ground [people say the same blessing]."

XV.

A.   [43B] Said R. Giddal said Rab, "For jasmine people say the blessing, 'Who creates various kinds of fragrant wood.'"

B.   Said R. Hananel said Rab, "As to sea-rush [Simon, p. 263, n. 4: which has stalks like flax], people say the blessing, 'Who creates various kinds of fragrant wood.'"

C.   Said Mar Zutra, "What is the pertinent verse of Scripture? 'She had brought them up to the roof and hid them with stalks of flax (Jos. 2:6).'"

D.   Said R. Mesharsheya, "For domestic narcissus people say the blessing, 'Who creates various kinds of fragrant wood.' For wild narcissus, 'Who creates fragrant herbs.'"

E.   Said R. Sheshet, "For violets people say the blessing, 'Who creates fragrant herbs.'"

F.   Said Mar Zutra, "Someone who smells an <u>etrog</u> or quince should say the blessing, 'Blessed is he who put a good smell into fruit.'"

G.   Said R. Judah, "One who goes out on spring days and sees the trees sprouting should say the blessing, 'Blessed is he who has left nothing that is needed out of his world, and who has created so many good things in creation, such as good trees, for the pleasure of humanity.'"

XVI.

A.   Said R. Zutra bar Tobiah said Rab, "How do we know that people are supposed to say a blessing over a good scent?

B.   "As it is said, 'Let the whole of the soul praise the Lord' (Ps. 150:6).

C.   "What is it from which the soul, and not the body, derives pleasure? One must say, it is a good smell."

D.   And R. Zutra bar Tobiah said Rab said, "The young men of Israel are destined to give forth a good smell like Lebanon.

E.   "For it is said, 'His branches shall spread, and his beauty shall be as the olive tree, and his fragrance as Lebanon' (Hos. 14:7)."

XVII.

A.   And R. Zutra bar Tobiah said Rab said, "What is the meaning of the Scriptural verse, 'He has made everything beautiful in its time' (Qoh. 3:11)?

B.   "It teaches that the Holy One, blessed be he, made each person's trade seem beautiful in his view."

C.   Said R. Pappa, "That is in line with what people say: 'Hang a palm's heart on a pig, and it will do its thing with it [taking it to a garbage dump].'"

XVIII.

A.   And R. Zutra bar Tobiah said Rab said, "[As to not walking alone because of fear of evil spirits,] a torch is equivalent to two people, and moonlight to three."

B.   The question was raised: Is the sense, then, that a torch is equivalent to two people including the one who carries it, or is it equivalent to two people besides him?

C.   Come and take note: "And moonlight is equivalent to three."

D.   Now if you say that the sense is, "Including the one who carries it," there is no problem.

E.   But if you say that the sense is, "Except for the one who carries it," then what need do I have for four [that is, three plus the man in question]?

F.   For has not a master stated, "To an individual person a demon will make an appearance and do damage, to two people it will make an appearance but not do damage. To three people it will not make an appearance at all."

G.   Does it not then follow that the sense is, "The torch is equivalent to two persons, <u>including</u> the one who carries it"?

H.   That indeed follows.

XIX.

A.   And R. Zutra bar Tobiah said Rab said, and some say R. Hana bar Bizna said R. Simeon, the pious, said, and some say, said R. Yohanan in the name of R. Simeon b.

Yohai, "It would be better for someone to throw himself into a fiery furnace rather than embarrass his fellow in public.

B.   "From whom do we learn that lesson? From Tamar.

C.   "For it is said, 'When she was brought forth...' (Gen. 38:25) [she did not identify Judah as the father of her child, even though it meant being put to death by burning.]"

XX.

A.   Our rabbis have taught on Tannaite authority:

B.   [If people] brought before a person oil and myrtle [Simon, p. 225, n. 3: oil for removing dirt from the hands, myrtle for scent],

C.   the House of Shammai say, "One says a blessing over the oil, and afterward one says a blessing over the myrtle."

D.   And the House of Hillel say, "One says a blessing over the myrtle, and afterward one says a blessing over the oil."

E.   Said Rabban Gamaliel, "I shall settle the matter [in favor of the position of the House of Shammai]. In the case of oil we have the pleasure of using it both for its scent and for anointing, while in the case of myrtle we enjoy it for its scent, but we do not enjoy it for use for anointing."

F.   Said R. Yohanan, "The law follows the view of him who settles the matter."

G.   R. Pappa came to the house of R. Huna, son of Iqa. The servants brought before them oil and myrtle. R. Pappa took them and said the blessing for the myrtle first, and then he said the blessing for the oil.

H.   He said to him, "Does the master not take the view that the law follows the opinion of the one who settles the matter?"

I.   He said to him, "This is what Raba said, 'The law follows the view of the House of Hillel.'"

J.   But that is not the fact. In fact, all he did was try to get himself out of it.

XXI.

A.   Our rabbis have taught on Tannaite authority:

B.   If at the end of the meal they brought before them oil and wine,

C.   The House of Shammai say, "[At the end of the meal] one holds the oil in his right hand and the wine in his left.

D.   "He recites the benediction over the oil and afterward recites the blessing over the wine."

E.   And the House of Hillel say, "One holds the wine in his right hand and the oil in his left.

F.   "He recites the benediction over the wine and then over the oil and smears it upon the head of the servant.

G.   "If the servant is a disciple of the sages, [then instead] one smears [the oil] on the wall,

H.   "for it is not befitting a disciple of the sages to go about perfumed" [T. Ber. 5:29A-F].

XXII.

A.   Our rabbis have taught on Tannaite authority:

B.   There are six things that are not befitting the dignity of a sage.

C.   He should not go out perfumed to the market place.

D.   He should not go out by himself at night.

E.   He should not go out in patched sandals.

F.   He should not talk with a woman in public.

G.   He should not recline in an eating club made up of ordinary people.

H.   He should not come last to the school house.

I.   And there are those who say, he should also not walk with giant steps.

J.   He should not go about stiffly erect.

K.   "He should not go out perfumed to the market place:"

L.   Said R. Abba, son of R. Hiyya bar Abba, said R. Yohanan, "That applies to a place in which people are suspect of pederasty."

M.   Said R. Sheshet, "The rule applies only to perfumed garments, but as to [perfuming] one's body, the perfume removes the smell of sweat [and is permitted]."

N.   Said R. Pappa, "One's hair is in the category of one's garment."

O.   And some say, "It is in the category of one's body."

P.   "He should not go out alone by night:"

Q.   That is on account of [bringing] suspicion [on himself]. And that rule applies only if he has no set engagement. But if he has a set engagement, people will know that he is going to that appointment.

R.   "He should not go out in patched sandals:"

S.   This supports the position of R. Hiyya bar Abba, for R. Hiyya bar Abba said, "It is a disgrace for a disciple to go out with patched sandals."

T.   Is that the case? And lo, R. Hiyya bar Abba went out [in such a way].

U.   Said Mar Zutra, son of R. Nahman, "The rule applies to those that have patches on the patches."

V.   And the rule applies only to a case in which the upper part is patched, but as to the sole, there is no objection.

W.   And this applies only to going out in such sandals to the public way, but as to wearing them in one's own house, there is no objection.

X.   And that applies only to the dry season, but as to the rainy season, there is no objection.

Y.   "He should not converse with a woman in the marketplace:"

Z.   Said R. Hisda, "That is the case even though it is his wife."

AA.   It has been taught on Tannaite authority along these same lines: "Even if it is his wife, even if it is his daughter, and even if it is his sister, since not everybody is expert in who are his women relatives."

BB.   "He should not recline in an eating club made up of ordinary people:"

CC.   What is the reason? So that he will not be drawn after them.

DD.   "And he should not come last to the study house:"

EE. It is because people will call him a transgressor [for wasting time].

FF. "And he should not walk with giant steps:"

GG. It is because a master has said, "Taking a giant step takes away one five-hundredth of a person's eyesight."

HH. What is the remedy?

IL. Let him restore it with the wine used for the recitation of the sanctification of the Sabbath on Friday evening.

JJ. "And he should not go about stiffly erect:"

KK. For a master has said, "He who walks about stiffly erect, even for four cubits, is as if he [Simon:] pushed against the heels of the Divine Presence [acted haughtily against God],

LL. "for it is written, 'The whole earth is full of his glory' (Is. 6:3)."

While somewhat protracted, the Talmudic passage before us focuses upon the exegesis of the Mishnah-paragraph or upon secondary expansion of what is given for that purpose. Units I-IV take up M. 6:5A. Unit V moves on to M. 6:5C-E, unit VI complemented by unit VII to M. 6:6A, unit VIII to M. 6:6B, IX to M. 6:6C, X to M. 6:6E. Then units XI, XII, XIII, XIV, XV, XVI, XVII proceed to develop the theme of blessings that are said for various good odors, e.g., incense. Units XVIII-XIX are joined for tradental reasons. Then unit XX reverts to the theme of blessings for sweet smells, now proceeding to the secondary issue of the choice to be made when a good odor comes along with some other occasion for a blessing; XXI is attached because of thematic congruence to the foregoing. The concluding unit, XXII, is added on account of XXI H.

6:7

A. [If] they brought before him a salted relish first and with it, a loaf [of bread],

B. [44A] he says a blessing over the salted relish and [thereby] exempts the loaf,

C. for the loaf is secondary to it.

D. This is the general rule: as to any primary [food] accompanied by a secondary [food], one says a blessing over the primary and exempts the secondary.

I.

A. Now can there be a case in which the salted food is the principal ingredient of a meal, and the bread is secondary to it?

B. Said R. Aha, son of R. Avira said R. Ashi, "The rule is taught with reference to those who eat fruit of Genessareth."

II.

A. Said Rabbah bar bar Hana, "When we would go to R. Yohanan to eat the fruit of Genessareth, when we were a hundred [disciples], we would each bring ten to him.

When we were ten, each one of us would bring him a hundred. And a hundred of them cannot be held by a basket that holds three seahs.

B. "And [Yohanan] would eat them all and swear that he had not had the taste of food."

C. Do you mean to say, "The taste of food"?

D. Rather, that he had not had a meal.

III.

A. R. Abbahu would eat them so much that a fly would slip off his forehead. [Simon: they made his skin so smooth that the fly could not obtain a footing.]

B. And R. Ammi and R. Assi would eat so many of them that their hair fell out.

C. R. Simeon b. Laqish would eat so many of them that his mind began to wander.

D. R. Yohanan reported that to the house of the patriarch, and R. Judah the Patriarch sent a band of officials after him to bring him home.

IV.

A. When R. Dimi came, he said, "King Yannai had a town in the Royal Mountain which produced sixty myriads of dishes of salted fish for those who were cutting figs from one week to the next."

B. When Rabin came, he reported, "King Yannai had a single tree in the royal mountain from which people would take down forty seahs of young pigeons from three broods month by month."

C. When R. Isaac came, he reported, "There was a town in the Land of Israel, called Gofnit, in which there were eighty sets of brothers, who were priests, married to eighty sets of sisters, who were priests[' daughters]."

D. Rabbis searched from Sura to Nehardea and found no equivalent case, except for that of the daughters of R. Hisda who were married to Rami bar Hama and Mar Uqba bar Hama. And while the women came from a priestly family, the men did not.

V.

A. Said Rab, "Any meal without salt is no meal."

B. Said R. Hiyya bar Abba said R. Yohanan, "Any meal without something sharp is no meal."

Once unit I has given an example to make M. 6:7A credible, the remainder, units II-IV, flows smoothly, expanding on the topic of the fruit mentioned in unit I, on the one side, or on salted fish, on the other, at units II-III, and IV respectively. Unit V continues the theme of salt.

6:8

A. "If one ate figs, grapes or pomegranates --

B. "he says after them [the Grace after Meals made up of] three blessings," the words of Rabban Gamaliel.

C. And sages say, "One blessing [which summarizes the three, in abbreviated form]"

D.   R. Aqiba says, "Even if one ate a cooked vegetable, if that was his
        meal," one says after it the three blessings."

E.   He who drinks water to quench his thirst says, "For everything was
        created at his word."

F.   R. Tarfon says, "Creator of [many] souls and their needs."

I.

A.   What is the scriptural basis for the view of Rabban Gamaliel?

B.   It is written, "A land of wheat and barley" (Deut. 8:8), and it is further written, "A
        land in which you shall eat bread without scarcity" (Deut. 8:9), and, finally, it is
        written, "And you shall eat and be satisfied and bless the Lord your God" (Deut.
        8:10). [Thus all foods listed at Deut. 8:8 and 8:9 are covered by Deut. 8:10.]

C.   And rabbis? There is a break marked off by the word "land," [so that the blessing to
        which Deut. 8:10 refers speaks only of eating bread, not the other produce for which
        the land is famed].

D.   And Rabban Gamaliel also should recognize that the word "land" marks a break in
        the passage.

E.   He requires that break [in the formulation of the verses to indicate that one who
        merely chews grain [does not have to say the requisite Grace after Meals, and that
        is the force of the exclusionary construction at hand].

II.

A.   Said R. Jacob b. Idi said R. Hanina, "For whatever derives from the five species [of
        cereals, wheat, barley, oats, rye, and spelt], beforehand one recites the blessing,
        'Who creates various kinds of food,' and after eating such a food, one recites the
        single blessing that abbreviates the three [of Grace after Meals]."

B.   Said Rabbah bar Meri said R. Joshua b. Levi, "For whatever derives from the seven
        species [listed at Deut. 8:8] beforehand one recites the blessing, 'Who creates the
        fruit of the tree,' and at the end one recites the simple blessing that summarizes the
        three [of Grace after Meals]."

III.

A.   Said Abayye to R. Dimi, "What is the single blessing that summarizes the three [of
        the Grace after Meals]?"

B.   He said to him, "For the fruit of the tree, one says, 'For the tree, for the fruit of
        the tree, for the produce of the field, for the pleasant, broad, and good land that you
        have given as an inheritance to our fathers, to eat of its fruit and to be satisfied of
        its goodness. Have mercy, Lord our God, on Israel, your people, on Jerusalem, your
        city, on your sanctuary and on your altar, and may Jerusalem, your holy city, be
        quickly rebuilt in our days, and take us up to it and give us joy in it, for you are good
        and do good.'

C.   "For the five species [of cereals]: 'For the provision, sustenance, the produce of the
        field...,' concluding, '... for the land and for sustenance.'"

D.   [In the case of fruit], how does one conclude the blessing?

E.   When R. Dimi came, he said Rab said, "One says at the conclusion, 'On the festival of the New Moon, one concludes, 'Blessed... who sanctifies Israel and the New Moons.'"

IV.

A.   Here what do we say [for produce]?

B.   R. Hisda said, "'For the land and for its fruit.'"

C.   R. Yohanan said, "'For the land and for fruit.'"

D.   Said R. Amram, "There is no contradiction between the two versions, for the one speaks of our circumstance [that is, Hisda's for Babylonia] and the other of theirs [in the land of Israel, that is, Yohanan's]."

E.   To this R. Nahman bar Isaac objected, "Are they to eat the produce, and we to say the blessing [with Babylonians blessing the land and _its_ fruit, which they have, in fact, not eaten]?"

F.   Rather, the opinions are to be reversed.

G.   "R. Hisda said, "For the land and for fruit."

H.   R. Yohanan said, "For the land and for _its_ fruit."

V.

A.   [44B] Said R. Isaac bar Abedimi in the name of our rabbi, "For eggs and for all sorts of meat, at the outset one says the blessing, 'By whose word....,' and at the end, 'Who creates many souls and fills their needs.'"

B.   "But as to vegetables, one does not [say a blessing afterward]."

C.   R. Isaac said, "Even for vegetables [one says a blessing afterward], but not for water."

D.   And R. Pappa said, "Even for water [one says a blessing afterward]."

E.   Mar Zutra acted in accord with the view of R. Isaac bar Abedimi, and R. Shimi bar Ashi, with R. Isaac.

F.   The mnemonic is one accords with two and two with one. [Simon, p. 270, n. 9: The authority who was mentioned alone, without his father (Mar Zutra) acted as prescribed by the authority who is mentioned with his father (R. Isaac b. Abedimi) and _vice versa_].

G.   Said R. Asha, "When I remember, I act in accord with all of them [thus saying a blessing after drinking water]."

H.   We have learned in the Mishnah:

I.   Whatever requires a blessing afterward requires a blessing beforehand, but there is that which requires a blessing beforehand and does not require a blessing afterward [M. Nid. 6:10].

J.   Now in the view of R. Isaac bar Abedimi, that concluding clause serves to exclude vegetables, and, in that of R. Isaac, water.

K.   But in R. Pappa's opinion, what does the concluding clause serve to exclude?

L.   It serves to exclude the case of carrying out religious duties [Simon, p. 271, n. 3: which require a blessing before the performance of them but not after, such as taking off the phylacteries, laying aside the palm branch, etc.]

M.   And in the case of the Westerners, who, after they remove their phylacteries, recite
      a blessing, "Who has sanctified us by his commandments and commanded us to keep
      his ordinances," what does it serve to exclude?

N.   It serves to exclude fragrances."

VI.

A.   Said R. Yannai, "To whatever is equivalent in volume to an egg, the egg nonetheless
      is superior [in food value (Simon)]."

B.   When Rabin came, he said, "An egg that is lightly roasted is superior to six measures
      of fine flour. An egg that is hard baked is superior to four. A boiled egg is superior
      to the equivalent volume of any other food except for meat."

VII.

A.   R. Aqiba says, "Even if he ate a cooked vegetable..." [M. 6:8D]:

B.   And is there any sort of boiled vegetable that may serve as the principal part of a
      meal?

C.   Said R. Ashi, "The authorities of the passage at hand referred to cabbage-stalks."

VIII.

A.   Our rabbis have taught on Tannaite authority:

B.   "Milt is good for the teeth and bad for the intestines.

C.   "Horse-beans are bad for the teeth and good for the intestines.

D.   "Every sort of raw vegetable makes a person pale.

E.   "Whatever is [eaten] not at full growth retards growth.

F.   "Whatever is alive [and eaten whole, (Simon:) like small fish] brings back vitality,
      and whatever parts of a beast derive from the area near the vital organs bring back
      vitality.

G.   "Cabbage is good to sustain life, and beets to heal.

H.   "Woe to the house [stomach] through which vegetables continually pass."

I.   A master said, "Milt is good for the teeth and bad for the intestines."

J.   What is the remedy? Chew it, then spit it out.

K.   "Horse beans are bad for the teeth and good for the intestines."

L.   What is the remedy? Boil them, then swallow them.

M.   "Every sort of raw vegetable makes a person pale."

N.   Said R. Isaac, "That statement applies to the first meal after blood letting."

O.   And said R. Isaac, "It is forbidden to talk with whoever eats vegetables before the
      fourth hour.

P.   What is the reason? Because of the odor.

Q.   And R. Isaac said, "It is forbidden for someone to eat fresh vegetables before the
      fourth hour."

R.   Amemar, Mar Zutra, and R. Ashi were in session. Before the fourth hour they
      brought before them fresh vegetables. Amemar and R. Ashi eat, while Mar Zutra
      did not eat them. They said to him, "What are you thinking? Is it because R. Isaac
      said, 'It is forbidden to talk with anybody who eats fresh vegetables before the
      fourth hour, on account of the bad odor'? But lo, we have been eating them and yet
      you are talking with us!"

S.   He said to them, "I concur with the other relevant statement of R. Isaac, for R. Isaac said, 'It is forbidden for a person to eat fresh vegetables before the fourth hour.'"

T.   "Whatever is not at full growth retards growth."

U.   Said R. Hisda, "Even a kid for a zuz [Simon: a good fat one]."

V.   But the cited rule applies only to one that has not attained a fourth of full growth. If it has attained a fourth of full growth, there is no objection.

W.   "Whatever is alive [and eaten whole] brings back vitality."

X.   Said R. Pappa, "Even little fishes that come from ponds."

Y.   "Whatever parts of a beast derive from the area near the vital organs bring back vitality."

Z.   Said R. Aha bar Jacob, "It is the neck."

AA.   Said Raba to his servant, "When you bring me a piece of meat, take the trouble to bring me from the part of the beast which is near the spot at which the blessing [when the beast is slaughtered] is said [namely, the neck]."

BB.   "Cabbage is good to sustain life, and beets to heal."

CC.   Is it the case, then, that cabbage is good as food but not as medicine?

DD.   And has it not been taught on Tannaite authority:

EE.   "There are six things that heal a sick person of his ailment in such a way as to effect a permanent cure: cabbage, beets, [Simon:] a decoction of dry poley, the maw, the womb, and the large lobe of the liver"?

FF.   Rather, I should say, "Cabbage serves also as food."

GG.   "Woe to the house through which vegetables continually pass."

HH.   Is that really so? And did not Raba say to his servant, "When you see vegetables in the market, do not ask me what will you wrap around your bread [but just buy the vegetables]"?

II.   Said Abayye, "The reference is to those cooked without meat."

JJ.   Said Raba, "It refers to those that are eaten without wine."

KK.   It has been stated on Amoraic authority:

LL.   Rab said, "It refers to those that are cooked without meat."

MM.   Samuel said, "It refers to those that are without wood [that is, not properly cooked]."

NN.   R. Yohanan said, "It refers to those that are eaten without wine."

OO.   Said Raba to R. Pappa, the brewer, "[Simon:] We neutralize it with meat and wine.

PP.   "As to you, who do not have a great deal of wine, how do you neutralize it?"

QQ.   He said to him, "With pieces [of wood]. [We cook it thoroughly.]"

RR.   That is illustrated by the action of R. Pappa's wife. When she cooked vegetables, she [Simon:] neutralized their evil effects with eighty twigs from Persian trees.

IX.

A.   Our rabbis have taught on Tannaite authority:

B.   Small salted fish at times may kill, specifically, on the seventh, the seventeenth, and the twenty-seventh day [after being salted].

C.   And some say, the twenty-third day.

D.   But the stated rule applies only to those that are not properly roasted.

E.   If they are properly roasted, there is no problem.

F.   And if it is not properly roasted, there is objection only if one does not drink beer afterward. But if one drinks beer afterward, there is no problem.

X.

A.   He who drinks water to quench his thirst [M. 6:8E]:

B.   What does the qualifying language exclude?

C.   Said R. Idi bar Abin, "It serves to exclude the case of one [45A] who is choking on meat."

XI.

A.   R. Tarfon says, "Creator of many souls and their needs" [M. 6:8F]:

B.   Said Raba bar R. Hanan to Abayye, and some say, to R. Joseph, "What is the law?

C.   He said to him, "Go and see what the people outside are doing."

Unit I provides a scriptural basis for the rule of M. 6:8A-B. Once we make reference to the catalogues of species of grain, we take up the issue of unit II. Unit III refers to M. 6:8B. Unit IV continues the same topic. Unit V deals with materials not included in the Mishnah but relevant to the topic of the Mishnah, namely, species of food that are subject to the same benedictions that the Mishnah takes up. Unit IV is tacked on to the foregoing. Unit VII treats M. 6:8D. Because of the reference to cabbage-stalks, unit VIII is tacked on, whole and complete. Unit IX is tacked on because of VIII F. Units X, XI then gloss the Mishnah-paragraph. So the entire set of materials either provides exegesis to the Mishnah-paragraph or complements the exegesis that is provided.

BAVLI BERAKHOT CHAPTER SEVEN

7:1-2

A.   Three who ate together are obligated to [appoint one] to invite [the others to recite the blessings over the meal].

B.   One who ate produce about which there is a doubt whether or not it was tithed, or first tithe from which heave-offering [of the title] was taken, or who ate second tithe or [produce which had been] dedicated [to the Temple] and then redeemed, or a servant who ate an olive's bulk [of food], or a Samaritan -- these may invite others [to say the blessings over the meal] on their account.

C.   But one who ate produce which is subject to the separation of tithes but not yet tithed, or who ate first tithe from which heave-offering [of the tithe] has not yet been taken, or [who ate] second tithe or [produce which had been] dedicated [to the Temple] but which was not redeemed, or a servant who ate less than an olive's bulk, or the Gentile -- they may not invite others [to say the blessing after the meal] on their account.

M. 7:2

A.   Women, slaves or minors [who ate together with adult Israelite males] -- they may not invite others [to recite Grace] on their account.

B.   What is the least [that one must eat in order to] invite others [to recite a blessing on his account]?

C.   At least an olive's bulk.

D.   Rabbi Judah says, "At least an egg's bulk."

M. 7:2

I.

A.   What is the scriptural source [of the rule that three who have eaten together publicly say Grace after Meals together as well]?

B.   Said R. Assi, "It is because Scripture has said, 'O [you] magnify the Lord with me, and let us exalt his name together' (Ps. 34:4).' [The use of the plural, besides the speaker, thus implies that there are at least three present.]"

C.   R. Abbahu said, "Proof derives from here: 'When I [who am one] proclaim the name of the Lord, you [who are two] ascribe greatness to our God' (Deut. 32:3)."

II.

A.   Said R. Hanan bar Raba, "How do we know that the one who replies by saying, 'Amen,' should not raise his voice above that of the one who says the blessing?

B.   "For it is said, 'O magnify the Lord with me, and let us exalt his name together' (Ps. 34:4) [that is, together, but not with one speaking louder than the other]."

C.   Said R. Simeon b. Pazzi, "How do we know that the one who pronounces the translation of Scripture should not raise his voice louder than that of the one who reads the Scripture out loud?

D.   "As it is said, 'Moses spoke and God answered by him by a voice' (Ex. 19:19). [Moses being the reader, God the one who recites the translation].

E.   "Scripture need not have added the words, 'by a voice,' and why, therefore, have those words been stated? To indicate that it was in accord with the voice of Moses [that the translator, God, modulated his voice]."

F.   It has been taught along these same lines on Tannaite authority:

G.   It is not allowed for the one who pronounces the translation of Scripture to raise his voice louder than that of the one who reads the Scripture out loud.

H.   But if it is not possible for the one who recites the translation to raise his voice to the level of that of the reader of Scripture, let the reader of Scripture moderate his voice when he reads Scripture.

III.

A.   It has been stated on Amoraic authority:

B.   As to the case of two who have eaten together [in the issue of whether the one should publicly invite the other to say grace, as is the case with three] there is a dispute between Rab and R. Yohanan.

C.   One of them said, "If the two of them wanted to designate one of them to invite the other to say Grace, they follow that procedure."

D.   And the other said, "If they wanted to have one of them invite the other to say Grace, they may not do so."

E.   We have learned in the Mishnah: Three who ate together are obligated to appoint one to invite the others to recite the blessings over the meal [M. 7:1A] -- three do it, two do not.

F.   There, the rule speaks of what is obligatory, here we address what is optional [and may be done, even though it is not obligatory to do it this way].

G.   Come and take note: Three who ate together are liable to appoint [one of the group to lead the others in Grace] and are not permitted to divide up -- thus three do it, two do not.

H.   No, that case is distinguished [from the present one], because to begin with the three people imposed an obligation upon themselves [which they must now carry out].

I.   Come and take note: In the case of a waiter who was serving two people, lo, this one eats with them, even though they have not given him the right to do so. If he was serving three people, lo, he may not eat with them unless they give him the right to do so. [In the former case we assume it is all right for the waiter to join the meal because we take for granted the others will wish to say Grace publicly, in which case they will need the third person's participation. In the latter case they do not need the third person, so the waiter may join in the meal only if asked. The assumption, then is that while two people do not say Grace publicly, three do.]

J. The case at hand is to be distinguished, [45B] because the diners approve, so that, [by joining in], the obligation [to say Grace publicly] is imposed, [and they want it that way].

K. Come and take note:

L. Women as a distinct group issue the invitation publicly to say Grace, and slaves as a distinct group do so. As to women, slaves, and minors, even if they wished to issue a public invitation to say Grace [as a collective group, with one another] they may not do so.

M. Now a hundred women are in the status of two men [so far as public recitation of Grace is concerned], and it is taught in the passage at hand, "Women as a group issue a public invitation to say Grace, and slaves as a group issue an invitation to say grace." [Simon, p. 276, n. 4: This proves that two by themselves are not sufficient to form a quorum for the public recitation of Grace.]

N. The case at hand is to be distinguished, for there are individual opinions [each of which matters, so (Simon:) therefore thanksgiving from three women is more valuable than from two men].

O. Then note the concluding clause: As to women, slaves, and minors, if they wished to issue a public invitation to say Grace, they may not do so.

P. Why not? Lo, here too, surely [Simon:] each has a mind!

Q. That case is different, because [we do not permit women and slaves to eat together and so say grace] because of the possibility of licentious behavior.

IV.

A. May one draw the conclusion that it is Rab who takes the view that, if [two] wanted to issue a public call to say Grace, [two] may not do so?

B. For R. Dimi bar Joseph said Rab said, "If three people ate together, and one of them went out to the market, they call him back and, depending upon him, recite a call to say Grace."

C. The reason is that they call him back. Lo, if they were not to call him back, they could not recite the Grace publicly. [So Rab would not allow two to do it.]

D. No, the case at hand is to be treated as different, because to begin with, the group has imposed upon itself the obligation to say grace publicly [so they must call the man back to reconstitute the group for the purpose of a quorum for reciting the Grace. But two could have done it by themselves, were it not for the special circumstance at hand].

E. Then draw the conclusion that it is R. Yohanan who takes the view that if two wished to issue a public invitation to say Grace, they may not do so.

F.   For Rabbah bar bar Hana said R. Yohanan said, "If two people ate together, one of
      them may carry out his obligation through the recitation of the blessing on the part
      of his fellow."

G.   Now we have to reflect on the statement at hand: What does the statement at hand
      tell us? We have learned on Tannaite authority, "If one has heard without respond-
      ing by saying, 'Amen,' he has nonetheless carried out his obligation."

H.   In this connection R. Zira said, "The point is that the call to say Grace may not be
      issued between only two. [It follows, however, that one may be exempted by the
      recitation of the other.]"

I.   You may therefore draw the conclusion [that R. Yohanan stands behind the cited
      position].

J.   Said Rab bar R. Huna to R. Huna, "And lo, the rabbis who come from the West say,
      'If they wished to issue a public call to recite the Grace after Meals, they may do
      so.' Now would they not have heard this ruling from R. Yohanan [who lived in the
      West]?"

K.   No, they heard it from Rab, before he came home to Babylonia.

V.

A.   Returning to the body of the foregoing passage:

B.   R. Dimi bar Joseph said Rab said, "If three people ate together and one of them
      went out to the market [leaving the meal], they call after him to form the quorum
      to say Grace depending upon him."

C.   Said Abayye, "[The fact that they call after him] applies only to a case in which the
      people call to him [as part of the quorum] and he responds [even though he has left
      the group]."

D.   Said Mar Zutra, "And the rule at hand applies only to a case in which there are only
      three persons [so he is needed]. But if there were ten, [the man is included] only if
      he actually comes back."

E.   To this point R. Ashi objected, "Quite to the contrary! The opposite view is more
      reasonable. Nine persons appear to be ten, while two do not appear to be three."

F.   But the decided law accords with the view of Mar Zutra.

G.   What is the reason?

H.   Since [the ten] are supposed to make mention of the name of heaven [in their
      quorum], fewer than ten persons would be improper [and hence we require that the
      man come all the way back and take his place, not merely responding to the call to
      worship with a distant "Amen."]

VI.

A.   Said Abayye, "We hold as a tradition:

B.   "In the case of two who have eaten together, it is a religious duty for them to
      separate [and for each to recite the Grace after Meals on his own]."

C.   We have a statement on Tannaite authority to the same effect:

D.   In the case of two who have eaten together, it is a religious duty for them to
      separate [and for each to recite the Grace after Meals on his own].

E.   Under what circumstances?

F.   When both of the men are scribes. But if one is a scribe and the other uninformed, the scribe says the blessing, and the uninformed person thereby carries out his obligation.

VII.

A.   Said Raba, "I report the following statement on my own, and it has been stated also along these same lines in the name of R. Zira:

B.   "In the case of three who have eaten together [and one of whom has not yet finished eating], one of them interrupts his meal to accommodate two [in order to respond to the call to worship and so form a quorum for saying grace], but two do not interrupt their meal to accommodate one."

C.   Do two not do so for one? And lo, R. Pappa interrupted [eating so as to accommodate] Abba Mar, his son, doing so along with another person [forming a quorum to say Grace].

D.   The case of R. Pappa is different, because he went beyond the strict requirement of the law.

VIII.

A.   Judah bar Maremar, Mar, son of R. Ashi, and R. Aha of Difta were eating bread together. One of them did not enjoy a higher standing than his fellow with regard to reciting the Grace after Meals for the lot of them.

B.   They said, "Lo, we have learned in the Mishnah, Three who ate together are obligated to appoint one to invite the others to recite the blessings over the meal [M. 7:1A].

C.   "That rule applies to a case in which a great authority is present. But in a case in which the people are more or less equal to one another, people should recite the blessings directly, each for himself."

D.   In consequence, each recited the blessing for himself.

E.   They came before Maremar. He said to them, "You have fulfilled your obligation to recite the Grace after Meals, but you have not fulfilled your obligation to appoint one of you to call the others to form a quorum to recite the Grace.

F.   "And if you should have in mind to go back and call a formal quorum, there is no possibility of calling a quorum after the fact."

IX.

A.   If someone came along and found people in the midst of reciting the Grace after Meals, what does one say after them?

B.   R. Zebid said, "'Blessed and to be blessed [be His name].'"

C.   R. Pappa said, "He responds, 'Amen.'"

D.   But the two do not differ. The one speaks of a case in which the person found the people saying, "Let us say the blessing."

E.   The other treats a case in which the man found the people saying, "Blessed."

F.   If one found the people saying, "Let us say the blessing," he says, "Blessed and to be blessed....'"

G.   If he found them saying, "Blessed...,' he answers, "Amen."

X.

A.   One Tannaite teaching holds, "He who responds, "Amen," after he has recited a blessing -- lo, this one is to be praised.

B.   Another Tannaite teaching maintains: Lo, this is a disgrace.

C.   And there is no contradiction, for the one speaks of the blessing, "Who builds Jerusalem," [to which the one who recites the blessing himself adds the word, "Amen,"] and the other speaks of other benedictions.

D.   Abayye would give the response [Amen] in a loud voice, so that the workers [at their meal] should hear him and rise [to go to work after their meal, treating the benedictions that follow is secondary].

E.   For the blessing [in the Grace after Meals] "Who is good and does good" does not derive from the authority of the Torah. [So the workers should go back to work without reciting the additional parts of the Grace].

F.   R. Ashi would give the response [Amen] in a whisper, so as not to cause disregard for [the blessing] "Who is good and who does good."

XI.

A.   [46A] R. Zira was sick, so R. Abbahu came to see him. [Abbahu] took upon himself [the vow], "If the little one with burned legs gets better, I shall make a festival-celebration for the rabbis."

B.   [The sick man] got better. [Abbahu] made a banquet for all the rabbis.

C.   When the time came to start [the meal], he said to R. Zira, "Will the master begin for us [by breaking bread]?"

D.   He said to him, "Does the master not concur with the statement of R. Yohanan, who said, 'The master of the household is the one who breaks bread'?"

E.   [Abbahu] commenced the meal [by breaking bread].

F.   When the time came to recite the blessing [of the Grace after meals], [Abbahu] said to [Zira], "Will the master say the blessing for us?"

G.   He said to him, "Does the master not concur with the statement of R. Huna of Babylonia, who said, 'The one who breaks bread says the blessing'?"

H.   And whose view does [Abbahu] take? It is in accord with what R. Yohanan said in the name of R. Simeon b. Yohai, "The master of the household breaks bread, and a guest is the one who says the blessing.

I.   "The master of the household breaks bread, so that he pass out food liberally, and the guest says the blessing, so that he may include in his blessing words for the householder."

J.   What is the blessing [that the guest] says?

K.   "May it please [God] that the householder not be ashamed in this world or humiliated in the world to come."

L.   Rabbi adds other matters: "And may he greatly prosper in all his property, and may his and our property prosper and be near town.

M.   "And may Satan not have power over what he does or over what we do. And may neither he nor we confront any temptation to sin or transgress or commit a sin now or forever."

XII.

A.   To what point does the blessing involved in calling to worship for the purpose of reciting Grace extend? [Simon, pp. 279-280, n. 8: This question refers to the statement above that one person may interrupt his meal to join two others in the call to a quorum. The question is now asked, How long must he wait before resuming his meal?] [I regret to say I can make no sense of this unit.]

B.   R. Nahman said, "Up to, 'Let us say a blessing.'"

C.   And R. Sheshet said, "To, '... who sustains.'"

D.   May we say that at issue is the matter subject to Tannaite debate, for one Tannaite authority repeats, "The Grace after Meals encompasses two or three blessings."

E.   Another Tannaite authority states, "It encompasses three or four blessings."

F.   In the assumption that the blessing, "Who is good and does good," does not derive from the authority of the Torah, would they not then dispute about the following matter:

G.   The one who has said, "Two or three," takes the view that [the time encompassed by the interruption of the man's meal is up to] the blessing, "Who feeds...."

H.   The one who said, "It is three or four benedictions" takes the view that it is only up to, "Let us say a blessing."

I.   No, R. Nahman explains [the two statements] in a way consistent with his view, and likewise does R. Sheshet.

J.   R. Nahman responds in a way consistent with his views. In his view all parties concur that it is up to "Let us say a blessing." The one who says, "Three or four" poses no difficulty. As to the one who says, "Two or three," he may tell you, "Here we deal with the Grace after Meals recited by workers. [That Grace, we recall, is abbreviated.]

K.   For a master has said, "[In the Grace after Meals said by workers,] one begins with, 'Who sustains...,' and includes the blessing, 'Who builds Jerusalem,' in the blessing for the Land."

L.   R. Sheshet responds in a manner consistent with his view. He holds that all parties concur that the matter lasts until the recitation of the blessing ending, "Who sustains." The one who says, "Two or three" poses no problems.

M.   The one who says "Three or four" takes the view that the blessing "Who is good and does good" rests upon the authority of the Torah.

XIII.

A.   Said R. Joseph, "You may know that the blessing of the Grace after Meals marked by the formula 'Who is good and does good,' does not rest on the authority of the Torah.

B.   "For lo, workers [when they recite the Grace] omit it."

C.   Said R. Isaac bar Samuel bar Marta in the name of Rab, "You may know that the blessing, 'Who is good and does good,' does not rest on the authority of the Torah, for lo, one begins that paragraph with the word, 'Blessed,' but does not conclude it with the word, 'Blessed.'"

D.   That accords with the following teaching on Tannaite authority:

E.   The formulation of all blessings begins with the word "Blessed," and ends with the word, "Blessed," except for the blessing that one says for produce, the blessing that one says for unleavened bread, a blessing that is juxtaposed to another, the final blessing that is recited in the Recitation of the <u>Shema</u>. There are some which begin with the word "Blessed," and do not end with the word, "Blessed" [46B]. There are those which end with the word, "Blessed" and do not begin with the word, "Blessed."

F.   And the blessing, "Who is good and does good" begins with the word, "Blessed," but does not end with the word, "Blessed."

G.   That formulation indicates that the blessing [under discussion] stands as a separate blessing.

XIV.

A.   And R. Nahman bar Isaac said, "You may know that the blessing, 'Who is good and does good,' does not stand upon the authority of the Torah.

B.   "For lo, they omit it when Grace after Meals is said in the house of a mourner."

C.   For it has been taught on Tannaite authority:

D.   What do people recite as Grace in the house of a mourner?

E.   "Blessed... who is good and does good."

F.   R. Aqiba says, "'Blessed is the true judge.'"

G.   [Is it the case, then, that in the view of the former of the two authorities] one says, "Who is good and does good" but does <u>not</u> say, "The true judge"?

H.   Rather, I should formulate it as, "<u>Also</u>, 'Who is good and does good."

XV.

A.   Mar Zutra visited R. Ashi, who had a death in the family.

B.   He began [in the Grace after Meals] with the blessing, "Who is good and does good, true God, true judge, righteous justice, who takes with justice and rules over his world to do with it in accord with his fill.

C.   "For all his ways are justice, for all things are his. We are his people and his servants, and in all things we are obligated to thank him and to bless him. He heals the breaches in Israel.

D.   "May he heal this breach in Israel -- for life."

XVI.

A.   [If one has broken off eating to join two others in a quorum for saying Grace,] where does he begin again [when he repeats Grace for himself]?

B.   R. Zebid in the name of Abayye said, "He goes back to the beginning [and recites the entire Grace].

C.   And rabbis say, "He goes back to the point at which he broke off [and resumed his meal, having said the Grace with the others]."

D.   And the decided law is that he goes back to the place at which he broke off [in the recitation of the Grace earlier on].

XVII.

A. Said the exilarch to R. Sheshet, "Even though you are authoritative sages, the Persians are more expert than are you in matters having to do with proper conduct at a meal.

B. "When there are two couches [for reclining at a meal], the more important person sits at the head, and the one second to him sits beyond him. When there are three couches, the most important person reclines in the middle, and the one second to him above him, and the one third in importance below him."

C. He said to him, "But that means that when the most important person wants to talk with the one above, he has to sit upright so as to talk with him."

D. He said to him, "The Persians are different [and it will not matter to them] because they gesticulate when they talk."

E. [Sheshet] asked,] "As to the water passed before the meal, with whom do they begin?"

F. He said to him, "With the most important person present."

G. "Then he will have to sit and keep his hands clean until all of them have washed their hands!"

H. He said to him, "No, [that is not a problem], because they bring him a tray right away."

I. "Where do they begin when they pass water around at the end of the meal [for the people to wash their hands]?

J. He said to him, "They begin with the least important person present."

K. "And will the most important person present have to sit with dirty hands until all the others have washed up?"

L. He said to him, "They do not remove the table from before him until they bring him water."

XVIII.

A. Said R. Sheshet, "I have a teaching on Tannaite authority on this subject."

B. What is the order for reclining [when several eat together]? [cf. T. Ber. 4:8, M. Ber. 6:6].

C. When there are two couches,

D. the greatest [in importance] among them reclines at the head of the first,

E. the second [in importance] to him reclines below him.

F. When there are three couches,

G. the greatest [in importance] reclines at the head of the middle [couch],

H. the second [in importance] to him [reclines] above him, the third [in importance] below him.

I. [B. omits:] In this manner they would go on and arrange the rest of the guests in order [T. Ber. 5:5].

J. [B. omits: What is the order] for washing hands at the beginning of the meal?

K. They begin with the most important person.

L. At the end of the meal,

M. [If there are in the group] up to five people,

N. they begin with the greatest [in importance],

O. [If there are] more than five [B.: a hundred], they begin with the least [important]
    and proceed until they reach the fifth (person), then they begin again with the
    greatest.

P. And (the person who is seated) at the place where the water (for washing hands)
    after (the meal) comes back (after circulating around the table) recites the
    benediction (i.e., the one who washes last after the meal has the honor of reciting
    the benediction) [T. Ber. 5:6A-D].

Q. The cited passage supports the view of Rab.

R. For R. Hiyya bar Ashi said Rab said, "Whoever washes his hands last at the beginning
    of the meal is the one who is designated to call the group to form a quorum for
    reciting the blessing after the meal."

S. Rab and R. Hiyya were sitting at a banquet before Rabbi. Rabbi said to Rab, "Go
    and wash your hands."

T. He saw him trembling.

U. He said to him, "Son of the aristocracy, review the Grace after Meals is what he
    meant to tell you."

XIX.

A. Our rabbis have taught on Tannaite authority:

B. People do not pay honor to one another [in politely asking another to take prece-
    dence] when out on the road or when on a bridge [47A], or in the matter of washing
    dirty hands [at the end of a meal].

XX.

A. Rabin and Abayye were going along the road. Rabin's ass got in front of Abayye's,
    and [Rabin] did not say to him, "Will the master not go ahead."

B. He said, "Since this one of the rabbis came up from the West [the Holy Land], he has
    become arrogant."

C. When they got to the door of the synagogue, he said to him, "Will the master not
    enter first?"

D. He said to him, "And up to now was I not the master?"

E. He said to him, "This is what R. Yohanan said, 'People pay honor to one another [in
    asking one to take precedence over the other] only before a donor on which there is
    a mezuzah.'"

F. Is it the case that one does so where there is a mezuzah and does not do so where
    there is none?

G. Then how do you deal with the case of the synagogue and school house, neither of
    which has a mezuzah? Should it be the case that there too people do not pay honor
    to one another?

H. Rather, I formulate the matter in this way: Before a door which is suitable for a
    mezuzah [that is, not a gate or a bridge].

XXI.

A.   Said R. Judah, son of Samuel bar Shilat, in the name of Rab, "People who have assembled for a meal are not permitted to eat anything until the one who breaks bread has eaten."

B.   R. Safra went into session and stated, "What has been formulated is, 'to _taste_.'"

C.   What difference does it make?

D.   It indicates only that a person is liable to repeat a teaching in the exact language of his master.

XXII.

A.   Our rabbis have taught on Tannaite authority:

B.   **Two wait for one another [to begin eating] with regard to [partaking of food from] a single plate.**

C.   **Three do not wait.**

D.   **The one who recites the benediction stretches forth his hand first [to partake of the food].**

E.   **If he wished to honor his master or someone else who is more important than himself [by letting him take the first piece of food], he may do so [T. Ber. 5:7].**

F.   Rabbah bar bar Hanah made a marriage feast for his son in the house of R. Samuel bar Qatina. Beforehand he went into session and repeated the rule for his son, "The one who breaks bread [at the coming banquet, the son himself] is not permitted to break the bread before the word, 'Amen,' has been fully enunciated by those who respond to the blessing that he has said.'"

G.   R. Hisda said, "It is only for the majority of those who respond."

H.   Said to him Rami b. Hama, "What difference does it make if the majority has not yet said, 'Amen'? It is because the blessing has not yet been completed. But the same is the case if only a minority has not yet finished saying the blessing."

I.   He said to him, "It is because I say, 'Whoever says too long an "Amen" only makes a mistake by doing so.'"

XXIII.

A.   Our rabbis have taught on Tannaite authority:

B.   **They do not respond, "Amen," in a way that is hasty [and slurred], nor curtailed [without the N], nor "as an orphan," [that is, if one has not actually heard the blessing], nor should one toss a blessing out of his mouth.**

C.   **Ben Azzai says, "Whoever answers, 'Amen,' as an orphan — his children will be orphans. If he does so 'cut off,' his years will be cut off. If he does so in a hurried way, his days will be hurried away. If he does so by drawing out the word, 'Amen,' they will lengthen his days and his years" [T. Meg. 3:27D-E].**

XXIV.

A.   Rab and Samuel were in session at a meal. R. Shimi bar Hiyya came along. He ate in a rush [wanting to join them when they said the Grace].

B.   Rab said to him, "What are you thinking? Is it to join us? We have already eaten."

C. Samuel said to him, "If people were to bring mushrooms for me and pigeons for Abba [Rab], would we not eat them? [So we really have not finished, and he can join us when he is done.]"

XXV.

A. The disciples of Rab were in session at a meal. R. Aha came in. They said, "A great authority has come to say Grace for us."

B. He said to them, "Do you think that the great authority present says Grace? The one who was at the meal from the beginning is the one who says Grace."

C. But the decided law is that the greatest authority present says Grace, even though he came at the end.

XXVI.

A. If one has eaten produce about which there is a doubt [M. 7:1B]:

B. But the type of food at hand [listed at M. 7:1B] is not suitable food [so why should one say Grace for the others]?

C. If the man wants, he may declare his property ownerless and so enter the category of a poor man, in which case the food at hand is suitable for him.

D. For we have learned in the Mishnah: People may feed doubtfully tithed produce to the poor and to billeted soldiers [M. Dem. 3:1].

E. And R. Huna said, "On Tannaite authority it is taught: The House of Shammai say, 'People do not feed doubtfully tithed produce to the poor and to billeted soldiers.'"

XXVII.

A. First tithe from which heave-offering had been removed [M. 7:1B]:

B. That is self-evident.

C. No, it has to be made clear to cover the case in which a Levite got there first [and took away the first tithe inhering in] the ears of corn and separated heave-offering of tithe, but did not separate the greater heave-offering.

D. And the given rule accords with the view of R. Abbahu.

E. For R. Abbahu said R. Simeon b. Laqish said, "In the case of first tithe, for which [the Levite] got there first [and took away the first tithe] in the ears of corn, the ears of corn are exempt from the requirement that great heave-offering be set aside from them as well.

F. "For it is said, 'You shall offer up a heave-offering of it for the Lord, even a tenth part of the tithe' (Num. 18:26).

G. "'A tenth part of the tithe is what I have instructed you to designate, and not both great heave-offering and also heave-offering separated from a tenth part of the tithe.'"

H. Said R. Pappa to Abayye, "If so, then even if the Levite got there first at the heap of grain [once it has been winnowed but has not yet been ground], the rule should be the same."

I. He said to him, "On that account Scripture has said, '[47B] Out of all your tithes you shall offer' (Num. 18:29)."

J. [Simon:] But still what reason have you (for including corn in the ear and not grain) [when it is in the pile]?

K.   One has been turned into corn, the other not [and it is only from what can be called grain that heave-offering has to be given].

XXVIII.

A.   Second tithe or produce which had been dedicated to the Temple and then redeemed [M. 7:1B]:

B.   That is self-evident.

C.   With what sort of case do we deal here?

D.   It is one in which, in redeeming the produce, one has already paid for the principal but has not yet paid the added fifth.

E.   Then we are informed that not paying the added fifth does not present an obstacle [for the use of the produce as ordinary food].

XXIX.

A.   A servant who ate an olive's bulk of food [M. 7:1B]:

B.   That is self-evident.

C.   What might you have said? Since the servant is not part of the organized meal, [he should not be included].

D.   So we are informed that that is not the case.

XXX.

A.   As to a Samaritan -- they invite others [to say the blessings over the meal] on (their) account [M. 7:1B]:

B.   Why is this the case? He should be no more than an ignoramus.

C.   And it has been taught on Tannaite authority:

D.   People do not include an ignoramus in the quorum for the public call to recite the Grace.

E.   Abayye said, "We speak here of a Samaritan who is an associate [and reliable in the keeping of cultic cleanness of food]."

F.   Raba said, "Even if you say that it is a Samaritan who is an ignoramus, here we deal with an ignoramus as defined by rabbis who differ on the matter with the view of R. Meir."

G.   For it has been taught on Tannaite authority:

H.   Who is deemed an ignoramus?

I.   "It is anyone who does not eat his unconsecrated food in conditions of cultic cleanness," the words of R. Meir.

J.   And sages say, "It is anyone who does not properly separate tithes" [T. A.Z. 3:10C-E].

K.   The Samaritans under discussion here properly tithe their food, for, in any matter which is written in the Torah, Samaritans are most punctilious.

L.   For a master has said, "In the case of any religious duty that the Samaritans have adopted for themselves, they are most meticulous, more so even than Israelites."

XXXI.

A.   Our rabbis have taught on Tannaite authority:

B.   What is the definition of an ignoramus?

C.   "It is anyone who does not recite the Shema evening and morning," the words of R. Eliezer.

D.   R. Joshua says, "It is anyone who does not put on phylacteries."

E.   Ben Azzai says, "It is anyone who does not have show-fringes on his garment."

F.   R. Nathan says, "It is anyone who does not have a mezuzah on his door."

G.   R. Nathan bar Joseph says, "It is anyone who has children and does not raise them to study Torah."

H.   Others say, "Even if one has studied Scripture and repeated Mishnah-traditions, if he has not served as attendant upon a disciple of a sage, lo, such a one is an ignoramus."

I.   Said R. Huna, "The decided law accords with 'others.'"

XXXII.

A.   Rami bar Hama did not count in a quorum for the purpose of a public call to recite the Grace after Meals R. Menassia bar Tahalipa, who had learned to repeat Sifra, Sifre, and various laws.

B.   When Rami bar Hama died, Raba said, "Rami bar Hama died only because he would not count R. Menassia bar Tahalipa in the quorum."

C.   But has it not been taught on Tannaite authority,

D.   Others say, "Even if one has studied Scripture and learned to recite Mishnah-traditions, if he has not served as attendant upon a disciple of a sage, lo, this one is an ignoramus"?

E.   [Raba replies,] "The case of R. Menassia bar Tahalipa is different, because in point of fact he did attend upon rabbis, and it was Rami bar Hama who had failed carefully to investigate his standing."

F.   Another version: He had heard traditions from the mouths of rabbis and memorized them, so he was in the status of a rabbinical neophyte.

XXXIII.

A.   If one ate produce which is subject to the separation of tithes but not yet tithed, or first tithe... [M. 7:1C]:

B.   The matter of produce that is liable to tithes but has not yet been tithed is self-evident.

C.   No, it was necessary to make it explicit to cover the case of produce in the status of being subject to tithed but not yet tithed only by the authority of rabbis.

D.   What would be such a case?

E.   It would be produce grown in a pot that has no hole on the bottom [and therefore is not attached to the ground and subject to the laws governing produce grown from the ground. Rabbis are the ones who declare it is nonetheless liable to tithing, and a rule for such a case had to be made explicit].

XXXIV.

A.   First tithe [from which heave-offering of the tithe had not been taken [M. 7:1C]:

B.   That is self-evident.

C.   No, it was necessary to make it explicit, for the case of a Levite's having gotten to the grain heap before the [priest].

D.   What might you have supposed? It is that the law follows the premise of R. Pappa's address to Abayye.

E.   This indicates that the law follows the answer given by Abayye.

XXXV.

A.   Second tithe [that had not been redeemed] [M. 7:1C]:

B.   That is self-evident.

C.   No, it was necessary to cover the case of that which had been redeemed but not in accord with the relevant law.

D.   In the case of second tithe, it would involve the case in which one had redeemed the produce in exchange for an unminted coin. But the All-Merciful has said, "You shall bind up the silver in your hand" (Deut. 14:25), speaking of silver that has a clear mark of binding [that is, has been minted and so bound to a given reign].

E.   In the case of produce that had been consecrated to the Temple, it would involve produce that one had secularized through an exchange with real estate rather than with money, while the All-Merciful has said, "He shall give money and it shall be assured unto him" (Lev. 27:9). [Hence money, not real estate, is what has to be used to redeem the produce from the Temple.]

XXXVI.

A.   A servant who ate less than an olive's bulk [M. 7:1C]:

B.   That is self-evident.

C.   [To be sure, but] since the framer of the passage made mention of an olive's bulk of food in the opening clause, he matched it, in the closing clause, by a reference to "less than an olive's bulk of food."

XXXVII.

A.   And a gentile -- they may not invite others to say the blessing after the meal on their account [M. 7:1C]:

B.   That is self-evident.

C.   With what category do we deal [in the specification of M. 7:1C about a gentile]? It concerns a gentile convert who had already been circumcised but not yet immersed [so completing his entry into the status of sanctification].

D.   For R. Zira said R. Yohanan said, "Under no circumstances does a man become a full proselyte until he both is circumcised and also immersed in a ritual pool.

E.   "And so long as he has not immersed, he remains a gentile."

XXXVIII.

A.   Women, slaves, or minors who ate together with adult Israelite males -- they may not invite others to recite Grace on their account [M. 7:2A]:

B.   Said R. Yose, "A minor in his crib may be included in the quorum for public recitation of Grace."

C.   And lo, we have learned in the Mishnah: Women, slaves, or minors who ate together with adult Israelite males -- they may not invite others to recite Grace on their account!

D.   He has ruled in accord with what R. Joshua b. Levi said

E.   For R. Joshua b. Levi said, "Even though they have said, 'In the case of a minor who is lying in his crib, they do not include him in a quorum for purposes of public recitation of Grace,' nonetheless, they treat him as an addition to reach the quorum of ten."

XXXIX.

A.   And R. Joshua b. Levi said, "Nine and a slave join together [to make up a quorum of ten]."

B.   An objection was raised:

C.   There was the precedent involving R. Eliezer, who came into the synagogue and did not find a quorum of ten, so he freed his slave and thereby completed the necessary quorum of ten.

D.   Thus if he freed him, he would be [counted], but if he did not free him, he would not [be counted].

E.   What he needed was two [there being only eight], so he freed one slave and made do with one, thus reaching the requisite number of ten.

F.   But how could he have acted in this way?

G.   For has not R. Judah said, "Whoever frees his slave violates an affirmative, for it is said, 'They shall be your slaves for ever' (Lev. 25:46)."

H.   For carrying out a religious duty [in this case, reaching the necessary quorum], the law is different.

I.   But is this not the accomplishment of a religious duty through the commission of a transgression??

J.   Accomplishing a religious duty for the community at large falls into a separate category [from any other, and that is permitted even under the present circumstances].

XL.

A.   And R. Joshua b. Levi said, "A person should always get up early to go to the synagogue, so that he will derive the merit of being counted among the first ten.

B.   "For even if a hundred people come after him, he receives for himself the reward that is coming to all of them."

C.   Do you think that he takes over the reward that is coming to all of them!

D.   Rather, I should say, "They assign to him a reward equivalent to that which is coming to all of them."

XLI.

A.   Said R. Huna, "Nine men and the ark join together to make up the requisite quorum."

B.   Said to him R. Nahman, "Is the ark a man?"

C.   Rather, said R. Huna, "Nine that appear to be ten join together to form the necessary quorum."

D.   There are those who say that that is when they are packed together, and there are those who say that that is when they are widely scattered [in the room].

XLII.

A.   Said R. Ammi, "Two and the Sabbath join together to form the necessary quorum [to recite Grace after Meals aloud]."

B. Said to him R. Nahman, "And is the Sabbath a man?"

C. Rather, said R. Ammi, "Two disciples of sages who sharpen one another's wits in the law join together."

D. R. Hisda gave as an instance, "For example, R. Sheshet and me."

E. R. Sheshet gave as an instance, "For example, R. Hisda and me."

XLIII.

A. Said R. Yohanan, "A minor who has produced puberty-signs before the age of thirteen years and one day is included in a quorum for the public recitation of Grace."

B. It has been taught on Tannaite authority to the same effect:

C. A minor who has produced two pubic hairs is included in a quorum for the public recitation of Grace, and one who has not produced two pubic hairs is not counted in the quorum for the public recitation of Grace. And people are not meticulous about a minor boy.

D. Now there is a contradiction in the foregoing formulation of the rule.

E. You have said that if he has produced two pubic hairs, he is included, and if he has not produced two pubic hairs, he is not included.

F. And then one goes and teaches, "People are not meticulous about a minor boy."

G. What would this clause serve to encompass? Is it not [48A] to encompass a minor boy who has produced puberty-signs prior to thirteen years and one day?

H. And the law is not in accord with all of these traditions, but rather it accords with that which R. Nahman said, "A minor who knows to whom the blessing is addressed is included in the quorum for the public call to the recitation of Grace."

XLIV.

A. Abayye and Raba were in session before Rabbah. Rabbah said to them, "To whom do we recite blessings?"

B. They said to him, "To the All-Merciful."

C. "And where does the All-Merciful dwell?"

D. Raba pointed upward to the roof.

E. Abayye went out and pointed to heaven.

F. Rabbah said to them, "The two of you will become rabbis."

G. That is in line with what people say: "You can tell a pumpkin from its stalk."

XLV.

A. Said R. Judah, son of R. Samuel bar Shilat, in the name of Rab, "If nine people ate grain and one ate vegetables, they join together [to form a quorum of ten for purposes of public recitation of Grace]."

B. Said R. Zira, "I asked R. Judah about the law for eight, about the law for seven.

C. "He said to me, 'It makes no difference.'

D. "But certainly, as to the case of six, I assuredly did not raise a question."

E. Said to him R. Jeremiah, "Did you do well in not raising the question at all? What is the operative consideration there? It is because a majority of those present [had eaten the corn]. Here too is there not a majority?"

F. But he took the view that a majority that is readily recognized is what we require.

XLVI.

A. King Yannai and the queen broke bread together. It was after he had killed the rabbis, so there was no one around to recite the blessing for them. He said to his wife, "Who will bring us a man to say the blessing for us?"

B. She said to him, "Take an oath to me that if I bring you someone, you will not give him any trouble."

C. He took the oath for her.

D. She brought him Simeon b. Shatah, her brother, seating him between him and her. [Yannai] said to [Simeon], "Do you see how much I honor you?"

E. He said to him, "You are not the one who honors me, but it is the Torah that honors me, for it is written, 'Exalt her and she will promote you, [she will bring you to honor when you embrace her]' (Prov. 4:8)."

F. [Yannai] said to her [his wife], "Don't you see that he does not accept [my] authority!"

G. They gave him a cup for the recitation of a blessing.

H. He said, "How shall I say a blessing? 'Blessed be what Yannai and his fellows have eaten of His'?"

I. He drank that cup and they gave him another and he said a blessing.

J. Said R. Abba son of R. Hiyya bar Abba, "Simeon b. Shetah acted in accord with his own view.

K. "For this is what R. Hiyya bar Abba said R. Yohanan said, 'A person can never carry out the obligation [of reciting the Grace] on behalf of the community unless he eats an olive's bulk of grain [with them]." [Simon had eaten nothing but only drunk the wine.]

XLVII.

A. So it has been taught:

B. Rabban Simeon b. Gamaliel says, "If one has gone in and reclined with the group, even though he dipped a little food into brine with them and ate with them only a single dried fig, he joins with them [to form a quorum]."

C. He joins with them to form a quorum, but he can fulfill the obligation of the group to recite Grace only if he eats an olive's bulk of grain.

D. It has been stated on Amoraic authority along these same lines:

E. Said R. Hana bar Judah in the name of Raba, "Even if one [48B] has dipped only a little bit of food in brine, or eaten with them only a dried fig, he joins with them [to form a quorum]. But he can carry out the obligation of the group by reciting the Grace after meals in their behalf only if he will eat an olive's bulk of grain."

F. Said R. Hana bar Judah in the name of Raba, "The decided law is this:

G. "If one has eaten a vegetable leaf or drunk a cup of wine, he joins with the group to form a quorum.

H. "But he is not able to carry out the obligation of the group to recite the Grace after meals unless he eats an olive's bulk of grain."

XLVIII.

A.   Said R. Nahman, "Moses ordained for Israel the blessing of the Grace after meals ending, 'Who feeds all,' when manna came down for them.

B.   "Joshua ordained for them the benediction [in the Grace after Meals] for the land, when they entered the land.

C.   "David and Solomon ordained for them, 'Who builds Jerusalem.'

D.   "David ordained the passage, 'For Israel, your people, and for Jerusalem, your city,' and Solomon ordained, 'For the great and holy house.'

E.   "The blessing, 'Who is good and does good' was ordained in Yabneh on account of those who had been killed at Betar.'"

F.   For R. Mattena said, "On the day on which those had been killed at Betar were committed for burial, they ordained in Yabneh the benediction 'Who is good and does good.'

G.   "'Who is good' that the bodies had not rotted.

H.   "'And who does good' that they were handed over for burial."

XLIX.

A.   Our rabbis have taught on Tannaite authority:

B.   This is the order of the Grace after Meals.

C.   The first blessing is the one ending, "Who feeds all."

D.   The second is the blessing of the land.

E.   The third is, "Who builds Jerusalem."

F.   The fourth is, "Who is good and does good."

G.   And on the Sabbath, [the third blessing] begins with words of consolation and ends that way, and one makes mention of the sanctification of the day in the middle of that blessing.

H.   R. Eliezer says, "If one wants to say it in the blessing for consolation, one does so, and if one wants to include it in the blessing of the land does so. Or one can make mention of it in the blessing which the sages ordained in Yabneh [the fourth one]."

I.   And sages say, "One may say it only in the blessing of consolation alone."

J.   Then sages [I] say exactly what the first authority [G] at hand says.

K.   At issue between them is a case in which one did it in another passage [Simon, p. 292, n. 9: in which case the first Tanna insists that it must be said again in the proper place.]

L.

A.   Our rabbis have taught on Tannaite authority:

B.   How do we know that the invitation to recite the benediction after meals has a scriptural basis?

C.   It is as Scripture states, "And you shall eat and be full, and you shall bless [the Lord your God for the good land which he has given you]" (Deut. 8:10) -- this [refers to] the blessing, "Who feeds all."

D.   "... the Lord your God..." -- this refers to the invitation to say Grace.

E.   "... for the [good] land..." -- this refers to the benediction for the Land [the second benediction of the series].

F.   "... the good [land]..." -- this refers to "Who builds Jerusalem" [the third benediction],

G.   and so it is said, "that goodly hill country and Lebanon" (Deut. 3:25).

H.   "... which the Lord has given you..." -- this refers to [the fourth benediction, which contains the words] "who is good and does good."

I.   "I thus know that one says Grace after Meals. From what [scriptural verse do we learn] that just as you recite benedictions after it [the meal], so you recite a benediction before it?

J.   It is an argument a fortiori: If when one is satisfied, one says a blessing, when he is hungry, should he not all the more so [say a blessing]?

K.   Rabbi says, "Such an argument is unnecessary. 'And you shall eat and be satisfied and bless' (Deut. 8:10) refers to the blessing ending, 'Who feeds all.'

L.   "But the blessing of calling the group to say Grace derives from this verse: 'O magnify the Lord with me' (Ps. 34:4).

M.   "'For the land' refers to the blessing of the land.

N.   "That is good' refers to the blessing, 'Who builds Jerusalem.'

O.   "And so Scripture says, 'This goodly mountain and Lebanon' (Deut. 3:25).

P.   "'Who is good and does good' did they ordain in Yabneh.

Q.   "I know only that one must say a blessing after a meal. How on the basis of Scripture do we know that one must say a blessing before it?

R.   "Scripture says, 'Which he has given you', meaning, 'As soon as he gives it to you' [Simon, p. 292, n. 4: even before partaking thereof.']"

S.   R. Isaac says, "It is not necessary [to use the proof just now outlined]. Lo, Scripture says, 'And he will bless your bread and your water' (Ex. 23:25).

T.   "Do not read 'and he shall bless' but rather 'and you say a blessing.'

U.   "And when is it called 'bread'? It is before it is eaten."

V.   R. Nathan says, "It is not necessary to resort to that argument. For lo, Scripture says, 'As soon as you have come into the city, you shall find him right away, before he goes up to the high place to eat, for the people will not eat until he comes, because he blesses the sacrifice and afterwards those who are united eat...' (1 Sam. 9:13)."

W.   Why so much [an account of the matter]? It is because women are talkative.

X.   Samuel said, "'It was so as to continue to gaze upon Saul's handsome face, for it is written, 'From his shoulders and upward he was taller than any of the people' (1 Sam. 9:2)."

Y.   R. Yohanan said, "It was because one regime may not touch the period assigned to another by even so much as a hair."

LI.

A.   I now have proved that the Grace after Meals rests upon the authority of Scripture. How may I show that the same foundation sustains the requirement to say a blessing over Torah-study?

B.   Said R. Ishmael, "It is an argument a fortiori. If one says a blessing for what sustains the life of the moment, how much the more so should one say a blessing over what sustains the life of the world to come!"

C.   R. Hiyya bar Nahmani, disciple of R. Ishmael, says in the name of R. Ishmael, "It is not necessary [to derive proof from that argument].

D.   "Lo, Scripture says, 'For the good land which he has given you' (Deut. 8:10). And elsewhere it says, 'And I will give you the tables of stone and Torah and commandments' (Ex. 24:12). [So if a blessing is required for the one gift, it is required for the other.]"

LII.

A.   R. Meir says, "How do we know on the basis of Scripture that, just as one says a blessing over good things that happen, so one says a blessing over bad things?

B.   "Scripture says, 'Which the Lord your God has given you' (Deut. 8:10) -- that is, your judge.

C.   "In every judgment with which he judges you, whether it is out of the measure of good or out of the measure of punishment, [one has to say a blessing]."

LIII.

A.   R. Judah b. Beterah says, "It is not necessary to resort to that argument. Lo, Scripture says, 'The good' while it could have said merely, 'Good.'

B.   "'Good' refers to Torah, as it says, 'For I give you a good doctrine' (Prov. 4:2).

C.   "'The good' refers to the building of Jerusalem, and so it says, 'This good mount and Lebanon' (Deut. 3:25)."

LIV.

A.   It has been taught on Tannaite authority:

B.   R. Eliezer says, "Whoever has not said, 'A broad and good and pleasant land' when reciting the blessing for the land, and has not referred to the dominion of the house of David in the blessing, 'Who builds Jerusalem,' has not carried out his obligation [to recite the Grace after Meals]."

C.   Nahum the Elder says, "It is necessary to mention the covenant in [the Grace after Meals]."

D.   R. Yose says, "It is necessary to mention the Torah."

E.   Pelimo says, "It is necessary to make mention of the covenant before mentioning the Torah, for the Torah was handed over on account of only three covenants [Sinai, Gerizim, and at the plains of Moab],

F.   "[49A] while the covenant was handed over with thirteen [Simon, p. 294, n. 6: the word of 'covenant' occurring thirteen times in the section of the circumcision of Abraham, Gen. 17:1-14]."

G.   R. Abba says, "It is necessary to express thanks at the beginning and at the end, and he who does less should not do it less than one time [at either the start or the conclusion].

H.   "And whoever does it less than one time -- lo, such a one is disgraceful.

I.   "And whoever concludes the blessing of the land with, 'Who gives lands as an inheritance.'

J.   "And whoever concludes, 'Who builds Jerusalem,' with the phrase, 'who saves Israel,' -- lo, such a one is ignorant.

K.   "And whoever does not refer to the covenant and the Torah in the blessing for the land, and the dominion of the house of David in the blessing ending, 'Who builds Jerusalem,' has not carried out his obligation [to recite the Grace after Meals]."

L.   The statement at hand supports the position of R. Ilaa, for R. Ilaa said R. Jacob bar Aha said in the name of our master, "Whoever has not made mention of the covenant and of the Torah in the blessing for the land, and the dominion of the house of David in the blessing ending, 'Who builds Jerusalem,' has not carried out his obligation."

M.   There is a dispute about this matter between Abba Yose b. Dosetai and rabbis.

N.   One said, "'Who is good and does good' requires the mention of divine rule."

O.   And the other said, "It does not require the mention of divine rule."

P.   He who says that it must be included takes the view that the blessing at hand rests only on the authority of rabbis.

Q.   And the one who says that it is not necessary to mention it holds that it rests on the authority of the Torah.

LV.

A.   Our rabbis have taught on Tannaite authority:

B.   What is the concluding phrase for the blessing "Who builds Jerusalem"?

C.   R. Yose b. R. Judah says, "'Who saves Israel.'"

D.   Should one say "Who saves Israel" and not "Who builds Jerusalem"?

E.   Rather, I should say, "<u>Also</u>, 'Who saves Israel' [is to be said]."

LVI.

A.   Rabbah bar R. Huna came to the house of the exilarch. He mentioned one item [Israel or Jerusalem] at the beginning [of the third blessing], and both of them at the end of that same blessing.

B.   Said R. Hisda, "Is it better to conclude with reference to both [Israel and Jerusalem]?

C.   "Has it not been taught on Tannaite authority: Rabbi says, 'People do not conclude [the blessing] by referring to both [Israel and Jerusalem]'?"

LVII.

A.   Reverting to the body of the text just now cited:

B.   Rabbi says, "People do not conclude [the blessing] by referring to both [Israel and Jerusalem]."

C.   Levi objected to Rabbi, "[Why not refer to both matters in concluding a blessing? For lo, at the end of the second blessing, we refer to thanks] 'For the land <u>and</u> for food.'"

D.   "It is for the land that produces the food."

E.   "For the land and for produce."

F.   "It is the land that produces the produce."

G.   "Who consecrates Israel and the holy seasons."

H.   "It is Israel that consecrates the seasons."

I.   "Who consecrates Israel and the new moons."

J.   "It is Israel that [by formal proclamation] consecrates the new moons."

K.   "Who consecrates the Sabbath, Israel, and the holy seasons."

L.   "Except for that case. [Simon, p. 296, n. 2: Israel does not sanctify the Sabbath by means of a formal proclamation, hence we cannot here apply the same explanation as in the case of festivals and New Moons]."

M.   "Why is this case any different?"

N.   "Here it is a single act [by which God sanctifies Israel and the Sabbath], while in the other cases it is two acts, each one distinct unto itself. [That is, saving Israel and building Jerusalem are separate acts.]"

O.   "And what is the reason, in any event, that people do not conclude by mentioning two separate matters?"

P.   "It is because we do not bundle religious duties together [and deal with them wholesale]."

Q.   What is the upshot of the matter?

R.   Said R. Sheshet, "If one begins by saying, 'Have mercy on your people, Israel,' then one concludes with, 'Who builds Jerusalem.'"

S.   "If one opens with, 'Who shows mercy to Jerusalem,' he concludes with, 'Who builds Jerusalem.'"

T.   And R. Nahman said, "Even if one opens with, 'Have mercy on Jerusalem,' he closes with, 'Who builds Jerusalem.'

U.   "For it is said, 'The Lord builds up Jerusalem, he gathers together the dispersed of Israel' (Ps. 147:2).

V.   "When does the Lord build Jerusalem? When he gathers the dispersed of Israel."

LVIII.

A.   Said R. Zira to R. Hisda, "Will the master come and repeat [the rules of Grace, so that we may learn them]?"

B.   He said to him, "I have not yet learned the rules covering the Grace after Meals, should I then repeat it on Tannaite authority?"

C.   He said to him, "How so?"

D.   He said to him, "I went to the household of the exilarch, and I said the Grace after the Meal, and R. Sheshet stretched his neck out to me like a snake. Why so? Because I did not mention either the covenant or the Torah or the kingship [of David]."

E.   "And why did you not do so?"

F.   "It was in accord with what R. Hananel said Rab said.

G.   "For R. Hananel said Rab said, 'If one has not made mention of the covenant, Torah, and divine sovereignty in the Grace after meals, he nonetheless has carried out his obligation.

H.   "'The covenant, because it does not apply to women.

I.   "'Torah and divine dominion, because they do not apply either to women or to slaves.'"

J.   "But have you abandoned the views of all these other Tannaite and Amoraic authorities and acted in accord with Rab?!"

LIX.

A. Said Rabbah b. b. Hana said R. Yohanan, "It is necessary to make mention of divine sovereignty in the blessing, 'Who is good and does good.'"

B. What [new point] does the foregoing statement supply? Is it that any blessing that lacks mention of divine sovereignty does not fall into the category of a blessing at all? R. Yohanan has already said that once.

C. Said R. Zira, "It is that [in 'Who is good...'] one has to make mention of divine sovereignty twice, once for the blessing itself, the other for the reference to 'Who builds Jerusalem.' [The benediction, 'Who is good and does good,' begins with, 'Blessed... king of the universe.' The benediction ending, 'Who builds Jerusalem,' by contrast does not include the formula, 'King of the universe.']"

D. If so, we should require the inclusion of reference to divine sovereignty three times, one for itself, one for "Who builds Jerusalem," and the third in the blessing of the land.

E. Then what is the reason that the blessing for the land does not require [reference to divine sovereignty]?

F. It is because it is a blessing that is juxtaposed closely to one that comes before it [where the concept is made explicit].

G. If that is the operative consideration, then the blessing ending, "Who builds Jerusalem," also should not require the inclusion of a reference to divine sovereignty, because there too, the matter is contained in a blessing that is closely juxtaposed to it.

H. That indeed is the rule, for even the blessing, "Who builds Jerusalem," also does not require [the inclusion of reference to divine sovereignty]. But since the text make reference to the sovereignty of the house of David, it would not be proper not to make mention, also, of the sovereignty of heaven.

I. R. Pappa said, "This indeed is the sense [of Yohanan's statement]: It is necessary to make mention [in 'Who is good and does good'] of sovereignty twice, in addition to the inclusion of reference to divine sovereignty in the blessing itself."

LX.

A. R. Zira sat behind R. Giddal, and R. Giddal sat before R. Huna, and, in session, stated, "If one made an error and did not include in the Grace after Meals the matter of the Sabbath, he says, 'Blessed is he who gave Sabbaths for rest to his people Israel, in love, as a sign and a covenant. Blessed is he who sanctifies the Sabbath.'"

B. He said to him, "Who made this statement?"

C. "Rab."

D. He went back into session and stated, "If one made a mistake and did not include a reference to the festival day [in his recitation of the Grace after Meals], he says, 'Blessed is he who gave festival days to his people Israel for rejoicing and for a memorial. Blessed is he who sanctifies Israel and the seasons.'"

E. He said to him, "Who said this?"

F.   "Rab."

G.   He went back into session and stated, "If one made an error and did not make mention of the new moon, he says, 'Blessed is he who gave new moons to his people, Israel, as a memorial.'

H.   "But [Zira continues] I do not know whether he included in that statement a reference to rejoicing or not.

I.   "I do not know whether he included a benediction as a formula of conclusion in that statement or not.

J.   "I do not know whether it was a formulation of his own or of his master [Rab]."

LXI.

A.   Giddal bar Minyomi was standing before R. Nahman. R. Nahman made an error [49B] and went back to the beginning [of the recitation of Grace after Meals]. He said to him, "Why did the master do this?"

B.   He said to him, "It is because R. Shila said Rab said, 'If one makes a mistake, he goes back to the beginning.'"

C.   [He replied,] "But lo, R. Huna said Rab said, 'If one made a mistake, he says, 'Blessed be he who gave....'"

D.   He said to him, "But has it not been stated on Amoraic authority on that passage: 'Said R. Menassia bar Tahalipa said Rab, "That has been taught only in a case in which one has not yet begun reciting, 'Who is good and does good.' But if one has begun reciting 'Who is good and does good' [and then discovers the mistake], he goes back to the beginning."'"

LXII.

A.   Said R. Idi bar Abin said R. Amram said R. Nahman said Samuel, "If one made a mistake in reciting the Prayer and did not make mention of the new moon, they have him go back.

B.   "If this was in the recitation of the Grace after Meals, they do not have him go back."

C.   Said R. Abin to R. Amram, "What is the difference between the recitation of the Prayer and that of the Grace after Meals?"

D.   He said to him, "That problem troubles me too, and I asked R. Nahman, and he said to me, 'I have heard nothing from the master, Samuel, on the subject.

E.   "'But let us see for ourselves. The recitation of the Prayer, which is obligatory, is a case in which people make a person go back. But as to the case of a meal in which, if one wants, he eats, and if one wants, he does not eat, they do not make him go back.'"

F.   [He replied,] "But what about the case of Sabbaths and festivals, in which it would not suffice [for observance] if one did not eat. [So eating is obligatory.] Would you say here too that if one made a mistake, he has to go back?"

G.   He said to him, "That is indeed the case. For R. Shila said Rab said, 'If one made a mistake, he has to go back to the beginning.'"

H.   [He replied,] "But lo, R. Huna said Rab said, 'If one made a mistake, he has to say, 'Blessed be he who gave....'"

I.   [He replied,] "Has it not been stated on Amoraic authority in that connection:

J.   "'That rule applies only in a case in which one has not yet begun to recite the blessing, "Who is good and does good."

K.   "'But if one has begun to recite the blessing, "Who is good and does good," he has to go back to the beginning'"?"

LXIII.

A.   What is the least that one must eat in order to invite others to recite a blessing on his account [M. 7:2B]:

B.   Does the passage at hand bear the implication that R. Meir [who stands behind the anonymous formulation of the rule and hence would regard an olive's bulk of food as sufficient] defines the minimum standard at an olive's bulk, while R. Judah [at M. 7:2C] requires an egg's bulk of food [for a person to fall into the category of having eaten a meal]?

C.   And lo, we have a tradition that the positions are reversed.

D.   For we have learned in the Mishnah:

E.   He who went forth from Jerusalem and remembered that he had in hand meat in the status of Holy Things, if he had already passed Mount Scopus, he burns it right where he is. But if not, let him go back and burn it before the Temple-pile with wood which has been set aside for the altar-hearth.

F.   And for how much [leaven or meat of Holy Things do they return]?

G.   R. Meir says, "This and that are subject to the measure of an egg's bulk."

H.   R. Judah says, "This and that are subject to the measure of an olive's bulk" [M. Pes. 3:8A-F].

I.   Said R. Yohanan, "The assigned opinions are to be reversed."

J.   Abayye said, "Under no circumstances should you reverse matters.

K.   "What is at issue in the present matter is the sense of verses of Scripture.

L.   "R. Meir takes the view that the sense of, 'You shall eat' (Deut. 8:10) is to refer to eating, and, 'You shall be satisfied,' refers to drinking. And an act of eating involves consuming at least an olive's bulk of food.

M.   "R. Judah takes the view that 'You shall eat and be satisfied' (Deut. 8:10) refers to eating that involves full satisfaction. And how much food is involved for that purpose? It is food in the volume of an egg's bulk.

N.   "In the other passage [involving leaven on Passover and Holy Things] what is at issue is a matter of reasoning.

O.   "R. Meir takes the view that one has to go back for the same volume as is involved in receiving or imparting uncleanness. Just as food receives or imparts uncleanness only if it is of the volume of an egg, so one has to return on account of food only if it is of the volume of an egg.

P.   "R. Judah theorizes that one has to go back for that same volume of food as is subjected, to begin with, to a prohibition. Just as one is prohibited to consume as much as an olive's bulk of food [whether of leaven on Passover or of Holy Things], so one has to go back [in the case described in the cited paragraph of the Mishnah] also for so much as an olive's bulk of [leaven or Holy Things]. [So there is reason for each party to take the distinct position he does in each case.]"

The protracted passage of the Talmud serving M. 7:1-2 may be divided into three categories. These are, first, exegesis of a clause or sentence of the Mishnah-paragraph; second, expansion of such an exegetical passage; third, secondary issues suggested by the Mishnah's themes or issues but not framed in terms of Mishnah-exegesis. I have tried to divide this third group into two subdivisions, (A) secondary issues suggests by Mishnah's themes or rules, and (B) thematic constructions essentially autonomous of Mishnah-exegesis. But the materials that fall into the respective categories overlap, so I doubt that the distinction can be sustained. I find no units of discourse completely out of relationship to the themes of the Mishnah-paragraph. In all, a review of the long passage suggests a very careful and principled selection and arrangement of units of discourse. The divisions are as follows:

1. Exegesis of a sentence in the Mishnah-paragraph: I, III-VI, XXVI, XXVII, XXVIIII, XXIX, XXX; XXXIII, XXXIV, XXXV, XXXVI, XXXVII, XXXVIII; LXIII.

2. Expansion of an exegetical passage serving the Mishnah paragraph: II, VII; VIII; XXXI, XXXII (to XXX); XXXIX-XLV (to XXXVIII):

3A. Secondary issues suggested by the themes or rules of the Mishnah: IX, X, XI, XII, XVI, XLVI, XLVII (joining a quorum); rules of the Grace after meals: LXVIII-L; LIV-LVIII: rules of the paragraph, "Who is good:" LIX-LXII.

3B. Thematic constructions autonomous of Mishnah-exegesis: XIII-XV (the standing of "Who is good and does good"); XVII-XVIII (who sits there); VIX-XX (taking precedence); XXI-XXV (who recites Grace, with supplement); LI-LIII (joined to proofs of Grace after meals;

4. Units of discourse unrelated to the Mishnah's themes: none.

7:3

A. How do they invite [others to join in the blessing after the meal]?
B. For three [who ate together, the leader] says, "Let us bless."
    For three [others] and himself [i.e., four], he says, "[All of you] bless."
C. For ten he says, "Let us bless our God."
    For ten and himself he says, "[All of you] bless."
D. The same [rule applies for] ten and for ten thousand.
E. For one hundred he says, "Let us bless the Lord our God."
    For one hundred and himself he says, "[All of you] bless."
F. For one thousand he says, "Let us bless the Lord our God, God of Israel."
    For one thousand and himself he says, "[All of you] bless."

G. For ten thousand he says, "Let us bless the Lord our God, God of Israel, God of the Hosts, who sits upon the cherubim, for the food we have eaten."

For ten thousand and himself he says, "[All of you] bless."

H. In terms of the blessing that he says, so do they answer after him:

I. "Blessed is the Lord our God, God of Israel, God of the Hosts, who sits upon the cherubim, for the food we have eaten."

J. R. Yose the Galilean says, "According to the size of the congregation, [so] they bless, as it says, 'In gathering bless God the Lord from the source of Israel' (Ps. 48:27)."

K. Said R. Aqiba, "Just as we find concerning the synagogue, that, whether there are many or few, one says, 'Bless the Lord,' [so is the rule for the Grace after meals]."

L. R. Ishmael says, "Bless the Lord who is blessed."

I.

A. Said Samuel, "A person should never remove himself from the group in general [and so should always say, 'Let us say a blessing.'"

B. We have learned in the Mishnah: For three others and himself, he says, "All of you bless..." [M. 7:3B].

C. I should say [50A], "Also [one may say], 'All of you bless,' but nonetheless, the language, 'Let us bless' is preferable."

D. For R. Adda bar Ahbah said that they say at the house of R. Rab, "It is taught on Tannaite authority: In the case of six persons up to ten, the group may divide [to form groups of three or four. But ten may not do so, since they lose the opportunity of adding the language, 'Our God.']"

E. Now if you say that the language, "Let us bless" is preferable, that is the reason that people may divide up [into several groups, so as to repeat the preferable language].

F. But if you say that the formulation, "All of you bless..." is preferable, why should people want to divide up?" [Simon, p. 301, n. 2: Rashi reads: "Why should six divide?" If they form two groups of three, neither can say, "All of you bless..."]

G. Does that not bear the implication that the language, "Let us bless," is preferable?

H. It does indeed bear that implication.

II.

A. It has been taught on Tannaite authority along these same lines:

B. Whether one has said, "All of you bless...," and whether one has said, "Let us bless...," people do not hold a person accountable.

C. But people who are meticulous do hold such a one accountable.

D. And from the way a person recites his blessings, one may discern whether he is a disciple of a sage or not.

E. How so?

F. Rabbi says, "If one says, 'By his goodness,' lo, such a one is a disciple of a sage. If he said, 'And from his goodness,' lo, such a one is an ignoramus."

G. Said Abayye to R. Dimi, "And is it not written, 'And <u>from</u> your blessing let the house of your servant be blessed for ever' (2 Sam. 7:29)?"

H. "When one supplicates, the rule is different."

I. "But in the case of a supplication, also is it not written, 'Open your mouth wide and I will fill it' (Ps. 81:11)?"

J. "That passage refers to teachings of Torah."

III.

A. It has been taught on Tannaite authority, "If one says, 'By his goodness do we live,' lo, such a one is a disciple of a sage.

B. "If he says, 'By his goodness do <u>they</u> live,' lo, such a one is an ignoramus."

C. The sages of Nahar Bel repeat the matter in the opposite formulation, but the law does not follow the view of the sages of Nahar Bel.

IV.

A. Said R. Yohanan, "If one said, 'Let us bless him out of whose bounty we have eaten,' lo, such a one is a disciple of a sage.

B. "'Let us bless the <u>one</u> out of whose bounty we have eaten,' lo, such a one is an ignoramus.

C. Said R. Aha, son of Raba, to R. Ashi, "But lo, we say, 'To the <u>one</u> who has done for our fathers and ourselves all these miracles.'"

D. He said to him, "In that case, the facts of the matter itself prove one's intent. For who is it who did the miracles? It is the Holy One, blessed be he."

E. Said R. Yohanan, "If one said, 'Blessed is he out of whose bounty we have eaten,' lo, such a one is a disciple of a sage.

F. "'For the <u>food</u> which we have eaten,' lo, this one is an ignoramus."

G. Said R. Huna, son of R. Joshua, "The cited rule applies only in a case in which there are three present, for, in such a case, the name of heaven is not invoked.

H. "But if there are ten present, in which case the name of heaven is invoked, then the facts speak for themselves [and the formulations just now specified make no difference].

I. "For we have learned in the Mishnah: <u>In terms of the blessing that he says, so do they answer after him: 'Blessed is the Lord our God, God of Israel, God of the Hosts, who sits upon the cherubim, for the food we have eaten' [M. 7:3H-I]</u>."

V.

A. <u>The same rule applies for ten and for ten thousand [M. 7:3D]</u>:

B. Now there is a contradiction in the passage itself.

C. You have said: <u>The same rule applies for ten and for ten thousand [M. 7:3D]</u>.

D. Thus all fall into a single category [under the same rule].

E. And then the passage goes and states, <u>For one hundred he says..., For one thousand he says..., For ten thousand he says...</u>.

F. Said R. Joseph, "There is no contradiction. The one formulation represents the view of R. Yose the Galilean, the other the view of R. Aqiba.

G. For we have learned in the Mishnah:

H. R. Yose the Galilean says, "According to the size of the congregation, so they bless, as it is said, 'In gatherings bless God...' (Ps. 48:27)" [M. 7:3J].

VI.

A. Said R. Aqiba, "Just as we find concerning the synagogue [that, whether there are many or few, one says, 'Bless the Lord,' [so is the rule for the Grace after Meals]" [M. 7:3K]:

B. How does R. Aqiba deal with the verse of Scripture cited by R. Yose the Galilean?

C. He makes use of it for the purpose indicated in the following teaching on Tannaite authority:

D. R. Meir would say, "How do we know that even the babes in the bellies of their mothers sang a song at the shore of the sea?

E. "As it is said, 'Bless you the Lord in full assemblies, even the Lord, you that are from the fountain of Israel' (Ps. 68:27)."

F. And the other party?

G. He derives the lesson from the word, "From the source...."

VII.

A. Said Raba, "The decided law follows the view of R. Aqiba."

B. Rabina and R. Hama bar Buzzi came to the house of the exilarch. R. Hama got up and started counting up to a hundred.

C. Rabina said to him, "It is not necessary to do so. Lo, said Raba, 'The decided law follows the opinion of R. Aqiba.'"

VIII.

A. Said Raba, "When we eat bread at the house of the exilarch, we say the blessing [of the Grace after Meals] in groups of three."

B. And why not say it in groups of ten?

C. The exilarch will hear and be angry [that the rabbis did not wait for him to participate].

D. And why not carry out one's obligation through the blessing that will [later on be recited for the meal by] the exilarch himself?

E. Since everyone present would recite in a loud voice, they will not hear [the Grace as he recites it].

IX.

A. Said Rabbah Tosfaah, "As to the case of three who broke bread together, and one of them finished earlier than the others and said the Grace after Meals for himself, the other two are able to carry out their obligation to do so through the quorum called together in his behalf. But he is not able to carry out his obligation through the quorum called together in their behalf.

B. "The reason is that there cannot be a quorum called together that applies retroactively."

X.

A. R. Ishmael says [M. 7:3L]:

B. Rafram bar Pappa came to the synagogue at Abi Gibbar. He got up and read in the
Scroll of the Torah and said, "Bless the Lord" and then he fell silent, not adding [the
required phrase], "Who is to be blessed."

C. Everybody cried out, "Bless the Lord who is to be blessed!"

D. Said Raba, "Black pot! What business do you have getting involved in disputes.

E. "And furthermore, the entire world follows the practice defined by R. Ishmael [so
why should you have varied from it]?"

Unit I intersects with the Mishnah-paragraph and interprets its language. Units II,
III, IV, complement the foregoing. Units V, VI, VII deal with the Mishnah-paragraph, and
unit VIII complements the foregoing. Unit IX then continues unit VIII's interest in the
case of forming a quorum for Grace independent of the group as a whole. Unit X then
deals with the Mishnah-paragraph. So the whole follows familiar rules of composition and
organization.

7:4-5

A. Three who ate together may not divide up.

B. And so too four, and so too five.

C. Six to ten may divide up [into two or three groups].

D. And ten may not divide up -- up to twenty.

M. 7:4

A. Two eating associations which were eating in one room --

B. when some [members] of each group face one another, lo, they may
combine as an invited group [i.e., a single group which together says the
blessing over the meal].

C. And if not, each invites [members of its own group to bless] for
themselves.

D. "They do not say a blessing over wine until one puts water into it [so that
it may be drunk]," the words of R. Eliezer.

E. And sages say, "They bless [in any event]."

M. 7:5

I.

A. Of what new facts does [M. 7:4A] inform us. On Tannaite authority we already have
learned:

B. Three who have eaten together are obligated to issue a call to the quorum [to recite the Grace after Meals].

C. What we learn in the present instance accords with that which R. Abba said Samuel said, "Three who have sat down to eat together and have not yet eaten [nonetheless] are not permitted to separate [from one another. They have to eat together so as to form a quorum for the public call to say Grace and so must carry out their intent.]"

D. Another version: Said R. Abba said Samuel, "This is the meaning of that which has been repeated on Tannaite authority:

E. "Three who have sat down together to eat, even though each one eats from his own loaf of bread, are not permitted to part from one another [but must form a quorum for the public recitation of Grace]."

F. An alternative [in answer to A] is that it teaches a rule along the lines of what R. Huna said.

G. For R. Huna said, "Three people, who came from three different eating associations, are not permitted to separate [from one another, but must form a quorum, once they have come together]."

H. Said R. Hisda, "That rule applies if the three of them came from three already established eating groups of three individuals each, [Simon, p. 304, n. 4: so that each of them was under the obligation of participating in a quorum]."

I. Said Raba, "[50B] But that rule applies only if the other eating associations have not already gone ahead and counted these individuals as part of the quorum for reciting Grace in their former locations.

J. "But if they had already counted on them in their original place, the obligation to participate in a quorum for the recitation of Grace has already left them."

K. Said Raba, "How do I know that that is the case?

L. "It is because we have learned in the Mishnah:

M. "A bed half of which was stolen, or half of which was lost, or which brothers divided into half as an inheritance, or which partners divided into half, is [useless and therefore] insusceptible to uncleanness. If they put it back together, it becomes susceptible to uncleanness from that point on [but whatever uncleanness had adhered to it has vanished] [M. Kel. 18:9A-B].

N. "For the future it indeed [is susceptible], but retroactively it is not.

O. "Therefore, once people have divided the bed, the capacity to receive and retain uncleanness has gone forth from it.

P. "Hereto, once the group has included the individuals in a quorum, the obligation to participating in a quorum has gone from them [having been carried out and they need not do so again elsewhere]."

II.

A. Two eating associations [M. 7:5A]:

B. It has been taught on Tannaite authority: If there is a waiter between the two groups [serving them both], the waiter serves to join them together [into a single quorum].

III.

A.   <u>They do not say a blessing over wine [M. 7:5D]:</u>

B.   Our rabbis have taught on Tannaite authority:

C.   "As to undiluted wine [i.e., wine in its natural, pure state] -- they do not recite over it the benediction, 'Creator of the fruit of the vine' but 'Creator of the fruit of the tree,'

D.   "and they may wash their hands in it [as in any fruit juice].

E.   "Once one has diluted it with water, they recite over it the benediction, 'Creator of the fruit of the vine' [cf. M. Ber. 6:1B-C],

F.   "and they may not wash their hands with it," the words of R. Eliezer.

G.   And sages say, "In either case they recite over it the benediction, 'Creator of the fruit of the vine,'

H.   "and they may not wash their hands with it" [cf. M. Ber. 7:5D-F] [T. Ber. 4:3A-G].

I.   In accord with which of the two authorities at hand is the statement of Samuel, "A person may carry out all his needs [e.g., may wipe his hands] using a piece of bread"?

J.   In accord with whom? In accord with R. Eliezer.

K.   Said R. Yose b. R. Hanina, "Sages concede to R. Eliezer in the case of a cup of wine over which a blessing is to be said, that one may not say a blessing over it before water is put in [to dilute the wine]."

L.   What is the reason for that concession?

M.   Said R. Oshiaia, "We require the fulfillment of the religious duty at hand through the most elegant possible means."

N.   And, so far as rabbis are concerned, what good is undiluted wine anyhow?

O.   Said R. Zira, "It is good for mixing with <u>karyotis</u> [Simon, p. 305, n. 4: a kind of date with the shape of a nut, used for medicinal purpose]."

IV.

A.   Our rabbis have taught on Tannaite authority:

B.   Four rules have been stated with regard to bread:

C.   People do not leave raw meat on bread.

D.   People do not pass a full cup over bread.

E.   People may not throw bread.

F.   People may not use bread to support a cup.

V.

A.   Amemar, Mar Zutra, and R. Ashi broke bread together. They brought before them dates and pomegranates. Mar Zutra took some and tossed some before R. Ashi as his portion.

B.   He said to him, "Does not the master take the view of the following teaching on Tannaite authority: 'People may not throw food?"

C.   "That was taught explicitly in regard to bread."

D.   But has it not been taught on Tannaite authority: 'Just as people may not throw bread, so they may not throw other food'?"

E.   He said to him, "And has it not been taught on Tannaite authority, 'Even though people may not throw bread, they may throw other food'?

F.   "But in point of fact there is no contradiction between the two statements. The one speaks of foods that can spoil [if they are thrown], the other to things that will not spoil [if they are thrown]."

VI.

A.   Our rabbis have taught on Tannaite authority:

B.   **They lead wine and oil through pipes before grooms and brides** [T. Shab. 7:16A], and they toss before them roasted ears of corn and nuts, in the dry season but not in the rainy season.

C.   And as to cakes, they may not do so either in the dry season or in the rainy season.

VII.

A.   Said R. Judah, "If one forgot and put food into his mouth without reciting a blessing, he puts the food to one side and says the blessing."

B.   One teaching on Tannaite authority says: "One swallows the food."

C.   Another such teaching reads: "One spits it out."

D.   And a third version: "One puts them to one side."

E.   There is no contradiction among the several versions.

F.   When we repeat the tradition as "swallows," it speaks of liquid.

G.   When we repeat the tradition as "spits it out," it speaks of something that will not spoil [if it is spit out].

H.   And when it is taught, "One puts the food to one side," it speaks of something that would be spoiled [if it is spit out].

I.   [51A] But as to something that will not be spoiled [if it is spit out], why not also put that to one side of the mouth and say the blessing?

J.   R. Isaac Qasqasaah explained the matter before R. Yose bar Abin in the name of R. Yohanan, "It is because it is said, 'My mouth shall be filled with your praise' (Ps. 81:8). [Simon, p. 306, n. 6: There should be no room for anything besides the benediction.]"

VIII.

A.   They asked before R. Hisda, "If someone ate and drank and did not say the blessing, what is the law as to his going back and saying the blessing later on?"

B.   He said to them, "If someone ate garlic and his breath stinks, should he go and eat more garlic so that his breath should stink more? [Simon, p. 306, n. 7: Having made one mistake, should he make another by not saying a blessing over the part he has still to eat?]"

C.   Said Rabina, "Therefore [since one says in the middle the blessing he did not say to begin with] even if one has completed his meal, he should go and recite the blessing.

D.   "For it has been taught on Tannaite authority:

E.   "If one has immersed and come up out of the water, he recites when he comes up, 'Blessed... who has sanctified us by his commandments and commanded us concerning immersion."

F. But that is not parallel. In that case, [to begin with] the man was not in fit condition [to recite the blessing], while in the present case, the man to begin with is in fit condition to say the blessing. Therefore, since the blessing has been set aside, it has been set aside [and cannot be made up later on].

IX.

A. Our rabbis have taught on Tannaite authority:

B. Asparagus-brew is good for the heart and good for the eyes, and all the more so, for the belly.

C. And he who takes it regularly will find that it is good for his entire body.

D. But he who gets drunk from it will find that it is bad for his entire body.

E. Since it has been taught, "It is good for the heart," it must follow that we deal with a kind of wine.

F. But it further teaches, And all the more so for the belly.

G. And yet has it not been taught on Tannaite authority, "It is good for the heart, eyes, and milt, and it is bad for the head, belly, and piles"?

H. When the statement at hand was taught, it concerned vintage wine.

I. As we have learned in the Mishnah:

J. If one said, "Qonam be wine, because it is bad for the belly," and they told him, "But isn't old wine good for the belly?" -- [M. Ned. 9:8A-B], and the person then was silent -- he is permitted to drink vintage wine but forbidden to drink new wine.

K. That proves the point.

X.

A. Our rabbis have taught on Tannaite authority:

B. There are six rules that have been stated with reference to asparagus-brew:

C. People may drink it only when it is undiluted, from a full cup, which one holds in the right hand and then from which one drinks holding the cup in his left hand. One should not talk after drinking it, or stop in the middle of drinking it. One gives the cup back only to the person who gave it to him. One spits after drinking it. And after drinking it, one should eat next only something of the same species.

D. But has it not been taught on Tannaite authority: "After drinking it, one should next have only bread"?

E. There is no contradiction.

F. The one speaks of asparagus-brew made from wine, the other of asparagus-brew made from beer.

G. It has been taught on Tannaite authority: It is good for the heart, eyes, and milt, and it is bad for the head, belly, and piles.

H. And another Tannaite authority taught: It is good for the head, belly, and piles, and bad for the heart, eyes, and milt.

I. There is no contradiction, the one speaks of asparagus-brew made from wine, the other of asparagus-brew made from beer.

J. One Tannaite tradition says, "One who spits after drinking will suffer," and another Tannaite authority states, "If one does not spit after drinking it, he will suffer,"

K.   There is no contradiction, since the one speaks of asparagus-brew made from wine, the other of asparagus-brew made from beer.

L.   Said R. Ashi, "Now that you have said, 'If one did not spit after drinking it, he will suffer,' one should pour out the fluid of it even in the presence of the king."

XI.

A.   Said R. Ishmael b. Elisha, "Three things did Suriel, the prince of the divine presence, tell me:

B.   "'In the morning do not take your cloak from your servant's hand and put it on.

C.   "'And do not take water for washing your hands from someone who has not washed his hands.

D.   "'And return a cup of asparagus-brew only to the one who gave it to you.

E.   "'For [Simon:] a company of demons, and some say, a band of destroying angels, lies in wait for a man, and they say, "When will this man fall into one of these traps and be taken."'"

F.   Said R. Joshua b. Levi, "Three things did the angel of death report to me:

G.   "'In the morning do not take your cloak from your servant's hand and put it on.

H.   "'And do not take water for washing your hands from someone who has not washed his hands.

I.   "'And do not stand in front of women when they are coming back from [burying a] corpse, because I am dancing back and forth before them, with my sword in my hand, and I have every right to inflict injury.'"

J.   And if someone has met them, what is his remedy?

K.   Let him move away four cubits: if there is a river, let him cross it; if there is another road, let him take it; if there is a wall, let him hide behind it; and if not, let him at least turn his face away, and say, "And the Lord said to Satan, The Lord rebuke you, O Satan" (Zech. 3:2).

L.   [This should be done] until the women have passed by him.

XII.

A.   Said R. Zira said R. Abbahu, and some say that it was repeated as a Tannaite tradition, "Ten things have been stated with respect to the cup that is used for the blessing of wine prior to the recitation of Grace after Meals:

B.   "It has to be rinsed and washed.

C.   "The wine has to be undiluted and filled up to the top. It has to be crowned and cloaked.

D.   "One takes it with his two hands and puts it in his right hand and raises it a handbreadth above the ground and gazes upon it."

E.   And some say, "One has also to send it as a gift to the members of his household."

F.   R. Yohanan said, "We have only four of these teachings alone, those involving rinsing and washing, the undiluted wine, and that it be filled up."

G.   On Tannaite authority it was stated: Rinsing is of the inside, and washing is of the outside.

H.   Said R. Yohanan, "Whoever recites a blessing over a full cup is given an unlimited inheritance.

I.   "For it is said, 'And full with the blessing of the Lord, possess the sea and the south' (Deut. 33:23)."

J.   R. Yose b. R. Hanina says, "He has the merit of inheriting both worlds, this world and the world to come."

K.   As to the meaning of "crowned" [said above]:

L.   R. Judah "crowned" it by surrounding it with disciples.

M.   R. Hisda "crowned" it with cups.

N.   [Simon:] "And undiluted:"

O.   R. Sheshet said, "[It is left undiluted] up to the blessing of the land."

P.   "Cloaked:"

Q.   R. Pappa would cloak himself and take his seat."

R.   R. Assi would spread a cloth on his head.

S.   "One takes it with his two hands:"

T.   Said R. Hinena bar Pappa, "What verse of Scripture indicates it? 'Lift up your hands in holiness and bless the Lord' (Ps. 134:2)."

U.   "And puts it in his right hand:"

V.   Said R. Hiyya bar Abba said R. Yohanan, "The ancients asked, 'What is the law about having the left hand support the right hand?'"

W.   Said R. Ashi, "Since to the ancients this was a problem which they could not solve, [51B] we should follow the strict ruling. [The left hand may not be used to support the right hand.]"

X.   "And raises it a handbreadth above the ground:"

Y.   Said R. Aha bar Hinena, "What is the relevant verse of Scripture? 'I will lift up the cup of salvation and call upon the name of the Lord' (Ps. 116:13)."

Z.   "And gaze upon it:"

AA.   That is so that one may not be distracted from concentrating on it.

BB.   "One has also to send it as a gift to the members of his household:"

CC.   That is so that his wife may be blessed too.

XIII.

A.   Ulla came to the house of R. Nahman. They broke bread and he said the grace. He handed the cup of blessing [to be taken with the Grace after the Meal] to R. Nahman.

B.   R. Nahman said to him, "Will the master [now] send the cup that is to be blessed to Yalta [Nahman's wife]?"

C.   He said to him, "Thus said R. Yohanan, 'The fruit of the body [belly] of a woman is blessed only through the fruit of the body of a man.'

D.   "For it is said, 'He will also bless the fruit of your body' (Deut. 7:13).

E.   "'The fruit of her body' is not what is said, but rather, 'the fruit of your body.'"

F.   It has been taught on Tannaite authority as well:

G.   R. Nathan says, "How do we know that the fruit of the body of a woman is blessed only through the fruit of the body of a man?

H.   "As it is said, 'He will also bless the fruit of your body' (Deut. 7:13).

I.   "'The fruit of her body' is not what is said, but rather, the 'fruit of your body.'"

J.   Meanwhile Yalta heard [that Ulla would not send the cup to her], and she lost her temper and went up to the wine shed and broke four hundred denars' worth of wine.

K.   Said R. Nahman to him, "Will the master send her another cup of wine?"

L.   He sent her [the wine] with the message, "All that wine is for a blessing."

M.   She retorted to him, "[Simon:] Gossip comes from peddlers, and vermin from rags."

XIV.

A.   Said R. Assi, "People are not to chatter over the cup for the blessing [at the Grace after Meals]."

B.   And R. Assi said, "People do not say a blessing over a cup of punishment."

C.   What is a "cup of punishment"?

D.   Said R. Nahman bar Isaac, "The second cup of wine [since two is an unlucky number]."

E.   It has been taught on Tannaite authority along these same lines:

F.   He who drinks in pairs [an even number of cups of wine] should not say the blessing [Grace].

G.   For it says, "Prepare to meet your God, Israel" (Amos 4:12). But this one is not prepared."

XV.

A.   Said R. Abbahu, and some say that it was taught on Tannaite authority:

B.   "He who eats as he walks along says the Grace after Meals while he is standing up.

C.   "If someone eats while standing, he should say the blessing [after the meal] while he is seated.

D.   "And when he reclines and eats, he sits and says the blessing."

E.   And the decided law in all settings is that one sits down to recite the blessing [of the Grace after Meals].

The explanation of the Mishnah-paragraph occupies the center of attention at units I-III. Unit IV is attached because of III, and units V, VI, VII, are tacked on because of the theme, introduced in the complementary units, of not permitting food to spoil. I am not sure why unit VIII is added, though the concluding allusion, at unit VII, to having one's mouth "filled with praise" may have struck a redactor as sufficient reason to introduce the matter. In fact the issue becomes important in Chapter Eight, to follow. I am equally puzzled by the introduction of units IX, X, XI, a miscellany if there ever was one, and XII, which tells us about a topic of no interest at all to the Mishnah-paragraph. But the matter of the recitation of the Grace after Meals is entirely pertinent to the chapter at hand. The same theme occupies units XIII, XIV, XV. Perhaps there was a policy of gathering up loose ends at the end of a chapter -- hence the miscellany above -- and concluding with a sustained essay on a theme characteristic of the chapter as a whole, but not of any particular statement within the chapter. I have no better way of accounting for the inclusion of the concluding group, XII-XV, on the one side, or of VIII-XI, on the other. At the same time, we have no problem in explaining the principle of conglomeration that made the joining of the two groups, respectively, perfectly self-evident to the people who made them up. What that means -- no surprise by this point in our inquiry -- is that out of all relationship to the tasks of either Mishnah- or Scripture-exegesis people were making up enormous, sustained, and important units of thought.

8:1-8

A.   These are the things which are between the House of Shammai and the House of Hillel in [regard to] the meal:

B.   The House of Shammai say, "One blesses over the day, and afterward one blesses over the wine."

C.   And the House of Hillel say, "One blesses over the wine, and afterward one blesses over the day."

<u>M. 8:1</u>

A.   The House of Shammai say, "They wash the hands and afterward mix the cup."

B.   And the House of Hillel say, "They mix the cup and afterward wash the hands."

<u>M. 8:2</u>

A.   The House of Shammai say, "He dries his hands on the cloth and lays it on the table."

B.   And the House of Hillel say, "On the pillow."

<u>M. 8:3</u>

A.   The House of Shammai say, "They clean the house, and afterward they wash the hands."

B.   And the House of Hillel say, "They wash the hands, and afterward they clean the house."

<u>M. 8:4</u>

A.   The House of Shammai say, "Light, and food, and spices, and Havdalah."

B.   And the House of Hillel say, "Light, and spices, and food, and Havdalah."

C.   The House of Shammai say, "Who created the light of the fire."

D.   And the House of Hillel say, "Who creates the lights of the fire."

<u>M. 8:5</u>

A.   They do not bless over the light or the spices of gentiles, nor the light or the spices of the dead, nor the light or the spices which are before an idol.

B.   And they do not bless over the light until they make use of its illumi-
      nation.

M. 8:6

A.   He who ate and forgot and did not bless [say Grace] --
B.   The House of Shammai say, "He should go back to his place and bless."
C.   And the House of Hillel say, "He should bless in the place in which he
      remembered."
D.   Until when does he bless? Until the food has been digested in his bowels.

M. 8:7

A.   Wine came to them after the meal, and there is there only that cup --
B.   The House of Shammai say, "He blesses the wine, and afterward he
      blesses the food."
C.   And the House of Hillel say, "He blesses the food, and afterward he
      blesses the wine."
D.   They respond Amen after an Israelite who blesses, and they do not
      respond Amen after a Samaritan who blesses, until hearing the entire
      blessing.

M. 8:8

I.

A.   Gemara: Our rabbis have taught:
B.   The things which are between the House of Shammai and the House of Hillel in
      [regard to] a meal:
C.   The House of Shammai say, "One blesses over the day and afterward blesses over the
      wine, for the day causes the wine to come, and the day has already been sactified,
      while the wine has not yet come."
D.   And the House of Hillel say, "He blesses over the wine and afterward blesses over
      the day, for the wine causes the Sanctification to be said.
E.   "Another matter: The blessing over the wine is perpetual, and the blessing over the
      day is not perpetual. Between that which is perpetual and that which is not
      perpetual, that which is perpetual takes precedence" [T. Ber. 5:25].
D.   And the law is in accordance with the words of the House of Hillel.
E.   What is the purpose of "another matter"?
F.   If you should say that there [in regard to the opinion of the House of Shammai] two
      [reasons are given] and here [in regard to the opinion of the House of Hillel] one,
      here too [in respect to the House of Hillel], there are two [reasons, the second
      being]: "The blessing of the wine is perpetual and the blessing of the day is not
      perpetual. That which is perpetual takes precedence over that which is not
      perpetual."
G.   And the law is in accord with the opinion of the House of Hillel.

H. This is obvious [that the law is in accord with the House of Hillel], for the echo has gone forth [and pronounced from heaven the decision that the law follows the opinion of the House of Hillel].

I. If you like, I can argue that [this was stated] before the echo.

J. And if you like, I can argue that it was after the echo, and [the passage was formulated in accord with the] opinion of [52A] R. Joshua, who stated, "They do not pay attention to an echo [from heaven]."

II.

A. And is it the reasoning of the House of Shammai that the blessing of the day is more important?

B. But has a Tanna not taught: "He who enters his house at the close of the Sabbath blesses over the wine and the light and the spices and afterward he says Havdalah. And if he has only one cup, he leaves it for after the food and then says the other blessings in order after it." [Havdalah is the blessing of the day, yet comes last!]

C. But lo, on what account [do you say] this is the view of the House of Shammai? Perhaps it is the House of Hillel['s opinion]?

D. Let [such a thought] not enter your mind, for the Tanna teaches: "Light and afterward spices." And of whom have you heard who holds this opinion? The House of Shammai, as a Tanna has taught:

E. R. Judah said, "The House of Shammai and the House of Hillel did not differ concerning the [blessing of the] food, that it is first, and the Havdalah, that it is at the end.

F. "Concerning what did they dispute? Concerning the light and the spices.

G. "For the House of Shammai say, 'Light and afterward spices.'

H. "And the House of Hillel say, 'Spices and afterward the light'" [T. Ber. 5:30].

I. And on what account [do you suppose that] it is the House of Shammai as [interpreted by] R. Judah? Perhaps it is [a teaching in accord with] the House of Hillel [as interpreted by] R. Meir?

J. Do not let such a thing enter your mind, for lo, a Tanna teaches here in our Mishnah: The House of Shammai say, "Light and food and spices and Havdalah."

K. And the House of Hillel say, "Light and spices, food and Havdalah."

L. But there, in the teaching on Tannaite authority, lo he has taught: "If he has only one cup, he leaves it for after the food and then says the other blessings in order after it."

M. From this it is to be inferred that it is the House of Shammai's teaching, according to the [interpretation] of R. Judah.

N. In any event there is a problem [for the House of Shammai now give precedence to reciting a blessing for the wine over blessing the day].

O. The House of Shammai suppose that the coming of the holy day is to be distinguished from its leaving. As to the coming of the [holy] day, the earlier one may bring it in, the better. As to the leaving of the festival day, the later one may take leave of it, the better, so that it should not seem to us as a burden.

P. And do the House of Shammai hold the opinion that Grace requires a cup [of wine]? And lo, we have learned: [If] wine came to them after the food, and there is there only that cup, the House of Shammai say, "He blesses over the wine and afterward blesses over the food" [M. Ber. 8:8]. [So Grace is said without the cup.]

Q. Does this not mean that he blesses it and drinks [it]?

R. No. He blesses it and leaves it.

S. But has not a master said, "He that blesses must [also] taste [it]."

T. He does taste it.

U. And has not a master said, "Tasting it is spoiling it."

V. He tastes it with his hand [finger].

W. And has not a master said, "The cup of blessing requires a [fixed] measure." And lo, he diminishes it from its fixed measure.

X. [We speak of a situation in which] he has more than the fixed measure.

Y. But lo, has it not been taught: If there is there only that cup... [so he has no more].

Z. There is not enough for two, but more than enough for one.

AA. And has not R. Hiyya taught: The House of Shammai say, "He blesses over the wine and drinks it, and afterward he says Grace."

BB. Then we have two Tannas' [traditions] in respect to the opinion of the House of Shammai.

IV.

A. The House of Shammai say [They wash the hands and afterward mix the cup]... [M. 8:2A].

B. Our rabbis have taught:

C. The House of Shammai say, "They wash the hands and afterward mix the cup, for if you say they mix the cup first, [against this view is] a [precautionary] decree to prevent the liquids on the outer sides of the cup, which are unclean by reason of his hands' [touching them], from going back and making the cup unclean" [T. Ber. 5:26].

D. But will not the hands make the cup itself unclean [without reference to the liquids]?

E. The hands are in the second remove of uncleanness, and the [object unclean in] the second remove of uncleanness cannot [then] render [another object unclean] in the third [remove] in respect to profane foods, [but only to Heave-offering]. But [this happens] only by means of liquids [unclean in the first remove].

F. And the House of Hillel say, "They mix the cup and afterward wash the hands, for if you say they wash the hands first, [against this view is] a [precautionary] decree lest the liquids which are [already] on the hands become unclean on account of the cup and go and render the hands unclean."

G. But will not the cup [itself] make the hands unclean?

H. A vessel cannot render a man unclean.

I. But will they [the hands] not render the liquids which are in it [the cup] unclean?

J. Here we are dealing with a vessel the outer part of which has been made unclean by liquid. The inner part is clean but the outer part is unclean. Thus we have learned:

K. [If] a vessel is made unclean on the outside by liquid, the outside is unclean, [52B] but its inside and its rim, handle, and haft are clean. If, however, the inside is unclean, the whole [cup] is unclean.

L.   What, then, do they [the Houses] dispute?

M.   The House of Shammai hold that it is prohibited to make use of a vessel whose outer parts are unclean by liquids, as a decree on account of the drippings. [There is] no [reason] to decree lest the liquids on the hands be made unclean by the cup.

N.   And the House of Hillel reckon that it is permitted to make use of a vessel whose outer part is made unclean by liquids, for drippings are unusual. But there is reason to take care lest the liquids which are on the hands may be made unclean by the cup.

IV.

A.   Another matter: [So that] immediately upon the washing of the hands [may come] the meal [itself].

B.   What is the reason for this additional explanation?

C.   This is what the House of Hillel said to the House of Shammai: "According to your reasoning, in saying that it is prohibited to make use of a cup whose outer parts are unclean, we decree on account of the drippings. But even so, [our opinion] is better, for immediately upon the washing of the hands [should come] the meal."

VI.

A.   The House of Shammai say, "He dries his hand on the napkin..." [M. 8:3A].

B.   Our rabbis have taught:

C.   The House of Shammai say, "He wipes his hands with the napkin and lays it on the table, for if you say, 'on the cushion,' [that view is wrong, for it is a precautionary] decree lest the liquids which are on the napkin become unclean on account of the cushion and go back and render the hands unclean" [T. Ber. 5:27].

D.   And will not the cushion [itself] render the napkin unclean?

E.   A vessel cannot make a vessel unclean.

F.   And will not the cushion [itself] make the man unclean?

G.   A vessel cannot make a man unclean.

H.   And the House of Hillel say, "'On the cushion,' for if you say, 'on the table,' [that opinion is wrong, for it is a] decree lest the liquids become unclean on account of the table and go and render the food unclean" [T. Ber. 5:27].

I.   But will not the table render the food which is on it unclean?

J.   We here deal with a table which is unclean in the second remove, and something unclean in the second remove does not render something unclean in the third remove in respect to unconsecrated food, except by means of liquids [which are always unclean in the first remove].

K.   What [principle] do they dispute?

L.   The House of Shammai reckon that it is prohibited to make use of a table unclean on the second remove, as a decree on account of those who eat Heave-offering [which is rendered unfit by an object unclean in the second remove].

M.   And the House of Hillel reckon that it is permitted to make use of a table unclean in the second remove, for those who eat Heave-offering [the priests] are careful.

N.   Another matter: There is no Scriptural requirement to wash the hands before eating unconsecrated food.

O. What is the purpose of "another explanation"?

P. This is what the House of Hillel said to the House of Shammai: If you ask what is the difference in respect to food, concerning which we take care, and in respect to the hands, concerning which we do not take care -- even in this regard [our opinion] is preferable, for there is no Scriptural requirement concerning the washing of the hands before eating unconsecrated food.

Q. It is better that the hands should be made unclean, for there is no Scriptural basis for [washing] them, and let not the food be made unclean, concerning which there is a Scriptural basis [for concern about its uncleanness].

VI.

A. The House of Shammai say, "They clean house and afterward wash the hands..." [M. 8:4A].

B. Our rabbis have taught:

C. The House of Shammai say, "They clean the house and afterward wash the hands, for if you say, 'They wash the hands first,' it turns out that you spoil the food" [T. Ber. 5:28].

D. But the House of Shammai do not reckon that one washes the hands first.

E. What is the reason?

F. On account of the crumbs.

G. And the House of Hillel say, "If the servant is a disciple of a sage, he takes the crumbs which are as large as an olive [in bulk] and leaves the crumbs which are not so much as an olive [in bulk]."

H. (This view supports the opinion of R. Yohanan, for R. Yohanan said, "Crumbs which are not an olive in bulk may be deliberately destroyed.")

I. In what do they differ?

J. The House of Hillel reckon that it is prohibited to employ a servant who is an ignorant man, and the House of Shammai reckon that it is permitted to employ a servant who is an ignorant man.

K. R. Yose bar Hanina said in the name of R. Huna, "In our entire chapter the law is in accord with the House of Hillel, excepting this matter, in which the law is in accord with the House of Shammai."

L. And R. Oshaia taught the matter contrariwise. And in this matter too the law is in accord with the House of Hillel.

VII.

A. The House of Shammai say, "Light and food..." [M. 8:5A].

B. R. Huna bar Judah happened by the house of Rava. He saw that Rava blessed the spices first.

C. He said to him, "Now the House of Shammai and the House of Hillel did not dispute concerning the light, [it should come first].

D. "For it was taught: The House of Shammai say, 'Light, and food, spices, and Havdalah,' and the House of Hillel say, 'Light, and spices, and food, and Havdalah.'

E. Rava answered him, "This is the opinion [= version] of R. Meir, but R. Judah says, 'The House of Shammai and the House of Hillel did not differ concerning the food, that it comes first, and concerning the Havdalah, that it is at the end.

F. "'Concerning what did they differ?'

G. "'Concerning the light and the spices.'

H. "For the House of Shammai say, 'The light and afterward the spices.'

I. "And the House of Hillel say, 'The spices and afterward the light.'

J. And R. Yohanan said, "The people were accustomed to act in accord with the House of Hillel as presented by R. Judah."

VIII.

A. The House of Shammai say, "Who created..." [M. 8:5C].

B. Rava said, "Concerning the word 'bara' [created] everyone agrees that 'bara' implies [the past tense]. They differ concerning 'boré' [creates]. The House of Shammai reckon that 'boré' means, 'Who will create in the future.' And the House of Hillel reckon that 'boré' also means what was created [in the past]."

C. R. Joseph objected, "'Who forms light and creates darkness' [Isaiah 45:7], 'Creates mountains and forms the wind' [Amos 4:13], 'Who creates the heavens and spreads them out'" [Isaiah 42:5].

D. "But," R. Joseph said, "Concerning 'bara' and 'boré' everyone agrees that [the words] refer to the past. They differ as to whether one should say 'light' or 'lights.'

E. "The House of Shammai reckon there is one light in the fire.

F. "And the House of Hillel reckon that there are many lights in the fire."

G. We have a Tannaite teaching along the same lines:
The House of Hillel said to the House of Shammai, "There are many illuminations in the light."

IX.

A. A blessing is not said... [M. 8:6A].

B. Certainly, [in the case of] the light [of idolators, one should not say a blessing] because it did not rest on the Sabbath. But what is the reason that for spices [one may not say the blessing]?

C. R. Judah said in the name of Rav, "We here deal with a banquet held by idolators, because the run-of-the-mill banquet held by idolators is for the sake of idolatry."

D. But since it has been taught at the end of the clause, "Or over the light or spices of idolatry," we must infer that the beginning of the clause does not deal with idolatry.

E. R. Hanina from Sura said, "What is the reason is what it explains, namely, what is the reason that they do not bless the light or spices of idolators? Because the run-of-the-mill banquet held by idolators is for the sake of idolatry."

X.

A. Our rabbis have taught:

B. One may bless a light which has rested on the Sabbath, but one may not bless a light which has not rested on the Sabbath.

C. And what is the meaning of "which has not rested on the Sabbath"?

D.   [53A] Shall we say it has not rested on the Sabbath on account of the work [which has been done with it, including] even work which is permitted?

E.   And has it not been taught: They do bless the light [kindled on the Sabbath for] a woman in confinement or a sick person.

F.   R. Nahman bar Isaac said, "What is the meaning of 'which enjoyed Sabbath-rest'? Which enjoyed Sabbath-rest on account of work, the doing of which is a trangression [on the Sabbath]."

G.   We have learned likewise on Tannaite authority:

H.   They may bless a lamp which has been burning throughout the day to the conclusion of the Sabbath.

XI.

A.   Our rabbis have taught:

B.   They bless [a light] kindled by a gentile from an Israelite, or by an Israelite from a gentile, but they do not bless [a light] kindled by a gentile from a gentile.

C.   What is the reason one does not do so [from a light kindled by] a gentile from a gentile?

D.   Because it did not enjoy Sabbath-rest.

E.   If so, lo, [a light kindled by] an Israelite from a gentile also has not enjoyed Sabbath-rest.

F.   And if you say this prohibited [light] has vanished, and the one [in hand] is another and was born in the hand of the Israelite, [how will you deal] with this teaching?

G.   He who brings out a flame to the public way [on the Sabbath] is liable [for violating the Sabbath rule against carrying from private to public property].

H.   Now why should he be liable? What he raised up he did not put down, and what he put down he did not raise up.

I.   But [we must conclude] that the prohibited [flame] is present, but when he blesses, it is over the additional [flame], which is permitted, that he blesses.

J.   If so, a gentile['s flame kindled] from a gentile['s flame] also [should be permitted].

K.   That is true, but [it is prohibited by] decree, on account of the original gentile and the original flame [of light kindled on the Sabbath by the gentile].

XII.

A.   Our rabbis have taught:

B.   [If] one was walking outside the village and saw a light, if the majority [of the inhabitants of the village] are gentiles, he does not bless it. If the majority are Israelites, he blesses it.

C.   Lo, the statement is self-contradictory. You have said, "If the majority are gentiles, he does not bless it." Then if they were evenly divided, he may bless it.

D.   But then it teaches, "If the majority are Israelites, he may bless." Then if they evenly divided, he may not bless it.

E.   Strictly speaking, even if they are evenly divided, he may bless. But since in the opening clause [the language is], "The majority are gentiles," in the concluding clause, [the same language is used:] "A majority are Israelites."

XIII.

A.　Our rabbis have taught:

B.　[If] a man was walking outside of a village and saw a child with a torch in his hand, he makes inquiries about him. If he is an Israelite, he may bless [the light]. If he is a gentile, he may not bless.

C.　Why do we speak of a child? Even an adult also [would be subject to the same rule].

D.　Rav Judah said in the name of Rav, "In this case we are dealing with [a time] near sunset. As to a gentile, it will be perfectly clear that he certainly is a gentile [for an Israelite would not use the light immediately after sunset]. If it is a child, I might say it is an Israelite child who happened to take up [the torch]."

XIV.

A.　Our rabbis have taught:

B.　[If] one was walking outside of a village and saw a light, if it was as thick as the opening of a furnace, he may bless it, and if not, he may not bless it.

C.　One Tanna [authority] [says], "They may bless the light of a furnace," and another Tanna [says], "They may not bless it."

D.　There is no difficulty. The first speaks at the beginning [of the fire], the other at the end.

E.　One authority says, "They may bless the light of an oven or a stove," and another authority says, "They may not bless it."

F.　There is no problem. The former speaks of the beginning, the latter of the end.

G.　One authority says, "They may bless the light of the synagogue and the schoolhouse," and another authority says, "They may not bless it."

H.　There is no problem. The former speaks [of a case in which] an important man is present, the latter [of a case in which] an important man is not present.

I.　And if you want, I shall explain both teachings as applying to a case in which an important man is present. There still is no difficulty. The former [teaching speaks of a case in which] there is a beadle [who eats in the synagogue], the latter in which there is none.

J.　And if you want, I shall explain both teachings as applying to a case in which a beadle is present. There still is no difficulty. The former teaching [speaks of a case in which] there is moonlight, the latter in which there is no moonlight.

XV.

A.　Our rabbis have taught:

B.　[If] they were sitting in the schoolhouse, and light was brought before them --

C.　The House of Shammai say, "Each one blesses for himself."

D.　And the House of Hillel say, "One blesses for all of them, as it is said, 'In the multitude of people is the King's glory'" [Proverbs 14:28].

E.　Certainly [we can understand the position of the House of Hillel because] the House of Hillel explain their reason.

F.　But what is the reason of the House of Shammai?

G. They reckon [it as they do] on account of [avoiding] interruption in [Torah study] in the schoolhouse.

H. We have a further Tannaitic tradition to the same effect:

I. The members of the house of Rabban Gamaliel did not say [the blessing] "Good health" [after a sneeze] in the schoolhouse on account of the interruption [of study] in the schoolhouse.

XVI.

A. They say a blessing neither on the light nor on the spices of the dead... [M. 8:6A].

B. What is the reason?

C. The light is made for the honor [of the deceased], the spices to remove the bad smell.

D. Rav Judah in the name of Rav said, ["Light made for] whoever [is of such importance that] they take out [a light] before him both by day and by night is not blessed. [And light made for] whoever [is not important, so that] they take out [a light] before him only by night, is blessed."

E. R. Huna said, "They do not bless spices of the privy and oil made to remove the grease."

F. Does this saying imply that wherever [spice] is not used for smell, they do not bless over it? It may be objected:

G. He who enters the stall of a spice dealer and smells the odor, even though he sat there all day long, blesses only one time. He who enters and goes out repeatedly blesses each time.

H. And lo, here is a case in which it is not used for the scent, and still he blesses.

I. Yes, but it also is used for the odor -- so that people will smell and come and purchase it.

XVII.

A. Our rabbis have taught:

B. If one was walking outside of a village and smelled a scent, if most of the inhabitants are idolators, he does not bless it. If most are Israelites, he blesses it.

C. R. Yose says, "Even if most are Israelites, he still may not bless, because Israelite women use incense for witchcraft."

D. But do they "all" burn incense for witchcraft!

E. A small part is for witchcraft and a small part is also for scenting garments, which yields a larger part not used for scent, and wherever the majority [of the incense] is not used for scent, one does not bless it.

F. R. Hiyya bar Abba said in the name of R. Yohanan, "He who walks on the eve of the Sabbath in Tiberias and at the end of the Sabbath in Sepphoris and smells an odor does not bless it, because it is presumed to have been made only to perfume garments."

G. Our rabbis taught: If one was walking in the gentiles' market and was pleased to scent the spices, he is a sinner.

XVIII.

A. [53B] They do not recite a blessing over the light until it has been used.. [M. 8:6B]:

B.   Rav Judah said in the name of Rav, "Not that he has actually used it, but if anyone stood near enough so that he might use the light, even at some distance, [he may say the blessing]."

C.   So too R. Ashi said, "We have learned this teaching even [concerning] those at some distance."

D.   It was objected [on the basis of the following teaching]: If one had a light hidden in the folds of his cloak or in a lamp, or saw the flame but did not make use of its light, or made use of the light but did not [actually] see the flame, he may not say the blessing. [He may say the blessing only when] he [both] sees the flame and uses its light.

E.   Certainly one finds cases in which one may use the light and not see the flame. This may be when the light is in a corner.

F.   But where do you find a case in which one may see the flame and not make use of its light? Is it not when he is at a distance?

G.   No, it is when the flame keeps on flickering.

XIX.

A.   Our rabbis have taught:

B.   They may say a blessing over glowing coals, but not over dying coals ('omemot).

C.   What is meant by glowing coals?

D.   R. Hisda said, "If one puts a chip into them and it kindles on its own, [these are] all [glowing coals]."

E.   It was asked: Is the word 'omemot ['alef] or 'omemot ['ayin]?

F.   Come and hear, for R. Hisda b. Abdimi said, "'The cedars in the garden of God could not darken ['amamuhu] it'" [Ezekiel 31:8].

G.   And Rava said, "He must make actual use of it."

H.   And how [near must one be]?

I.   Ulla said, "So that he may make out the difference between an issar and a pundion [two small coins]."

J.   Hezekiah said, "So that he may make out the difference between a meluzma [a weight] of Tiberias and one of Sepphoris."

K.   Rav Judah would say the blessing [for the light of the] house of Adda the waiter [which was nearby].

L.   Rava would say the blessing [for the light of the] house of Guria bar Hama.

M.   Abayye would say the blessing [for the light of the] house of Bar Abbuha.

N.   R. Judah said in the name of Rav, "They do not go looking for the light in the way they go looking for [means to carry out other] commandments."

O.   R. Zera said, "At the outset, I used to go looking [for light]. Now that I have heard this teaching of R. Judah in the name of Rav, I too will not go searching, but if one comes my way, I shall say the blessing over it."

XX.

A.   He who ate [and did not say Grace]... [M. 8:7A]:

B.   R. Zevid, and some say, R. Dimi bar Abba, said, "The dispute [between the Houses] applies to a case of forgetfulness, but in a case in which a person deliberately [omitted Grace], all agree that he should return to his place and say the blessing."

C.   This is perfectly obvious. It is [explicitly] taught, "And he forgot."

D.   What might you have said? That is the rule even where it was intentional, but the reason that the Tanna taught, "And he forgot," is to tell you how far the House of Shammai were willing to go [in requiring the man to go back to where he ate. They did so even if a man accidentally forgot]. Thus we are taught [the contrary. Even if one forgot, unintentionally, he must go back].

XXI.

A.   It was taught:

B.   The House of Hillel said to the House of Shammai, "According to your opinion, someone who ate on the top of the Temple Mount and forgot and went down without saying Grace should go back to the top of the Mount and say the blessing."

C.   The House of Shammai said to the House of Hillel, "According to your opinion, someone who forgot a purse on the top of the Temple Mount would not go back and retrieve it.

D.   "For his own sake, he [assuredly] will go back. For the sake of Heaven [should he] not all the more so [go back]?"

E.   There were these two disciples. One did it [forgot Grace] accidentally, and, following the rule of the House of Shammai, [went back to bless], and found a purse of gold. And one did it deliberately [omitted Grace], and following the rule of the House of Hillel [did not go back to say it], and a lion ate him.

F.   Rabbah bar bar Hanna was traveling in a caravan. He ate and was sated but [forgot and] did not say Grace.

G.   He said, "What shall I do? If I tell the men [of the caravan with me] that I forgot to bless, they will say to me, 'Bless here. Wherever you say the blessing, you are saying the blessing to the Merciful [God].' It is better that I tell them I have forgotten a golden dove."

H.   So he said to them, "Wait for me, for I have forgotten a golden dove."

I.   He went back and blessed and found a golden dove.

J.   And why was a dove so important?

K.   Because the community of Israel is compared to a dove, as it is written, "The wings of the dove are covered with silver, and her pinions with the shimmer of gold" [Psalm 68:14]. Just as the dove is saved only by her wings, so Israel is saved only by the commandments.

XXII.

A.   <u>Until when can he say the Grace? Until the food is digested in his bowels... [M. 8:7D]:</u>

B.   How long does it take to digest the food?

C.   R. Yohanan said, "As long as one is no longer hungry."

D.   Resh Laqish said, "As long as one [still] is thirsty on account of his meal."

E. R. Yemar bar Shelamia said to Mar Zutra -- and some say, Rav Yemar bar Shizbi said to Mar Zutra -- "Did Resh Laqish really say this? And did not R. Ammi say in the name of Resh Laqish, 'How long does it take to digest a meal? The time it takes to go four miles.'"

F. There is no problem: Here [we speak of] a big meal, there [we speak of] a small meal.

XXIII.

A. If wine came to them... [M. 8:8A]:

B. This implies that in the case of an Israelite['s saying Grace], even though one has not heard the entire blessing, he responds [Amen].

C. But if he has not heard [the whole Grace], how can he have performed his duty by doing so [assuming he has eaten also]?

D. Hiyya bar Rav said, "[We speak of a case] in which he did not eat with them."

E. So too did R. Nahman say in the name of Rabbah bar Abbuha, "[We speak of a case] in which he did not eat with them."

F. Rav said to Hiyya his son, "My son, seize [the cup] and bless."

G. So did R. Huna say to Rabbah his son, "Seize and bless."

H. This implies that he who says the blessing is better than he who answers Amen. But has it not been taught:

I. R. Yose says, "The one who answers Amen is greater than the one who says the blessing."

J. R. Nehorai said to him, "By heaven! It is so. You should know it, for behold, common soldiers go ahead and open the battle, but the heroes go in and win it."

K. It is a matter of dispute between Tannaites, as it has been taught:

L. Both the one who says the blessing and the one who answers Amen are implied [in the Scripture (Nehemiah 9:5)]. But the one who says the blessing is more quickly [answered] than he who answers Amen.

XXIV.

A. Samuel asked Rav, "Should one answer [Amen] after [the blessings of] children in the schoolhouse?"

B. He said to him, "They answer Amen after everyone except children in the schoolhouse, since they are [saying blessings solely] for the sake of learning."

C. And this applies when it is not the time for them to say the "Haftarah," but in the time to say "Haftarah," they do respond [Amen].

XXV.

A. Our rabbis have taught:

B. "The absence of oil holds up the blessing [Grace]," the words of Rabbi Zilai.

C. R. Zivai says, "It does not hold it up."

D. R. Aha says, "[The absence of] good oil holds it up."

E. R. Zuhamai says, "Just as a dirty person [mezuham] is unfit for the Temple service, so dirty hands are unfit for the blessing."

F.   R. Nahman Bar Isaac said, "I know neither Zilai nor Zivai nor Zuhamai. But I know a
      teaching which R. Judah said in the name of Rav, and some say it was taught on
      Tannaite authority:

G.   "'And be you holy' [Leviticus 20:7] -- this refers to washing the hands before the
      meal.

H.   "'And you shall be holy' -- this refers to the washing after the meal.

I.   "'For holy' -- this refers to the oil.

J.   "'Am I the Lord your God' -- this refers to the blessing [Grace]."

While the Talmud as printed presents the whole of the Mishnah for the entire
chapter at hand, in fact the layout of the Talmud leaves no doubt as to the intent of any
unit of discourse. Nearly all of the materials at hand either clarify the reasoning behind a
rule in the Mishnah-paragraph or expand upon the theme of that same statement. Unit I
cites the Tosefta's amplification of the Mishnah. Unit II carries forward that same
matter. Unit III moves on to the next clause in the Mishnah-paragraph. Units IV, V-IX
gloss aspects of the Mishnah-paragraph. Unit X amplifies M. 8:6A, as is clear, and units
XI-XV simply cite Tannaite materials that expand upon the same theme. Then unit XVII
stands in relationship to unit XVI as units XI-XV do to unit X. Unit XVIII once more
reverts to cite the Mishnah and gloss its statement. Unit XIX enriches the foregoing.
Unit XX again cites the Mishnah-paragraph, with a complement at XXI. XXII, XXIII gloss
the Mishnah's language. XXIV, XXV provide a simple supplement. So, in all, the entire
chapter of the Talmud consists of glosses of the Mishnah or secondary supplements and
expansions of the topic of the Mishnah, little else.

CHAPTER NINE
BAVLI BERAKHOT CHAPTER NINE

9:1-5

A.   [54A] One who sees a place where miracles were performed for Israel
      says, "Blessed is he who performed miracles for our fathers in this place."
B.   [One who sees] a place from which idolatry was uprooted says, "Blessed
      is he who uprooted idolatry from our land."

M. 9:1

A.   For meteors, earth tremors, lightning, thunder, and wind, one says,
      "Blessed... whose power and might fill the world."
B.   For mountains, hills, seas, rivers, and deserts, he says, "Blessed... the
      maker of [all of] creation."
C.   R. Judah says, "He who sees the Great [Mediterranean] Sea says,
      'Blessed... who made the Great Sea,'
D.   "when he sees it at intervals."
E.   For the rain and for good tidings, he says, "Blessed... who is good and
      does good."
F.   And for bad tidings he says, "Blessed... the true judge."

M. 9:2

A.   One who built a new house, or bought new clothes says, "Blessed... [who
      kept us alive and] brought us to this occasion."
B.   One [who] blesses over evil [with the blessing used] for good, or [who
      blesses] over good [with the blessing used] for evil
C.   [or] one who cries out about the past --
D.   lo, this is a vain prayer.
E.   [How so?] If one's wife was pregnant and he prayed, "May it be thy will
      that she give birth to a male" -- lo, this is a vain prayer.
F.   If one was coming along the road and he heard a noise of crying in the
      city and he said, "May it be thy will that those [who are crying] are not
      members of my household" -- lo, this is a vain prayer.

M. 9:3

A.   One who enters a town prays two [prayers] -- one upon his entry and one upon his exit.

B.   B. Azzai says, "[He prays] four prayers -- two upon his entry and two upon his exit.

C.   "And he gives thanks for the past, and cries out for the future."

M. 9:4

A.   One is obligated to bless over evil as one blesses over the good,

B.   as it is said, "And you shall love the Lord your God with all your heart, with all your soul, and with all your might" (Deut. 6:5).

C.   "With all your heart" -- with both of your inclinations, with the good inclination and with the evil inclination.

D.   "And with all your soul" -- even if He takes your soul.

E.   "And with all your might" -- with all of your money.

F.   Another matter: With all your might (m'dk) -- with each and every measure that he measures out for you, thank him much [a play of words: mydh, mwdd, mwdh, m'd].

G.   One should not act light-headedly while facing the Eastern Gate [of the Temple in Jerusalem] for it faces toward the Chamber of the Holy of Holies.

H.   One should not enter the Temple Mount with his walking stick, his shoes, his money bag, or with dust on his feet.

I.   And one should not use [the Temple Mount] for a shortcut.

J.   And spitting [there likewise is forbidden, as is proven by an argument] a minori ad majus.

K.   [At one time] all blessings in the Temple concluded with "from time immemorial."

L.   When the sectarians corrupted their ways and claimed, "There is but one world [and no word to come],"

M.   they ordained that they should say, "From time immemorial and forever" [which suggests the existence of a time to come].

N.   [And] they instituted the practice that an individual should greet his fellow with God's name.

O.   As it is said, "And behold Boaz came from Bethlehem; and he said to the reapers, 'The Lord be with you' And they answered, 'The Lord bless you'"(Ruth 2:4).

P.   And Scripture says, "The Lord is with you you mighty man of valor" (Judges 6:12).

Q.   And it says, "Do not despise your mother when she is old" (Proverbs 23:22).

R.   And it says, "It is the time for the Lord to act for they have violated
      your teaching" (Psalms 119:126).

S.   R. Nathan says, "They have violated your teaching. It is time "to act"
      for the Lord."

M. 9:5

I.

A.   How on the basis of Scripture do we know [that one says a blessing on account of a
      miracle, M. 9:1A]?

B.   Said R. Yohanan, "It is in line with the following verse of Scripture: 'And Jethro
      said, Blessed be the Lord who has delivered you' (Ex. 18:10)."

C.   Now do we say a blessing on account only of a miracle performed for the community
      but not for one performed for an individual?

D.   And lo, there was the case of a certain man, who was going along the way in Eber
      Yamina. A lion attacked him. A miracle was done for him, and he was saved from
      it. He came before Raba, who said to him, "Whenever you come to that place, say
      the blessing: 'Blessed is he who did a miracle for me in this place.'"

E.   Mar, son of Rabina, was going along the way in the valley of Arabot and was
      thirsty. A miracle was done for him. A well of water was created for him, and he
      drank.

F.   And on another occasion he was walking along the way in the Manor of Mahoza,
      when a wild camel attacked him. Just then a wall of a nearby house fell down, and
      he took refuge inside it. When he came to Arabot, he would say the blessing,
      "Blessed is he who did a miracle for me in Arabot and in the matter of the camel."
      When he came by the Manor of Mahoza he would say the blessing, "Blessed is he who
      did a miracle for me in the matter of the camel and in Arabot."

G.   Hence one should conclude that, for a miracle done for the community, everyone is
      liable to say a blessing.

H.   For a miracle done for an individual, the individual is liable to say a blessing [but the
      community is not].

II.

A.   Our rabbis have taught on Tannaite authority:

B.   He who sees the place where [Israel] crossed the sea, the place where [Israel]
      crossed the Jordan, the place where [Israel] crossed the streams of the Arnon, hail
      stones in the descent of Bet Horon, the stone that Og, the king of Bashan, wanted to
      throw at Israel, the stone on which Moses sat when Joshua made war against
      Amalek, the wife of Lot, the wall of Jericho that was swallowed where it stood --

C.   "in all these instances, one has to give thanks and praise before the Omnipresent."

D.   Now there is no issue with respect to the place at which the Israelites crossed the
      sea, for it is written, "And the children of Israel went into the midst of the sea upon
      the dry ground" (Ex. 14:22).

E. Likewise the fords of the Jordan: "And the priests that carried the ark of the covenant of the Lord stood firm on dry ground in the midst of the Jordan, while all Israel passed over on dry ground until all the nation was passed clean over the Jordan" (Jos. 3:17).

F. But how do we know that that is the rule for the place where [Israel] crossed the streams of the Arnon?

G. As it is written, "Therefore it is said in the book of the Wars of the Lord, [Simon:] Eth and Heb in the rear" (Num. 21:14).

H. On Tannaite authority it was taught: "Eth and Heb in the rear" refers to two men afflicted with saraat. They were walking behind, at the end of the camp of Israel. When the Israelites were going to pass through, the Amorites came [54B] and made holes [in the rocks] and hid in them, saying, "When the Israelites come by here, we shall kill them."

I. They did not know that the ark was going before Israel and leveling the mountains before them. Once the ark came by, the mountains cleaved to one another and killed [the Amorites in the caves], and their blood flowed into the streams of Arnon.

J. Now when Eth and Heb came along, they saw the blood oozing forth from the mountains. They came and told the Israelites, who recited a song.

K. That is in line with what is written: "And he poured forth the streams which inclined toward the seat of Ar and leaned upon the border of Moab" (Jos. 3:15).

L. "Hailstones:" What are hailstones?

M. It was taught on Tannaite authority: They are stones which remain suspended for "the man" or come down for "the man."

N. "They remain suspended for the man" -- that is, for Moses, for it is written, "Now the man Moses was very meek" (Num. 12:3). And it is written, "And the thunder and hail ceased, and the rain did not pour upon the earth" (Ex. 9:33).

O. "They come down for the sake of the man" -- that is, for Joshua, for it is written, "Take you Joshua, the son of Nun, the man in whom there is spirit" (Num. 27:18). And it is written, "And it came to pass as they fled from before Israel, while they were at the descent of Beth Horon, that the Lord cast down great stones" (Jos. 10:11).

P. "The stone that Og, king of Bashan, wanted to throw at Israel:"

Q. It is taught on the basis of tradition:

R. [Og] said, "How large is the camp of Israel? It is three parasangs. I shall go and uproot a mountain three parasangs in size and toss it at them and kill them."

S. He went and uprooted a mountain three parasangs in size and brought it along on his head. The Holy One, blessed be he, brought ants on it, which bored a hole into it, so it fell down around his neck. He tried to raise it up, but because his teeth projected on either side, he could not pull it off.

T. That is in line with what is written, "You have broken the teeth of the wicked" (Ps. 3:8).

U.   And that verse is to be explained in accord with the interpretation of R. Simeon b. Laqish.

V.   For R. Simeon b. Laqish said, "What is the meaning of the verse, 'You have broken the teeth of the wicked' (Ps. 3:8)?

W.   "Do not read the word as 'you have broken' but 'you have lengthened.'"

X.   How tall was Moses? He was ten cubits tall. He took an axe ten cubits long, jumped ten cubits into the air, hit him on his ankle, and killed him.

Y.   "The stone on which Moses sat:"

Z.   As it is written, "But Moses' hands were heavy, and they took a stone and put it under him and he sat on it" (Ex. 17:12).

AA. "Lot's wife:" as it is said, "But his wife looked back from behind him and she became a pillar of salt" (Gen. 19:26).

BB. "The wall of Jericho that was swallowed where it stood:" so it is written, "And the wall fell down flat" (Jos. 6:20).

CC. Now as to all of these other miracles, there is no problem [since all of them were indeed beneficial], but the matter of Lot's wife was punishment [and not a miracle], in which case, one says, "Blessed be the true judge." But as we noted above, one is supposed to recite words of thanksgiving and praise. [So there is a problem.]

DD. It has been taught on Tannaite authority:

EE. In connection with Lot and his wife, people say two blessings. For his wife, one says, "Blessed is the true judge." And for Lot one says, "Blessed is he who remembers the righteous."

FF. Said R. Yohanan, "Even when he is angry, the Holy One, blessed be he, remembers the righteous, for it is said, 'And it came to pass when God destroyed the cities of the Plain, that God remembered Abraham and sent Lot out of the midst of the overthrow' (Gen. 19:29)."

GG. "The wall of Jericho that was swallowed where it stood:" And was the wall of Jericho swallowed up? Lo, it fell down, as it is said, "And it came to pass, when the people heard the sound of the horn, that the people shouted with a great shout, and the wall fell down flat" (Jos. 6:20).

HH. Since the breadth and height of the wall were equal, on that account it was swallowed up.

III.

A.   Said R. Judah said Rab, "Four sorts of people have to give thanks: those who go down to the sea, those who wander far in the deserts, he who was sick and got better, and he who was in prison and came forth."

B.   How do we know that that is the case for those who go down to the sea? As it is written, "They who go down to the sea in ships... these saw the works of the Lord... he raised the stormy wind... they mounted up to the heaven, they went down to the deeps... they reeled to and fro and staggered like a drunken man... they cried to the Lord in their trouble, and he brought them out of their distress. He made the storm a calm... then were they glad because they were quiet... Let them give thanks to the

Lord for his mercy and for his wonderful works to the children of men" (Ps. 107:23-31).

C. How do we know that that is the case for those who wander far in the deserts? As it is written, "They wandered in the wilderness in a desert way; they found no city of habitation... Then they cried to the Lord... and he led them by a straight way... Let them give thanks to the Lord for his mercy" (Ps. 107:4-8).

D. How do we know that that is the case for someone who was sick and got better? As it is written, "Crazed because of the way of their transgression and afflicted because of their iniquities, their soul abhorred all manner of food... They cried to the Lord in their trouble. He sent his word to them... Let them give thanks to the Lord for his mercy" (Ps. 107:17-21).

E. How do we know that that is the case for him who was in prison and came forth? As it is said, "Such as sat in darkness and in the shadow of death... Because they rebelled against the words of God... Therefore he humbled their heart with travail... They cried to the Lord in their trouble... He brought them out of darkness and the shadow of death... Let them give thanks to the Lord for his mercy" (Ps. 107:10-15).

F. What blessing does one say?

G. Said R. Judah, "Blessed is he who bestows acts of lovingkindness."

H. Abayye said, "And one has to give thanks in the presence of a quorum of ten men, for it is written, 'Let them exalt him in the assembly of the people' (Ps. 107:32)."

I. Mar Zutra said, "And two of them have to be rabbis, as it is said, 'And praise him in the seat of elders' (Ps. 107:32)."

J. R. Ashi objected to this proposition, "And must I say that all of them must be rabbis? For is it written, 'In the assembly of the elders'? What is written is, 'In the assembly of the people.'"

K. Then I may say, "In the presence of ten common folk and also two rabbis."

L. It remains a problem.

IV.

A. R. Judah was sick and got better. R. Hana of Bagdad and rabbis came to him. They said to him, "Blessed is the All-Merciful, who gave you back to us and did not hand you over to the dirt."

B. He said to him, "You have freed me of any further obligation to give thanks."

C. But has not Abayye said that one has to give thanks in the presence of ten men?

D. There were ten men present.

E. But he was not the one who gave thanks?

F. It was not necessary, because he answered, "Amen," after what they said.

V.

A. Said R. Judah, "Three sorts of people have to be watched carefully: a sick person, a groom, and a bride."

B. In Tannaite tradition it is repeated: A sick person, a midwife, a groom, and a bride.

C. Some say, "Also a mourner."

D. Some say, "Also disciples of sages by night."

VI.

A.   And R. Judah says, "Three things there are, which, if one lengthens the process of doing them, will lengthen his days and years.

B.   "He who lengthens the process of reciting his prayer.

C.   "He who lengthens the process of eating at table.

D.   "And he who lengthens his stay in the privy."

E.   Is lengthening one's prayer a virtue?

F.   And has not R. Hiyya bar Abba said R. Yohanan said, [55A], "Whoever lengthens the process of reciting his Prayer and [Simon:] expects therefore its fulfillment, will end up with heart ache.

G.   "For it is said, 'Hope deferred makes the heart sick' (Prov. 13:12)."

H.   And R. Isaac said, "Three things call to mind the sins a person has committed.

I.   "And these are they: a shaky wall, [Simon:] expectation of the fulfillment of prayer, and one who hands over his claim against his fellow to Heaven."

J.   There is no contradiction [between these views and Judah's]. The one speaks of one who expects his prayer to be fulfilled, the other of one who does not count on it.

K.   What does the former do? He simply offers up many prayers of supplication.

L.   "He who lengthens the process of eating at table."

M.   Perhaps a poor man may come along, and the householder will [have the merit of] giving him food.

N.   For it is written, "The altar of wood three cubits high... and he said to me, This is the table that is before the Lord" (Ez. 41:22).

O.   The verse begins by referring to the altar and concludes by referring to a table.

P.   Both R. Yohanan and R. Eleazar say, "So long as the house of the sanctuary stood, the altar atoned for Israel. Now a person's table atones for him."

Q.   "He who lengthens his stay in the privy."

R.   Is this a virtue? And has it not been taught on Tannaite authority:

S.   Ten things cause piles: he who eats leaves of reeds, leaves of vines, sprouts of vines, the rough parts of the meat of an animal, the backbone of a fish, salted fish not properly cooked, he who drinks wine lees, he who wipes himself with lime, potters' clay, or pebbles used by someone else.

T.   Some say, He who strains himself in the privy too much.

U.   There is no contradiction [between the statement at hand and the concluding prescription]: the one speaks of one who stays a long time, and strains himself, the other [regarding it as beneficial] is one who stays a long time but does not strain himself.

V.   That is in line with what a matron said to R. Judah bar Ilai, "Your face is [red] like that of people who raise pigs and lend on interest."

W.   He said to her, "By my faith! Both such occupations are forbidden in my view. But there are twenty-four privies between my inn and the school, and, when I go along, I try myself out in each of them."

VII.

A.   And R. Judah said, "Three things shorten a person's days and years:

B.   "A person to whom they hand over a scroll of the Torah to read but who does not agree to read.

C.   "A person to whom they hand over a cup for reciting the blessing [of the Grace after Meals] and who declines to say the blessing.

D.   "And he who puts on airs of authority."

E.   "A person to whom they hand over a scroll of the Torah to read but who does not agree to read:" as it is written, "For that is your life and the length of your days" (Deut. 30:20).

F.   "A person to whom they hand over a cup for reciting the blessing [of the Grace after Meals] and who declines to say the blessing:" as it is written, "I will bless them who bless you" (Gen. 12:3).

G.   "And he who puts on airs of authority:" As R. Hama b. Hanina said, "Why did Joseph die before his brothers did? Because he put on airs of authority."

VIII.

A.   And R. Judah said R. Rab said, "There are three things which require [God's] mercy [Simon: for which one should supplicate]:

B.   "A good king, a good year, and a good dream."

C.   "A good king:" as it is written, "A king's heart is in the hands of the Lord as the water-courses" (Prov. 21:1).

D.   "A good year:" as it is written, "The eyes of the Lord your God are always upon it, from the beginning of the year even to the end of the year" (Deut. 11:12).

E.   "A good dream:" as it is written, "Wherefore causes me to dream and make me live" (Is. 38:16).

IX.

A.   Said R. Yohanan, "There are three things about which the Holy One, blessed be he, makes a proclamation himself [and not through an intermediary], and these are they: famine, plenty, and a good leader."

B.   "Famine:" as it is written, "The Lord has called for a famine" (2 Kgs. 8:1).

C.   "Plenty:" as it is written, "I will call for the corn and will increase it" (Ez. 36:29).

D.   "A good leader:" as it is written, "And the Lord spoke to Moses saying, See I have called by name Bezalel, son of Uri" (Ex. 31:1).

X.

A.   Said R. Isaac, "People do not appoint a leader over the community unless they have consulted the community.

B.   "For it is said, 'See, the Lord has called by name Bezalel, son of Uri' (Ex. 5:30).

C.   "Said the Holy One, blessed be he, to Moses, 'Moses, is Bezalel acceptable to you?'

D.   "He said to him, 'Lord of the Universe, if he is acceptable to you, how much more so to me!'

E.   "He said to him, 'Nonetheless, go and report the matter to them.'

F.   "He went and reported the matter to Israel, 'Is Bezalel acceptable to you?'

G.   "They said to him, 'If to the Holy One, blessed be he, and to you, he is acceptable, how much the more so to us!'"

XI.

A.   Said R. Samuel bar Nahmani said R. Jonathan, "Bezalel was so named because of his wisdom. When the Holy One, blessed be he, said to Moses, 'Go to Bezalel and say to him, "Make me a tabernacle, an ark, and utensils,"' Moses went and got things confused and said to him, 'Make an ark, utensils, and a tabernacle.'

B.   "He said to him, 'Moses, our master, the custom of the world is that a person builds a house and afterward he brings in the utensils. But you say, "Make me an ark and utensils and then a tabernacle." As to the utensils that I am going to make, where shall I bring them? Is it possible, then, that the Holy One, blessed be he, told you to make a tabernacle, and ark, and then utensils!'

C.   "He said to him, 'Is it possible that you have been in the shadow of God (besel el), that you should know all this?'"

XII.

A.   Said R. Judah said Rab, "Bezalel knew how to join together the letters by which the heaven and the earth were made.

B.   "Here it is written, 'And he has filled him with the spirit of God, in wisdom and in understanding and in knowledge' (Ez. 35:31), and elsewhere it is written, 'The Lord by wisdom founded the earth, by understanding he established the heavens' (Prov. 3:19), and it is written, 'By his knowledge the depths were broken up' (Prov. 3:20)."

XIII.

A.   Said R. Yohanan, "The Holy One, blessed be he, gives wisdom only to someone who has wisdom.

B.   "For it is said, 'It is said, 'He gives wisdom to the wise and knowledge to those who know understanding' (Dan. 2:21)."

C.   R. Tahalipa, who comes from the West, heard this and stated it before R. Abbahu.

D.   He said to him, "You derive the proof-text from that passage, and we derive the proof-text from the following verse of Scripture, 'In the hearts of all that are wise-hearted I have put wisdom' (Ex. 31:6)."

XIV.

A.   Said R. Hisda, "Any dream but not one about a fast."

B.   And said R. Hisda, "A dream left without interpretation is like a letter left unread."

C.   And said R. Hisda, "A good dream is never fully realized, and a bad dream is never fully realized."

D.   And said R. Hisda, "A bad dream is better than a good dream."

E.   And said R. Hisda, "As to a bad dream, the sadness that it causes is enough for it, and as to a happy dream, the pleasure that it causes is enough for it. [Simon, p. 337, n. 6: There is no need for them to be fulfilled.]"

F.   Said R. Joseph, "As to a good dream, even for me [a blind man] the pleasure caused by such a dream [Simon:] nullifies it."

G. And said R. Hisda, "A bad dream is harder to take than a flogging, for it is said, 'God has so made it that men should fear before him' (Qoh. 3:14), in which regard Rabbah b. b. Hana said in the name of R. Yohanan, 'This speaks of a bad dream.'"

XV.

A. "The prophet who has a dream let him tell a dream, and he who has my word let him faithfully speak my word. What has straw got to do with wheat, says the Lord" (Jer. 23:28).

B. What have straw and wheat got to do with a dream?

C. But, said R. Yohanan in the name of R. Simeon b. Yohai, "Just as it is not possible to have wheat without straw, so it is not possible to have dreams without little nonsense."

D. Said R. Berekhiah, "As to a dream, even though part of it may come true, the whole of it will never come true.

E. "How do we know it? From the case of Joseph, for it is written, 'And behold, the sun and the moon [and eleven stars bowed down to me]' (Gen. 37:9).

F. [55B] "But at that time his mother was no longer alive [so the moon was absent]."

G. Said R. Levi, "A person should always keep the hope that a good dream [will come true], even for twenty-two years.

H. "How do we know it? It is from the case of Joseph.

I. "For it is written, 'These are the generations of Jacob. Joseph was seventeen years old' (Gen. 37:11).

J. "And it is written, 'And Joseph was thirty years old when he stood before Pharaoh' (Gen. 41:46).

K. "How many years are there from seventeen to thirty? It is thirteen. Then there were the seven years of plenty and the two of famine, thus twenty-two in all [until the brothers came and bowed down before Joseph]."

XVI.

A. Said R. Huna, "To a good person a good dream is not shown, and to a bad person, a bad one."

B. It has been taught along these same lines on Tannaite authority:

C. In David's entire life he did not see a good dream, and in Ahitophel's entire life he never saw a bad one.

D. But has it not been written, "There shall no evil befall you" (Ps. 91:10)? And in this connection, said R. Hisda said R. Jeremiah bar Abba, "It is that you will not be disturbed either by bad dreams or by bad fantasies."

E. "Neither shall any plague come near to your tent" (Ps. 91:10). [This means that] when you come home from a trip you will never find that your wife may be in doubt as to whether or not she is menstruating.

F. [Reverting to the matter of David, the point is that] while he does not see [bad dream about himself], others may see a bad one [about him].

G. And if a person never sees a bad dream about himself, is this a good thing?

H. And has not R. Zeira said, "Whoever sleeps for seven successive days without a seeing a dream is called wicked,

I. "for it is said, 'He shall abide satisfied, he shall not be visited by evil' (Prov. 19:23) -- do not read the word as 'satisfied' but rather as 'seven'"?

J. But this is the sense of the matter: One may see but he does not [later on] know what he has seen.

XVII.

A. Said R. Huna bar Ammi said R. Pedat said R. Yohanan, "He who has a dream and is upset about it should go and seek an interpretation of the dream before three people."

B. Should he indeed have it interpreted? And has not R. Hisda said, "A dream left uninterpreted is like a letter left unread"?

C. But rather I should repeat the matter as, "He should have the dream improved in the presence of three."

D. [How so?] Let him bring three people and tell them, "I saw a good dream."

E. And they will then say to him, "It is indeed good and may it be good, and may the All-Merciful make it good, seven times may they make a decree for you for good from him, so that it may be good, and it should be good." And let them repeat three verses of Scripture with the word "turn," three with the word "redeem," and three with the word "peace."

F. Three with the word "Turn:"

G. "You turned for me my mourning into dancing, you loosened my sack-cloth and girded me with gladness" (Ps. 30:12).

H. "Then shall the virgin rejoice in the dance and the young men and the old together, for I will turn their mourning into joy and comfort them and make them rejoice from their sorrow" (Jer. 31:13).

I. "Nevertheless the Lord your God would not hearken to Balaam, but the Lord your God turned the curse into a blessing for you" (Deut. 23:6).

J. Three verses with the word redeem:

K. "He has redeemed my soul in peace, so that none came near me" (Ps. 55:19).

L. "And the redeemed of the Lord shall return and come with singing unto Zion... and sorrow and sighing shall flee away" (Is. 35:10).

M. "And the people said to Saul, Shall Jonathan die who has wrought this great salvation in Israel? So the people redeemed Jonathan, that he died not" (1 Sam. 14:45).

N. Three with the word "peace:"

O. "Peace, peace to him who is far off and to him that is near, says the Lord who creates the fruit of the lips, and I will heal him" (Is. 57:19).

P. "Then the spirit clothed Amasai who was chief of the captains: We are yours, David, and on your side, O son of Jesse: Peace, peace be to you and peace be to your helpers, for your God helps you" (1 Chr. 12:19).

Q. "Thus you shall say, All hail! and peace be both to you and peace be to your house and peace be to all that you have" (1 Sam. 25:6),

XVIII.

A. Amemar, Mar Zutra, and R. Ashi were in session together. They said, "Let each one of us say something that the others have not heard."

B. One of them commenced, saying, "If someone has seen a dream and does not know what he saw, let him stand before the priests at the time that they spread out their hands [in the priestly blessing] and say this prayer, 'Lord of the world, I belong to you, and my dreams belong to you. I dreamed a dream, and I do not know what it is.

C. "'Whether it is a dream that I myself dreamed about myself, or whether it is a dream that my friends have dreamed about me, or whether I have had a dream about others, if they are good dreams, make them as strong and effective as the dreams of Joseph. And if they need healing, heal them as the waters of Marah were healed by Moses, our master, as Miriam was healed from her saraat, as Hezekiah was healed from his ailment, and as the water of Jericho was healed by Elisha.

D. "'And just as you turned the wicked Balaam's curse into a blessing, so turn all of my dreams into good for me.'

E. "And let him complete this prayer along with the priests, so that the community will respond, 'Amen.'

F. "And if he cannot do it this way, let him say the following: 'He who is mighty on high, dwelling in strength, you are peace and your name is peace. May it please you to give peace to us.'"

G. The second commenced by saying, "He who goes somewhere and fears on account of the evil eye should take the thumb of his right hand in his left hand and the thumb of his left hand in his right hand and say, 'I, Mr. So-and-so, son of So-and-so, come from the seed of Joseph, over which the evil eye has no power.'"

H. For it is said, "Joseph is a fruitful vine, a fruitful vine by a fountain" (Gen. 39:22). Do not read the words "by a fountain" but "overcoming the evil eye."

I. R. Yose bar Hanina said, "The proof derives from the following verse: 'And let them grow many, like fish in the midst of the earth' (Gen. 48:16).

J. "Just as, in the case of fish in the sea, water covers them so that the evil eye has no control over them, so the seed of Joseph is such that the evil eye has no control over them."

K. [Continuing where we left off:] "And if the man is afraid of his own evil eye, [Simon:] he should look at the side of his left nostril."

L. The third commenced by saying, "If someone gets sick, on the first day [of his sickness] he should not tell anyone, so as not to have bad luck.

M. "From that point onward, let him tell people."

N. That conforms to the practice of Raba. When he was sick, on the first day he would not tell anyone. From that point he would tell his servant, "Go out and tell people, 'Raba is sick. Whoever loves him should pray for mercy for him. And whoever hates him should rejoice over him.'"

O. For it is written, "Rejoice not when your enemy falls, and let not your heart be glad when he stumbles, lest the Lord see it and it displease him, and he turn away his wrath from him" (Prov. 24:17).

XIX.

A.   When Samuel would have a bad dream, he would say, "Dreams speak falsely" (Zech. 10:2).

B.   When he had a good dream, he would say, "Do dreams speak falsely? For it is written, 'I speak with him in a dream' (Num. 12:6)."

C.   Raba contrasted these two verses: "'I speak with him in a dream' (Num. 12:6), but it also is written, 'Dreams speak falsely' (Zech. 10:2).

D.   "But [Raba said] there is no contradiction. In the one case we speak of a message in a dream brought by an angel, in the other one brought by a shade."

XX.

A.   Said R. Bizna bar Zabeda, said R. Aqiba, said R. Paneda, said R. Nahum, said R. Birim in the name of a sage, and who is it? it is R. Benaah, "There were twenty-four dream-interpreters in Jerusalem.

B.   "Once I had a dream and I went to each one of them, and what one of them said by way of interpretation did not correspond to what the next one told me, but all of them came true for me.

C.   "That serves to illustrate what is said: 'All dreams accord with what people have to say about them.'"

D.   Is it the case that the view that all things follow what is said in interpretation of them rests upon the Scripture?

E.   Indeed so, in accord with what R. Eleazar said, for R. Eleazar said, "How do we know [on the basis of Scripture] that all dreams accord with what people have to say about them?

F.   "For it is said, 'And it came to pass, as he interpreted the dreams to us, so it was' (Gen. 41:13)."

G.   Said Raba, "That is the case if the interpretation of the dream has something to do with the dream,

H.   "as it is said, 'To each man according to his dream he did interpret' (Gen. 41:12)."

I.   "When the chief baker saw that the interpretation was good" (Gen. 40:16):

J.   How did he know that it was good?

K.   Said R. Eleazar, "This teaches that to each of them was shown both his own dream and the interpretation of the dream of his fellow."

XXI.

A.   Said R. Yohanan, "If someone got up and a verse of Scripture came to mind [his mouth], lo, this constitutes a minor form of prophecy."

B.   And R. Yohanan said, "Three dreams come true:

C.   "A dream that one has in the morning, and a dream that someone's friend had about him, and a dream that is interpreted through a dream."

D.   Some say, "Also a dream that comes again, as it says, 'And for that the dream was doubled to Pharaoh twice' (Gen. 41:32)."

XXII.

A.   Said R. Samuel bar Nahmani said R. Jonathan, "What a man is shown [in a dream] is only his own fantasy [Simon: what is suggested by his own thoughts].

B.   "For it is said, 'As for you, O King, your thoughts come into your mind upon your bed' (Dan. 2:29).

C.   "If you prefer, I offer proof from the following verse: 'That you may know the thoughts of your heart' (Den. 2:30)."

D.   Said Raba, "You may know that that is so, for people are not shown in dreams [such impossibilities as] either a golden palm tree or an elephant going through the eye of a needle."

XXIII.

A.   [56A] Said Caesar to R. Joshua b. Hananiah, "You say that you are very smart. Tell me what I shall see in my dream."

B.   He said to him, "You will see that the Persians are making you do forced labor, humiliating you, and making you feed unclean animals with a crook of gold."

C.   He thought about it all day long, and at night he saw it.

XXIV.

A.   Said King Shapur to Samuel, "You say that you are very smart. Tell me what I am going to see in my dream."

B.   He said to him, "You will see that the Romans are coming, and they will capture you and make you grind date-pits in a mill of gold."

C.   He thought about it all day long and at night, he saw it.

XXV.

A.   Bar Hedya was a dream-interpreter. If someone gave him a fee, he would interpret his dream in a good way, and if someone did not pay him a fee, he interpreted it in a bad way.

B.   Abayye and Raba had dreams. Abayye paid him a fee of a _zuz_, and Raba did not give him anything.

C.   They said to him, "In our dream we recited the verse, 'Your ox shall be slain before your eyes' (Deut. 28:31)."

D.   To Raba he said, "You will go bankrupt and will not even want to eat because of depression."

E.   To Abayye he said, "You will make a killing, and you will not want to eat because of excitement."

F.   They said to him, "We recited [in our dreams] the verse, 'You shall beget sons and daughters but they will not be yours' (Deut. 28:41)."

G.   To Raba he said that it is an unfavorable sign.

H.   To Abayye he said, "Your sons and daughters will be many. Your daughters will get married to others and it will seem to you as if they go into captivity."

I.   "We recited, 'Your sons and your daughters will be given to another people' (Deut. 28:32)."

J.   To Abayye he said, "Your sons and daughters will be many. You will want to marry them to your relations, and your wife will want to marry them off to hers, and she will force you to give them to her relations, so that it will seem as if it is to another people."

K.   To Raba he said, "Your wife will die, and your sons and daughters will fall into the hands of another woman [when you remarry]."

L.   For Raba said R. Jeremiah bar Abba said Rab said, "What is the meaning of the verse of Scripture, 'Your sons and your daughters will be given to another people' (Deut. 23:32)?

M.   "This speaks of a step-mother."

N.   "We recited in our dreams: 'Go your way, eat your bread with joy' (Qoh. 9:7)."

O.   To Abayye he said, "You will make a killing and eat and drink and recite that verse out of great joy."

P.   To Raba he said, "You will go bankrupt. You will

.   "We recited this verse: 'You shall carry much seed out into the field [and gather little in, for the locusts will consume it]' (Deut. 28:38)."

R.   To Abayye he cited the first half of the verse, to Raba, the second half.

S.   "We recited, 'You shall have olive trees throughout your borders [but you shall not anoint yourself]' (Deut. 28:40)."

T.   To Abayye he cited the first half of the verse, to Raba the second half.

U.   "We recited, 'And all the peoples of the earth shall see that the name of the Lord is called upon you' (Deut. 28:10)."

V.   To Abayye he said, "Your reputation will go forth as head of a court, and respect for you will fall upon everybody."

W.   To Raba he said, "The royal treasury will be broken into, and you will be arrested as a thief, and everyone will make an argument a fortiori based upon you [Simon: If Raba is suspect, how much more so are we]."

X.   The next day the royal treasury was broken into, and they came and arrested Raba.

Y.   They said to [Bar Hedya], "We saw lettuce on the mouth of the jar."

Z.   To Abayye he said, "Your profits will double like lettuce."

AA. To Raba he said, "Your business will be as bitter as lettuce."

BB. They said to him, "We saw meat on the mouth of the jar."

CC. To Abayye he said, "Your wine will be sweet, and everyone will come to buy meat and wine from you."

DD. To Raba he said, "Your wine will turn, and everyone will come to buy meat to eat with it [as a cheap condiment]."

EE. They said, "We saw a cask hanging on a palm."

FF. To Abayye he said, "Your business will thrive like a palm."

GG. To Raba he said, "Your merchandise will be as sweet as dates [to the customers, who will find it very cheap]."

HH. They said to him, "We saw a pomegranate growing on the mouth of a jar."

II. To Abayye he said, "Your goods will fetch high prices like pomegranates."

JJ. To Raba he said, "Your merchandise will turn stale, like a [dry] pomegranate."

KK. They said to him, "We saw a cask fall into a pit,"

LL. To Abayye he said, "Your merchandise will fetch a good market, as in the saying, 'The madder has fallen into a well and cannot be found. [Simon, p. 344, n. 4: Your goods will be in demand like something which has fallen into a pit.]"

MM. To Raba he said, "Your merchandise will spoil and be thrown into a pit."

NN. They said to him, "We saw a young ass standing by our pillow and braying."

OO. To Abayye he said, "You will become king and an Amora will stand at your side [to repeat in a loud voice what you say]."

PP. To Raba he said, "The words, 'The first born of an ass' [a passage written in the phylacteries] have been erased from your phylactery."

QQ. [Raba then] said to him, "I examined them, and those words are there."

RR. He said to him, "The letter W from the word '[first born of] an ass' certainly has been erased from your phylactery."

SS. In the end Raba came by himself to [Bar Hedya]. He said to him, "I saw that the outer door fell down."

TT. He said to him, "Your wife will die."

UU. He said to him, "I saw that my front and back teeth fell out."

VV. He said to him, "Your sons and daughters will die."

WW. He said to him, "I saw two pigeons flying away."

XX. He said to him, "You will divorce two wives."

YY. He said to him, "I saw two turnip tops."

ZZ. He said to him, "You will be hit twice with a club."

AAA. That day Raba went and stayed at the session of the school house all day long. He came upon two blind men fighting with one another. Raba went to separate them, and they hit Raba twice. They were going to hit him again, but he said, "Two are enough. That is all that I saw in my dream."

BBB. In the end Raba came and paid [Bar Hedya] a fee. He said to him, "I saw a wall fall down."

CCC. He said to him, "Goods without limit you will get."

DDD. He said to him, "I saw Abayye's house fall down and get covered with dirt."

EEE. He said to him, "Abayye will die and his entire court will come to you."

FFF. He said to him, "I saw my house fall down and everybody came and took a brick."

GGG. He said to him, "Your traditions will be scattered [and known] everywhere."

HHH. He said to him, "I saw that my skull was split open and my brains fell out."

III. He said to him, "The stuffing will come out of your pillow."

JJJ. He said to him, "In my dream I recited the Hallel-Psalms for [the exodus from] Egypt."

KKK. He said to him, "A miracle will happen to you."

LLL. [Bar Hedya] was going along with [Raba] on a boat. [Bar Hedya] said [to himself], "What business do I have traveling with someone for whom a miracle will be done? [It will be necessary to save us all, but only he will be saved]."

MMM. As he got off the boat, a scroll fell from his hand. Raba found it and saw that written in it were the words, "All dreams accord with the interpretation [that someone gives to them]."

NNN. He said, "Wicked one! It was your fault that the dreams came true as they did, and you made all this trouble for us. I forgive you for everything except for what happened to the daughter of R. Hisda [my wife, who died on your account]. May it be God's will that that man [you] be handed over to the government, and that the government have no pity for you."

OOO. He said, "What shall I do? It is a tradition that a curse of a sage, even if it is for nothing, comes true. That is all the more so the case with Raba's curse, for he cursed me quite justly."

PPP. He said, "I'll go and escape into exile. For a master has said, 'Exile atones for sin.'"

QQQ. He went and into exile, to Roman territory. He went and sat at the door of the [Simon:] keeper of the king's wardrobe. The wardrobe keeper had a dream. He said to him, "I had a dream that a needle pricked my finger."

RRR. He said to him, "Pay me a zuz."

SSS. The other would not hand it over to him, so he would not say anything to him.

TTT. He said to him, "I saw in a dream that a worm fell between my two fingers."

UUU. He said to him, "Pay me a zuz."

VVV. The other would not hand it over to him, so he would not say anything to him.

WWW. He said to him, "I saw in a dream that a worm fell in my hand."

XXX. He said to him, "Worms have fallen all over the silks [of the wardrobe]."

YYY. The word spread throughout the palace, and they took the wardrobe keeper to kill him. He said to them, "Why are you taking me? You should take the one who knew what was going on and said nothing."

ZZZ. They took Bar Hedya and said to him, "On account of your zuz the king's silks have been ruined [56B]. They tied together two cedar trees with a rope. They tied one of his legs to one cedar and the other to the other one. Then they cut the cedars loose, and he split into two. Each tree popped up, and he lost his head and split into two.

XXVI.

A. Ben Dama, son of R. Ishmael's sister, asked R. Ishmael, "I saw in a dream that both my jaws fell out."

B. He said to him, "Two Roman officers have conspired against you, but they have died."

XXVII.

A. Said Bar Qappara to Rabbi, "I saw in a dream that my nose fell off."

B. He said to him, "Divine wrath has gone away from you."

C. He said to him, "I saw both my hands cut off."

D. He said to him, "You will not need to work for a living."

E. He said to him, "I saw both my legs cut off."

F. He said to him, "You'll be riding a horse."

G. "I saw [in my dream] people saying to me, 'You're going to die in Adar and you will never see Nisan.'"

H. He said to him, "You will die full of honor [adruta] and not suffer temptation [nisayon]."

XXVII.

A. A certain min said to R. Ishmael, "I saw in my dream that I was pouring oil into olives."

B. He said to him, "He has had sexual relations with his mother."

C. He said to him, "I saw that I picked a star."

D. He said to him, "You have stolen an Israelite."

E. He said to him, "I saw that I swallowed a star."

F. He said to him, "You have sold an Israelite and consumed the proceeds."

G. He said to him, "I saw that my eyes were kissing one another."

H. He said to him, "He has had sexual relations with his sister."

I. He said to him, "I saw that I kissed the moon."

J. He said to him, "He has had sexual relations with the wife of an Israelite."

K. He said to him, "I saw that I was walking along in the shade of a myrtle."

L. He said to him, "He has had sexual relations with a betrothed girl."

M. He said to him, "I saw shade above me and yet also below me."

N. He said to him, "You have had unnatural sexual relations."

O. He said to him, "I saw ravens hovering around my bed."

P. He said to him, "Your wife has played the whore with many men."

Q. He said to him, "I saw pigeons hovering around my bed."

R. He said to him, "You have made many women unclean."

S. He said to him, "I saw that I held two pigeons and they flew off."

T. He said to him, "You married two women and sent them off without a writ of divorce."

U. He said to him, "I saw that I was shelling eggs."

V. He said to him, "You have been stripping the dead."

W. He said to him, "Everything you have said in fact applies to me, except for that one item, which does not apply."

X. Meanwhile a woman came along and said to him, "This cloak which you are wearing belonged to Mr. So-and-so, who died. You have stripped it from him."

Y. He said to him, "I saw that people said to me, 'Your father has left you property in Cappadocia.'"

Z. He said to me, "Do you have property in Cappadocia?

AA. He said to him, "No."

BB. "Has your father ever gone to Cappadocia?"

CC. He said to him, "No."

DD. "If so then the kappa stands for a beam, and dika stands for ten. Go and look at the beam that stands at the head of ten, for it is full of money."

EE. He went and found it full of money.

XXVIII.

A. Said R. Hanina, "He who sees a well in a dream will see peace.

B.   "For it is said, 'And Isaac's servants dug in the valley and there found a well of living water' (Gen. 26:19)."

C.   R. Nathan says, "It means he has found Torah.

D.   "For it is said, 'For whoever finds me finds life' (Prov. 8:35), and here it says, 'A well of living water' (Gen. 26:19)."

E.   Raba said, "It means, literally, life."

XXIX.

A.   Said R. Hanan, "Three signs of peace [in a dream] are these: seeing a river, a bird, and a pot.

B.   "A river: 'Behold I will extend peace to her like a river' (Is. 66:12).

C.   "A bird: 'As birds hovering, so will the Lord of hosts protect Jerusalem' (Is. 31:5).

D.   "A pot: 'Lord, you will establish peace for us' (Is. 26:12)."

E.   Said R. Hanina, "But that statement applies to seeing in a dream a pot in which there is no meat: 'They chop them in pieces, as that which is in the pot and as flesh within the cauldron' (Mic. 3:3)."

XXX.

A.   Said R. Joshua b. Levi, "He who in a dream sees a river, when he gets up should say, 'Behold I will extend peace to her like a river' (Is. 66:12). [This he should do] lest some other verse should come to mind before that one, such as, 'For distress will come in like a river' (Is. 59:19).

B.   "He who in a dream sees a bird, when he gets up should say, 'As birds hovering, so will the Lord of hosts protect' (Is. 31:5). [This he should do] lest some other verse should come to mind before that one, such as, 'As a bird that wanders from her nest, so is a man who wanders from his place' (Prov. 27:8).

C.   "He who in a dream sees a pot, when he gets up should say, 'Lord, you will establish peace for us' (Is. 26:12), lest some other verse should come to mind before that one, such as 'Set on the pot, set it on' (Ez. 24:3).

D.   "He who in a dream sees grapes, when he gets up should say, 'I found Israel like grapes in the wilderness' (Hos. 9:10), lest some other verse should come to mind before that one, such as, 'Their grapes are grapes of wrath' (Deut. 32:32).

E.   "He who in a dream sees a mountain, when he gets up should say, 'How beautiful upon the mountains are the feet of the messenger of good tidings' (Is. 52:7), lest some other verse should come to mind before that one, such as, 'For the mountains will I take up a weeping and wailing' (Jer. 9:9).

F.   "He who in a dream sees a horn, when he gets up should say, 'And it shall come to pass in that day that a great horn shall be blown' (Is. 27:13), lest some other verse should come to mind before that one, such as, 'Blow you the horn of Gibeah' (Hos. 5:8).

G.   "He who in a dream sees a dog, when he gets up should say, 'But against any of the children of Israel shall not a dog whet his tongue' (Ex. 11:7), lest some other verse should come to mind before that one, such as, 'Yes, the dogs are greedy' (Is. 56:11).

H. "He who in a dream sees a lion, when he gets up should say, 'The lion has roared, who will not fear' (Amos. 3:8), lest another verse should come to mind first, such as, 'A lion is gone up from his thicket' (Jer. 4:7).

I. "He who in a dream sees [himself] shaving, when he gets up should say, 'And Joseph shaved himself and changed his raiment' (Gen. 41:14), lest another verse should come to mind before that one, such as, 'If I be shaven, then my strength will go from me' (Jud. 16:17).

J. "He who in a dream sees a well, when he gets up should say, 'A well of living waters' (Song. 4:15), lest another verse should come to mind first, such as, 'As a cistern wells with her waters, so she wells with her wickedness' (Jer. 6:7).

K. "He who in a dream sees a reed, when he gets up should say, 'A bruised reed shall he not break' (Is. 52:3), lest another verse should come to mind first, such as, 'Behold you rely upon the staff of this bruised reed' (Is. 36:6).

XXXI.

A. Our rabbis have taught on Tannaite authority:

B. He who in a dream sees a reed should hope for wisdom, as it says, "Get [Using the letters of the word for reed] wisdom" (Prov. 4:5).

C. [If he sees a number of] reeds, he may hope for understanding, as it says, "With all your getting get understanding" (Prov. 4:7).

D. Said R. Zira, "A pumpkin, a palm-heart, wax, and a reed -- all of them are good signs in a dream."

E. It has been taught on Tannaite authority:

F. Only one who fears heaven with all his power is shown a pumpkin in his dream.

G. He who in a dream sees an ox, when he gets up should say, "His firstling bullock, majesty is his" (Deut. 33:17), lest another verse come to mind first, such as, "If an ox gore a man" (Ex. 21:28).

XXXII.

A. Our rabbis have taught on Tannaite authority:

B. Five things have been stated with regard to an ox [seen in a dream]:

C. He who [in his dream] is eating from its flesh will get rich.

D. [If he is] gored by the ox [in his dream], he will have sons who are great "gorers" in Torah-study.

E. [If the ox] bites him, it is a sign that troubles will come upon him.

F. [If the ox] kicks him, it is a sign that a long journey is prepared for him.

G. [If he rode] on it, he will rise to greatness.

H. But has it not been taught on Tannaite authority:

I. "If he [dreamed that he] rode on it, it is a sign that he will die"?

J. There is no contradiction, for in the one case, he dreams that he is riding on the ox, and in the other, the ox is riding on him.

XXXIII.

A. He who sees an ass in a dream may hope for salvation,

B. for it is said, "Behold your king comes to you, he is triumphant and victorious, lowly and riding on an ass" (Zech. 9:9).

C. He who sees a cat in a dream, in a place in which they call it a shunra, will find that a lovely song [shirah naah] has been prepared for him. If it is in a place where it is called shinra, a bad change has been prepared for him.

D. He who sees grapes in a dream, if they are white, whether in season or not in season, will find it is a good sign.

E. If they are black, if they are in season, it is a good sign, but not in season, it is a bad sign.

F. He who sees a white horse, whether ambling or galloping, will find that it is a good sign for him.

G. [If it is] a red horse, if it is ambling, it is a good sign for him. If it is galloping, it is a bad sign for him.

H. He who sees Ishmael in a dream will find that his prayer is heard.

I. But that is, in particular, Ishmael, the son of Abraham. But if it is an ordinary Tai [Arab], that is not the case.

J. He who sees a camel in a dream will find that the penalty of death has been imposed upon him from Heaven, but he has been saved from it.

K. Said R. Hama b. R. Hanina, "What is the proof-text? 'I will go down with you to Egypt and I will also surely bring you up again' (Gen. 46:4)."

L. R. Nahman bar Isaac said, "Proof is from the following: 'The Lord also has put away your sin, you will not die' (2 Sam. 12:13)."

M. He who sees Phineas in a dream will find that a miracle is done for him.

N. He who sees an elephant (pil) in a dream will find that wonders (pilaot) will be done for him.

O. If he sees elephants, he will find that wonderful miracles are going to be done for him.

P. And has it not been taught on Tannaite authority:

Q. "All sorts of wild beasts are good signs in a dream except for an elephant and an ape"?

R. There is no contradiction, [57A] for the one speaks of a saddled elephant, the other an elephant without a saddle.

S. He who sees Huna in a dream will find that a miracle is done for him.

T. He who sees Hanina, Hanania, or Yohanan will find that wonderful miracles are done for him.

U. He who sees a lamentation in a dream will find that from Heaven he has been shown pity and been redeemed. But that is the case only if it is in writing.

V. He who [in a dream] answers, "May the Great Name be blessed" may be assured that he is going to be party to the world to come.

W. He who [in a dream] recites the Shema is worthy of having the Presence of God rest upon him, though his generation does not have the merit that such a thing [should happen in its time].

X. He who puts on phylacteries in a dream may look forward to greatness,

Y. for it is said, "And all the peoples of the earth shall see that the name of the Lord is called upon you, and they shall fear you" (Deut. 28:10).

Z.   And in this connection it has been taught on Tannaite authority:

AA.   R. Eliezer the Great says, "This refers to the phylacteries that one puts on the head."

BB.   He who in a dream sees himself praying will find that that is a good sign for him.

CC.   But that is so only if in the dream he did not complete the prayer.

DD.   "He who in a dream has sexual relations with his mother may expect to come to understanding.

EE.   For it is said, "Yes, you shall call understanding mother" (Prov. 2:3).

FF.   He who has sexual relations with a betrothed girl in a dream may expect to master Torah.

GG.   For it is said, "Moses commanded us a law an inheritance of the congregation of Jacob" (Deut. 33:4). Do not read the word for "inheritance" as such but rather read it as "betrothed."

HH.   He who in a dream has sexual relations with his sister may expect to attain wisdom, for it is said, "Say to wisdom, You are my sister" (Prov. 7:4).

II.   He who in a dream has sexual relations with a married woman may be assured that he has a share in the world to come.

JJ.   But that principle applies if he did not know her, and if he did not fantasize about her in the prior evening.

XXXIV.

A.   Said R. Hiyya bar Abba, "He who sees wheat in a dream will see peace.

B.   "For it is said, 'He makes your borders peace, he gives you in plenty the fat of wheat' (Ps. 147:14).

C.   "If one sees barley, his sins will leave.

D.   "For it is said, 'Your iniquity is taken away and your sin expiated' (Is. 6:7)."

E.   Said R. Zira, "I did not go up from Babylonia to the Land of Israel until in a dream I saw barley."

F.   [Hiyya continues,] "He who in a dream sees a vine that is laden [will find that] his wife will not abort.

G.   "For it is said, 'Your wife shall be as a fruitful vine' (Ps. 128:3).

H.   "[He who in a dream sees] a choice vine may expect [to witness the coming of] the Messiah.

I.   "For it is said, 'Binding his foal to the vine and his ass's colt to a choice vine' (Gen. 49:11).

J.   "He who in a dream sees a fig will find that his knowledge of Torah will be fully protected within him.

K.   "For it is said, 'He who keeps the fig tree shall eat the fruit thereof' (Prov. 27:18).

L.   "He who in a dream sees pomegranates, if they are small, will find that his trading will prove as fruitful as a pomegranate. If they are large, he will find that his trading will increase like a pomegranate. If they are split open, if he is a disciple of a sage, he may hope for knowledge of Torah.

M.   "For it is said, 'I would cause you to drink of spiced wine, of the juice of my pomegranate' (Song 8:2).

N.   "If he is an ordinary person, he may look forward to the accomplishment of religious duties.

O.   "For it is said, 'Your temples are like a pomegranate split open' (Song 4:3)."

P.   What is the meaning of "your temples"?

Q.   Even the empty heads among you will be full of religious deeds like a pomegranate.

R.   [Hiyya continues,] "He who in a dream sees olives, if they are small, may expect that his business dealings will be fruitful and multiply and endure like olives. And that is the case if he sees the fruit of olive trees. But if he sees olive <u>trees</u>, he will have many sons,

S.   "For it is said, 'Your children like olive plants round about your table' (Ps. 128:3)."

T.   There are those who say, "He who sees an olive in a dream will find that a good name about him will circulate.

U.   "For it is said, 'The Lord called your name a leafy olive-tree, fair and goodly fruit' (Jer. 11:6)."

V.   [Hiyya continues,] "He who in a dream sees olive oil may expect to attain the light of Torah-learning.

W.   "For it is said, 'That they bring you pure olive oil beaten for the light' (Ex. 27:20).

X.   "He who in a dream sees date trees may expect that his sins have been brought to an end.

Y.   "For it says, 'The punishment of your sin is accomplished, O daughter of Zion' (Lam. 4:22)."

XXXV.

A.   Said R. Joseph, "He who in a dream sees a goat may expect that the year will be blessed for him. [If he sees] goats, he may expect that several years will be blessed for him.

B.   "For it is said, 'And there will be goat's milk enough for your food' (Prov. 27:27).

C.   "He who in a dream sees a myrtle will find that his property will bring him success, and if he has no property, an inheritance will fall to him from some other source."

D.   Said Ulla, and some say it was repeated in a Tannaite statement, "And that rule applies only if he sees it on its stem."

E.   [Joseph continues,] "He who in a dream sees a pomegranate will find that he is honored before his creator.

F.   "For it says, 'The fruit of citrons, branches of palm trees' (Lev. 23:40).

G.   "He who in a dream sees a palm branch [may know] that he is completely sincere in relationship to his father in heaven.

H.   "He who in a dream sees a goose may expect to attain wisdom.

I.   "For it is said, 'Wisdom cries aloud in the street' (Prov. 1:20).

J.   "[And he who in a dream sees] that he has sexual relations [with a goose] will become the head of a session."

K.   Said R. Ashi, "I saw one in a dream and had sexual relations with it and I rose to a high position."

L. [Joseph continues,] "He who in a dream sees a rooster may look forward to having a male child. If he sees roosters, he may look forward to male children. If he sees hens, he may look forward to a fine garden and rejoicing.

M. "He who in a dream sees eggs will find [Simon that] his petition remains in suspense [Simon, p. 353, n. 10: like the contents of the egg, of which one is doubtful as long as the shell is unbroken].

N. "If the eggs are broken, it means that his petition has been granted, and so is the rule for nuts, cucumbers, all sorts of glass utensils, and everything of the same sort that will break.

O. "[He who in a dream sees himself] entering a town will find that his desires have been carried out.

P. "For it is said, 'And he led them to their desired haven' (Ps. 107:30).

Q. "He who in a dream shaves his head will find that it is a good omen for him.

R. "If it is his head and his beard, then it is a good omen for him and his entire family.

S. "He who [in a dream] is sitting in a small boat, it means that a good name will circulate for him. If it is in a big boat, the good name will be both for himself and for his entire family.

T. "And that is the case if it is on the high sea.

U. "He who dreams that he is defecating will find that it is a good omen for him.

V. "For it is said, 'He who is bent down shall speedily be loosed' (Is. 51:14).

W. "But that is the case only if he in his dream did not wipe himself.

X. "He who in a dream sees that he goes up to a roof will go up to a high position. If he sees that he goes down, it means he will go down from his high position."

Y. Both Abayye and Raba say, "Once one has gone up, he has gone up [and will not come down]."

Z. [Joseph continues,] "He who in a dream sees himself tearing his clothes will find that a decree against him has been torn up.

AA. "He who in a dream is standing naked, if it is in Babylonia, may know that he is standing without sin.

BB. "If it is in the land of Israel, however, it means that he will be naked of religious duties.

CC. "He who in a dream is arrested by the police may know that protection has been arranged for him.

DD. "If he was put into a neck-iron, it means that additional protection has been arranged for him.

EE. "That is the case if he dreams of a neck-iron. But if he dreams of rope in general, that is not the case.

FF. "He who in a dream goes into a swamp -- it means he will be made head of a session.

GG. "If he goes into a forest, it means he will be made head of those who attend the annual sessions [as mature sages]."

XXXVI.

A. R. Pappa and R. Huna, son of R. Joshua, gave [things] in dreams. R. Pappa saw that he went into a swamp. He was made head of the session.

B.   R. Huna, son of R. Joshua, saw that he went into a forest. He became head of those who attend the annual sessions.

C.   There are those who say that both of them saw that they went into a swamp.

D.   But R. Pappa, who [saw himself] carrying a drum [Simon, p. 354, n. 8: such as was used for announcing the approach of a man of distinction] was made head of the session.

E.   R. Huna, son of R. Joshua, who [in his dream] was not carrying a drum, was made head of those who attend the annual sessions.

F.   Said R. Ashi, "I dreamt that I went into a swamp and was carrying a drum and made a racket with it."

XXXVII.

A.   A Tannaite authority repeated the following tradition before R. Nahman bar Isaac, "He who in a dream sees himself letting blood may know that his sins have been forgiven for him."

B.   But has it not been taught on Tannaite authority: "... that his sins are laid out [and recorded]"?

C.   What is the sense of "laid out"? It is, "laid out so as to be forgiven."

XXXVIII.

A.   A Tannaite authority repeated the following tradition before R. Sheshet: "He who in a dream sees a snake may know that his living has been prepared for him.

B.   "If he was bitten, it means that his living has been doubled for him.

C.   "If he killed the snake, it means that his living has been lost."

D.   Said R. Sheshet to him, "All the more so it must mean that his living has been doubled for him."

E.   But that is not the case. R. Sheshet was the one who saw a snake in his dream, and he killed it.

XXXIX.

A.   A Tannaite authority repeated the following tradition before R. Yohanan, "Seeing all sorts of drinks are a good omen in a dream, except for seeing wine.

B.   "There is he who in a dream drinks it and it is a good omen for him, and there is he who in a dream drinks it and it is a bad omen for him.

C.   "There is he who drinks it and it is a good omen for him, as it is said, 'Wine makes glad the heart of man' (Ps. 104:15).

D.   "There is he who drinks it and it is a bad omen for him, as it is said, 'Give strong drink to him who is ready to perish, and wine to the bitter in soul' (Prov. 31:6)."

E.   Said to him R. Yohanan, "Repeat in the following language on Tannaite authority: 'In the case of a disciple of a sage it is always a good omen for him.

F.   "'For it is said, "Come eat of my bread and drink of the wine which I have mixed" (Prov. 9:5).'"

G.   [57B] Said R. Yohanan, "If one got up in the morning and a particular verse of Scripture came to mind, lo, that is a minor mode of prophecy."

XL.

A. Our rabbis have taught on Tannaite authority:

B. There are three kings [who constitute omens if seen in dreams].

C. He who in a dream sees David may expect to attain piety, Solomon, wisdom, and Ahab, punishment.

D. There are three such prophets.

E. He who in a dream sees the book of Kings may expect to attain a high position, Ezekiel, wisdom, Isaiah, consolation, Jeremiah, punishment.

F. There are three relevant items among the larger books of the Writings.

G. He who in a dream sees the book of Psalms may look forward to attaining piety, Proverbs, wisdom, Job, punishment.

H. There are three relevant items among the smaller books of Writings.

I. He who in a dream sees the Song of Songs may look forward to attaining piety, Qohelet, wisdom, and Lamentations, punishment.

J. He who in a dream sees the scroll of Esther may know that a miracle has been carried out for him.

K. There are three sages [in this same context].

L. He who in a dream sees Rabbi may look forward to wisdom, Eleazar b. Azariah, riches, R. Ishmael b. Elisha, punishment.

M. There are three disciples of sages in this same context.

N. He who in a dream sees Ben Azzai may look forward to attaining piety, Ben Zoma, wisdom, and Aher [Elisha b. Abbuyah], punishment.

XLI.

A. Seeing in a dream all sorts of wild beasts is a good omen, except for seeing an elephant, monkey, and long-tailed ape.

B. But has not a master said, "He who in a dream sees an elephant may know that a miracle has been done for him"?

C. There is no contradiction, the one speaks of seeing an elephant that is saddled, the other, one that is not saddled.

D. Seeing all sorts of metal objects in a dream is a good omen, except for seeing a hoe, mattock, and hatchet.

E. But that is the case only if they are seen in their hafts.

F. Seeing in a dream all sorts of fruit is a good omen, except for unripe dates.

G. Seeing in a dream all sorts of vegetables is a good omen, except for turnip tops.

H. But did not Rab say, "I become rich only after I dreamed of turnip tops"?

I. When he saw them, it was with their tops.

J. Seeing in a dream any sort of color is a good omen, except for the color blue.

K. Seeing in a dream all sorts of fowl is a good omen, except for seeing the owl, horned owl, and bat.

XLII.

A. There are three things which enter the body, and from which the body gains nothing:

B. melilot, date-berries, and unripe dates.

C. There are three things which do not enter the body, but from which the body benefits:

D. washing, anointing, and exercise.

E. There are three things that are a reflection of the world to come, and these are they:

F. the Sabbath, the sun, and exercise.

G. What sort of exercise? If one should say, exercise in bed [sexual relations], lo, that weakens a person. It must then be making use of the bodily apertures.

H. There are three things that restore a person's mind: sound, sight, and smell.

I. There are three things that make a person generous in heart, and there are they: a good house, a good wife, and good clothes.

XLIII.

A. Five things are one-sixtieth [of something else], and these are they:

B. fire, honey, the Sabbath, sleeping, and dreaming.

C. Fire is one-sixtieth of Gehenna.

D. Honey is one-sixtieth of manna.

E. The Sabbath is one-sixtieth of the world to come.

F. Sleep is one-sixtieth of death.

G. Dreaming is one-sixtieth of prophecy.

XLIV.

A. Six things are a good omen for a sick person, and these are they:

B. sneezing, sweating, good bowel movements, seminal emission, sleeping, and dreaming.

C. Sneezing, as it is written, "His sneezings flash forth light" (Job 41:10).

D. Sweating, as it is written, "In the sweat of your face you shall eat bread" (Gen. 3:19).

E. Good bowel movements, as it is written, "If he that is bent down hastens to be loosed, he shall not go down dying to the pit" (Is. 51:14).

F. Seminal emission, as it is written, "Seeing seed, he will prolong his days" (Is. 53:10).

G. Sleeping, as it is written, "I should have slept, then should I have been at rest" (Job 3:13).

H. Dreaming, as it is said, "You caused me to dream and made me live" (Is. 38:16).

XLV.

A. Six things heal a sick person from his ailment, and the remedy serves as a permanent one, and these are they:

B. cabbage, beets, [Simon:] a decoction of dried poley, the maw, womb, and large lobe of the liver.

C. There are those who say, "Also small fish. And not only so, but small fish make the person fruitful and [Simon:] invigorate a man's whole body."

XLVI.

A. There are ten things that make a person sick again, and the sickness takes a severe form, and these are they:

B. eating beef, fat meat, roasted meat, fowl, roasted egg; shaving; [eating] cress, milk, cheese; and bathing.

C.   There are those who say, "Also nuts."

D.   There are those who say, "Also cucumbers."

E.   It was taught on Tannaite authority at the house of R. Ishmael "Why is it that cucumbers are called that [qishuim]? Because they are as hard [qashim] for the body as are swords."

F.   Is that the case? And has it not been written, "And the Lord said to her, Two nations are in your womb" (Gen. 25:23). Do not read the word as "nations" but as "lords," in which connection said R. Judah said Rab, "This refers to Antoninus and Rabbi, from whose table there never were absent either radishes, lettuce, or cucumbers, not in the dry season nor in the rainy season."

G.   There is no contradiction, for the one speaks of large [cucumbers], and the other of small ones.

XLVII.

A.   Our rabbis have taught on Tannaite authority:

B.   [If someone dreams that there is] a corpse in the house, it means there will be peace in the house.

C.   If he dreams that he ate and drank in the house, it is a good omen for the house.

D.   If one dreams that he took clothing from the house, it is a bad omen for the house.

E.   R. Pappa interpreted this to refer, in particular, to shoes or sandals.

F.   Whatever [in a dream one sees] a dead person removing is a good omen, except for shoes and sandals.

G.   Whatever a dead person [in a dream is seen] to bring into a house is a good omen, except for dirt and mustard.

XLVIII.

A.   One who sees a place from which idolatry was uprooted [says, "Blessed is he who uprooted idolatry from our land"] [M. 9:1B]:

B.   Our rabbis have taught on Tannaite authority:

C.   He who sees a statue of Mercury says, "Blessed is he who has granted patience to those who violate his will" [cf. T. Ber. 6:2A].

D.   He who sees a place from which an idol has been uprooted says, "Blessed is he who uprooted idolatry from our land. And just as it has been uprooted from this place, so may it be uprooted from all of the places in which Israel dwells. And return the hearts of those who serve them to your service."

E.   And abroad it is not necessary to say, "And return the hearts of those that serve them to your service," because the majority of the people there are idolators anyhow.

F.   R. Simeon b. Eleazar says, "Even abroad one has to add that language, for they are going to convert, as it is said, 'For then I will turn to the peoples a pure language' (Zeph. 3:9)." [T. Ber. 6:2B-C].

XLIX.

A.   Said R. Hamnuna, "He who sees wicked Babylon has to say these five blessings.

B.   "If he saw Babylon, he says, 'Blessed is he who has destroyed wicked Babylon.'

C.   "If he saw the palace of Nebuchadnezzar, he says, 'Blessed is he who has destroyed the palace of the wicked Nebuchadnezzar.'

D.   "If he saw the lion's den or the fiery furnace, he says, 'Blessed is he who did miracles for our fathers in this place.'

E.   "If he saw a statue of Mercury, he says, 'Blessed is he who has granted patience to those who trangress his will.'

F.   "If he saw the place used for a quarry [for dirt and stone for building elsewhere], he says, 'Blessed is he who makes a statement and does it, who makes a decree and carries it out.'"

G.   When Raba would see asses bearing dirt, would pat them on their behinds and say, "Run, righteous ones, to do the will of your Master."

H.   When Mar, son of Rabina, would come to Babylonia, he would take some dirt in his scarf and throw it outside, to carry out the verse of Scripture, "I will sweep it with the broom of destruction" (Is. 14:23).

I.   Said R. Ashi, "I had never heard this statement of R. Hamnuna, but on my own reasoning I framed and said all of these blessings."

J.   [58A] Said R. Jeremiah b. Eleazar, "When Babylonia was cursed, its neighbors were cursed, but when Samaria was cursed, its neighbors were blessed.

K.   "When Babylonia was cursed, its neighbors were cursed, as it is written, 'I will also make it a possession for the bittern and pools of water' (Is. 14:23).

L.   "But when Samaria was cursed, its neighbors were blessed, as it is written, 'Therefore I will make Samaria a heap in the field, a place for planting vineyards' (Mic. 1:6)."

M.   And R. Hamnuna said, "He who sees a large crowd of Israelites says, 'Blessed is the one who is wise in knowing secrets.'

N.   "He who sees large crowds of pagans says, 'Your mother shall be ashamed' (Jer. 50:12)."

L.

A.   Our rabbis have taught on Tannaite authority:

B.   **He who sees large crowds of Israelites says, "Blessed is he who is wise in knowing secrets.**

C.   **"For the opinions of these people are not equivalent, and they do not look alike"** [T. Ber. 6:2D-E].

D.   [When] Ben Zoma saw a crowd on steps of the Temple Mount, he said, "Blessed is he who is wise in knowing secrets. Blessed is he who created [all] these [people] to serve me."

E.   He would say, "How hard did Adam toil before he could taste a morsel [of food]: he seeded, plowed, reaped, sheaved, threshed, winnowed, separated, ground, sifted, kneaded, and baked, and only then could he eat. But I arise in the morning and find all these [foods ready] before me.

F.   "How hard did Adam toil before he could put on a garment: he sheared, bleached, separated, dyed, spun, and wove, and only then could he put it on. But I arise in the morning and find all these [garments ready] before me.

G.   "How many skilled craftsmen are industrious and rise early [to their work] at my door. And I arise in the morning and find all these [ready] before me."

H.   And so [Ben Zoma] would say, "What does a good guest say? '[May my host be remembered [by God] for good!] How much trouble did he take for me! How many kinds of wine did he bring before us! How many kinds of cuts [of meat] did he bring before us! How many kinds of cakes did he bring before me! And all the trouble that he took he took for me!'

I.   "But what does a bad guest say? How little trouble did this household take. [And what have I eaten of his?] I ate only a loaf of his bread. I drank only a cup of his wine. He went to all this trouble only to provide for his wife and children' [T. Ber. 6:2F-J].

J.   What does Scripture say about a good guest? "Remember to magnify his works, of which men have sung" (Job 36:24).

K.   And of a bad guest it is written, "Men therefore fear him [he regards not any of those who are wise of heart" (Job 37:24).

LI.

A.   And the man was an old man in the days of Saul, stricken in years among men" (1 Sam. 17:12).

B.   Raba, and some say, R. Zebid, and some say, R. Oshaia, said, "This refers to Jesse, father of David, who went out with an escort and came in with an escort and gave expositions with an escort."

C.   Said Ulla, "We have in hand the tradition that there is no escort [accorded to sages] in Babylonia."

D.   It has been taught on Tannaite authority:

E.   An escort can add up to no less than sixty myriads.

LII.

A.   Our rabbis have taught on Tannaite authority:

B.   One sees Israelite sages say, "Blessed is he who has given a share of his wisdom to those who fear him."

C.   [He who sees] gentile sages says, "Blessed is he who has given some of his wisdom to those whom he has created."

D.   He who sees Israelite kings says, "Blessed be he who has given some of his honor to those who fear him."

E.   [If he sees] gentile kings, he says, "Blessed is he who has given some of his honor to those who fear him."

F.   Said R. Yohanan, "A person should always try to run to greet Israelite kings, and not Israelite kings alone, but also gentile kings, so that if a person should have the merit [to witness the Messianic coming], he will know the difference between Israelite and gentile kings."

LIII.

A.   R. Sheshet was blind. Everyone was running to give a reception to the king. R. Sheshet got up and went with them. A min said to him, "Whole jugs go to the river [for water], where do broken ones go?"

B.   He said to him, "Come and you will see that I know more than you."

C.   The first troop came by. When a cry arose, the <u>min</u> said to him, "The king is coming."

D.   R. Sheshet said to him, "He is not coming."

E.   The second troop came by. At the outcry, the <u>min</u> said to him, "Now the king is coming."

F.   Said R. Sheshet to him, "The king is not coming."

G.   The third troop passed by. When the crowds became hushed, R. Sheshet said to him, "Now the king is assuredly coming."

H.   The <u>min</u> said to him, "How do you know?"

I.   He said to him, "Because earthly royalty is like the royalty of the firmament.

J.   "For it is written, 'Go forth and stand upon the mount before the Lord. And behold, the Lord passed by and a great and strong wind broke the mountains and shattered the rocks before the Lord, but the Lord was not in the wind. And after the wind an earthquake, but the Lord was not in the earthquake. And after the earthquake a fire, but the Lord was not in the fire. And after the fire a still small voice' (1 Kgs. 19:11-12)."

K.   When the king came by, R. Sheshet said a blessing for him.

L.   Said the <u>min</u> to him, "Are you going to say a blessing for someone whom you cannot see?"

M.   What was the fate of that <u>min</u>?

N.   There are those who say his friends put out his eyes, and there are those who say that R. Sheshet laid eyes against him, and he turned into a mountain of bones.

LIV.

A.   R. Shila administered a flogging to a certain man who had sexual relations with an "Egyptian" [= gentile] woman. The man went and informed against him to the royal government. He said, "There is a man among the Jews who judges cases without royal authorization. The government sent investigators. When they came, they said to him, "Why did you administer a flogging to that man?"

B.   He said to them, "Because he had sexual relations with a she-ass."

C.   They said to him, "Do you have witnesses?"

D.   He said to them, "Yes."

E.   Elijah came and appeared to him in the form of a man and gave testimony.

F.   They said to him, "If that is the case, he surely would be subject to the death penalty!"

G.   He said to them, "As to us, from the day on which we were exiled from our land, we have not had the right to impose the death penalty. But as for you, what you wish, do to him."

H.   While the investigators were considering the matter, R. Shila recited the verse, "Yours, Lord, are the greatness and the power" (1 Chr. 29:11).

I.   They said to him, "What were you saying?"

J.   He said to them, "This is what I was saying: 'Blessed is the All-Merciful who has made earthly royalty like the royalty of the firmament, and given you power and [made you] lovers of justice."

K.   They said, "Are you so solicitous of the honor owing to the government?"

L.   They gave him a sash [of office], saying to him, "You may judge cases."

M.   When they had left, that man [who had been flogged] said to him, "Does the All-Merciful do miracles for liars?"

N.   He said to him, "Wicked one! Are they not called asses? For it is written, 'Whose flesh is as the flesh of asses' (Ez. 23:20)."

O.   [Shila] saw that the man was going to go and report this to them, saying that he had called them asses. [Shila] said, "This man is a persecutor, and the Torah has said that if one comes to kill you, forestall matters by killing him first [cf. Ex. 22:1]." He hit him with his sash and killed him.

P.   [Shila] said, "Since a miracle has been done for me through the particular verse of Scripture that I cited, I shall expound the whole of it:

Q.   "'Yours O Lord is the greatness' -- this refers to the works of creation, and so Scripture says, 'Who does great things past finding out' (Job 9:10).

R.   "'And the power' -- this refers to the Exodus from Egypt, as it is said, 'And Israel saw the great work' (Ex. 14:31).

S.   "'And the glory' -- this refers to the sun and moon, standing still for Joshua, as it is said, 'And the sun stood still and the moon stayed' (Jos. 10:13).

T.   "'And the victory' -- this speaks of the fall of Rome, and so it says, 'And their life-blood is dashed against my garments' (Is. 63:3).

U.   "'And the majesty' -- this speaks of the battle of the valleys of Arnon, as it is said, 'Wherefore it is said in the book of the Wars of the Lord: Vaheb in Supah and the valleys of Arnon' (Num. 21:14).

V.   "'For all that is in heaven and earth' -- this speaks of the war of Sisera, as it is said, 'They fought from heaven, the stars in their courses fought against Sisera' (Jud. 5:20).

W.   "'Yours is the kingdom, O Lord' -- this refers to the war of Gog and Magog, and so it is said, 'Behold I am against you, Gog, chief prince of Meshech and Tubal' (Ez. 38:3)."

Y.   "Head above all" (1 Chr. 29:1):

Z.   Said R. Hanan bar Raba said R. Yohanan, "Even the designation of who will be in charge of the irrigation well is decided in heaven."

AA.   In a teaching on Tannaite authority it has been taught in the name of R. Aqiba, "'Yours, Lord, is the greatness' refers to the splitting of the sea of Reeds.

BB.   "'And the power' refers to the blow against the first-born.'

CC.   "'And the glory' refers to the giving of the Torah.

DD.   "'And the victory' refers to Jerusalem.

EE.   "'And the majesty' refers to the Temple."

LV.

A.   [58B] Our rabbis have taught on Tannaite authority:

B. He who sees Israelite homes, if they are inhabited, says, "Blessed is he who establishes the boundary of the widow [Jerusalem]."

C. If they are in ruins, he says, "Blessed be the true judge."

D. When he sees gentile houses, if they are inhabited, says, 'The Lord will pluck up the house of the proud' (Prov. 15:25)."

E. If they are in ruins, he says, "'O Lord, you God, to whom vengeance belongs, you, God, to whom vengeance belongs, shine forth' (Ps. 94:1)."

LVI.

A. Ulla and R. Hisda were going along the way. When they got to the gate of the house of R. Hana bar Hanilai, R. Hisda broke down and signed.

B. Said to him Ulla, "Why are you sighing? Has not Rab said, 'A sigh breaks half the body of a man, as it is said, "Sigh, therefore, you son of man, with the breaking of your loins" (Ex. 21:11).' And R. Yohanan [Ulla continues] has said, 'Even the whole of a man's body, as it is said, "And it shall be, when they say to you, Why are you sighing, you shall say, Because of the news, for it comes, and every heart shall melt" (Ez. 21:12).'"

C. He said to him, "Now should I not sigh? For here is a house in which there were sixty cooks by day and sixty by night, and they would cook for everyone in need.

D. "And [Hana] did not take his hand away from his purse, thinking that a poor man, son of good parents, may come, and while [Huna] was reaching for his purse, the poor man might be ashamed.

E. "And furthermore, this house had four doors, facing the four points of the compass, and whoever came in empty would go out full.

F. "And they would toss wheat and barley out in years of famine, so that whoever might find the matter shameful to come and take by day could come and take by night.

G. "Now it has all fallen into ruins, and should I not sigh?"

H. He said to him, "This is what R. Yohanan said, 'Since the day on which the house of sanctuary was destroyed, a decree has been issued against the households of the righteous, that they should be destroyed.

I. "'For it is said, "In my ears, said the Lord of hosts, Of a truth many houses shall be desolate, even great and fair, without inhabitants" (Is. 5:9).

J. "[But, he continued,] R. Yohanan also said, 'The Holy One, blessed be he, is going to restore those houses to full habitation, as it is said, "A song of ascents. They that trust in the Lord are as Mount Zion" (Ps. 125:1). Just as the Holy One, blessed be he, is going to restore Mount Zion to full habitation, so the houses of the righteous will the Holy One, blessed be he, restore to full habitation.'"

K. He saw that he was not really comforted. He said to him, "It is sufficient that a servant should be in the status of his master [and that Israel's houses should be in the status of the Lord's house]."

LVII.

A. Our rabbis have taught on Tannaite authority:

B. He who sees Israelite graves says, "Blessed is he who has created you in justice, fed you in justice, sustained you in justice, gathered you in justice, and is going to raise you up in justice.'"

C. Mar, son of Rabina, completed the passage, in the name of R. Nahman, as follows: "'And who knows the numbers of you all, and who is going to bring you back to life and to establish you. Blessed is he who brings the dead to life.'"

D. [If one sees] gentile graves, he says, "'Your mother shall be sore ashamed' (Jer. 50:12)."

LVIII.

A. Said R. Joshua b. Levi, "He who sees his friend after an interval of thirty days says, "Blessed is he who has kept us in life and sustained us and brought us to this time."

B. If it is after an interval of twelve months, he says, "Blessed is he who brings the dead back to life."

C. Said Rab, "The deceased is forgotten from the heart [so that mourning ends] only after twelve months, for it is said, 'I am forgotten as a dead man out of mind, I am like a lost vessel' (Ps. 31:13). [Simon, p. 364, n. 5: A thing is not given up as lost till after twelve months]."

LIX.

A. R. Pappa and R. Huna, son of R. Joshua, were going along the way. They met R. Hanina, son of R. Iqa. They said to him, "Now that we see you, we may say two blessings in your regard:

B. "'Blessed is he who shared his wisdom with those who fear him,' and, '... who has kept us in life....'"

C. He said to them, "As to me, now that I see you, I regard it as the same as seeing sixty myriads of Israel, so I recite in your regard [not two but] three blessings!

D. "These two [which you have said], and also, 'Blessed is the one who understands mysteries.'"

E. They said to him, "Are you so smart!"

F. They cast their eyes against him and he dropped dead.

LX.

A. Said R. Joshua b. Levi, "He who sees a pock-marked person says the blessing, 'Blessed is he who varies the creatures [that he has made].'"

B. An objection was raised by citing the following:

C. One who sees a Negro, [a man] red-spotted in the face, or [a man] white-spotted in the face [a man afflicted with psoriasis, or elephantiasis], or a hunchback, or a dwarf [or a dropsical person] says, "Blessed [are you, Lord...] who creates such varied creatures."

D. [One who sees] an amputee, a blind man, flatheaded man, a lame man, or a man afflicted with boils, says, "Blessed be the true judge" [cf. M. Ber. 9:2] [T. Ber. 6:3A-B].

E. There is no contradiction [between the two positions on what blessing is to be said with reference to a pock-marked person], for the one speaks of what is to be said on the occasion of seeing such a person afflicted from birth, the other, a person afflicted only afterward.

F.   You may see this very distinction if you closely examine the formulation of the passage, for the latter falls into the category of one who has had a leg amputated [and so has been affected by divine judgment and is not in his condition by nature].

LIX.

A.   Our rabbis have taught on Tannaite authority:

B.   He who sees an elephant, ape, long-tailed ape, says, "Blessed be he who varies the creatures [that he has made]."

C.   **One who sees attractive people or attractive trees says, "Praised be He who has [made] such attractive creations" [T. Ber. 6:4A].**

LX.

A.   For shooting stars [M. Ber. 9:   ]:

B.   What are shooting stars?

C.   Said Samuel, "Comets."

D.   And said Samuel, "The paths of heaven are as clear to me as the paths of Nehardea, except for the orbit of the shooting star, which I do not know."

E.   And there is a tradition that it does not pass through the constellation of Orion,

F.   And if it is passed through the constellation of Orion, the world would be destroyed.

G.   But lo, we see that it does pass through that constellation!

H.   It is its orb that passes through, and it appears as if it itself passed through [but it did not].

I.   R. Huna, son of R. Joshua, said, "The Veil [the lowest of seven firmament (Simon, p. 365, n. 3)] was torn up and rolled away, revealing the brightness of the firmament."

J.   R. Ashi said, "There was a star that was removed from one side of the constellation of Orion and its mate made an appearance on the other side of the same constellation, and that caused confusion so that people thought that a star had passed through."

LXI.

A.   Samuel contrasted these verses: "It is written, 'Who makes the Bear, Orion, and the Pleiades' (Job 9:9).

B.   "And elsewhere it is written, 'Who makes Pleiades and Orion' (Amos 5:8) [thus in different order].

C.   "How so? If it were not for the heat of Orion the world could not stand the cold caused by Pleiades, and if it were not for the cold of Pleiades, the world could not stand the heat caused by Orion.

D.   "[Simon:] There is a tradition that were it not that the tail of the Scorpion has been placed in the Stream of Fire [Dan 7:10], no one who has ever been stung by a scorpion could live.

E.   "This is in line with what the All-Merciful said to Job, 'Can you bind the chains of Pleiades or loose the bands of Orion' (Job 38:31)."

F.   What is the sense of Kimah [the Hebrew name for Pleiades]?

G.   Said Samuel, "It is made up of about a hundred (kemeah) stars."

H.   There are those who say that they are packed together, and there are those who say that they are scattered.

I.   What is the sense of Ash [the Hebrew name for the Bear]?

J.   Said R. Judah, "Yuta."

K.   What is Yuta?

L.   Some say, "It is the tail of the Ram, others, it is the head of the Calf.

M.   The one who says that it is the tail of the Ram is in the more likely position, for it is written, "Ayish will be comforted for her children" (Job 38:32). Therefore it lacks something and appears [59A] like something that has been torn off [Simon, p. 366, n. 10: and then stuck on artificially]."

N.   And as to its going after her, it is as if it is saying to her, "Give me back my children."

O.   For at the moment that the Holy One, blessed be he, proposed to bring the flood on the world, he took two stars from Kimah [Pleiades] and brought the flood upon the world. When he wished to stop the flood, he took two stars from the Bear and stopped it.

P.   But why not put the two stars back?

Q.   A pit cannot be refilled by what is taken out of it.

R.   Or, alternatively, what has served as evidence for the prosecution cannot then serve as evidence for the defense.

S.   And why not create two new stars for it?

T.   "There is nothing new under the sun" (Qoh. 1:9).

U.   Said R. Nahman, "The Holy One, blessed be he, is going to put them back.

V.   "For it is said, 'And the Bear will be comforted for her children' (Job 38:32)."

LXII.

A.   And for earthquakes [M. Ber. 9:   ]:

B.   What are earthquakes?

C.   Said R. Qattina, "Rumbling."

D.   R. Qattina was going along the way. When he got to the gate of the house of a necromancer, there was a rumbling in the deep.

E.   [Qattina] said, "Can this necromancer possibly know what causes this rumbling in the deep?"

F.   [The necromancer] raised a voice after him, "Qattina, Qattina, why should I not know?

G.   "When the Holy One, blessed be he, reflects that his children are plunged in distress among the nations of the world, he drops two tears into the Great Sea, and the sound is heard from one end of the world to the other, and that is the rumbling."

H.   Said R. Qattina, "The necromancer is a liar and what he says are lies. For if it were as he says, there should be one rumble, then another rumble."

I.   But that [4] is not really proof. [For] there actually is one rumble and, after, another, and the reason that he did not concede to him [that he knew what he was talking about] was so that people should not go astray after him.

J.   And R. Qattina himself said, "[God] claps hands, as it is said, 'I will also smite my hands together and I will satisfy my anger' (Ez. 21:22)."

K.   R. Nathan says, "God sighs, as it is said, 'I will satisfy my anger upon them and I will be eased' (Ez. 5:13)."

L.   And rabbis say, "[God] treads on the firmament, as it is said, 'He gives a noise as they that tread grapes against all the inhabitants of the earth' (Jer. 25:30)."

M.   R. Aha bar Jacob said, "He pushes his feet together under the throne of glory, as it is said, 'So says the Lord, The heaven is my throne and the earth is my footstool' (Is. 66:1)."

LXIII.

A.   And over thunder [M. Ber. 9:2]:

B.   What is thunder?

C.   Said Samuel, "Clouds in a whirl, as it is said, 'The voice of your thunder was in the whirlwind, the lightning lighted up the world, the earth trembled and shook' (Ps. 77:19)."

D.   And rabbis say, "Clouds pouring water into one another, as it is said, 'At the sound of his pouring a multitude of waters in the heavens' (Jer. 10:13)."

E.   R. Aha bar Jacob said, "A strong flash of lightning that hits the clouds and breaks off hailstones."

F.   R. Ashi said, "Clouds are puffed out, and [Simon:] a blast of wind comes and blows across the mouth of them and it makes a sound like wind blowing across the mouth of a jar."

G.   And the most likely view is that of R. Aha bar Jacob, for where lightning flashes, the clouds rumble, and then it rains.

LXIV.

A.   And for storms [M. Ber. 9:2]:

B.   Where are "storms"?

C.   Said Abayye, "Hurricanes."

D.   And said Abayye, "There is a tradition that a hurricane does not come at night."

E.   But lo, we see that they do come at night!

F.   In such a case it starts by day [and continues].

G.   And said Abayye, "There is a tradition that a hurricane does not go on for two hours, so carrying out that which is said, 'Troubles shall not rise up the second time' (Nah. 1:9)."

H.   But we see that hurricanes do last longer than that.

I.   But there is an interruption in the middle.

LXV.

A.   For lightning, one says, "Blessed is he whose strength and power fill the world" [M. 9:2]:

B.   What is lightning?

C.   Said Raba, "A flash of light."

D. And said Raba, "A single flash of light, white light, blue light, clouds rising in the west, clouds coming from the south, two clouds that rise facing one another -- all signify trouble."

E. What difference does such an omen make?

F. So that one should pray for mercy.

G. And that rule applies to these phenomena appearing at night, but if they come by day, they mean nothing.

H. Said R. Samuel bar Isaac, "Clouds that come by day have no significance [Simon: do not portend a good fall of rain], for it is said, 'Your goodness is as a morning cloud' (Hos. 6:4)."

I. Said R. Pappa, to Abayye, "But lo, people say, 'When you open your door to find rain, ass-driver, put down your sack and sleep on it'" [Simon, p. 368, n. 4: because corn will be cheap on account of abundant rain].' [So would that not mean morning clouds bring rain?]"

J. There is no contradiction. One saying speaks of a case in which the clouds are thick, the other, light.

LXVI.

A. Said R. Alexandri said R. Joshua b. Levi, "Clouds were created only to [Simon:] straighten out the crookedness of the heart.

B. "As it is said, 'God has so made it that men should bear before him' (Qoh. 3:14)."

C. And said R. Alexandri said R. Joshua b. Levi, "He who sees a rainbow in the clouds has to fall on his face, as it is said, 'As the appearance of the bow that is in the cloud, and, when I saw it, I fell upon my face' (Ez. 1:28)."

D. In the West they curse one who does this, because it looks as if he is bowing down to the rainbow.

E. But someone [who sees a rainbow] assuredly should say a blessing.

F. What blessing does he say?

G. "Blessed is he who remembers the covenant."

H. In a Tannaite teaching it is taught:

I. R. Ishmael, son of R. Yohanan b. Beroqa, says, "'... who is faithful to his covenant and carries out his word.'"

J. Said R. Pappa, "Therefore let us say both of those blessings: 'Blessed is he who remembers the covenant,' and '... who is faithful to his covenant and carries out his word.'"

LXVII.

A. For mountains and hills [M. Ber. 9:2]:

B. But are not all the things that we have listed to this point not in the category of the works of creation [that only at this point we should make mention of the works of creation]?

C. And has it not been written, "For he makes lightnings for the rain" (Ps. 135:7)?

D. Said Abayye, "Combine both and repeat them [as a double blessing]."

E. Said Raba, "In the earlier case one says two blessings, 'Blessed is he whose power fills the world' and 'who accomplishes the works of creation.'

F.   "But here one says, 'Who accomplishes the works of creation,' but one does not say, 'Whose power fills the world.'"

LXVIII.

A.   Said R. Joshua b. Levi, "He who sees the firmament in its purity says, 'Blessed is he who accomplishes creation.'"

B.   When does one say so?

C.   Said Abayye, "It is when it rains all night, and, in the morning, the north wind comes and [clears away the clouds and] reveals the heavens."

D.   They differ on the statement of Rafram bar Pappa in R. Hisda's name.

E.   For Rafram bar Pappa said R. Hisda said, "From the day on which the house of the sanctuary was destroyed, the firmament has never appeared in all its purity.

F.   "For it is said, 'I clothe the heavens with blackness and I made sackcloth for their covering' (Is. 50:3)."

LXIX.

A.   [59B] Our rabbis have taught on Tannaite authority:

B.   [What follows produces verbatim the translation of Simon, pp. 369-70, with the notes of W. M. Feldman, p. 369, n. 6, and pp. 370-371, n.s 1-6.] He who sees the sun at its turning point [in its apparent motion in the ecliptic, the sun has four 'turning points' which mark the beginnings of the four respective seasons. These points are generically referred to as the tekufoth (sing. tekufah). They are: the two equinoctial points when the sun crosses the equator at the beginning of spring and autumn respectively, and 'turns' from one side of the equator to the other; and the two solstices, when the sun is at its maximum distance, or declination, from the equator, at one or other side of it, at the beginning of summer and winter respectively, and instead of progressively increasing its declination it 'turns' to decrease it progressively. (It may be mentioned that the term 'tekufah' is also used not only for the beginning of a season but for the whole of the season itself.)], the moon in its power [As the sun and moon were created to rule the day and night respectively (Gen. I, 16), they are necessarily endowed with the attribute of power (cf. Sabbath Liturgy). In this passage, however, 'the moon in its power' may have a special significance, because at the Nisan, or spring equinox, the spring tides are greatest, owing to the combined action of the sun and the moon in conjunction, or new moon. The moon in its power to cause tides (a fact known to Pliny and Aristotle, and referred to by Maimonides (Guide II, 10), although never directly mentioned in the Talmud), is therefore best seen at this time], the planets in their orbits [The orbits of the planets which are now known to be ellipses, were, on the Ptolemaic system, which prevailed at that time, assumed to be traced out by a most ingenious combination of eccentric circles and epicycles (v. for instance, the epicyclic theory of the moon in Feldman W.M., Rabbinical Mathematics and Astronomy, London, 1931, pp. 132ff). Hence the contemplation of the planets in their orbits was an adequate reason for pronouncing the blessing], and the signs of the zodiac in their orderly progress [The vernal or autumnal equinox is not a fixed point in relation to

the signs of the zodiac, but keeps on changing its position to the extent of 50.1"
(50.1 seconds of arc) per year. This movement which is called 'precession of the
equinoxes' is due to the continual shifting of the point of intersection of the ecliptic
with the equator, but was believed by the ancients to be due to the progressive
movement of the signs of the zodiac. As the result of precession, the equinoctial
point which 2,000 years ago was the beginning of the sign Ram (first point of Aries)
has since shifted 30° to the sign Pisces, although it is still spoken of as the first
point of Aries], should say, "Blessed be he who has wrought the work of creation."

C. And when does this happen? [The reference is to the sun at its turning point (Rashi).]

D. Said Abayye, "Every twenty-eight years, when the cycle [This means here the Big or
Solar Cycle. Taking a Samuel, or Julian, year to consist of 365 1/4 days or 52 weeks
1/14 days, every tekufah occurs 1 1/4 days later in the week every consecutive year,
so that after 4 years it occurs at the same time of the day but (1 1/4 x 4 =) 5 days
later in the week. After 28, or 4 x 7 years, the tekufah will recur not only at the
same time of the day, but also on the same day of the week. V. Feldman, op. cit. p.
199] begins again and the Nisan [spring] equinox falls in Saturn on the evening of
Tuesday [As the sun and moon were created on the 4th day, the beginning of the 28
years cycle is always on a Wednesday which begins at the vernal equinox at 6 p.m.
on Tuesday. This, according to computation coincides with the rise of Saturn, v.
Rashi], going into Wednesday.

LXX.

A. R. Judah says, "He who sees the Great Sea..." [M. Ber. 9:2]:

B. What are the intervals?

C. Said Rami bar Abba said R. Isaac, "Every thirty days."

D. And said Rami bar Abba said R. Isaac, "He who sees the Euphrates at the bridge at
Babylon says, 'Blessed is he who accomplishes creation.'"

E. These days, however, that the Persians have shifted [the course of the river by
making canals], it is only if one sees the Euphrates from Be Shabur and beyond [that
the blessing is called for].

F. R. Joseph says, "From Ihi Deqira and beyond."

G. And said Rami bar Abba, "He who sees the Tigris at the bridge of Shabistana says,
'Blessed is he who accomplishes creation.'"

H. What is "the Tigris" [hideqqel]?

I. Said R. Ashi, "It is so called because its water is sharp and swift [had, qal]."

J. What is "the Euphrates"? [Perat]?

K. It is so called because its waters are fruitful [parim] and multiply.

L. And said Raba, "The reason that the people who live in Mahoza are sharp is that
they brink the waters of the Tigris.

M. "The reason that they have red spots is that they have sexual relations in daylight.

N. "The reason that their eyes blink is that they live in dark houses."

<u>LXXI.</u>

A.   <u>For rain [M. Ber. 9:2]</u>:

B.   And for rain is the blessing, "Who is good and does good"?

C.   And has not R. Abbahu said, and some say it was repeated in a Tannaite teaching, "From what point in the year do people say a blessing for rain? From the time at which the husband goes forth to greet the bride [which is to say, when the drops of rain fall so hard that they rebound from the earth (Simon, p. 371, n. 8)]."

D.   "What is the blessing that people say?

E.   "Said R. Judah, 'We give thanks to you for every drop of rain that you bring down for us.'"

F.   And R. Yohanan concludes the blessing in the following way, "'Were our mouths as full of song as the sea..., we could not suffice to give thanks to you, Lord our God,' up to, 'shall prostrate itself before you. Blessed are you, to whom many words of thanksgiving are due.'"

G.   <u>Many</u> words of thanksgiving and not <u>all</u> words of thanksgiving?

H.   Said Raba, "Phrase it, 'God who is to be thanked.'"

I.   Said R. Pappa, "Therefore let us say both versions. 'Many words of thanksgiving and God who is to be thanked.'"

J.   In any event there is a problem [in the diverse traditions, B, E, on what blessing is to be said for rain].

K.   There is no problem. The one speaks of the moment at which one has heard [that it has rained] [at which point one says, "Who is good and does good"], and the other blessing is said when one actually sees the rain.

L.   But when one hears about the rain, that is simply hearing good news, and we have learned in the Mishnah, <u>On hearing good news, one says, "Blessed is he who is good and who does good" [M. Ber. 9:2]</u>.

M.   Rather, both blessings apply to a case in which one has actually seen the rain, and there still is no contradiction. The one applies when just a little rain has come, the other when much rain has fallen.

N.   If you like, I shall say that both of the benedictions apply to the case in which a great deal of rain has fallen, and there still is no contradiction. The one blessing is said by someone who has land, the other by someone who does not have land.

O.   Is it the case, then, that the one who has land says, "Who is good and does good"?

P.   And it has been taught on Tannaite authority:

Q.   <u>If one has built a new house, bought new clothing, he says, "Blessed is he who has kept us in life and brought us to this time" [M. Ber. 9:3]</u>.

R.   If it is both his and other peoples' property, he says, "Who is good and does good." [We assume that the landowner owns the land on his own, in which case we would expect the former blessing, "Kept us in life" to apply to him.]

S.   There is no contradiction. In the one case ["Who is good and does good"] the blessing applies if the person is in a partnership, the other ["he has kept us alive"] applies where there is no partnership.

T.   For has it not been taught on Tannaite authority:

U.   The upshot of the matter is this: For something that belongs to oneself, one says, "Blessed... who has kept us in life and sustained us...,"

V.   and for something that belongs both to the person himself and also to someone else, he says, "Blessed is he who is good and does good"?

W.   But is it the case that wherever there is no one else [in partnership along with a person], one does not say the blessing, "Who is good and does good"?

X.   And has it not been taught on Tannaite authority:

Y.   If people told someone that his wife has produced a male child, he says, "Blessed is he who is good and does good"?

Z.   But in that case, too, his wife is with him as a partner. For she is glad to have a male child.

AA.   Come and take note of the following:

BB.   If one's father died and he is the heir, to begin with he says, "Blessed is the true judge." Then he says, "Blessed is he who is good and does good."

CC.   Here too there are brothers who inherit along with him.

DD.   Come and take note of the following:

EE.   Concerning a new kind of wine [which one tastes for the first time] it is not necessary to say a blessing.

FF.   Concerning a move to a new place, it is necessary to say a blessing.

GG.   And said R. Joseph b. Abba said R. Yohanan, "Even though they have said, 'Concerning a new kind of wine it is not necessary to say a blessing,' one does, nonetheless, say, 'Blessed is he who is good and does good.'" [Where is there a partnership here?]

HH.   In that case too, there are others who are members of the same eating club, who drank the wine with him.

LXXII.

A.   If one has built a new house or bought new clothes [M. 9:3A]:

B.   Said R. Huna, "That rule applies only in a case in which the person does not have similar items. But if he has similar items, it is not necessary to say a blessing."

C.   And R. Yohanan said, "Even if he has similar items, it is necessary to say a blessing."

D.   [60A] This then bears the implication that if someone bought something and went and bought some more, all parties concur that he does not have to say a blessing.

E.   And there are those who report the matter as follows:

F.   Said R. Huna, "The rule applies only to one who did not buy and then go back and buy more. But if one bought and went back and bought more, it is not necessary to say a blessing."

G.   And R. Yohanan said, "Even if one bought and went back and bought some more, it is necessary to say a blessing."

H.   The foregoing bears the implication that if someone has [some items] and went and bought [some more], all parties concur that he does have to say a blessing.

I.   An objection was raised on the basis of the following statement:

J.   "If one bought a house and has no other like it, bought new clothes and has no others like them, he has to say a blessing. But if he has others like them, he does not have to say a blessing," the words of R. Meir.

K.   R. Judah says, "One way or the other, he has to say a blessing."

L.   Now with respect to the first of the two versions of the matter, R. Huna accords with R. Meir and R. Yohanan with R. Judah.

M.   But as to the second of the two versions of the matter, while R. Huna concurs with R. Judah, with whom does R. Yohanan rule? It cannot be in accord with either R. Meir or R. Judah.

N.   R. Yohanan [in the second version] may reply to you, "In point of fact, in R. Judah's view as well, if one bought something and went back and bought some more, he also has to say a blessing. And where there is a dispute, it pertains to a case in which the man has something but has gone out and bought [some more].

O.   "This then tells you the full extent of the position taken by R. Meir, that even if one has bought something and has that some object already, he does not have to say a blessing, and all the more so if he bought something and went and bought some more, in which case, likewise, one does not have to say a blessing."

P.   But let the two differ as to a case in which one has bought something and gone back and bought some more, in which case, one does not have to say a blessing, so indicating the full extent of the position taken by R. Judah?

Q.   It is better to show the full extent of the position of the person who takes the lenient position.

LXXIII.

A.   One says a blessing over evil [M. Ber. 9:5A]:

B.   For example?

C.   For instance if a flood took one's land. Even though eventually it will be a good thing, because his land [Simon:] is covered with alluvium and becomes more fertile, now, for the moment, however, it is a bad thing.

LXXIV.

A.   And over good [M. 9:5A]:

B.   For example?

C.   For instance if one found something. Even though it is a disadvantage to him because, if the government hears about it, it will confiscate the object from him, still, for the moment, it is a good thing.

LXXV.

A.   If one's wife is pregnant and he says, "May it be pleasing that she bear... lo, this is a vain prayer [M. 9:3E]:

B.   And will not such a prayer make a difference?

C.   R. Joseph objected, "'And afterwards she bore a daughter and called her name Dinah' (Gen. 30:21)."

D.   What is the meaning of "and afterwards"?

E. Said Rab, "After Leah had judged herself, saying, 'Twelve tribes are destined to come forth from Jacob, six from me, four from the handmaidens, so there are now ten. If this one should be a male, then my sister, Rachel, will not even be equivalent to one of the handmaidens.' Forthwith the baby was turned into a girl.

F. "For it is said, 'And she called her name Dina' (Gen. 30:21) [that is, judgment]."

G. [In constructing an argument] people may not call as evidence what is in fact a miracle.

H. And if you like, I shall say that the matter involving Leah took place within forty days of conception [before the sex of the child had been determined].

I. This is in line with that which has been taught on Tannaite authority:

J. For the first three days [after sexual relations] a man should pray that [the semen] not putrefy. From the third day to the fortieth he should pray for mercy that the child be male. From the fortieth day to the end of the third month he should pray for mercy that it not be an abortion resembling a fish. From the end of the third month through the sixth, he should pray for mercy that there not be a miscarriage. From the sixth to the ninth he should pray for mercy that the baby should come forth whole.

K. But does a prayer [for a male child] actually make a difference?

L. And has not R. Isaac, son of R. Ammi, said, "If the man reaches orgasm first, the wife will produce a female, if the woman reaches orgasm first, the child will be a male.

M. "For it is said, 'When a woman reaches orgasm, she will produce a male' (Lev. 12:1). [Hence prayer has nothing to do with the issue.]"

N. With what case do we deal [when we claim that prayer will help]? For instance, if the two of them reached orgasm simultaneously [in which case prayer can make a difference].

LXXVI.

A. If someone was coming along the way [M. 9:3F]:

B. Our rabbis have taught on Tannaite authority:

C. There was the case involving Hillel, the elder, who was coming along the way and heard the sound of an outcry in town. He said, "I am confident that this is not coming from my house."

D. And concerning him Scripture says, "He shall not be afraid of evil tidings, his heart is steadfast, trusting in the Lord" (Ps. 112:7).

E. Said Raba, "When you give an exposition of this verse of Scripture, you may explain it so the second clause explains the first, or so that the first clause explains the second.

F. "So the second clause explains the first: 'He will not fear evil tidings' because 'His heart is steadfast, trusting in the Lord.'

G. "The first clause explains the second: 'His heart is steadfast, trusting in the Lord' because 'He will not bear evil tidings.'"

LXXVII.

A. There was a disciple who was walking along in the market place of Zion behind R. Ishmael, son of R. Yose. [Ishmael] saw that [the disciple] was trembling. He said to him, "You are a sinner, for it is written, 'Sinners in Zion are afraid' (Is. 33:14)."

B. He said to him, "But it is written, 'Happy is the man who is always afraid' (Prov. 28:14)."

C. He said to him, "That refers to words of Torah [which one should fear losing]."

LXXVIII.

A. Judah bar Nathan would follow after R. Hamnuna. [Once time] he sighed. [Hamnuna] said to him, "That man wants trouble to come upon him, for it is written, 'For the thing which I feared is come upon me, and that of which I was afraid has overtaken me' (Job 3:25)."

B. He said to him, "It is written, 'Happy is the man who is always afraid' (Prov. 28:14)."

C. He said to him, "That refers to words of Torah."

LXXIX.

A. He goes through a city [M. Ber. 9:4A]:

B. Our rabbis have taught on Tannaite authority:

C. When he goes in, what does he say?

D. "May it please you, Lord my God, that you bring me into this city whole."

E. Once he has entered, he says, "I thank you, Lord my God, that you have brought me into this city whole."

F. When he plans to leave, he says, "May it please you, Lord my God and God of my fathers, that you take me from this city whole."

G. When he has gone forth, he says, "I thank you, Lord my God, that you have taken me from this city whole.

H. "And just as you have taken me out whole, so may you bring me along whole, support me whole, guide my steps whole and save me from the power of every sort of enemy and ambush by the way."

I. Said R. Mattena, "That teaching applies only to a city in which they do not judge and execute criminals, but in a city in which they judge and execute criminals, there is no need [for such a prayer]."

J. There are those who state: Said R. Mattena, "Even in a city in which they judge and execute criminals [such a prayer should be said, for] there may be times that one may not find someone who will plead his case."

LXXX.

A. Our rabbis have taught on Tannaite authority:

B. He who goes into a bath house says, "May it please you, Lord my God, that you will save me from this [place] and those like it, and may no humiliation or sin befall me, and if a humiliation or sin befall me, may my death serve as atonement for all my sins."

C. Said Abayye, "A person should not say this, lest he give Satan an opportunity."

D. For R. Simeon b. Laqish said, and so it has been taught on Tannaite authority in the name of R. Yose, "A person should never give Satan an opportunity."

E.   Said R. Joseph, "What verse of Scripture indicates it? It is that which is written, 'We should have been as Sodom, we should have been like unto Gomorrah' (Is. 1:9). What did he then say to them? 'Hear the word of the Lord, you rulers of Sodom' (Is. 1:10)."

F.   When one leaves the bath house, what does he say?

G.   Said R. Aha, "I thank you, Lord my God, that you have saved me from the fire."

LXXXI.

A.   R. Abbahu went into a bath house, and the floor of the bath house collapsed underneath him.

B.   A miracle was done for him, and he stood on a pillar and saved a hundred and one men on one arm.

C.   He said, "That is in line with what R. Aha said [LXXX G].

LXXXII.

A.   He who goes in to have blood let says, "May it please you, Lord my God, that this procedure serve as healing for me, and that you may heal me. For you are a God who heals faithfully, and your healing is truth. For in point of fact mortals do not have the power to heal, but they merely do what is customary."

B.   Said Abayye, "A person should not say such a prayer.

C.   "For it has been taught by a Tanna of the house of R. Ishmael, 'He shall cause him to be thoroughly healed' (Ex. 21:19).

D.   "'On the basis of this verse of Scripture we learn that the right is given to a physician to heal [patients].' [So the sentiment of the foregoing prayer, that physicians do not heal, is wrong.]"

E.   When one arises [after the blood letting], what does he say?

F.   Said R. Aha, "Blessed is [God], who heals for nothing."

LXXXIV.

A.   [60B] He who goes into a privy says, "Be most honored, you honored and holy ones, those who serve the Most High. Give honor to the God of Israel. Wait on me until I go in and do what I wish and come back to you. [So guard me from the evil spirits at the privy.]"

B.   Said Abayye, "A person should not say such a prayer, lest [the guardian angels] leave him and go their way.

C.   "But this is what he should say: 'Guard me, guard me. Help me, help me. Support me, support me. Wait for me, wait for me, until I go in and come out. For this is the way of mortals."

D.   When he comes out, he should say, "Blessed are you... who has formed man with wisdom and created in him various sorts of holes and apertures. It is entirely clear before your glorious throne that if one of them [that should remain closed] should open up, or if one of them [that should remain open] should close up, it will not be possible to arise before you."

E.   How does one conclude the blessing?

F.   Said Rab, "'... who heals the sick.'"

G. Said Samuel, "In this way Abba [Rab] turns the whole world into invalids! Rather: 'Who heals all flesh.'"

H. R. Sheshet said, "'Who does wonders.'"

I. Said R. Pappa, "Therefore let us say them both: 'Who heals all flesh and who does wonders.'"

LXXXV.

A. He who is going to sleep in his bed says from "Hear O Israel" to "And it shall come to pass if you diligently listen."

B. Then he says, "Blessed... who sets the bonds of sleep on my eyes and drowsiness on my eyelids and illuminates the apple of my eye. May it please you, Lord my God, to make me lie down in peace, give me my lot in your Torah, make it my custom to do religious duties, do not make it my custom to do transgressions nor bring me into the power of sin, violation, temptation, or humiliation. May the impulse to do good control me, and may the impulse to do evil not control me. And save me from unfortunate accidents and ailments. Do not let bad dreams or fantasies confuse me. Let my bed be whole before you, and illuminate my eyes lest I sleep to die. Blessed are you, Lord, who illuminates the whole world in his glory."

C. When someone gets up, he says, "My God, the soul that you put in me is pure. You formed it in me. You breathed it into me. You keep it in me. You will take it from me one day but restore it to me in the time to come. So long as the soul is in me, I thank you, Lord my God and God of my fathers, master of all ages, lord of all souls. Blessed are you, Lord, who restores souls to dead corpses."

D. When one hears the cock crow, he says, "Blessed is he who has given the cock understanding to know the difference between day and night."

E. When one opens his eyes, he says, "Blessed is he who opens the eyes of the blind."

F. When one stretches and sits up, he says, "Blessed is he who frees those who are tied up."

G. When one gets dressed, he says, "Blessed is he who puts clothing on the naked."

H. When he stands up straight, he says, "Blessed is he who straightens up those who are bowed down."

I. When he puts his foot on the ground, he says, "Blessed is he who stretches out the earth over the water."

J. When he begins to walk, he says, "Blessed is he who makes man's steps firm."

K. When he ties his shoes, he says, "Blessed is he who has done for me everything I need."

L. When he fastens his belt, he says, "Blessed is he who girds Israel with might."

M. When he spreads a cloth over his head, he says, "Blessed is he who crowns Israel with glory."

N. When he wraps himself in his cloak containing show-fringes, he says, "Blessed... who has sanctified us by his commandments and commanded us to wrap ourselves in a cloak containing show-fringes."

O.   When he puts his phylactery on his arm, he says, "Blessed is he who has sanctified us by his commandments and commanded us concerning the religious duty of phylacteries."

P.   When he washes his hands, he says, "Blessed is he who has sanctified us by his commandments and commanded us concerning hand-washing."

Q.   When he washes his face, he says, "Blessed is he who has taken away the bonds of sleep from my eyes and drowsiness from my eyelids. May it please you, Lord my God, to make study of your Torah a habit for me, and may you make me closely follow your commandments. Do not bring me into the power of sin, transgression, temptation, or humiliation. Subdue my impulse so as to be subservient to you. Take far away from me bad men and bad companions. Make me cleave to the good impulse and to a good companion in your world. Today and every day, in your view and in the view of everyone who sees me, let me have grace, lovingkindness, and mercy, and bestow on me lovingkindness. Blessed are you, who bestows loving kindness on his people, Israel."

LXXXVI.

A.   One is obligated to say a blessing for evil [M. Ber. 9:5A]:

B.   What is the meaning of the statement, One is obligated to say a blessing for evil just as he is obligated to say a blessing for good?

C.   Should I say that, just as one says a blessing over good, "Who is good and does good," so one says a blessing over evil, "Who is good and does good"?

D.   But have we not learned in the Mishnah: For good news one says, "Who is good and who does good," while for bad news, one says the blessing, "Blessed is the true judge" [M. Ber. 9:2E-F]?

E.   Said Raba, "It was necessary [to make the statement in the Mishnah-clause at hand] only to indicate that one must accept [evil] with gladness."

F.   Said R. Aha in the name of R. Levi, "What is the relevant verse of Scripture? 'I will sing of mercy and justice to you, O Lord, I will sing praises' (Ps. 101:1).

G.   "Whether it is mercy or justice, I will sing."

H.   R. Samuel bar Nahmani said, "Proof derives from here: 'In the Lord I will praise his word, in God I will praise his word' (Ps. 66:11).

I.   "'In the Lord I will praise his word' speaks of his meting out of goodness.

J.   "'In God I will praise his word' speaks of his meting out of punishment."

K.   Said R. Tanhum, "Proof derives from here: 'I will lift up the cup of salvation and call on the name of the Lord' (Ps. 116:13). 'I found trouble and sorrow, but I called upon the name of the Lord' (Ps. 116:3)."

L.   Rabbis say, "From here: 'The Lord gave and the Lord has taken away, blessed be the name of the Lord' (Job 1:21)."

LXXXVII.

A.   Said R. Huna said Rab in the name of R. Meir, and so it was taught on Tannaite authority in the name of R. Aqiba, "A person should always make it a habit of saying, 'Whatever the All-Merciful does he does for the good.'"

B.   That is illustrated by the case of R. Aqiba, who was walking along the way. He came to a certain place and looked for room at the inn, but none gave him any. He said, "'Whatever the All-Merciful does he does for good.'"

C.   He went and spent the night in an open field. He had with him a cock, an ass, and a lamp. The wind came and put out the lamp, a weasel came and ate the cock, a lion came and ate the ass. He said, "'Whatever the All-Merciful does, he does for good.'"

D.   On that night a marauding troop came to that town and took into captivity everyone in the town.

E.   He said to them, "Did I not tell you, 'Whatever the Holy One, blessed be he, does is [61A] for the good'?"

LXXXVIII.

A.   Said R. Huna said Rab in the name of R. Meir, "A person's words before the Holy One, blessed be he, should always be few,

B.   "for it is said, 'Be not rash with your mouth, and let not your heart be hasty to utter a word before God. For God is in heaven and you are on earth, therefore let your words be few' (Qoh. 5:1)."

LXXXIX.

A.   R. Nahman bar R. Hisda interpreted the verse, "What is the meaning of that which is written, 'Then the Lord God formed man' (Gen. 2:7)?

B.   "The word 'formed' is written with two Ys to indicate that the Holy One, blessed be he, formed two impulses [in the Hebrew, a word beginning with Y], one Y standing for the impulse to do good, the other, the impulse to do evil."

C.   To this R. Nahman bar Isaac objected, "But how about the domesticated cattle, concerning which the word is not written with two Ys [at Gen. 2:19, 'And the Lord God formed all the beasts of the field']? Does it then mean that these beasts do not have an impulse to do evil? Yet we see that such beasts injure and bite and kick. Rather, matters accord with R. Simeon b. Pazzi."

D.   For Simeon b. Pazzi said, "Woe is me because of my Creator (yosri) and woe is me because of my inclination to do evil (yisri)."

E.   Or also, it would accord with what R. Jeremiah b. Eleazar said.

F.   For R. Jeremiah b. Eleazar said, "God created two faces in the first man, as it is said, 'Behind and before you have formed me' (Ps. 89:5)."

XC.

A.   "And the rib which the Lord God had taken from man made he a woman" (Gen. 2:22):

B.   Rab and Samuel:

C.   One said, "[The rib] was a face."

D.   The other said, "It was a tail."

E.   Now there is no problem for the one who has said that it was a face, for that is in line with what is written, "Behind and before have you formed me" (Ps. 39:5).

F.   But from the viewpoint of him who said that it was a tail, what is the meaning of the verse, "Behind and before have you formed me" (Ps. 39:5)?

G.   It accords with what R. Ammi said.

H.   For R. Ammi said, "'Behind' [last] in the order of the works of creation, and 'before' [first] as to punishment."

I.   Now to be sure man was "behind" as to creation, for he was created only at the very eve of the Sabbath. But as to "before" for punishment, what sort of punishment?

J.   If one should say that it was the punishment affecting the snake, has it not been taught on Tannaite authority:

K.   Rabbi says, "[In the order of passing out positions of] greatness they begin with the great one. In the order of passing out a curse, they begin with the unimportant one.

L.   "In passing out positions of greatness, they begin with the great man, for it is written, 'And Moses spoke to Aaron and to Eleazar and to Ithamar his sons that were left. Take the meal-offering that remains' (Lev. 10:12). [Thus Aaron comes first].

M.   "In the order of passing out a curse, they begin from the unimportant one: first the snake was cursed, then Eve, and, in the end, Adam"?

N.   [Hence the punishment to which man was subjected first] was the punishment of the flood.

O.   For it is written, "And he blotted out every living substance which was upon the face of the ground, both man and cattle" (Gen. 3:14ff.) -- first man, then beast.

P.   Now from the viewpoint of him who said it was a face, that is in line with what is written, "And he created" (Gen. 2:7), with two Ys. But in the viewpoint of him who has said that it was a tail, why write "and he created" with two Ys?

Q.   It accords with what R. Simeon b. Pazzi said.

R.   For R. Simeon b. Pazzi said, "Woe is me on account of my creator, woe is me on account of my impulse to do evil."

S.   Now from the viewpoint of him who has said that it was a face, that is in line with what is written: "Male and female created he them" (Gen. 5:2).

T.   But from the viewpoint of him who has said that it was a tail, what is the sense of "Male and female created he them" (Gen. 5:2)?

U.   It accords with what R. Abbahu said.

V.   For R. Abbahu contrasted two verses: "It is written, 'Male and female created he them' (Gen. 5:2), and it further is written, 'For in the image of God made he man' (Gen. 9:6).

W.   "How so? To begin with, he had had the intention to create two, but in the end only one was created."

X.   Now from the viewpoint of him who has said that it was a face, that is in line with what is written, "He closed up the place with flesh instead thereof'" (Gen. 2:21).

Y.   But in the view of him who said that it was a tail, what is the sense of "He closed up the place with flesh instead thereof" (Gen. 2:21)?

Z.   Said R. Jeremiah, and some say, R. Zebid, and some say, R. Nahman bar Isaac, "That statement refers solely to the place of the cut."

AA. Now from the viewpoint of him who said that it was a tail, that is in line with what is written, "And the God built" (Gen. 2:22).

BB. But from the viewpoint of him who says that it was a face, what is the sense of "And God built"?

CC. It accords with what R. Simeon b. Menassia said.

DD. For R. Simeon b. Menassia expounded, "What is the meaning of the verse of Scripture, 'And the Lord built the rib' (Gen. 2:22)?

EE. "It teaches that the Holy One, blessed be he, made up Eve's hair and brought her to the first Man. For so in the overseas cities they call 'hair dressing' 'building up.'"

FF. Another explanation: "And he built" (Gen. 2:22):

GG. Said R. Hisda, and some say it was repeated on Tannaite authority: "This teaches that the Holy One, blessed be he, built up Eve just like a storehouse.

HH. "Just as a storehouse is narrow on top and wide on the bottom so that it can hold the produce, so Eve is narrow on top and wide on the bottom, so as to hold the foetus."

II. "And brought her to Adam" (Gen. 2:22):

JJ. Said R. Jeremiah b. Eleazar, "This teaches that the Holy One, blessed be he, served as the groomsman for the first Man.

KK. "From this passage the Torah taught the lesson of proper conduct, indicating that a great man should serve a less important one as a groomsman and not regard it as inappropriate."

LL. Now in the view of him who has said that it was a face, which of the two faces [of which the first man was formed, before Eve was made] went before?

MM. Said R. Nahman bar Isaac, "It is logical to suppose that the male face went first.

NN. "For so it has been taught on Tannaite authority:

OO. "'A man should not follow after a woman on the way, even if it is his wife who happens to come in front of him on a bridge, in which case he should put her off to the side.

PP. "'And whoever passes behind a woman over a river will have no share in the world to come.'"

XCI.

A. Our rabbis have taught on Tannaite authority:

B. He who counts out coins into a woman's hand from his own in order to have a chance to stare at her, even if such a one has in hand Torah and good deeds like Moses, our master, will not be quit of the judgment of Gehenna.

C. "For it is said, "Hand to hand, he shall not escape from evil" (Prov. 11:21). He shall not escape from the judgment of Gehenna."

XCII.

A. Said R. Nahman, "Manoah was an ignorant man.

B. "For it is written, 'And Manoah went after his wife' (Jud. 13:11)."

C. To this statement R. Nahman bar Isaac objected, "But does the same judgment apply to Elkanah. For it is written [sic], 'And Elkanah went after his wife,' [no such verse exists], and, with respect to Elisha, does this judgment apply, for it is written, 'And he rose and went after her' (2 Kgs. 4:30)?

D. "Is the meaning then that he literally went after her? But what it means was that he followed her views and her counsel. Here too he followed her views and her counsel."

E. Said R. Ashi, "Now in regard to the view of R. Nahman that Manoah was an ignorant man, he had not learned as much Scripture as someone who is in the house of a master [as a beginner in Scripture-studies].

F. "For it is said, 'And Rebekah arose and her maidens, and they rode upon the camels and followed the man' (Gen. 24:61). Thus [they went] after the man, not before him."

XCIII.

A. Said R. Yohanan, "[Walk] after a lion but not after a woman,

B. "after a woman but not after a gentile,

C. "after a gentile but not behind a synagogue when the community is saying prayers.

D. "What we have said applies only if one is not carrying a load, but if one is carrying a load, there is no objection.

E. "And what we have said applies only if there is no other door [into the synagogue], but if there is another door, there is no objection.

F. "And what we have said applies only if one is not riding an ass, but if one is riding an ass, there is no objection.

G. "And what we have said applies only if one has not put on phylacteries. But if one is wearing phylacteries, there is no objection."

XCIV.

A. Said Rab, "The impulse to do evil is like a fly. It sits between the two doors of the heart, as it is said, 'Dead flies make the ointment of the perfumes fetid and putrid' (Qoh. 10:1)."

B. And Samuel said, "It is like a grain of wheat, as it is said, 'Sin couches at the door' (Gen. 4:7)."

XCV.

A. Our rabbis have taught on Tannaite authority:

B. Man has two kidneys, one counseling him to do good, the other counseling him to do evil.

C. And it is reasonable to suppose that the one for good is at the right side and for evil at the left.

D. For it is written, "A wise man's understanding is at his right hand, but a fool's understanding is at his left" (Qoh. 10:2).

XCVI.

A. Our rabbis have taught on Tannaite authority:

B. The kidneys counsel, the heart discerns, the tongue shapes [words], the mouth expresses them, the gullet admits and gives out all sorts of food, the wind-pipe produces sound, [61B] the lungs take in all sorts of liquids, the liver produces anger, the gall drops a drop into it and calms it, the milt makes one laugh, the large intestine grinds food, the maw induces sleep, the nose wakes one up.

C. If what produces wakening sleeps, or what produces sleep wakes one up, a person will pine away.

D. It has been taught on Tannaite authority:

E. If both of them produce sleep or both of them wakes one up, one forthwith dies.

XCVII.

A.   It has been taught on Tannaite authority:

B.   R. Yose the Galilean says, "As to the righteous, the impulse to do good produces their judgments [of what to do or not to do], for it is said, 'My heart is slain within me' (Ps. 109:22).

C.   "As to the wicked, the impulse to do evil produces their judgments [of what to do or not to do], for it is said, 'Transgression speaks to the wicked, I think, there is no fear of God before his eyes' (Ps. 36:2).

D.   "As to people who fall in the middle, both impulses produce their judgments [of what to do or not to do], for it is said, 'Because he stands at the right hand of the needy, to save him from them that judge his soul' (Ps. 109:31)."

E.   Said Raba, "People such as we fall in the middle."

F.   Said Abayye to him, "The master has not allowed anyone else to live [if so righteous a man is only middling]."

G.   And Raba said, "The world was created only for those who are completely wicked or for those who are completely righteous."

H.   Said Raba, "A person should know concerning himself whether he is completely righteous or not."

I.   Said Raba, "The world was created only for Ahab son of Omri, and for R. Hanina b. Dosa, this world for Ahab son of Omri, and the world to come for R. Hanina b. Dosa."

XCVIII.

A.   "You shall love the Lord your God" [M. 9:5B]:

B.   It has been taught on Tannaite authority:

C.   R. Eliezer says, "If it is said, 'With all your soul,' why is it also said, 'With all your might'? And if it is said, 'With all your might,' why is it also said, 'With all your soul'?

D.   "But if there is someone who places greater value on his body than on his possessions, for such a one it is said, 'With all your soul.'

E.   "And if there is someone who places greater value on his possessions than on his life, for such a one it is said, 'With all your might.'"

F.   R. Aqiba says, "'With all your soul' -- even if he takes your soul.'"

XCIX.

A.   Our rabbis have taught on Tannaite authority:

B.   The wicked government once made a decree that the Israelites should not take up the study of Torah. Pappos b. Judah came and found R. Aqiba gathering crowds in public and taking up the study of Torah.

C.   He said to him, "Aqiba, aren't you afraid of the government?"

D.   He said to him, "I shall show you a parable. What is the matter like? It is like the case of a fox who was going along the river and saw fish running in swarms place to place."

E.   He said to them, "Why are you running away?"

F.   They said to him, 'Because of the nets people cast over us.'

G.   "He said to him, 'Why don't you come up on dry land, and you and I can live in peace as my ancestors lived in peace with yours?'

H.   "They said to him, 'Are you the one they call the cleverest of all wild beasts? You are not clever, you're a fool. Now if in the place in which we can live, we are afraid, in a place in which we perish, how much the more so [should we fear]!'

I.   "Now we too, if when we are in session and taking up the study of Torah, in which it is written, 'For it is your life and the length of your days' (Deut. 30:20), things are as they are, if we should go and abandon it, how much the more so [shall we be in trouble]!"

J.   They say that only a few days passed before they arrested and imprisoned R. Aqiba. They arrested and imprisoned Pappos b. Judah nearby. He said to him, "Pappos, who brought you here?"

K.   He said to him, "Happy are you, Aqiba, because you were arrested on account of teachings of Torah. Woe is Pappos, who was arrested on account of nonsense."

L.   The hour at which they brought R. Aqiba out to be put to death was the time for reciting the Shema. They were combing his flesh with iron combs while he was accepting upon himself [in the recitation of the Shema] the yoke of the Kingdom of Heaven.

M.   His disciples said to him, "Our master, to such an extent?"

N.   He said to them, "For my whole life I have been troubled about this verse, 'With all your soul' [meaning] even though he takes your soul. I wondered when I shall have the privilege of carrying out this commandment. Now that it has come to hand, should I not carry it out?"

O.   He held on to the word, "One," until his soul expired [as he said the word] "one." An echo came forth and said, "Happy are you, Rabbi Aqiba, that your soul expired with the word 'one.'"

P.   The serving angels said before the Holy One, blessed be he, "Is this Torah and that the reward? 'From them that die by your hand, O Lord' (Ps. 17:14) [ought to have been his lot]."

Q.   He said to them, "'Their portion is in life' (Ps. 17:14)."

R.   An echo went forth and proclaimed, "Happy are you, R. Aqiba, for you are selected for the life of the world to come."

C.

A.   One should not act in a silly way while facing the eastern gate [of the Temple of Jerusalem] for it faces toward the chamber of the holy of holies [M. 9:5G]:

B.   Said R. Judah said Rab, "That rule applies only to the area on the inner side of Mount Scopus [toward the Temple] and within sight [of the Temple]."

C.   It has also been stated on Amoraic authority:

D.   Said R. Abba, son of R. Hiyya bar Abba, "This is what R. Yohanan said: 'That rule applies only to the area on the inner side of Mount Scopus [toward the Temple] and within sight [of the Temple], and where there is no intervening fence, and at the time at which the Presence of God rests [upon the Temple] [but not when the Temple is in ruins]."

CI.

A. Our rabbis have taught on Tannaite authority:

B. In Judah one who defecates should not do so on an east-west axis but on a north-south axis, and in Galilee he should defecate only on an east-west axis.

C. But R. Yose permits [doing so in the other direction].

D. For R. Yose would say, "The prohibition applies only within sight, in a place in which there is no fence, and when the Presence of God rests [on the Temple]."

E. But sages prohibit doing so [as specified].

F. Now are not the sages [E] in exactly the position of the original authority [B]?

G. The difference between them is with regard to the side-[parts of Judea and Galilee, not due east or due north of Jerusalem. The first Tanna prohibits the specified axis even in these parts, since they speak of the whole of Judea, whereas the sages permit, referring as they do only to Yose's statement (Simon, p. 387, n. 6)].

H. A further teaching on Tannaite authority:

I. In Judea he who defecates should not defecate on an east-west axis but on a north-south axis, and for him who does so in Galilee a north-south axis is forbidden, an east-west axis is permitted.

J. And R. Yose declares it permitted [in any event].

K. For R. Yose would say, "The prohibition applies only within sight [of the Temple]."

L. R. Judah says, "When the house of the sanctuary stands, it is forbidden. When the house of the sanctuary does not stand, it is permitted."

M. R. Aqiba forbids in every place.

N. R. Aqiba says the same thing as the first [anonymous] Tannaite authority.

O. At issue between them is conduct outside of the land [entirely].

P. Rabbah would have bricks set up for him east and west. Abayye went and placed them on a north-south axis. Rabbah went and rearranged them. He said, "Who is giving me this trouble? I take the view of R. Aqiba, who has said, 'In every place it is forbidden [to defecate on a north-south axis].'"

CII.

A. [62A] It has been taught on Tannaite authority:

B. Said R. Aqiba, "I once went after R. Joshua to the privy and I learned the three things from him.

C. "I learned that people defecate not on an east-west axis but on a north-south axis.

D. "I learned that one urinates not standing but sitting.

E. "And I learned that one wipes not with the right hand but with the left."

F. Said Ben Azzai to him, "Do you behave that insolently toward your master?"

G. He said to him, "It is a matter of Torah, which I need to learn."

H. It has been taught on Tannaite authority:

I. Ben Azzai says, "I once followed R. Aqiba into the privy, and I learned three things from him:

J.   "I learned that people defecate not on an east-west axis but on a north-south axis.

K.   "And I learned that people urinate not standing up but sitting down.

L.   "And I learned that people wipe themselves not with the right hand but with the left."

M.   Said R. Judah to him, "Do you behave all that insolently toward your master?"

N.   He said to him, "It is a matter of Torah, which I need to learn."

CIII.

A.   R. Kahana went and hid under Rab's bed. He heard [Rab and his wife] "conversing" and laughing and doing what comes naturally. He said to him, "It appears that Abba's mouth has never before tasted the dish."

B.   He said, "Kahana, are you here! Get out! That's disgraceful!"

C.   He said to him, "It is a matter of Torah, which I need to learn."

CIV.

A.   On what account do people wipe not with the right hand but with the left?

B.   Said Raba, "Because the Torah was given with the right hand, as it is said, 'At his right hand was a fiery law unto them' (Deut. 33:2)."

C.   Said Rabbah bar bar Hana, "It is because [the right hand] is nearer to the mouth."

D.   And R. Simeon b. Laqish said, "It is because with [the right hand] one ties on the phylacteries [onto the left arm]."

E.   R. Nahman bar Isaac said, "Because with [the right hand] one points out the letters of the Torah."

F.   The matter is subject to dispute among Tannaite authorities:

G.   R. Eliezer says, "It is because one eats with it."

H.   R. Joshua says, "It is because one writes with it."

I.   R. Aqiba says, "It is because one points out with it the letters of the Torah."

CV.

A.   Said R. Tanhum bar Hanilai, "Whoever behaves modestly in the privy is saved from three things: snakes, scorpions, and destructive spirits."

B.   Some say, "Also his dreams rest easy on him."

CVI.

A.   There was a privy in Tiberias, into which, even if two people entered and, even by day, they would be harmed.

B.   R. Ammi and R. Assi went in one by one but were not injured.

C.   Rabbis said to them, "Are you not afraid?"

D.   They said to them, "We have learned a tradition: the lesson for [dealing with] the privy is modesty and silence, the lesson for [dealing with] suffering is silence and prayer."

CVII.

A.   Abayye's mother trained a lamb to go with him into a privy.

B.   Why not train a goat for him?

C.   It might turn into a satyr.

CVIII.

A. Before Raba became head, the daughter of R. Hisda [his wife] would rattle nuts in a brass dish [to frighten away spirits].

B. After he came to power, she made a little window for him and put her hand on his head.

CIX.

A. Said Ulla, "If it is behind a fence, one may defecate right away. If it is in an open field, one may do so long as he can fart without his fellow's hearing it."

B. Issi b. Nathan repeated the statement on Tannaite authority in this way: "If it is behind a fence, one may do so so long as he can fart without his fellow's hearing it, but in an open field, he can do so, so long as his fellow cannot see him."

C. An objection was raised from the following:

D. [Those who watch the olive-press to see that no cause of uncleanness affects it] go outside the door of the olive-press and defecate behind the wall and [the olives] are not affected by uncleanness. [How far are they to go and have the olives remain unaffected? So far that one may still see them [M. Toh. 10:2H-J].

E. In matters affecting preservation of cultic cleanness a more lenient rule applies.

F. Come and take note:

G. How far are they to go and yet [have the olives] remain unaffected [by uncleanness]? So far that one may still see them [M. Toh. 10:2I-J]. [Simon, p. 389, n. 12: But no further, so that he would himself still be visible. This refutes Issi.]

H. The case involving food prepared in conditions of cultic cleanness is subject to a lenient rule, for in that matter rabbis imposed a lenient ruling.

I. R. Ashi said, "What is the meaning of the phrase, 'So long as his fellow cannot see him,' as R. Issi bar Nathan used that phrase?

J. "His meaning is, 'So long as his fellow cannot see his body naked.' But his fellow nonetheless may see the man [as he defecates, but only from a distance, without violating the rule as Issi gives it]."

CX.

A. There was a funeral orator who went down before R. Nahman [to speak], and made the statement, "The deceased was modest in his ways."

B. Said R. Nahman to him, "Did you go with him to the privy that you know whether he was modest or not modest?

C. "For it has been taught on Tannaite authority: 'People are called modest only in respect to modesty in the privy.'"

D. And what difference did it make to R. Nahman?

E. Because it has been taught on Tannaite authority:

F. "Just as punishment is exacted from the dead, so punishment is exacted from those who lament the dead and those who respond, ['Amen'] after them."

CXI.

A. Our rabbis have taught on Tannaite authority:

B. Who is regarded as modest? It is one who defecates by night in a place in which one would be permitted to defecate by day.

C.   Is this so?

D.   And has not R. Judah said Rab said, "A person should always conduct himself [in defecating] both morning and night so that he does not have to go any distance"?

E.   And, furthermore, by day Raba would go a <u>mil,</u> and by night he would say to his attendant, "Clear a place for me right in the street of the town."

F.   And so said R. Zira to his attendant, "See if anyone is behind the house of the associates [the school house], since I want to defecate."

G.   Rather, phrase the teaching not as "in the place" but "in the manner" as he does by day.

H.   R. Ashi said, "You may preserve the phrasing, 'in the place.' The sense is that what is required only is to go into a private corner."

CXII.

A.   Reverting to the body of the text:

B.   Said R. Judah said Rab, "A person should always conduct himself [in defecating] both morning and night so that he does not have to go any distance."

C.   It has been taught on Tannaite authority along these same lines:

D.   Ben Azzai says, "Get up early [before dawn] and go forth, go to bed late [after dark] and go forth, so that [since it will be nearby] you do not have to go a distance.

E.   "Test yourself and then sit down, but do not sit down and then test yourself, for whoever sits down and then tests himself, even if people carry out witchcraft against him so far away as Aspamea, will suffer the consequences."

F.   And if someone should sit down and then test himself, what is his remedy?

G.   When he gets up he should say this, "Not to me, not to me, not <u>tahim</u> nor <u>tahtim</u>, not these nor any part of these, nor sorceries of sorcerers nor sorceries of female sorceresses."

CXIII.

A.   [62B] It has been taught on Tannaite authority:

B.   Ben Azzai says, "Sleep on anything except for the ground.

C.   "Sit on anything except on a beam."

D.   Said Samuel, "Urinating at dawn is like a steel edge to iron, defecation at dawn is like a steel edge to iron."

E.   Bar Qappara would sell wise sayings for pennies: "When you're hungry, eat, when you're thirsty, drink, when the pot is still boiling [and you have to defecate] pour it out. When the horn is sounded in Rome, son of the fig-seller, sell your father's figs [and don't wait for your father to come and do it.]"

F.   Said Abayye to rabbis, "When you are going through the streets of Mahoza to go out to the fields, do not look this way or that, lest be women sitting around, for it would not be proper to stare at them."

CXIV.

A.   R. Safra went into a privy. R. Aba came and cleared his throat at the door. He said to him, "Let the master come in."

B. After he had gone forth, [Abba] said to him, "Up to now you have not turned into a satyr but you have learned the wisdom of satyrs. Have we not learned in the Mishnah:

C. "There was a fire there, and a privy in good taste. And this was its good taste: if one found it locked, he knew that someone was there; if he found it open, he knew that no one was there [M. Tam. 1:1N-P].

D. "Therefore it is not proper [for more than one person to be in a privy at one time]."

E. But R. Safra took the view that it would be dangerous [if he kept Abba waiting].

F. For so it has been taught on Tannaite authority:

G. Rabban Simeon b. Gamaliel says, "If one holds in fecal discharge it brings a person dropsie, and if one holds in urine it brings a person jaundice."

CXV.

A. R. Eleazar went into a privy. A Roman [= Edomite] came along and pushed him away. R. Eleazar got up and left.

B. A snake came and tore out the [Roman's] gut.

C. R. Eleazar recited in connection with that man the following verse: "'Therefore will I give a man for you' (Is. 43:4). Do not read, 'A man,' but an Edomite [Edom for Adam]."

CXVI.

A. "And he thought to kill you but he spared you" (1 Sam. 24:11):

B. Rather than saying, "He thought," [since it is David speaking of what he himself did not do], it should read, "And I thought..."

C. "He spared" likewise should be "I spared."

D. Said R. Eleazar, "Said David to Saul, On the basis of the rules of the Torah, you are liable to be put to death, for lo, you are in pursuit of me, and the Torah has said, "If someone comes to kill you, rise and kill him first."

E. "'But the modesty that you displayed is what brought pity on you.

F. "'And what is it? It is in accord with what is written, "And he came to the fences by the way, where there was a cave, and Saul went in to cover his feet" (1 Sam. 24:4).'"

G. It was taught on Tannaite authority:

H. There was a fence inside of a fence, and a cave inside of a cave.

I. "To cover" (SK): Said R. Eleazar, "This teaches that he covered himself like a sukkah."

CXVII.

A. "Then David arose and cut off the skirt of Saul's robe privily" (1 Sam. 24:5):

B. Said R. Yose bar Hanina, "Whoever treats clothing without care in the end will not get any benefit from it.

C. "For it is said, 'Now King David was old, stricken in years, and they covered him with clothes, but he could get no heat' (1 Kgs. 1:1)."

CXVIII.

A. "If it be the Lord who has stirred you up against me, let him accept an offering" (1 Sam. 26:19):

B. Said R. Eleazar, "Said the Holy One, blessed be he, to David, 'Will you then use the language of "stir up" in my regard? Lo, I am going to make you stumble through a matter which even school children know.'

C. "For it is written, 'When you take the sum of the children of Israel according to their number, then shall they give every man a ransom for his soul unto the Lord... [that there be no plague among them]' (Ex. 30:12).

D. "Forthwith: 'Satan stood up against Israel' (1 Chr. 31:1).

E. "And it is further written, 'He stirred up David against them saying, Go number Israel' (2 Sam. 24:1).

F. "But when he counted them, he did not take a ransom from them, for it is written, 'So the Lord sent a pestilence upon Israel from morning even to the time appointed' (2 Sam. 24:15)."

G. What is this "time appointed"?

H. Said Samuel the elder, son in law of R. Hanina, in the name of R. Hanina, "It was from the time at which the daily whole offering was slaughtered until the time that its blood was sprinkled."

I. R. Yohanan said, "It was actually up to mid day."

CXIX.

A. "And he said to the angel that destroyed the people, it is great" (2 Sam. 24:16):

B. Said R. Eleazar, "Said the Holy One, blessed be he, to the angel, 'Take for me the great man among them, from whom may be exacted the penalty for many sins for [all of] them. At that moment Abishai, son of Zeruiah, died, who was in himself worth the better part of the sanhedrin."

CXX.

A. "And as he was about to destroy, the Lord saw and changed his mind" (1 Chr. 21:15):

B. What did he see?

C. Said Rab, "He saw Jacob, our father.

D. "For it is written, 'And Jacob said when he beheld them' (Gen. 32:3)."

E. Samuel said, "He saw the ashes of [the ram of] Isaac, as it says, 'God will see to the lamb for himself' (Gen. 22:8)."

F. R. Isaac Nappaha said, "He saw the atonement-money, as it is said, 'And you shall take the atonement money from the children of Israel and it shall be a memorial' (Ex. 30:16)."

G. R. Yohanan said, "He saw the house of the sanctuary, as it is said, 'In the mount where the Lord will see' (Gen. 22:14)."

H. R. Jacob bar Idi and R. Samuel bar Nahmani debated the matter.

I. One of them said, "He saw the atonement money."

J. The other said, "He saw the house of the sanctuary."

K. And the more reasonable position accords with the view of him who said that he saw the house of the sanctuary, for it is said, "As it will be said on that day in the mountain where the Lord sees" (Gen. 22:14).

CXXI.

A. <u>One should not enter the Temple Mount with his walking stick, [his shoes, his money bag, or with dust on his feet] [M. 9:5H]</u>:

B. What is a walking stick?

C. Said Raba, "Just what its name implies."

D. And R. Hana bar Ada in the name of Rab Sama, son of R. Mari, said, "[Simon:] It is as if a man said, 'Instead of going round the blocks, I will go in here.'"

CXXII.

A. Said R. Nahman said Rabbah bar Abuha, "He who goes into a synagogue not intending to make it a shortcut is permitted to make it a shortcut."

B. R. Abbahu said, "If it was a path to begin with, it is permitted [to use it as such]."

C. Said R. Helbo said R. Huna, "He who enters a synagogue in order to say his prayers is permitted to make it a short cut, as it is said, 'But when the people of the land shall come before the Lord in the appointed seasons [he who enters by the north gate shall go forth by the south gate]' (Ez. 46:9)."

CXXIII.

A. <u>And spitting there likewise is forbidden, as is proven by an argument a minori ad magus [M. 9:5J]</u>:

B. Said R. Bibi said R. Joshua b. Levi, "Whoever at this time spits on the Temple mount is as if he spit in the pupil of God's eye, since it is said, 'And my eyes and my heart shall be there forever' (1 Kgs. 9:3)."

C. Said Raba, "Spitting in the synagogue is permitted, parallel to the matter of the shoe. Just as wearing shoes on the Temple mount is forbidden but in a synagogue is permitted, so spitting on the Temple mount is where it is forbidden, but in the synagogue it is permitted."

D. Said R. Pappa to Raba, and some say Rabina to Raba, and some say R. Ada bar Mattena to Raba, "Instead of deriving the lesson from the case of the shoe, let us derive it from the case of the shortcut."

E. He said to him, "On Tannaite authority it is derived from the shoe, and you want to derive it from the short cut?"

F. What is the reference at hand?

G. It is as has been taught on Tannaite authority:

H. A person should not enter the Temple mount either with his walking stick in his hand or with his shoe on his foot or with his money tied up in his cloth or with his wallet slung over his shoulder, and he should not make it a shortcut, and, as to spitting, the prohibition derives from an argument a fortiori from the matter of the shoe.

I. Just as in the matter of the shoe, which, in general, is not regarded as a disgrace, Scripture has said, 'Put off your shoes from off your feet' (Ex. 3:5), all the more so should spitting [be forbidden], which is regarded as a matter of disgrace!

J. R. Jose b. R. Judah says, "It is not necessary to construct an argument on that basis. Lo, Scripture states, 'For none might enter within the king's gate clothed in sackcloth' (Est. 4:2). Now is it not a matter of an argument a fortiori? If the matter of sack cloth, which is not regarded as distasteful before mortals, by a mortal king [is forbidden], spitting, which is regarded as distasteful, all the more so should be regarded as forbidden before the King of kings of kings" [T. Ber. 6:19A-E].

K.   [Papa] said to [Raba], "This is what I meant to say: Let us impose a strict rule here and a strict rule there. [63A] Thus I might propose the following: The rule [prohibiting spitting] on the Temple mount is parallel to the rule governing wearing shoes [and so is forbidden on the Temple mount]. But as to the synagogue, in which wearing a shoe is permitted, instead of deriving the rule from the wearing a shoe and so permitting the matter, let us derive the rule from the prohibition against turning the synagogue into a shortcut and so, too, forbid spitting as well."

L.   Rather, said Raba, "It may be compared to one's view of his own house. Just as, in one's own home, one will object to having the house turned into a short cut, but he will not object to either wearing shoes or spitting, so in the synagogue turning it into a short cut is what is forbidden, but spitting and wearing a shoe are permitted."

CXXIV.

A.   At one time all blessings in the Temple concluded with, "From time immemorial." [When sectarians corrupted their ways and claimed there is but one world and no world to come, they ordained that they should say, "From time immemorial and forever" [M. 9:5K-M].

B.   Why [did they conclude with, "From time immemorial"]?

C.   Because people do not answer, "Amen," in the sanctuary.

D.   And how do we know that people are not to answer, "Amen" in the sanctuary?

E.   As it is said, "Stand up and bless the Lord your God from everlasting to everlasting" (Neh. 9:5), and, the text proceeds, "And let them say, Blessed be your glorious name that is exalted above every blessing and praise" (Neh. 9:5).

F.   Might I suppose that in the case of all blessings, one word of praise should suffice [Simon, p. 295, n. 7: that one response should be made at the end of all the blessings]?

G.   Scripture says, "Above every blessing and praise," meaning, for every blessing give praise to him [not only at the end].

CXXV.

A.   And they instituted the practice that an individual should greet his fellow with God's name [M. 9:5N]:

B.   What is the need of the additional proof-text [at M. 9:5P]?

C.   If you should take the view that Boaz did so on his own, come and take note: "The Lord be with you, you mighty man of valor" (Jud. 6:12).

D.   And should you say that it was merely an angel who spoke in this way to Gideon,

E.   come and take note of the further verse of Scripture: "Do not despise your mother when she is old" (Prov. 23:22).

CXXVI.

A. And it says, "It is time to act for the Lord, for they have violated your teaching" (Ps. 119:126) [M. 9:5R]:

B. Said Raba, "In this verse one may interpret the second clause in light of the first, or the first in light of the second.

C. "The second in light of the first: 'It is time to act for the Lord.' Why? 'For they have violated your teaching.'

D. "The first in light of the second: 'They have violated your teaching.' Why? 'Because it is time for the Lord to act.' [One should violate the Torah if it is in behalf of the Lord.]"

CXXVII.

A. It has been taught on Tannaite authority:

B. Hillel the Elder says, "At the time of ingathering, scatter; at the time of scattering, gather in.

C. "When you see a generation for whom the Torah is beloved, [then] scatter it [i.e., disseminate it freely; teach it widely],

D. "as Scripture states, One man gives freely, yet grows all the richer (Prov. 11:24).

E. "[But] when you see that a generation for whom the Torah is not beloved, [then] gather it in [viz., preserve it among yourselves],

F. "as Scripture states, It is time for the Lord to act (ibid.) [i.e., 'it is time to act for the Lord']."

CXXVIII.

A. Bar Qappara gave an exposition, "When prices are low, put your funds together and buy.

B. "In a place in which there is no man [to teach Torah], there be a man."

C. Said Abayye, "Does that then imply that in a place where there is a man [to teach Torah], there you do not have to be a man?

D. "That is self-evident.

E. "It is necessary to make that point to cover a place in which two men are equivalent [in capacity]."

CXXIX.

A. Bar Qappara gave an exposition, "What short passage of Scripture contains the principals of the Torah?

B. "'In all your ways know him and he will direct your paths' (Prov. 3:6)."

C. Said Raba, "Even to a transgression! [Simon, p. 397, n. 2: Weigh the pros and cons of it. This must be linked with the foregoing principle which permits the violation of the law when the exigencies of the time demand it.]"

D. Bar Qappara gave an exposition, "A person should always try to teach his son a clean and easy trade.

E. What would it be?

F. Said R. Hisda, "Needle-stitching."

CXXX.

A. It has been taught on Tannaite authority:

B. Rabbi says, "A person should never bring many friends into his house.

C. "For it is said, 'There are friends that one has to his own hurt' (Prov. 18:24)."

D. It has been taught on Tannaite authority:

E. Rabbi says, "A person should not appoint a steward over his own house.

F. "For had not Potiphar appointed Joseph as steward in his house, he would not have come to that unfortunate incident."

G. It has been taught on Tannaite authority:

H. Rabbi says, "Why was the passage on the Nazirite [Num. 6] placed side by side with the passage on the accused wife [Num. 6]?

I. "It is to tell you that whoever sees an accused wife in her disgrace should take the vow of a Nazirite upon himself, not to drink wine."

J. Said Hezekiah, son of R. Parnak, said R. Yohanan, "Why was the passage dealing with the accused wife [Num. 5] joined to the passage dealing with the designation of portions of the crop as priestly rations and tithes?

K. "It is to tell you that there may be someone who has designated portions of his crop for priestly rations and tithes but does not hand them over to a priest. In the end he will have to consult a priest on account of his wife.

L. "For it is said, 'Every man's holy things shall be his' (Num. 5:10, and, near at hand, 'And the man shall bring his wife' (Num. 5:15).

M. "Even more, in the end, he shall be in need of them, as it says, 'Every man's holy things shall be his' [Simon, p. 397, n. 13: in the form of poor man's tithe]."

N. Said R. Nahman bar Isaac, "And if one does hand over [the rations and tithes], in the end, he will get rich.

O. "For it is said, 'Whatever a man gives to the priest he shall have' (Num. 5:10) -- he will have a great deal of money."

CXXXI.

A. Said R. Huna bar Berekhiah in the name of R. Eleazar Haqappar, "Whoever joins the Name of heaven with his suffering [praying on that account] will find that his living will be doubled.

B. "For it is said, 'And the Almighty shall be in your distress, and you shall have double silver' (Job 27:24)."

C. R. Samuel bar Nahmani said, "His living will fly to him like a bird, as it is said, 'Silver shall fly to you' (Job 27:25)."

CXXXII.

A. Said R. Tabi said R. Josiah, "Whoever [Simon:] is faint in studying Torah will have not the strength to withstand the day of trouble.

B. "For it is said, 'You who are faint in the day of adversity, your strength will be small' (Prov. 24:10)."

C. Said R. Ammi bar Mattenah said Samuel, "And even if only in carrying out a single religious duty, as it says, 'If you faint' -- in any event."

CXXXIII.

A.   Said R. Safra, R. Abbahu would tell the following tale,

B.   "When Hanina, nephew of R. Joshua, went down to the Exile, he would intercalate years and designate the beginnings of the new month abroad.

C.   "They sent to him the disciples of sages. R. Yose b. Kippar and the grandson of Zechariah b. Qebuttal.

D.   "When he saw them, he said to them, 'Why have you come?'

E.   "They said to him, 'We have come to study Torah.'

F.   "He made a public announcement concerning them, saying, 'These men are the great men of the generation, and their ancestors served in the house of the sanctuary, in line with that which we have learned: Zechariah b. Qubuttal said, "Many times I read before [the high priest, on the night prior to the Day of Atonement], in the Book of Daniel."'

G.   "He began to declare objects under dispute to be susceptible to uncleanness, while they declared them insusceptible.

H.   "He declared a given action prohibited, and they declared it permitted.

I.   "He made a public announcement concerning them, 'These men are worthless, of no account.'

J.   "They said to him, 'You have already built [us up], and you cannot now destroy [us], you have already made a fence, and you cannot now destroy it.'

K.   He said to them, 'On what account is it the case that when I declare an object insusceptible to uncleanness, you declare it susceptible, and when I declare an act forbidden, you declare it permitted?'

L.   "They said to him, 'Because abroad [outside of the Land] you intercalate the year [adding an additional month] and also declare the beginning of the new months. [But this should be done only in the Land].'

M.   "He said to them, 'But did not Aqiba b. Joseph outside of the land intercalate the year and declare when the new month began?'

N.   "They said to him, 'Omit reference to R. Aqiba, who did not leave his equivalent in the Land of Israel.'

O.   "He said to them, 'I too did not leave my equivalent in the Land of Israel!'

P.   "They said to him, 'The lambs that you left behind have become rams -- with horns! And they have sent us to you and so have they said to us, "Go and say to him in our name, 'If you obey, well and good, and if not, then be excommunicated!'"

Q.   "'[They said to us,]'[63B] Say to our brothers in the Exile, 'If you obey, well and good, and if not, then go up to a mountain. Ahayah will build the altar, and Hananiah will play on the harp, and let all of them deny [God] and say, "We have no share in the God of Israel!""'"

R.   "Forthwith [Abbahu continues], all of the people broke out into weeping, saying, 'God forbid! We do have a portion in the God of Israel.'

S.   "Why all this?

T.   "Because it is said, 'For out of Zion shall the Torah go forth, and the word of the

Lord from Jerusalem' (Is. 2:3)."

U. Now we can understand why, if he declared something insusceptible, they would declare it susceptible, so that a more strict ruling should be imposed.

V. But if he declared an object susceptible and they declared it insusceptible to uncleanness, how is this possible?

W. For it has been taught on Tannaite authority:

X. In the case of a sage who declared an object susceptible to uncleanness, his fellow has not got the right to declare the object insusceptible.

Y. If he prohibited an act, his fellow has not got the right to permit it.

Z. They took the view that [they should act as they did] so that the people would not follow him, [an example of violating the law so as to work for the Lord].

CXXXIV.

A. Our rabbis have taught on Tannaite authority:

B. When our rabbis came into the vineyard at Yavneh, present were R. Judah, R. Yose, R. Nehemiah, and R. Eliezer, son of R. Yose the Galilee. All of them commenced discourse by speaking concerning the honor that is owing to hospitality and gave expositions [on that theme].

C. R. Judah, who speaks first under all circumstances, spoke about the honor owing to the Torah.

D. He interpreted the verse, "Now Moses used to take the tent and pitch it without the camp" (Ex. 33:7).

E. [He said,] "Is this not an argument a fortiori. Now if the ark of the Lord, which was only twelve mil distant, is such that the Torah has said [in praise of those who approached it], 'Everyone who sought the Lord went out to the tent of meeting' (Ex. 33:7), how much the more so [is the title, 'one who seeks the Lord,' owing to] disciples of sages, who go from town to town and province to province to study Torah!"

F. "And the Lord spoke to Moses face to face" (Ex. 33:11):

G. Said R. Isaac, "Said the Holy One, blessed be he, to Moses, 'Moses, you and I will come face and face in discourse on the law.'"

H. Some say, "This is what the Holy One, blessed be he, said to Moses, 'Just as I have shown favor to you, so you show favor to Israel, and bring the tent back to its place.'"

I. "And he would return to the camp" (Ex. 33:11):

J. Said R. Abbahu, "Said the Holy One, blessed be he, to Moses, 'Now people will say that the master is angry, the disciple is angry, and what will happen to the Israelites! If you return the tent to its place, well and good, and if not, Joshua b. Nun, your disciple, will serve in your place.'

K. "And that is in line with what is written, 'And he would return to the camp.'"

L. Said Raba, "Even so, the statement was hardly null, for it says, 'But his minister, Joshua, son of Nun, a young man, did not depart out of the tent' (Ex. 3:11). [He succeeded Moses, just as God said.]"

CXXXV.

A. Further, R. Judah commenced discourse with a statement about the honor owing to the Torah, interpreting matters as follows: "'Attend and hear O Israel, this day you have become a people to the Lord your God' (Deut. 27:9).

B. "Now was that the day on which the Torah was given to Israel? Was it not the day marking the end of the forty years?

C. "But it serves to teach you that Torah is precious to those who study it every day, just as it was on the day on which it was given at Mount Sinai."

D. Said R. Tanhum, son of R. Hiyya of Kefar Akko, "You may know that that is the case. For lo, a person recites the Shema morning and night. If on a given evening he does not recite it, it is as if he has never recited the Shema."

E. As to the meaning of the Hebrew word for "attend," it can be read as "Make yourselves into groups to study the Torah [Simon], for knowledge of Torah is attained only in association with others [studying together].

F. This is in accord with what R. Yose b. R. Hanina said.

G. For R. Yose b. R. Hanina said, "What is the meaning of the verse of Scripture, 'A sword is upon the boasters and they shall become fools' (Jer. 50:36)?

H. "A sword smite the (enemies of) disciples of sages, who go into session, each by himself, while studying Torah! And not only so, but they grow stupid.

I. "Here it is written, 'And they shall become fools' (Jer. 50:36), and elsewhere it is written, 'And we have done foolishly' (Num. 12:11) [using the same verb].

J. "Not only so, but they sin, for it is said, 'And we have sinned' (Num. 12:11).

K. "If you wish, I shall prove the proposition from the following: 'The princes of Zoan have become fools' (Is. 19:13)."

L. A further interpretation of the word used for "attend and hear O Israel" (Deut. 27:9):

M. Cut yourself on account of studying the teachings of the Torah, in line with what R. Simeon b. Laqish said.

N. For R. Simeon b. Laqish said, "How do we know on the basis of Scripture that teachings of Torah endure only for him who offers his life on that account? As it is said, 'This is the Torah. When a man shall die in a tent' (Num. 19:14)."

O. Another interpretation for "Attend and hear, O Israel" (Deut. 27:9):

P. "Be quiet and then analyze" [Simon, p. 401, n. 7: First listen to the teacher, and then discuss what he has said]. That accords with what Raba said.

Q. For said Raba, "A person should always first of all learn the teaching of the Torah and only afterward reflect on it."

CXXXVI.

A. In the house of R. Yannai they say, "What is the meaning of the verse of Scripture, 'For the churning of milk brings forth curd, and the wringing of the nose brings forth blood, so the forcing of wrath brings forth strife' (Prov. 30:33)?

B. "With whom do you find the cream of the Torah? With him who throws up [upon it] the milk that he sucks from his mother's breasts.

C.   "'The wringing of the nose brings forth blood:' Any disciple who keeps his peace on the first occasion on which his master expresses anger at him will have the merit of knowing the difference between unclean and clean blood.

D.   "'So the forcing of wrath brings forth strife:' Any disciple who keeps his peace on the first and second occasions on which his master expresses anger at him will have the merit of knowing the difference between monetary cases and capital cases."

E.   For we have learned in the Mishnah:

F.   R. Ishmael says, "Whoever wants to get smart had best get busy with commercial law, for you have no specialty in the Torah greater than those laws, for they are like an ever-bubbling spring" [M. B.B. 10:8/O-Q].

G.   Said R. Samuel bar Nahmani, "What is the meaning of the verse of Scripture, 'If you have done foolishly in lifting up yourself, or if you have planned devices, put your hand on your mouth' (Prov. 30:32)?

H.   "Whoever humbles himself for the purpose of studying teachings of the Torah in the end will be exalted, but if one [Simon:] muzzles himself, his hand will be upon his mouth. [Simon, p. 402, n. 3: He will be unable to answer questions put to him.]"

CXXXVII.

A.   [Reverting to CXXXIV B:] R. Nehemiah commenced discourse speaking on the honor owing to hospitality. He gave this exposition: "What is the meaning of the verse of Scripture, 'And Saul said to the Kenites, Go, depart, get you down from among the Amalekites, lest I destroy you with them, for you showed kindness to all the children of Israel when they came up out of Egypt' (1 Sam. 15:6)?

B.   "Now is it not an argument a fortiori? If Jethro, who drew Moses near himself only for his own honor, is treated in this way, he who makes a disciple of a sage a guest in his home and feeds him and gives him drink and supports him from his prosperity, how much the more so [will such a one be blessed]!"

CXXXVIII.

A.   R. Yose commenced discourse, speaking on the honor owing to hospitality. He gave this exposition: "'You shall not abhor an Edomite, for he is your brother, you shall not abhor an Egyptian, because you were a stranger in his land' (Deut. 23:8).

B.   "Now is it not an argument a fortiori? Now if the Egyptians, who drew the Israelites near only for their own purposes, as it is said, 'And if you know any able men among them, then make them rulers over my cattle' (Gen. 47:6), [are treated in this way], he who makes a disciple of a sage a guest in his home and feeds him and gives him drink and supports him from his property -- how much the more so [will such a one be blessed]!"

CXXXIX.

A.   R. Eliezer, son of R. Yose the Galilean, commenced discourse, speaking on the honor owing to hospitality. He gave this exposition: "'And the Lord blessed Obed Edom and all his house... because of the ark of God' (2 Sam. 6:12).

B.   "Now is it not an argument a fortiori? Now if the ark, which ate and drank nothing, but required only that one sweep and lay the dust, [produced such a reward], he who makes a disciple of a sage a guest in his home and feeds him and gives him drink and supports him from his property -- how much the more so [will such a one be blessed]!"

C. What was the blessing with which [God] blessed [Obed Edom]?

D. Said R. Judah bar Zabida, "This refers to Hamoth and her eight daughters-in-law, each of whom produced six children at a birth, [64A], as it is said, 'Peullethai, the eighth son for God blessed him' (1 Chr. 26:5), and it is written, 'All these were of the sons of Obed-Edom, they and their sons and their brethren, able men in the strength for the service, threescore and two of Obed Edom' (1 Chr. 26:5). [Simon, p. 403, n. 4: The sixty-two are made up of the eight sons mentioned, six more to his wife at one birth, and six to each of his eight daughters-in-law.]"

CXL.

A. Said R. Abin the Levite, "Whoever tries to take advantage of an occasion will find that the occasion takes advantage of him, and whoever forgoes the occasion will find that the occasion is forgone on his account."

B. This [matter derives from the case of] Rabbah and R. Joseph.

C. For R. Joseph was Sinai, and Rabbah was one who uproots mountains. The occasion came on which they were needed [for high office]. They sent over there [to the Land of Israel, to ask], "As between Sinai and one who uproots mountains, which takes precedence?"

D. They replied, "Sinai takes precedence, for everyone needs the sustenance of the one who owns the wheat."

E. Even so, R. Joseph did not accept office, because the Chaldean [astrologers] told him that he would rule for only two years.

F. Rabbah did indeed rule twenty-two years, and after him, R. Joseph ruled for two and a half years.

G. All the time that Rabbah ruled, he did not call to his house even a blood-letter.

CXLI.

A. And R. Abin the Levite said, "What is the meaning of that which is written, 'The Lord answer you in the day of trouble, the name of the God of Jacob set you up on high' (Ps. 20:2)?

B. "'The God of Jacob" and not the God of Abraham and Isaac?

C. "On the basis of this statement we learn that the owner of a beam should insert the thickest [and heaviest] part of the beam [into the ground, as the best support. Simon, p. 404, n. 1: So the name of Jacob would be more efficacious in prayer because he was the more immediate ancestor of the Jewish people.]"

CXLII.

A. And R. Abin the Levite said, "Whoever enjoys a banquet at which a disciple of a sage is ensconced is as if he enjoys the splendor of the Presence of God.

B. "For it says, 'And Aaron came and all the elders of Israel to eat bread with Moses' father-in-law before God' (Ex. 18:12).

C. "Now did they eat before God? And was it not before Moses that they ate?

D.   "But this tells you: Whoever enjoys a banquet at which a disciple of a sage is
       ensconced is as if he enjoys the splendor of the Presence of God."

CXLIII.

A.   And said R. Abin the Levite, "He who takes leave of his fellow should not say to
       him, 'Go in peace,' but, 'Go to peace.' For lo, Jethro is the one to whom Moses said,
       'Go to peace' (Ex. 4:18), and he rose high and succeeded. But Absalom, to whom
       David said, 'Go in peace' (2 Sam. 15:9) went and got himself hanged."

B.   And said R. Abin the Levite, "He who takes leave of the deceased should not say to
       him, 'Go to peace,' but, 'Go in peace,'

C.   "for it is said, 'And you shall go to your fathers in peace' (Gen. 15:15)."

CXLIV.

A.   Said R. Levi bar Hiyya, "He who leaves a synagogue and goes into a study-house and
       takes up study of Torah enjoys such merit as to receive the face of the Presence of
       God.

B.   "For it is said, 'They go from strength to strength, every one of them appears before
       God in Zion' (Ps. 84:8)."

C.   Said R. Hiyya bar Ashi said Rab, "Disciples of sages enjoy no repose either in this
       world or in the world to come.

D.   "For it is said, 'They go from struggle to struggle, every one of them appears before
       God in Zion' (Ps. 84:8)."

CXLV.

A.   Said R. Eleazar said R. Hanina, "Disciples of sages increase peace in the world.

B.   "For it is said, 'And all your children shall be taught of the Lord, and great shall be
       the peace of your children' (Is. 54:13).

C.   "Read not 'your children' but 'your builders.'"

CXLVI.

A.   "Great peace have they who love your Torah, and there is no stumbling for them"
       (Ps. 119:165).

B.   "Peace be within your walls and prosperity within your palaces" (Ps. 122:7).

C.   "For my brethren and companions' sake I will now say, 'Peace be within you'" (Ps.
       122:8).

D.   "For the sake of the house of the Lord our God I will seek your good" (Ps. 122:9).

E.   "The Lord will give strength to his people, the Lord will bless his people with peace"
       (Ps. 29:11).

       Let us begin by surveying the way in which the composers of the chapter have laid
out the materials, starting with their treatment of the sentences of the Mishnah-paragraphs, then accounting for sizable tracts of materials not devoted to those sentences.

Mishnah-exegesis

I.   Saying a blessing in a place in which miracles were performed (M. 9:1A):
       A.   Miracles I-V

      B.   Idolatry was uprooted: XLVIII-XLIX

      C.   Other such occasions for blessings: L-LIX

II.   Saying a blessing on seeing mountains, hills, and other natural wonders (M. 9:2): LX-LXX

III.   Saying a blessing for rain, for good news (M. 9:2E-F): LXXI

IV.   Saying a blessing for a new house, new clothes (M. 9:2A): LXXII

V.   Saying a blessing for good as for evil (M. 9:3B): LXXIII-LXXIV

VI.   A vain prayer (M. 9:3C-F): LXXV-LXXVI

VII.   Saying a prayer upon entering, leaving a town (M. 9:4): LXXIX-LXXXIV

VIII. Saying a blessing for evil as for good, reciting the <u>Shema</u> (M. 9:5A-F): LXXXV-XC; XCVIII-XCIX

IX.   Conduct on the Temple mount (M. 9:5H-M): C-CII and CIII, CXXI-CXXIII

X.   Changes in the law made on account of crisis (M. 9:5N-S): CXXIV-CXXIX, CXXXIII

XI.   Sayings on Torah, honoring disciples: CXXXIV-CXLVI

The layout of these units completely conforms to the order of the sentences of the Mishnah.

Topical tracts

Groups of units of discourse formed on principles other than those dictated by the order and topics of the Mishnah-paragraph:

1.   <u>Enumeration-sayings</u> (three sorts, three things, etc.: V-IX. (Extension of issue of IX: X-XIII);

2.   <u>The interpretation of dreams</u>: XIV-XLVII

3.   <u>Avoiding licentious contact with women</u>: XCI-XCVII

4.   <u>Privy-sayings</u> (joined to the theme of conduct <u>vis à vis</u> the Temple mount): CIV-CXX

5.   <u>Miscellaneous</u>: CXXX-CXXXII

We see therefore that the layout of the Talmud follows the order of the Mishnah, even though the printers have not given the several Mishnah-paragraphs in full prior to the Talmud's discussion of those paragraphs. The result of their failure to do so is the impression of a somewhat prolix and disorganized discussion. But, as in the opening chapter, once we recognize that the Talmud's organizers carefully followed the sequence of topics of the Mishnah paragraph, but also inserted, whole and complete, fully framed units in addition, we see the true state of affairs. Virtually nothing is miscellaneous. Protracted and autonomous discussions, e.g., enumeration-sayings, dream-interpretation sayings (no fewer than 33 complete and length units of discourse!), sayings about the privy (a dozen and a half) and the like, fill up the chapter. There is a concluding unit of sayings on Torah-study and honoring disciples, something we can hardly find surprising. So, in all, the chapter's composition proves entirely orderly and rational, following rules we can discern.

BROWN JUDAIC STUDIES SERIES